THE HOLY CATHOLIC CHURCH

THE HOLY CATHOLIC CHURCH

BOOK FOURTH

INSTITUTES OF THE CHRISTIAN RELIGION

JOHN CALVIN

A New Translation by Henry Beveridge, Esq.

Alachua, Florida 32615

Bridge-Logos
Alachua, FL 32615 USA

The Holy Catholic Church
by John Calvin

Translation by Henry Beveridge, Esq.

Printed in the United States of America.

Library of Congress Catalog Card Number: 2013953468
International Standard Book Number 978-1-61036-003-6

Unless otherwise indicated, Scripture quotations in this book are from the *King James Version* of the Bible.

General Index of Chapters

BOOK FOUR

OF THE HOLY CATHOLIC CHURCH

Foreword

To read John Calvin is to study the work of some of the finest minds and sharpest pens in Christendom. Calvin was extremely well read and drew heavily from the writings of Turtullian, Origen, the Apostles, Saint Augustine, and Bernard, to name only a few. Befitting his training as an attorney and his passion as a Christian, Calvin devoted years to writing and rewriting his *Institutes of the Christian Religion*, deftly weaving the ideas of his predecessors with his own into a brilliant case for reformation.

That other scholars have enjoined this discussion is no surprise. In the spirit of this partnership of elite brothers that has spanned centuries, the biography of John Calvin in this volume was written by John Foxe (1516-1587), author of *Foxes' Book of Martyrs*. At the end of his piece, we have included some insights from Calvin's personal friends to give you insight into the character of this very human man. Additionally, Charles Haddon Spurgeon (1850-1892), author of *Morning by Morning* and *Evening by Evening*, contributes his treatise, *A Defense of Calvinism*.

We have maintained as much of the original vocabulary as we dare. Calvin wrote in a time when books were rare and owned by only a few. Since Calvin's day, and with the ever widening availability of books and other written media, our culture has developed a distinction between the spoken word and the written word. Their styles are sharply different, with rules that govern each. But Calvin and his contemporaries had no concept of "written" word. That would evolve with readers over the next several centuries. Their work was "spoken" word put to paper. As a consequence, it tends to be oratory in style, filled with flourish and flare. To further complicate the matter of unfamiliar style, Calvin was a Frenchman who wrote in Latin. The work we have today has been translated with careful intention of honoring Calvin's words. If, as a present-day reader, you get tangled up in an occasional sentence that seems to meander maddeningly through a peppering of punctuation marks, merely read it out loud. You will become clear about the meaning, and moreover, you will "hear" Calvin as he thunders. We beg your indulgence, and assure you that the occasional challenge is well worth the result.

Welcome to the mind of Calvin.

The Original Translator's Preface

PREFIXED TO THE FOURTH EDITION 1581 AND REPRINTED VERBATIM IN ALL THE SUBSEQUENT EDITIONS. THOMAS NORTON, THE TRANSLATOR TO THE READER.

Good reader, here is now offered you, the fourth time printed in English, M. Calvin's book of the Institutes of the Christian Religion; a book of great labor to the author, and of great profit to the Church of God. M. Calvin first wrote it when he was a young man, a book of small volume, and since that season he has at sundry times published it with new increases, still protesting at every edition himself to be one of those qui scribendo proficiunt, et proficiendo scribunt, which with their writing do grow in profiting, and with their profiting do proceed in writing. At length having, in many [of] his other works, traveled about exposition of sundry books of the Scriptures, and in the same finding occasion to discourse of sundry common-places and matters of doctrine, which being handled according to the occasions of the text that were offered him, and not in any other method, were not so ready for the reader's use, he therefore entered into this purpose to enlarge this book of Institutions, and therein to treat of all those titles and commonplaces largely, with this intent, that whensoever any occasion fell in his other books to treat of any such cause, he would not newly amplify his books of commentaries and expositions therewith, but refer his reader wholly to this storehouse and treasure of that sort of divine learning. As age and weakness grew upon him, so he hastened his labor; and, according to his petition to God, he in manner ended his life with his work, for he lived not long after.

So great a jewel was meet to be made most beneficial, that is to say, applied to most common use. Therefore, in the very beginning of the Queen's Majesty's most blessed reign, I translated it out of Latin into English for the commodity of the Church of Christ, at the special request of my dear friends of worthy memory, Reginald Wolfe and Edward Whitchurch, the one her Majesty's printer for the Hebrew, Greek, and Latin tongues, the other her Highness' printer of the books of Common Prayer. I performed my work in the house of my said friend, Edward Whitchurch, a man well known of upright heart and dealing, an ancient zealous gospeller, as plain and true a friend as ever I knew living, and as desirous to do anything to common good, especially by the advancement of true religion.

At my said first edition of this book, I considered how the author thereof had of long time purposely labored to write the same most exactly, and to pack great plenty of matter in small room of words; yea, and those so circumspectly and precisely ordered, to avoid the cavillations of such as for enmity to the truth therein contained would gladly seek and abuse all advantages which might be found by any oversight in penning of it, that the sentences were thereby become so full as nothing might well be added without idle superfluity, and again so highly pared, that nothing could be diminished without taking away some necessary substance of matter therein expressed.

This manner of writing, beside the peculiar terms of arts and figures, and the difficulty of the matters themselves, being throughout interlaced with the school men's controversies, made a great hardness in the author's own book, in that tongue wherein otherwise he is both plentiful and easy, insomuch that it sufficeth not to read him once, unless you can be content to read in vain. This consideration encumbered me with great doubtfullness for the whole order and frame of my translation. If I should follow the words, I saw that of necessity the hardness in the translation must needs be greater than was in the tongue wherein it was originally written. If I should leave the course of words, and grant myself liberty after the natural manner of my own tongue, to say that in English which I conceived to be his meaning in Latin, I plainly perceived how hardly I might escape error, and on the other side, in this matter of faith and religion, how perilous it was to err. For I durst not presume to warrant myself to have his meaning without his words. And they that knew what it is to translate well and faithfully, especially in matters of religion, do know that not the only grammatical construction of words sufficeth, but the very building and order to observe all advantages of vehemence or grace, by placing or accent of words, maketh much to the true setting forth of a writer's mind.

In the end, I rested upon this determination, to follow the words so near as the phrase of the English tongue would suffer me. Which purpose I so performed, that if the English book were printed in such paper and letter as the Latin is, it should not exceed the Latin in quantity. Whereby, beside all other commodities that a faithful translation of so good a work may bring, this one benefit is moreover provided for such as are desirous to attain some knowledge of the Latin tongue (which is, at this time, to be wished in many of those men for whose profession this book most fitly serveth), that they shall not find any more English than shall suffice to construe the Latin withal, except in such few places where the great difference of the phrases of the languages enforced me: so that, comparing the one with the other, they shall both profit in good matter, and furnish themselves with understanding of that speech, wherein the greatest treasures of knowledge are disclosed.

In the doing hereof, I did not only trust mine own wit or ability, but examined my whole doing from sentence to sentence throughout the whole book with conference and overlooking of such learned men, as my translation being allowed by their Judgment, I did both satisfy mine own conscience that I had done truly, and their approving of it might be a good warrant to the reader that nothing should herein be delivered him but sound, unmingled, and uncorrupted doctrine, even in such sort as the author himself had first framed it. All that I wrote, the grave, learned, and virtuous man, M. David Whitehead (whom I name with honorable remembrance), did, among others, compare with the Latin, examining every sentence throughout the whole book. Beside all this, I privately required many, and generally all men with whom I ever had any talk of this matter, that if they found anything either not truly translated, or not plainly Englished, they would inform me thereof, promising either to satisfy them or to amend it. Since which time, I have not been advised by any man of anything, which they would require to be altered. Neither had I myself, by reason of my profession, being otherwise occupied, any leisure to peruse it. And that is the cause, why not only at the second and third time, but also at this impression, you have no change at all in the work, but altogether as it was before.

Indeed, I perceived many men well-minded and studious of this book, to require a table for their ease and furtherance. Their honest desire I have fulfilled in the second edition, and have added thereto a plentiful table, which is also here inserted, which I have translated out of the Latin, wherein the principal matters discoursed in this book are named by their due titles in order of alphabet, and under every title is set forth a brief sum of the whole doctrine taught in this book concerning the matter belonging to that title or common-place; and therewith is added the book, chapter, and section or division of the chapter, where the same doctrine is more largely expressed and proved. And for the easier finding thereof, I have caused the number of the chapters to be set upon every leaf in the book, and quoted the sections also by their due numbers with the usual figures of algorism. And now at this last publishing, my friends, by whose charge it is now newly imprinted in a Roman letter and smaller volume, with divers other Tables which, since my second edition, were gathered by M. Marlorate, to be translated and here added for your benefit.

Moreover, whereas in the first edition the evil manner of my scribbling hand, the interlining of my copy, and some other causes well known among workmen of that faculty, made very many faults to pass the printer, I have, in the second impression, caused the book to be composed by the printed copy, and corrected by the written; whereby it must needs be that it was much more truly done than the other was, as I myself do know above three hundred faults amended. And now at this last printing, the composing after a printed copy bringeth some ease, and the diligence used about the correction having been right faithfully looked unto, it cannot be but much more truly set forth. This also is performed, that the volume being smaller, with a letter fair and legible, it is of more easy price, that it may be of more common use, and so to more large communicating of so great a treasure to those that desire Christian knowledge for instruction of their faith, and guiding of their duties. Thus, on the printer's behalf and mine, your ease and commodity (good readers) provided for. Now resteth your own diligence, for your own profit, in studying it.

To spend many words in commending the work itself were needless; yet thus much I think, I may both not unruly and not vainly say, that though many great learned men have written books of common-places of our religion, as Melancthon, Sarcerius, and others, whose works are very good and profitable to the Church of God, yet by the consenting Judgment of those that understand the same, there is none to be compared to this work of Calvin, both for his substantial sufficiency of doctrine, the sound declaration of truth in articles of our religion, the large and learned confirmation of the same, and the most deep and strong confutation of all old and new heresies; so that (the Holy Scriptures excepted) this is one of the most profitable books for all students of Christian divinity. Wherein (good readers), as I am glad for the glory of God, and for your benefit, that you may have this profit of my travel, so I beseech you let me have this use of your gentleness, that my doings may be construed to such good end as I have meant them; and if you dislike anything by reason of hardness, or any other cause that may seem to be my fault, you will not forthwith condemn the work, but read it after; in which doing you will find (as many have confessed to me that they have found by experience) that those things which at the first reading shall displease you for hardness, shall be found so easy as so hard matter would suffer, and, for the most part, more easy than some other phrase which should with greater looseness and smoother sliding away deceive your understanding. I confess, indeed, it is not finely and pleasantly written, nor carrieth with it such delightful grace of speech as some great wise men have bestowed upon some foolisher things, yet it containeth sound truth set forth with faithful plainness, without wrong done to the author's meaning; and so, if you accept and use it, you shall not fail to have great profit thereby, and I shall think my labor very well employed.

Thomas Norton.

The Printers to the Readers

hereas some men have thought and reported it to be [very great negligence in us for that we have so long kept back from you this,] being so profitable a work for you, namely before the master J[ohnne] Dawes had translated it and delivered it into our hands more than a twelvemonth past: you shall understand for our excuse in that behalf, that we could not well imprint it sooner. For we have been by diverse necessary causes constrained with our earnest entreatance to procure an other frede or oures to translate it whole again. This translation, we trust, you shall well allow. For it hath not only been faithfully done by the translator himself, but also hath been wholly perused by such men, whose ingement and credit all the godly learned in England well know I estheme. But since it is now come forth, we pray you accept it, and see it. If any faults have passed us by oversight, we beseech you let us have your patience, as you have had our diligence.

The Institutes of the Christian Religion, written in Latin by M. John Calvin, and translated into English according to the Author's last edition, with sundry Tables to find the principal matters entreated of in this book, and also the declaration of places of Scripture therein expounded, by Thomas Norton. Whereunto there are newly added in the margen of the book, notes containing in briefs the substance of the matter handled in each Section.

Originally printed at London by Arnold Hatfield, for Bonham Norton. 1599

Prefactory Address

TO HIS MOST CHRISTIAN MAJESTY, THE MOST MIGHTY AND ILLUSTRIOUS MONARCH, FRANCIS, KING OF THE FRENCH, HIS SOVEREIGN; JOHN CALVIN PRAYS PEACE AND SALVATION IN CHRIST.

Sire, when I first engaged in this work, nothing was further from my thoughts than to write what should afterwards be presented to your Majesty. My intention was only to furnish a kind of rudiment, by which those who feel some interest in religion might be trained to true godliness. And I toiled at the task chiefly for the sake of my countrymen, the French multitudes of whom I perceived to be hungering and thirsting after Christ, while very few seemed to have been duly imbued with even a slender knowledge of Him. That this was the object, which I had in view, is apparent from the work itself, which is written in a simple and elementary form adapted for instruction.

But when I perceived that the fury of certain bad men had risen to such a height in your realm, that there was no place in it for sound doctrine, I thought it might be of service if I were in the same work both to give instruction to my countrymen, and also lay before your Majesty a Confession from which you may learn what the doctrine is that so inflames the rage of those madmen who are this day, with fire and sword, troubling your kingdom. For I fear not to declare that what I have here given may be regarded as a summary of the very doctrine, which, they shout, ought to be punished with confiscation, exile, imprisonment, and flames, as well as exterminated by land and sea.

Indeed, I am aware of how, in order to render our cause as hateful to your Majesty as possible, they have filled your ears and mind with atrocious insinuations; but you will be pleased, of your clemency, to reflect that neither in word nor deed could there be any innocence, were it sufficient merely to accuse. When anyone with the view of exciting prejudice observes that this doctrine, of which I am endeavoring to give your Majesty an account, has been condemned by the suffrages of all the estates, and was long ago stabbed again and again by partial sentences of courts of law, he undoubtedly says nothing more than that it has sometimes been violently oppressed by the power and faction of adversaries, and sometimes fraudulently and insidiously overwhelmed by lies, cavils, and calumny. While a cause is unheard, it is violence to pass sanguinary sentences against it; it is fraud to charge it, contrary to its deserts, with sedition and mischief.

That no one may suppose we are unjust in thus complaining, you yourself, most illustrious Sovereign, can bear us witness with what lying calumnies it is daily traduced in your presence, as aiming at nothing else than to wrest the scepters of kings out of their hands, to overturn all tribunals and seats of justice, to subvert all order and government, to disturb the peace and quiet of society, to abolish all laws, to destroy the distinctions of rank and property, and, in short, to turn all things upside down. And yet, that which you hear is but the smallest portion of what is said; for among the common people are disseminated certain horrible insinuations—insinuations which, if well founded, would justify the whole world in condemning the doctrine with its authors to a thousand fires and gibbets. Who can wonder that the popular hatred is inflamed against it, when credit is given to those most iniquitous accusations? See why all ranks unite with one accord in condemning our persons and our doctrine!

Carried away by this feeling, those who sit in judgment merely give utterance to the prejudices, which they have imbibed at home, and who think they have duly performed their part if they do not order punishment to be inflicted on anyone until convicted, either on his own confession, or on legal evidence. But of what crime convicted? "Of that condemned doctrine," is the answer. But with what justice condemned? The very essence of the defense was not to abjure the doctrine itself, but to maintain its truth. On this subject, however, not a whisper is allowed!

Justice, then, most invincible Sovereign, entitles me to demand that you will undertake a thorough investigation of this cause, which has hitherto been tossed about in any kind of way, and handled in the most irregular manner, without any order of law, and with passionate heat rather than judicial gravity.

Let it not be imagined that I am here framing my own private defense with the view of obtaining a safe return to my native land. Though I cherish towards it the feelings, which become me as a man, still, as matters now are, I can be absent from it without regret. The cause, which I plead, is the common cause of all the godly, and therefore the very cause of Christ—a cause which, throughout your realm, now lies in despair—torn and trampled upon in all kinds of ways, and that more through the tyranny of certain Pharisees than any sanction from yourself. But it matters not to inquire how the thing is done; the fact that it is done cannot be denied. For so far have the wicked prevailed, that the truth of Christ, if not utterly routed and dispersed, lurks as if it were ignobly buried; while the poor Church, either wasted by cruel slaughter or driven into exile or intimidated and terror—struck, scarcely ventures to breathe. Still her enemies press on with their wonted rage and fury over the ruins, which they have made, strenuously assaulting the wall, which is already giving way. Meanwhile, no man comes forth to offer his protection against such furies. Any who would be thought most favorable to the truth, merely talk of pardoning the error and imprudence of ignorant men, for so those modest personages speak: giving the name of *error and imprudence* to that which they know to be the infallible truth of God, and of *ignorant men* to those whose intellect they see that Christ has not despised, seeing He has deigned to entrust them with the mysteries of His heavenly wisdom. Thus, all are ashamed of the Gospel.

Your duty, most serene Prince, is to not shut either your ears or mind against a cause involving such mighty interests as these: how the glory of God is to be maintained on the Earth inviolate, how the truth of God is to preserve its dignity, how the kingdom of Christ is to continue amongst us compact and secure. The cause is worthy of your ear, worthy of your investigation, worthy of your throne.

The characteristic of a true sovereign is to acknowledge that in the administration of his kingdom, he is a minister of God. He, who does not make his reign subservient to the divine glory, acts the part not of a king, but a robber. He, moreover, deceives himself who anticipates long prosperity to any kingdom, which is not ruled by the scepter of God—that is, by His divine word. For the heavenly oracle is infallible which has declared, "where there is no vision the people perish" (Proverbs 29:18).

Let not a contemptuous idea of our insignificance dissuade you from the investigation of this cause. We, indeed, are perfectly conscious how poor and abject we are: in the presence of God we are miserable sinners, and in the sight of men most despised—we are, if you will, the mere dregs and off—scouting of the world, or worse, if worse can be named: so that before God there remains nothing of which we can glory save only His mercy, by which, without any merit of our own, we are admitted to the hope of eternal salvation: and before men not even this much remains, since we can glory only in our infirmity, a thing which, in the estimation of men, it is the greatest ignominy even tacitly to confess. But our doctrine must stand sublime above all the glory of the world, and invincible by all its power, because it is not ours, but that of the living God and His Anointed, whom the Father has appointed King, that He may rule from sea to sea, and from the rivers even to the ends of the Earth; and so rule as to smite the whole earth and its strength of iron and brass, its splendor of gold and silver, with the mere rod of his mouth, and break them in pieces like a potter's vessel; according to the magnificent predictions of the prophets respecting his kingdom (Daniel 2:34, Isaiah 11:4, Psalm 2:9).

Our adversaries, indeed, clamorously maintain that our appeal to the word of God is a mere pretext—that we are, in fact, its worst corrupters. How far this is not only malicious calumny, but also shameless effrontery, you will be able to decide of your own knowledge by reading our Confession. Here, however, it may be necessary to make some observations which may dispose, or at least assist, you to read and study it with attention.

When Paul declared that all prophecy ought to be according to the analogy of faith (Romans 12:6), he laid down the surest rule for determining the meaning of Scripture. Let our doctrine be tested by this rule, and our victory is secure. For what accords better and more aptly with faith than to acknowledge ourselves divested of all virtue that we may be clothed by God, devoid of all goodness, that we may be filled by Him; the slaves of sin, that He may give us freedom; blind, that He may enlighten; lame, that He may cure; and feeble, that He may sustain us; to strip ourselves of all ground of glorying, that He alone may shine forth glorious, and we be glorified in Him? When these things and others to the same effect are said by us, they interpose and querulously complain, that in this way we overturn some blind light of nature, fancied preparations, free will, and works meritorious of eternal salvation, with their own supererogation also; because they cannot bear that the entire praise and glory of all goodness, virtue, justice, and wisdom should remain with God. But we read not of any having been blamed for drinking too much of the fountain of living water; on the contrary, those are severely reprimanded who "have Hewed them out cisterns, broken cisterns, that can hold no water" (Jeremiah 2:13). Again, what more agreeable to faith than to feel assured that God is a propitious Father when Christ is acknowledged as a brother and propitiator, than confidently to expect all prosperity and gladness from Him, whose ineffable love towards us was such that He "spared not his own Son, but delivered Him up for us all" (Romans 8:32), than to rest in the sure hope of salvation and eternal life whenever Christ, in whom such treasures are hid, is conceived to have been given by the Father? Here they attack us, and loudly maintain that this sure confidence is not free from arrogance and presumption. But as nothing is to be presumed of ourselves, so all things are to be presumed of God; nor are we stripped of vainglory for any other reason than that we may learn to glory in the Lord. Why go further? Take but a cursory view, most valiant King, of all the parts of our cause, and count us of all wicked men the most iniquitous, if you do not discover plainly, that "therefore we both labor and suffer reproach because we trust in the living God" (1 Timothy 4:10); because we believe it to be "life eternal" to know "the only true God, and Jesus Christ," whom He has sent (John 17:3). For this hope some of us are in bonds, some beaten with rods, some made a gazingstock, some proscribed, some most cruelly tortured, some obliged to flee; we are all pressed with straits, loaded with dire execrations, lacerated by slanders, and treated with the greatest indignity.

Look now to our adversaries (I mean the priesthood, at whose beck and pleasure others ply their enmity against us), and consider with me for a little by what zeal they are actuated. The true religion which is delivered in the Scriptures, and which all ought to hold, they readily permit both themselves and others to be ignorant of, to neglect and despise; and they deem it of little moment what each man believes concerning God and Christ, or disbelieves, provided he submits to the judgment of the Church with what they call implicit faith; nor are they greatly concerned though they should see the glory of God dishonored by open blasphemies, provided not a finger is raised against the primacy of the Apostolic See and the authority of holy mother Church. Why, then, do they war for the mass, purgatory, pilgrimage, and similar follies, with such fierceness and acerbity, that though they cannot prove one of them from the Word of God, they deny godliness can be safe without faith in these things—faith drawn out, if I may so express it, to its utmost stretch? Why? Just because their belly is their God, and their kitchen their religion, and they believe that if these were away they would not only not be Christians, but not even men. For although some wallow in luxury, and others feed on slender crusts, still they all live by the same pot, which without that fuel might not only cool, but altogether freeze. He, accordingly, who is most anxious about his stomach, proves the fiercest champion of his faith. In short, the object on which all to a man are bent, is to keep their kingdom safe or their belly filled; not one gives even the smallest sign of sincere zeal.

Nevertheless, they cease not to assail our doctrine, and to accuse and defame it in what terms they may, in order to render it either hated or suspected. They call it new, and of recent birth; they complain about it as doubtful and uncertain; they bid us tell by what miracles it has been confirmed; they ask if it be fair to receive it against the consent of so many holy Fathers and the most ancient custom; they urge us to confess either that it is schismatical in giving battle to the Church, or that the Church must have been without life during the many centuries in which nothing of the kind was heard. Lastly, they say there is little need of argument, for its quality may be known by its fruits: namely, the large number of sects, the many seditious disturbances, and the great licentiousness, which it has produced. No doubt, it is a very easy matter for them, in presence of an ignorant and credulous multitude, to insult over an undefended cause; but were an opportunity of mutual discussion afforded, that acrimony which they now pour out upon us in frothy torrents, with as much license as impunity, would assuredly boil dry.

1 First, in calling it new, they are exceedingly injurious to God, whose sacred Word deserved not to be charged with novelty. To them, indeed, I very little doubt it is new, as Christ is new, and the Gospel new; but those who are acquainted with the old saying of Paul, that Christ Jesus "died for our sins, and rose again for our justification" (Romans 4:25), will not detect any novelty in us. That it long lay buried and unknown is the guilty consequence of man's impiety; but now when, by the kindness of God, it is restored to us, it ought to resume its antiquity just as the returning citizen resumes his rights.

2 It is owing to the same ignorance that they hold it to be doubtful and uncertain; for this is the very thing of which the Lord complains by his prophet, "The ox knoweth his owner, and the ass his master's crib; but Israel doth not know, my people doth not consider" (Isaiah 1:3). But however they may sport with its uncertainty, had they to seal their own doctrine with their blood, and at the expense of life, it would be seen what value they put upon it. Very different is our confidence—a confidence that is not appalled by the terrors of death, and therefore not even by the judgment seat of God.

3 In demanding miracles from us, they act dishonestly. For we have not coined some new gospel, but retain the very one the truth of which is confirmed by all the miracles which Christ and the apostles ever wrought. But they have a peculiarity, which we have not—they can confirm their faith by constant miracles down to the present day! Way rather, they allege miracles, which might produce wavering in minds otherwise well disposed; they are so frivolous and ridiculous, so vain and false. But were they even exceedingly wonderful, they could have no effect against the truth of God, whose name ought to be hallowed always, and everywhere, whether by miracles, or by the natural course of events. The deception would

perhaps be more specious if Scripture did not admonish us of the legitimate end and use of miracles. Mark tells us (Mark 16:20) that the signs which followed the preaching of the apostles were wrought in confirmation of it; so Luke also relates that the Lord "gave testimony to the word of his grace, and granted signs and wonders to be done" by the hands of the apostles (Acts 14:3). Very much to the same effect are those words of the apostle, that salvation by a preached gospel was confirmed, "The Lord bearing witness with signs and wonders, and with divers miracles" (Hebrews 2:4). Those things that we are told are seals of the gospel, shall we pervert to the subversion of the gospel? What was destined only to confirm the truth, shall we misapply to the confirmation of lies? The proper course, therefore, is, in the first instance, to ascertain and examine the doctrine, which is said by the Evangelist to precede; then after it, has been proved, but not until then, it may receive confirmation from miracles. But the mark of sound doctrine given by our Savior himself is its tendency to promote the glory not of men, but of God (John 7:18, 8:50). Our Savior having declared this to be test of doctrine, we are in error if we regard as miraculous, works, which are used for any other purpose than to magnify the name of God. And it becomes us to remember that Satan has his miracles, which, although they are tricks rather than true wonders, are still such as to delude the ignorant and unwary. Magicians and enchanters have always been famous for miracles, and miracles of an astonishing description have given support to idolatry: these, however, do not make us converts to the superstitions either of magicians or idolaters. In old times, too, the Donatists used their power of working miracles as a battering ram, with which they shook the simplicity of the common people. We now give to our opponents the answer, which Augustine then gave to the Donatists, "The Lord put us on our guard against those wonder—workers, when he foretold that false prophets would arise, who, by lying signs and divers wonders, would, if it were possible, deceive the very elect" (Matthew 24:24). Paul, too, gave warning that the reign of antichrist would be "with all power, and signs, and lying wonders" (2 Thessalonians 2:9).

But our opponents tell us that their miracles are wrought not by idols, not by sorcerers, not by false prophets, but by saints: as if we did not know it to be one of Satan's wiles to transform himself "into an angel of light" (2 Corinthians 11:14). The Egyptians, in whose neighborhood Jeremiah was buried, anciently sacrificed and paid other divine honors to him. Did they not make an idolatrous abuse of the holy prophet of God? And yet, in recompense for so venerating his tomb, they thought that they were cured of the bite of serpents. What, then, shall we say but that it has been, and always will be, a most just punishment of God, to send on those who do not receive the truth in the love of it, "strong delusion, that they should believe a lie?" (2 Thessalonians 2:11). We, then, have no lack of miracles, sure miracles, that cannot be questioned; but those to which our opponents lay claim are mere delusions of Satan, inasmuch as they draw off the people from the true worship of God to vanity.

4 It is slanderous to represent us as opposed to the Fathers (I mean the ancient writers of a purer age), as if the Fathers were supporters of their impiety. Were the contest to be decided by such authority (to speak in the most moderate terms), the better part of the victory would be ours. While there is much that is admirable and wise in the writings of those Fathers, and while in some things it has fared with them as with ordinary men; these pious sons, truth, with the peculiar acuteness of intellect, and judgment, and soul, which belongs to them, adore only their slips and errors, while those things which are well said they either overlook, or disguise, or corrupt; so that it may be truly said their only care has been to gather dross among gold. Then, with dishonest clamor, they assail us as enemies and despisers of the Fathers. So far are we from despising them, that if this were the proper place, it would give us no trouble to support the greater part of the doctrines, which we now hold by their suffrages. Still, in studying their writings, we have endeavored to remember (1 Corinthians 3:21-23), that all things are ours, to serve, not lord it over us, but that we boast Christ's only, and must obey him in all things without exception. He who does not draw this distinction will not have any fixed principles in religion; for those holy men were ignorant of many things, are often opposed to each other, and are sometimes at variance with themselves.

It is not without cause (remark our opponents) we are thus warned by Solomon, "Remove not the ancient landmarks which thy fathers have set" (Proverbs 22:28). But the same rule applies not to the measuring of fields and the obedience of faith. The rule applicable to the latter is, "Forget also thine own people, and thy father's house" (Psalm 45:10). But if they are so fond of allegory, why do they not understand the apostles, rather than any other class of Fathers, to be meant by those whose landmarks it is unlawful to remove? This is the interpretation of Jerome, whose words they have quoted in their canons. But as regards those to whom they apply the passage, if they wish the landmarks to be fixed, why do they, whenever it suits their purpose, so freely overleap them?

Among the Fathers there were two, the one of whom said, "Our God neither eats nor drinks, and therefore has no need of chalices and salvers;" and the other, "Sacred rites do not require gold, and things which are not bought with gold, please not by gold." They step beyond the boundary; therefore, when in sacred matters they are so much delighted with gold, driver, ivory, marble, gems, and silks, that unless everything is overlaid with costly show, or rather insane luxury, they think God is not duly worshipped.

It was a Father, who said, "He ate flesh freely on the day on which others abstained from it, because he was a Christian." They overleap the boundaries, therefore, when they doom to perdition every soul that, during Lent, shall have tasted flesh.

There were two Fathers, the one of whom said, "A monk not laboring with his own hands is no better than a violent man and a robber;" and the other, "Monks, however assiduous they may be in study, meditation, and prayer, must not live by others." This boundary, too, they transgressed, when they placed lazy gormandizing monks in dens and stews, to gorge themselves on other men's substance.

It was a Father, who said, "It is a horrid abomination to see in Christian temples a painted image either of Christ or of any saint." Nor was this pronounced by the voice era single individual; but an Ecclesiastical Council also decreed, "Let nothing that is worshipped be depicted on walls." Very far are they from keeping within these boundaries when they leave not a corner without images.

Another Father counseled, "That after performing the office of humanity to the dead in their burial, we should leave them at rest." These limits they burst through when they keep up a perpetual anxiety about the dead.

It is a Father, who testified, "That the substance of bread and wine in the Eucharist does not cease but remains, just as the nature and substance of man remains united to the Godhead in the Lord Jesus Christ." This boundary they pass in pretending that, as soon as the words of our Lord are pronounced, the substance of bread and wine ceases and is transubstantiated into body and blood.

They were Fathers, who, as they exhibited only one Eucharist to the whole Church, and kept back from it the profane and flagitious; so they, in the severest terms, censured all those who, being present, did not communicate. How far have they removed these landmarks, in filling not churches only, but also private houses, with their masses, admitting all and sundry to be present, each the more willingly the more largely he pays, however wicked and impure he may be—not inviting anyone to faith in Christ and faithful communion in the sacraments, but rather vending their own work for the grace and merits of Christ!

There were two Fathers, the one of whom decided that those were to be excluded altogether from partaking of Christ's sacred supper, who, contented with communion in one kind, abstained from the other; while the other Father strongly contends that the blood of the Lord ought not to be denied to the Christian people, who, in confessing him, are enjoined to shed their own blood. These landmarks, also, they removed, when, by an unalterable law, they ordered the very thing, which the former Father punished with excommunication, and the latter condemned for a valid reason.

It was a Father, who pronounced it rashness in an obscure question, to decide in either way without clear and evident authority from Scripture. They forgot this landmark when they enacted so many constitutions, so many canons, and so many dogmatic decisions, without sanction from the Word of God.

It was a Father, who reproved Montanus, among other heresies, for being the first who imposed laws of fasting. They have gone far beyond this landmark also in enjoining fasting under the strictest laws.

It was a Father, who denied that the ministers of the Church should be prohibited from marrying, and pronounced married life to be a state of chastity; and there were other Fathers, who assented to his decision. These boundaries they overstepped in rigidly binding their priests to celibacy.

It was a Father who thought that Christ only should be listened to, from its being said, "Hear him," and that regard is due not to what others before us have said or done, but only to what Christ, the head of all, has commanded. This landmark they neither observe themselves nor allow to be observed by others, while they subject themselves and others to any master whatever, rather than Christ.

There is a Father, who contends that the Church ought not to prefer herself to Christ, who always judges truly, whereas ecclesiastical judges, who are but men, are generally deceived. Having burst through this barrier also, they hesitate not to suspend the whole authority of Scripture on the judgment of the Church.

All the Fathers with one heart execrated, and with one mouth protested against, contaminating the Word of God with subtleties of sophists, and involving it in the brawls of dialecticians. Do they keep within these limits when the sole occupation of their lives is to entwine and entangle the simplicity of Scripture with endless disputes, and worse than sophistical jargon? So much so, that were the Fathers to rise from their graves, and listen to the brawling art which bears the name of speculative theology, there is nothing they would suppose it less to be than a discussion of a religious nature.

But my discourse would far exceed its just limits were I to show, in detail, how petulantly those men shake off the yoke of the Fathers, while they wish to be thought their most obedient sons. Months, nay, years would fail me; and yet so deplorable and desperate is their effrontery, that they presume to chastise us for overstepping the ancient landmarks!

5 Then, again, it is to no purpose they call us to the bar of custom. To make everything yield to custom would be to do the greatest injustice. Were the judgments of mankind correct, custom would be

regulated by the good. But it is often far otherwise in point of fact; for, whatever the many are seen to do, forthwith obtains the force of custom. But human affairs have scarcely ever been so happily constituted as that the better course pleased the greater number. Hence, the private vices of the multitude have generally resulted in public error, or rather that common consent in vice which these worthy men would have to be law. Anyone with eyes may perceive that it is not one flood of evils, which has deluged us; that many fatal plagues have invaded the globe; that all things rush headlong; so that either the affairs of men must be altogether despaired of, or we must not only resist, but boldly attack prevailing evils. The cure is prevented by no other cause than the length of time during which we have been accustomed to the disease. But be it so that public error must have a place in human society, still, in the Kingdom of God, we must look and listen only to His eternal truth, against which no series of years, no custom, no conspiracy, can plead prescription. Thus Isaiah formerly taught the people of God, "Say ye not, A confederacy, to all to whom this people shall say, A confederacy;" i.e. do not unite with the people in an impious consent; "neither fear ye their fear, nor be afraid. Sanctify the Lord of hosts himself; and let him be your fear, and let him be your dread" (Isaiah 8:12). Now, therefore, let them, if they will, object to us both past ages and present examples; if we sanctify the Lord of hosts, we shall not be greatly afraid. Though many ages should have consented to like ungodliness, He is strong who taketh vengeance to the third and fourth generation; or the whole world should league together in the same iniquity. He taught experimentally what the end is of those who sin with the multitude, when He destroyed the whole human race with a flood, saving Noah with his little family, who, by putting his faith in Him alone, "condemned the world" (Hebrews 11:7). In short, depraved custom is just a kind of general pestilence in which men perish not the less that they fall in a crowd. It would be well, moreover, to ponder the observation of Cyprian: that those who sin in ignorance, though they cannot be entirely exculpated, seem, however, to be, in some sense, excusable; whereas those who obstinately reject the truth, when presented to them by the kindness of God, have no defense to offer.

6 Their dilemma does not push us so violently as to oblige us to confess, either that the Church was a considerable time without life, or that we have now a quarrel with the Church. The Church of Christ assuredly has lived, and will live, as long as Christ shall reign at the right hand of the Father. By His hand it is sustained, by His protection defended, by His mighty power preserved in safety. For what He once undertook He will undoubtedly perform, He will be with iris people always, "even to the end of the world" (Matthew 28:20). With the Church we wage no war, since, with one consent, in common with the whole body of the faithful, we worship and adore one God, and Christ Jesus the Lord, as all the pious have always adored Him. But they themselves err not a little from the truth in not recognizing any church but that which they behold with the bodily eye, and in endeavoring to circumscribe it by limits, within which it cannot be confined.

The hinges on which the controversy turns are these: first, in their contending that the form of the Church is always visible and apparent; and, secondly, in their placing this form in the see of the Church of Rome and its hierarchy. We, on the contrary, maintain, both that the Church may exist without any apparent form, and, moreover, that the form is not ascertained by that external splendor which they foolishly admire, but by a very different mark, namely, by the pure preaching of the Word of God, and the due administration of the sacraments. They make an outcry whenever the Church cannot be pointed to with the finger. But how oft was it the fate of the Church among the Jews to be so defaced that no comeliness appeared? What do we suppose to have been the splendid form when Elijah complained that he was left alone? (1 Kings 19:14). How long after the advent of Christ, did it lie hid without form? How often since has it been so oppressed by wars, seditions, and heresies, that it was nowhere seen in splendor? Had they lived at that time, would they have believed there was any Church? But Elijah learned that there remained seven thousand men, who had not bowed the knee to Baal; nor ought we to doubt that Christ has always reigned on Earth ever since he ascended to Heaven. Had the faithful at that time required some discernible form, must they not have forthwith given way to despondency? And, indeed, Hilary accounted it a very great fault in his day that men were so possessed with a foolish admiration of Episcopal dignity as not to perceive the deadly hydra lurking under that mask. His words are, "One advice I give: Beware of Antichrist; for, unhappily, a love of walls has seized you; unhappily, the Church of God which you venerate exists in houses and buildings; unhappily, under these you find the name of peace. Is it doubtful that in these Antichrist will have his seat? Safer to me are mountains, and woods, and lakes, and dungeons, and whirlpools; since in these prophets, dwelling or immersed, did prophesy."

And what is it at the present day that the world venerates in its horned bishops, unless that it imagines those who are seen presiding over celebrated cities to be holy prelates of religion? Away, then, with this absurd mode of judging! Let us rather reverently admit that, as God alone knows who are His, so He may sometimes withdraw the external manifestation of His Church from the view of men. This, I allow, is a fearful punishment, which God sends on the Earth; but if the wickedness of men so deserves, why do we strive to oppose the just vengeance of God? It was thus that God, in past ages, punished the ingratitude of men; for after they had refused to obey His truth, and had extinguished his light, He allowed them, when blinded by sense, both to be deluded by lying vanities and plunged in thick darkness, so that no face of a true Church appeared. Meanwhile, however, though His own people were dispersed and concealed amidst errors and darkness, He saved them from destruction. No wonder; for He knew how to preserve them even in the confusion of Babylon and the flame of the fiery furnace.

But as to the wish that the form of the Church should be ascertained by some kind of vain pomp, how perilous it is I will briefly indicate, rather than explain, that I may not exceed all bounds. What they say is, that the Pontiff, who holds the Apostolic See, and the priests who are anointed and consecrated by him, provided they have the insignia of fillets and miters, represent the Church, and ought to be considered as in the place of the Church, and therefore cannot err. Why so? Because they are pastors of the Church, and consecrated to the Lord. And were not Aaron and other prefects of Israel pastors? But Aaron and his sons, though already set apart to the priesthood, erred notwithstanding when they made the calf (Exodus 32:4). Why, according to this view, should not the four hundred prophets who lied to Ahab represent the Church? (1 Kings 22:11), etc.). The Church, however, stood on the side of Micaiah. He was alone, indeed, and despised, but from his mouth, the truth proceeded. Did not the prophets also exhibit both the name and face of the Church, when, with one accord, they rose up against Jeremiah, and with menaces boasted of it as a thing impossible that the law should perish from the priest, or counsel from the wise, or the word from the prophet? (Jeremiah 19:18). In opposition to the whole body of the prophets, Jeremiah is sent alone to declare from the Lord (Jeremiah 4:9), that a time would come when the law would perish from the priest, counsel from the wise, and the word from the prophet. Was not like splendor displayed in that council when the chief priests, scribes, and Pharisees assembled to consult how they might put Jesus to death? Let them go, then, and cling to the external mask, while they make Christ and all the prophets of God schismatics, and, on the other hand, make Satan's ministers the organs of the Holy Spirit!

But if they are sincere, let them answer me in good faith, —in what place, and among whom, do they think the Church resided, after the Council of Basle degraded and deposed Eugenius from the popedom, and substituted Amadeus in his place? Do their utmost, they cannot deny that that Council was legitimate as far as regards external forms, and was summoned not only by one Pontiff, but by two. Eugenius, with the whole herd of cardinals and bishops who had joined him in plotting the dissolution of the Council, was there condemned of contumacy, rebellion, and schism. Afterwards, however, aided by the favor of princes, he got back his popedom safe. The election of Amadeus, duly made by the authority of a general holy synod, went to smoke; only he himself was appeased with a cardinal's cap, like a piece of offal thrown to a barking dog. Out of the lap of these rebellious and contumacious schismatics proceeded all future popes, cardinals, bishops, abbots, and presbyters. Here they are caught, and cannot escape. For, on which party will they bestow the name of Church? Will they deny it to have been a general Council, though it lacked nothing as regards external majesty, having been solemnly called by two bulls, consecrated by the legate of the Roman See as its president, constituted regularly in all respects, and continuing in possession of all its honors to the last? Will they admit that Eugenius, and his whole train, through whom they have all been consecrated, were schismatic? Let them, then, either define the form of the Church differently, or, however numerous they are, we will hold them all to be schismatics in having knowingly and willingly received ordination from heretics. But had it never been discovered before that the Church is not tied to external pomp, we are furnished with a lengthened proof in their own conduct, in proudly vending themselves to the world under the specious title of Church, notwithstanding that they are the deadly pests of the Church. I speak not of their manners and of those tragic atrocities with which their whole life teems, since it is said that they are Pharisees who should be heard, not imitated. By devoting some portion of your leisure to our writings, you will see, not obscurely, that their doctrine—the very doctrine to which they say it is owing that they are the Church—is a deadly murderer of souls, the firebrand, ruin, and destruction of the Church.

7 Lastly, they are far from candid when they invidiously number up the disturbances, tumults, and disputes, which the preaching of our doctrine has brought in its train, and the fruits which, in many instances, it now produces; for the doctrine itself is undeservedly charged with evils which ought to be ascribed to the malice of Satan. It is one of the characteristics of the divine Word, that whenever it appears, Satan ceases to slumber and sleep. This is the surest and most unerring test for distinguishing it from false doctrines, which readily betray themselves, while they are received by all with willing ears, and welcomed by an applauding world. Accordingly, for several ages, during which all things were immersed in profound darkness, almost all mankind were mere jest and sport to the god of this world, who, like any Sardanapalus, idled and luxuriated undisturbed. For what else could he do but laugh and sport while in tranquil and undisputed possession of his kingdom? But when light beaming from above somewhat dissipated the darkness—when the strong man arose and aimed a blow at his kingdom—then, indeed, he began to shake off his wonted torpor, and rush to arms. And first he stirred up the hands of men, that by them he might violently suppress the dawning

truth; but when this availed him not, he turned to snares, exciting dissensions and disputes about doctrine by means of his Catabaptists, and other portentous miscreants, that he might thus obscure, and, at length, extinguish the truth. And now he persists in assailing it with both engines, endeavoring to pluck up the true seed by the violent hand of man, and striving, as much as in him lies, to choke it with his tares, that it may not grow and bear knit. But it will be in vain, if we listen to the admonition of the Lord, who long ago disclosed his wiles, that we might not be taken unawares, and armed us with full protection against all his machinations. But how malignant to throw upon the Word of God itself the blame either of the seditions which wicked men and rebels, or of the sects which impostors stir up against it! The example, however, is not new. Elijah was asked if it had been he, who troubled Israel. Christ was seditious, according to the Jews; and the apostles were charged with the crime of popular commotion. What else do those who, in the present day, impute to us all the disturbances, tumults, and contentions, which break out against us? Elijah, however, has taught us our answer (1 Kings 18:17, 18). It is not we who disseminate errors or stir up tumults, but they who resist the mighty power of God.

But while this single answer is sufficient to rebut the rash charges of these men, it is necessary, on the other hand, to consult for the weakness of those who take the alarm at such scandals, and not infrequently waver in perplexity. But that they may not fall away in this perplexity, and forfeit their good degree, let them know that the apostles in their day experienced the very things, which now befall us. There were then unlearned and unstable men who, as Peter tells us (2 Peter 3:16), wrested the inspired writings of Paul to their own destruction. There were despisers of God, who, when they heard that sin abounded in order that grace might more abound, immediately inferred, "We will continue in sin that grace may abound" (Romans 6:1); when they heard that believers were not under the law, but under grace, forthwith sung out, "We will sin because we are not under the law, but under grace" (Romans 6:15). There were some who charged the apostle with being the minister of sin. Many false prophets entered in privately to pull down the churches, which he had reared. Some preached the gospel through envy and strife, not sincerely (Philippians

1:15)—maliciously even—thinking to add affliction to his bonds. Elsewhere the gospel made little progress. All sought their own, not the things which were Jesus Christ's. Others went back like the dog to his vomit, or the sow that was washed to her wallowing in the mire. Great numbers perverted their spiritual freedom to carnal licentiousness. False brethren crept in to the imminent danger of the faithful. Among the brethren themselves various quarrels arose. What, then, were the apostles to do? Were they either to dissemble for the time, or rather lay aside and abandon that gospel which they saw to be the seedbed of so many strifes, the source of so many perils, the occasion of so many scandals? In straits of this kind, they remembered that "Christ was a stone of stumbling, and a rock of offense," "set up for the fall and rising again of many," and "for a sign to be spoken against" (Luke 2:34); and, armed with this assurance, they proceeded boldly through all perils from tumults and scandals. It becomes us to be supported by the same consideration, since Paul declares that it is a never failing characteristic of the gospel to be a "savor of death unto death in them that perish" (2 Corinthians 2:16), although rather destined to us for the purpose of being a savor of life unto life, and the power of God for the salvation of believers. This we should certainly experience it to be, did we not by our ingratitude corrupt this unspeakable gift of God, and turn to our destruction what ought to be our only saving defense.

But to return, Sire. Be not moved by the absurd insinuations with which our adversaries are striving to frighten you into the belief that nothing else is wished and aimed at by this new gospel (for so they term it), than opportunity for sedition and impunity for all kinds of vice. Our God is not the author of division, but of peace; and the Son of God, who came to destroy the works of the devil, is not the minister of sin. We, too, are undeservedly charged with desires of a kind for which we have never given even the smallest suspicion. We, forsooth, meditate the subversion of kingdoms; we, whose voice was never heard in faction, and whose life, while passed under you, is known to have been always quiet and simple; even now, when exiled from our home, we nevertheless cease not to pray for all prosperity to your person and your kingdom. We, forsooth, are aiming after an unchecked indulgence in vice, in whose manners, though there is much to be blamed, there is nothing which deserves such an imputation; nor (thank God) have we profited so little in the gospel that our life may not be to these slanderers an example of chastity, kindness, pity, temperance, patience, moderation, or any other virtue. It is plain, indeed, that we fear God sincerely, and worship Him in truth, since, whether by life or by death, we desire His name to be hallowed; and hatred herself has been forced to bear testimony to the innocence and civil integrity of some of our people on whom death was inflicted for the very thing which deserved the highest praise. But if any, under pretext of the gospel, excite tumults (none such have as yet been detected in your realm), if any use the liberty of the grace of God as a cloak for licentiousness (I know of numbers who do), there are laws and legal punishments by which they may be punished up to the measure of their deserts—only, in the mean time, let not the Gospel of God be evil spoken of because of the iniquities of evil men.

Sire, That you may not lend too credulous an ear to the accusations of our enemies, their virulent injustice has been set before you at sufficient length; I fear even more than sufficient, since this preface has grown almost to the bulk of a full apology. My object, however, was not to frame a defense, but only with a view to the hearing of our cause, to mollify your mind, now indeed turned away and estranged from us—I add, even inflamed against us—but whose good will, we are confident, we should regain, would you but once, with calmness and composure, read this our Confession, which we desire your Majesty to accept instead of a defense. But if the whispers of the malevolent so possess your ear, that the accused are to have no opportunity of pleading their cause; if those vindictive furies, with your connivance, are always to rage with bonds, scourging, torture, maiming, and burnings, we, indeed, like sheep doomed to slaughter, shall be reduced to every extremity; yet so that, in our patience, we will possess our souls, and wait for the strong hand of the Lord, which, doubtless, will appear in its own time, and show itself armed, both to rescue the poor from affliction, and also take vengeance on the despisers, who are now exulting so securely.

Most illustrious King, may the Lord, the King of kings, establish your throne in righteousness, and your scepter in equity.

Epistle to the Reader

[Prefixed to the last edition, revised by the author.]

In the First Edition of this work, having not the least expectation of the success which God, in His boundless goodness, has been pleased to give it, I had, for the greater part, performed my task in a perfunctory manner (as is usual in trivial undertakings); but when I understood that it had been received, by almost all the pious with a favor which I had never dared to ask, far less to hope for, the more I was sincerely conscious that the reception was beyond my deserts, the greater I thought my ingratitude would be, if, to the very kind wishes which had been expressed towards me, and which seemed of their own accord to invite me to diligence, I did not endeavor to respond, at least according to my humble ability. This I attempted not only in the Second Edition, but in every subsequent one the work has received some improvement. But though I do not regret the labor previously expended, I never felt satisfied until the work was arranged in the order in which it now appears. Now I trust it will approve itself to the Judgment of all my readers. As a clear proof of the diligence with which I have labored to perform this service to the Church of God, I may be permitted to mention, that last winter, when I thought I was dying of quartan ague, the more the disorder increased, the less I spared myself, in order that I might leave this book behind me, and thus make some return to the pious for their kind urgency. I could have wished to give it sooner, but it is soon enough if good enough. I shall think it has appeared in good time when I see it more productive of benefit than formerly to the Church of God. This is my only wish.

And truly it would fare ill with me if, not contented with the approbation of God alone, I were unable to despise the foolish and perverse censures of ignorant as well as the malicious and unjust censures of ungodly men. For although, by the blessing of God, my most ardent desire has been to advance his Kingdoms and promote the public good, —although I feel perfectly conscious, and take God and His angels to witness, that ever since I began to discharge the office of teacher in the Church, my only object has been to do good to the Church, by maintaining the pure doctrine of godliness, yet I believe there never was a man more assailed, stung, and torn by calumny [as well by the declared enemies of the truth of God, as by many worthless persons who have crept into His Church—as well by monks who have brought forth their frocks from their cloisters to spread infection wherever they come, as by other miscreants not better than they]. After this letter to the reader was in the press, I had undoubted information that, at Augsburg, where the Imperial Diet was held, a rumor of my defection to the papacy was circulated, and entertained in the courts of the princes more readily than might have been expected. This, forsooth, is the return made me by those who certainly are aware of numerous proofs of my constancy—proofs which, while they rebut the foul charge, ought to have defended me against it, with all humane and impartial judges. But the devil, with all his crew, is mistaken if he imagines that, by assailing me with vile falsehoods, he can either cool my zeal, or diminish my exertions. I trust that God, in His infinite goodness, will enable me to persevere with unruffled patience in the course of His holy vocation. Of this, I give the pious reader a new proof in the present edition.

I may further observe, that my object in this work has been, so to prepare and train candidates for the sacred office, for the study of the sacred volume, that they may both have an easy introduction to it, and be able to prosecute it with unfaltering step; for, if I mistake not, I have given a summary of religion in all its parts, and digested it in an order which will make it easy for anyone, who rightly comprehends it, to ascertain both what he ought chiefly to look for in Scripture, and also to what head he ought to refer whatever is contained in it. Having thus paved the way, as it will be unnecessary, in any Commentaries on Scripture which I may afterwards publish, to enter into long discussions of doctrinal points, and enlarge on commonplaces, I will compress them into narrow compass. In this way much trouble and fatigue will be spared to the pious reader, provided he comes prepared with a knowledge of the present work as an indispensable prerequisite. The system here followed being set forth as in a mirror in all my Commentaries, I think it better to let it speak for itself than to give any verbal explanation of it.

Farewell, kind reader: if you derive any benefit from my labors, aid me with your prayers to our heavenly Father.

Geneva, 1*st August* 1559.

The zeal of those whose cause I undertook,
Has swelled a short defense into a book.

"I profess to be one of those who, by profiting, write, and by writing profit." —*Augustine*, Epist. 7.

The Reverend Dr. Wisner, in his late discourse at Plymouth, on the anniversary of the landing of the Pilgrims, made the following assertion:

"Much as the name of Calvin has been scoffed at and loaded with reproach by many sons of freedom, there is not an historical proposition more susceptible of complete demonstration than this, that no man has lived to whom the world is under greater obligations for the freedom it now enjoys, than John Calvin."

✣

An Account of the Life of John Clavin

by John Foxe

excerpted from *The Foxe's Book of Martyrs*

The reformer John Calvin was born in France at Noyon in Picardy, July 10, 1509. He was instructed in grammar in Paris under Maturinus Corderius, and studied philosophy in the College of Montaign under a Spanish professor.

Young John's father noticed his son's marks of early piety (particularly in His reprehensions of the vices of his companions), reared him for the church, and got him presented on May 21, 1521, to the chapel of Notre Dame de la Gesine in the Church of Noyon. In 1527, John was presented to the rectory of Marseville, which he exchanged in 1529 for the rectory of Point l'Eveque near Noyon. His father afterward changed his resolution and would have him study law. John readily consented. By that time, through reading the Scriptures, he had grown to dislike the superstitions of popery. He gladly resigned the chapel in 1534. He made a great progress in law, and improved no less in the knowledge of divinity by his private studies. At Bourges he studied Greek under the direction of Professor Wolmar.

His father's death called him back to Noyon, where he stayed only a short time before he ventured on to Paris. It was there that he furnished materials for a speech delivered by Nicholas Cop, rector of the University of Paris. The speech greatly displeased the Sorbonne and the parliament, and gave rise to a persecution against the Protestants in general and Calvin in particular. He narrowly escaped being taken in the College of Forteret, and was forced to flee to Xaintonge after having had the honor of being introduced to the queen of Navarre, who had raised this first storm against the Protestants.

Calvin returned to Paris in 1534. This year the reformed met with severe treatment. He determined that he would have to leave France, particularly after publishing a treatise against those who believed that departed souls are in a kind of sleep. He retired to Basel, where he studied Hebrew: at this time he published his *Institutions of the Christian Religion*; a work well adapted to spread his fame, though he himself was desirous of living in obscurity. It is dedicated to the French king, Francis I.

Calvin next wrote an apology for the Protestants who were burned for their religion in France. After the publication of this work, Calvin went to Italy to pay a visit to the duchess of Ferrara, a lady of eminent piety, by whom he was very kindly received.

From Italy he returned to France, and having settled his private affairs, proposed to go to Strassburg or Basel with his sole surviving brother, Antony Calvin. The roads were not safe because of the war. The exception was a road that ran through the duke of Savoy's territories. The Calvin brothers chose that road. "This was a particular direction of Providence," says Bayle, "It was his destiny that he should settle at Geneva, and when he was wholly intent upon going farther, he found himself detained by an order from Heaven, if I may so speak."

At Geneva, Calvin therefore was obliged to comply with the choice, which the consistory and magistrates made of him, with the consent of the people: to be one of their ministers and a professor of divinity. He wanted to serve only as a professor of divinity, but in the end he was obliged to take both offices upon him in August 1536. The year following, he made all the people declare, upon oath, their assent to the confession of faith, which contained a renunciation of popery. He next intimated that he could not submit to a regulation, that the canton of Berne had made. The syndics of Geneva summoned an assembly of the people, and it was ordered that Calvin, Farel, and another minister should leave the town in a few days for refusing to administer the Sacrament.

Calvin retired to Strassburg and established a French church in that city, of which he was the first minister. He was also appointed to be professor of divinity there. Meanwhile the people of Geneva entreated him so earnestly to return to them that at last he consented, and arrived September 13, 1541, to the great satisfaction both of the people and the magistrates. The first thing he did after his arrival was to establish a form of church discipline, and a consistorial jurisdiction, invested with power of inflicting censures and canonical punishments, as far as excommunication, inclusively.

It has long been the delight of both infidels and some professed Christians, when they wish to bring odium upon the opinions of Calvin, to refer to his participation in the death of Michael Servetus. Those who are unable to overthrow his opinions use this as a conclusive argument against his whole system. A certain class of reasoners use, "Calvin burned Servetus! Calvin burned Servetus!" as good proof that the doctrine of the Trinity is not true, that divine sovereignty is against Scripture, and that Christianity a cheat.

We have no wish to palliate any act of Calvin's, which is manifestly wrong. All his proceedings in relation to the unhappy affair of Servetus, we think, cannot be defended. Still it should be remembered that the true principles of religious toleration were very little understood in the time of Calvin. All the other reformers then living approved of Calvin's conduct. Even the gentle and amiable Melancthon expressed himself in relation to this affair in the following manner. In a letter addressed to Bullinger, he says, "I have read your statement respecting the blasphemy of Servetus, and praise your piety and judgment; and am persuaded that the Council of Geneva has done right in putting to death this obstinate man, who would never have ceased his blasphemies. I am astonished that any one can be found to disapprove of this proceeding." Farel expressly says, "Servetus deserved a capital punishment." Bucer did not hesitate to declare, "Servetus deserved something worse than death."

The truth is, although Calvin had some hand in the arrest and imprisonment of Servetus, he was unwilling that he should be burned at all. "I desire," said he, "that the severity of the punishment should be remitted.... We endeavored to commute the kind of death, but in vain."

"By wishing to mitigate the severity of the punishment," said Farel to Calvin, "you discharge the office of a friend towards your greatest enemy."

"That Calvin was the instigator of the magistrates that Servetus might be burned," says Turritine, "historians neither anywhere affirm, nor does it appear from any considerations. Nay, it is certain, that he, with the college of pastors, dissuaded from that kind of punishment."

It has been often asserted that Calvin possessed so much influence with the magistrates of Geneva that he might have obtained the release of Servetus had he not wanted his destruction. This, however, is not true. So far from it, that Calvin was himself once banished from Geneva by these very magistrates and often opposed their arbitrary measures in vain. Calvin was so against the death of Servetus that he warned him of his danger, and suffered him to remain several weeks at Geneva before he was arrested. But his language, which was then accounted blasphemous, was the cause of his imprisonment. When in prison, Calvin visited him and used every argument to persuade him to retract his horrible blasphemies without reference to his peculiar sentiments. This was the extent of Calvin's agency in this unhappy affair.

It cannot, however, be denied that in this instance, Calvin acted contrary to the kind and gracious spirit of the Gospel. It is better to drop a tear over the inconsistency of human nature and to bewail those infirmities that cannot be justified. He declared that he acted conscientiously, and publicly justified the act.

It was the opinion, that erroneous religious principles are punishable by the civil magistrate that did the mischief, whether at Geneva, in Transylvania, or in Britain. To this, rather than to Trinitarianism or Unitarianism, it ought to be imputed.

After the death of Luther, Calvin exerted great sway over the men of that notable period. He was influential in France, Italy, Germany, Holland, England, and Scotland. Two thousand one hundred and fifty reformed congregations were organized, receiving from him their preachers.

Calvin, triumphant over all his enemies, felt his death drawing near. Yet he continued to exert himself in every way with youthful energy. When about to lie down in rest, he drew up his will, saying:

> I do testify that I live and purpose to die in this faith which God has given me through His Gospel, and that I have no other dependence for salvation than the free choice which is made of me by Him. With my whole heart I embrace His mercy, through which all my sins are covered, for Christ's sake, and for the sake of His death and sufferings. According to the measure of grace granted unto me, I have taught this pure, simple Word by sermons, by deeds, and by expositions of this Scripture. In all my battles with the enemies of the truth I have not used sophistry, but have fought the good fight squarely and directly.

May 27, 1564, was the day of his release and blessed journey home. He was in his fifty-fifth year.

That a man who had acquired so great a reputation and such an authority should have had but a salary of one hundred crowns, and refuse to accept more; and after living fifty-five years with the utmost frugality should leave but three hundred crowns to his heirs, including the value of his library, which sold very dear, is something so heroic, that one must have lost all feeling not to admire.

When Calvin took his leave of Strassburg, to return to Geneva, they wanted to continue to him the privileges of a freeman of their town, and the revenues of a prebend, which had been assigned to him; the former he accepted, but absolutely refused the other. He carried one of the brothers with him to Geneva, but he never took any pains to get him preferred to an honorable post, as any other possessed of his credit would have done. He took care indeed of the honor of his brother's family, by getting him freed from an adulteress, and obtaining leave to him to marry again; but even his enemies relate that he made him learn the trade of a bookbinder, which he followed all his life after.

John Calvin was buried in the cemetery of Plain Palais, and at his own request, no monument was set up to mark his grave. The exact spot is unknown to this day.

Other historians and biographers offer personal insight into John Calvin, the man.

ERNEST RENAN, educated for the Romish priesthood, but later a skeptic, pays this striking tribute to Calvin's character:

> Calvin was one of those absolute men, cast complete in one mold, who is taken in wholly at a single glance: one letter, one action, suffices for a judgment of him. There were no folds in that inflexible soul, which never knew doubt or hesitation. Careless of wealth, of titles, of honors, indifferent to pomp, modest in his life, transparently humble, sacrificing everything to the desire of making others like himself, I hardly know of a man, save Ignatius Loyola, who could match him.... Lacking that vivid, deep, sympathetic ardor which was one of the secrets of Luther's success, lacking the charm, the languishing tenderness of Francis of Sales, Calvin succeeded, in an age and in a country which called for a reaction towards Christianity, simply because he was the most Christian man of his generation.

GUIZOT, the French historian, concludes his biography:

> Calvin is great by reason of his marvelous powers, his enduring labors, and the moral height and purity of his character. Earnest in faith, pure in motive, austere in his life, and mighty in his works, Calvin is one of those who deserve their great fame. Three centuries separate us from him, but it is impossible to examine his character and history without feeling, if not affection and sympathy, at least profound respect and admiration for one of the great Reformers of Europe and one of the great Christians of France.

THEODORE BEZA, Calvin's close friend, confidante, and successor, offers an intimate look at a beloved man:

> Calvin was not of large stature: his complexion was pale, and rather brown: even to his last moments his eyes were peculiarly bright, and indicative of his penetrating genius. He knew nothing of luxury in his outward life, but was fond

of the greatest neatness, as became his thorough simplicity. His manner of living was so arranged that he showed himself equally averse to extravagance and meanness. He took so little nourishment, such being the weakness of his stomach, that for many years he contented himself with one meal a day. Of sleep he had almost none. His memory was incredible; he immediately recognized, after many years, those whom he had once seen; and when he had been interrupted for several hours, in some work about which he was employed, he could immediately resume and continue it, without reading again what he had written. Of the numerous details connected with the business of his office, he never forgot even the most trifling, and this notwithstanding the multitude of his affairs.

His judgment was so acute and correct in regard to the most opposite concerns about which his advice was asked, that he often seemed to possess the gift of looking into the future. I never remember to have heard that anyone who followed his counsel went wrong. He despised fine speaking, and was rather abrupt in his language; but he wrote admirably, and no theologian of his time expressed himself so clearly, so impressively and acutely as he; and yet he labored as much as any one of his contemporaries, or of the fathers. For this fluency he was indebted to the several studies of his youth, and to the natural acuteness of his genius, which had been still further increased by the practice of dictation, so that proper and dignified expressions never failed him, whether he was writing or speaking. He never, in any wise, altered the doctrine, which he first adopted, but remained true to it to the last.

Although nature had endowed Calvin with a dignified seriousness, both in manner and character, no one was more agreeable than he in ordinary conversation. He could bear, in a wonderful manner, with the failings of others, when they sprang from mere weakness. Thus he never shamed anyone by ill-timed reproofs, or discouraged a weak brother; while, on the other hand, he never spared or overlooked willful sin. An enemy to all flattery, he hated dissimulation, especially every dishonest sentiment in reference to religion. He was therefore as powerful and strong an enemy to vices of this kind as he was a devoted friend to truth, simplicity and uprightness. His temperament was naturally choleric, and his active public life had tended greatly to increase this failing; but the Spirit of God had so taught him to moderate his anger, that no word ever escaped him unworthy of a righteous man. Still less did he ever commit aught unjust towards others. It was then only, indeed, when the question concerned religion, and when he had to contend against hardened sinners, that he allowed himself to be moved and excited beyond the bounds of moderation.

Let us take but a single glance at the history of those men who, in any part of the world, have been distinguished for their virtues, and no one will be surprised at finding that the great and noble qualities which Calvin exhibited, both in his private and public life, excited against him a host of enemies. We ought not indeed to feel any wonder that so powerful a champion of pure doctrine, and so stern a teacher of sound morals, as well at home as in the world, should be so fiercely assailed. Rather ought we to let our admiration dwell on the fact that, standing alone as he did, he was sufficiently mighty to avail himself of that strongest of weapons, the Word of God. Thus, however numerous the adversaries, whom Satan roused against him (for he never had any but such as had declared war against piety and virtue), the Lord gave His servant sufficient strength to gain the victory over all.

Having been for sixteen years a witness of his labors, I have pursued the history of his life and death with all fidelity; and I now unhesitatingly testify that every true Christian may find in this man the noble pattern of a truly Christian life and Christian death; a pattern, however, which it is as easy to calumniate as it would be difficult to follow.

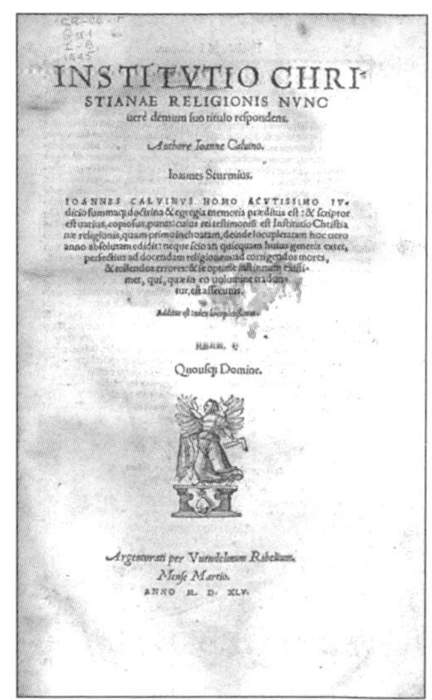

INSTITUTIO CHRISTIANAE RELIGIONIS NUNC uere demum suo titulo respondens.

Authore Ioanne Caluino.

Ioannes Sturmius.

IOANNES CALVINUS HOMO ACUTISSIMO IUdicio summaq; doctrina & egregia memoria praeditus est: & scriptor est uarius, copiosus, purus: cuius rei testimonium est Institutio Christianae religionis, quam primo inchoatam, deinde locupletatam hoc uero anno absolutam edidit: neque scio an quicquam huius generis extet, perfectius ad docendam religionem, ad corrigendos mores, & tollendos errores: & se optime institutum existimet, qui, quae in eo uolumine traduntur, est assecutus.

Additus est index locupletissimus.

[illegible]

Quousq; Domine.

Argentorati per Vuendelinum Rihelium.
Mense Martio.
ANNO M. D. XLV.

John Calvin's Magnum Opus: The Institutes of the Christian Religion

Various depictions of John Calvin

St. Peter's Church in Geneva.

John Calvin preaching at St. Peter's Church in Geneva.

Left: Theodore Beza, Calvin's close friend, and confidante
Middle: Michael Servetus and John Calvin debating before the Council of Geneva.
Below: Calvin's friend, Evangelist William Farel, stands before the death bed of Calvin.

Institutes of the Christian Religion

Book Fourth

Book Fourth

OF THE HOLY CATHOLIC CHURCH

ARGUMENT

In the former books, an exposition has been given of the three parts of the Apostles' Creed concerning God the Creator, the Redeemer, and the Sanctifier. In this last book, it now remains to teach the Church and the Communion of Saints, or the external means or helps by which God invites us to fellowship with Christ, and keeps us in it.

The next twenty Chapters may be conveniently reduced to three particular heads–viz. I. Of the Church. II. Of the Sacraments. III. Of Civil Government.

The first head occupies the first thirteen chapters; but these may all be reduced to four–viz. I. Of the marks of the Church, or the means by which the Church may be discerned, since it is necessary to cultivate unity with the Church. This is considered in Chapters 1 and 2–II. Of the rule or government of the Church. The order of government, Chapter 3. The form in use in the primitive Church, Chapter 4. The form at present existing in the Papacy, Chapter 5. The primacy of the Pope, Chapter 6. The gradual rise of his usurpation, Chapter 7–III. Of the power of the Church. The power in relation to doctrine as possessed either by individuals, Chapter 8; or universally as in Councils, Chapter 9. The power of enacting laws, Chapter 10. The extent of ecclesiastical jurisdiction, Chapter 11–IV. Of the discipline of the Church. The chief use of discipline, Chapter 12. The abuse of it, Chapter 13.

The second general head, Of the Sacraments, comprehends three particulars,–I. Of the Sacraments in general, Chapter 14–II. Of the two Sacraments in particular. Of Baptism, Chapter 15. Of

Paedobaptism, Chapter 16. Of the Lord's Supper, Chapter 17. Of profaning the Lord's Supper, Chapter 18. Of the five Sacraments falsely so called, Chapter 19.

The third general head, Of Civil Government. This considered first generally, and then under the separate heads of Magistrates, Laws, and People.

Chapter 1

DUTY OF CULTIVATING UNITY WITH HER, AS THE MOTHER OF ALL THE GODLY.

The three divisions of this chapter are,–I. The article of the Creed concerning the Holy Catholic Church and the Communion of Saints briefly expounded. The grounds on which the Church claims our reverence, sections 1-6. II. Of the marks of the Church, sections 7-9. III. The necessity of cleaving to the Holy Catholic Church and the Communion of Saints. Refutation of the errors of the Novatians, Anabaptists, and other schismatics, in regard to this matter, sections 10-29.

Sections

1. The Church now to be considered. With her God has deposited whatever is necessary to faith and good order. A summary of what is contained in this book. Why it begins with the Church.

2. In what sense the article of the Creed concerning the Church is to be understood. Why we should say, "I believe the Church," not "I believe in the Church." The purport of this article. Why the Church is called Catholic or Universal.

3. What is meant by the Communion of Saints. Whether it is inconsistent with various gifts in the saints, or with civil order. Uses of this article concerning the Church and the communion of saints. Must the Church be visible in order to maintain unity with her?

4. The name of Mother given to the Church shows how necessary it is to know her. No salvation out of the Church.

5. The Church is our mother, inasmuch as God has committed to her the kind office of bringing us up in the faith until we attain full age. This method of education is not to be despised. Useful to us in two ways. This utility destroyed by those who despise the pastors and teachers of the Church. The petulance of such despisers repressed by reason and Scripture. For this education of the Church, her children enjoined to meet in the sanctuary. The abuse of churches both before and since the advent of Christ. Their proper use.

6. Her ministry effectual, but not without the Spirit of God. Passages in proof of this.

7. Second part of the chapter. Concerning the marks of the Church. In what respect the Church is invisible. In what respect she is visible.

8. God alone knoweth them that are His. Still He has given marks to discern His children.

9. These marks are the ministry of the Word, and administration of the sacraments instituted by Christ. The same rule is not to be followed in judging of individuals and of churches.

10. We must on no account forsake the Church distinguished by such marks. Those who act otherwise are apostates, deserters of the truth and of the household of God, deniers of God and Christ, violators of the mystical marriage.

11. These marks to be the more carefully observed, because Satan strives to efface them, or to make us revolt from the Church. The twofold error of despising the true, and submitting to a false Church.

12. Though the common profession should contain some corruption, this is not a sufficient reason for forsaking the visible Church. Some of these corruptions specified. Caution necessary. The duty of the members.

13. The immoral lives of certain professors is no ground for abandoning the Church. Error on this head of the ancient and modern Cathari. Their first objection. Answer to it from three of our Savior's parables.

14. Second objection. Answer from a consideration of the state of the Corinthian Church, and the Churches of Galatia.

15. Third objection and answer.

16. The origin of these objections. A description of Schismatics. Their portraiture by Augustine. A pious counsel respecting these scandals, and a safe remedy against them.

17. Fourth objection and answer. Answer confirmed by the divine promises.

18. Another confirmation from the example of Christ and of the faithful servants of God. The appearance of the Church in the days of the prophets.

19. Appearance of the Church in the days of Christ and the apostles, and their immediate followers.

20. Fifth objection. Answer to the ancient and modern Cathari, and to the Novatians, concerning the forgiveness of sins

21. Answer to the fifth objection continued. By the forgiveness of sins, believers are enabled to remain perpetually in the Church.

22. The keys of the Church given for the express purpose of securing this benefit. A summary of the answer to the fifth objection.

23. Sixth objection, formerly advanced by the Novatians, and renewed by the Anabaptists. This error confuted by the Lord's Prayer.

24. A second answer, founded on some examples under the Old Testament.

25. A third answer, confirmed by passages from Jeremiah, Ezekiel, and Solomon. A fourth answer, derived from sacrifices.

26. A fifth answer, from the New Testament. Some special examples.

27. General examples. A celebrated passage. The arrangement of the Creed.

28 Objection, that voluntary transgression excludes from the Church.

29. Last objection of the Novatians, founded on the solemn renewal of repentance required by the Church for more heinous offenses. Answer.

1 The Church now to be considered. With her, God has deposited whatever is necessary to faith and good order. A summary of what is contained in this book. Why it begins with the Church.

In the last book, it has been shown that by the faith of the gospel, Christ becomes ours, and we are made partakers of the salvation and eternal blessedness procured by Him. But because our ignorance and sloth (I may add, the vanity of our mind) stand in need of external helps, by which faith may be begotten in us and may increase and make progress until its consummation, God, in accommodation to our infirmity, has added such helps and secured the effectual preaching of the gospel by depositing this treasure with the Church. He has appointed pastors and teachers, by whose lips He might edify His people (see Ephesians 4:11); He has invested them with authority, and, in short, omitted nothing that might conduce to holy consent in the faith, and to right order. In particular, He has instituted sacraments, which we feel by experience to be most useful helps in fostering and confirming our faith. For seeing we are shut up in the prison of the body, and have not yet attained to the rank of angels, God, in accommodation to our capacity and in His admirable providence, has provided a method by which, though widely separated, we might still draw near to Him. Wherefore, due order requires that we first treat of the Church, of its government, orders, and power; next, of the Sacraments; and, lastly, of civil government–at the same time guarding pious readers against the corruptions of the papacy, by which Satan has adulterated all that God had appointed for our salvation.

I will begin with the Church, into whose bosom God is pleased to collect His children, not only that by her aid and ministry they may be nourished so long as they are babes and children, but may also be guided by her maternal care until they grow up to manhood, and, finally, attain to the perfection of faith. What God has thus joined, let not man put asunder (See Mark 10:9): to those to whom He is a Father, the Church must also be a mother. This was true not merely under the Law, but even now after the advent of Christ; since Paul declares that we are the children of a new, even a heavenly Jerusalem. (See Galatians 4:26.)

2 In what sense the article of the Creed concerning the Church is to be understood. Why we should say, "I believe the Church," not "I believe in the Church." The purport of this article. Why the Church is called Catholic or Universal.

When in the Creed we profess to believe the Church, reference is made not only to the visible Church of which we are now treating, but also to all the elect of God, including in the number even those who have departed this life. And, accordingly, the word used is "believe," because oftentimes no difference can be observed between the children of God and the profane, between His proper flock and the untamed herd. The particle *in* is often interpolated, but without any probable ground. I confess, indeed, that it is the more usual form, and is not unsupported by antiquity, since the Nicene Creed, as quoted in *Ecclesiastical History*, adds the preposition. At the same time, we may perceive from early writers, that the expression received without controversy in ancient times was to believe "the Church," and not "in the Church." This is not only the expression used by Augustine, and that ancient writer, whoever he may have been, whose treatise, *De Symboli Expositione*, is extant under the name of Cyprian, but they distinctly remark that the addition of the preposition would make the expression improper, and they give good grounds for so thinking. We declare that we believe in God, because both our mind reclines upon Him as true, and our confidence is fully satisfied in Him.

This cannot be said of the Church, just as it cannot be said of the forgiveness of sins, or the resurrection of the body. Wherefore, although I am unwilling to dispute about words, yet I would rather keep to the proper form, as better fitted to express the thing that is meant, than affect terms by which the meaning is causelessly obscured. The object of the expression is to teach us, that though the devil leaves no stone unturned in order to destroy the grace of Christ, and the enemies of God rush with insane violence in the same direction, it cannot be extinguished–the blood of Christ cannot be rendered barren, and prevented from producing fruit.

Hence, regard must be had both to the secret election and to the internal calling of God, because He alone "knoweth them that are his" (2 Timothy 2:19); and as Paul expresses it, holds them enclosed under His seal, although, at the same time, they wear His insignia, and are thus distinguished from the reprobate. But as they are a small and despised number, concealed in an immense crowd, as if a few grains of wheat buried among a heap of chaff, to God alone must be left the knowledge of His Church, of which His secret election forms the foundation. Nor is it enough to embrace the number of the elect in thought and intention merely. By the unity of the Church, we must understand a unity into which we feel persuaded that we are truly engrafted. For unless we are united with all the other members under Christ our head, no hope of the future inheritance awaits us.

Hence, the Church is called Catholic or Universal, for two or three cannot be invented without dividing Christ; and this is impossible. All the elect of God are so joined together in Christ that as they depend on one head, so they are compacted into one body. They are made truly one by living together under the same Spirit of God in one faith, hope, and charity. They are called not only to the same inheritance of eternal life, but also to participation in one God and Christ. For although the sad devastation which everywhere meets our view may proclaim that no Church remains, let us know that the death of Christ produces fruit, and that God wondrously preserves His Church, while placing it in concealment. Thus, it was said to Elijah, "Yet I have left me seven thousand in Israel" (1 Kings 19:18).

3 What is meant by the Communion of Saints. Whether it is inconsistent with various gifts in the saints, or with civil order. Uses of this article concerning the Church and the communion of saints. Must the Church be visible in order to maintain unity with her?

Moreover, this article of the Creed relates in some measure to the external Church, that everyone of us must maintain brotherly concord with all the children of God, give due authority to the Church, and, in short, conduct ourselves as sheep of the flock. Hence the additional expression, the "communion of saints." This clause, though usually omitted by ancient writers, must not be overlooked. It admirably expresses the quality of the Church, just as if it had been said that saints are united in the fellowship of Christ on this condition, and that all the blessings, which God bestows upon them, are mutually communicated to each other. This, however, is not incompatible with a diversity of graces, for we know that the gifts of the Spirit are variously distributed; nor is it incompatible with civil order, by which each is permitted privately to possess his own means, it being necessary for the preservation of peace among men that distinct rights of property should exist among them. Still a community is asserted, such as Luke describes when he says, "The multitude of them that believed were of one heart and of one soul" (Acts 4:32); and Paul, when he reminds the Ephesians, "There is one body, and one Spirit, even as ye are called in one hope of your calling" (Ephesians 4:4). For if they are truly persuaded that God is the common Father of them all, and Christ their common head, they cannot but be united together in brotherly love, and mutually impart their blessings to each other. Then it is of the highest importance for us to know what benefit thence redounds to us. For when we believe the Church, it is in order that we may be firmly persuaded that we are its members. In this way our salvation rests on a foundation so firm and sure, that though the whole fabric of the world were to give way, it could not be destroyed.

First, it stands with the election of God, and cannot change or fail, any more than His eternal providence. Next, it is in a manner united with the stability of Christ, who will no more allow His faithful followers to be dissevered from Him, than He would allow His own members to be torn to pieces. We may add that so long as we continue in the bosom of the Church, we are sure that the truth will remain with us. Lastly, we feel that we have an interest in such promises as these, "In Mount Zion and in Jerusalem shall be deliverance" (Joel 2:32; Obadiah 17); "God is in the midst of her, she shall not be moved" (Psalm 46:5).

So available is communion with the Church to keep us in the fellowship of God. In the very term communion, there is great consolation; because, while we are assured that everything, which God bestows on His members, belongs to us, all the blessings conferred upon them confirm our hope. But in order to embrace the unity of the Church in this manner, it is not necessary, as I have observed, to see it with our eyes, or feel it with our hands. Nay, rather from its being placed in faith, we are reminded that our thoughts are to dwell upon it, as much when it escapes our perception as when it openly appears. Nor is our faith the worse for apprehending what is unknown, since we are not enjoined here to distinguish between the elect and the reprobate. This belongs not to us, but to God only. We are to feel firmly assured in our minds that all those who, by the mercy of God the Father and through the efficacy of the Holy Spirit, have become partakers with Christ, are set apart as the proper and peculiar possession of God. As we are of the number, we are also partakers of this great grace.

4 The name of Mother given to the Church shows how necessary it is to know her. No salvation out of the Church.

But as it is now our purpose to discuss the visible Church, let us learn from her single title of "Mother," how useful, nay, how necessary the knowledge of her is. There is no other means of entering into life unless she conceives us in the womb and gives us birth, unless she nourishes us at her breasts, and, in short, keeps us under her charge and government until, divested of mortal flesh, we become like the angels. (See Matthew 22:30.) For our weakness does not permit us to leave the school until we have spent our whole lives as scholars. Moreover, beyond the pale of the Church no forgiveness of sins, no salvation, can be hoped for, as Isaiah and Joel testify. (See Isaiah 37:32; Joel 2:32.) To their testimony Ezekiel subscribes, when he declares, "They shall not be in the assembly of my people, neither shall they be written in the writing of the house of Israel" (Ezekiel 3:9); as, on the other hand, those who turn to the cultivation of true piety are said to inscribe their names among the citizens of Jerusalem. For which reason it is said in the psalm, "Remember me, O Lord, with the favor that thou bearest unto thy people: O visit me with thy salvation; that I may see the good of thy chosen, that I may rejoice in the gladness of thy nation, that I may glory with thine inheritance" (Psalm 106:4, 5). By these words the paternal favor of God and the special evidence of spiritual life are confined to His peculiar people, and hence the abandonment of the Church is always fatal.

5 The Church is our mother, inasmuch as God has committed to her the kind office of bringing us up in the faith until we attain full age. This method of education not to be despised. Useful to us in two ways. This utility destroyed by those who despise the pastors and teachers of the Church. The petulance of such despisers repressed by reason and Scripture. For this education of the Church, her children enjoined to meet in the sanctuary. The abuse of churches both before and since the advent of Christ. Their proper use.

But let us proceed to a full exposition of this view. Paul says that our Savior "ascended far above all heavens, that He might fill all things. He gave some, apostles; and some, prophets; and some, evangelists; and some, pastors and teachers. This He did for the perfecting of the saints, for the work of the ministry, and for the edifying of the body of Christ until we all come in the unity of the faith and the knowledge of the Son of God, unto a perfect man, unto the measure of the stature of the fullness of Christ" (Ephesians 4:10-13).

We see that God, who might perfect His people in a moment, chooses not to bring them to manhood in any other way than by the education of the Church. We see the mode of doing it expressed; the preaching of celestial doctrine is committed to pastors. We see that all without exception are brought into the same order, that with meek and docile spirits, they may allow themselves to be governed by teachers appointed for this purpose.

Isaiah had long before given this as the characteristic of the Kingdom of Christ: "My Spirit that is upon thee, and my words which I have put in thy mouth, shall not depart out of thy mouth, nor out of the mouth of thy seed, nor out of the mouth of thy seed's seed, saith the Lord, from henceforth and forever" (Isaiah 59:21).

Hence, it follows, that all who reject the spiritual food of the soul divinely offered to them by the hands of the Church, deserve to perish of hunger and famine. God inspires us with faith, but it is by the instrumentality of His Gospel, as Paul reminds us, "Faith cometh by hearing" (Romans 10:17).

God reserves to himself the power of maintaining it, but it is by the preaching of the Gospel, as Paul also declares, that He brings it forth and unfolds it. With this view, it pleased Him in ancient times that sacred meetings should be held in the sanctuary, that consent in faith might be nourished by doctrine proceeding from the lips of the priest. Those magnificent titles, as when the temple is called God's rest, His sanctuary, and His habitation, and when He is said to dwell between the cherubim (see Psalm 32:13, 14; 80:1), are used for no other purpose than to procure respect, love, reverence, and dignity to the ministry of heavenly doctrine, to which otherwise the appearance of an insignificant human being might be derogatory. Therefore, to teach us that the treasure offered to us in earthen vessels is of inestimable value (see 2 Corinthians 4:7), God himself appears and, as the author of this ordinance, requires His presence to be recognized in his own institution. Accordingly, after forbidding His people to give heed to familiar spirits, wizards, and other superstitions (see Leviticus 19:30, 31), He adds, that He will give what ought to be sufficient for all–namely, that He will never leave them without prophets. For, as He did not commit his ancient people to angels, but raised up teachers on the Earth to perform a truly angelical office, so He is pleased to instruct us in the present day by human means.

But as anciently He did not confine himself to the law merely, but added priests as interpreters, from whose lips the people might inquire after His true meaning, so in the present day He would not only have us to be attentive to reading, but has appointed masters to give us their assistance. In this, there is a twofold advantage. On the one hand, by an admirable test, He proves our obedience when we listen to His ministers just as we would to himself.

On the other hand and at the same time, He consults our weakness in being pleased to address us after the manner of men by means of interpreters, that He may thus allure us to himself, instead of driving us away by His thunder. How well this familiar mode of teaching is suited to us all the godly are aware, from the dread with which the divine majesty justly inspires them.

Those who think that the authority of the doctrine is impaired by the insignificance of the men who are called to teach, betray their ingratitude. Among the many noble endowments with which God has adorned the human race, one of the most remarkable is that He deigns to consecrate the mouths and tongues of men to His service, making His own voice heard in them. Wherefore, let us not on our part decline obediently to embrace the doctrine of salvation, delivered by His command and mouth; because, although the power of God is not confined to external means, He has, however, confined us to His ordinary method of teaching, which method, when fanatics refuse to observe, they entangle themselves in many fatal snares. Pride, or fastidiousness, or emulation, induces many to persuade themselves that they can profit sufficiently by reading and meditating in private, and thus to despise public meetings, and deem preaching superfluous.

But since as much as in them lies they loose or burst the sacred bond of unity, none of them escapes the just punishment of this impious divorce, but become fascinated with pestiferous errors, and the foulest delusions. Wherefore, in order that the pure simplicity of the faith may flourish among us, let us not decline to use this exercise of piety, which God by His institution of it has shown to be necessary, and which He so highly recommends. None, even among the most petulant of men, would venture to say, that we are to shut our ears against God, but in all ages prophets and pious teachers have had a difficult contest to maintain with the ungodly, whose perverseness cannot submit to the yoke of being taught by the lips and ministry of men. This is just the same as if they were to destroy the impression of God as doctrine exhibits it. For no other reason were believers anciently enjoined to seek the face of God in the sanctuary (see Psalm 105:4) (an injunction so often repeated in the Law), than because the doctrine of the Law, and the exhortations of the prophets, were to them a living image of God. Thus, Paul declares, that in his preaching the glory of God shone in the face of Jesus Christ. (See 2 Corinthians 4:6.) The more detestable are the apostates who delight in producing schisms in churches, just as if they wished to drive the sheep from the fold, and throw them into the jaws of wolves. Let us hold, agreeably to the passage we quoted from Paul, that the Church can only be edified by external preaching, and that there is no other bond by which the saints can be kept together than by uniting with one consent to observe the order which God has appointed in His Church for learning and making progress. For this end, as I have observed, believers were anciently enjoined under the Law to flock together to the sanctuary.

When Moses speaks of the habitation of God, He at the same time calls it the place of the name of God, the place where He will record his name (see Exodus 20:24); thus plainly teaching that no use could be made of it without the doctrine of godliness.

And there can be no doubt that, for the same reason, David complains with great bitterness of soul, that by the tyrannical cruelty of his enemies he was prevented from entering the tabernacle. (See Psalm 84.) To many the complaint seems childish, as if no great loss were sustained, not much pleasure lost, by exclusion from the temple, provided other amusements were enjoyed. David, however, laments this one deprivation, as filling him with anxiety and sadness, tormenting, and almost destroying him. This he does because there is nothing on which believers set a higher value than on this aid, by which God gradually raises His people to Heaven. For it is to be observed, that he always exhibited himself to the holy patriarchs in the mirror of His doctrine in such a way as to make their knowledge spiritual. Whence the temple is not only styled His face, but also, for removing all superstition, is termed His footstool. (See Psalm 132:7; 99:5.) Herein is the unity of the faith happily realized, when all, from the highest to the lowest, aspire to the head. All the temples which the Gentiles built to God with a different intention were a mere profanation of His worship—a profanation into which the Jews also fell, though not with equal grossness. With this Stephen upbraids them in the words of Isaiah when he says, "Howbeit the

Most High dwelleth not in temples made with hands; as saith the Prophet, Heaven is my throne" (Acts 7:48).

For God only consecrates temples to their legitimate use by His word. And when we rashly attempt anything without His order, immediately setting out from a bad principle, we introduce adventitious fictions, by which evil is propagated without measure. It was inconsiderate in Xerxes when, by the advice of the magians, he burnt or pulled down all the temples of Greece, because he thought it absurd that God, to whom all things ought to be free and open, should be enclosed by walls and roofs, as if it were not in the power of God in a manner to descend to us, that He may be near to us, and yet neither change His place nor affect us by earthly means, but rather, by a kind of vehicles, raise us aloft to His own heavenly glory, which, with its immensity, fills all things, and in height is above the heavens.

6 Her ministry effectual, but not without the Spirit of God. Passages in proof of this.

Moreover, as at this time there is a great dispute as to the efficacy of the ministry, some extravagantly overrating its dignity, and others erroneously maintaining, that what is peculiar to the Spirit of God is transferred to mortal man, when we suppose that ministers and teachers penetrate to the mind and heart, so as to correct the blindness of the one, and the hardness of the other; it is necessary to place this controversy on its proper footing. The arguments on both sides will be disposed of without trouble, by distinctly attending to the passages in which God, the author of preaching, connects His Spirit with it, and then promises a beneficial result; or, on the other hand, to the passages in which God, separating himself from external means, claims for himself alone both the commencement and the whole course of faith.

The office of the second Elias was, as Malachi declares, to "turn the heart of the fathers to the children, and the heart of the children to their fathers" (Malachi 4:6). Christ declares that He sent the apostles to produce fruit from His labors. (See John 15:16.) What this fruit is Peter briefly defines, when he says that we are begotten again of incorruptible seed. (See 1 Peter 1:23.)

Hence, Paul glories, that by means of the Gospel he had begotten the Corinthians, who were the seals of his apostleship (see 1 Corinthians 4:15); moreover, that his was not a ministry of the letter, which only sounded in the ear, but that the effectual agency of the

Spirit was given to him, in order that his doctrine might not be in vain. (See 1 Corinthians 9:2; 2 Corinthians 3:6.) In this sense, he elsewhere declares that his Gospel was not in word, but in power. (See 1 Thessalonians 1:5.) He also affirms that the Galatians received the Spirit by the hearing of faith. (See Galatians 3:2.)

In short, in several passages he not only makes himself a fellow-worker with God, but also attributes to himself the province of bestowing salvation (1 Corinthians 3:9). All these things he certainly never uttered with the view of attributing to himself one iota apart from God, as he elsewhere briefly explains. "For this cause also thank we God without ceasing, because, when ye received the Word of God which ye heard of us, ye received it not as the word of men, but (as it is in truth) the Word of God, which effectually worketh also in you that believe" (1 Thessalonians 2:13). Again, in another place, "He that wrought effectually in Peter to the apostleship of the circumcision, the same was mighty in me toward the Gentiles" (Galatians 2:8). And that He allows no more to ministers is obvious from other passages. "So then neither is he that planteth anything, neither he that watereth; but God that giveth the increase" (1 Corinthians 3:7). Again, "I labored more abundantly than they all: yet not I, but the grace of God which was with me" (1 Corinthians 15:10). And it is indeed necessary to keep these sentences in view, since God, in ascribing to himself the illumination of the mind and renewal of the heart, reminds us that it is sacrilege for man to claim any part of either to himself. Still everyone who listens with docility to the ministers whom God appoints, will know by the beneficial result, that for good reason God is pleased with this method of teaching, and for good reason has laid believers under this modest yoke.

7 Second part of the chapter. Concerning the marks of the Church. In what respect the Church is invisible. In what respect she is visible.

The judgment, which ought to be formed concerning the visible Church, which comes under our observation, must, I think, be sufficiently clear from what has been said. I have observed that the Scriptures speak of the Church in two ways. Sometimes when they speak of the Church they mean the Church as it really is before God—the Church into which none are admitted but those who by the gift of adoption are sons of God and by the sanctification of the Spirit true members of Christ. In this case, it not only comprehends the saints who dwell on the Earth, but all the elect who have existed from the beginning of the world. Often, too, by the name of Church is designated the whole body of mankind scattered throughout the world, who profess to worship one God and Christ, who by baptism are initiated into the faith; by partaking of the Lord's Supper profess unity in true doctrine and charity, agree in holding the Word of the Lord, and observe the ministry which Christ has appointed for the preaching of it. In this Church there is a very large mixture of hypocrites, who have nothing of Christ but the name and outward appearance: of ambitious, avaricious, envious, evil-speaking men, some also of impurer lives, who are tolerated for a time, either because their guilt cannot be legally established, or because due strictness of discipline is not always observed. Hence, as it is necessary to believe the invisible Church, which is manifest to the eye of God only, so we are also enjoined to regard this Church, which is so called with reference to man, and to cultivate its communion.

8 God alone knoweth them that are His. Still He has given marks to discern His children.

Accordingly, inasmuch as it was of importance to us to recognize it, the Lord has distinguished it by certain marks, and symbols. It is, indeed, the special prerogative of God to know those who are His, as Paul declares in the passage already quoted (2 Timothy 2:19). And doubtless, it has been so provided as a check on human rashness, the experience of every day reminding us how far His secret judgments surpass our apprehension. For even those who seemed most abandoned, and who had been completely despaired of, are by His goodness recalled to life, while those who seemed most stable often fall.

Hence, as Augustine says, "In regard to the secret predestination of God, there are very many sheep without, and very many wolves within." He knows and has His mark on those who know neither Him nor themselves. Of those again who openly bear His badge, His eyes alone see who of them are sincerely holy, and will persevere even to the end, which alone is the completion of salvation.

On the other hand, foreseeing that it was in some degree expedient for us to know who are to be regarded by us as His sons, in this matter He has accommodated himself to our capacity. But as here full certainty was not necessary, He has in its place substituted the judgment of charity, by which we acknowledge all as members of the Church who by confession of faith, regularity of conduct, and participation in the sacraments, unite with us in acknowledging the same God and Christ. The knowledge of His body, inasmuch as He knew it to be more necessary for our salvation, He has made known to us by surer marks.

9 These marks are the ministry of the word, and administration of the sacraments instituted by Christ. The same rule not to be followed in judging of individuals and of churches.

Hence, the form of the Church appears and stands forth conspicuous to our view. Wherever we see the Word of God sincerely preached and heard, wherever we see the sacraments administered according to the institution of Christ, we cannot doubt that the Church of God has some existence, since His promise cannot fail, "Where two or three are gathered together in my name, there am I in the midst of them" (Matthew 18:20). But that we may have a clear summary of this subject, we must proceed by the following steps: –The Church universal is the multitude collected out of all nations, who, though dispersed and far distant from each other, agree in one truth of divine doctrine, and are bound together by the tie of a common religion. In this way, it comprehends single churches, which exist in different towns and villages, according to the wants of human society, so that each of them justly obtains the name and authority of the Church. It also comprehends single individuals, who by a religious profession are accounted to belong to such churches, although they are in fact aliens from the Church, but have not been cut off by a public decision.

There is, however, a slight difference in the mode of judging of individuals and of churches. For it may happen in practice that those whom we deem not altogether worthy of the fellowship of believers, we yet ought to treat as brethren, and regard as believers, on account of the common consent of the Church in tolerating and bearing with them in the Body of Christ. Such persons we do not approve by our suffrage as members of the Church, but we leave them the place, which they hold among the people of God, until they are legitimately deprived of it. With regard to the general body, we must feel differently; if they have the ministry of the Word, and honor the administration of the sacraments, they are undoubtedly entitled to be ranked with the Church, because it is certain that these things are not without a beneficial result. Thus we both maintain the Church universal in its unity, which malignant minds have always been eager to dissever, and deny not due authority to lawful assemblies distributed as circumstances require.

10 We must on no account forsake the Church distinguished by such marks. Those who act otherwise are apostates, deserters of the truth and of the household of God, deniers of God and Christ, violators of the mystical marriage.

We have said that the symbols by which the Church is discerned are the preaching of the Word and the observance of the sacraments, for these cannot anywhere exist without producing fruit and prospering by the blessing of God. I say not that wherever the Word is preached fruit immediately appears; but that in every place where it is received, and has a fixed abode, it uniformly displays its efficacy.

Be this as it may, when the preaching of the gospel is reverently heard and the sacraments are not neglected, then the face of the Church appears without deception or ambiguity. No man may with impunity spurn her authority, or reject her admonitions, or resist her counsels, or make sport of her censures, far less revolt from her, and violate her unity (see Chapter 2, sections 1, 10, and Chapter 8, section 12).

For such is the value which the Lord sets on the communion of His Church, that all who contumaciously alienate themselves from any Christian society, in which the true ministry of His Word and sacraments is maintained, He regards as deserters of religion. So highly does He recommend her authority, that when it is violated He considers that his own authority is impaired. For there is no small weight in the designation given to her, "the house of God," and "the pillar and ground of the truth" (1 Timothy 3:15). By these words Paul intimates, that to prevent the truth from perishing in the world. The Church is its faithful guardian, because God has been pleased to preserve the pure preaching of His Word by her instrumentality, and to exhibit himself to us as a parent while He feeds us with spiritual nourishment, and provides whatever is conducive to our salvation.

Moreover, no mean praise is conferred on the Church when she is said to have been chosen and set apart by Christ as His spouse, "not having spot or wrinkle, or any such thing" (Ephesians 5:27), as "his body, the fullness of him that filleth all in all" (Ephesians 1:23). Whence it follows, that revolt from the Church is denial of God and Christ. Wherefore there is the more necessity to beware of a dissent so iniquitous; for seeing by it we aim as far as in us lies at the destruction of God's truth, we deserve to be crushed by the full thunder of His anger. No crime can be imagined more atrocious than that of sacrilegiously and perfidiously violating the sacred marriage, which the only begotten Son of God has condescended to contract with us.

11 These marks to be the more carefully observed, because Satan strives to efface them, or to make us revolt from the Church. The twofold error of despising the true, and submitting to a false Church.

Wherefore, let these marks be carefully impressed upon our minds, and let us estimate them as in the sight of the Lord. There is nothing on which Satan is more intent than to destroy and efface one or both of them—at one time to delete and abolish these marks, and thereby destroy the true and genuine distinction of the Church; at another, to bring them into contempt, and so hurry us into open revolt from the Church. To his wiles, it owed that for several ages the pure preaching of the word disappeared, and now, with the same dishonest aim, he labors to overthrow the ministry, which, however, Christ has so ordered in His Church, that if it is removed the whole edifice must fall. How perilous, then, nay, how fatal the temptation, when we even entertain a thought of separating ourselves from that assembly in which are beheld the signs and badges which the Lord has deemed sufficient to characterize His Church! We see how great caution should be employed in both respects. That we may not be imposed upon by the name of Church, every congregation, which claims the name, must be brought to that test as to a Lydian stone. If it holds the order instituted by the Lord in Word and sacraments, there will be no deception. We may safely pay it the honor due to a church. On the other hand, if it exhibits itself without Word and sacraments, we must in this case be no less careful to avoid the imposture than we were to shun pride and presumption in the other.

12 Though the common profession may contain some corruption, this is not a sufficient reason for forsaking the visible Church. Some of these corruptions specified. Caution necessary. The duty of the members.

When we say that the pure ministry of the Word and pure celebration of the sacraments is a fit pledge and earnest, so that we may safely recognize a church in every society in which both exist, our meaning is, that we are never to discard it so long as these remain, though it may otherwise teem with numerous faults. Nay, even in the administration of Word and sacraments defects may creep in which ought not to alienate us from its communion. For all the heads of true doctrine are not in the same position. Some are so necessary to be known, that all must hold them to be fixed and undoubted as the proper essentials of religion: for instance, that God is one, that Christ is God, and the Son of God, that our salvation depends on the mercy of God, and the like.

Others, again, which are the subject of controversy among the churches, do not destroy the unity of the faith. Why should it be regarded as a ground of dissension between churches, if one, without any spirit of contention or perverseness in dogmatizing, holds that the soul on quitting the body flies to Heaven, and another, without venturing to speak positively as to the abode, holds it for certain that it lives with the Lord?

The words of the Apostle are, "Let us therefore, as many as be perfect, be thus minded: and if in anything ye be otherwise minded, God shall reveal even this unto you" (Philippians 3:15). Does he not sufficiently intimate that a difference of opinion as to these matters which are not necessary, ought not to be a ground of dissension among Christians?

The best thing, indeed, is to be perfectly agreed, but seeing there is no man who is not involved in some mist of ignorance, we must either have no church at all, or pardon delusion in those things of which one may be ignorant, without violating the substance of religion and forfeiting salvation.

Here, however, I have no wish to patronize even the minutest errors, as if I thought it right to foster them by flattery or connivance. What I say is that we are not because every minute difference to abandon a church, provided it retains sound and unimpaired that doctrine in which the safety of piety consists, and keeps the use of the sacraments instituted by the Lord.

Meanwhile, if we strive to reform what is offensive, we act in the discharge of duty. To this effect are the words of Paul, "If anything be revealed to another that sitteth by, let the first hold his peace" (1 Corinthians 14:30). From this it is evident that to each member of the Church, according to his measure of grace, the study of public edification has been assigned, provided it is done decently and in order. In other words, we must neither renounce the communion of the Church, nor, continuing in it, disturb peace and discipline when duly arranged.

13 The immoral lives of certain professors is no ground for abandoning the Church. Error on this head of the ancient and modern Cathari. Their first objection. Answer to it from three of our Savior's parables.

Our indulgence ought to extend much further in tolerating imperfection of conduct. Here there is great danger of falling, and Satan employs all his machinations to ensnare us. For there always have been persons who, imbued with a false persuasion of absolute holiness, as if they had already become a kind of aerial spirits, spurn the society of all in whom they see that something human still remains. Such of old were the Cathari and the Donatists, who were similarly infatuated. Such in the present day are some of the Anabaptists, who would be thought to have made superior progress. Others, again, sin in this respect, not so much from that insane pride as from inconsiderate zeal. Because among those to whom the gospel is preached, the fruit produced is not in accordance with the doctrine, they forthwith conclude that there no church exists. The offense is indeed well founded, and it is one to which in this most unhappy age we give far too much occasion.

It is impossible to excuse our accursed sluggishness, which the Lord will not leave unpunished, as He is already beginning sharply to chastise us. Woe then to us who, by our dissolute license of wickedness, cause weak consciences to be wounded! Still those of whom we have spoken sin in their turn, by not knowing how to set bounds to their offense. For where the Lord requires mercy, they omit it, and give themselves up to immoderate severity. Thinking there is no church where there is not complete purity and integrity of conduct, they, through hatred of wickedness, withdraw from a genuine church, while they think they are shunning the company of the ungodly. They allege that the Church of God is holy.

But that they may at the same time understand that it contains a mixture of good and bad, let them hear from the lips of our Savior that parable in which He compares the Church to a net in which all kinds of fishes are taken, but not separated until they are brought ashore. Let them hear it compared to a field, planted with good seed, which is by the fraud of an enemy mingled with tares, and is not freed of them until the harvest is brought into the barn. Let them hear, in fine, that it is a threshing floor in which the collected wheat lies concealed under the chaff, until, cleansed by the fanners and the sieve, it is at length laid up in the granary. If the Lord declares that the Church will labor under the defect of being burdened with a multitude of wicked until the day of judgment, it is in vain to look for a church altogether free from blemish. (See Matthew 13.)

14 Second objection. Answer from a consideration of the state of the Corinthian Church, and the Churches of Galatia.

They exclaim that it is impossible to tolerate the vice, which everywhere stalks abroad like a pestilence. What if the apostle's sentiment applies here also? Among the Corinthians, it was not a few that erred, but almost the whole body had become tainted; there was not one species of sin merely, but a multitude, and those not trivial errors, but some of them execrable crimes. There was not only corruption in manners, but also in doctrine.

What course was taken by the holy apostle, in other words, by the organ of the heavenly Spirit, by whose testimony the Church stands and falls? Does he seek separation from them? Does he discard them from the Kingdom of Christ? Does he strike them with the thunder of a final anathema? He not only does none of these things, but he acknowledges and heralds them as a Church of Christ, and a society of saints.

If the Church remains among the Corinthians, where envy, division, and contention rage; where quarrels, lawsuits, and avarice prevail; where a crime, which even the Gentiles would execrate, is openly approved; where the name of Paul, whom they ought to have honored as a father, is petulantly assailed; where some hold the resurrection of the dead in derision, though with it the whole gospel must fall; where the gifts of God are made subservient to ambition, not to charity; where many things are done neither decently nor in order: If there the Church still remains, simply because the ministration of Word and sacrament is not rejected, who will presume to deny the title of church to those to whom a tenth part of these crimes cannot be imputed? How, I ask, would those who act so morosely against present churches have acted to the Galatians, who had done all but abandon the gospel (see Galatians 1:6), and yet among them the same apostle found churches?

15 Third objection and answer.

They also object, that Paul sharply rebukes the Corinthians for permitting an heinous offender in their communion, and then lays down a general sentence, by which he declares it unlawful even to eat bread with a man of impure life. (See 1 Corinthians 5:11, 12.) Here they exclaim, If it is not lawful to eat ordinary bread, how can it be lawful to eat the Lord's bread?

I admit that it is a great disgrace if dogs and swine are admitted among the children of God–much more if the sacred body of Christ is prostituted to them. And, indeed, when churches are well regulated, they will not bear the wicked in their bosom, nor will they admit the worthy and unworthy indiscriminately to that sacred feast. But because pastors are not always sedulously vigilant, are sometimes also more indulgent than they ought, or are prevented from acting so strictly as they could wish; the consequence is, that even the openly wicked are not always excluded from the fellowship of the saints. This I admit to be a vice, and I have no wish to extenuate it, seeing that Paul sharply rebukes it in the Corinthians. But although the Church fails in her duty, it does not therefore follow that every private individual is to decide the question of separation for himself.

I deny not that it is the duty of a pious man to withdraw from all private intercourse with the wicked, and not entangle himself with them by any voluntary tie; but it is one thing to shun the society of the wicked, and another to renounce the communion of the Church through hatred of them.

Those who think it sacrilege to partake the Lord's bread with the wicked, are in this more rigid than Paul. For when he exhorts us to pure and holy communion, he does not require that we should examine others, or that everyone should examine the whole church, but that each should examine himself (1 Corinthians 11:28, 29). If it were unlawful to communicate with the unworthy, Paul would certainly have ordered us to take heed that there would be no individual in the whole body by whose impurity we might be defiled. But now, he only requires each to examine himself. He shows that it does no harm to us, though some who are unworthy present themselves along with us. To the same effect he afterwards adds, "He that eateth and drinketh unworthily, eateth and drinketh damnation to himself." He says not *to others*, but *to himself*. And justly; for the right of admitting or excluding ought not to be left to the decision of individuals. Cognizance of this point, which cannot be exercised without due order, as shall afterwards be more fully shown, belongs to the whole church. It would therefore be unjust to hold any private individual as polluted by the unworthiness of another, whom he neither can nor ought to keep back from communion.

16 The origin of these objections. A description of Schismatics. Their portraiture by Augustine. A pious counsel respecting these scandals, and a safe remedy against them.

Still, however, even the good are sometimes affected by this inconsiderate zeal for righteousness, though we shall find that this excessive moroseness is more the result of pride and a false idea of sanctity, than genuine sanctity itself, and true zeal for it. Accordingly, those who are the most forward, and leaders in producing revolt from the Church, have, for the most part, no other motive than to display their own superiority by despising all other men.

Well and wisely, therefore, does Augustine say, "Seeing that pious reason and the mode of ecclesiastical discipline ought specially to regard the unity of the Spirit in the bond of peace, which the Apostle enjoins us to keep, by bearing with one another (for if we keep it not, the application of medicine is not only superfluous, but pernicious, and therefore proves to be no medicine); those bad sons who, not from hatred of other men's iniquities, but zeal for their own contentions, attempt altogether to draw away, or at least to divide, weak brethren ensnared by the glare of their name, while swollen with pride, stuffed with petulance, insidiously calumnious, and turbulently seditious, use the cloak of a rigorous severity, that they may not seem devoid of the light of truth, and pervert to sacrilegious schism, and purposes of excision, those things which are enjoined in the Holy Scriptures (due regard being had to sincere love, and the unity of peace), to correct a brother's faults by the appliance of a moderate cure."

To the pious and placid, his advice is mercifully to correct what they can, and to bear patiently with what they cannot correct, in love lamenting and mourning until God either reforms or corrects, or at the harvest root up the tares, and scatter the chaff. Let all the godly study to provide themselves with these weapons, lest, while they deem themselves strenuous and ardent defenders of righteousness, they revolt from the Kingdom of Heaven, which is the only kingdom of righteousness. For as God has been pleased that the communion of His Church shall be maintained in this external society, anyone who, from hatred of the ungodly, violates the bond of this society, enters on a downward course, in which he incurs great danger of cutting himself off from the communion of saints. Let them reflect, that in a numerous body there are several who may escape their notice, and yet are truly righteous and innocent in the eyes of the Lord. Let them reflect, that of those who seem diseased, there are many who are far from taking pleasure or flattering themselves in their faults, and who, always aroused by a serious fear of the Lord, aspire to greater integrity. Let them reflect, that they have no right to pass judgment on a man for one act, since the holiest sometimes make the most grievous fall. Let them reflect, that in the ministry of the Word and participation of the sacraments, the power to collect the Church is too great to be deprived of all its efficacy, by the fault of some ungodly men. Lastly, let them reflect, that in estimating the Church, divine is of more force than human judgment.

17 Fourth objection and answer. Answer confirmed by the divine promises.

Since they also argue that there is good reason for the Church being called holy, it is necessary to consider what the holiness is in which it excels, lest by refusing to acknowledge any church, save one that is perfect, we leave no church at all. It is indeed true, as Paul says, that Christ "loved the church, and gave himself for it, that he might sanctify and cleanse it with the washing of water by the word, that he might present it to himself a glorious church, not having spot, or wrinkle, or any such thing; but that it should be holy and without blemish" (Ephesians 5:25-27). Nevertheless, it is true, that the Lord is daily smoothing its wrinkles, and wiping away its spots. Hence, it follows, that its holiness is not yet perfect. Such, then, is the holiness of the Church: it makes daily progress, but is not yet perfect; it daily advances, but as yet has not reached the goal, as will elsewhere be more fully explained. Therefore, when the Prophets foretell, "Then shall Jerusalem be holy, and there shall no strangers pass through her any more;"—"It shall be called, The way of holiness; the unclean shall not pass over it" (Joel 3:17; Isaiah 35:8), let us not understand it as if no blemish remained in the members of the Church: but only that with their whole heart they aspire after holiness and perfect purity.

Hence, that purity, which they have not yet fully attained, by the kindness of God, is attributed to them. And though the indications of such a kind of holiness existing among men are too rare, we must understand, that at no period since the world began has the Lord been without His Church, nor ever shall be until the final consummation of all things. For although, at the very outset, the whole human race was vitiated and corrupted by the sin of Adam, yet of this kind of polluted mass He always sanctifies some vessels to honor, that no age may be left without experience of His mercy. This He has declared by sure promises, such as the following: "I have made a covenant with my chosen, I have sworn unto David my servant, Thy seed will I establish forever, and build up thy throne to all generations" (Psalm 89:3, 4). "The Lord hath chosen Zion; he hath desired it for his habitation. This is my rest forever; here will I dwell" (Psalm 132:13, 14). "Thus saith the Lord, which giveth the sun for a light by day, and the ordinances of the moon and of the stars for a light by night, which divideth the sea when the waves thereof roar; The Lord of hosts is his name: If those ordinances depart from before me, saith the Lord, then the seed of Israel also shall cease from being a nation before me forever" (Jeremiah 31:35, 36).

18 Another confirmation from the example of Christ and of the faithful servants of God. The appearance of the Church in the days of the prophets.

On this head, Christ himself, His apostles, and almost all the prophets, have furnished us with examples. Fearful are the descriptions in which Isaiah, Jeremiah, Joel, Habakkuk, and others, deplore the diseases of the Church of Jerusalem. In the people, the rulers, and the priests, corruption prevailed to such a degree, that Isaiah hesitates not to liken Jerusalem to Sodom and Gomorrah. (See Isaiah 1:10.) Religion was partly despised, partly adulterated, while in regard to morals, we everywhere meet with accounts of theft, robbery, perfidy, murder, and similar crimes. The prophets, however, did not therefore either form new churches for themselves or erect new altars on which they might have separate sacrifices. Instead, whatever their countrymen might be, reflecting that the Lord had deposited His word with them and instituted the ceremonies by which He was then worshipped, they stretched out pure hands to Him, though amid the company of the ungodly. Certainly, had they thought that they thereby contracted any pollution, they would have died a hundred deaths sooner than suffered themselves to be dragged thither. Nothing, therefore, prevented them from separating themselves, but a desire of preserving unity. But if the holy prophets felt no obligation to withdraw from the Church because of the very numerous and heinous crimes of almost everyone, we arrogate too much to ourselves if we then withdraw from the communion of the Church, because the lives of all accord not with our judgment, or even with the Christian profession.

19 Appearance of the Church in the days of Christ and the apostles, and their immediate followers.

Then, what kind of age was that of Christ and the apostles? Yet could neither the desperate impiety of the Pharisees, nor the dissolute licentiousness of manners, which everywhere prevailed, prevent them from using the same sacred rites with the people, and meeting in one common temple for the public exercises of religion. And why so, but just because they knew that those who joined in these sacred rites with a pure conscience were not at all polluted by the society of the wicked? If anyone is little moved by prophets and apostles, let him at least defer to the authority of Christ. Well, therefore, does Cyprian say, "Although tares or unclean vessels are seen in the Church, that is no reason that we ourselves should withdraw from the Church; we must only labor that we may be able to be wheat; we must give our endeavor, and strive as far as we can, to be vessels of gold or silver. But to break the earthen vessels belongs to the Lord alone, to whom a rod of iron has been given: let no one arrogate to himself what is peculiar to the Son alone, and think himself sufficient to winnow the floor and cleanse the chaff, and separate all the tares by human judgment. What depraved zeal thus assumes to itself is proud obstinacy and sacrilegious presumption." Therefore, let both points be regarded as fixed.

First, there is no excuse for him who spontaneously abandons the external communion of a church in which the Word of God is preached and the sacraments are administered. *Secondly*, notwithstanding the faults of a few or of many, there is nothing to prevent us from there duly professing our faith in the ordinances instituted by God, because a pious conscience is not injured by the unworthiness of another, whether he is a pastor or a private individual.

Sacred rites are not less pure and salutary to a man who is holy and upright, from being at the same time handled by the impure.

20 Fifth objection. Answer to the ancient and modern Cathari, and to the Novatians, concerning the forgiveness of sins

Their moroseness and pride proceed even to greater lengths. Refusing to acknowledge any church that is not pure from the minutest blemish, they take offense at sound teachers for exhorting believers to make progress, and so teaching them to groan during their whole lives under the burden of sin, and flee for pardon. For they pretend that in this way believers are led away from perfection. I admit that we are not to labor feebly or coldly in urging perfection, far less to desist from urging it; but I hold that it is a device of the devil to fill our minds with a confident belief of it while we are still in our course. Accordingly, in the Creed forgiveness of sins is appropriately subjoined to belief as to the Church, because none obtain forgiveness but those who are citizens, and of the household of the Church, as we read in the Prophet. (See Isaiah 33:24.)

The first place, therefore, should be given to the building of the heavenly Jerusalem, in which God afterwards is pleased to wipe away the iniquity of all who betake themselves to it. I say, however, that the Church must first be built; not that there can be any church without forgiveness of sins, but because the Lord has not promised His mercy save in the communion of saints. Therefore, our first entrance into the Church and the Kingdom of God is by forgiveness of sins, without which we have neither covenant nor union with God. For thus He speaks by the Prophet, "In that day will I make a covenant for them with the beasts of the field, and with the fowls of heaven, and with the creeping things of the ground: and I will break the bow, and the sword, and the battle, out of the earth, and will make them to lie down safely. And I will betroth thee unto me forever; yea, I will betroth thee unto me in righteousness, and in judgment, and in loving-kindness, and in mercies" (Hosea 2:18, 19). We see in what way the Lord reconciles us to himself by His mercy. So, in another passage, where He foretells that the people whom He had scattered in anger will again be gathered together, "I will cleanse them from all their iniquity, whereby they have sinned against me" (Jeremiah 33:8). Wherefore, our initiation into the fellowship of the Church is, by the symbol of ablution, to teach us that we have no admission into the family of God, unless by His goodness our impurities are previously washed away.

21 Answer to the fifth objection continued. By the forgiveness of sins, believers are enabled to remain perpetually in the Church.

Nor by remission of sins does the Lord only once for all elect and admit us into the Church, but by the same means, He preserves and defends us in it. For what would it avail us to receive a pardon of which we were afterwards to have no use? That the mercy of the Lord would be vain and delusive if only granted once, all the godly can bear witness; for there is none who is not conscious, during his whole life, of many infirmities which stand in need of divine mercy. And truly, it is not without cause that the Lord promises this gift especially to His own household, nor in vain that He orders the same message of reconciliation to be daily delivered to them. Wherefore, as during our whole lives we carry about with us the remains of sin, we could not continue in the Church one single moment were we not sustained by the uninterrupted grace of God in forgiving our sins.

On the other hand, the Lord has called His people to eternal salvation, and therefore they ought to consider that pardon for their sins is always ready. Hence, let us surely hold that if we are admitted and engrafted into the Body of the Church, the forgiveness of sins has been bestowed, and is daily bestowed on us, in divine liberality, through the intervention of Christ's merits, and the sanctification of the Spirit.

22 The keys of the Church given for the express purpose of securing this benefit. A summary of the answer to the fifth objection.

To impart this blessing to us, the keys have been given to the Church (See Matthew 16:19; 18:18.) For when Christ gave the command to the apostles, and conferred the power of forgiving sins, He not merely intended that they should loose the sins of those who should be converted from impiety to the faith of Christ; but, moreover, that they should perpetually perform this office among believers. This Paul teaches, when he says that the embassy of reconciliation has been committed to the ministers of the Church, that they may always exhort the people to be reconciled to God in the name of Christ. (See 2 Corinthians 5:20.) Therefore, in the communion of saints our sins are constantly forgiven by the ministry of the Church, when presbyters or bishops, to whom the office has been committed, confirm pious consciences, in the hope of pardon and forgiveness by the promises of the gospel, and that as well in public as in private, as the case requires. For there are many who, from their infirmity, stand in need of special pacification, and Paul declares that he testified of the grace of Christ not only in the public assembly, but from house to house, reminding each individually of the doctrine of salvation (See Acts 20:20, 21.)

Three things are here to be observed. First, whatever be the holiness, which the children of God possess, it is always under the condition, that so long as they dwell in a mortal body, they cannot stand before God without forgiveness of sins. Secondly, this benefit is so peculiar to the Church, that we cannot enjoy it unless we continue in the communion of the Church. Thirdly, it is dispensed to us by the ministers and pastors of the Church, either in the preaching of the gospel or the administration of the Sacraments, and herein is especially manifested the power of the keys, which the Lord has bestowed on the company of the faithful.

Accordingly, let each of us consider it his duty to seek forgiveness of sins only where the Lord has placed it. Of the public reconciliation, which relates to discipline, we shall speak at the proper place.

23 Sixth objection, formerly advanced by the Novatians, and renewed by the Anabaptists. This error confuted by the Lord's Prayer.

But since those frantic spirits of whom I have spoken attempt to rob the Church of this the only anchor of salvation, consciences must be more firmly strengthened against this pestilential opinion. The Novatians, in ancient times, agitated the churches with this dogma, but in our day, not unlike the Novatians are some of the Anabaptists, who have fallen into the same delirious dreams. For they pretend that in baptism, the people of God are regenerated to a pure and angelical life, which is not polluted by any carnal defilement. But if a man sin after baptism, they leave him nothing except the inexorable judgment of God.

In short, to the sinner who has lapsed after receiving grace they give no hope of pardon, because they admit no other forgiveness of sins save that by which we are first regenerated. But although no falsehood is more clearly refuted by Scripture, yet as these men find means of imposition (as Novatus also of old had very many followers), let us briefly show how much they rave, to the destruction of both themselves and others.

In the first place, since by the command of our Lord the saints daily repeat this prayer, "Forgive us our debts" (Matthew 6:12), they confess that they are debtors. Nor do they ask in vain, for the Lord has only enjoined them to ask what He will give. Nay, while He has declared that the whole prayer will be heard by His Father, He has sealed this absolution with a peculiar promise. What more do we wish? The Lord requires of His saints confession of sins during their whole lives, and that without ceasing, and promises pardon. How presumptuous, then, to exempt them from sin, or when they have stumbled, to exclude them altogether from grace? Then whom does He enjoin us to pardon seventy and seven times? Is it not our brethren? (See Matthew 18:22.) And why has He so enjoined but that we may imitate His clemency? He therefore pardons not once or twice only, but as often as we feel alarmed under a sense of our faults. Sighing, we call upon Him.

24 A second answer, founded on some examples under the Old Testament.

And to begin almost with the very first commencement of the Church: the Patriarchs had been circumcised, admitted to a participation in the covenant, and doubtless instructed by their father's care in righteousness and integrity, when they conspired to commit fratricide. The crime was one, which the most abandoned robbers would have abominated. At length, softened by the remonstrance of Judah, they sold him; this also was intolerable cruelty. Simeon and Levi took a nefarious revenge on the sons of Sychem, one, too, condemned by the judgment of their father. Reuben, with execrable lust, defiled his father's bed. Judah, when seeking to commit whoredom, sinned against the law of nature with his daughter-in-law. But so far are they from being expunged from the chosen people, that they are rather raised to be its heads. What, moreover, of David? When on the throne of righteousness, with what iniquity did he make way for blind lust, by the shedding of innocent blood? He had already been regenerated, and, as one of the regenerated, received distinguished approbation from the Lord. But he perpetrated a crime at which even the Gentiles would have been horrified, and yet obtained pardon. And not to dwell on special examples, all the promises of divine mercy extant in the Law and the Prophets are so many proofs that the Lord is ready to forgive the offenses of His people. For why does Moses promise a future period, when the people who had fallen into rebellion should return to the Lord? "Then the Lord thy God will turn thy captivity, and have compassion upon thee, and will return and gather thee from all the nations whither the Lord thy God hath scattered thee" (Deuteronomy 30:3).

25 A third answer, confirmed by passages from Jeremiah, Ezekiel, and Solomon. A fourth answer, derived from sacrifices.

But I am unwilling to begin an enumeration, which never could be finished. The prophetical books are filled with similar promises, offering mercy to a people covered with innumerable transgressions. What crime is more heinous than rebellion? It is styled divorce between God and the Church, and yet, by His goodness, it is surmounted. They say, "If a man put away his wife, and she go from him, and become another man's, shall he return unto her again? Shall not that land be greatly polluted? But thou hast played the harlot with many lovers; yet return again unto me, saith the Lord." "Return, thou backsliding Israel, saith the Lord; and I will not cause mine anger to fall upon you; for I am merciful, saith the Lord, and I will not keep anger forever" (Jeremiah 3:1, 12). And surely, He could not have a different feeling who declares, "I have no pleasure in the death of him that dieth;" "Wherefore turn yourselves, and live ye" (Ezekiel 18:23, 32). Accordingly, when Solomon dedicated the temple, one of the uses for which it was destined was that prayers offered up for the pardon of sins might there be heard.

"If they sin against thee (for there is no man that sinneth not), and thou be angry with them, and deliver them to the enemy, so that they carry them away captive unto the land of the enemy, far or near; yet if they shall bethink themselves in the land whither they were carried captives, and repent, and make supplication unto thee in the land of them that carried them captives, saying, We have sinned, and have done perversely, we have committed wickedness; and so return unto thee with all their heart, and with all their soul, in the land of their enemies which led them away captive, and pray unto thee towards their land, which thou gavest unto their fathers, the city which thou hast chosen, and the house which I have built for thy name: then hear thou their prayer and their supplication in heaven thy dwelling place, and maintain their cause, and forgive thy people that have sinned against thee, and all their transgressions wherein they have transgressed against thee" (1 Kings 8:46-50). Nor in vain in the Law did God ordain a daily sacrifice for sins. Had He not foreseen that His people were constantly to labor under the disease of sin, He never would have appointed these remedies.

26 A fifth answer, from the New Testament. Some special examples.

Did the advent of Christ, by which the fullness of grace was displayed, deprive believers of this privilege of supplicating for the pardon of their sins? If they offended against the Lord, were they not to obtain any mercy? What were it but to say that Christ came not for the salvation, but for the destruction of His people, if the divine indulgence in pardoning sin, which was constantly provided for the saints under the Old Testament, is now declared to have been taken away? But if we give credit to the Scriptures, when distinctly proclaiming that in Christ alone the grace and loving kindness of the Lord have fully appeared, the riches of His mercy been poured out, reconciliation between God and man accomplished (see Titus 2:11; 3:4; 2 Timothy 1:9, 10), let us not doubt that the clemency of our heavenly Father, instead of being cut off or curtailed, is in much greater exuberance. Nor are proofs of this wanting. Peter, who had heard our Savior declare that he who did not confess His name before men would be denied before the angels of God, denied him thrice in one night, and not without execration; yet, he is not denied pardon. (See Mark 8:38.) Those who lived disorderly among the Thessalonians, though chastised, are still invited to repentance. (See 2 Thessalonians 3:6.) Not even is Simon Magus thrown into despair. He is rather told to hope, since Peter invites him to have recourse to prayer (Acts 8:22).

27 General examples. A celebrated passage. The arrangement of the Creed.

What shall we say to the fact, that occasionally whole churches have been implicated in the grossest sins, and yet Paul, instead of giving them over to destruction, rather mercifully extricated them? The defection of the Galatians was no trivial fault; the Corinthians were still less excusable, the iniquities prevailing among them being more numerous and not less heinous, yet neither is excluded from the mercy of the Lord. Nay, the very persons who had sinned above others in uncleanness and fornication are expressly invited to repentance. The covenant of the Lord remains, and ever will remain, inviolable. That covenant He solemnly ratified with Christ, the true Solomon, and His members, in these words: "If his children forsake my law, and walk not in my judgments; if they break my statutes, and keep not my commandments; then will I visit their transgression with the rod, and their iniquity with stripes. Nevertheless, my loving-kindness will I not utterly take from him" (Psalm 89:30-33). In short, by the very arrangement of the Creed, we are reminded that forgiveness of sins always resides in the Church of Christ, for after the Church is constituted, forgiveness of sins is subjoined.

28 Objection, that voluntary transgression excludes from the Church.

Some persons who have somewhat more discernment, seeing that the dogma of Novatus is so clearly refuted in Scripture, do not make every fault unpardonable, but that voluntary transgression of the Law into which a man falls knowingly and willingly. Those who speak thus allow pardon to those sins only that have been committed through ignorance. But since the Lord has in the Law ordered some sacrifices to be offered in expiation of the voluntary sins of believers, and others to redeem sins of ignorance (Leviticus 4), how perverse is it to concede no expiation to a voluntary sin? I hold nothing to be more plain, than that the one sacrifice of Christ avails to remit the voluntary sins of believers, the Lord having attested this by carnal sacrifices as emblems. Then how is David, who was so well instructed in the Law, to be excused by ignorance? Did David, who was daily punishing it in others, not know how heinous a crime murder and adultery was? Did the patriarchs deem fratricide a lawful act? Had the Corinthians made so little proficiency as to imagine that God was pleased with lasciviousness, impurity, whoredom, hatred, and strife? Was Peter, after being so carefully warned, ignorant how heinous it was to forswear his Master? Therefore, let us not by our malice shut the door against the divine mercy, when so benignly manifested.

29 Last objection of the Novatians, founded on the solemn renewal of repentance required by the Church for more heinous offenses. Answer.

I am aware, that by the sins which are daily forgiven to believers, ancient writers have understood the lighter errors which creep in through the infirmity of the flesh, while they thought that the formal repentance which was then exacted for more heinous crimes was no more to be repeated than baptism. This opinion is not to be viewed as if they wished to plunge those into despair who had fallen from their first repentance, or to extenuate those errors as if they were of no account before God. For they knew that the saints often stumble through unbelief, that superfluous oaths occasionally escape them, that they sometimes boil with anger, nay, break out into open invectives, and labor under other evils that are greatly offensive to the Lord. But they so called them to distinguish them from public crimes, which came under the cognizance of the Church, and produced much scandal. The great difficulty they had in pardoning those who had done something that called for ecclesiastical animadversion, was not because they thought it difficult to obtain pardon from the Lord, but by this severity they wished to deter others from rushing precipitately into crimes, which, by their demerit, would alienate them from the communion of the Church. Still the Word of the Lord, which here ought to be our only rule, certainly prescribes greater moderation, since it teaches that the rigor of discipline must not be stretched so far as to overwhelm with grief the individual for whose benefit it should specially be designed (2 Corinthians 2:7), as we have above discoursed at greater length.

Chapter 2

COMPARISON BETWEEN THE FALSE CHURCH AND THE TRUE.

The divisions of the chapter are,–I. Description of a spurious church, resembling the Papacy vaunting of personal succession, of which a refutation is subjoined, sections 1-4. II. An answer, in name of the orthodox Churches, to the popish accusations of heresy and schism. A description of the churches existing at present under the Papacy.

Sections

1. Recapitulation of the matters treated in the previous chapter. Substance of the present chapter—viz. Where lying and falsehood prevail, no church exists. There is falsehood wherever the pure doctrine of Christ is not in vigor.

2. This falsehood prevails under the Papacy. Hence, the Papacy is not a church. Still the Papists extol their own church, and charge those who dissent from it with heresy and schism. They attempt to defend their vaunting by the name of personal succession. A succession, which abandons the truth of Christ, proved to be of no importance.

3. This proof confirmed, A. By examples and passages of Scripture; B. By reason and the authority of Augustine.

4. Whatever the Papists may pretend, there is no church where the Word of God appears not.

5. The objection of personal succession, and the charge of heresy and schism, refuted, both from Scripture and Augustine.

6. The same thing confirmed by the authority of Cyprian. The anathemas of the Papists of no consequence.

7. The churches of the Papists are in the same situation as those of the Israelites, which revolted to superstition and idolatry under Jeroboam.

8. The character of those Israelitish churches.

9. Hence, the Papists act unjustly when they would compel us to communion with their church. Their two demands. Answer to the first. Sum of the question. Why we cannot take part in the external worship of the Papists.

10. Second demand of the Papists answered.

11. Although the Papacy cannot properly be called a church, still, against the will of Antichrist himself, there is some vestige of a church in the Papacy, as baptism and some other remnants.

12. The name of church not conceded to the Papacy, though under its domination there have been some kind of churches. Herein is a fulfillment of Paul's prophecy, that Antichrist would sit in the temple of God. Deplorable condition of such churches. Summary of the chapter.

1 Recapitulation of the matters treated in the previous chapter. Substance of the present chapter—viz. Where lying and falsehood prevail, no church exists. There is falsehood wherever the pure doctrine of Christ is not in vigor.

How much the ministry of the Word and sacraments should weigh with us, and how far reverence for it should extend, to be a perpetual badge for distinguishing the church, has been explained. We have shown, first, that wherever it exists entire and unimpaired, neither errors of conduct nor defects should prevent us from giving the name of church. Secondly, trivial errors in this ministry ought not to make us regard it as illegitimate. Moreover, we have shown that the errors to which such pardon is due, are those by which the fundamental doctrine of religion is not injured, and by which those articles of religion, in which all believers should agree, are not suppressed while, in regard to the sacraments, the defects neither destroy nor impair the legitimate institution of their Author.

But as soon as falsehood has forced its way into the citadel of religion, as soon as the sum of necessary doctrine is inverted, and the use of the sacraments is destroyed, the death of the church undoubtedly ensues, just as the life of man is destroyed when his throat is pierced, or his vitals mortally wounded. This is clearly evinced by the words of Paul when he says, that the Church is "built upon the foundation of the apostles and prophets, Jesus Christ himself being the chief cornerstone" (Ephesians 2:20). If the Church is founded on the doctrine of the apostles and prophets, by which believers are enjoined to place their salvation in Christ alone, then if that doctrine is destroyed, how can the Church continue to stand? The Church must necessarily fall whenever that sum of religion, which alone can sustain it, has given way. Again, if the true Church is "the pillar and ground of the truth" (1 Timothy 3:15), it is certain that there is no church where lying and falsehood have usurped the ascendancy.

2 This falsehood prevails under the Papacy. Hence, the Papacy is not a church. Still the Papists extol their own Church, and charge those who dissent from it with heresy and schism. They attempt to defend their vaunting by the name of personal succession. A succession, which abandons the truth of Christ, proved to be of no importance.

Since this is the state of matters under the Papacy, we can understand how much of the church there survives. There, instead of the ministry of the Word, prevails a perverted government, compounded of lies, a government, which partly extinguishes, partly suppresses, the pure light. In place of the Lord's Supper, the foulest sacrilege has entered, the worship of God is deformed by a varied mass of intolerable superstitions; doctrine (without which Christianity exists not) is wholly buried and exploded, the public assemblies are schools of idolatry and impiety. Wherefore, in declining fatal participation in such wickedness, we run no risk of being dissevered from the Church of Christ. The communion of the Church was not instituted to be a chain to bind us in idolatry, impiety, ignorance of God, and other kinds of evil, but rather to retain us in the fear of God and obedience of the truth.

They, indeed, vaunt loudly of their church, as if there was not another in the world; and then, as if the matter were ended, they make out that all are schismatics who withdraw from obedience to that church which they thus depict, that all are heretics who presume to whisper against its doctrine. (See section 5.) But by what arguments do they prove their possession of the true church? They appeal to ancient records, which formerly existed in Italy, France, and Spain. They pretend to derive their origin from those holy men who, by sound doctrine, founded and raised up churches, confirmed the doctrine, and reared the edifice of the Church with their blood. They pretend that the Church, thus consecrated by spiritual gifts and the blood of martyrs, was preserved from destruction by a perpetual succession of bishops. They dwell on the importance, which Irenaeus, Tertullian, Origen, Augustine, and others attached to this succession. (See section 3.)

How frivolous and plainly ludicrous these allegations are, I will enable any, who will for a little consider the matter with me, to understand without any difficulty. I would also exhort our opponents to give their serious attention, if I had any hope of being able to benefit them by instruction.

But since they have laid aside all regard to truth, and make it their only aim to prosecute their own ends in whatever way they can, I will only make a few observations by which good men and lovers of truth may disentangle themselves from their quibbles. First, I ask them why they do not quote Africa, and Egypt, and all Asia, just because in all those regions there was a cessation of that sacred succession, by the aid of which they vaunt of having continued churches. They therefore fall back on the assertion, that they have the true church, because ever since it began to exist it was never destitute of bishops, because they succeeded each other in an unbroken series. But what if I bring Greece before them? Therefore, I again ask them, Why they say that the church perished among the Greeks, among whom there never was any interruption in the succession of bishops—a succession, in their opinion, the only guardian and preserver of the church? They make the Greeks schismatics. Why? Because, by revolting from the Apostolic See, they lost their privilege. What? Do not those who revolt from Christ much more deserve to lose it? It follows, therefore, that the pretence of succession is vain, if posterity do not retain the truth of Christ, which was handed down to them by their fathers, safe and uncorrupted, and continue in it.

3 This proof confirmed, A. By examples and passages of Scripture; B. By reason and the authority of Augustine.

In the present day, therefore, the presence of the Romanists is just the same as that which appears to have been formerly used by the Jews, when the prophets of the Lord charged them with blindness, impiety, and idolatry. For as the Jews proudly vaunted of their temple, ceremonies, and priesthood, by which, with strong reason, as they supposed, they measured the Church, so, instead of the Church, we are presented by the Romanists with certain external masks, which often are far from being connected with the Church, and without which the Church can perfectly exist. Wherefore, we need no other argument to refute them than that with which Jeremiah opposed the foolish confidence of the Jews–namely, "Trust ye not in lying words, saying, The temple of the Lord, The temple of the Lord, The temple of the Lord are these" (Jeremiah 7:4).

The Lord recognizes nothing as His own, save when His Word is heard and religiously observed. Thus, though the glory of God sat in the sanctuary between the cherubim (see Ezekiel 10:4), and He had promised that He would there have His stated abode, still when the priests corrupted His worship by depraved superstitions, He transferred it elsewhere, and left the place without any sanctity. If that temple which seemed consecrated for the perpetual habitation of God, could be abandoned by God and become profane, the Romanists have no ground to pretend that God is so bound to persons or places, and fixed to external observances, that He must remain with those who have only the name and semblance of a church. This is the question, which Paul discusses in the Epistle to the Romans, from the ninth to the twelfth chapter.

Weak consciences were greatly disturbed, when those who seemed to be the people of God not only rejected, but also even persecuted the doctrine of the gospel. Therefore, after expounding doctrine, he removes this difficulty, denying that those Jews, the enemies of the truth, were the Church, though they wanted nothing which might otherwise have been desired to the external form of the Church. The ground of his denial is that they did not embrace Christ. In the Epistle to the Galatians, when comparing Ishmael with Isaac, he says still more expressly, that many hold a place in the Church to whom the inheritance does not belong, because they were not the offspring of a free parent. From this he proceeds to draw a contrast between two Jerusalems, because as the Law was given on Mount Sinai, but the gospel proceeded from Jerusalem. Consequently, many born and brought up in servitude confidently boast that they are the sons of God and of the Church. Nay, while they are themselves degenerate, they proudly despise the genuine sons of God.

Let us also, in like manner, when we hear that it was once declared from Heaven, "Cast out the bondmaid and her son," trust to this inviolable decree, and boldly despise their unmeaning boasts. For if they plume themselves on external profession, Ishmael also was circumcised: if they found on antiquity, he was the firstborn. Yet, we see that he was rejected. If the reason is asked, Paul assigns it (Romans 9:6), that those only are accounted sons who are born of the pure and legitimate seed of doctrine. On this ground, God declares that He was not astricted to impious priests, though He had made a covenant with their father Levi to be their angel or interpreter. (See Malachi 2:4.) Nay, He retorts the false boast by which they were wont to rise against the Prophets–namely, that the dignity of the priesthood was to be held in singular estimation. This He himself willingly admits: and He disputes with them, on the ground that He is ready to fulfill the covenant, while they, by not fulfilling it on their part, deserve to be rejected. Here, then, is the value of succession when not conjoined with imitation and corresponding conduct. Posterity, as soon as they are convicted of having revolted from their origin, are deprived of all honor, unless we are prepared to say that because Caiaphas succeeded many pious priests (nay, the series from Aaron to him was continuous), that accursed assembly deserved the name of church. Even in earthly governments, no one would bear to see the tyranny of Caligula, Nero, Heliogabalus, and the like, described as the true condition of a republic, because they succeeded such men as Brutus, Scipio, and Camillus.

That in the government of the Church especially, nothing is more absurd than to disregard doctrine, and place succession in persons. Nor, indeed, was anything further from the intention of the holy teachers, whom they falsely obtrude upon us, than to maintain distinctly that churches exist, as by hereditary right, wherever bishops have been uniformly succeeded by bishops. But while it was without controversy that no change had been made in doctrine from the beginning down to their day, they assumed it a sufficient refutation of all their errors, that they were opposed to the doctrine maintained constantly, and with unanimous consent, even by the apostles themselves. They have, therefore, no longer any ground for proceeding to make a gloss of the name of the Church, which we regard with due reverence; but when we come to definition, not only (to use the common expression) does the water adhere to them, but they stick in their own mire, because they substitute a vile prostitute for the sacred spouse of Christ. That the substitution may not deceive us, let us, among other admonitions, attend to the following from Augustine. Speaking of the Church, he says, "She herself is sometimes obscured, and beclouded by a multitude of scandals; sometimes, in a time of tranquility, she appears quiet and free; sometimes she is covered and tossed by the billows of tribulation and trial." As instances, he mentions that the strongest pillars of the Church often bravely endured exile for the faith, or lay hid throughout the world.

4 Whatever the Papists may pretend, there is no church where the Word of God appears not.

In this way, the Romanists assail us in the present day, and terrify the unskillful with the name of church, while they are the deadly adversaries of Christ. Therefore, although they exhibit a temple, a priesthood, and other similar masks, the empty glare by which they dazzle the eyes of the simple should not move us in the least to admit that there is a church where the Word of God appears not. The Lord furnished us with an unfailing test when He said, "Everyone that is of the truth heareth my voice" (John 18:37). Again, "I am the good shepherd, and know my sheep, and am known of mine." "My sheep hear my voice, and I know them, and they follow me." A little before He had said, when the shepherd "putteth forth his own sheep, he goeth before them, and the sheep follow him; for they know his voice. And a stranger will they not follow, but will flee from him: for they know not the voice of strangers" (John 10:14, 4, 5).

Why then do we, of our own accord, form such an infatuated estimate of the Church, since Christ has designated it by a sign in which is nothing in the least degree equivocal? This sign is seen everywhere, the existence of which infallibly proves the existence of the Church, while its absence proves the absence of everything that properly bears the name of Church. Paul declares that the Church is not founded either upon the judgments of men or the priesthood, but upon the doctrine of the Apostles and Prophets (Ephesians 2:20). Nay, Jerusalem is to be distinguished from Babylon, the Church of Christ from a conspiracy of Satan, by the discriminating test which our Savior has applied to them, "He that is of God, heareth God's words: ye therefore hear them not, because ye are not of God" (John 8:47). In short, since the Church is the Kingdom of Christ, and He reigns only by His word, can there be any doubt as to the falsehood of those statements by which the Kingdom of Christ is represented without His scepter, in other words, without His sacred word?

5 The objection of personal succession, and the charge of heresy and schism, refuted, both from Scripture and Augustine.

As to their charge of heresy and schism, because we preach a different doctrine, and submit not to their laws, and meet apart from them for prayer, baptism, the administration of the Supper, and other sacred rites, it is indeed a very serious accusation, but one which needs not a long and labored defense. The name of heretics and schismatics is applied to those who, by dissenting from the Church, destroy its communion. This communion is held together by two chains–viz. consent in sound doctrine and brotherly charity.

Hence, the distinction, which Augustine makes between heretics and schismatics, is that the former corrupt the purity of the faith by false dogmas, whereas the latter sometimes, even while holding the same faith, break the bond of union. But the thing to be observed is, that this union of charity so depends on unity of faith, as to have within its beginning and its end–in fine, its only rule. Let us therefore remember, that whenever ecclesiastical unity is commended to us, the thing required is, that while our minds consent in Christ, our wills also be united together by mutual goodwill in Christ. Accordingly, Paul, when he exhorts us to it, takes for his fundamental principle that there is "one God, one faith, one baptism" (Ephesians 4:5). Nay, when he tells us to be "of one accord, of one mind," he immediately adds, "Let this mind be in you which was also in Christ Jesus" (Philippians 2:2, 5); intimating, that where the Word of the Lord is not, it is not a union of believers, but a faction of the ungodly.

6 The same thing confirmed by the authority of Cyprian. The anathemas of the Papists of no consequence.

Cyprian, also, following Paul, derives the fountain of ecclesiastical concord from the one bishopric of Christ. He afterwards adds, "There is one Church, which by increase from fruitfulness is more widely extended to a multitude, just as there are many rays of the sun, but one light, and many branches of a tree, but one trunk upheld by the tenacious root. When many streams flow from one fountain, though there seems wide spreading numerosity from the overflowing copiousness of the supply, yet unity remains in the origin. Pluck a ray from the body of the sun, and the unity sustains no division. Break a branch from a tree, and the branch will not germinate. Cut off a stream from a fountain, that which is thus cut off dries up. So the

Church, pervaded by the light of the Lord, extends over the whole globe, and yet the light which is everywhere diffused is one."

Words could not more elegantly express the inseparable connection, which all the members of Christ have with each other. We see how He constantly calls us back to the head. Accordingly, He declares that when heresies and schisms arise, it is because men return not to the origin of the truth, because they seek not the head, because they keep not the doctrine of the heavenly Master. Let them now go and clamor against us as heretics for having withdrawn from their church, since the only cause of our estrangement is that they cannot tolerate a pure profession of the truth. I say nothing of their having expelled us by anathemas and curses. The fact is more than sufficient to excuse us, unless they would also make schismatics of the apostles, with whom we have a common cause.

Christ, I say, forewarned His apostles, "they shall put you out of the synagogues" (John 16:2). The synagogues of which he speaks were then held to be lawful churches. Seeing then it is certain that we were cast out, and we are prepared to show that this was done for the name of Christ, the cause should first be ascertained before any decision is given either for or against us. This, however, if they choose, I am willing to leave to them; to me it is enough that we behooved to withdraw from them in order to draw near to Christ.

7 The churches of the Papists are in the same situation as those of the Israelites, which revolted to superstition and idolatry under Jeroboam.

The place which we ought to assign to all the churches on which the tyranny of the Romish idol has seized will better appear if we compare them with the ancient Israelitish Church, as delineated by the prophets. So long as the Jews and Israelites persisted in the laws of the covenant, a true Church existed among them; in other words, they by the kindness of God obtained the benefits of a Church. True doctrine was contained in the law, and the ministry of it was committed to the prophets and priests. They were initiated in religion by the sign of circumcision, and by the other sacraments trained and confirmed in the faith. There can be no doubt that the titles with which the Lord honored His Church were applicable to their society. After they forsook the law of the Lord, and degenerated into idolatry and superstition, they partly lost the privilege. For who can presume to deny the title of the Church to those with whom the Lord deposited the preaching of His Word and the observance of His mysteries?

On the other hand, who may presume to give the name of church, without reservation, to that assembly by which the Word of God is openly and with impunity trampled under foot—where His ministry, its chief support, and the very soul of the Church, is destroyed?

8 The character of those Israelitish churches.

Some will say, What then? Was there not a particle of the Church left to the Jews from the date of their revolt to idolatry? The answer is easy. First, I say that in the defection itself there were several gradations, for we cannot hold that the lapses by which both Judah and Israel turned aside from the pure worship of God were the same. Jeroboam corrupted religion entirely when he fabricated the calves against the express prohibition of God and dedicated an unlawful place for worship. The Jews became degenerate in manners and superstitious opinions before they made any improper change in the external form of religion. For although they had adopted many perverse ceremonies under Rehoboam, yet, as the doctrine of the law and the priesthood, and the rites which God had instituted, continued at Jerusalem, the pious still had the Church in a tolerable state.

In regard to the Israelites, matters that, up to the time of Ahab, had certainly not been reformed then became worse. Those who succeeded him, until the overthrow of the kingdom, were partly like him, and partly (when they wished to be somewhat better) followed the example of Jeroboam, while all, without exception, were wicked and idolatrous. In Judea, different changes now and then took place, some kings corrupting the worship of God by false and superstitious inventions, and others attempting to reform it, until, at length, the priests themselves polluted the temple of God by profane and abominable rites.

9 Hence, the Papists act unjustly when they would compel us to communion with their church. Their two demands. Answer to the first. Sum of the question. Why we cannot take part in the external worship of the Papists.

Now then let the Papists, in order to extenuate their vices as much as possible, deny, if they can, that the state of religion is as much vitiated and corrupted with them as it was in the kingdom of Israel under Jeroboam. They have a grosser idolatry, and in doctrine are not one whit more pure; rather, perhaps, they are even still more impure. God, nay, even those possessed of a moderate degree of judgment, will bear me witness, and the thing itself is too manifest to require me to enlarge upon it. When they would force us to the communion of their church, they make two demands upon us—first, that we join in their prayers, their sacrifices, and all their ceremonies; and, secondly, that whatever honor, power, and jurisdiction, Christ has given to His Church, the same we must attribute to theirs.

In regard to the first, I admit that all the prophets who were at Jerusalem, when matters there were very corrupt, neither sacrificed apart nor held separate meetings for prayer. For they had the command of God, which enjoined them to meet in the temple of Solomon, and they knew that the Levitical priests, whom the Lord had appointed over sacred matters, and who were not yet discarded, how unworthy soever they might be of that honor, were still entitled to hold it (Exodus 24:9).

But the principal point in the whole question is, that they were not compelled to any superstitious worship, nay, they undertook nothing but what had been instituted by God. But in these men, I mean the Papists, where is the resemblance? Scarcely can we hold any meeting with them without polluting ourselves with open idolatry. Their principal bond of communion is undoubtedly in the Mass, which we abominate as the greatest sacrilege.

Whether this is justly or rashly done will be elsewhere seen. (See chapter 18; see also Book 2, chapter 15, section 6). It is now sufficient to show that our case is different from that of the prophets, who, when they were present at the sacred rites of the ungodly, were not obliged to witness or use any ceremonies but those which were instituted by God.

But if we would have an example in all respects similar, let us take one from the kingdom of Israel. Under the ordinance of Jeroboam, circumcision remained, sacrifices were offered, the law was deemed holy, and the God whom they had received from their fathers was worshipped; but in consequence of invented and forbidden modes of worship, everything which was done there God disapproved and condemned. Show me one prophet or pious man who once worshipped or offered sacrifice in Bethel. They knew that they could not do it without defiling themselves with some kind of sacrilege. We hold, therefore, that the communion of the Church ought not to be carried so far by the godly as to lay them under a necessity of following it when it has degenerated to profane and polluted rites.

10 Second demand of the Papists answered.

With regard to the second point, our objections are still stronger. For when the church is considered in that particular point of view as the church, whose judgment we are bound to revere, whose authority acknowledge, whose admonitions obey, whose censures dread, whose communion religiously cultivate in every respect, we cannot concede that they have a church, without obliging ourselves to subjection and obedience. Still we are willing to concede what the Prophets conceded to the Jews and Israelites of their day, when with them matters were in a similar, or even in a better condition. For we see how they uniformly exclaim against their meetings as profane conventicles, to which it is not more lawful for them to assent than to abjure God (Isaiah 1:14). And certainly if those were churches, it follows, that Elijah, Micaiah, and others in Israel, Isaiah, Jeremiah, Hosea, and those of like character in Judah, whom the prophets, priests, and people of their day, hated and execrated more than the uncircumcised, were aliens from the Church of God. If those were churches, then the Church was no longer the pillar of the truth, but the stay of falsehood, not the tabernacle of the living God, but a receptacle of idols. They were, therefore, under the necessity of refusing consent to their meetings, since consent was nothing else than impious conspiracy against God. For this same reason, should anyone acknowledge those meetings of the present day, which are contaminated by idolatry, superstition, and impious doctrine, as churches, full communion with which a Christian must maintain so far as to agree with them even in doctrine, he will greatly err. For if they are churches, the power of the keys belongs to them, whereas the keys are inseparably connected with the Word which they have put to flight. Again, if they are churches, they can claim the promise of Christ, "Whatsoever ye bind," etc.; whereas, on the contrary, they discard from their communion all who sincerely profess themselves the servants of Christ. Therefore, either the promise of Christ is vain, or in this respect, at least, they are not churches.

In fine, instead of the ministry of the Word, they have schools of impiety, and sinks of all kinds of error. Therefore, in this point of view, either they are not churches, or no badge will remain by which the lawful meetings of the faithful can be distinguished from the meetings of Turks.

11 Although the Papacy cannot properly be called a church, still, against the will of Antichrist himself, there is some vestige of a church in the Papacy, as baptism and some other remnants.

Still, as in ancient times, there remained among the Jews certain special privileges of a Church, so in the present day we deny not to the Papists those vestiges of a Church, which the Lord has allowed to remain among them amid the dissipation. When the Lord had once made His covenant with the Jews, it was preserved not so much by them as by its own strength, supported by which it withstood their impiety. Such, then, is the certainty and constancy of the divine goodness, that the covenant of the Lord continued there and His faith could not be obliterated by their betrayal; nor could circumcision be so profaned by their impure hands as not still to be a true sign and sacrament of His covenant. Hence, the children who were born to them the Lord called His own (Ezekiel 16:20), though, unless by special blessing, they in no respect belonged to Him. So having deposited His covenant in Gaul, Italy, Germany, Spain, and England, when these countries were oppressed by the tyranny of Antichrist, in order that His covenant might remain inviolable, He first preserved baptism there as an evidence of the covenant; –baptism, which, consecrated by His lips, retains its power in spite of human depravity. Secondly, he provided that there should be other remains also to prevent the Church from utterly perishing. But as in pulling down buildings, the foundations and ruins are often permitted to remain, so He did not suffer Antichrist either to subvert His Church from its foundation, or to level it with the ground, but was pleased that amid the devastation the edifice should remain, though half in ruins. Although, to punish the ingratitude of men who had despised His Word, he allowed a fearful shaking and dismembering to take place.

12 The name of church not conceded to the Papacy, though under its domination there have been some kind of churches. Herein is a fulfillment of Paul's prophecy, that Antichrist would sit in the temple of God. Deplorable condition of such churches. Summary of the chapter.

Therefore, while we are unwilling simply to concede the name of church to the Papists, we do not deny that there are churches among them. The question we raise only relates to the true and legitimate constitution of the church, implying communion in sacred rites, which are the signs of profession, and especially in doctrine. Daniel and Paul foretold that Antichrist would sit in the temple of God (Daniel 9:27; 2 Thessalonians 2:4). We regard the Roman Pontiff as the leader and standard-bearer of that wicked and abominable kingdom. By placing his seat in the temple of God, it is intimated that his kingdom would not be such as to destroy the name either of Christ or of His Church. Hence, then, it is obvious that we do not at all deny that churches remain under his tyranny. Churches, however, which by sacrilegious impiety he has profaned, by cruel domination has oppressed, by evil and deadly doctrines like poisoned potions has corrupted and almost slain; churches where Christ lies half buried, the gospel is suppressed, piety is put to flight, and the worship of God almost abolished; where, in short, all things are in such disorder as to present the appearance of Babylon rather than the holy city of God. In one word, I call them churches, inasmuch as the Lord there wondrously preserves some remains of His people, though miserably torn and scattered, and inasmuch as some symbols of the Church still remain–symbols especially whose efficacy neither the craft of the devil nor human depravity can destroy. But as, on the other hand, those marks to which we ought especially to have respect in this discussion are effaced; I say that the whole body, as well as every single assembly, wants the form of a legitimate Church.

Chapter 3

OF THE TEACHERS AND MINISTERS OF THE CHURCH. THEIR ELECTION AND OFFICE.

The three heads of this chapter are,—I. A few preliminary remarks on Church order, on the end, utility, necessity, and dignity of the Christian ministry, sections 1-3. II. A separate consideration of the persons performing Ecclesiastical functions, sections 4-10. III. Of the Ordination or calling of the ministers of the Church, sections 10-16.

Sections

1. *Summary of the chapter. Reasons why God, in governing the Church, uses the ministry of men. A. To declare His condescension. B. To train us to humility and obedience. C. To bind us to each other in mutual charity. These reasons confirmed by Scripture.*

2. *This ministry of men most useful to the whole Church. Its advantages enumerated.*

3. *The honorable terms in which the ministry is spoken of. Its necessity established by numerous examples.*

4. *Second part of the chapter, treating of ecclesiastical office-bearers in particular. Some of them, as apostles, prophets, and evangelists, temporary. Others, as pastors and teachers, perpetual and indispensable.*

5. *Considering the office of evangelist and apostle as one, we have pastors corresponding with apostles, and teachers with prophets. Why the name of apostles specially conferred on the twelve.*

6. *As to the apostles, so also to pastors the preaching of the Word and the administration of the sacraments has been committed. How the Word should be preached.*

7. Regularly, every pastor should have a separate church assigned to him. This, however, admits of modification, when duly and regularly made by public authority.

8. Bishops, presbyters, pastors, and ministers, are used by the apostles as one and the same. Some functions, as being temporary, are omitted. Two—namely, those of elders and deacons—as pertaining to the ministry of the Word, are retained.

9. Distinction between deacons. Some employed in distributing alms, others in taking care of the poor.

10. Third part of the chapter, treating of the ordination or calling of the ministers of the Church.

11. A twofold calling—viz. an external and an internal. Mode in which both are to be viewed.

12. A. Who are to be appointed ministers? B. Mode of appointment.

13. C. By whom the appointment is to be made. Why the apostles were elected by Christ alone. Of the calling and election of St. Paul.

14. Ordinary pastors are designated by other pastors. Why certain of the apostles also were designated by men.

15. The election of pastors does not belong to one individual. Other pastors should preside, and the people consent and approve.

16. Form in which the ministers of the Church are to be ordained. No express precept, but one. Laying on of hands.

1 Summary of the chapter. Reasons why God, in governing the Church, uses the ministry of men. A. To declare His condescension. B. To train us to humility and obedience. C. To bind us to each other in mutual charity. These reasons confirmed by Scripture.

We are now to speak of the order in which the Lord has been pleased that His Church should be governed. It is right that He alone should rule and reign in the Church, that He should preside and be conspicuous in it, and that its government should be exercised and administered solely by His word. Yet, as He does not dwell among us in visible presence and declare His will to us by His own lips. He uses the ministry of men by making them His substitutes, not by transferring His right and honor to them, but only doing His own work by their lips, just as an artificer uses a tool for any purpose. That which I have previously expounded (Chapter 1, section 5), I am again forced to repeat. God might have acted, in this respect, by himself, without any aid or instrument, or might even have done it by angels; but there are several reasons why He rather chooses to employ men.

First, in this way He declares His condescension towards us, employing men to perform the function of His ambassadors in the world, to be the interpreters of his secret will; in short, to represent His own person. Thus, He shows by experience that it is not to no purpose He calls us His temples, since by man's mouth He gives responses to men as from a sanctuary.

Secondly, it forms a most excellent and useful training to humility, when He accustoms us to obey His word though preached by men like ourselves, or, it may be, our inferiors in worth. Did He himself speak from Heaven, it would be no wonder if His sacred oracles were received by all ears and minds reverently and immediately. For who would not dread His present power? Who would not fall prostrate at the first view of His great majesty? Who would not be overpowered by that immeasurable splendor? But when a feeble man, sprung from the dust, speaks in the name of God, we give the best proof of our piety and obedience, by listening with docility to His servant, though not in any respect our superior. Accordingly, He hides the treasure of His heavenly wisdom in frail earthen vessels (2 Corinthians 4:7), that He may have a more certain proof of the estimation in which it is held by us.

Moreover, nothing was fitter to cherish mutual charity than to bind men together by this tie, appointing one of them as a pastor to teach the others who are enjoined to be disciples, and receive the common doctrine from a single mouth. For did every man suffice for himself, and stand in no need of another's aid (such is the pride of the human intellect), each would despise all others, and be in his turn despised.

The Lord, therefore, has astricted His Church to what He foresaw would be the strongest bond of unity when He deposited the doctrine of eternal life and salvation with men, that by their hands He might communicate it to others. To this Paul had respect when he wrote to the Ephesians, "There is one body, and one Spirit, even as ye are called in one hope of your calling; one Lord, one faith, one baptism, one God and Father of all, who is above all, and through all, and in you all. But unto every one of us is given grace according to the measure of the gift of Christ. Wherefore He saith, When He ascended up on high, He led captivity captive, and gave gifts unto men. (Now that He ascended, what is it but that He also descended first into the lower parts of the Earth? He that descended is the same also that ascended far above all heavens, that He might fill all things.) And He gave some, apostles; and some, prophets; and some, evangelists; and some, pastors and teachers; for the perfecting of the saints, for the work of the ministry, for the edifying of the Body of Christ: until we all come in the unity of the faith, and of the knowledge of the Son of God, unto a perfect man, unto the measure of the stature of the fullness of Christ: that we henceforth be no more children, tossed to and fro, and carried about with every wind of doctrine, by the sleight of men, and cunning craftiness, whereby they lie in wait to deceive; but speaking the truth in love, may grow up into Him in all things, which is the head, even Christ: from whom the whole body fitly joined together and compacted by that which every joint supplieth, according to the effectual working in the measure of every part, maketh increase of the body unto the edifying of itself in love" (Ephesians 4:4-16).

2 This ministry of men most useful to the whole Church. Its advantages enumerated.

By these words, He shows that the ministry of men, which God employs in governing the Church, is a principal bond by which believers are kept together in one body. He also intimates, that the Church cannot be kept safe, unless supported by those guards to which the Lord has been pleased to commit its safety. Christ "ascended far above all heavens, that he might fill all things" (Ephesians 4:10). The mode of filling is this: By the ministers to whom He has committed this office, and given grace to discharge it, He dispenses and distributes His gifts to the Church, and thus exhibits himself as in a manner actually present by exerting the energy of His Spirit in this His institution, so as to prevent it from being vain or fruitless. In this way, the renewal of the saints is accomplished, and the Body of Christ is edified; in this way we grow up in all things unto Him who is the Head, and unite with one another; in this way we are all brought into the unity of Christ, provided prophecy flourishes among us, provided we receive His apostles, and despise not the doctrine which is administered to us.

Whoever, therefore, studies to abolish this order and kind of government of which we speak, or disparages it as of minor importance, plots the devastation, or rather the ruin and destruction, of the Church. For neither are the light and heat of the sun, nor meat and drink, so necessary to sustain and cherish the present life, as is the apostolical and pastoral office to preserve a Church in the Earth.

3 The honorable terms in which the ministry is spoken of. Its necessity established by numerous examples.

Accordingly, I have observed above, that God has repeatedly commended its dignity by the titles, which He has bestowed upon it, in order that we might hold it in the highest estimation, as among the most excellent of our blessings. He declares, that in raising up teachers, He confers a special benefit on men, when He bids His prophet exclaim, "How beautiful upon the mountains are the feet of him that bringeth good tidings, that publisheth peace" (Isaiah 52:7); when He calls the apostles the light of the world and the salt of the earth (Matthew 5:13, 14). Nor could the office be more highly eulogized than when He said, "He that heareth you heareth me; and he that despiseth you despiseth me" (Luke 10:16).

But the most striking passage of all is that in the Second Epistle to the Corinthians, where Paul treats as it would be professedly of this question. He contends that there is nothing in the Church more noble and glorious than the ministry of the Gospel, seeing it is the administration of the Spirit of righteousness and eternal life. These and similar passages should have the effect of preventing that method of governing and maintaining the Church by ministers, a method which the Lord has ratified forever, from seeming worthless in our eyes, and at length becoming obsolete by contempt. How very necessary it is, He has declared not only by words but also by examples. When He was pleased to shed the light of His truth in greater effulgence on Cornelius, He sent an angel from Heaven to dispatch Peter to him (Acts 10:3). When He was pleased to call Paul to the knowledge of himself, and engraft him into the Church, He does not address him with His own voice, but sends him to a man from whom he may both obtain the doctrine of salvation and the sanctification of baptism (see Acts 9:6-20). If it was not by mere accident that the angel, who is the interpreter of God, abstains from declaring the will of God, and orders a man to be called to declare it; that Christ, the only Master of believers, commits Paul to the teaching of a man, that Paul whom He had determined to carry into the third heaven, and honor with a wondrous revelation of things that could not be spoken (see 2 Corinthians 12:2), who will presume to despise or disregard as superfluous that ministry, whose utility God has been pleased to attest by such evidence?

4 Second part of the chapter, treating of ecclesiastical office-bearers in particular. Some of them, as apostles, prophets, and evangelists, temporary. Others, as pastors and teachers, perpetual and indispensable.

Those who preside over the government of the Church, according to the institution of Christ, are named by Paul, first, *apostles*; secondly, *prophets*; thirdly, *evangelists*; fourthly, *pastors*; and, lastly, *teachers*. (See Ephesians 4:11.) Of these, only the two last have an ordinary office in the Church. The Lord raised up the other three at the beginning of His Kingdom, and still occasionally raises them up when the necessity of the times requires. The nature of the apostolic function is clear from the command, "Go ye into all the world, and preach the gospel to every creature" (Mark 16:15). No fixed limits are given them, but the whole world is assigned to be reduced under the obedience of Christ, that by spreading the gospel as widely as they could, they might everywhere erect His Kingdom. Accordingly, Paul, when he would approve his apostleship, does not say that he had acquired some one city for Christ, but had propagated the gospel far and wide–had not built on another man's foundation, but planted churches where the name of his Lord was unheard.

The apostles, therefore, were sent forth to bring back the world from its revolt to the true obedience of God, and everywhere establish His Kingdom by the preaching of the gospel; or, if you choose, they were like the first architects of the Church, to lay its foundations throughout the world.

By *prophets*, he means not all interpreters of the divine will, but those who excelled by special revelation; none such now exist, or they are less manifest. By *evangelists*, I mean those who, while inferior in rank to the apostles, were next to them in office, and even acted as their substitutes. Such were Luke, Timothy, Titus, and the like, perhaps, also, the seventy disciples whom our Savior appointed in the second place to the apostles (Luke 10:1). According to this interpretation, which appears to me consonant both to the words and the meaning of Paul, those three functions were not instituted in the Church to be perpetual, but only to endure so long as churches were to be formed where none previously existed, or at least where churches were to be transferred from Moses to Christ; although I deny not, that afterward God occasionally raised up apostles, or at least evangelists, in their stead, as has been done in our time. For such were needed to bring back the Church from the revolt of Antichrist. The office I nevertheless call extraordinary, because it has no place in churches duly constituted.

Next come *pastors* and *teachers*, with whom the Church never can dispense, and between whom, I think, there is this difference, that teachers preside not over discipline, or the administration of the sacraments, or admonitions, or exhortations, but the interpretation of Scripture only, in order that pure and sound doctrine may be maintained among believers. But all these are embraced in the pastoral office.

5 Considering the office of evangelist and apostle as one, we have pastors corresponding with apostles, and teachers with prophets. Why the name of apostles specially conferred on the twelve.

We now understand what offices in the government of the Church were temporary, and what offices were instituted to be of perpetual duration. But if we class evangelists with apostles, we shall have two like offices in a manner corresponding to each other. For the same resemblance which our teachers have to the ancient prophets pastors have to the apostles. The prophetical office was excellent in respect of the special gift of revelation, which accompanied it, but the office of teachers was almost of the same nature, and had altogether the same end.

In like manner, the twelve, whom the Lord chose to publish the new preaching of the gospel to the world (see Luke 6:13), excelled others in rank and dignity. For although, from the nature of the case, and etymology of the word, all ecclesiastical officers may be properly called apostles, because they are all sent by the Lord and are His messengers, yet as it was of great importance that a sure attestation should be given to the mission of those who delivered a new and extraordinary message, it was right that the twelve (to the number of whom Paul was afterwards added) should be distinguished from others by a peculiar title. The same name, indeed, is given by Paul to Andronicus and Junia, who, he says, were "of note among the apostles" (Romans 16:7); but when he would speak properly, he confines the term to that primary order. And this is the common use of Scripture. Still pastors (except that each has the government of a particular church assigned to him) have the same function as apostles. The nature of this function let us now see still more clearly.

6 As to the apostles, so also to pastors the preaching of the Word and the administration of the sacraments has been committed. How the Word should be preached.

When our Lord sent forth the apostles, He gave them a commission (as has been lately said) to preach the Gospel, and baptize those who believed for the remission of sins. He had previously commanded that they should distribute the sacred symbols of His body and blood after His example. (See Matthew 28:19; Luke 22:19.) Such is the sacred, inviolable, and perpetual law, enjoined on those who succeed to the place of the apostles–they receive a commission to preach the gospel and administer the sacraments. Whence we infer that those who neglect both of these falsely pretend to the office of apostles. But what shall we say of pastors? Paul speaks not of himself only but of all pastors, when he says, "Let a man so account of us, as of the ministers of Christ, and stewards of the mysteries of God" (1 Corinthians 4:1). Again, in another passage, he describes a bishop as one "holding fast the faithful word as he hath been taught, that he may be able by sound doctrine both to exhort and convince the gainsayers" (Titus 1:9).

From these and similar passages which everywhere occur, we may infer that the two principal parts of the office of pastors are to preach the gospel and administer the sacraments. But the method of teaching consists not merely in public addresses; it extends also to private admonitions.

Thus, Paul takes the Ephesians to witness, "I kept back nothing that was profitable to you, but have showed you, and have taught you publicly, and from house to house, testifying both to the Jews, and also to the Greeks, repentance toward God, and faith toward our Lord Jesus Christ." A little after he says, "Remember, that, for the space of three years, I ceased not to warn everyone night and day with tears" (Acts 20:20, 31).

Our present purpose, however, is not to enumerate the separate qualities of a good pastor, but only to indicate what those profess who call themselves pastors–viz. that in presiding over the Church, they have not an indolent dignity, but must train the people to true piety by the doctrine of Christ, administer the sacred mysteries, preserve and exercise right discipline. To those who are set as watchmen in the Church, the Lord declares, "When I say unto the wicked, Thou shalt surely die; and thou givest him not warning, nor speakest to warn the wicked from his wicked way, to save his life; the same wicked man shall die in his iniquity; but his blood will I require at thine hand" (Ezekiel 3:18). What Paul says of himself is applicable to all pastors: "For though I preach the gospel, I have nothing to glory of: for necessity is laid upon me; yea, woe is unto me if I preach not the Gospel" (1 Corinthians 4:16). In short, what the apostles did to the whole world, every pastor should do to the flock over which he is appointed.

7 **Regularly, every pastor should have a separate church assigned to him. This, however, admits of modification, when duly and regularly made by public authority.**

While we assign a church to each pastor, we deny not that he who is fixed to one church may assist other churches, whether any disturbance has occurred which requires his presence, or his advice is asked on some doubtful matter. But because that policy is necessary to maintain the peace of the Church, each has his proper duty assigned, lest all should become disorderly, run up and down without any certain vocation, flock together promiscuously to one spot, and capriciously leave the churches vacant, being more solicitous for their own convenience than for the edification of the Church. This arrangement ought, as far as possible, to be commonly observed, that not everyone, content with his own limits, may encroach on another's province. Nor is this a human invention. It is an ordinance of God. For we read that Paul and Barnabas appointed presbyters over each of the churches of Lystra, Antioch, and Iconium (see Acts 14:23); and Paul himself enjoins Titus to ordain presbyters in every town. (See

Titus 1:5.) In like manner, he mentions the bishops of the Philippians, and Archippus, the bishop of the Colossians. (See Philippians 1:1; Colossians 4:17.) And in the Acts, we have his celebrated address to the presbyters of the Church of Ephesus. (See Acts 20:28.)

Let everyone, then, who undertakes the government and care of one church, know that he is bound by this law of divine vocation, not that he is astricted to the soil (as lawyers speak), that is, enslaved and fixed, unable to move a foot if public utility so requires, and the thing is done duly and in order; but he who has been called to one place ought not to think of removing, nor seek to be set free when he deems it for his own advantage. Again, if it is expedient for anyone to be transferred to another place, he ought not to attempt it of his own private motive, but to wait for public authority.

8 Bishops, presbyters, pastors, and ministers, are used by the apostles as one and the same. Some functions, as being temporary, are omitted. Two—namely, those of elders and deacons—as pertaining to the ministry of the Word, are retained.

In giving the name of bishops, presbyters, and pastors, indiscriminately to those who govern churches, I have done it on the authority of Scripture, which uses the words as synonymous. To all who discharge the ministry of the word it gives the name of bishops. Thus Paul, after enjoining Titus to ordain elders in every city, immediately adds, "A bishop must be blameless," etc. (See Titus 1:5, 7.) So, in another place he salutes several bishops in one church. (See Philippians 1:1.) And in the Acts, the elders of Ephesus, whom he is said to have called together, he, in the course of his address, designates as bishops. (See Acts 20:17.) Here it is to be observed, that we have hitherto enumerated those offices only which consist in the ministry of the Word; nor does Paul make mention of any others in the passage which we have quoted from the fourth chapter of the Epistle to the Ephesians.

But in the Epistle to the Romans, and the First Epistle to the Corinthians, he enumerates other offices, as powers, gifts of healing, interpretation, government, care of the poor. (See Romans 12:7; 1 Corinthians 12:28.) As to those, which were temporary, I say nothing, for it is not worthwhile to dwell upon them. But there are two of perpetual duration–viz. government and care of the poor. By these governors, I understand seniors selected from the people to unite with the bishops in pronouncing censures and exercising discipline. For this is the only meaning which can be given to the passage, "He that ruleth with diligence" (Romans 12:8).

From the beginning, therefore, each church had its senate, composed of pious, grave, and venerable men, in whom was lodged the power of correcting faults. Of this power we shall afterwards speak. Moreover, experience shows that this arrangement was not confined to one age, and therefore we are to regard the office of government as necessary for all ages.

9 Distinction between deacons. Some employed in distributing alms, others in taking care of the poor.

The care of the poor was committed to deacons, of whom two classes are mentioned by Paul in the Epistle to the Romans, "He that giveth, let him do it with simplicity;" "he that showeth mercy, with cheerfulness" (Romans 12:8). As it is certain that he is here speaking of public offices of the Church, there must have been two distinct classes. If I mistake not, he in the former clause designates deacons, who administered alms, in the latter, those who had devoted themselves to the care of the poor and the sick. Such were the widows of whom he makes mention in the Epistle to Timothy. (See 1 Timothy 5:10.) For there was no public office, which women could discharge save that of devoting themselves to the service of the poor. If we admit this (and it certainly ought to be admitted), there will be two classes of deacons, the one serving the Church by administering the affairs of the poor, the other, by taking care of the poor themselves.

For although the term in Greek translations of Scripture has a more extensive meaning, it specially gives the name of deacons to those whom the Church appoints to dispense alms, and take care of the poor, constituting them stewards of the public treasury of the poor. Their origin, institution, and office, is described by Luke. (See Acts 6:3.) When a murmuring arose among the Greeks, because in the administration of the poor their widows were neglected, the apostles, excusing themselves that they were unable to discharge both offices, to preach the Word and serve tables, requested the multitude to elect seven men of good report, to whom the office might be committed. Such deacons as the Apostolic Church had, it becomes us to have after her example.

10 Third part of the chapter, treating of the ordination or calling of the ministers of the Church.

Now seeing that in the sacred assembly all things ought to be done decently and in order (see 1 Corinthians 14:40), there is nothing in which this ought to be more carefully observed than in settling government, irregularity in any respect being nowhere more perilous. Wherefore, lest restless and turbulent men should presumptuously push themselves forward to teach or rule (an event which actually was to happen), it was expressly provided that no one should assume a public office in the Church without a call. (See Hebrews 5:4; Jeremiah 17:16.)

Therefore, if anyone would be deemed a true minister of the Church, he must *first* be duly called; and, *secondly*, he must answer to his calling; that is, undertake and execute the office assigned to him.

This may often be observed in Paul, who, when he would approve his apostleship, usually alleges a call, together with his fidelity in discharging the office. If so great a minister of Christ dares not arrogate to himself authority to be heard in the Church, unless as having been appointed to it by the command of his Lord, and faithfully performing what has been entrusted to him, how great the effrontery for any man, devoid of one or both of them, to demand for himself such honor. But as we have already touched on the necessity of executing the office, let us now treat only of the call.

11 A twofold calling—viz. an external and an internal. Mode in which both are to be viewed.

The subject is comprehended under four heads–viz. *who* are to be appointed ministers, *in what way, by whom*, and *with what rite or initiatory ceremony*. I am speaking of the external and formal call that relates to the public order of the Church. I say nothing of that secret call of which every minister is conscious before God, but has not the Church as a witness of it. I mean the good testimony of our heart, that we undertake the offered office from neither ambition nor avarice, nor any other selfish feeling, but a sincere fear of God and desire to edify the Church. This, as I have said, is indeed necessary for every one of us, if we would approve our ministry to God. Still, however, a man may have been duly called by the Church, though he may have accepted with a bad conscience, provided his wickedness is not manifest. It is usual also to say, that private men are called to the ministry when they seem fit and apt to discharge it; that is, because learning, conjoined with piety and the other endowments of a good pastor, is a kind of preparation for the office. For those whom the Lord has destined for this great office he previously provides with the armor, which is requisite for the discharge of it, that they may not come empty and unprepared. Hence, Paul, in the First Epistle to the Corinthians, when treating of the offices, first enumerates the gifts in which those who performed the offices ought to excel. But as this is the first of the four heads, which I mentioned, let us now proceed to it.

12 A. Who are to be appointed ministers? B. Mode of appointment.

What persons should be elected bishops is treated at length by Paul in two passages (Titus 1:7; 1 Timothy 3:1). The substance is, that none are to be chosen save those who are of sound doctrine and holy lives, and not notorious for any defect which might destroy their authority and bring disgrace on the ministry. The description of deacons and elders is entirely similar (see Chapter 4 section 10-13). We must always take care that they are not unfit for or unequal to the burden imposed upon them; in other words, that they are provided with the means which will be necessary to fulfill their office. Thus our Savior, when about to send His apostles, provided them with the arms and instruments, which were indispensably requisite.

And Paul, after portraying the character of a good and genuine bishop, admonishes Timothy not to contaminate himself by choosing an improper person for the office. The expression, *in what way*, I use not in reference to the rite of choosing, but only to the religious fear, which is to be observed in election. Hence, the fasting and prayers which Luke narrates that the faithful employed when they elected presbyters (Acts 14:23). For, understanding that the business was the most serious in which they could engage, they did not venture to act without the greatest reverence and solicitude. But above all, they were earnest in prayer, imploring from God the spirit of wisdom and discernment.

13 C. By whom the appointment is to be made. Why the apostles were elected by Christ alone. Of the calling and election of St. Paul.

The third division, which we have adopted, is, *by whom* ministers are to be chosen. A certain rule on this head cannot be obtained from the appointment of the apostles, which was somewhat different from the common call of others. As theirs was an extraordinary ministry, in order to render it conspicuous by some more distinguished mark, those who were to discharge it behooved to be called and appointed by the mouth of the Lord himself. It was not, therefore, by any human election, but at the sole command of God and Christ, that they prepared themselves for the work.

Hence, when the apostles were desirous to substitute another in the place of Judas, they did not venture to nominate anyone certainly, but brought forward two, that the Lord might declare by lot which of them He wished to succeed. (See Acts 1:23.) In this way, we ought to understand Paul's declaration, that he was made an apostle, "not of men, neither by man, but by Jesus Christ, and God the Father" (Galatians 1:1). The former–viz. *not of men* he had in common with all the pious ministers of the Word, for no one could duly perform the office unless called by God. The other was proper and peculiar to him. And while he glories in it, he boasts that he had not only what pertains to a true and lawful pastor, but he also brings forward the insignia of his apostleship. For when there were some among the Galatians who, seeking to disparage his authority, represented him as some ordinary disciple, substituted in place of the primary apostles, he, in order to maintain unimpaired the dignity of his ministry, against which he knew that these attempts were made, felt it necessary to show that he was in no respect inferior to the other apostles. Accordingly, he affirms that he was not chosen by the judgment of men, like some ordinary bishop, but by the mouth and manifest oracle of the Lord himself.

14 Ordinary pastors are designated by other pastors. Why certain of the apostles also were designated by men.

But no sober person will deny that the regular mode of lawful calling is that bishops should be designated by men, since there are numerous passages of Scripture to this effect. Nor, as has been said, is there anything contrary to this in Paul's protestation. He was not sent either of man or by man, seeing he is not there speaking of the ordinary election of ministers, but claiming for himself what was peculiar to the apostles, although the Lord, in selecting Paul by special privilege, subjected him in the meantime to the discipline of an ecclesiastical call. Luke relates, "As they ministered to the Lord, and fasted, the Holy Ghost said, Separate me Barnabas and Saul for the work whereunto I have called them" (Acts 13:2). Why this separation and laying on of hands after the Holy Spirit had attested their election, unless that ecclesiastical discipline might be preserved in appointing ministers by men? God could not give a more illustrious proof of His approbation of this order, than by causing Paul to be set apart by the Church after He had previously declared that He had appointed him to be the Apostle of the Gentiles. The same thing we may see in the election of Matthias. As the apostolic office was of such importance that they did not venture to appoint anyone to it of their own judgment, they bring forward two, on one of whom the lot might fall, that thus the election might have a sure testimony from heaven, and, at the same time, the policy of the Church might not be disregarded.

15 The election of pastors does not belong to one individual. Other pastors should preside, and the people consent and approve.

The next question is, Whether a minister should be chosen *by the whole Church*, or only by *colleagues* and *elders*, who have the charge of discipline; or whether they may be appointed by the authority of one individual? Those who attribute this right to one individual quote the words of Paul to Titus "For this cause left I thee in Crete, that thou shouldest set in order the things that are wanting, and ordain elders in every city" (Titus 1:5); and also to Timothy, "Lay hands suddenly on no man" (1 Timothy 5:22). But they are mistaken if they suppose that Timothy so reigned at Ephesus, and Titus in Crete, as to dispose of all things at their own pleasure. They only presided by previously giving good and salutary counsels to the people, not by doing alone whatever pleased them, while all others were excluded.

Lest this should seem to be a fiction of mine, I will make it plain by a similar example. Luke relates that Barnabas and Paul ordained elders throughout the churches, but he at the same time marks the plan or mode when he says that it was done by suffrage. They therefore selected two, but the whole body, as was the custom of the Greeks in elections, declared by a show of hands which of the two they wished to have.

Thus it is not uncommon for Roman historians to say, that the consul who held the comitia elected the new magistrates, for no other reason but because he received the suffrages, and presided over the people at the election. Certainly, it is not credible that Paul conceded more to Timothy and Titus than he assumed to himself. Now we see that his custom was to appoint bishops by the suffrages of the people. We must therefore interpret the above passages, so as not to infringe on the common right and liberty of the Church. Rightly, therefore, does Cyprian contend for it as of divine authority, that the priest be chosen in presence of the people, before the eyes of all, and be approved as worthy and fit by public judgment and testimony. Indeed, we see that by the command of the Lord, the practice in electing the Levitical priests was to bring them forward in view of the people before consecration. Nor is Matthias enrolled among the number of the apostles, nor are the seven deacons elected in any other way, than at the sight and approval of the people. (See Acts 6:2.)

"Those examples," says Cyprian, "show that the ordination of a priest behooved not to take place, unless under the consciousness of the people assisting, so that that ordination was just and legitimate which was vouched by the testimony of all." We see, then, that ministers are legitimately called according to the Word of God, when those who may have seemed fit are elected on the consent and approbation of the people. Other pastors, however, ought to preside over the election, lest any error should be committed by the general body through either levity, or bad passion, or tumult.

16 Form in which the ministers of the Church are to be ordained. No express precept, but one. Laying on of hands.

It remains to consider the form of ordination, to which we have assigned the last place in the call. (See Shapter 4, section 14, 15.) It is certain, that when the apostles appointed anyone to the ministry, they used no other ceremony than the laying on of hands. This form was derived, I think, from the custom of the Jews, who, by the laying on of hands, in a manner presented to God whatever they wished to be blessed and consecrated. Thus Jacob, when about to bless Ephraim and Manasseh, placed his hands upon their heads. (See Genesis 48:14.) The same thing was done by our Lord, when He prayed over the little children. (See Matthew 19:15.) With the same intent (as I imagine), the Jews, according to the injunction of the law, laid hands upon their sacrifices. Wherefore, the apostles, by the laying on of hands, intimated that they made an offering to God of him whom they admitted to the ministry; though they also did the same thing over those on whom they conferred the visible gifts of the Spirit. (See Acts 8:17; 19:6.)

However this is, it was the regular form, whenever they called anyone to the sacred ministry. In this way they consecrated pastors and teachers; in this way they consecrated deacons. But though there is no fixed precept concerning the laying on of hands, yet as we see that it was uniformly observed by the apostles, this careful observance ought to be regarded by us in the light of a precept. (See Chapter 14, section 20; Chapter 19, section 31.) And it is certainly useful, that by such a symbol the dignity of the ministry should be commended to the people, and he who is ordained, reminded that he is no longer his own, but is bound in service to God and the Church.

Besides, it will not prove an empty sign, if it be restored to its genuine origin. For if the Spirit of God has not instituted anything in the Church in vain, this ceremony of his appointment we shall feel not to be useless, provided it be not superstitiously abused.

Lastly, it is to observed, that it was not the whole people, but only pastors, who laid hands on ministers, though it is uncertain whether or not several always laid their hands: it is certain, that in the case of the deacons, it was done by Paul and Barnabas, and some few others (See Acts 6:6; 13:3.) But in another place, Paul mentions that he himself, without any others, laid hands on Timothy. "Wherefore, I put thee in remembrance, that thou stir up the gift of God which is in thee, by the putting on of my hands" (2 Timothy 1:6). For what is said in the First Epistle, of the *laying on of the hands of the presbytery*, I do not understand as if Paul were speaking of the college of Elders. By the expression, I understand the ordination itself; as if he had said, Act so, that the gift, which you received by the laying on of hands, when I made you a presbyter, may not be in vain.

Chapter 4

OF THE STATE OF THE PRIMITIVE CHURCH, AND THE MODE OF GOVERNMENT IN USE BEFORE THE PAPACY.

The divisions of this chapter are,–I. The mode of government in the primitive Church, sections 1-10. II. The formal ordination of Bishops and Ministers in the primitive Church, sections 10-15.

Sections

1. The method of government in the primitive Church. Not in every respect conformable to the rule of the Word of God. Three distinct orders of Ministers.

2. First, the Bishop, for the sake of preserving order, presided over the Presbyters or Pastors. The office of Bishop. Presbyter and Bishop the same. The institution of this order ancient.

3. The office of Bishop and Presbyters. Strictly preserved in the primitive Church.

4. Of Archbishops and Patriarchs. Very seldom used. For what end instituted. Hierarchy an improper name, and not used in Scripture.

5. Deacons, the second order of Ministers in the primitive Church. Their proper office. The Bishop their inspector. Subdeacons, their assistants. Archdeacons, their presidents. The reading of the Gospel, an adventitious office conferred in honor on the Deacons.

6. Mode in which the goods of the Church were anciently dispensed. A. The support of the poor. B. Due provision for the ministers of the Church.

7. The administration at first free and voluntary. The revenues of the Church afterwards classed under four heads.

8. A third part of the revenues devoted to the fabric of churches. To this, however, when necessary, the claim of the poor was preferred. Sayings, testimonies, and examples to this effect from Cyril, Acatius, Jerome, Exuperius, Ambrose.

9. The Clerici, among whom were the Doorkeepers and Acolytes, were the names given to exercises used as a kind of training for tyros.

10. Second part of the chapter, treating of the calling of Ministers. Some error introduced in course of time in respect to celibacy from excessive strictness. In regard to the ordination of Ministers, full regard not always paid to the consent of the people. Why the people less anxious to maintain their right. Ordinations took place at stated times.

11. In the ordination of Bishops, the liberty of the people maintained.

12. Certain limits afterwards introduced to restrain the inconsiderate license of the multitude.

13. This mode of election long prevailed. Testimony of Gregory. Nothing repugnant to this in the decretals of Gratian.

14. The form of ordination in the ancient Church.

15. This form gradually changed.

1 The method of government in the primitive Church. Not in every respect conformable to the rule of the word of God. Three distinct orders of Ministers.

Hitherto, we have discoursed of the order of Church government as delivered to us in the pure Word of God, and of ministerial offices as instituted by Christ. (See Chapter 1, sections 5, 6; Chapter 3.) Now that the whole subject may be more clearly and familiarly explained, and also better fixed in our minds, it will be useful to attend to the form of the early Church, as this will give us a kind of visible representation of the divine institution. For although the bishops of those times published many canons, in which they seemed to express more than is expressed by the sacred volume, yet they were so cautious in framing all their economy on the Word of God, the only standard, that it is easy to see that they scarcely in any respect departed from it. Even if something may be wanting in these enactments, still, as they were sincerely desirous to preserve the divine institution, and have not strayed far from it, it will be of great benefit here briefly to explain what their observance was.

As we have stated that three classes of ministers are set before us in Scripture, so the early Church distributed all its ministers into three orders. For from the order of presbyters, part were selected as pastors and teachers, while to the remainder was committed the censure of manners and discipline. To the deacons belonged the care of the poor and the dispensing of alms. Readers and Acolytes were not the names of certain offices; but those whom they called clergy, they accustomed from their youth to serve the Church by certain exercises, that they might the better understand for what they were destined, and afterwards come better prepared for their duty, as I will shortly show at greater length. Accordingly, Jerome, in setting forth five orders in the Church, enumerates Bishops, Presbyters, Deacons, Believers, Catechumens: to the other Clergy and Monks he gives no proper place.

2 First, the Bishop, for the sake of preserving order, presided over the Presbyters or Pastors. The office of Bishop. Presbyter and Bishop the same. The institution of this order ancient.

All, therefore, to whom the office of teaching was committed, they called presbyters, and in each city these presbyters selected one of their number to whom they gave the special title of bishop, lest, as usually happens, from equality dissension should arise. The bishop, however, was not so superior in honor and dignity as to have dominion over his colleagues, but as it belongs to a president in an assembly to bring matters before them, collect their opinions, take precedence of others in consulting, advising, exhorting, guide the whole procedure by his authority, and execute what is decreed by common consent, a bishop held the same office in a meeting of presbyters. And the ancients themselves confess that this practice was introduced by human arrangement, according to the exigency of the times.

Thus Jerome, on the Epistle to Titus, chapter 1, says, "A bishop is the same as a presbyter. And before dissensions were introduced into religion by the instigation of the devil, and it was said among the people, I am of Paul, and I of Cephas, churches were governed by a common council of presbyters. Afterwards, that the seeds of dissension might be plucked up, the whole charge was devolved upon mendatory rescripts, preventions, and the like. But they all conduct one.

Therefore, as presbyters know that by the custom of the Church they are subject to him who presides, so let bishops know that they are greater than presbyters more by custom than in consequence of our Lord's appointment, and ought to rule the Church for the common good."

In another place, he shows how ancient the custom was. For he says that at Alexandria, from Mark the Evangelist, as far down as Heraclas and Dionysius, presbyters always placed one, selected from themselves, in a higher rank, and gave him the name of bishop. Each city, therefore, had a college of presbyters, consisting of pastors and teachers. For they all performed to the people that office of teaching, exhorting, and correcting, which Paul enjoins on bishops (Titus 1:9); and that they might leave a seed behind them, they made it their business to train the younger men who had devoted themselves to the sacred warfare. To each city was assigned a certain district, which took presbyters from it, and was considered incorporated into that church. Each presbyter, as I have said, merely to preserve order and peace, was under one bishop, who, though he excelled others in dignity, was subject to the meeting of the brethren. But if the district, which was under his bishopric, was too large for him to be able to discharge all the duties of bishop, presbyters were distributed over it in certain places to act as his substitutes in minor matters. These were called Chorepiscopi (rural bishops), because they represented the bishops throughout the province.

3 The office of Bishop and Presbyters. Strictly preserved in the primitive Church.

But, in regard to the office of which we now treat, the bishop as well as the presbyters behooved to employ themselves in the administration of word and sacraments. For, at Alexandria only (as Arius had there troubled the Church), it was enacted, that no presbyter should deliver an address to the people, as Socrates says, Tripartit. Jerome does not conceal his dissatisfaction with the enactment. It certainly would have been deemed monstrous for one to give himself out as a bishop, and yet not show himself a true bishop by his conduct. Such, then, was the strictness of those times, that all ministers were obliged to fulfill the office as the Lord requires of them. Nor do I refer to the practice of one age only, since not even in the time of Gregory, when the Church had almost fallen (certainly had greatly degenerated from ancient purity), would any bishop have been tolerated who abstained from preaching. In some part of his twenty-fourth Epistle he says, "The priest dies when no sound is heard from him: for he calls forth the wrath of the unseen Judge against him if he walks without the sound of preaching." Elsewhere he says, "When Paul testifies that he is pure from the blood of all men (Acts 20:26), by his words, we, who are called priests, are charged, are arraigned, are shown to be guilty, since to those sins which we have of our own we add the deaths of other men, for we commit murder as often as lukewarm and silent we see them daily going to destruction" (Ezekiel 11:26). He calls himself and others silent when less assiduous in their work than they ought to be. Since he does not spare even those who did their duty partially, what do you think he would do in the case of those who entirely neglected it? For a long time, therefore, it was regarded in the Church as the first duty of a bishop to feed the people by the Word of God, or to edify the Church, in public and private, with sound doctrine.

4 Of Archbishops and Patriarchs. Very seldom used. For what end instituted. Hierarchy an improper name, and not used in Scripture.

As to the fact, that each province had an archbishop among the bishops (see Chapter 7, section 15), and, moreover, that, in the Council of Nice, patriarchs were appointed to be superior to archbishops, in order and dignity, this was designed for the preservation of discipline, although, in treating of the subject here, it ought not to be omitted, that the practice was very rare. The chief reason for which these orders were instituted was, that if anything occurred in any church which could not well be explicated by a few, it might be referred to a provincial synod. If the magnitude or difficulty of the case demanded a larger discussion, patriarchs were employed along with synods, and from them there was no appeal except to a General Council. To the government thus constituted some gave the name of Hierarchy—a name, in my opinion, improper, certainly one not used by Scripture. For the Holy Spirit designed to provide that no one should dream of primacy or domination in regard to the government of the Church. But if, disregarding the term, we look to the thing, we shall find that the ancient bishops had no wish to frame a form of church government different from that which God has prescribed in His Word.

5 Deacons, the second order of Ministers in the primitive Church. Their proper office. The Bishop their inspector. Subdeacons, their assistants. Archdeacons, their presidents. The reading of the Gospel, an adventitious office conferred in honor on the Deacons.

Nor was the case of deacons then different from what it had been under the apostles. (See Chapter 3, section 6.) For they received the daily offerings of the faithful, and the annual revenues of the Church, that they might apply them to their true uses; in other words, partly in maintaining ministers, and partly in supporting the poor; at the sight of the bishop, however, to whom they every year gave an account of their stewardship. For, although the canons uniformly make the bishop the dispenser of all the goods of the Church, this is not to be understood as if he by himself undertook that charge, but because it belonged to him to prescribe to the deacons who were to be admitted to the public alimony of the Church, and point out to what persons, and in what portions, the residue was to be distributed, and because he was entitled to see whether the deacon faithfully performed his office. Thus, in the canons, which they ascribe to the apostles, it is said, "We command that the bishop have the affairs of the Church under his control. For if the souls of men, which are more precious, have been entrusted to him, much more is he entitled to have the charge of money matters, so that under his control all may be dispensed to the poor by the presbyters and deacons, that the ministration may be made reverently and with due care."

And in the Council of Antioch, it was decreed that bishops, who inter-meddled with the effects of the Church, without the knowledge of the presbyters and deacons, should be restrained. But there is no occasion to discuss this point further, since it is evident, from many of the letters of Gregory, that even at that time, when the ecclesiastical ordinances were otherwise much vitiated, it was still the practice for the deacons to be, under the bishops, the stewards of the poor.

It is probable that at the first subdeacons were attached to the deacons, to assist them in the management of the poor; but the distinction was gradually lost. Archdeacons began to be appointed when the extent of the revenues demanded a new and more exact method of administration, though Jerome mentions that it already existed in his day. To them belonged the amount of revenues, possessions, and furniture, and the charge of the daily offerings.

Hence, Gregory declares to the Archdeacon Solitanus, that the blame rested with him, if any of the goods of the Church perished through his fraud or negligence. The reading of the Word to the people, and exhortation to prayer, was assigned to them, and they were permitted, moreover, to give the cup in the sacred Supper; but this was done for the purpose of honoring their office, that they might perform it with greater reverence, when they were reminded by such symbols that what they discharged was not some profane stewardship, but a spiritual function dedicated to God.

6 Mode in which the goods of the Church were anciently dispensed. A. The support of the poor. B. Due provision for the ministers of the Church.

Hence, also, we may judge what was the use, and of what nature was the distribution of ecclesiastical goods. You may everywhere find both from the decrees of synods, and from ancient writers, that whatever the Church possessed, either in lands or in money, was the patrimony of the poor. Accordingly, the saying is always sounded in the ears of bishops and deacons, Remember that you are not handling your own property, but that destined for the necessities of the poor; if you dishonestly conceal or dilapidate it, you will be guilty of blood. Hence, they are admonished to distribute them to those to whom they are due, with the greatest fear and reverence, as in the sight of God, without respect of persons.

Hence, also, in Chrysostom, Ambrose, Augustine, and other like bishops, those grave obtestations in which they assert their integrity before the people. But since it is just in itself, and was sanctioned by a divine law, that those who devote their labor to the Church shall be supported at the public expense of the Church, and some presbyters in that age having consecrated their patrimony to God, had become voluntarily poor, the distribution was so made that aliment was afforded to ministers, and the poor were not neglected. Meanwhile, it was provided that the ministers themselves, who ought to be an example of frugality to others, should not have so much as might be abused for luxury or delicacy; but only what might be needful to support their wants: "For those clergy, who can be supported by their own patrimony," says Jerome, "commit sacrilege if they accept what belongs to the poor, and by such abuse eat and drink judgment to themselves."

7 The administration at first free and voluntary. The revenues of the Church afterwards classed under four heads.

At first, the administration was free and voluntary, when bishops and deacons were faithful of their own accord, and when integrity of conscience and purity of life supplied the place of laws. Afterwards, when, from the cupidity and depraved desires of some, bad examples arose, canons were framed, to correct these evils, and divided the revenues of the Church into four parts, assigning one to the clergy, another to the poor, another to the repair of churches and other edifices, a fourth to the poor, whether strangers or natives. For though other canons attribute this last part to the bishop, it differs in no respect from the division, which I have mentioned. For they do not mean that it is his property, which he may devour alone or squander in any way he pleases, but that it may enable him to use the hospitality which Paul requires in that order. (See 1 Timothy 3:2.) This is the interpretation of Gelasius and Gregory. For the only reason that Gelasius gives–that the bishop should claim anything to himself, is that he may be able to bestow it on captives and strangers.

Gregory speaks still more clearly. "It is the custom of the Apostolic See," says he, "to give command to the bishop who has been ordained, to divide all the revenues into four portions–namely, one to the bishop and his household for hospitality and maintenance, another to the clergy, a third to the poor, a fourth to the repair of churches."

The bishop, therefore, could not lawfully take for his own use more than was sufficient for moderate and frugal food and clothing. When anyone became wanton in either luxury or ostentation and show, he was immediately reprimanded by his colleagues, and if he obeyed not, was deprived of his honors.

8 A third part of the revenues devoted to the fabric of churches. To this, however, when necessary, the claim of the poor was preferred. Sayings, testimonies, and examples to this effect from Cyril, Acatius, Jerome, Exuperius, Ambrose.

Moreover, the sum expended on the adorning of churches was at first very trifling, and even afterwards, when the Church had become somewhat more wealthy, they in that matter observed mediocrity. Still, whatever money was then collected was reserved for the poor, when any greater necessity occurred. Thus, Cyril, when a famine prevailed in the province of Jerusalem and the want could not otherwise be supplied, took the vessels and robes, and sold them for the support of the poor. In like manner, Acatius, Bishop of Amida, when a great multitude of the Persians were almost destroyed by famine, having assembled the clergy, and delivered this noble address, "Our God has no need either of chalices or salvers, for He neither eats nor drinks," melted down the plate to be able to furnish food and obtain the means of ransoming the miserable. Jerome also, while inveighing against the excessive splendor of churches, relates that Exuperius, Bishop of Tholouse, in his day, though he carried the body of the Lord in a wicker basket, and his blood in a glass, nevertheless suffered no poor man to be hungry.

What I lately said of Acatius, Ambrose relates of himself. For when the Arians assailed him for having broken down the sacred vessels for the ransom of captives, he made this most admirable excuse: "He who sent the apostles without gold has also gathered churches without gold. The Church has gold not to keep but to distribute, and give support in necessity. What need is there of keeping what is of no benefit? Are we ignorant how much gold and silver the Assyrians carried off from the temple of the Lord? Is it not better for a priest to melt them for the support of the poor, if other means are wanting, than for a sacrilegious enemy to carry them away? Would not the Lord say, Why have you suffered so many poor to die of hunger, and you certainly had gold wherewith to minister to their support? Why have so many captives been carried away and not redeemed? Why have so many been slain by the enemy? It had been better to preserve living than metallic vessels. These charges you will not be able to answer: for what could you say? I feared lest the temple of God should want ornament. He would answer, Sacraments require not gold, and things which are not bought with gold please not by gold. The ornament of the Sacraments is the ransom of captives."

In a word, we see the exact truth of what he elsewhere says–viz. that whatever the Church then possessed was the revenue of the needy. Again, A bishop has nothing but what belongs to the poor.

9 The Clerici, among whom were the Doorkeepers and Acolytes, were the names given to exercises used as a kind of training for tyros.

We have now reviewed the ministerial offices of the ancient Church. For others, of which ecclesiastical writers make mention, were rather exercises and preparations than distinct offices. These holy men, that they might leave a nursery of the Church behind them, received young men, who, with the consent and authority of their parents, devoted themselves to the spiritual warfare under their guardianship and training, and so formed them from their tender years, that they might not enter on the discharge of the office as ignorant novices. All who received this training were designated by the general name of Clerks.

I could wish that some more appropriate name had been given them, for this appellation had its origin in error, or at least improper feeling, since the whole Church is by Peter denominated clerus, that is, the inheritance of the Lord. (See 1 Peter 5:3.) It was in itself, however, a most sacred and salutary institution, that those who wished to devote themselves and their labor to the Church should be brought up under the charge of the bishop; so that no one should minister in the Church unless he had been previously well trained, unless he had in early life imbibed sound doctrine, unless by stricter discipline he had formed habits of gravity and severer morals, been withdrawn from ordinary business, and accustomed to spiritual cares and studies. For as tyros in the military art are trained by mock fights for true and serious warfare, so there was a rudimental training by which they were exercised in clerical duty before they were actually appointed to office.

First, then, they entrusted them with the opening and shutting of the Church, and called them Ostiarii. Next, they gave the name of Acolytes to those who assisted the bishop in domestic services, and constantly attended him, first, as a mark of respect; and, secondly, that no suspicion might arise. Moreover, that they might gradually become known to the people, and recommend themselves to them, and at the same time might learn to stand the gaze of all, and speak before all, that they might not, when appointed presbyters, be overcome with shame when they came forward to teach, the office of reading in the desk was given them.

In this way they were gradually advanced, that they might prove their carefulness in separate exercises, until they were appointed subdeacons. All I mean by this is that these were rather the rudimentary exercises of tyros than functions, which were accounted among the true ministries of the Church.

10 Second part of the chapter, treating of the calling of Ministers. Some error introduced in course of time in respect to celibacy from excessive strictness. In regard to the ordination of Ministers, full regard not always paid to the consent of the people. Why the people less anxious to maintain their right. Ordinations took place at stated times.

In regard to what we have set down as the first and second heads in the calling of ministers–viz. the persons to be elected and the religious care to be therein exercised–the ancient Church followed the injunction of Paul, and the examples of the apostles. For they were accustomed to meet for the election of pastors with the greatest reverence, and with earnest prayer to God. Moreover, they had a form of examination by which they tested the life and doctrine of those who were to be elected by the standard of Paul (1 Timothy 3:2); only here they sometimes erred from excessive strictness, by exacting more of a bishop than Paul requires, and especially, in process of time, by exacting celibacy: but in other respects their practice corresponded with Paul's description.

In regard to our third head, however–viz. Who were entitled to appoint ministers? –They did not always observe the same rule. Anciently none were admitted to the number of the clergy without the consent of the whole people: and hence Cyprian makes a labored apology for having appointed Aurelius a reader without consulting the Church, because, although done contrary to custom, it was not done without reason. He thus premises: "In ordaining clergy, dearest brethren, we are wont previously to consult you, and weigh the manners and merits of each by the common advice." But as in these minor exercises, there was no great danger, inasmuch as they were appointed to a long probation and unimportant function, the consent of the people ceased to be asked.

Afterwards, in other orders also, with the exception of the bishopric, the people usually left the choice and decision to the bishop and presbyters, who thus determined who were fit and worthy, unless, perhaps, when new presbyters were appointed to parishes, for then the express consent of the inhabitants of the place behooved to be given. Nor is it strange that in this matter the people were not very anxious to maintain their right, for no subdeacon was appointed who had not given a long proof of his conduct in the clerical office, agreeably to the strictness of discipline then in use. After he had approved himself in that degree, he was appointed deacon, and thereafter, if he conducted himself faithfully, he attained to the honor of a presbyter. Thus, none were promoted whose conduct had not, in truth, been tested for many years under the eye of the people. There were also many canons for punishing their faults, so that the Church, if she did not neglect the remedies, was not burdened with bad presbyters or deacons. In the case of presbyters, indeed, the consent of the citizens was always required, as is attested by the canon (*Primus Distinct.* 67), which is attributed to Anacletus.

In fine, all ordinations took place at stated periods of the year, that none might creep in stealthily without the consent of the faithful, or be promoted with too much facility without witnesses.

11 In the ordination of Bishops, the liberty of the people maintained.

In electing bishops, the people long retained their right of preventing anyone from being intruded who was not acceptable to all. Accordingly, it was forbidden by the Council of Antioch to induct anyone on the unwilling. This also Leo carefully confirms. Hence, these passages: "Let him be elected whom the clergy and people or the majority demand." Again. "Let him who is to preside over all be elected by all." He, therefore, who is appointed while unknown and unexamined, must of necessity be violently intruded. Again, "Let him be elected who is chosen by the clergy, and called by the people, and let him be consecrated by the provincials with the judgment of the metropolitan." So careful were the holy fathers that this liberty of the people should on no account be diminished, that when a general council assembled at Constantinople and ordaining Nectarius, they declined to do it without the approbation of the whole clergy and people, as their letter to the Roman synod testified. Accordingly, when any bishop nominated his successor, the act was not ratified without consulting the whole people. Of this, you have not only an example, but also the form in Augustine in the nomination of Eradius. And Theodoret, after relating that Peter was the successor nominated by Athanasius, immediately adds, that the sacerdotal order ratified it, that the magistracy, chief men, and whole people, by their acclamation approved.

12 Certain limits afterwards introduced to restrain the inconsiderate license of the multitude.

It was, indeed, decreed (and I admit on the best grounds) by the Council of Laodicea that the election should not be left to crowds. For it scarcely ever happens that so many heads, with one consent, settle any affair well. It generally holds true, *"Incertum scindi studia in contraria vulgus;"*—"Opposing wishes rend the fickle crowd." For, first, the clergy alone selected, and presented him whom they had selected to the magistrate, or senate, and chief men. These, after deliberation, put their signature to the election, if it seemed proper, if not, they chose another whom they more highly approved. The matter was then laid before the multitude, which, although not bound by those previous proceedings, was less able to act tumultuously. Or, if the matter began with the multitude, it was only that it might be known whom they were most desirous to have; the wishes of the people being heard, the clergy at length elected. Thus, it was neither lawful for the clergy to appoint whom they chose, nor were they, however, under the necessity of yielding to the foolish desires of the people. Leo sets down this order, when he says, "The wishes of the citizens, the testimonies of the people, the choice of the honorable, the election of the clergy, are to be waited for." Again, "Let the testimony of the honorable, the subscription of the clergy, the consent of the magistracy and people, be obtained; otherwise (says he) it must on no account be done." Nor is anything more intended by the decree of the Council of Laodicea, than that the clergy and rulers were not to allow themselves to be carried away by the rash multitude, but rather by their prudence and gravity to repress their foolish desires whenever there was occasion.

13 This mode of election long prevailed. Testimony of Gregory. Nothing repugnant to this in the decretals of Gratian.

This mode of election was still in force in the time of Gregory, and probably continued to a much later period. Many of his letters which are extant clearly prove this, for whenever a new bishop is to be elected, his custom is to write to the clergy, magistrates, and people; sometimes also to the governor, according to the nature of the government. But if, because of the unsettled state of the Church, he gives the oversight of the election to a neighboring bishop, he always requires a formal decision confirmed by the subscriptions of all. Nay, when one Constantius was elected Bishop of Milan, and in consequence of the incursions of the Barbarians, many of the Milanese had fled to Genoa, he thought that the election would not be lawful unless they too were called together and gave their assent. Nay, five hundred years have not elapsed since Pope Nicholas fixed the election of the Roman Pontiff in this way, first, that the cardinals should precede; next, that they should join to themselves the other clergy; and, lastly, that the election should be ratified by the consent of the people. And in the end he recites the decree of Leo, which I lately quoted, and orders it to be enforced in future. But should the malice of the wicked so prevail that the clergy are obliged to quit the city, in order to make a pure election, he, however, orders that some of the people shall, at the same time, be present.

The suffrage of the Emperor, as far as we can understand, was required only in two churches, those of Rome and Constantinople, these being the two seats of empire. For when Ambrose was sent by Valentinianus to Milan with authority to superintend the election of a new bishop, it was an extraordinary proceeding, in consequence of the violent factions, which raged among the citizens. But at Rome, the authority of the Emperor in the election of the bishop was so great, that Gregory says he was appointed to the government of the Church by his order, though he had been called by the people in regular form. The custom, however, was, that when the magistrates, clergy, and people, nominated anyone, he was forthwith presented to the Emperor, who either by approving ratified, or by disapproving annulled the election. There is nothing contrary to this practice in the decretals, which are collected by Gratian. Where all that is said is, that it was on no account to be tolerated, that canonical election should be abolished, and a king should at pleasure appoint a bishop, and that one thus promoted by violent authority was not to be consecrated by the metropolitans. For it is one thing to deprive the Church of her right, and transfer it entirely to the caprice of a single individual; it is another thing to assign to a king or emperor the honor of confirming a legitimate election by his authority.

14 The form of ordination in the ancient Church.

It now remains to treat of the form by which the ministers of the ancient Church were initiated to their office after election. This was termed by the Latins, Ordination, or consecration. The Greeks termed it a mode of election by which suffrages are declared by a show of hands. There is still in existence a decree of the Council of Nice, to the effect that the metropolitans, with all the bishops of the province, were to meet to ordain him who was chosen. But if, from distance, or sickness, or any other necessary cause, part were prevented, three at least should meet, and those who were absent signify their consent by letter. And this canon, after it had fallen into desuetude, was afterwards renewed by several councils. All, or at least all who had not an excuse, were enjoined to be present, in order that a stricter examination might be had of the life and doctrine of him who was to be ordained; for the thing was not done without examination. And it appears, from the words of Cyprian, that, in old time, they were not wont to be called after the election, but to be present at the election, and with the view of their acting as moderators, that no disorder might be committed by the crowd. For after saying that the people had the power either of choosing worthy or refusing unworthy priests, he immediately adds, "For which reason, we must carefully observe and hold by the divine and apostolic tradition (which is observed by us also, and almost by all the provinces), that for the due performance of ordinations all the nearest bishops of the province should meet with the people over whom the person is proposed to be ordained, and the bishop should be elected in presence of the people." But as they were sometimes too slowly assembled, and there was a risk that some might abuse the delay for purposes of intrigue, it was thought that it would be sufficient if they came after the designation was made, and on due investigation consecrated him who had been approved.

15 This form gradually changed.

While this was done everywhere without exception, a different custom gradually gained ground—namely, that those who were elected should go to the metropolitan to obtain ordination. This was owing more to ambition, and the corruption of the ancient custom, than to any good reason. And not long after, the authority of the Romish See being now increased, another still worse custom was introduced, of applying to it for the consecration of the bishops of almost all Italy. This we may observe from the letters of Gregory. The ancient right was preserved only by a few cities, which had not yielded so easily, for instance, Milan. Perhaps metropolitan sees only retained their privilege. For, in order to consecrate an archbishop, it was the practice for all the provincial bishops to meet in the metropolitan city. The form used was the laying on of hands. (See Chapter 19, section 28, 31.) I do not read that any other ceremonies were used, except that, in the public meeting, the bishops had some dress to distinguish them from the other presbyters. Presbyters, also, and deacons, were ordained by the laying on of hands; but each bishop, with the college of presbyters, ordained his own presbyters. But though they all did the same act, yet because the bishop presided, and the ordination was performed under his auspices, it was said to be his. Hence, ancient writers often say that a presbyter does not differ in any respect from a bishop except in not having the power of ordaining.

Chapter 5

THE ANCIENT FORM OF GOVERNMENT UTTERLY CORRUPTED BY THE TYRANNY OF THE PAPACY.

This chapter consists of two parts,–I. Who are called to the ministry under the Papacy, their character, and the ground of their appointment, sections 1-7. II. How far they fulfill their office, sections 8-19.

Sections

1. Who and what kind of persons are uniformly appointed bishops in the Papacy. A. No inquiry into doctrine. B. In regard to character, the unlearned and dissolute, boys, or men of wicked lives, chosen.

2. The right of the people taken away, though maintained by Leo, Cyprian, and Councils. It follows that there is no Canonical election in the Papacy. Two objections answered. Papal elections, what. Kind of persons elected.

3. A fuller explanation of the answer to the second objection, unfolding the errors of people, bishops, and princes.

4. No election of Presbyters and Deacons in the Papacy. A. Because they are ordained for a different end. B. Contrary to the command of Scripture and the Council of Chalcedon, no station is assigned them. C. Both the name and thing adulterated by a thousand frauds.

5. Refutation of those corruptions. Proper end of ordination. Of trial, and other necessary things. For these, wicked and sanguinary men have substituted vain show and deplorable blindness.

6. Second corruption relating to the assignation of benefices, which they call collation. Manifold abuses here exposed. Why the offices of priests are in the Papacy called benefices.

7. One individual appointed over five or six churches. This most shameful corruption severely condemned by many Councils.

8. Second part of the chapter—viz. how the office is discharged. Monks who have no place among Presbyters. Objection answered.

9. Presbyters divided into beneficiaries and mercenaries. The beneficiaries are bishops, parsons, canons, chaplains, abbots, and priors. The mercenaries condemned by the Word of God.

10. The name of beneficiaries given to idle priests who perform no office in the church. Objection answered. What kind of persons the canons should be. Another objection answered. The beneficiaries not true Presbyters.

11. The Bishops and rectors of parishes, by deserting their churches, glory only in an empty name.

12. The seeds of this evil in the age of Gregory, who inveighs against mercenaries. More sharply rebuked by Bernard.

13. The supreme Popish administration described. Ridiculous allegation of those so-called Ministers of the church. Answer.

14. Their shameful morals. Scarcely one who would not have been excommunicated or deposed by the ancient canons.

15. No true diaconate existing in the Papacy, though they have still the shadow of it. Corruption of the practice of the primitive Church in regard to deacons.

16. Ecclesiastical property, which was formerly administered by true deacons, plundered by Bishops and Canons, in defraud of the poor.

17. Blasphemous defense of these robbers. Answer. Kings doing homage to Christ. Theodosius. A saying of Ambrose.

18. Another defense with regard to the adorning of churches. Answer.

19. Concluding answer, showing that the diaconate is completely subverted by the Papacy.

1 Who and what kind of persons are uniformly appointed Bishops in the Papacy. A. No inquiry into doctrine. B. In regard to character, the unlearned and dissolute, boys, or men of wicked lives, chosen.

It may now be proper to bring under the eye of the reader the order of church government observed by the Roman See and all its satellites, and the whole of that hierarchy, which they have perpetually in their mouths, and compare it with the description we have given of the primitive and early Church, that the contrast may make it manifest what kind of church those have who plume themselves on the very title, as sufficient to outweigh, or rather overwhelm us. It will be best to begin with the call, that we may see who are called to the ministry, with what character, and on what grounds. Thereafter we will consider how far they faithfully fulfill their office. We shall give the first place to the bishops if they could claim the honor of holding the first rank in this discussion!

But the subject does not allow me even to touch it lightly, without exposing their disgrace. Still, let me remember in what kind of writing I am engaged, and not allow my discourse, which ought to be framed for simple teaching, to wander beyond its proper limits. But let any of them, who have not laid aside all modesty, tell me what kinds of bishops are uniformly elected in the present day. Any examination of doctrine is too old fashioned, but if any respect is had to doctrine, they make choice of some lawyer who knows better how to plead in the forum than to preach in the church.

This much is certain, that for a hundred years, scarcely one in a hundred has been elected who had any acquaintance with sacred doctrine. I do not spare former ages because they were much better, but because the question now relates only to the present church. If morals are inquired into, we shall find almost none whom the ancient canons would judge worthy. If one was not a drunkard, he was a fornicator; if one was free from this vice, he was either a gambler or sportsman, or a loose liver in some respect. For there are lighter faults which, according to the ancient canons, exclude from the episcopal office.

But the most absurd thing of all is, that even boys scarcely ten years of age are, by the permission of the Pope, made bishops. Such is the effrontery and stupidity to which they have arrived, that they have no dread even of that last and monstrous iniquity, which is altogether abhorrent even from natural feeling. Hence, it appears what kind of elections these must have been, when such supine negligence existed.

2 The right of the people taken away, though maintained by Leo, Cyprian, and Councils. It follows that there is no Canonical election in the Papacy. Two objections answered. Papal elections, what. Kind of persons elected.

Then, in election, the whole right has been taken from the people. Vows, assents, subscriptions, and all things of this sort, have disappeared; the whole power has been given to the canons alone. First, they confer the episcopal office on whomsoever they please; by-and-by they bring him forth into the view of the people, but it is to be adored, not examined. But Leo protests that no reason permits this, and declares it a violent imposition. Cyprian, after declaring it to be of divine authority, that election should not take place without the consent of the people, shows that a different procedure is at variance with the Word of God.

Numerous decrees of councils most strictly forbid it to be otherwise done, and if done, order it to be null. If this is true, there is not throughout the whole Papacy in the present day any canonical election in accordance either with divine or ecclesiastical law. Now, were there no other evil in this, what excuse can they give for having robbed the church of her right? But the corruption of the times required (they say), that since hatred and party spirit prevailed with the people and magistrates in the election of bishops more than right and sound judgment, the determination should be confined to a few. Allow that this was the last remedy in desperate circumstances. When the cure was seen to be more hurtful than the disease, why was not a remedy provided for this new evil? But it is said that the course, which the canons must follow, is strictly prescribed.

But can we doubt, that even in old times the people, on meeting to elect a bishop, were aware that they were bound by the most sacred laws, when they saw a rule prescribed by the Word of God? That one sentence in which God describes the true character of a bishop ought justly to be of more weight than ten thousand canons. Nevertheless, carried away by the worst of feelings, they had no regard to law or equity. So, in the present day, though most excellent laws have been made, they remain buried in writing.

Meanwhile, the general and approved practice is (and it is carried on systematically), that drunkards, fornicators, gamblers, are everywhere promoted to this honor; nay, this is little: bishoprics are the rewards of adulterers and panders: for when they are given to hunters and hawkers, things may be considered at the best. To excuse such unworthy procedure in any way would be wicked over much. The people had a most excellent canon prescribed to them by the Word of God–viz. that a bishop must be blameless, apt to teach, not a brawler, etc. (See 1 Timothy 3:2.) Why, then, was the province of electing transferred from the people to these men? Just because among the tumults and factions of the people the Word of God was not heard. And, on the other hand, why is it not in the present day transferred from these men, who not only violate all laws, but having cast off shame, libidinously, avariciously, and ambitiously, mix and confound things human and divine?

3 A fuller explanation of the answer to the second objection, unfolding the errors of people, bishops, and princes.

But it is not true to say that the thing was devised as a remedy. We read, that in old times tumults often arose in cities at the election of bishops; yet no one ever ventured to think of depriving the citizens of their right: for they had other methods by which they could either prevent the fault, or correct it when committed. I will state the matter as it truly is. When the people began to be negligent in making their choice, and left the business, as less suited to them, to the presbyters, these abused the opportunity to usurp a domination, which they afterwards established by putting forth new canons. Ordination is now nothing else than a mere mockery. For the kind of examination of which they make a display is so empty and trifling, that it even entirely wants the semblance. Therefore, when sovereigns, by pact with the Roman Pontiffs, obtained for themselves the right of nominating bishops, the church sustained no new injury, because the canons were merely deprived of an election, which they had seized without any right, or acquired, by stealth. Nothing, indeed, can be more disgraceful, than that bishops should be sent from courts to take possession of churches, and pious princes would do well to desist from such corruption. For there is an impious spoliation of the church whenever any people have a bishop intruded whom they have not asked, or at least freely approved. But that disorderly practice, which long existed in churches, gave occasion to sovereigns to assume to themselves the presentation of bishops. They wished the benefice to belong to themselves, rather than to those who had no better right to it, and who equally abused it.

4 No election of Presbyters and Deacons in the Papacy. A. Because they are ordained for a different end. B. Contrary to the command of Scripture and the Council of Chalcedon, no station is assigned them. C. Both the name and thing adulterated by a thousand frauds.

Such is the famous call, because of which bishops boast that they are the successors of the apostles. They say, moreover, that they alone can competently appoint presbyters. But herein they most shamefully corrupt the ancient institution that they by their ordination appoint not presbyters to guide and feed the people, but priests to sacrifice. In like manner, when they consecrate deacons, they pay no regard to their true and proper office, but only ordain to certain ceremonies concerning the cup and patent. On the contrary, the Council of Chalcedon decreed that there should be no absolute ordinations—that is, ordinations without assigning to the ordained a place where they were to exercise their offices. This decree is most useful for two reasons.

First, churches may not be burdened with superfluous expense, nor idle men receive what ought to be distributed to the poor.

Secondly, those who are ordained may consider that they are not promoted merely to an honorary office, but entrusted with a duty that they are solemnly bound to discharge.

But the Roman authorities (who think that nothing is to be cared for in religion but their belly) consider the first title to be revenue adequate to their support, whether it is from their own patrimony or from the priesthood. Accordingly, when they ordain presbyters or deacons, without any anxiety as to where they ought to minister, they confer the order, provided those ordained are sufficiently rich to support themselves. But what man can admit that the title, which the decree of the council requires, is annual revenue for sustenance? Again, when canons that are more recent made bishops liable in the support of those whom they had ordained without a fit title, that they might thus repress too great facility, a method was devised of eluding the penalty. For he who is ordained promises that whatever is the title named he will be contented with it. In this way, he is precluded from an action for aliment.

I say nothing of the thousand frauds, which are here committed, as when some falsely claim the empty titles of benefices, from which they cannot obtain a sixpence of revenue, and others by secret stipulation obtain a temporary appointment, which they promise that they will immediately restore, but sometimes do not. There are still more mysteries of the same kind.

5 Refutation of those corruptions. Proper end of ordination. Of trial, and other necessary things. For these, wicked and sanguinary men have substituted vain show and deplorable blindness.

But although these grosser abuses were removed, is it not at all times absurd to appoint a presbyter without assigning him a locality? For when they ordain it is only to sacrifice. But the legitimate ordination of a presbyter is to the government of the Church, while deacons are called to the charge of alms. It is true, many pompous ceremonies are used to disguise the act, that mere show may excite veneration in the simple; but what effect can these semblances have upon men of sound minds, when beneath them there is nothing solid or true? They used ceremonies either borrowed from Judaism or devised by themselves; from these it would be better if they would abstain. Of the trial (for it is unnecessary to say anything of the shadow which they retain), of the consent of the people, of other necessary things, there is no mention. By shadow, I mean those ridiculous gesticulations framed in inept and frigid imitation of antiquity.

The bishops have their vicars, who, before ordination, inquire into doctrine. But what is the inquiry? Is it whether they are able to read their Missals, or whether they can decline some common noun, which occurs in the lesson, conjugate a verb, or give the meaning of some one word? For it is not necessary to give the sense of a single sentence. And yet, even those who are deficient in these puerile elements are not repelled, provided they bring the recommendation of money or influence. Of the same nature is the question which is thrice put in an unintelligible voice, when the persons who are to be ordained are brought to the altar–viz. Are they worthy of the honor? One (who never saw them, but has his part in the play, that no form may be wanting) answers, They are worthy. What can you accuse in these venerable fathers save that, by indulging in such sacrilegious sport, they shamelessly laugh at God and man? But as they have long been in possession of the thing, they think they have now a legal title to it. For anyone who ventures to open his lips against these palpable and flagrant iniquities is hurried off to a capital trial, like one who had in old time divulged the mysteries of Ceres. Would they act thus if they had any belief in a God?

6 Second corruption relating to the assignation of benefices, which they call collation. Manifold abuses here exposed. Why the offices of priests are in the Papacy called benefices.

Then, in the collation of benefices (which was formerly conjoined with ordination, but is now altogether separate), how much better do they conduct themselves? But they have many reasons to give, for it is not bishops alone who confer the office of priests (and even in their case, where they are called Collators, they have not always the full right), but others have the presentation, while they only retain the honorary title of collations. To these are added nominations from schools, resignations, and either simple or by way of exchange, commendatory rescripts, preventions, and the like. But they all conduct themselves in such a way that one cannot upbraid another.

I maintain that, in the Papacy in the present day, scarcely one benefice in a hundred is conferred without simony, as the ancients have defined it. I say not that all purchase for a certain sum; but show me one in twenty who does not attain to the priesthood by some sinister method. Some owe their promotion to kindred or affinity, others to the influence of their parents, while others procure favor by obsequiousness. In short, the end for which the offices are conferred is that provision may be made not for churches, but for those who receive them. Accordingly, they call them benefices, by which name they sufficiently declare, that they look on them in no other light than as the largesse by which princes either court the favor or reward the services of their soldiers. I say nothing of the fact that these rewards are conferred on barbers, cooks, grooms, and dross of that sort. At present, indeed, there are no cases in law courts which make a greater noise than those concerning sacerdotal offices, so that you may regard them as nothing else than game set before dogs to be hunted. Is it tolerable even to hear the name of pastors given to those who have forced their way into the possession of a church as into an enemy's country? Who have evicted it by forensic brawls? Who have bought it for a price? Who have labored for it by sordid sycophancy? Who, while scarcely lisping boys, have obtained it like heritage from uncles and relatives? Sometimes even bastards obtain it from their fathers.

7 One individual appointed over five or six churches. This most shameful corruption severely condemned by many Councils.

Was the licentiousness of the people, however corrupt and lawless, ever carried to such a height? But a more monstrous thing still is that one man (I say not what kind of man, but certainly one who cannot govern himself) is appointed to the charge of five or six churches. In the courts of princes in the present day, you may see youths who are thrice abbots, twice bishops, and once archbishops. Everywhere are canons loaded with five, six, or seven cures, of not one of which they take the least charge, except to draw the income.

I will not object that the Word of God cries aloud against this: it has long ceased to have the least weight with them. I will not object that many councils denounce the severest punishment against this dishonest practice; these, too, when it suits them, they boldly contemn. But I say that it is monstrous wickedness, altogether opposed to God, nature, and ecclesiastical government, that one thief should lie brooding over several churches, that the name of pastor should be given to one who, even if he were willing, could not be present among his flock, and yet (such is their impudence) they cloak these abominations with the name of church, that they may exempt them from all blame. Nay, if you please, in these iniquities is contained that sacred succession to which, as they boast, it is owing that the church does not perish.

8 Second part of the chapter—viz. how the office is discharged. Monks who have no place among Presbyters. Objection answered.

Let us now see, as the second mark for estimating a legitimate pastor, how faithfully they discharge their office. Of the priests who are there elected, some are called monks, others seculars. The former herd was unknown to the early Church; even to hold such a place in the church is so repugnant to the monastic profession, that in old times, when persons were elected out of monasteries to clerical offices, they ceased to be monks. And, accordingly, Gregory, though in his time there were many abuses, did not suffer the offices to be thus confounded. For he insists that those who have been appointed abbots shall resign the clerical office, because no one can be properly at the same time a monk and a clerk, the one being an obstacle to the other.

Now, were I to ask how he can well fulfill his office who is declared by the canons to be unfit, what answer, pray, will they give? They will quote those abortive decrees of Innocent and Boniface, by which monks are admitted to the honor and power of the priesthood, though they remain in their monasteries. But is it at all reasonable that any unlearned ass, as soon as he has seized upon the Roman See, may by one little word overturn all antiquity? But of this matter afterwards, let it now suffice, that in the purer times of the Church it was regarded as a great absurdity for a monk to hold the office of priest. For Jerome declares that he does not the office of priest while he is living among monks, and ranks himself as one of the people to be governed by the priests. But to concede this to them, what duty do they perform? Some of the mendicants preach, while all the other monks chant or mutter masses in their cells, as if either our Savior had wished, or the nature of the office permits, presbyters to be made for such a purpose. When Scripture plainly testifies that it is the duty of a presbyter to rule his own church (see Acts 20:28), is it not impious profanation to transfer it to another purpose, nay, altogether to change the sacred institution of God? For when they are ordained, they are expressly forbidden to do what God enjoins on all presbyters. For this is their cant, let a monk, contented with his cell, neither presume to administer the sacraments, nor hold any other public office. Let them deny, if they can, that it is open mockery of God when anyone is appointed a presbyter in order to abstain from his proper and genuine office, and when he who has the name is not able to have the thing.

9 Presbyters divided into Beneficiaries and Mercenaries. The Beneficiaries are Bishops, Parsons, Canons, Chaplains, Abbots, and Priors. The Mercenaries condemned by the Word of God.

I come to the seculars, some of whom are (as they speak) beneficiaries; that is, have offices by which they are maintained, while others let out their services, day by day, to chant or say masses, and live in a manner on a stipend thus collected. Benefices either have a care of souls, as bishoprics and parochial charges, or they are the stipends of delicate men, who gain a livelihood by chanting: as prebends, canonries, parsonships, deaneries, chaplainships, and the like. Although, things being now turned upside down, the offices of abbot and prior are not only conferred on secular presbyters, but on boys also by privilege—that is, by common and usual custom. In regard to the mercenaries who seek their food from day to day, what else could they do than they actually do, in other words, prostitute themselves in an illiberal and disgraceful manner for gain, especially from the vast multitude of them with which the world now teems? Hence, as they dare not beg openly, or think that in this way they would gain little, they go about like hungry dogs, and by a kind of barking importunity extort from the unwilling what they may deposit in their hungry stomachs. Were I here to attempt to describe how disgraceful it is to the church, that the honor and office of a presbyter should come to this, I should never have done. My readers, therefore, must not expect from me a discourse, which can fully represent this flagitious indignity. I briefly say that if it is the office of a presbyter (and this both the Word of God prescribes [see 1 Corinthians 4:1] and the ancient canons enjoin) to feed the Church and administer the spiritual Kingdom of Christ, all those priests who have no work or stipend, save in the traffic of masses, not only fail in their office, but have no lawful office to discharge. No place is given them to teach, they have no people to govern. In short, nothing is left them but an altar on which to sacrifice Christ; this is to sacrifice not to God but to demons, as we shall afterwards show. (See Chapter 18, sections 3, 9, 14.)

10 The name of Beneficiaries given to idle Priests who perform no office in the church. Objection answered. What kind of persons the canons should be. Another objection answered. The Beneficiaries not true Presbyters.

I am not here touching on extraneous faults, but only on the intestine evil, which lies at the root of the very institution. I will add a sentence which will sound strange in their ears, but which, as it is true, it is right to express, that canons, deans, chaplains, provosts, and all who are maintained in idle offices of priesthood, are to be viewed in the same light. For what service can they perform to the church? The preaching of the Word, the care of discipline, and the administration of the Sacraments, they have shaken off as burdens too grievous to be borne. What then remains on which they can plume themselves as being true presbyters? Merely chanting and pompous ceremonies. But what is this to the point? If they allege custom, use, or the long prescription, I, on the contrary, appeal to the definition by which our Savior has described true presbyters, and shown the qualities of those who are to be regarded as presbyters. But if they cannot endure the hard law of submitting to the rule of Christ, let them at least allow the cause to be decided by the authority of the primitive Church. Their condition will not be one whit improved when decided according to the ancient canons. Those who have degenerated into canons ought to be presbyters, as they formerly were, to rule the Church in common with the bishop, and be his colleagues in the pastoral office. What they call deaneries of the chapter have no concern with the true government of the Church, much less chaplainships and other similar worthless names. In what light then are they all to be regarded? Assuredly, both the Word of Christ and the practice of the primitive Church exclude them from the honor of presbyters. They maintain, however, that they are presbyters; but we must unmask them, and we shall find that their whole profession is most alien from the office of presbyters, as that office is described to us by the apostles, and was discharged in the primitive Church. All such offices, therefore, by whatever titles they are distinguished, as they are novelties, and certainly not supported either by the institution of God or the ancient practice of the Church, ought to have no place in a description of that spiritual government which the Church received, and was consecrated by the mouth of the Lord himself. Or (if they would have me express it in ruder and coarser terms), since chaplains, canons, deans, provosts, and such like lazy bellies, do not even, with one finger, touch a particle of the office, which is necessarily required in presbyters, they must not be permitted falsely to usurp the honor, and thereby violate the holy institution of Christ.

11 The bishops and rectors of parishes, by deserting their churches, glory only in an empty name.

There still remain bishops and rectors of parishes; and I wish that they would contend for the maintenance of their office. I would willingly grant that they have a pious and excellent office if they would discharge it; but when they desert the churches committed to them, and throwing the care upon others, would still be considered pastors, they just act as if the office of pastor were to do nothing. If any usurer, who never stirs from the city, were to give himself out as a ploughman or vine dresser; or a soldier, who has constantly been in the field or the camp, and has never seen books or the forum, to pass for a lawyer, who could tolerate the absurdity? Much more absurdly do those act who would be called and deemed lawful pastors of the church, and are unwilling so to be. How few are those who in appearance even take the superintendence of their church? Many spend their lives in devouring the revenues of churches, which they never visit even for the purpose of inspection. Some once a year go themselves or send a steward, that nothing may be lost in the letting of them. When the corruption first crept in, those who wished to enjoy this kind of vacation pleaded privilege, but it is now a rare case for anyone to reside in his church. They look upon them merely in the light of farms, over which they appoint their vicars as grieves or husbandmen. But it is repugnant to common sense to regard him as a shepherd who has never seen a sheep of his flock.

12 The seeds of this evil in the age of Gregory, who inveighs against mercenaries. More sharply rebuked by Bernard.

It appears that in the time of Gregory, some of the seeds of this corruption existed. The rulers of churches had begun to be more negligent in teaching. He thus bitterly complains: "The world is full of priests, and yet laborers in the harvest are rare, for we indeed undertake the office of the priesthood, but we perform not the work of the office." Again, "As they have no bowels of love, they would be thought lords, but do not at all acknowledge themselves to be fathers. They change a post of humility into the elevation of ascendancy." Again, "But we, O pastors! What are we doing, we who obtain the hire but are not laborers? We have fallen off to extraneous business; we undertake one thing, we perform another; we leave the ministry of the Word, and, to our punishment, as I see, are called bishops, holding the honor of the name, not the power." Since he uses such bitterness of expression against those who were only less diligent or sedulous in their office, what, pray, would he have said if he had seen that very few bishops, if any at all, and scarcely one in a hundred of the other clergy, mounted the pulpit once in their whole lifetime? For to such a degree of infatuation have men come, that it is thought beneath the episcopal dignity to preach a sermon to the people. In the time of Bernard, things had become still worse. Accordingly, we see how bitterly he inveighs against the whole order, and yet there is reason to believe that matters were then in a much better state than now.

13 The supreme Popish administration described. Ridiculous allegation of those so-called Ministers of the Church. Answer.

Whoever will duly examine and weigh the whole form of ecclesiastical government as now existing in the Papacy, will find that there is no kind of spoliation in which robbers act more licentiously, without law or measure. Certainly all things are so unlike, nay, so opposed to the institution of Christ, have so degenerated from the ancient customs and practices of the Church, are so repugnant to nature and reason, that a greater injury cannot be done to Christ than to use His name in defending this disorderly rule. We (say they) are the pillars of the church, the priests of religion, the vicegerents of Christ, the heads of the faithful, because the apostolic authority has come to us by succession. As if they were speaking to stocks, they perpetually plume themselves on these absurdities. Whenever they make such boasts, I, in my turn, will ask, What have they in common with the apostles? We are not now treating of some hereditary honor which can come to men while they are asleep, but of the office of preaching, which they so greatly shun. Similarly, when we maintain that their kingdom is the tyranny of Antichrist, they immediately object that their venerable hierarchy has often been extolled by great and holy men—as if the holy fathers, when they commended the ecclesiastical hierarchy or spiritual government handed down to them by the apostles, ever dreamed of that shapeless and dreary chaos where bishoprics are held for the most part by ignorant asses, who do not even know the first and ordinary rudiments of the faith, or occasionally by boys who have just left their nurse; or if any are more learned (this, however, is a rare case), they regard the episcopal office as nothing else than a title of magnificence and splendor; where the rectors of churches no more think of feeding the flock than a cobbler does of plowing, where all things are so confounded by a confusion worse than that of Babel, that no genuine trace of paternal government is any longer to be seen.

14 Their shameful morals. Scarcely one who would not have been excommunicated or deposed by the ancient canons.

But if we descend to conduct, where is that light of the world which Christ requires, where is the salt of the earth, where is that sanctity which might operate as a perpetual censorship? In the present day, there is no order of men more notorious for luxury, effeminacy, delicacy, and all kinds of licentiousness; in no order are more apt or skillful teachers of imposture, fraud, treachery, and perfidy; nowhere is there more skill or audacity in mischief, to say nothing of ostentation, pride, rapacity, and cruelty. In bearing these, the world is so disgusted, that there is no fear lest I seem to exaggerate. One thing I say, which even they themselves will not be able to deny: Among bishops there is scarcely an individual, and among the parochial clergy not one in a hundred, who, if sentence were passed on his conduct according to the ancient canons, would not deserve to be excommunicated, or at least deposed from his office. I seem to say what is almost incredible, so completely has that ancient discipline which enjoined strict censure of the morals of the clergy become obsolete; but such the fact really is. Let those who serve under the banner and auspices of the Romish See now go and boast of their sacerdotal order. It is certain that that which they have is neither from Christ, nor His apostles, nor the fathers, nor the early Church.

15 No true diaconate existing in the Papacy, though they have still the shadow of it. Corruption of the practice of the primitive Church in regard to deacons.

Let the deacons now come forward and show their most sacred distribution of ecclesiastical goods (see Chapter 19, section 32). Although their deacons are not at all elected for that purpose, for the only injunction which they lay upon them is to minister at the altar, to read the gospel, or chant and perform I know not what frivolous acts. Nothing is said of alms, nothing of the care of the poor, and nothing at all of the function, which they formerly performed. I am speaking of the institution itself; for if we look to what they do, theirs, in fact, is no office, but only a step to the priesthood. In one thing, those who hold the place of deacons in the mass exhibit an empty image of antiquity, for they receive the offerings before consecration. Now, the ancient practice was, that before the communion of the Supper the faithful mutually kissed each other, and offered alms at the altar; thus declaring their love, first by symbol, and afterwards by an act of beneficence. The deacon, who was steward of the poor, received what was given that he might distribute it. Now, of these, alms do not come to the poor any more than if they were cast into the sea. They, therefore, delude the Church by that lying deaconship. Assuredly in this, they have nothing resembling the apostolical institution or the ancient practice. The very distribution of goods they have transferred elsewhere, and have so settled it that nothing can be imagined more disorderly. For as robbers, after murdering their victims, divide the plunder, so these men, after extinguishing the light of God's Word, as if they had murdered the Church, have imagined that whatever had been dedicated to pious uses was set down for prey and plunder. Accordingly, they have made a division, each seizing for himself as much as he could.

16 Ecclesiastical property, which was formerly administered by true Deacons, plundered by Bishops and Canons, in defraud of the poor.

All those ancient methods, which we have explained, are not only disturbed but altogether disguised and expunged. The chief part of the plunder has gone to bishops and city presbyters, who, having thus enriched themselves, have been converted into canons. That the partition was a mere scramble is apparent from this, that even to this day they are litigating as to the proportions. Be this as it may, the decision has provided that out of all the goods of the Church not one penny shall go to the poor, to whom at least the half belonged. The canons expressly assign a fourth part to them, while the other fourth they destine to the bishops, that they may expend it in hospitality and other offices of kindness. I say nothing as to what the clergy ought to do with their portion, or the use to which they ought to apply it, for it has been clearly shown that what is set apart for churches, buildings, and other expenditure, ought in necessity to be given to the poor. If they had one spark of the fear of God in their heart, could they, I ask, bear the consciousness that all their food and clothing is the produce of theft, nay, of sacrilege? But as they are little moved by the judgment of God, they should at least reflect that those whom they would persuade that the orders of their Church are so beautiful and well arranged as they are wont to boast, are men endued with sense and reason. Let them briefly answer whether the diaconate is a license to rob and steal. If they deny this, they will be forced to confess that no diaconate remains among them, since the whole administration of their ecclesiastical resources has been openly converted into sacrilegious depredation.

17 Blasphemous defense of these robbers. Answer. Kings doing homage to Christ. Theodosius. A saying of Ambrose.

But here they use a very fair gloss, for they say that the dignity of the church is not unbecomingly maintained by this magnificence. And some of their sect are so impudent as to dare to boast openly that thus only are fulfilled the prophecies, in which the ancient prophets describe the splendor of Christ's Kingdom, and where the sacerdotal order is exhibited in royal attire; that it was not without cause that God made the following promises to His Church: "All kings shall fall down before him: all nations shall serve him" (Psalm 72:11). "Awake, awake; put on thy strength, O Zion; put on thy beautiful garments, O Jerusalem, the holy city" (Isaiah 52:1). "All they from Sheba shall come; they shall bring gold and incense, and they shall show forth the praises of the Lord. All the flocks of Kedar shall be gathered together unto thee" (Isaiah 60:6, 7). I fear I should seem childish were I to dwell long in refuting this dishonesty. I am unwilling, therefore, to use words unnecessarily. I ask, however, if any Jew were to misapply these passages, what answer would they give? They would rebuke his stupidity in making a carnal and worldly application of things spiritually said of Christ's spiritual Kingdom. For we know that under the image of earthly objects, the prophets have delineated to us the heavenly glory, which ought to shine in the Church. For in those blessings with these words literally express, the Church never less abounded than under the apostles; and yet all admit that the power of Christ's Kingdom was then most flourishing.

What, then, is the meaning of the above passages? That everything, which is precious, sublime, and illustrious, ought to be made subject to the Lord. As to its being said expressly of kings, that they will submit to Christ, that they will throw their diadems at His feet, that they will dedicate their resources to the Church, when was this more truly and fully manifested than when Theodosius, having thrown aside the purple and left the insignia of empire, like one of the people humbled himself before God and the Church in solemn repentance? Than when he and other like pious princes made it their study and their care to preserve pure doctrine in the Church, to cherish and protect sound teachers? But that priests did not then luxuriate in superfluous wealth is sufficiently declared by this one sentence of the Council of Aquileia, over which Ambrose presided, Poverty in the priests of the Lord is glorious." It is certain that the bishops then had some means by which they might have rendered the glory of the Church conspicuous, if they had deemed them the true ornaments of the Church. But knowing that nothing was more adverse to the duty of pastors than to plume themselves on the delicacies of the table, on splendid clothes, numerous attendants, and magnificent places, they cultivated and followed the humility and modesty, nay, the very poverty, which Christ has consecrated among His servants.

18 Another defense with regard to the adorning of churches. Answer.

But not to be tedious, let us again briefly sum up, and show how far that distribution, or rather squandering, of ecclesiastical goods, which now exists, differs from the true diaconate, which both the Word of God recommends and the ancient Church observed. (See Book 1 chapter 11, sections 7, 13; Book 3, chapter 20, section 30; supra, chapter 4, section 8.) I say, that what is employed on the adorning of churches is improperly laid out, if not accompanied with that moderation which the very nature of sacred things prescribes, and which the apostles and other holy fathers prescribed, both by precept and example. But is anything like this seen in churches in the present day? Whatever accords (I do not say with that ancient frugality, but with decent mediocrity) is rejected. Nothing pleases but what savors of luxury and the corruption of the times. Meanwhile, so far are they from taking due care of living temples, that they would allow thousands of the poor to perish sooner than break down the smallest cup or platter to relieve their necessity. That I may not decide too severely at my own hand, I would only ask the pious reader to consider what Exuperius, the Bishop of Thoulouse, whom we have mentioned, what Acatius, or Ambrose, or anyone like minded, if they were to rise from the dead, would say? Certainly, while the necessities of the poor are so great, they would not approve of their funds being carried away from them as superfluous; not to mention that, even were there no poor, the uses to which they are applied are noxious in many respects and useful in none. But I appeal not to men. These goods have been dedicated to Christ, and ought to be distributed at His pleasure. In vain, however, will they make that to be expenditure for Christ, which they have squandered contrary to His commands, though, to confess the truth, the ordinary revenue of the church is not much curtailed by these expenses. No bishoprics are so opulent, no abbacies so productive, in short, no benefices so numerous and ample, as to suffice for the gluttony of priests. But while they would spare themselves, they induce the people by superstition to employ what ought to have been distributed to the poor in building temples, erecting statues, buying plate, and providing costly garments. Thus, the daily alms are swallowed up in this abyss.

19 Concluding answer, showing that the diaconate is completely subverted by the Papacy.

Of the revenue, which they derive from lands and property, what else can I say than what I have already said, and is manifest before the eyes of all? We see with what kind of fidelity the greatest portion is administered by those who are called bishops and abbots. What madness is it to seek ecclesiastical order here? Is it becoming in those whose life ought to have been a singular example of frugality, modesty, continence, and humility, to rival princes in the number of their attendants, the splendor of their dwellings, the delicacies of dressing and feasting? Can anything be more contrary to the duty of those whom the eternal and inviolable edict of God forbids to long for filthy lucre, and orders to be contented with simple food, not only to lay hands on villages and castles, but also invade the largest provinces, and even seize on empire itself? If they despise the Word of God, what answer will they give to the ancient canons of councils, which decree that the bishop shall have a little dwelling not far from the church, a frugal table, and furniture? What answer will they give to the declaration of the Council of Aquileia, in which poverty in the priests of the Lord is pronounced glorious? For, the injunction, which Jerome gives to Nepotian, to make the poor and strangers acquainted with his table, and have Christ with them as a guest, perhaps they would repudiate as too austere. What he immediately adds it would shame them to acknowledge–viz. that the glory of a bishop is to provide for the sustenance of the poor, that the disgrace of all priests is to study their own riches. This they cannot admit without covering themselves with disgrace. But it is unnecessary here to press them so hard, since all we wished was to demonstrate that the legitimate order of deacons has long ago been abolished, and that they can no longer plume themselves on this order in commendation of their Church. This, I think, has been completely established.

Chapter 6

OF THE PRIMACY OF THE ROMISH SEE.

The divisions of this chapter are,–I. Question stated, and an argument for the primacy of the Roman Pontiff drawn from the Old Testament refuted, sections 1, 2. II. Reply to various arguments in support of the Papacy founded on the words, "Thou art Peter," etc., sections 3-17.

Sections

1. Brief recapitulation. Why the subject of primacy is not yet mentioned. Represented by Papists as the bond of ecclesiastical unity. Setting out with this axiom, they begin to debate about their hierarchy.

2. Question stated. An attempted proof from the office of High Priest among the Jews. Two answers.

3. Arguments for primacy from the New Testament. Two answers.

4. Another answer. The keys given to the other apostles as well as to Peter. Other two arguments answered by passages of Cyprian and Augustine.

5. Another argument answered.

6. Answer to the argument that the Church is founded on Peter, from its being said, "Upon this rock I will build my Church."

7. Answer confirmed by passages of Scripture.

8. Even allowing Peter's superiority in some respect, this is no proof of the primacy of the Roman Pontiff. Other arguments answered.

9. Distinction between civil and ecclesiastical government. Christ alone the Head of the Church. Argument that there is still a ministerial head answered.

10. Paul, in giving a representation of the Church, makes no mention of this ministerial head.

11. Even though Peter was ministerial head, it does not follow that the Pope is so also. Argument founded on Paul's having lived and died at Rome.

12. On the hypothesis of the Papists, the primacy belongs to the Church of Antioch.

13. Absurdity of the Popish hypothesis.

14. Peter was not the Bishop of Rome.

15. Same subject continued.

16. Argument that the unity of the Church cannot be maintained without a supreme head on Earth. Answer, stating three reasons why great respect was paid in early times to the See of Rome.

17. Opinion of early times on the subject of the unity of the Church. No primacy attributed to the Church of Rome. Christ alone regarded as the Head of the Universal Church.

1 Brief recapitulation. Why the subject of primacy is not yet mentioned. Represented by Papists as the bond of ecclesiastical unity. Setting out with this axiom, they begin to debate about their hierarchy.

Hitherto, we have reviewed those ecclesiastical orders, which existed in the government of the primitive Church. But afterwards corrupted by time, and increasingly vitiated, they now only retain the name in the Papal Church, and are, in fact, nothing but mere masks. The contrast will enable the pious reader to judge what kind of church that is, for revolting from which we are charged with schism. But, on the head and crown of the whole matter, I mean the primacy of the Roman See, from which they undertake to prove that the Catholic Church is to be found only with them, we have not yet touched, because it did not take its origin either in the institution of Christ, or the practice of the early Church, as did those other parts, in regard to which we have shown, that though they were ancient in their origin, they in process of time altogether degenerated, nay, assumed an entirely new form. And yet, they endeavor to persuade the world that the chief and only bond of ecclesiastical unity is to adhere to the Roman See, and continue in subjection to it. I say, the prop on which they chiefly lean, when they would deprive us of the Church, and arrogate it to themselves, is that they retain the head on which the unity of the Church depends, and without which it must necessarily be rent and go to pieces. For they regard the Church as a kind of mutilated trunk if it be not subject to the Romish See as its head. Accordingly, when they debate about their hierarchy they always set out with the axiom: The Roman Pontiff (as the vicar of Christ, who is the Head of the Church) presides in his stead over the universal Church, and the Church is not rightly constituted unless that See hold the primacy over all others. Therefore, the nature of this claim must be considered. We may not omit anything, which pertains to the proper government of the Church.

2 Question stated. An attempted proof from the office of High Priest among the Jews. Two answers.

The question, then, may be thus stated, Is it necessary for the true order of the hierarchy (as they term it), or of ecclesiastical order, that one See should surpass the others in dignity and power, so as to be the head of the whole body? We subject the Church to unjust laws if we lay this necessity upon her without sanction from the Word of God. Therefore, if our opponents would prove what they maintain, it behooves them first to show that this economy was instituted by Christ. For this purpose, they refer to the office of High Priest under the law, and the supreme jurisdiction, which God appointed at Jerusalem. But the solution is easy, and it is manifold if one does not satisfy them. First, no reason obliges us to extend what was useful in one nation to the whole world; nay, the cases of one nation and of the whole world are widely different. Because the Jews were hemmed in on every side by idolaters, God fixed the seat of His worship in the central region of the Earth, that they might not be distracted by a variety of religions; there He appointed one priest to whom they might all look up, that they might be the better kept in unity. But now when the true religion has been diffused over the whole globe, who does not see that it is altogether absurd to give the government of East and West to one individual? It is just as if one were to contend that the whole world ought to be governed by one prefect, because one district has not several prefects. But there is still another reason that that institution ought not to be drawn into a precedent. Everyone knows that the High Priest was a type of Christ; now, the priesthood being transferred, that right must also be transferred. To whom, then, was it transferred? Certainly not to the Pope, as he dares impudently to boast when he arrogates this title to himself, but to Christ, who, as He alone holds the office without vicar or successor, does not resign the honor to any other. For this priesthood consists not in doctrine only, but in the propitiation which Christ made by His death, and the intercession, which He now makes with the Father (Hebrews 7:11).

3 Arguments for primacy from the New Testament. Two answers.

That example, therefore, which is seen to have been temporary, they have no right to bind upon us as by a perpetual law. In the New Testament, there is nothing, which they can produce in confirmation of their opinion, but its having been said to one, "Thou art Peter, and upon this rock I will build my Church" (Matthew 16:18). Again, "Simon, son of Jonas, lovest thou me?" "Feed my lambs" (John 21:15). But to give strength to these proofs, they must, in the first place, show, that to him who is ordered to feed the flock of Christ power is given over all churches, and that to bind and loose is nothing else than to preside over the whole world. But as Peter had received a command from the Lord, so he exhorts all other presbyters to feed the Church (1 Peter 5:2). Hence, we are entitled to infer, that, by that expression of Christ, nothing more was given to Peter than to the others, or that the right, which Peter had received, he communicated equally to others. But not to argue to any purpose, we elsewhere have, from the lips of Christ himself, a clear exposition of what it is to bind and loose. It is just to retain and remit sins (John 10:23). The mode of loosing and binding is explained throughout Scripture: but especially in that passage in which Paul declares that the ministers of the gospel are commissioned to reconcile men to God, and at the same time to exercise discipline over those who reject the benefit (2 Corinthians 5:18; 10:16).

4 Another answer. The keys given to the other apostles as well as to Peter. Other two arguments answered by passages of Cyprian and Augustine.

How unbecomingly they wrest the passages of binding and loosing I have elsewhere glanced at, and will in a short time more fully explain. It may now be worthwhile merely to see what they can extract from our Savior's celebrated answer to Peter. He promised him the keys of the Kingdom of Heaven, and said, that whatever things he bound on Earth should be bound in Heaven. (See Matthew 16:19.) The moment we are agreed as to the meaning of the keys, and the mode of binding, all dispute will cease. For the Pope will willingly omit that office assigned to the apostles, which, full of labor and toil, would interfere with his luxuries without giving any gain. Since Heaven is opened to us by the doctrine of the gospel, it is by an elegant metaphor distinguished by the name of keys. Again, the only mode in which men are bound and loosed is, in the latter case, when they are reconciled to God by faith, and in the former, more strictly bound by unbelief. Were this all that the Pope arrogated to himself, I believe there would be none to envy him or stir the question. But because this laborious and very far from lucrative succession is by no means pleasing to the pope, the dispute immediately arises as to what it was that Christ promised to Peter. From the very nature of the case, I infer that nothing more is denoted than the dignity, which cannot be separated from the burden of the apostolic office. For, admitting the definition, which I have given (and it cannot without effrontery be rejected), nothing is here given to Peter that was not common to him with his colleagues.

On any other view, not only would injustice be done to their persons, but the very majesty of the doctrine would be impaired. They object; but what, pray, is gained by striking against this stone? The utmost they can make out is that as the preaching of the same gospel was enjoined on all the apostles, so the power of binding and loosing was bestowed upon them in common. Christ (they say) constituted Peter prince of the whole Church when He promised to give him the keys. But what He then promised to one He elsewhere delivers, and hands over, to all the rest. If the same right, which was promised to one, is bestowed upon all, in what respect is that one superior to his colleagues? He excels (they say) in this, that he receives both in common, and by himself, what is given to the others in common only. What if I should answer with Cyprian, and Augustine, that Christ did not do this to prefer one to the other, but in order to commend the unity of His Church? For Cyprian thus speaks: "In the person of one man He gave the keys to all, that He might denote the unity of all; the rest, therefore, were the same that Peter was, being admitted to an equal participation of honor and power, but a beginning is made from unity that the Church of Christ may be shown to be one."

Augustine's words are, "Had not the mystery of the Church been in Peter, our Lord would not have said to him, I will give thee the keys. For if this was said to Peter, the Church has them not; but if the Church has them, then when Peter received the keys he represented the whole Church." Again, "All were asked, but Peter alone answers, Thou art the Christ; and it is said to him, I will give thee the keys; as if he alone had received the power of loosing and binding; whereas he both spoke for all, and received in common with all, being the representative of unity. One received for all, because there is unity in all."

5 Another argument answered.

But we nowhere read of its being said to any other, "Thou art Peter, and upon this rock I will build my Church"! (Matthew 16:18); as if Christ then affirmed anything else of Peter, than Paul and Peter himself affirm of all Christians. (See Ephesians 2:20; 1 Peter 2:5.) The former describes Christ as the chief cornerstone, on whom are built all who grow up into a holy temple in the Lord; the latter describes us as living stones who are founded on that elect and precious stone, and being so joined and compacted, are united to our God, and to each other. Peter (they say) is above others, because the name was specially given to him. I willingly concede to Peter the honor of being placed among the first in the building of the Church, or (if they prefer it) of being the first among the faithful; but I will not allow them to infer from this that he has a primacy over others. For what kind of inference is this? Peter surpasses others in fervid zeal, in doctrine, in magnanimity; therefore, he has power over them: as if we might not with greater plausibility infer, that Andrew is prior to Peter in order, because he preceded him in time, and brought him to Christ (see John 1:40, 42); but this I omit. Let Peter have the preeminence; still there is a great difference between the honor of rank and the possession of power. We see that the apostles usually left it to Peter to address the meeting, and in some measure take precedence in relating, exhorting, admonishing, but we nowhere read anything at all of power.

6 Answer to the argument that the Church is founded on Peter, from its being said, "Upon this rock I will build my Church."

Though we are not yet come to that part of the discussion, I would merely observe at present, how futilely those argue who, out of the mere name of Peter, would rear up a governing power over the whole Church. For the ancient quibble which they at first used to give a color–viz. The Church is founded upon Peter, because it is said, "On this rock," etc.–is undeserving of notice, not to say of refutation. Some of the Fathers so expounded! But when the whole of Scripture is repugnant to the exposition, why is their authority brought forward in opposition to God? Nay, why do we contend about the meaning of these words, as if it were obscure or ambiguous, when nothing can be more clear and certain? Peter had confessed in his own name, and that of his brethren, that Christ was the Son of God. (See Matthew 16:16.).

On this rock, Chrit builds His Church, because it is the only foundation; as Paul says, "Other foundation than this can no man lay" (1 Corinthians 3:11). Therefore, I do not here repudiate the authority of the Fathers, because I am destitute of passages from them to prove what I say, if I were disposed to quote them. As I have observed, I am unwilling to annoy my readers by debating so clear a matter, especially since the subject has long ago been fully handled and expounded by our writers.

7 Answer confirmed by passages of Scripture.

And yet, in truth, none can solve this question better than Scripture, if we compare all the passages in which it shows what office and power Peter held among the apostles, how he acted among them, how he was received by them. (See Acts 15:7.) Run over all these passages, and the utmost you will find is that Peter was one of twelve, their equal and colleague, not their master. He indeed brings the matter before the council when anything is to be done, and advises as to what is necessary, but he, at the same time, listens to the others, not only conceding to them an opportunity of expressing their sentiments, but allowing them to decide; and when they have decided, he follows and obeys. When he writes to pastors, he does not command authoritatively as a superior, but makes them his colleagues, and courteously advises as equals are wont to do. (See 1 Peter 5:1.) When he is accused of having gone in to the Gentiles, though the accusation is unfounded, he replies to it, and clears himself. (See Acts 11:3.) Being ordered by his colleagues to go with John into Samaria, he declines not. (See Acts 8:14.) The apostles, by sending him, declare that they by no means regard him as a superior, while he, by obeying and undertaking the embassy committed to him, confesses that he is associated with them, and has no authority over them. But if none of these facts existed, the one Epistle to the Galatians would easily remove all doubt, there being almost two chapters in which the whole for which Paul contends is, that in regard to the honor of the apostleship, he is the equal of Peter. (See Galatians 1:18; 2:8.)

Hence, he states that he went to Peter, not to acknowledge subjection, but to make their agreement in doctrine manifest to all. He states that Peter himself asked no acknowledgment of the kind, but gave him the right hand of fellowship, that they might be common laborers in the vineyard; that not less grace was bestowed on him among the Gentiles than on Peter among the Jews. In fine, when he was not acting with strict fidelity, Peter was rebuked by him, and submitted to the rebuke. (See Galatians 2:11.) All these things make it manifest, either that there was an equality between Paul and Peter, or, at least, that Peter had no more authority over the rest than they had over him. This point, as I have said, Paul handles professedly, in order that no one might give a preference over him, in respect of apostleship, to Peter or John, who were colleagues, not masters.

8 Even allowing Peter's superiority in some respect, this is no proof of the primacy of the Roman Pontiff. Other arguments answered.

But were I to concede to them what they ask with regard to Peter—viz. that he was the chief of the apostles, and surpassed the others in dignity—there is no ground for making a universal rule out of a special example, or wresting a single fact into a perpetual enactment, seeing that the two things are widely different. One was chief among the apostles, just because they were few in number. If one man presided over twelve, will it follow that one ought to preside over a hundred thousand? That twelve had one among them to direct all is nothing strange. Nature admits, the human mind requires that in every meeting, though all are equal in power, there should be one as a kind of moderator to whom the others should look up. There is no senate without a consul, no bench of judges without a president or chancellor, no college without a provost, no company without a master. Thus, there would be no absurdity were we to confess that the apostles had conferred such a primacy on Peter. But an arrangement, which is effectual among a few, must not be forthwith transferred to the whole world, which no one man is able to govern. But (say they) it is observed that not less in nature as a whole, than in each of its parts, there is one supreme head. Proof of this it pleases them to derive from cranes and bees, which always place themselves under the guidance of one, not of several.

I admit the examples, which they produce; but do bees flock together from all parts of the world to choose one queen? Each queen is contented with her own hive. So, among cranes, each flock has its own king. What can they prove from this, except that each church ought to have its bishop? They refer us to the examples of states, quoting from Homer, "a many-headed rule is not good;" and other "passages to the same effect from heathen writers in commendation of monarchy. The answer is easy. Monarchy is not lauded by Homer's Ulysses, or by others, as if one individual ought to govern the whole world; but they mean to intimate that one kingdom does not admit of two kings, and that empire, as one expresses it, cannot bear a partner.

9 Distinction between civil and ecclesiastical government. Christ alone is the Head of the Church. Argument that there is still a ministerial head answered.

Be it, however, as they will have it (though the thing is most absurd; be it), that it would be good and useful for the whole world to be under one monarchy, I will not, therefore, admit that the same thing should take effect in the government of the Church. Her only Head is Christ, under whose government we are all united to each other, according to that order and form of policy which He himself has prescribed. Wherefore they offer an egregious insult to Christ, when under this pretext they would have one man to preside over the whole Church, seeing the Church can never be without a head, "even Christ, from whom the whole body fitly joined together, and compacted by that which every joint supplieth, according to the effectual working in the measure of every part, maketh increase of the body" (Ephesians 4:15, 16).

See how all men, without exception, are placed in the Body, while the honor and name of Head is left to Christ alone. See how to each member is assigned a certain measure, a finite and limited function, while both the perfection of grace and the supreme power of government reside only in Christ.

I am aware of the caviling objection which they are wont to urge—viz. that Christ is properly called the only Head, because He alone reigns by His own authority and in His own name; but that there is nothing in this to prevent what they call another ministerial head from being under Him, and acting as His substitute. But this cavil cannot avail them, until they previously show that this office was ordained by Christ. For the apostle teaches that, the whole subministration is diffused through the members while the power flows from one celestial Head. Or, more plainly, since Scripture testifies that Christ is Head, and claims this honor for himself alone, it ought not to be transferred to any other than him whom Christ himself has made His vicegerent. But not only is there no passage to this effect, but it can be amply refuted by many passages.

10 Paul, in giving a representation of the Church, makes no mention of this ministerial head.

Paul sometimes depicts a living image of the Church, but makes no mention of a single head. On the contrary, we may infer from his description, that it is foreign to the institution of Christ. Christ, by His ascension, took away His visible presence from us, and yet He ascended that He might fill all things: now, therefore, He is present in the Church, and always will be. When Paul would show the mode in which He exhibits himself, he calls our attention to the ministerial offices which He employs: "Unto everyone of us is given grace according to the measure of the gift of Christ;" "And he gave some, apostles; and some, prophets; and some, evangelists; and some, pastors and teachers." Why does he not say that one presided over all to act as his substitute? The passage particularly required this, and it ought not on any account to have been omitted if it had been true. Christ, he says, is present with us. How? By the ministry of men whom He appointed over the government of the Church. Why not rather by a ministerial head whom He appointed his substitute? He speaks of unity, but it is in God and in the faith of Christ. He attributes nothing to men but a common ministry, and a special mode to each. Why, when thus commending unity, does he not, after saying, "one body, one Spirit, even as ye are called in one hope of your calling, one Lord, one faith, one baptism" (Ephesians 4:4), immediately add, one Supreme Pontiff to keep the Church in unity? Nothing could have been said more aptly if the case had really been so. Let that passage be diligently pondered, and there will be no doubt that Paul there meant to give a complete representation of that sacred and ecclesiastical government to which posterity have given the name of hierarchy. Not only does he not place a monarchy among ministers, but even intimates that there is none.

There can also be no doubt that he meant to express the mode of connection by which believers unite with Christ the Head. There he not only makes no mention of a ministerial head, but attributes a particular operation to each of the members, according to the measure of grace distributed to each. Nor is there any ground for subtle philosophical comparisons between the celestial and the earthly hierarchy. For it is not safe to be wise above measure with regard to the former, and in constituting the latter, the only type, which it behooves us to follow, is that which our Lord himself has delineated in His own Word.

11 Even though Peter was ministerial head, it does not follow that the Pope is so also. Argument founded on Paul's having lived and died at Rome.

I will now make them another concession, which they will never obtain from men of sound mind–viz. that the primacy of the Church was fixed in Peter, with the view of remaining forever by perpetual succession. Still how will they prove that his seat of bishopric was so fixed at Rome, that whosoever becomes bishop of that city is to preside over the whole world? By what authority do they annex this dignity to a particular place, when it was given without any mention of place? Peter, they say, lived and died at Rome. What did Christ himself do? Did He not discharge His episcopate while He lived, and complete the office of the priesthood by dying at Jerusalem? The Prince of pastors, the chief Shepherd, the Head of the Church, could not procure honor for a place, and Peter, so far his inferior, could! Is not this worse than childish trifling? Christ conferred the honor of primacy on Peter. Peter had his cathedral at Rome; therefore, he fixed the seat of the primacy there. In this way, the Israelites of old must have placed the seat of the primacy in the wilderness, where Moses, the chief teacher and prince of prophets, discharged his ministry and died.

12 On the hypothesis of the Papists, the primacy belongs to the Church of Antioch.

Let us see, however, how admirably they reason. Peter, they say, had the first place among the apostles; therefore, the church in which he sat ought to have the privilege. But where did he first sit? At Antioch, they say. Therefore, the church of Antioch justly claims the primacy. They acknowledge that she was once the first, but that Peter, by removing from it, transferred the honor, which he had brought with him to Rome. For there is extant, under the name of Pope Marcellus, a letter to the presbyters of Antioch, in which he says, "The See of Peter, at the outset, was with you, and was afterwards, by the order of the Lord, translated hither." Thus the church of Antioch, which was once the first, yielded to the See of Rome. But by what oracle did that good man learn that the Lord had so ordered? For if the question is to be determined in regular form, they must say whether they hold the privilege to be personal, or real, or mixed. One of the three it must be. If they say personal, then it has nothing to do with place; if real, then when once given to a place it is not lost by the death or departure of the person. It remains that they must hold it to be mixed; then the mere consideration of place is not sufficient unless the person also correspond. Let them choose which they will, I will forthwith infer, and easily prove, that Rome has no ground to arrogate the primacy.

13 Absurdity of the Popish hypothesis.

However, be it so. Let the primacy have been (as they vainly allege) transferred from Antioch to Rome. Why did not Antioch retain the second place? For if Rome has the first, simply because Peter had his See there at the end of his life, to which place should the second be given sooner than to that where he first had his See? How comes it, then, that Alexandria takes precedence of Antioch? How can the church of a disciple be superior to the See of Peter? If honor is due to a church according to the dignity of its founder, what shall we say of other churches? Paul names three individuals who seemed to be pillars–viz. James, Peter, and John. (See Galatians 2:9.) If, in honor of Peter, the first place is given to the Roman See, do not the churches of Ephesus and Jerusalem, where John and James were fixed, deserve the second and third places? But in ancient times, Jerusalem held the last place among the Patriarchates, and Ephesus was not able to secure even the lowest corner. Other churches too have passed away, churches, which Paul founded, and over which the apostles presided. The See of Mark, who was only one of the disciples, has obtained honor. Let them either confess that that arrangement was preposterous, or let them concede that it is not always true that each church is entitled to the degree of honor, which its founder possessed.

14 Peter was not the Bishop of Rome.

But I do not see that any credit is due to their allegation of Peter's occupation of the Roman See. Certainly, it is that the statement of Eusebius, that he presided over it for twenty-five years, is easily refuted. For it appears from the first and second chapters of Galatians, that he was at Jerusalem about twenty years after the death of Christ, and afterwards came to Antioch. How long he remained here is uncertain; Gregory counts seven, and Eusebius twenty-five years. But from our Savior's death to the end of Nero's reign (under which they state that he was put to death), will be found only thirty-seven years. For our Lord suffered in the eighteenth year of the reign of Tiberius. If you cut off the twenty years, during which, as Paul testifies, Peter dwelt at Jerusalem, there will remain at most seventeen years; and these must be divided between his two episcopates. If he dwelt long at Antioch, his See at Rome must have been of short duration. This we may demonstrate still more clearly. Paul wrote to the Romans while he was on his journey to Jerusalem, where he was apprehended and conveyed to Rome. (See Romans 15:15, 16.) It is therefore probable that this letter was written four years before his arrival at Rome. Still there is no mention of Peter, as there certainly would have been if he had been ruling that church. Nay, in the end of the Epistle, where he enumerates a long list of individuals whom he orders to be saluted, and in which it may be supposed he includes all who were known to him, he says nothing at all of Peter. To men of sound judgment, there is no need here of a long and subtle demonstration; the nature of the case itself, and the whole subject of the epistle, proclaims that he ought not to have passed over Peter if he had been at Rome.

15 Same subject continued.

Paul is afterwards conveyed as a prisoner to Rome. Luke relates that he was received by the brethren, but says nothing of Peter. From Rome, he writes to many churches. He even sends salutations from certain individuals, but does not by a single word intimate that Peter was then there. Who, pray, will believe that he would have said nothing of him if he had been present? Nay, in the Epistle to the Philippians, after saying that he had no one who cared for the work of the Lord so faithfully as Timothy, he complains, "all seek their own" (Philippians 2:21). And to Timothy he makes the more grievous complaint, that no man was present at his first defense, that all men forsook him. (See 2 Timothy 4:16.) Where then was Peter? If they say that he was at Rome, how disgraceful the charge that Paul brings against him of being a deserter of the gospel! For he is speaking of believers, since he adds, "The Lord lay it not to their charge." At what time, therefore, and how long, did Peter hold that See? The uniform opinion of authors is that he governed that church until his death. But these authors are not agreed as to who was his successor. Some say Linus, others Clement. And they relate many absurd fables concerning a discussion between him and Simon Magus. Nor does Augustine, when treating of superstition, disguise the fact, that owing to an opinion rashly entertained, it had become customary at Rome to fast on the day on which Peter carried away the palm from Simon Magus. In short, the affairs of that period are so involved from the variety of opinions that credit is not to be given rashly to anything we read concerning it. And yet, from this agreement of authors, I do not dispute that he died there, but that he was bishop, particularly for a long period, I cannot believe. However, I do not attach much importance to the point, since Paul testifies, that the apostleship of Peter pertained especially to the Jews, but his own especially to us. Therefore, in order that that compact which they made between themselves, nay, that the arrangement of the Holy Spirit may be firmly established among us, we ought to pay more regard to the apostleship of Paul than to that of Peter, since the Holy Spirit, in allotting them different provinces, destined Peter for the Jews and Paul for us. Let the Romanists, therefore, seek their primacy somewhere else than in the Word of God, which gives not the least foundation for it.

16 Argument that the unity of the Church cannot be maintained without a supreme head on Earth. Answer, stating three reasons why great respect was paid in early times to the See of Rome.

Let us now come to the Primitive Church, that it may also appear that our opponents plume themselves on its support, not less falsely and unadvisedly than on the testimony of the Word of God. When they lay it down as an axiom—that the unity of the Church cannot be maintained unless there be one supreme head on Earth whom all the members should obey; and that, accordingly, our Lord gave the primacy to Peter, and thereafter, by right of succession, to the See of Rome, there to remain even to the end—they assert that this has always been observed from the beginning. But since they improperly wrest many passages, I would first premise, that I deny not that the early Christians uniformly give high honor to the Roman Church, and speak of it with reverence. This, I think, is owing chiefly to three causes. The opinion that had prevailed (I know not how), that that Church was founded and constituted by the ministry of Peter, had great effect in procuring influence and authority. Hence, in the East, it was, as a mark of honor, designated the Apostolic See.

Secondly, as the seat of empire was there, and it was for this reason to be presumed, that the most distinguished for learning, prudence, skill, and experience, were there more than elsewhere, account was justly taken of the circumstance, lest the celebrity of the city, and the much more excellent gifts of God also, might seem to be despised. To these was added a third cause, that when the churches of the East, of Greece and of Africa, were kept in a constant turmoil by differences of opinion, the Church of Rome was calmer and less troubled. To this it was owing, that pious and holy bishops, when driven from their sees, often betook themselves to Rome as an asylum or haven. For as the people of the West are of a less acute and versatile turn of mind than those of Asia or Africa, so they are less desirous of innovations. It therefore added very great authority to the Roman Church, that in those dubious times it was not so much unsettled as others, and adhered more firmly to the doctrine once delivered, as shall immediately be better explained. For these three causes, I say, she was held in no ordinary estimation, and received many distinguished testimonies from ancient writers.

17 Opinion of early times on the subject of the unity of the Church. No primacy attributed to the Church of Rome. Christ alone regarded as the Head of the Universal Church.

But since on this our opponents would rear up a primacy and supreme authority over other churches, they, as I have said, greatly err. That this may better appear, I will first briefly show what the views of early writers are as to this unity, which they so strongly urge. Jerome, in writing to Nepotian, after enumerating many examples of unity, descends at length to the ecclesiastical hierarchy. He says, "Every bishop of a church, every archpresbyter, every archdeacon, and the whole ecclesiastical order, depends on its own rulers."

Here a Roman presbyter speaks and commends unity in ecclesiastical order. Why does he not mention that all the churches are bound together by one Head as a common bond? There was nothing more appropriate to the point in hand, and it cannot be said that he omitted it through forgetfulness; there was nothing he would more willingly have mentioned, if permitted. He therefore undoubtedly owns, that the true method of unity is that which Cyprian admirably describes in these words: "The episcopate is one, part of which is held entire by each bishop, and the Church is one, which, by the increase of fecundity, extends more widely in numbers. As there are many rays of the sun and one light, many branches of a tree and one trunk, upheld by its tenacious root, and as very many streams flow from one fountain, and though numbers seem diffused by the largeness of the overflowing supply, yet unity is preserved entire in the source, so the Church, pervaded with the light of the Lord, sends her rays over the whole globe, and yet is one light, which is everywhere diffused without separating the unity of the body, extends her branches over the whole globe, and sends forth flowing streams; still the head is one, and the source one." Afterwards he says, "The spouse of Christ cannot be an adulteress: she knows one house, and with chaste modesty keeps the sanctity of one bed." See how he makes the bishopric of Christ alone universal, as comprehending under it the whole Church: See how he says that part of it is held entire by all who discharge the episcopal office under this head. Where is the primacy of the Roman See, if the entire bishopric resides in Christ alone, and a part of it is held entire by each? My object in these remarks is, to show the reader, in passing, that that axiom of the unity of an earthly kind in the hierarchy, which the Romanists assume as confessed and indubitable, was altogether unknown to the ancient Church.

Chapter 7

OF THE BEGINNING AND RISE OF THE ROMISH PAPACY, TILL IT ATTAINED A HEIGHT BY WHICH THE LIBERTY OF THE CHURCH WAS DESTROYED, AND ALL TRUE RULE OVERTHROWN.

There are five heads in this chapter. I. The Patriarchate given and confirmed to the Bishop of Rome, first by the Council of Nice, and afterwards by that of Chalcedon though by no means approved of by other bishops, was the commencement of the Papacy, sections 1-4. II. The Church at Rome, by taking pious exiles under its protection, and also thereby protecting wicked men who fled to her, helped forward the mystery of iniquity, although at that time neither the ordination of bishops, nor admonitions and censures, nor the right of convening Councils, nor the right of receiving appeals, belonged to the Roman Bishop, whose profane meddling with these things was condemned by Gregory, sections 5-13. III. After the Council of Turin, disputes arose as to the authority of Metropolitans. Disgraceful strife between the Patriarchs of Rome and Constantinople. The vile assassin Phocas put an end to these brawls at the instigation of Boniface, sections 14-18. IV. To the dishonest arts of Boniface succeeded fouler frauds devised in more modern times, and expressly condemned by Gregory and Bernard. sections 19-21. V. The Papacy at length appeared complete in all its parts, the seat of Antichrist. Its impiety, execrable tyranny, and wickedness, portrayed, sections 23-30.

Sections

1. First part of the chapter, in which the commencement of the Papacy is assigned to the Council of Nice. In subsequent Councils, other bishops presided. No attempt then made to claim the first place.

2. Though the Roman Bishop presided in the Council of Chalcedon, this was owing to special circumstances. The same right not given to his successors in other Councils.

3. The ancient Fathers did not give the title of Primate to the Roman Bishop.

4. Gregory was vehement in opposition to the title when claimed by the Bishop of Constantinople, and did not claim it for himself.

5. Second part of the chapter, explaining the ambitious attempts of the Roman See to obtain the primacy. Their reception of pious exiles. Hearing the appeals and complaints of heretics. Their ambition in this respect offensive to the African Church.

6. The power of the Roman Bishops in ordaining bishops, appointing councils, deciding controversies, etc., confined to their own Patriarchate.

7. If they censured other bishops, they themselves were censured in their turn.

8. They had no right of calling provincial councils except within their own boundaries. The calling of a universal council belonged solely to the Emperor.

9. Appeal to the Roman See not acknowledged by other bishops. Stoutly resisted by the Bishops of France and Africa. The impudence and falsehood of the Roman Pontiff detected.

10. Proof from history that the Roman had no jurisdiction over other churches.

11. The decretal epistles of no avail in support of this usurped jurisdiction.

12. The authority of the Roman Bishop extended in the time of Gregory. Still it only consisted in aiding other bishops with their own consent, or at the command of the Emperor.

13. Even the extent of jurisdiction, thus voluntarily conferred, objected to by Gregory as interfering with better duties.

14. Third part of the chapter, showing the increase of the power of the Papacy in defining the limits of Metropolitans. This gave rise to the decree of the Council of Turin. This decree haughtily annulled by Innocent.

15. Hence, the great struggle for precedence between the Sees of Rome and Constantinople. The pride and ambition of the Roman Bishops unfolded.

16. Many attempts of the Bishop of Constantinople to deprive the Bishop of Rome of the primacy.

17. Phocas murders the Emperor, and gives Rome the primacy.

18. The Papal tyranny shortly after established. Bitter complaints by Bernard.

19. Fourth part of the chapter. Altered appearance of the Roman See since the days of Gregory.

20. The present demands of the Romanists not formerly conceded. Fictions of Gregory IX. and Martin.

21. Without mentioning the opposition of Cyprian, of councils, and historical facts, the claims now made were condemned by Gregory himself.

22. The abuses of which Gregory and Bernard complained now increased and sanctioned.

23. The fifth and last part of the chapter, containing the chief answer to the claims of the Papacy—viz. that the Pope is not a bishop in the house of God. This answer confirmed by an enumeration of the essential parts of the episcopal office.

24. A second confirmation by appeal to the institution of Christ. A third confirmation e contrario—viz. that in doctrine and morals the Roman Pontiff is altogether different from a true bishop. Conclusion, that Rome is not the Apostolic See, but the Papacy.

25. Proof from Daniel and Paul that the Pope is Antichrist.

26. Rome could not now claim the primacy, even though she had formerly been the first See, especially considering the base trafficking in which she has engaged.

27. Personal character of Popes. Irreligious opinions held by some of them.

28. John XXII. heretical in regard to the immortality of the soul. His name, therefore, ought to be expunged from the catalogue of Popes, or rather, there is no foundation for the claim of perpetuity of faith in the Roman See.

29. Some Roman Pontiffs atheists, or sworn enemies of religion. Their immoral lives. Practice of the Cardinals and Romish clergy.

30. Cardinals were formerly merely presbyters of the Roman Church, and far inferior to bishops. As they now are, they have no true and legitimate office in the Church. Conclusion.

1 First part of the chapter, in which the commencement of the Papacy is assigned to the Council of Nice. In subsequent Councils, other bishops presided. No attempt then made to claim the first place.

In regard to the antiquity of the primacy of the Roman See, there is nothing in favor of its establishment more ancient than the decree of the Council of Nice, by which the first place among the Patriarchs is assigned to the Bishop of Rome, and he is enjoined to take care of the suburban churches. While the council, in dividing between him and the other Patriarchs, assigns the proper limits of each, it certainly does not appoint him head of all, but only one of the chiefs. Vitus and Vincentius attended on the part of Julius, who then governed the Roman Church, and to them the fourth place was given. I ask, if Julius were acknowledged the head of the Church, would his legates have been consigned to the fourth place? Would Athanasius have presided in the council where a representative of the hierarchal order should have been most conspicuous? In the Council of Ephesus, it appears that Celestinus (who was then Roman Pontiff) used a cunning device to secure the dignity of his See. For when he sent his deputies, he made Cyril of Alexandria, who otherwise would have presided, his substitute.

Why that commission, but just that his name might stand connected with the first See? His legates sit in an inferior place, are asked their opinion along with others, and subscribe in their order, while, at the same time, his name is coupled with that of the Patriarch of Alexandria. What shall I say of the second Council of Ephesus, where, while the deputies of Leo were present, the Alexandrian Patriarch Dioscorus presided as in his own right? They will object that this was not an orthodox council, since by it the venerable Flavianus was condemned, Eutyches acquitted, and his heresy approved.

Yet, when the council was met, and the bishops distributed the places among themselves, the deputies of the Roman Church sat among the others just as in a sacred and lawful Council. Still they contend not for the first place, but yield it to another: this they never would have done if they had thought it their own by right. For the Roman bishops were never ashamed to stir up the greatest strife in contending for honors, and for this cause alone, to trouble and harass the Church with many pernicious contests; but because Leo saw that it would be too extravagant to ask the first place for his legates, he omitted to do it.

2 Though the Roman Bishop presided in the Council of Chalcedon, this was owing to special circumstances. The same right not given to his successors in other Councils.

Next came the Council of Chalcedon, in which, by concession of the Emperor, the legates of the Roman Church occupied the first place. But Leo himself confesses that this was an extraordinary privilege; for when he asks it of the Emperor Marcian and Pulcheria Augusta, he does not maintain that it is due to him, but only pretends that the Eastern bishops who presided in the Council of Ephesus had thrown all into confusion, and made a bad use of their power. Therefore, seeing there was need of a grave moderator, and it was not probable that those who had once been so fickle and tumultuous would be fit for this purpose, he requests that, because of the fault and unfitness of others, the office of governing should be transferred to him. That which is asked as a special privilege, and out of the usual order, certainly is not due by a common law. When it is only pretended that there is need of a new president, because the former ones had behaved themselves improperly, it is plain that the thing asked was not previously done, and ought not to be made perpetual, being done only in respect of a present danger. The Roman Pontiff, therefore, holds the first place in the Council of Chalcedon, not because it is due to his See, but because the council is in want of a grave and fit moderator, while those who ought to have presided exclude themselves by their intemperance and passion. This statement the successor of Leo approved by his procedure. For when he sent his legates to the fifth Council, that of Constantinople, which was held long after, he did not quarrel for the first seat, but readily allowed Mennas, the patriarch of Constantinople, to preside.

In like manner, in the Council of Carthage, at which Augustine was present, we perceive that not the legates of the Roman See, but Aurelius, the archbishop of the place, presided, although there was then a question as to the authority of the Roman Pontiff. Nay, even in Italy itself, a universal council was held (that of Aquileia), at which the Roman Bishop was not present. Ambrose, who was then in high favor with the Emperor, presided, and no mention is made of the Roman Pontiff. Therefore, owing to the dignity of Ambrose, the See of Milan was then more illustrious than that of Rome.

3 The ancient Fathers did not give the title of Primate to the Roman Bishop.

In regard to the mere title of primate and other titles of pride, of which that pontiff now makes a wondrous boast, it is not difficult to understand how and in what way they crept in. Cyprian often makes mention of Cornelius, nor does he distinguish him by any other name than that of brother, or fellow bishop, or colleague. When he writes to Stephen, the successor of Cornelius, he not only makes him the equal of himself and others, but addresses him in harsh terms, charging him at one time with presumption, at another with ignorance. After Cyprian, we have the judgment of the whole African Church on the subject. For the Council of Carthage enjoined that none should be called chief of the priests, or first bishop, but only bishop of the first See. But anyone who will examine the more ancient records will find that the Roman Pontiff was then contented with the common appellation of brother. Certainly, as long as the true and pure form of the Church continued, all these names of pride on which the Roman See afterwards began to plume itself, were altogether unheard of; none knew what was meant by the supreme Pontiff, and the only head of the Church on Earth. Had the Roman Bishop presumed to assume any such title, there were right-hearted men who would immediately have repressed his folly. Jerome, seeing he was a Roman presbyter, was not slow to proclaim the dignity of his church, in as far as fact and the circumstances of the times permitted, and yet we see how he brings it under due subordination. "If authority is asked, the world is greater than a city. Why produce to me the custom of one city? Why vindicate a small number with whom superciliousness has originated against the laws of the Church? Wherever the bishop be, whether at Rome, or Eugubium, or Constantinople, or Rhegium, the merit is the same, and the priesthood the same. The power of riches, or the humbleness of poverty, do not make a bishop superior or inferior."

4 Gregory was vehement in opposition to the title when claimed by the Bishop of Constantinople, and did not claim it for himself.

The controversy over the title of universal bishop arose at length in the time of Gregory, and was occasioned by the ambition of John of Constantinople. He wished to make himself universal, a thing that no other had ever attempted. In that controversy, Gregory does not allege that he is deprived of a right, which belonged to him, but he strongly insists that the appellation is profane, nay, blasphemous, nay the forerunner of Antichrist. "The whole Church falls from its state, if he who is called universal falls." Again, "It is very difficult to bear patiently that one who is our brother and fellow bishop should alone be called bishop, while all others are despised. But his pride, what else is intimated but that the days of Antichrist are already near? For he is imitating him, who, despising the company of angels, attempted to ascend the pinnacle of greatness." He elsewhere says to Eulogius of Alexandria and Anastasius of Antioch: "None of my predecessors ever desired to use this profane term: for if one patriarch is called universal, it is derogatory to the name of patriarch in others.

But far be it from any Christian mind to wish to arrogate to itself that which would in any degree, however slight, impair the honor of his brethren." "To consent to that impious term is nothing else than to lose the faith." "What we owe to the preservation of the unity of the faith is one thing, what we owe to the suppression of pride is another. I speak with confidence, for everyone that calls himself, or desires to be called, universal priest, is by his pride a forerunner of Antichrist, because he acts proudly in preferring himself to others." Thus, again, in a letter to Anastasius of Antioch, "I said, that he could not have peace with us unless he corrected the presumption of a superstitious and haughty term which the first apostate invented; and (to say nothing of the injury to your honor) if one bishop is called universal, the whole Church goes to ruin when that universal bishop falls." But when he writes that this honor was offered to Leo in the Council of Chalcedon, he says bears no semblance of truth. Nothing of the kind is found among the acts of that council.

And Leo himself, who, in many letters, impugns the decree, which was then made in honor of the See of Constantinople, undoubtedly would not have omitted this argument, which was the most plausible of all, if it was true that he himself repudiated what was given to him. One, who, in other respects, was rather too desirous of honor, would not have omitted what would have been to his praise. Gregory, therefore, is incorrect in saying that the title was conferred on the Roman See by the Council of Chalcedon; not to mention how ridiculous it is for him to say that it proceeded from that sacred council, and yet to term it wicked, profane, nefarious, proud, and blasphemous, nay, devised by the devil, and promulgated by the herald of Antichrist. And yet he adds, that his predecessor refused it, lest by that which was given to one individually, all priests should be deprived of their due honor. In another place, he says, "None ever wished to be called by such a name; none arrogated this rash name to himself, lest, by seizing on the honor of supremacy in the office of the Pontificate, he might seem to deny it to all his brethren."

5 Second part of the chapter, explaining the ambitious attempts of the Roman See to obtain the primacy. Their reception of pious exiles. Hearing the appeals and complaints of heretics. Their ambition in this respect offensive to the African Church.

I come now to jurisdiction, which the Roman Pontiff asserts as an incontrovertible proposition that he possesses over all churches. I am aware of the great disputes, which anciently existed on this subject: for there never was a time when the Roman See did not aim at authority over other churches. And here it will not be out of place to investigate the means by which she gradually attained to some influence. I am not now referring to that unlimited power which she seized at a comparatively recent period. The consideration of that we shall defer to its own place. But it is worthwhile here briefly to show in what way, and by what means, she formerly raised herself, to arrogate some authority over other churches. When the churches of the East were troubled and rent by the factions of the Arians, under the Emperors Constantius and Constans, sons of Constantine the Great; and Athanasius, the principal defender of the orthodox faith, had been driven from his see, the calamity obliged him to come to Rome, in order that by the authority of this see he might both repress the rage of his enemies, and confirm the orthodox under their distress. He was honorably received by Julius, who was then bishop, and engaged those of the West to undertake the defense of his cause. Therefore, when the orthodox stood greatly in need of external aid, and perceived that their chief protection lay in the Roman See, they willingly bestowed upon it all the authority they could. But the utmost extent of this was that its communion was held in high estimation, and it was deemed ignominious to be excommunicated by it. Dishonest bad men afterwards added much to its authority, for when they wished to escape lawful tribunals, they betook themselves to Rome as an asylum. Accordingly, if any presbyter was condemned by his bishop, or if any bishop was condemned by the synod of his province, he appealed to Rome. These appeals the Roman bishops received more eagerly than they ought, because it seemed a species of extraordinary power to interpose in matters with which their connection was so very remote.

Thus, when Eutyches was condemned by Flavianus, Bishop of Constantinople, he complained to Leo that the sentence was unjust. He, willingly and no less presumptuously than abruptly, undertook the patronage of a bad cause, and inveighed bitterly against Flavianus, as having condemned an innocent man without due investigation.

Thus the effect of Leo's ambition was that for some time the impiety of Eutyches was confirmed. It is certain that in Africa, the same thing repeatedly occurred, for whenever any miscreant had been condemned by his ordinary judge, he fled to Rome, and brought many calumnious charges against his own people. The Roman See was always ready to interpose. This dishonesty obliged the African bishops to decree that no one should carry an appeal beyond sea under pain of excommunication.

6 The power of the Roman Bishops in ordaining bishops, appointing councils, deciding controversies, etc., confined to their own Patriarchate.

Be this as it may, let us consider what right or authority the Roman See then possessed. Ecclesiastical power may be reduced to four heads—viz. ordination of bishops, calling of councils, hearing of appeals (or jurisdiction), inflicting monitory chastisements or censures. All ancient councils enjoin that bishops shall be ordained by their own Metropolitans; they nowhere enjoin an application to the Roman Bishop, except in his own patriarchate. Gradually, however, it became customary for all Italian bishops to go to Rome for consecration, with the exception of the Metropolitans, who did not allow themselves to be thus brought into subjection; but when any Metropolitan was to be ordained, the Roman Bishop sent one of his presbyters merely to be present, but not to preside. An example of this kind is still in existence in Gregory, in the consecration of Constantius of Milan, after the death of Laurence.

I do not, however, think that this was a very ancient custom. At first, as a mark of respect and good will, they sent deputies to one another to witness the ordination, and attest their communion. What was thus voluntary afterwards began to be regarded as necessary. However this be, it is certain that anciently the Roman Bishop had no power of ordaining except within the bounds of his own patriarchate, that is, as a canon of the Council of Nice expresses it, in suburban churches.

To ordination was added the sending of a synodical epistle, but this implied no authority. The patriarchs were accustomed, immediately after consecration, to attest their faith by a formal writing, in which they declared that they assented to sacred and orthodox councils. Thus, by rendering an account of their faith, they mutually approved of each other. If the Roman Bishop had received this confession from others, and not given it, he would therein have been acknowledged superior; but when it behooved to give as well as to receive, and to be subject to the common law, this was a sign of equality, not of lordship. Of this, we have an example in a letter of Gregory to Anastasius and Cyriac of Constantinople, and in another letter to all the patriarchs together.

7 If they censured other bishops, they themselves were censured in their turn.

Next, come admonitions or censures. These the Roman Bishops anciently employed towards others, and in their turn received. Irenaeus sharply rebuked Victor for rashly troubling the Church with a pernicious schism, for a matter of no moment. He submitted without objecting. Holy bishops were then wont to use the freedom as brethren, of admonishing and rebuking the Roman Prelate when he happened to err. He in his turn, when the case required, reminded others of their duty, and reprimanded them for their faults. For Cyprian, when he exhorts Stephen to admonish the bishops of France, does not found on his larger power, but on the common right, which priests have, in regard to each other. I ask if Stephen had then presided over France, would not Cyprian have said, "Check them, for they are yours"? But his language is very different. "The brotherly fellowship which binds us together requires that we should mutually admonish each other." And we see with what severity of expression, a man otherwise of a mild temper, inveighs against Stephen himself, when he thinks him chargeable with insolence. Therefore, it does not yet appear in this respect that the Roman Bishop possessed any jurisdiction over those who did not belong to his province.

8 They had no right of calling provincial councils except within their own boundaries. The calling of a universal council belonged solely to the Emperor.

In regard to calling of councils, it was the duty of every Metropolitan to assemble a provincial synod at stated times. Here the Roman Bishop had no jurisdiction, while the Emperor alone could summon a general council. Had any of the bishops attempted this, not only would those out of the province not have obeyed the call, but a tumult would instantly have arisen. Therefore, the Emperor gave intimation to all alike to attend. Socrates, indeed, relates that Julius expostulated with the Eastern bishops for not having called him to the Council of Antioch, seeing it was forbidden by the canons that anything should be decided without the knowledge of the Roman Bishop. But who does not perceive that this is to be understood of those decrees, which bind the whole Church? At the same time, it is not strange if, in deference both to the antiquity and largeness of the city, and the dignity of the see, no universal decree concerning religion should be made in the absence of the Bishop of Rome, provided he did not refuse to be present. But what has this to do with the dominion of the whole Church? For we deny not that he was one of the principal bishops, though we are unwilling to admit what the Romanists now contend for–viz. that he had power over all.

9 Appeal to the Roman See not acknowledged by other bishops. Stoutly resisted by the Bishops of France and Africa. The impudence and falsehood of the Roman Pontiff detected.

The fourth remaining species of power is that of hearing appeals. It is evident that the supreme power belongs to him to whose tribunal appeals are made. Many had repeatedly appealed to the Roman Pontiff. He also had endeavored to bring causes under his cognizance, but he had always been derided whenever he went beyond his own boundaries. I say nothing of the East and of Greece, but it is certain, that the bishops of France stoutly resisted when he seemed to assume authority over them. In Africa, the subject was long disputed, for in the Council of Milevita, at which Augustine was present, when those who carried appeals beyond seas were excommunicated, the Roman Pontiff attempted to obtain an alteration of the decree, and sent legates to show that the privilege of hearing appeals was given him by the Council of Nice.

The legates produced acts of the council drawn from the armory of their church. The African bishops resisted, and maintained, that credit was not to be given to the Bishop of Rome in his own cause; accordingly, they said that they would send to Constantinople, and other cities of Greece, where less suspicious copies might be had. It was found that nothing like what the Romanists had pretended was contained in the acts, and thus the decree, which abrogated the supreme jurisdiction of the Roman Pontiff, was confirmed. In this matter was manifested the egregious effrontery of the Roman Pontiff. For when he had fraudulently substituted the Council of Sardis for that of Nice, he was disgracefully caught in a palpable falsehood.

But still greater and more impudent was the iniquity of those who added a fictitious letter to the Council, in which some Bishop of Carthage condemns the arrogance of Aurelius his predecessor, in promising to withdraw himself from obedience to the Apostolic See. Making a surrender of himself and his church, he suppliantly prays for pardon.

These are the noble records of antiquity on which the majesty of the Roman See is founded, while, under the pretext of antiquity, they deal in falsehoods so puerile that even a blind man might feel them. "Aurelius (says he), elated by diabolical audacity and contumacy, was rebellious against Christ and St. Peter, and, accordingly, deserved to be anathematized."

What does Augustine say? And what the many Fathers who were present at the Council of Milevita? But what need is there to give a lengthened refutation of that absurd writing, which not even Romanists, if they have any modesty left them, can look at without a deep feeling of shame? Thus Gratian, whether through malice or ignorance, I know not, after quoting the decree, That those are to be deprived of communion who carry appeals beyond seas, subjoins the exception, Unless, perhaps, they have appealed to the Roman See. What can you make of creatures like these, who are so devoid of common sense that they set down as an exception from the law the very thing because of which, as everybody sees, the law was made? For the Council, in condemning transmarine appeals, simply prohibits an appeal to Rome. Yet, this worthy expounder excepts Rome from the common law.

10 Proof from history that the Roman had no jurisdiction over other churches.

To end the question at once, one narrative will make manifest the kind of jurisdiction that belonged to the Roman Bishop. Donatus of Casa Nigra had accused Cecilianus the Bishop of Carthage. Cecilianus was condemned without a hearing: for, having ascertained that the bishops had entered into a conspiracy against him, he refused to appear. The case was brought before the Emperor Constantine, who, wishing the matter to be ended by an ecclesiastical decision; gave the cognizance of it to Melciades, the Roman Bishop, appointing as his colleagues some bishops from Italy, France, and Spain. If it formed part of the ordinary jurisdiction of the Roman See to hear appeals in ecclesiastical causes, why did he allow others to be conjoined with him at the Emperor's discretion? Nay, why does he undertake to decide more from the command of the Emperor than his own office? But let us hear what afterwards happened. Cecilianus prevails. Donatus of Casa Nigra is thrown in his calumnious action and appeals. Constantine devolves the decision of the appeal on the Bishop of Arles, who sits as judge, to give sentence after the Roman Pontiff. If the Roman See has supreme power not subject to appeal, why does Melciades allow himself to be so greatly insulted as to have the Bishop of Arles preferred to him? And who is the Emperor that does this? Constantine, who they boast not only made it his constant study, but employed all the resources of the empire to enlarge the dignity of that see. We see, therefore, how far in every way the Roman Pontiff was from that supreme dominion, which he asserts to have been given him by Christ over all churches, and which he falsely alleges that he possessed in all ages, with the consent of the whole world.

11 The decretal epistles of no avail in support of this usurped jurisdiction.

I know how many epistles there are, how many rescripts and edicts in which there is nothing, which the pontiffs do not ascribe and confidently arrogate to themselves. But all men of the least intellect and learning know, that the greater part of them are in themselves so absurd, that it is easy at the first sight to detect the forge from which they have come. Does any man of sense and soberness think that Anacletus is the author of that famous interpretation which is given in Gratian, under the name of Anacletus–viz. that Cephas is head? Numerous follies of the same kind, which Gratian has heaped together without judgment, the Romanists of the present day, employ against us in defense of their see. The smoke, by which, in the former days of ignorance, they imposed upon the ignorant, they would still vend in the present light. I am unwilling to take much trouble in refuting things, which, by their extreme absurdity, plainly refute themselves.

I admit the existence of genuine epistles by ancient Pontiffs, in which they pronounce magnificent eulogiums on the extent of their see. Such are some of the epistles of Leo. For as he possessed learning and eloquence, so he was excessively desirous of glory and dominion, but the true question is, whether or not, when he thus extolled himself, the churches gave credit to his testimony? It appears that many were offended with his ambition, and resisted his cupidity. He in one place appoints the Bishop of Thessalonica his vicar throughout Greece and other neighboring regions, and elsewhere gives the same office to the Bishop of Arles or some other throughout France. In like manner, he appointed Hormisdas, Bishop of Hispala, his vicar throughout Spain, but he uniformly makes this reservation, that in giving such commissions, the ancient privileges of the Metropolitans were to remain safe and entire. These appointments, therefore, were made on the condition, that no bishop should be impeded in his ordinary jurisdiction, no Metropolitan in taking cognizance of appeals, no provincial council in constituting churches. But what else was this than to decline all jurisdiction, and to interpose for settling discord only, as far as the law and nature of ecclesiastical communion admit?

12 The authority of the Roman Bishop extended in the time of Gregory. Still it only consisted in aiding other bishops with their own consent, or at the command of the Emperor.

In the time of Gregory, that ancient rule was greatly changed. The empire was convulsed and torn. France and Spain were suffering from the many disasters that they always received, Illyricum was laid waste, Italy was harassed, and Africa was almost destroyed by uninterrupted calamities. All this happened in order that, during these civil convulsions, the integrity of the faith might remain, or at least not entirely perish. The bishops in all quarters attached themselves more to the Roman Pontiff. In this way, not only the dignity, but also the power of the see, exceedingly increased, although I attach no great importance to the means, by which this was accomplished. It is certain, that it was then greater than in former ages. And yet, it was very different from the unbridled dominion of one ruling others as he pleased. Still the reverence paid to the Roman See was such, that by its authority it could guide and repress those whom their own colleagues were unable to keep to their duty; for Gregory is careful always to testify that he was not less faithful in preserving the rights of others, that in insisting that his own should be preserved. "I do not," says he, "under the stimulus of ambition, derogate from any man's right, but desire to honor my brethren in all things." There is no sentence in his writings in which he boasts more proudly of the extent of his primacy than the following: "I know not what bishop is not subject to the Roman See, when he is discovered in a fault." However, he immediately adds, "Where faults do not call for interference, all are equal according to the rule of humility." He claims for himself the right of correcting those who have sinned; if all do their duty, he puts himself on a footing of equality. He, indeed, claimed this right, and those who chose assented to it, while those who were not pleased with it would be at liberty to object with impunity; and it is known that the greater part did so. We may add, that he is then speaking of the primate of Byzantium, who, when condemned by a provincial synod, repudiated the whole judgment. His colleagues had informed the Emperor of his contumacy, and the Emperor had given the cognizance of the matter to Gregory. We see, therefore, that he does not interfere in any way with the ordinary jurisdiction, and that, in acting as a subsidiary to others, he acts entirely by the Emperor's command.

13 Even the extent of jurisdiction, thus voluntarily conferred, objected to by Gregory as interfering with better duties.

At this time, therefore, the whole power of the Roman Bishop consisted in opposing stubborn and ungovernable spirits, where some extraordinary remedy was required, and this in order to assist other bishops, not to interfere with them. Therefore, he assumes no more power over others than he elsewhere gives others over himself, when he confesses that he is ready to be corrected by all, amended by all. So, in another place, though he orders the Bishop of Aquileia to come to Rome to plead his cause in a controversy as to doctrine that had arisen between himself and others, he thus orders not of his own authority, but in obedience to the Emperor's command. Nor does he declare that he himself will be sole judge, but promises to call a synod, by which the whole business may be determined. But although the moderation was still such, that the power of the Roman See had certain limits which it was not permitted to overstep, and the Roman Bishop himself was not more above than under others, it appears how much Gregory was dissatisfied with this state of matters. For he always complains, that he, under the color of the episcopate, was brought back to the world, and was more involved in earthly cares than when living as a laic; that he, in that honorable office, was oppressed by the tumult of secular affairs. Elsewhere he says, "So many burdensome occupations depress me, that my mind cannot at all rise to things above. I am shaken by the many billows of causes, and after they are quieted, am afflicted by the tempests of a tumultuous life, so that I may truly say I am come into the depths of the sea, and the flood has overwhelmed me." From this I infer what he would have said if he had fallen on the present times. If he did not fulfill, he at least did the duty of a pastor. He declined the administration of civil power, and acknowledged himself subject, like others, to the Emperor. He did not interfere with the management of other churches, unless forced by necessity. And yet, he thinks himself in a labyrinth, because he cannot devote himself entirely to the duty of a bishop.

14 Third part of the chapter, showing the increase of the power of the Papacy in defining the limits of Metropolitans. This gave rise to the decree of the Council of Turin. This decree haughtily annulled by Innocent.

At that time, as has already been said, the Bishop of Constantinople was disputing with the Bishop of Rome for the primacy. For after the seat of the empire was fixed at Constantinople, the majesty of the empire seemed to demand that that church should have the next place of honor to that of Rome. And certainly, at the outset, nothing had tended more to give the primacy to Rome, than that it was then the capital of the empire. In Gratian, there is a rescript under the name of Pope Lucinus, to the effect that the only way in which the cities where Metropolitans and Primates ought to preside were distinguished, was by means of the civil government, which had previously existed. There is a similar rescript under the name of Pope Clement, in which he says, that patriarchs were appointed in those cities, which had previously had the first flamens [a Roman priest, one of a group of fifteen, each of whom oversaw the rituals connected with a particular deity]. Although this is absurd, it was borrowed from what was true. For it is certain, that in order to make as little change as possible, provinces were distributed according to the state of matters then existing, and Primates and Metropolitans were placed in those cities which surpassed others in honors and power. Accordingly, it was decreed in the Council of Turin, that the cities of every province, which were first in the civil government, should be the first sees of bishops. But if it should happen that the honor of civil government was transferred from one city to another, then the right of the metropolis should be at the same time transferred thither. But Innocent, the Roman Pontiff, seeing that the ancient dignity of the city had been decaying ever since the seat of empire had been transferred to Constantinople, and fearing for his see, enacted a contrary law, in which he denies the necessity of changing metropolitan churches as imperial metropolitan cities were changed. But the authority of a synod is justly to be preferred to the opinion of one individual, and Innocent himself should be suspected in his own cause. However this is, he by his caveat shows the original rule to have been, that Metropolitans should be distributed according to the order of the empire.

15 Hence, the great struggle for precedence between the Sees of Rome and Constantinople. The pride and ambition of the Roman Bishops unfolded.

Agreeably to this ancient custom, the first Council of Constantinople decreed that the bishop of that city should take precedence after the Roman Pontiff, because it was a new Rome. But long after, when a similar decree was made at Chalcedon, Leo keenly protested. And not only did he permit himself to set at nothing what six hundred bishops or more had decreed, but he even assailed them with bitter reproaches, because they had derogated from other sees in the honor which they had presumed to confer on the Church of Constantinople. What, pray, could have incited the man to trouble the world for so small an affair but mere ambition? He says, that what the Council of Nice had once sanctioned ought to have been inviolable; as if the

Christian faith was in any danger if one church was preferred to another; or as if separate Patriarchates had been established on any other grounds than that of policy. But we know that policy varies with times, nay, demands various changes. It is therefore futile in Leo to pretend that the See of Constantinople ought not to receive the honor, which was given to that of Alexandria, by the authority of the Council of Nice. For it is the dictate of common sense, that the decree was one of those which might be abrogated, in respect of a change of times. What shall we say to the fact, that none of the Eastern churches, though chiefly interested, objected? Proterius, who had been appointed at Alexandria instead of Dioscorus, was certainly present; other patriarchs whose honor was impaired were present. It belonged to them to interfere, not to Leo, whose station remained entire. While all of them are silent, many assent, and the Roman Bishop alone resists, it is easy to judge what it is that moves him, just because he foresaw what happened not long after, that when the glory of ancient Rome declined, Constantinople, not contented with the second place, would dispute the primacy with her. And yet, his clamor was not so successful as to prevent the decree of the council from being ratified. Accordingly, his successors seeing themselves defeated, quietly desisted from that petulance, and allowed the Bishop of Constantinople to be regarded as the second Patriarch.

16 Many attempts of the Bishop of Constantinople to deprive the Bishop of Rome of the primacy.

But shortly after, John, who, in the time of Gregory, presided over the church of Constantinople, went so far as to say that he was universal Patriarch. Here Gregory, that he might not be wanting to his See in a most excellent cause, constantly opposed. And certainly, it was impossible to tolerate the pride and madness of John, who wished to make the limits of his bishopric equal to the limits of the empire. This, which Gregory denies to another, he claims not for himself, but abominates the title by whomsoever used, as wicked, impious, and nefarious. Nay, he is offended with Eulogius, Bishop of Alexandria, who had honored him with this title. He says, "See in the address of the letter which you have directed to me, though I prohibited you, you have taken care to write a word of proud signification by calling me Universal Pope. What I ask is, that your holiness do not go further, because, whatever is given to another more than reason demands is withdrawn from you. I do not regard that as honor by which I see that the honor of my brethren is diminished. For my honor is the universal honor of the church, and entire prerogative of my brethren. If your holiness calls me universal Pope, it denies itself to be this whole which it acknowledges me to be." The cause of Gregory was indeed good and honorable; but John, aided by the favor of the Emperor Maurice, could not be dissuaded from his purpose. Cyriac also, his successor, never allowed himself to be spoken to on the subject.

17 Phocas murders the Emperor, and gives Rome the primacy.

At length Phocas, who had slain Maurice, and usurped his place (more friendly to the Romans, for what reason I know not, or rather because he had been crowned king there without opposition), conceded to Boniface III that which Gregory by no means demanded–viz. that Rome should be the head of all the churches. In this way, the controversy was ended. And yet this kindness of the Emperor to the Romans would not have been of very much avail had not other circumstances occurred. For shortly after Greece and all Asia were cut off from his communion, while all the reverence, which he received from France, was obedience only in so far as she pleased. She was brought into subjection for the first time when Pepin got possession of the throne. For Zachary, the Roman Pontiff, having aided him in his perfidy and robbery when he expelled the lawful sovereign, and seized upon the kingdom, which lay exposed as a kind of prey, was rewarded by having the jurisdiction of the Roman See established over the churches of France. In the same way as robbers are wont to divide and share the common spoil, those two worthies arranged that Pepin should have the worldly and civil power by spoiling the true prince, while Zachary should become the head of all the bishops, and have the spiritual power. This, though weak at the first (as usually happens with new power), was afterwards confirmed by the authority of Charlemagne for a very similar cause. For he too was under obligation to the Roman Pontiff, to whose zeal he was indebted for the honor of empire. Though there is reason to believe that the churches had previously been greatly altered, it is certain that the ancient form of the church was then only completely effaced in Gaul and Germany. There are still extant among the archives of the Parliament of Paris short commentaries on those times, which, in treating of ecclesiastical affairs, make mention of the compacts both of Pepin and Charlemagne with the Roman Pontiff. Hence, we may infer that the ancient state of matters was then changed.

18 The Papal tyranny shortly after established. Bitter complaints by Bernard.

From that time, while everywhere matters were becoming daily worse, the tyranny of the Roman Bishop was established, and always increased, and this partly by the ignorance, partly by the sluggishness, of the bishops. For while he was arrogating everything to himself, and proceeding more and more to exalt himself without measure, contrary to law and right, the bishops did not exert themselves so zealously as they ought in curbing his pretensions. And though they had not been deficient in spirit, they were devoid of true doctrine and experience, so that they were by no means fit for so important an effort. Accordingly, we see how great and monstrous were the profanation of all sacred things, and the dissipation of the whole ecclesiastical order at Rome, in the age of Bernard. He complains that the ambitious, avaricious, demoniacal, sacrilegious, fornicators, incestuous, and similar miscreants, flocked from all quarters of the world to Rome, that by apostolic authority they might acquire or retain ecclesiastical honors: that fraud, circumvention, and violence, prevailed. The mode of judging causes then in use he describes as execrable, as disgraceful, not only to the church, but the bar. He exclaims that the church is filled with the ambitious: that not one is more afraid to perpetrate crimes than robbers in their den when they share the spoils of the traveler. "Few (say he) look to the mouth of the legislator, but all to his hands. Not without cause, however: for their hands do the whole business of the Pope. What kind of thing is it when those are bought by the spoils of the church, who say to you, Well done, well done? The life of the poor is sown in the highways of the rich: silver glitters in the mire: they run together from all sides: it is not the poorer that takes it up, but the stronger, or, perhaps, he who runs fastest. That custom, however, or rather that death, comes not of you: I wish it would end in you. While these things are going on, you, a pastor, come forth robed in much costly clothing. If I might presume to say it, this is more the pasture of demons than of sheep. Peter, forsooth, acted thus; Paul sported thus. Your court has been more accustomed to receive good men than to make them. The bad do not gain much there, but the good degenerate." Then when he describes the abuses of appeals, no pious man can read them without being horrified. At length, speaking of the unbridled cupidity of the Roman See in usurping jurisdiction, he thus concludes, "I express the murmur and common complaint of the churches. Their cry is that they are maimed and dismembered. There are none, or very few, who do not lament or fear that plague. Do you ask what plague? Abbots are encroached upon by bishops, bishops by archbishops, etc. It is strange if this can be excused. By thus acting, you prove that you have the fullness of power, but not the fullness of righteousness. You do this because you are able; but whether you also ought to do it is the question. You are appointed to preserve, not to envy, the honor and rank of each." I have thought it proper to quote these few passages out of many, partly that my readers may see how grievously the church had then fallen, partly, too, that they may see with what grief and lamentation all pious men beheld this calamity.

19 Fourth part of the chapter. Altered appearance of the Roman See since the days of Gregory.

But though we were to concede to the Roman Pontiff of the present day the eminence and extent of jurisdiction, which his see had in the middle ages, as in the time of Leo and Gregory, what would this be to the existing Papacy? I am not now speaking of worldly dominion, or of civil power, which will afterwards be explained in their own place (see Chapter 11, section 8-14); but what resemblance is there between the spiritual government of which they boast and the state of those times? The only definition, which they give of the Pope, is that he is the supreme head of the church on Earth, and the universal bishop of the whole globe. The Pontiffs themselves, when they speak of their authority, declare with great superciliousness, that the power of commanding belongs to them–that the necessity of obedience remains with others–that all their decrees are to be regarded as confirmed by the divine voice of Peter–that provincial synods, from not having the presence of the Pope, are deficient in authority, –that they can ordain the clergy of any church, –and can summon to their See any who have been ordained elsewhere. Innumerable things of this kind are contained in the farrago of Gratian, which I do not mention, that I may not be tedious to my readers. The whole comes to this, that to the Roman Pontiff belongs the supreme cognizance of all ecclesiastical causes, whether in determining and defining doctrines, or in enacting laws, or in appointing discipline, or in giving sentences. It would be also tedious and superfluous to review the privileges, which they assume to themselves in what they call reservations. But the most intolerable of all things is their leaving no judicial authority in the world to restrain and curb them when they licentiously abuse their immense power. "No man (say they) is entitled to alter the judgment of this See, on account of the primacy of the Roman Church." Again, "The judge shall not be judged either by the emperor, or by kings, or by the clergy, or by the people." It is surely imperious enough for one man to appoint himself the judge of all, while he will not submit to the judgment of any. But what if he tyrannizes the people of God? If he dissipates and lays waste the Kingdom of Christ? If he troubles the whole church? If he converts the pastoral office into robbery? Nay, though he should be the most abandoned of all, he insists that none can call him to account. The language of Pontiffs is, "God has been pleased to terminate the causes of other men by men, but the Prelate of this See he has reserved unquestioned for his own judgment." Again, "The deeds of subjects are judged by us; ours by God only."

20 The present demands of the Romanists not formerly conceded. Fictions of Gregory IX. and Martin.

And in order that edicts of this kind might have more weight, they falsely substituted the names of ancient Pontiffs, as if matters had been so constituted from the beginning. Yet, it is absolutely certain that whatever attributes more to the Pontiff than we have stated to have been given to him by ancient councils, is new and of recent fabrication. Nay, they have carried their effrontery so far as to publish a rescript under the name of Anastasius, the Patriarch of Constantinople, in which he testifies that it was appointed by ancient regulations, that nothing should be done in the remotest provinces without being previously referred to the Roman See. Besides its extreme folly, who can believe it credible that such an eulogium on the Roman See proceeded from an opponent and rival of its honor and dignity? But doubtless it was necessary that those Antichrists should proceed to such a degree of madness and blindness, that their iniquity might be manifest to all men of sound mind who will only open their eyes. The decretal epistles collected by Gregory IX, also the Clementines and Extravagants of Martin, breathe still more plainly, and in more bombastic terms bespeak this boundless ferocity and tyranny of barbarian kings. But these are the oracles out of which the Romanists would have their Papacy judged. Hence, have sprung those famous axioms which have the force of oracles throughout the Papacy in the present day–viz. that the Pope cannot err; that the Pope is superior to councils; that the Pope is the universal bishop of all churches, and the chief Head of the church on Earth. I say nothing of the still greater absurdities, which are babbled by the foolish canonists in their schools, absurdities, however, which Roman theologians not only assent to, but even applaud in flattery of their idol.

21 Without mentioning the opposition of Cyprian, of councils, and historical facts, the claims now made were condemned by Gregory himself.

I will not treat with them on the strictest terms. In opposition to their great insolence, some would quote the language, which Cyprian used, to the bishops in the council over which he presided: "None of us styles himself bishop of bishops, or forces his colleagues to the necessity of obeying by the tyranny of terror." Some might object what was long after decreed at Carthage, "Let no one be called the prince of priests or first bishop;" and might gather many proofs from history, and canons from councils, and many passages from ancient writers, which bring the Roman Pontiff into due order. But these I omit, that I may not seem to press too hard upon them. However, let these worthy defenders of the Roman See tell me with what face they can defend the title of universal bishop, while they see it so often anathematized by Gregory. If effect is to be given to his testimony, then they, by making their Pontiff universal, declare him Antichrist. The name of head was not more approved. For Gregory thus speaks: "Peter was the chief member in the body, John, Andrew, and James, the heads of particular communities. All, however, are under one head members of the church: nay, the saints before the law, the saints under the law, the saints under grace, all perfecting the Body of the Lord, are constituted members: none of them ever wished to be styled universal." When the Pontiff arrogates to himself the power of ordering, he little accords with what Gregory elsewhere says. For

Eulogius, Bishop of Alexandria, having said that he had received an order from him, he replies in this manner: "This word order I beg you to take out of my hearing, for I know who I am, and who you are: in station you are my brethren, in character my fathers. I therefore did not order, but took care to suggest what seemed useful." When the Pope extends his jurisdiction without limit, he does great and atrocious injustice not only to other bishops, but to each single church, tearing and dismembering them, that he may build his see upon their ruins. When he exempts himself from all tribunals, and wishes to reign in the manner of a tyrant, holding his own caprice to be his only law, the thing is too insulting, and too foreign to ecclesiastical rule, to be on any account submitted to. It is altogether abhorrent, not only from pious feeling, but also from common sense.

22 The abuses of which Gregory and Bernard complained now increased and sanctioned.

So that I will not be forced to discuss and follow out each point individually, I again appeal to those who, in the present day, would be thought the best and most faithful defenders of the Roman See, if they are not ashamed to defend the existing state of the Papacy, which is clearly a hundred times more corrupt than in the days of Gregory and Bernard, though even then these holy men were so much displeased with it. Gregory everywhere complains that he was distracted above measure by foreign occupations. He say that under color of the episcopate, he was taken back to the world and subject to more worldly cares than he remembered to have ever had when a laic. He complains that he was so oppressed by the trouble of secular affairs that he was unable to raise his mind to things above; and so tossed by the many billows of causes and afflicted by the tempests of a tumultuous life, that he might well say, "I am come into the depths of the sea." It is certain, that amid these worldly occupations, he could teach the people in sermons, admonish in private, and correct those who required it; order the Church, give counsel to his colleagues, and exhort them to their duty. Moreover, some time was left for writing, and yet he deplores it as his calamity, that he was plunged into the very deepest sea. If the administration at that time was a sea, what shall we say of the present Papacy? For what resemblance is there between the periods? Now there are no sermons, no care for discipline, no zeal for churches, no spiritual function.

In short, there is nothing but the world. And yet, this labyrinth is lauded as if nothing could be found better ordered and arranged. What complaints also does Bernard pour forth, what groans does he utter, when he beholds the vices of his own age? What then would he have done on beholding this iron, or, if possible, worse than iron, age of ours? How dishonest, therefore, not only obstinately to defend as sacred and divine what all the saints have always with one mouth disapproved, but to abuse their testimony in favor of the Papacy, which, it is evident, was altogether unknown to them? Although I admit, in respect to the time of Bernard, that all things were so corrupt as to make it not unlike our own. But it betrays a want of all sense of shame to seek any excuse from that middle period–namely, from that of Leo, Gregory, and the like. It is just like vindicating the monarchy of the Caesars by lauding the ancient state of the Roman Empire–in other words, if one were to borrow the praises of liberty in order to eulogize tyranny.

23 The fifth and last part of the chapter, containing the chief answer to the claims of the Papacy—viz. that the Pope is not a bishop in the house of God. This answer confirmed by an enumeration of the essential parts of the episcopal office.

Lastly, although all these things were granted, an entirely new question arises, when we deny that there is at Rome a church in which privileges of this nature can reside; when we deny that there is a bishop to sustain the dignity of these privileges. Assume, therefore, that all these things are true (though we have already extorted the contrary from them). Assume that Peter, by the Words of Christ, was constituted head of the universal Church, and that the honor thus conferred upon him he deposited in the Roman See. Assume that this was sanctioned by the authority of the ancient Church, and confirmed by long use; that supreme power was always unanimously devolved by all on the Roman Pontiff; and that while he was the judge of all causes and all men, he was subject to the judgment of none. Let even more be conceded to them if they will, I answer, in one word, that none of these things avail if there be not a church and a bishop at Rome. They must concede to me that she is not a mother of churches who is not herself a church, that he cannot be the chief of bishops who is not himself a bishop. Would they then have the Apostolic See at Rome? Let them give me a true and lawful apostleship. Would they have a supreme pontiff, let them give me a bishop. But how? Where will they show me any semblance of a church? They, no doubt, talk of one, and have it ever in their mouths. But surely, the church is recognized by certain marks, and bishopric is the name of an office. I am not now speaking of the people but of the government, which ought perpetually to be conspicuous in the church. Where, then, is a ministry such as the institution of Christ requires? Let us remember what was formerly said of the duty of presbyters and bishops. If we bring the office of cardinals to that test, we will acknowledge that they are nothing less than presbyters. But I should like to know what one quality of a bishop the Pope himself has?

The first point in the office of a bishop is to instruct the people in the Word of God; the second and next to it is to administer the sacraments; the third is to admonish and exhort, to correct those who are in fault, and restrain the people by holy discipline. Which of these things does he do? Nay, which of these things does he pretend to do? Let them say, then, on what ground they will have him to be regarded as a bishop, who does not even in semblance touch any part of the duty with his little finger.

24 A second confirmation by appeal to the institution of Christ. A third confirmation *e contrario*—viz. that in doctrine and morals the Roman Pontiff is altogether different from a true bishop. Conclusion, that Rome is not the Apostolic See, but the Papacy.

It is not with a bishop as with a king; the latter, though he does not execute the proper duty of a king, nevertheless retains the title and the honor; but in deciding on a bishop, respect is had to the command of Christ, to which effect ought always to be given in the Church. Let the Romanists then untie this knot. I deny that their pontiff is the prince of bishops, seeing he is no bishop. This allegation of mine they must prove to be false if they would succeed in theirs. What then do I maintain? That he has nothing proper to a bishop, but is in all things the opposite of a bishop. But with what shall I here begin? With doctrine or with morals? What shall I say, what shall I pass in silence, or where shall I end? This I maintain: while in the present day the world is so inundated with perverse and impious doctrines, so full of all kinds of superstition, so blinded by error and sunk in idolatry, there is not one of them which has not emanated from the Papacy, or at least been confirmed by it. Nor is there any other reason that the pontiffs are so enraged against the reviving doctrine of the gospel, why they stretch every nerve to oppress it, and urge all kings and princes to cruelty, than just that they see their whole dominion tottering and falling to pieces the moment the Gospel of Christ prevails. Leo was cruel and Clement sanguinary, Paul is truculent. But in assailing the truth, it is not so much natural temper that impels them as the conviction that they have no other method of maintaining their power. Therefore, seeing they cannot be safe unless they put Christ to flight, they labor in this cause as if they were fighting for their altars and hearths, for their own lives and those of their adherents. What then? Shall we recognize the Apostolic See where we see nothing but horrible apostasy? Shall he be the vicar of Christ who, by his furious efforts in persecuting the gospel, plainly declares himself Antichrist? Shall he be the successor of Peter who goes about with fire and sword demolishing everything that Peter built? Shall he be the Head of the Church who, after dissevering the Church from Christ, her only true Head, tears and lacerates her members? Rome, indeed, was once the mother of all the churches, but since she began to be the seat of Antichrist, she ceased to be what she was.

25 Proof from Daniel and Paul that the Pope is Antichrist.

To some we seem slanderous and petulant, when we call the Roman Pontiff Antichrist. But those who think so perceive not that they are bringing a charge of intemperance against Paul, after whom we speak, nay, in whose very words we speak. But lest anyone object that Paul's words have a different meaning, and are wrested by us against the Roman Pontiff, I will briefly show that they can only be understood of the Papacy. Paul says that Antichrist would sit in the temple of God. (See 2 Thessalonians 2:4.) In another passage, the Spirit, portraying him in the person of Antiochus, says that his reign would be with great swelling words of vanity. (See Daniel 7:25.) Hence, we infer that his tyranny is more over souls than bodies, a tyranny set up in opposition to the spiritual Kingdom of Christ. Then his nature is such, that he abolishes not the name either of Christ or the Church, but rather uses the name of Christ as a pretext, and lurks under the name of Church as under a mask. But though all the heresies and schisms that have existed from the beginning belong to the kingdom of Antichrist, yet when Paul foretells that defection will come, he by the description intimates that that seat of abomination will be erected, when a kind of universal defection comes upon the Church, though many members of the Church scattered up and down should continue in the true unity of the faith. But when he adds, that in his own time, the mystery of iniquity, which was afterwards to be openly manifested, had begun to work in secret, we thereby understand that this calamity was neither to be introduced by one man, nor to terminate in one man. (See 2 Thessalonians 2:3; Daniel 7:9.) Moreover, when the mark by which he distinguishes Antichrist is, that he would rob God of His honor and take it to himself, he gives the leading feature which we ought to follow in searching out Antichrist; especially when pride of this description proceeds to the open devastation of the Church. Seeing then it is certain that the Roman Pontiff has impudently transferred to himself the most peculiar properties of God and Christ, there cannot be a doubt that he is the leader and standard-bearer of an impious and abominable kingdom.

26 Rome could not now claim the primacy, even though she had formerly been the first See, especially considering the base trafficking in which she has engaged.

Let the Romanists now go and oppose us with antiquity, as if, amid such a complete change in every respect, the honor of the See can continue where there is no See. Eusebius says that God, to make way for His vengeance, transferred the church, which was at Jerusalem to Pella. What we are told was once done may have been done repeatedly. Hence, it is too absurd and ridiculous to fix the honor of the primacy to a particular spot, so that he who is in fact the most inveterate enemy of Christ, the chief adversary of the gospel, the greatest devastator and waster of the church, and he most cruel slayer and murderer of the saints should be regarded as the vicegerent of Christ, the successor of Peter, and the first priest of the church, merely because he occupies what was formerly the first of all sees. I do not say how great the difference is between the chancery of the Pope and well-regulated order in the church; although this one fact might well set the question at rest. For no man of sound mind will include the episcopate in lead and bulls, much less in that administration of captions and circumscriptions, in which the spiritual government of the Pope is supposed to consist. It has therefore been elegantly said, that that vaunted Roman Church was long ago converted into a temporal court, the only thing that is now seen at Rome. I am not here speaking of the vices of individuals, but demonstrating that the Papacy itself is diametrically opposed to the ecclesiastical system.

27 Personal character of Popes. Irreligious opinions held by some of them.

But if we come to individuals, it is well known what kind of vicars of Christ we shall find. No doubt, Julius and Leo, and Clement and Paul, will be pillars of the Christian faith, the first interpreters of religion, though they knew nothing more of Christ than they had learned in the school of Lucian. But why give the names of three or four pontiffs? As if there were any doubt as to the kind of religion professed by pontiffs, with their College of Cardinals, and professors in the present day. The first head of the secret theology, which is in vogue among them, is that there is no God. Another: that whatever things have been written and are taught concerning Christ are lies and imposture. A third, that the doctrine of a future life and final resurrection is a mere fable. Not all think, few speak thus; I confess it. Yet, it is long since this began to be the ordinary religion of pontiffs. And though the thing is notorious to all who know Rome, Roman theologians continue to boast that by special privilege, our Savior has provided that the Pope cannot err, because it was said to Peter, "I have prayed for thee that thy faith fail not"(Luke 22:32). What, pray, do they gain by their effrontery, but to let the whole world understand that they have reached the extreme of wickedness, so as neither to fear God nor regard man?

28 John XXII. heretical in regard to the immortality of the soul. His name, therefore, ought to be expunged from the catalogue of Popes, or rather, there is no foundation for the claim of perpetuity of faith in the Roman See.

But let us suppose that the iniquity of these pontiffs whom I have mentioned is not known, as they have not published it either in sermons or writings, but betrayed it only at table or in their chamber, or at least within the walls of their court. But if they would have the privilege, which they claim to be confirmed, they must expunge from their list of pontiffs John XXII, who publicly maintained that the soul is mortal, and perishes with the body until the day of resurrection. And to show you that the whole See with its chief props then utterly fell, none of the Cardinals opposed his madness, only the Faculty of Paris urged the king to insist on a recantation. The king interdicted his subjects from communion with him, unless he would immediately recant, and published his interdict in the usual way by a herald. Thus necessitated, he abjured his error. This example relieves me from the necessity of disputing further with my opponents, when they say that the Roman See and its pontiffs cannot err in the faith, from its being said to Peter, "I have prayed for thee that thy faith fail not." Certainly by this shameful lapse he fell from the faith, and became a noted proof to posterity, that all are not Peters who succeed Peter in the episcopate; although the thing is too childish in itself to need an answer: for if they insist on applying everything that was said to Peter to the successors of Peter, it will follow, that they are all Satans, because our Lord once said to Peter, "Get thee behind me, Satan, thou art an offense unto me." It is as easy for us to retort the latter saying as for them to adduce the former.

29 Some Roman Pontiffs atheists, or sworn enemies of religion. Their immoral lives. Practice of the Cardinals and Romish clergy.

But I have no pleasure in this absurd mode of disputation, and therefore return to the point from which I digressed. To affix Christ and the Holy Spirit and the Church to a particular spot, so that everyone who presides in it, should he be a devil, must still be deemed vicegerent of Christ, and the head of the Church, because that spot was formerly the See of Peter, and is not only impious and insulting to Christ, but absurd and contrary to common sense. For a long period, the Roman Pontiffs have either been altogether devoid of religion, or been its greatest enemies. The See, which they occupy, therefore, no more makes them the vicars of Christ, than it makes an idol to become God when it is placed in the temple of God. (See 2 Thessalonians 2:4.) Then, if manners be inquired into, let the Popes answer for themselves, what there is in them that can make them be recognized for bishops. First, the mode of life at Rome, while they not only connive and are silent, but also tacitly approve, is altogether unworthy of bishops, whose duty it is to curb the license of the people by the strictness of discipline. But I will not be so rigid with them as to charge them with the faults of others. But when they with their household, with almost the whole College of Cardinals, and the whole body of their clergy, are so devoted to wickedness, obscenity, uncleanness, iniquity, and crime of every description, that they resemble monsters more than men, they herein betray that they are nothing less than bishops. They need not fear that I will make a further disclosure of their turpitude. For it is painful to wade through such filthy mire, and I must spare modest ears. But I think I have amply demonstrated what I proposed–viz. that though Rome was formerly the first of churches, she deserves not in the present day to be regarded as one of her minutest members.

30 Cardinals were formerly merely presbyters of the Roman Church, and far inferior to bishops. As they now are, they have no true and legitimate office in the Church. Conclusion.

In regard to those whom they call Cardinals, I know not how it happened that they rose so suddenly to such a height. In the age of Gregory, the name was applied to bishops only. For whenever he makes mention of cardinals, he assigns them not only to the Roman Church, but to every other church, so that, in short, a Cardinal priest is nothing else than a bishop. I do not find the name among the writers of a former age. I see, however, that they were inferior to bishops, whom they now far surpass. There is a well-known passage in Augustine: "Although, in regard to terms of honor which custom has fixed in the church, the office of bishop is greater than that of presbyter, yet in many things, Augustine is inferior to Jerome." Here, certainly, he is not distinguishing a presbyter of the Roman Church from other presbyters, but placing all of them alike after bishops. And so strictly was this observed, that at the Council of Carthage, when two legates of the Roman See were present, one a bishop, and the other a presbyter, the latter was put in the lowest place. But not to dwell too much on ancient times, we have account of a Council held at Rome, under Gregory, at which the presbyters sit in the lowest place, and subscribe by themselves, while deacons do not subscribe at all. And, indeed, they had no office at that time, unless to be present under the bishop, and assist him in the administration of word and sacraments. So much is their lot now changed, that they have become associates of kings and Caesars. And there can be no doubt that they have grown gradually with their head, until they reached their present pinnacle of dignity. This much it seemed proper to say in passing, that my readers may understand how very widely the Roman See, as it now exists, differs from the ancient See, under which it endeavors to cloak and defend itself.

But whatever they were formerly, as they have no true and legitimate office in the Church, they only retain a color and empty mask; nay, as they are in all respects the opposite of true ministers, the thing, which Gregory so often writes, must have befallen them. His words are, "Weeping, I say, groaning, I declare it; when the sacerdotal order has fallen within, it cannot long stand without." Nay, rather what Malachi says of such persons must be fulfilled in them: "Ye are departed out of the way; ye have caused many to stumble at the law; ye have corrupted the covenant of Levi, saith the Lord of hosts. Therefore have I also made you contemptible and base before all the people" (Malachi 2:8, 9). I now leave all the pious to judge what the supreme pinnacle of the Roman hierarchy must be, to which the Papists, with nefarious effrontery, hesitate not to subject the Word of God itself, that word which should be venerable and holy in Earth and Heaven, to men and angels.

Chapter 8

OF THE POWER OF THE CHURCH IN ARTICLES OF FAITH. THE UNBRIDLED LICENSE OF THE PAPAL CHURCH IN DESTROYING PURITY OF DOCTRINE.

This chapter is divided into two parts,—I. The limits within which the Church ought to confine herself in matters of this kind, sections 1-9. II. The Roman Church convicted of having transgressed these limits, sections 10-16.

Sections

1. The marks and government of the Church having been considered in the seven previous chapters, the power of the Church is now considered under three heads—viz. Doctrine, Legislation, and Jurisdiction.

2. The authority and power given to Church officers not given to themselves, but their office. This shown in the case of Moses and the Levitical priesthood.

3. The same thing shown in the case of the Prophets.

4. Same thing shown in the case of the Apostles, and of Christ himself.

5. The Church astricted to the written Word of God. Christ the only teacher of the Church. From His lips, ministers must derive whatever they teach for the salvation of others. Various modes of divine teaching. Personal revelations.

6. Second mode of teaching—viz. by the Law and the Prophets. The Prophets were in regard to doctrine, the expounders of the Law. To these were added Historical Narratives and the Psalms.

7. Last mode of teaching by our Savior himself manifested in the flesh. Different names given to this dispensation, to show that we are not to dream of anything more perfect than the written Word.

8. Nothing can be lawfully taught in the Church that is not contained in the writings of the Prophets and Apostles, as dictated by the Spirit of Christ.

9. Neither the Apostles, nor apostolic men, nor the whole Church, allowed to overstep these limits. This confirmed by passages of Peter and Paul. Argument a fortiori.

10. The Roman tyrants have taught a different doctrine—viz. that Councils cannot err, and, therefore, may coin new dogmas.

11. Answer to the Papistical arguments for the authority of the Church. Argument, that the Church is to be led into all truth. Answer. This promise made not only to the whole Church, but to every individual believer.

12. Answers continued.

13. Answers continued.

14. Argument, that the Church should supply the deficiency of the written word by traditions. Answer.

15. Argument founded on Matthew 18:17. Answer.

16. Objections founded on Infant Baptism, and the Canon of the Council of Nice, as to the consubstantiality of the Son. Answer.

1 The marks and government of the Church having been considered in the seven previous chapters, the power of the Church is now considered under three heads—viz. Doctrine, Legislation, and Jurisdiction.

We come now to the third division–viz. the Power of the Church, as existing either in individual bishops, or in councils, whether provincial or general. I speak only of the spiritual power which is proper to the Church, and which consists either in doctrine, or jurisdiction, or in enacting laws. In regard to doctrine, there are two divisions–viz. the authority of delivering dogmas, and the interpretation of them. Before we begin to treat of each in particular, I wish to remind the pious reader, that whatever is taught respecting the power of the Church, ought to have reference to the end for which Paul declares (see 2 Corinthians 10:8; 13:10) that it was given–namely, for edification, and not for destruction, those who use it lawfully deeming themselves to be nothing more than servants of Christ, and, at the same time, servants of the people in Christ. Moreover, the only mode by which ministers can edify the Church is, by studying to maintain the authority of Christ, which cannot be unimpaired, unless that which He received of the Father is left to Him–viz. to be the only Master of the Church. For it was not said of any other but of himself alone, "Hear him" (Matthew 17:5). Ecclesiastical power, therefore, is not to be mischievously adorned, but it is to be confined within certain limits, so as not to be drawn hither and thither at the caprice of men. For this purpose, it will be of great use to observe how it is described by prophets and apostles. For if we concede unreservedly to men all the power which they think proper to assume, it is easy to see how soon it will degenerate into a tyranny which is altogether alien from the Church of Christ.

2 The authority and power given to Church officers not given to themselves, but their office. This shown in the case of Moses and the Levitical priesthood.

Therefore, it is here necessary to remember, that whatever authority and dignity the Holy Spirit in Scripture confers on priests, or prophets, or apostles, or successors of apostles, is wholly given not to men themselves, but to the ministry to which they are appointed; or, to speak more plainly, to the Word, to the ministry of which they are appointed. For were we to go over the whole in order, we should find that, they were not invested with authority to teach or give responses, save in the name and Word of the Lord. For whenever they are called to office, they are enjoined not to bring anything of their own, but to speak by the mouth of the Lord. Nor does He bring them forward to be heard by the people, before He has instructed them what they are to speak, lest they should speak anything but His own Word. Moses, the prince of all the prophets, was to be heard in preference to others (Exodus 3:4; Deuteronomy 17:9); but he is previously furnished with his orders, that he may not be able to speak at all except from the Lord. Accordingly, when the people embraced his doctrine, they are said to have believed the Lord, and His servant Moses. (See Exodus 14:31.) It was also provided under the severest sanctions, that the authority of the priests should not be despised. (See Exodus 17:9.) But the Lord, at the same time, shows in what terms they were to be heard, when He says that He made His covenant with Levi, that the law of truth might be in his mouth. (See Malachi 2:4-6.) A little after he adds, "The priest's lips should keep knowledge, and they should seek the law at his mouth; for he is the messenger of the Lord of hosts." Therefore, if the priest would be heard, let him show himself to be the messenger of God; that is, let him faithfully deliver the commands, which he has received from his Maker. When the mode of hearing, then, is treated of, it is expressly said, "According to the sentence of the law which they shall teach thee" (Deuteronomy 17:11).

3 The same thing shown in the case of the Prophets.

The nature of the power conferred upon the prophets in general is elegantly described by Ezekiel: "Son of man, I have made thee a watchman unto the house of Israel: therefore hear the word at my mouth, and give them warning from me" (Ezekiel 3:17). Is not he who is ordered to hear at the mouth of the Lord prohibited from devising anything of himself? And what is meant by giving a warning from the Lord, but just to speak so as to be able confidently to declare that the word which he delivers is not his own but the Lord's? The same thing is expressed by Jeremiah in different terms, "The prophet that hath a dream, let him tell a dream; and he that hath my word, let him speak my word faithfully" (Jeremiah 23:28). Surely, God here declares the law to all, and it is a law, which does not allow anyone to teach more than he has been ordered. He afterwards gives the name of chaff to whatever has not proceeded from himself alone. Accordingly, none of the prophets opened his mouth unless preceded by the Word of the Lord. Hence, we so often meet with the expressions, "The word of the Lord, The burden of the Lord, Thus saith the Lord, The mouth of the Lord hath spoken it." And justly, for Isaiah exclaims that his lips are unclean (see Isaiah 6:5); and Jeremiah confesses that he knows not how to speak because he is a child (Jeremiah 1:6). Could anything proceed from the unclean lips of the one, and the childish lips of the other, if they spoke their own language, but what was unclean or childish? But their lips were holy and pure when they began to be organs of the Holy Spirit. The prophets, after being thus strictly bound not to deliver anything but what they received, are invested with great power and illustrious titles. For when the Lord declares, "See, I have this day set thee over the nations, and over the kingdoms, to root out, and to pull down, and to destroy, and to throw down, to build, and to plant," He at the same time gives the reason, "Behold, I have put my words in thy mouth" (Jeremiah 1:9,10).

4 Same thing shown in the case of the apostles, and of Christ himself.

Now, if you look to the apostles, they are commended by many distinguished titles, as the light of the world, and the salt of the Earth, to be heard in Christ's stead, whatever they bound or loosed on Earth being bound or loosed in Heaven. (See Matthew 5:13, 14; Luke 10:16; John 20:23.) But they declare in their own name what the authority was which their office conferred on them–viz. if they are apostles they must not speak their own pleasure, but faithfully deliver the commands of Him by whom they are sent. The words in which Christ defined their embassy are sufficiently clear, "Go ye, therefore, and teach all nations, teaching them to observe all things whatsoever I have commanded you" (Matthew 28:19, 20). Nay, that none might be permitted to decline this law, He received it and imposed it on himself. "My doctrine is not mine, but his that sent me" (John 7:16). He who always was the only and eternal counselor of the Father, who by the Father was constituted Lord and Master of all, yet because He performed the ministry of teaching, prescribed to all ministers by His example the rule which they ought to follow in teaching. The power of the Church, therefore, is not infinite, but is subject to the Word of the Lord, and included in it.

5 The Church astricted to the written Word of God. Christ the only teacher of the Church. From His lips, ministers must derive whatever they teach for the salvation of others. Various modes of divine teaching. Personal revelations.

But though the rule which always existed in the Church from the beginning, and ought to exist in the present day, is, that the servants of God are only to teach what they have learned from himself, yet, according to the variety of times, they have had different methods of learning. The mode, which now exists, differs very much from that of former times. First, if it is true, as Christ says, "Neither knoweth any man the Father save the Son, and he to whomsoever the Son will reveal him" (Matthew 11:27), then those who wish to attain to the knowledge of God behooved always to be directed by that eternal wisdom. For how could they have comprehended the mysteries of God in their minds, or declared them to others, unless by the teaching of Him, to whom alone the secrets of the Father are known? The only way, therefore, by which in ancient times holy men knew God, was by beholding Him in the Son as in a mirror. When I say this, I mean that God never manifested himself to men by any other means than by His Son, that is, His own only wisdom, light, and truth. From this fountain Adam, Noah, Abraham, Isaac, Jacob, and others, drew all the heavenly doctrine that they possessed. From the same fountain, all the prophets also drew all the heavenly oracles, which they published. For this wisdom did not always display itself in one manner. With the patriarchs, He employed secret revelations, but, at the same time, in order to confirm these, had recourse to signs to make it impossible for them to doubt that God spoke to them. What the patriarchs received they handed down to posterity, for God had, in depositing it with them, bound them thus to propagate it, while their children and descendants knew by the inward teaching of God, that what they heard was of Heaven and not of Earth.

6 Second mode of teaching—viz. by the Law and the Prophets. The prophets were in regard to doctrine, the expounders of the law. To these were added historical narratives and the Psalms.

But when God determined to give a more illustrious form to the Church, He was pleased to commit and consign His word to writing, that the priests might there seek what they were to teach the people, and every doctrine delivered be brought to it as a test. (See Malachi 2:7.) Accordingly, after the promulgation of the Law, when the priests are enjoined to teach from the mouth of the Lord, the meaning is, that they are not to teach anything extraneous or alien to that kind of doctrine which God had summed up in the Law, while it was unlawful for them to add to it or take from it. Next followed the prophets, by whom God published the new oracles, which were added to the Law, not so new, however, but that they flowed from the Law, and had respect to it. For in so far as regards doctrine, they were only interpreters of the Law, adding nothing to it but predictions of future events. With this exception, all that they delivered was pure exposition of the Law. But as the Lord was pleased that doctrine should exist in a clearer and more ample form, the better to satisfy weak consciences, He commanded the prophecies also to be committed to writing, and to be held part of His Word. To these at the same time were added historical details, which are also the composition of prophets, but dictated by the Holy Spirit; I include the Psalms among the prophecies, the quality that we attribute to the latter belonging also to the former. The whole body, therefore, composed of the Law, the Prophets, the Psalms, and Histories, formed the Word of the Lord to His ancient people. By it as a standard, priests and teachers, before the advent of Christ, were bound to test their doctrine. It was unlawful for them to turn aside either to the right hand or the left, because their whole office was confined to this–to give responses to the people from the mouth of God. This is gathered from a celebrated passage of Malachi, in which it is enjoined to remember the Law, and give heed to it until the preaching of the gospel. (See Malachi 4:4.) For He thus restrains men from all adventitious doctrines, and does not allow them to deviate in the least from the path which Moses had faithfully pointed out. And the reason that David so magnificently extols the Law and pronounces so many encomiums on it (see Psalm 19; 119), was, that the Jews might not long after any extraneous aid, all perfection being included in it.

7 Last mode of teaching by our Savior himself manifested in the flesh. Different names given to this dispensation, to show that we are not to dream of anything more perfect than the written Word.

But when at length the Wisdom of God was manifested in the flesh, He fully unfolded to us all that the human mind can comprehend, or ought to think of the heavenly Father. Now, therefore, since Christ, the Sun of Righteousness, has arisen, we have the perfect refulgence of divine truth, like the brightness of noonday, whereas the light was previously dim. It was no ordinary blessing which the apostle intended to publish when he wrote: "God, who at sundry times and in divers manners, spake in time past unto the fathers by the prophets, hath in these last days spoken unto us by his Son" (Hebrews 1:1, 2). He intimates, nay, openly declares, that God will not henceforth speak by this one and that one, that He will not add prophecy to prophecy, or revelation to revelation. God has so completed all the parts of teaching in the Son, that it is to be regarded as His last and eternal testimony. For which reason, the whole period of the new dispensation, from the time when Christ appeared to us with the preaching of His Gospel, until the Day of Judgment, is designated by the last hour, the last times, the last days. Contented with the perfection of Christ's doctrine, we may learn to frame no new doctrine for ourselves, or admit anyone devised by others. With good cause, therefore, the Father appointed the Son our teacher, with special prerogative, commanding that He and no human being should be heard. When he said, "Hear him" (Matthew 17:5), He commended His office to us in few words of more weight and energy than is commonly supposed. It is just as if He had withdrawn us from all doctrines of man, and confined us to Him alone, ordering us to seek the whole doctrine of salvation from Him alone, to depend on Him alone, and cleave to Him alone; in short (as the words express), to listen only to His voice. And, indeed, what can now be expected or desired from man, when the very Word of life has appeared before us, and familiarly explained himself? Nay, every mouth should be stopped when once He has spoken, in whom, according to the pleasure of our heavenly Father, "are hid all the treasures of wisdom and knowledge" (Colossians 2:3), and spoken as became the Wisdom of God (which is in no part defective) and the Messiah (from whom the revelation of all things was expected) (see John 4:25); in other words, has so spoken as to leave nothing to be spoken by others after Him.

8 Nothing can be lawfully taught in the Church that is not contained in the writings of the Prophets and Apostles, as dictated by the Spirit of Christ.

Let this then be a sure axiom–that there is no Word of God to which place should be given in the Church save that which is contained, first, in the Law and the Prophets; and, secondly, in the writings of the Apostles, and that the only due method of teaching in the Church is according to the prescription and rule of His word. Hence, also we infer that nothing else was permitted to the Apostles than was formerly permitted to the Prophets–namely, to expound the ancient Scriptures, and show that the things there delivered are fulfilled in Christ: this, however, they could not do unless from the Lord; that is, unless the Spirit of Christ went before, and in a manner dictated words to them. For Christ thus defined the terms of their embassy, when He commanded them to go and teach, not what they themselves had at random fabricated, but whatsoever He had commanded. (See Matthew 28:20.) And nothing can be plainer than His words in another passage, "Be not ye called Rabbi: for one is your Master, even Christ" (Matthew 23:8-10). To impress this more deeply in their minds, He in the same place repeats it twice. And because from ignorance they were unable to comprehend the things, which they had heard and learned from the lips of their Master, the Spirit of truth is promised to guide them unto all truth. (See John 114:26; 16:13.) The restriction should be carefully attended to. The office, which He assigns to the Holy Spirit, is to bring to remembrance what His own lips had previously taught.

9 Neither the Apostles, nor apostolic men, nor the whole Church, allowed to overstep these limits. This confirmed by passages of Peter and Paul. Argument a fortiori.

Accordingly, Peter, who was perfectly instructed by his Master as to the extent of what was permitted to him, leaves nothing more to himself or others than to dispense the doctrine delivered by God. "If any man speak, let him speak as the oracles of God" (1 Peter 4:11); that is, not hesitatingly, as those are wont whose convictions are imperfect, but with the full confidence which becomes a servant of God, provided with a sure message. What else is this than to banish all the inventions of the human mind (whatever be the head which may have devised them), so that the pure Word of God may be taught and learned in the Church of the faithful–than to discard the decrees, or rather fictions of men (whatever be their rank), that the decrees of God alone may remain steadfast? These are "the weapons of our warfare," which "are not carnal, but mighty through God to the pulling down of strongholds; casting down imaginations, and every high thing that exalteth itself against the knowledge of God, and bringing into captivity every thought to the obedience of Christ" (2 Corinthians 10:4, 5). Here is the supreme power with which pastors of the Church, by whatever name they are called, should be invested–namely, to dare all boldly for the Word of God, compelling all the virtue, glory, wisdom, and rank of the world to yield and obey its majesty; to command all from the highest to the lowest, trusting to its power to build up the house of Christ and overthrow the house of Satan; to feed the sheep and chase away the wolves; to instruct and exhort the docile, to accuse, rebuke, and subdue the rebellious and petulant, to bind and loose; in fine, if need be, to fire and fulminate, but all in the Word of God.

Although, as I have observed, there is this difference between the apostles and their successors, they were sure and authentic amanuenses of the Holy Spirit; and, therefore, their writings are to be regarded as the oracles of God, whereas others have no other office than to teach what is delivered and sealed in the holy Scriptures. We conclude, therefore, that it does not now belong to faithful ministers to coin some new doctrine, but simply to adhere to the doctrine to which all, without exception, are made subject.

When I say this, I mean to show not only what each individual, but what the whole Church, is bound to do. In regard to individuals, Paul certainly had been appointed an apostle to the Corinthians, and yet he declares that he has no dominion over their faith. (See 2 Corinthians 1:24.) Who will now presume to arrogate a dominion to which the apostle declares that he himself was not competent? But if he had acknowledged such license in teaching, that every pastor could justly demand implicit faith in whatever he delivered, he never would have laid it down as a rule to the Corinthians, that while two or three prophets spoke, the others should judge, and that, if anything was revealed to one sitting by, the first should be silent. (See 1 Corinthians 14:29, 30.) Thus, he spared none, but subjected the authority of all to the censure of the Word of God.

But it will be said, that with regard to the whole Church the case is different. I answer, that in another place Paul meets the objection also when he says, that faith cometh by hearing, and hearing by the Word of God. (See Romans 10:17.) In other words, if faith depends upon the word of God alone, if it regards and reclines on it alone, what place is left for any word of man? He who knows what faith is can never hesitate here, for it must possess a strength sufficient to stand intrepid and invincible against Satan, the machinations of hell, and the whole world. This strength can be found only in the word of God. Then the reason to which we ought here to have regard is universal: God deprives man of the power of producing any new doctrine, in order that He alone may be our master in spiritual teaching, as He alone is true, and can neither lie nor deceive. This reason applies not less to the whole Church than to every individual believer.

10 The Roman tyrants have taught a different doctrine—viz. that councils cannot err, and, therefore, may coin new dogmas.

But if this power of the Church which is here described be contrasted with that which spiritual tyrants, falsely styling themselves bishops and religious prelates, have now for several ages exercised among the people of God, there will be no more agreement than that of Christ with Belial. It is not my intention here to unfold the manner, the unworthy manner, in which they have used their tyranny; I will only state the doctrine which they maintain in the present day, first, in writing, and then, by fire and sword. Taking it for granted, that a universal council is a true representation of the Church, they set out with this principle, and, at the same time, lay it down as incontrovertible, that such councils are under the immediate guidance of the Holy Spirit, and therefore cannot err. But as they rule councils, nay, constitute them, they in fact claim for themselves whatever they maintain to be due to councils. Therefore, they will have our faith to stand and fall at their pleasure, so that whatever they have determined on either side must be firmly seated in our minds; what they approve must be approved by us without any doubt; what they condemn we also must hold to be justly condemned. Meanwhile, at their own caprice and in contempt of the Word of God, they coin doctrines to which they demand our assent by declaring that no man can be a Christian unless he assent to all their dogmas, because it belongs to the church to frame new articles of faith.

11 Answer to the Papistical arguments for the authority of the Church. Argument, that the Church is to be led into all truth. Answer. This promise made not only to the whole Church, but to every individual believer.

First, let us hear by what arguments they prove that this authority was given to the Church, and then we shall see how far their allegations concerning the Church avail them. The Church, they say, has the noble promise that she will never be deserted by Christ her spouse, but be guided by his Spirit into all truth. But of the promises, which they are wont to allege, many were given not less to private believers than to the whole Church. For although the Lord spoke to the twelve apostles, when he said, "Lo! I am with you alway, even unto the end of the world" (Matthew 28:20); and again, "I will pray the Father, and he shall give you another Comforter, that he may abide with you forever: even the Spirit of truth" (John 14:16, 17), He made these promises not only to the twelve, but to each of them separately, nay, in like manner, to other disciples whom He already had received, or was afterwards to receive. When they interpret these promises, which are replete with consolation, in such a way as if they were not given to any particular Christian but to the whole Church together, what else is it but to deprive Christians of the confidence which they ought thence to have derived, to animate them in their course? I do not deny that the whole body of the faithful is furnished with a manifold variety of gifts, and endued with a far larger and richer treasure of heavenly wisdom than each Christian apart. I do not mean that this was said of believers in general, as implying that all possess the spirit of wisdom and knowledge in an equal degree. We are not to give permission to the adversaries of Christ to defend a bad cause, by wresting Scripture from its proper meaning. Omitting this, however, I simply hold what is true–viz. that the Lord is always present with His people, and guides them by His Spirit. He is the Spirit, not of error, ignorance, falsehood, or darkness, but of sure revelation, wisdom, truth, and light, from whom they can, without deception, learn the things which have been given to them (see 1 Corinthians 2:12); in other words, "what is the hope of their calling, and what the riches of the glory of their inheritance in the saints" (Ephesians 1:18). But while believers, even those of them who are endued with more excellent graces, obtain in the present life only the first fruits and a foretaste of the Spirit, nothing better remains to them than, under a consciousness of their weakness, to confine themselves anxiously within the limits of the Word of God, lest, in following their own sense too far, they stray from the right path, being left without that Spirit, by whose teaching alone truth is discerned from falsehood. For all confess with Paul, "they have not yet reached the goal" (Philippians 3:12). Accordingly, they rather aim at daily progress than glory in perfection.

12 Answers continued.

But it will be objected, that whatever is attributed in part to any of the saints, belongs in complete fullness to the Church. Although there is some semblance of truth in this, I deny that it is true. God, indeed, measures out the gifts of His Spirit to each of the members, so that nothing necessary to the whole body is wanting, since the gifts are bestowed for the common advantage. The riches of the Church, however, are always of such a nature, that much is wanting to that supreme perfection of which our opponents boast. Still the Church is not left destitute in any part, but always has as much as is sufficient, for the Lord knows what her necessities require. But to keep her in humility and pious modesty, He bestows no more on her than He knows to be expedient. I am aware, it is usual here to object, that Christ hath cleansed the Church "with the washing of water by the word: that he might present it to himself a glorious Church, not having spot or wrinkle" (Ephesians 5:26, 27), and that it is therefore called the "pillar and ground of the truth" (1 Timothy 3:15). But the former passage rather shows what Christ daily performs in it, than what He has already perfected. For if He daily sanctifies all His people, purifies, refines them, and wipes away their stains, it is certain that they have still some spots and wrinkles, and that their sanctification is in some measure defective.

How vain and fabulous is it to suppose that the Church, all whose members are somewhat spotted and impure, is completely holy and spotless in every part? It is true, therefore, that the Church is sanctified by Christ, but here the commencement of her sanctification only is seen; the end and entire completion will be effected when Christ, the Holy of holies, shall truly and completely fill her with His holiness. It is true also, that her stains and wrinkles have been effaced, but so that the process is continued every day, until Christ at His advent will entirely remove every remaining defect. For unless we admit this, we shall be constrained to hold with the Pelagians, that the righteousness of believers is perfected in this life: like the Cathari and Donatists, we shall tolerate no infirmity in the Church.

The other passage, as we have elsewhere seen (see Chapter 1, section 10), has a very different meaning from what they put upon it. For when Paul instructed Timothy, and trained him to the office of a true bishop, he says, he did it in order that he might learn how to behave himself in the Church of God. And to make him devote himself to the work with greater seriousness and zeal, he adds, that the Church is the pillar and ground of the truth. And what else do these words mean, except that the truth of God is preserved in the Church? Truth is preserved by the instrumentality of preaching. As he elsewhere says, Christ "gave some, apostles; and some, prophets;

and some, evangelists; and some, pastors and teachers;" "that we henceforth be no more children, tossed to and fro, and carried about with every wind of doctrine, by the sleight of men, and cunning craftiness, whereby they lie in wait to deceive; but, speaking the truth in love, may grow up into him in all things, who is the head, even Christ" (Ephesians 4:11, 14, 15). Instead of being extinguished in the world, the truth remains unimpaired because God has the Church as a faithful guardian, by whose aid and ministry it is maintained. But if this guardianship consists in the ministry of the Prophets and Apostles, it follows, that the whole depends upon this–viz. that the Word of the Lord is faithfully preserved and maintained in purity.

13 Answers continued.

And that my readers may the better understand the hinge on which the question chiefly turns, I will briefly explain what our opponents demand, and what we resist. When they deny that the Church can err, their end and meaning are to this effect: Since the Church is governed by the Spirit of God, she can walk safely without the Word. In whatever direction she moves, she cannot think or speak anything but the truth, and hence, if she determines anything without or beside the Word of God, it must be regarded in no other light than if it were a divine oracle. If we grant the first point–viz. that the Church cannot err in things necessary to salvation–our meaning is that she cannot err, because she has altogether discarded her own wisdom, and submits to the teaching of the Holy Spirit through the Word of God. Here then is the difference. They place the authority of the Church without the Word of God; we annex it to the Word, and allow it not to be separated from it. And is it strange if the spouse and pupil of Christ is so subject to her Lord and Master as to hang carefully and constantly on His lips?

In every well-ordered house, the wife obeys the command of her husband; in every well-regulated school, the doctrine of the master only is listened to. Wherefore, let not the Church be wise in herself, nor think anything of herself, but let her consider her wisdom terminated when He ceases to speak. In this way she will distrust all the inventions of her own reason; and when she leans on the Word of God, will not waver in diffidence or hesitation but rest in full assurance and unwavering constancy. Trusting to the liberal promises, which she has received, she will have the means of nobly maintaining her faith, never doubting that the Holy Spirit is always present with her to be the perfect guide of her path. At the same time, she will remember the use, which God wishes to be derived from His Spirit. "When he, the Spirit of truth, is come, he will guide you into all truth" (John 16: 13). How? "He shall bring to your remembrance all things whatsoever I have said unto you." He declares, therefore, that nothing more is to be expected of His Spirit than to enlighten our minds to perceive the truth of His doctrine.

Hence, Chrysostom most shrewdly observes, "Many boast of the Holy Spirit, but with those who speak their own it is a false pretence. As Christ declared that He spoke not of himself (see John 12:50; 14:10), because He spoke according to the Law and the Prophets; so, if anything contrary to the gospel is obtruded under the name of the Holy Spirit, let us not believe it. For as Christ is the fulfillment of the Law and the Prophets, so is the Spirit the fulfillment of the gospel." We may now easily infer how erroneously our opponents act in vaunting of the Holy Spirit, for no other end than to give the credit of His name to strange doctrines, extraneous to the Word of God, whereas He himself desires to be inseparably connected with the Word of God; and Christ declares the same thing of Him, when He promises Him to the Church. And so indeed it is. The soberness, which our Lord once prescribed to His Church, He wishes to be perpetually observed. He forbade that anything should be added to His Word, and that anything should be taken from it. This is the inviolable decree of God and the Holy Spirit, a decree that our opponents endeavor to annul when they pretend that the Church is guided by the Spirit without the Word.

14 Argument, that the Church should supply the deficiency of the written Word by traditions. Answer.

Here again they mutter that the Church behooved to add something to the writings of the apostles, or that the apostles themselves behooved orally to supply what they had less clearly taught, since Christ said to them, "I have yet many things to say unto you, but ye cannot bear them now" (John 16:12), and that these are the points which have been received, without writing, merely by use and custom. But what effrontery is this? The disciples, I admit, were ignorant and almost indocile when our Lord thus addressed them, but were they still in this condition when they committed His doctrine to writing, so as afterwards to be under the necessity of supplying orally that which, through ignorance, they had omitted to write? If they were guided by the Spirit of truth unto all truth when they published their writings, what prevented them from embracing a full knowledge of the Gospel, and consigning it therein? But let us grant them what they ask, provided they point out the things, which behooved to be revealed without writing. Should they presume to attempt this, I will address, them in the words of Augustine, "When the Lord is silent, who of us may say, this is, or that is? Or if we should presume to say it, how do we prove it?" But why do I contend superfluously? Every child knows that in the writings of the apostles, which these men represent as mutilated and incomplete, is contained the result of that revelation which the Lord then promised to them.

15 Argument founded on Matthew 18:17. Answer.

What, say they, did not Christ declare that nothing which the Church teaches and decrees can be gainsayed, when He enjoined that everyone who presumes to contradict should be regarded as a heathen man and a publican? (Matthew 18:17.) First, there is here no mention of doctrine, but her authority to censure, for correction is asserted, in order that none who had been admonished or reprimanded might oppose her judgment. But to say nothing of this, it is very strange that those men are so lost to all sense of shame that they hesitate not to plume themselves on this declaration. For what, pray, will they make of it, but just that the consent of the Church, a consent never given but to the Word of God, is not to be despised? The Church is to be heard, say they. Who denies this since she decides nothing but according to the Word of God? If they demand more than this, let them know that the words of Christ give them no countenance. I ought not to seem contentious when I so vehemently insist that we cannot concede to the Church any new doctrine; in other words, allow her to teach and oracularly deliver more than the Lord has revealed in His Word. Men of sense see how great the danger is if so much authority is once conceded to men. They see also, how wide a door is opened for the jeers and cavils of the ungodly, if we admit that Christians are to receive the opinions of men as if they were oracles. We may add, that our Savior, speaking according to the circumstances of His times, gave the name of Church to the Sanhedrim, that the disciples might learn afterwards to revere the sacred meetings of the Church. Hence, it would follow, that single cities and districts would have equal liberty in coining dogmas.

16 Objections founded on infant baptism, and the Canon of the Council of Nice, as to the consubstantiality of the Son. Answer.

The examples, which they bring, do not avail them. They say that Paedobaptism proceeds not so much on a plain command of Scripture, as on a decree of the Church. It would be a miserable asylum if, in defense of Paedobaptism, we were obliged to betake ourselves to the bare authority of the Church; but it will be made plain enough elsewhere (chapter 16) that it is far otherwise. In like manner, when they object that we nowhere find in the Scriptures what was declared in the Council of Nice–viz. that the Son is consubstantial with the Father–they do a grievous injustice to the Fathers, as if they had rashly condemned Arius for not swearing to their words, though professing the whole of that doctrine which is contained in the writings of the Apostles and Prophets. I admit that the expression does not exist in Scripture, but seeing it is there so often declared that there is one God, and Christ is so often called true and eternal God, one with the Father, what do the Nicene Fathers do when they affirm that He is of one essence, than simply declare the genuine meaning of Scripture? Theodoret relates that Constantine, in opening their meeting, spoke as follows: "In the discussion of divine matters, the doctrine of the Holy Spirit stands recorded. The Gospels and Apostolical writings, with the oracles of the Prophets, fully show us the meaning of the Deity. Therefore, laying aside discord, let us take the exposition of questions from the words of the Spirit." There was none who opposed this sound advice; none who objected that the Church could add something of her own, that the Spirit did not reveal all things to the apostles, or at least that they did not deliver them to posterity, and so forth. If the point on which our opponents insist is true, Constantine, first, was in error in robbing the Church of her power; and, secondly, when none of the bishops rose to vindicate it, their silence was a kind of perfidy, and made them traitors to Ecclesiastical law. But since Theodoret relates that they readily embraced what the Emperor said, it is evident that this new dogma was then wholly unknown.

Chapter 9

OF COUNCILS AND THEIR AUTHORITY.

Since Papists regard their Councils as expressing the sentiment and consent of the Church, particularly as regards the authority of declaring dogmas and the exposition of them, it was necessary to treat of Councils before proceeding to consider that part of ecclesiastical power, which relates to doctrine. I. First, the authority of Councils in delivering dogmas is discussed, and it is shown that the Spirit of God is not so bound to the pastors of the Church as opponents suppose. Their objections refuted, sections 1-7. II. The errors, contradictions, and weaknesses, of certain Councils exposed. A refutation of the subterfuge, that those set over us are to be obeyed without distinction, sections 8-12. III. Of the authority of Councils, as regards the interpretation of Scripture, sections 13, 14.

Sections

1. The true nature of Councils.

2. Whence the authority of Councils is derived. What meant by assembling in the name of Christ.

3. Objection, that no truth remains in the Church if it is not in pastors and councils. Answer, showing by passages from the Old Testament that Pastors were often devoid of the spirit of knowledge and truth.

4. Passages from the New Testament showing that our times were to be subject to the same evil. This confirmed by the example of almost all ages.

5. All not pastors who pretend to be so.

6. Objection, that General Councils represent the Church. Answer, showing the absurdity of this objection from passages in the Old Testament.

7. Passages to the same effect from the New Testament.

8. Councils have authority only in so far as accordant with Scripture. Testimony of Augustine. Councils of Nice,

Constantinople, and Ephesus, Subsequent Councils more impure, and to be received with limitation.

9. Contradictory decisions of Councils. Those agreeing with divine truth to be received. Those at variance with it to be rejected. This confirmed by the example of the Council of Constantinople and the Council of Nice; also of the Council of Chalcedon, and second Council of Ephesus.

10. Errors of purer Councils. Four causes of these errors. An example from the Council of Nice.

11. Another example from the Council of Chalcedon. The same errors in Provincial Councils.

12. Evasion of the Papists. Three answers. Conclusion of the discussion as to the power of the Church in relation to doctrine.

13. Last part of the chapter. Power of the Church in interpreting Scripture. From what source interpretation is to be derived. Means of preserving unity in the Church.

14. Impudent attempt of the Papists to establish their tyranny refuted. Things at variance with Scripture sanctioned by their Councils. Instance in the prohibition of marriage and communion in both kinds.

1 The true nature of Councils.

Were I now to concede all that they ask concerning the Church, it would not greatly aid them in their object. For everything that is said of the Church, they immediately transfer to councils, which, in their opinion, represent the Church. Nay, when they contend so doggedly for the power of the Church, their only object is to devolve the whole, which they extort on the Roman Pontiff and his conclave. Before I begin to discuss this question, two points must be briefly premised. First, though I mean to be more rigid in discussing this subject, it is not because I set less value than I ought on ancient councils. I venerate them from my heart, and would have all to hold them in due honor. But there must be some limitation; there must be nothing derogatory to Christ. Moreover, it is the right of Christ to preside over all councils, and not share the honor with any man. Now, I hold that He presides only when He governs the whole assembly by His Word and Spirit. Secondly, in attributing less to councils than my opponents demand, it is not because I have any fear that councils are favorable to their cause and adverse to ours. For as we are amply provided by the Word of the Lord with the means of proving our doctrine and overthrowing the whole Papacy, and thus have no great need of other aid, so, if the case required it, ancient councils furnish us in a great measure with what might be sufficient for both purposes.

2 Whence the authority of Councils is derived. What meant by assembling in the name of Christ.

Let us now proceed to the subject itself. If we consult Scripture on the authority of councils, there is no promise more remarkable than that which is contained in these Words of our Savior, "Where two or three are gathered together in my name, there am I in the midst of them." But this is just as applicable to any particular meeting as to a universal council. And yet the important part of the question does not lie here, but in the condition, which is added–viz. that Christ will be in the midst of a council, provided it be assembled in His name. Wherefore, though our opponents should name councils of thousands of bishops it will little avail them; nor will they induce us to believe that they are, as they maintain, guided by the Holy Spirit, until they make it credible that they assemble in the name of Christ: since it is as possible for wicked and dishonest to conspire against Christ, as for good and honest bishops to meet together in His name. Of this we have a clear proof in very many of the decrees which have proceeded from councils. But this will be afterwards seen. At present, I only reply in one word, that our Savior's promise is made to those only who assemble in His name. How, then, is such an assembly to be defined? I deny that those assemble in the name of Christ who, disregarding His command by which He forbids anything to be added to the Word of God or taken from it, determine everything at their own pleasure, who, not contented with the oracles of Scripture, that is, with the only rule of perfect wisdom, devise some novelty out of their own head. (See Deuteronomy 4:2; Revelation 22:18.) Certainly, since our Savior has not promised to be present with all councils of whatever description, but has given a peculiar mark for distinguishing true and lawful councils from others, we ought not by any means to lose sight of the distinction. The covenant, which God anciently made with the Levitical priests, was to teach at His mouth. (See Malachi 2:7.) This He always required of the prophets, and we see that it was the law given to the apostles. On those who violate this covenant, God bestows neither the honor of the priesthood nor any authority. Let my opponents solve this difficulty if they would subject my faith to the decrees of man, without authority from the Word of God.

3 Objection, that no truth remains in the Church if it is not in pastors and councils. Answer, showing by passages from the Old Testament that pastors were often devoid of the spirit of knowledge and truth.

Their idea that the truth cannot remain in the Church unless it exists among pastors, and that the Church herself cannot exist unless displayed in general councils, is very far from holding true if the prophets have left us a correct description of their own times. In the time of Isaiah, there was a Church at Jerusalem, which the Lord had not yet abandoned. But of pastors He thus speaks: "His watchmen are blind; they are all ignorant, they are all dumb dogs, they cannot bark; sleeping, lying down, loving to slumber. Yea, they are greedy dogs which never have enough, and they are shepherds that cannot understand: they all look to their own way" (Isaiah 56:10, 11). In the same way Hosea says, "The watchman of Ephraim was with my God: but the prophet is a snare of a fowler in all his ways, and hatred in the house of his God" (Hosea 9:8). Here, by ironically connecting them with God, he shows that the pretext of the priesthood was vain. There was also a Church in the time of Jeremiah. Let us hear what he says of pastors: "From the prophet even unto the priest, everyone dealeth falsely." Again, "The prophets prophesy lies in my name: I sent them not, neither have I commanded them, neither spake unto them" (Jeremiah 6:13; 14:14). And not to be prolix with quotations, read the whole of his thirty-third and fortieth chapters. Then, on the other hand, Ezekiel inveighs against them in no milder terms. "There is a conspiracy of her prophets in the midst thereof, like a roaring lion ravening the prey; they have devoured souls." "Her priests have violated my law, and profaned mine holy things" (Ezekiel 22:25, 26). There is more to the same purpose. Similar complaints abound throughout the prophets; nothing is of more frequent recurrence.

4 Passages from the New Testament showing that our times were to be subject to the same evil. This confirmed by the example of almost all ages.

But perhaps, though this great evil prevailed among the Jews, our age is exempt from it. Would that it would be so; but the Holy Spirit declared that it would be otherwise. For Peter's words are clear, "But there were false prophets among the people, even as there shall be false teachers among you, who privily will bring in damnable heresies" (2 Peter 2:1). See how he predicts impending danger, not from ordinary believers, but from those who should plume themselves on the name of pastors and teachers. Besides, how often did Christ and His apostles foretell that the greatest dangers with which the Church was threatened would come from pastors? (See Matthew 24:11, 24.) Nay, Paul openly declares, that Antichrist would have his seat in the temple of God (see 2 Thessalonians 2:4); thereby intimating, that the fearful calamity of which he was speaking would come only from those who should have their seat in the Church as pastors. And in another passage, he shows that the introduction of this great evil was almost at hand. For in addressing the Elders of Ephesus, he says, "I know this, that after my departing shall grievous wolves enter in among you, not sparing the flock. Also of your own selves shall men arise, speaking perverse things, to draw away disciples after them" (Acts 20:29, 30). How great corruption might a long series of years introduce among pastors, when they could degenerate so much within so short a time? And not to fill my pages with details, we are reminded by the examples of almost every age, that the truth is not always cherished in the bosoms of pastors, and that the safety of the Church depends not on their state. It was becoming that those appointed to preserve the peace and safety of the Church should be its presidents and guardians; but it is one thing to perform what you owe, and another to owe what you do not perform.

5 All are not Pastors who pretend to be so.

Let no man, however, understand me as if I were desirous in everything rashly and unreservedly to overthrow the authority of pastors. All I advise is, to exercise discrimination, and not suppose, as a matter of course, that all who call themselves pastors are so in reality. But the Pope, with the whole crew of his bishops, for no other reason but because they are called pastors, shake off obedience to the Word of God, invert all things, and turn them hither and thither at their pleasure; meanwhile, they insist that they cannot be destitute of the light of truth, that the Spirit of God perpetually resides in them, that the Church subsists in them, and dies with them, as if the Lord did not still inflict His judgments, and in the present day punish the world for its wickedness, in the same way in which He punished the ingratitude of the ancient people–namely, by smiting pastors with astonishment and blindness. (See Zechariah 12:4.) These stupid men understand not that they are just chiming in with those of ancient times who warred with the Word of God. For the enemies of Jeremiah thus set themselves against the truth, "Come, and let us devise devices against Jeremiah; for the law shall not perish from the priest, nor counsel from the wise, nor the word from the prophet" (Jeremiah 18:18).

6 Objection, that General Councils represent the Church. Answer, showing the absurdity of this objection from passages in the Old Testament.

Hence, it is easy to reply to their allegation concerning general councils. It cannot be denied, that the Jews had a true Church under the prophets. But had a general council then been composed of the priests, what kind of appearance would the Church have had? We hear the Lord denouncing not against one or two of them, but the whole order: "The priests shall be astonished, and the prophets shall wonder" (Jeremiah 4:9). Again, "The law shall perish from the priest, and counsel from the ancients" (Ezekiel 7:26). Again, "Therefore night shall be unto you, that ye shall not have a vision; and it shall be dark unto you, that ye shall not divine; and the sun shall go down over the prophets, and the day shall be dark over them," etc. (Micah 3:6). Now, had all men of this description been collected together, what spirit would have presided over their meeting? Of this, we have a notable instance in the council, which Ahab convened. (See 1 Kings 22:6, 22.) Four hundred prophets were present. But because they had met with no other intention than to flatter the impious king, Satan is sent by the Lord to be a lying spirit in all their mouths. The truth is there unanimously condemned. Micaiah is judged a heretic, is smitten, and cast into prison. So was it done to Jeremiah, and so to the other prophets.

7 Passages to the same effect from the New Testament.

But there is one memorable example, which may suffice for all. In the council, which the priests and Pharisees assembled at Jerusalem against Christ (see John 11:47), what is wanting, as far as external appearance is concerned? Had there been no Church then at Jerusalem, Christ would never have joined in the sacrifices and other ceremonies. A solemn meeting is held; the High Priest presides; the whole sacerdotal order take their seats, and yet Christ is condemned, and His doctrine is put to flight. This atrocity proves that the Church was not at all included in that council. But there is no danger that anything of the kind will happen with us. Who has told us so? Too much security in a matter of so great importance lies open to the charge of sluggishness. Nay, when the Spirit, by the mouth of Paul, foretells, in distinct terms, that a defection will take place, a defection which cannot come until pastors first forsake God (see 2 Thessalonians 2:3), why do we spontaneously walk blindfold to our own destruction? Wherefore, we cannot on any account admit that the Church consists in a meeting of pastors, as to whom the Lord has nowhere promised that they would always be good, but has sometimes foretold that they would be wicked. When He warns us of danger, it is to make us use greater caution.

8 Councils have authority only in so far as accordant with Scripture. Testimony of Augustine. Councils of Nice, Constantinople, and Ephesus, Subsequent Councils more impure, and to be received with limitation.

What, then, you will say, is there no authority in the definitions of councils? Yes, indeed, for I do not contend that all councils are to be condemned, and all their acts rescinded, or, as it is said, made one complete erasure. But you are bringing them all (it will be said) under subordination, and so leaving everyone at liberty to receive or reject the decrees of councils as he pleases. By no means; but whenever the decree of a council is produced, the first thing I would wish to be done is, to examine at what time it was held, on what occasion, with what intention, and who were present at it; next I would bring the subject discussed to the standard of Scripture. And this I would do in such a way that the decision of the council should have its weight, and be regarded in the light of a prior judgment, yet not so as to prevent the application of the test which I have mentioned. I wish all had observed the method, which Augustine prescribes in his Third Book against Maximinus, when he wished to silence the cavils of this heretic against the decrees of councils, "I ought not to oppose the Council of Nice to you, nor ought you to oppose that of Ariminum to me, as prejudging the question. I am not bound by the authority of the latter, nor you by that of the former. Let thing contend with thing, cause with cause, reason with reason, on the authority of Scripture, an authority not peculiar to either, but common to all." In this way, councils would be duly respected, and yet the highest place would be given to Scripture, everything being brought to it as a test. Thus those ancient Councils of Nice, Constantinople, the first of Ephesus, Chalcedon, and the like, which were held for refuting errors, we willingly embrace, and reverence as sacred, in so far as relates to doctrines of faith, for they contain nothing but the pure and genuine interpretation of Scripture, which the holy Fathers with spiritual prudence adopted to crush the enemies of religion who had then arisen. In some later councils, also, we see displayed a true zeal for religion, and unequivocal marks of genius, learning, and prudence. But as matters usually become worse and worse, it is easy to see in more modern councils how much the Church gradually degenerated from the purity of that golden age. I doubt not, however, that even in those more corrupt ages, councils had their bishops of better character. But it happened with them as the Roman senators of old complained in regard to their decrees. Opinions being numbered, not weighed, the better were obliged to give way to the greater number. They certainly put forth many impious sentiments. There is no need here to collect instances, both because it would be tedious, and because it has been done by others so carefully, as not to leave much to be added.

9 Contradictory decisions of Councils. Those agreeing with divine truth to be received. Those at variance with it to be rejected. This confirmed by the example of the Council of Constantinople and the Council of Nice; also of the Council of Chalcedon, and second Council of Ephesus.

Moreover, why should I review the contests of council with council? Nor is there any ground for whispering to me, that when councils are at variance, one or other of them is not a lawful council. For how shall we ascertain this? Just, if I mistake not, by judging from Scripture that the decrees are not orthodox. For this alone is the sure law of discrimination. It is now about nine hundred years since the Council of Constantinople, convened under the Emperor Leo, determined that the images set up in temples were to be thrown down and broken to pieces. Shortly after, the Council of Nice, which was assembled by Irene, through dislike of the former, decreed that images were to be restored. Which of the two councils shall we acknowledge to be lawful? The latter has usually prevailed, and secured a place for images in churches. But Augustine maintains that this could not be done without the greatest danger of idolatry. Epiphanius, at a later period, speaks much more harshly. For he says, it is an unspeakable abomination to see images in a Christian temple. Could those who speak thus approve of that council if they were alive in the present day? But if historians speak true, and we believe their acts—not only images themselves, but the worship of them—were there sanctioned. It is plain that this decree emanated from Satan. Do they not show, by corrupting and wresting Scripture, that they held it in derision? This I have made sufficiently clear in a former part of the work (see Book I, chapter 11, section). Be this as it may, we shall never be able to distinguish between contradictory and dissenting councils, which have been many, unless we weigh them all in that balance for men and angels, I mean, the Word of God. Thus, we embrace the Council of Chalcedon, and repudiate the second of Ephesus, because the latter sanctioned the impiety of Eutyches, and the former condemned it. The judgment of these holy men was founded on the Scriptures, and while we follow it, we desire that the Word of God, which illuminated them, may now also illuminate us. Let the Romanists now go and boast after their manner, that the Holy Spirit is fixed and tied to their councils.

10 Errors of purer Councils. Four causes of these errors. An example from the Council of Nice.

Even in their ancient and purer councils there is something to be desiderated, either because the otherwise learned and prudent men who attended, being distracted by the business in hand, did not attend to many things beside; or because, occupied with grave and more serious measures, they winked at some of lesser moment; or simply because, as men, they were deceived through ignorance, or were sometimes carried headlong by some feeling in excess. Of this last case (which seems the most difficult of all to avoid), we have a striking example in the Council of Nice, which has been unanimously received, as it deserves, with the utmost veneration. For when the primary article of our faith was there in peril, and Arius, its enemy, was present, ready to engage anyone in combat, and it was of the utmost moment that those who had come to attack Arius should be agreed, they nevertheless, feeling secure amid all these dangers, nay forgetting their gravity, modesty, and politeness, laying aside the discussion which was before them (as if they had met for the express purpose of gratifying Arius), began to give way to intestine dissensions, and turn the pen, which should have been employed against Arius, against each other. Foul accusations were heard, libels flew up and down, and they never would have ceased from their contention until they had stabbed each other with mutual wounds, had not the Emperor Constantine interfered, and declaring that the investigation of their lives was a matter above his cognizance, repressed their intemperance by flattery rather than censure. In how many respects is it probable that councils, held subsequently to this, have erred? Nor does the fact stand in need of a long demonstration; anyone who reads their acts will observe many infirmities, not to use a stronger term.

11 Another example from the Council of Chalcedon. The same errors in Provincial Councils.

Even Leo, the Roman Pontiff, hesitates not to charge the Council of Chalcedon, which he admits to be orthodox in its doctrines, with ambition and inconsiderate rashness. He denies not that it was lawful, but openly maintains that it might have erred. Some may think me foolish in laboring to point out errors of this description, since my opponents admit that councils may err in things not necessary to salvation. My labor, however, is not superfluous. For although compelled, they admit this in word, yet by obtruding upon us the determination of all councils, in all matters without distinction, as the oracles of the Holy Spirit, they exact more than they had at the outset assumed. By thus acting what do they maintain but just that councils cannot err, of if they err, it is unlawful for us to perceive the truth, or refuse assent to their errors? At the same time, all I mean to infer from what I have said is, that though councils, otherwise pious and holy, were governed by the Holy Spirit, He yet allowed them to share the lot of humanity, lest we should confide too much in men. This is a much better view than that of Gregory Nanzianzen, who says that he never saw any council end well. In asserting that all, without exception, ended ill, he leaves them little authority. There is no necessity for making separate mention of provincial councils, since it is easy to estimate, from the case of general councils, how much authority they ought to have in framing articles of faith, and deciding what kind of doctrine is to be received.

12 Evasion of the Papists. Three answers. Conclusion of the discussion as to the power of the Church in relation to doctrine.

But our Romanists, when, in defending their cause, they see all rational grounds slip from beneath them, betake themselves to a last miserable subterfuge. Although they should be dull in intellect and counsel, and most depraved in heart and will, still the Word of the Lord remains, which commands us to obey those who have the rule over us. (See Hebrews 13:17.) Is it indeed so? What if I should deny that those who act thus have the rule over us? They ought not to claim for themselves more than Joshua had, who was both a prophet of the Lord and an excellent pastor. Let us then hear in what terms the Lord introduced him to his office. "This book of the law shall not depart out of thy mouth; but thou shalt meditate therein day and night, that thou mayest observe to do according to all that is written therein: for then shalt thou make thy way prosperous, and thou shalt have good success" (Joshua 1:7, 8). Our spiritual rulers, therefore, will be those who turn not from the law of the Lord to the right hand or the left. But if the doctrine of all pastors is to be received without hesitation, why are we so often and so anxiously admonished by the Lord not to give heed to false prophets? "Thus saith the Lord of Hosts, Hearken not unto the words of the prophets that prophesy unto you; they make you vain: they speak a vision of their own heart, and not out of the mouth of the Lord" (Jeremiah 23:16). Again, "Beware of false prophets, which come to you in sheep's clothing but inwardly they are ravening wolves" (Matthew 7:15).

In vain also would John exhort us to try the spirits whether they be of God (1 John 4:1). From this judgment, not even angels are exempted (Galatians 1:8); far less Satan with his lies. And what is meant by the expression, "If the blind lead the blind, both shall fall into the ditch"? (Matthew 15:14)

Does it not sufficiently declare that there is a great difference among the pastors who are to be heard, that all are not to be heard indiscriminately? Wherefore they have no ground for deterring us by their name, in order to draw us into a participation of their blindness, since we see, on the contrary, that the Lord has used special care to guard us from allowing ourselves to be led away by the errors of others, whatever be the mask under which they may lurk. For if the answer of our Savior is true, blind guides, whether high priests, prelates, or pontiffs, can do nothing more than hurry us over the same precipice with themselves. Wherefore, let no names of councils, pastors, and bishops (which may be used on false pretences as well as truly), hinder us from giving heed to the evidence both of words and facts, and bringing all spirits to the test of the divine Word, that we may prove whether they are of God.

13 Last part of the chapter. Power of the Church in interpreting Scripture. From what source interpretation is to be derived. Means of preserving unity in the Church.

Having proved that no power was given to the Church to set up any new doctrine, let us now treat of the power attributed to them in the interpretation of Scripture. We readily admit that when any doctrine is brought under discussion, there is not a better or surer remedy than for a council of true bishops to meet and discuss the controverted point. There will be much more weight in a decision of this kind, to which the pastors of churches have agreed in common after invoking the Spirit of Christ, than if each, adopting it for himself, should deliver it to his people, or a few individuals should meet in private and decide. Secondly, When bishops have assembled in one place, they deliberate more conveniently in common, fixing both the doctrine and the form of teaching it, lest diversity give offense. Thirdly, Paul prescribes this method of determining doctrine. For when he gives the power of deciding to a single church, he shows what the course of procedure should be in more important cases—namely, that the churches together are to take common cognizance. And the very feeling of piety tells us, that if anyone trouble the Church with some novelty in doctrine, and the matter be carried so far that there is danger of a greater dissension, the churches should first meet, examine the question, and at length, after due discussion, decide according to Scripture, which may both put an end to doubt in the people, and stop the mouths of wicked and restless men, so as to prevent the matter from proceeding further. Thus when Arius arose, the Council of Nice was convened, and by its authority both crushed the wicked attempts of this impious man, and restored peace to the churches which he had vexed, and asserted the eternal divinity of Christ in opposition to his sacrilegious dogma. Thereafter, when Eunomius and Macedonius raised new disturbances, their madness was met with a similar remedy by the Council of Constantinople; the impiety of Nestorius was defeated by the Council of Ephesus.

In short, this was from the first the usual method of preserving unity in the Church whenever Satan commenced his machinations. But let us remember, that all ages and places are not favored with an Athanasius, a Basil, a Cyril, and like vindicators of sound doctrine, whom the Lord then raised up. Nay, let us consider what happened in the second Council of Ephesus when the Eutychian heresy prevailed. Flavianus, of holy memory, with some pious men, was driven into exile, and many similar crimes were committed, because, instead of the Spirit of the Lord, Dioscorus, a factious man, of a very bad disposition, presided. But the Church was not there. I admit it; for I always hold that the truth does not perish in the Church though it is oppressed by one council, but is wondrously preserved by the Lord to rise again, and prove victorious in His own time. I deny, however, that every interpretation of Scripture is true and certain which has received the votes of a council.

14 Impudent attempt of the Papists to establish their tyranny refuted. Things at variance with Scripture sanctioned by their Councils. Instance in the prohibition of marriage and communion in both kinds.

But the Romanists have another end in view when they say that the power of interpreting Scripture belongs to councils, and that without challenge. For they employ it as a pretext for giving the name of an interpretation of Scripture to everything which is determined in councils. Of purgatory, the intercession of saints, and auricular confession, and the like, not one syllable can be found in Scripture. But as all these have been sanctioned by the authority of the Church, or, to speak more correctly, have been received by opinion and practice, every one of them is to be held as an interpretation of Scripture. And not only so, but whatever a council has determined against Scripture is to have the name of an interpretation. Christ bids all drink of the cup, which He holds forth in the Supper. The Council of Constance prohibited the giving of it to the people, and determined that the priest alone should drink. Though this is diametrically opposed to the institution of Christ (Matthew 26:26), they will have it to be regarded as His interpretation. Paul terms the prohibition of marriage a doctrine of devils (see 1 Timothy 4:1, 3); and the Spirit elsewhere declares, "marriage is honorable in all" (Hebrews 13:4). Having afterwards interdicted their priests from marriage, they insist on this as a true and genuine interpretation of Scripture, though nothing can be imagined more alien to it.

Should anyone venture to open his lips in opposition, he will be judged a heretic, since the determination of the Church is without challenge, and it is unlawful to have any doubt as to the accuracy of her interpretation. Why should I assail such effrontery? To point to it is to condemn it. Their dogma with regard to the power of approving Scripture I intentionally omit. For to subject the oracles of God in this way to the censure of men, and hold that they are sanctioned because they please men, is a blasphemy which deserves not to be mentioned. Besides, I have already touched upon it (Book 1, chapter 7; 8 section 9).

I will ask them one question, however. If the authority of Scripture is founded on the approbation of the Church, will they quote the decree of a council to that effect? I believe they cannot. Why, then, did Arius allow himself to be vanquished at the Council of Nice by passages adduced from the Gospel of John? According to these, he was at liberty to repudiate them, as they had not previously been approved by any general council. They allege an old catalogue, which they call the Canon, and say that it originated in a decision of the Church. But I again ask, In what council was that Canon published? Here they must be dumb. Besides, I wish to know what they believe that Canon to be. For I see that the ancients are little agreed with regard to it. If effect is to be given to what Jerome says: the Maccabees, Tobit, Ecclesiasticus, and the like must take their place in the Apocrypha, but this they will not tolerate on any account.

Chapter 10

OF THE POWER OF MAKING LAWS. THE CRUELTY OF THE POPE AND HIS ADHERENTS, IN THIS RESPECT, IN TYRANNICALLY OPPRESSING AND DESTROYING SOULS.

This chapter treats—I. Of human constitutions in general. Of the distinction between Civil and Ecclesiastical Laws. Of conscience, why and in what sense ministers cannot impose laws on the conscience, sections 1-8. II. Of traditions or Popish constitutions relating to ceremonies and discipline. The many vices inherent in them, sections 9-17. Arguments in favor of those traditions refuted, sections 17-26. III. Of Ecclesiastical constitutions that are good and lawful, sections 27-32.

Sections

1. *The power of the church in enacting laws. This made a source of human traditions. Impiety of these traditions.*
2. *Many of the Papistical traditions not only difficult, but impossible to be observed.*
3. *That the question may be more conveniently explained, nature of conscience must be defined.*
4. *Definition of conscience explained. Examples in illustration of the definition.*
5. *Paul's doctrine of submission to magistrates for conscience sake, gives no countenance to the Popish doctrine of the obligation of traditions.*
6. *The question stated. A brief mode of deciding it.*
7. *A perfect rule of life in the Law. God our only Lawgiver.*
8. *The traditions of the Papacy contradictory to the Word of God.*
9. *Ceremonial traditions of the Papists. Their impiety. Substituted for the true worship of God.*

10. Through these ceremonies, the commandment of God made void.

11. Some of these ceremonies useless and childish. Their endless variety. Introduce Judaism.

12. Absurdity of these ceremonies borrowed from Judaism and Paganism.

13. Their intolerable number condemned by Augustine.

14. Injury thus done to the church. They cannot be excused.

15. Mislead the superstitious. Used as a kind of show and for incantation. Prostituted to gain.

16. All such traditions liable to similar objections.

17. Arguments in favor of traditions answered.

18. Answer continued.

19. Illustration taken from the simple administration of the Lord's Supper, under the Apostles, and the complicated ceremonies of the Papists.

20. Another illustration from the use of Holy Water.

21. An argument in favor of traditions founded on the decision of the Apostles and elders at Jerusalem. This decision explained.

22. Some things in the Papacy may be admitted for a time for the sake of weak brethren.

23. Observance of the Popish traditions inconsistent with Christian liberty, torturing to the conscience, and insulting to God.

24. All human inventions in religion displeasing to God. Reason. Confirmed by an example.

25. An argument founded on the examples of Samuel and Menorah. Answer.

26. Argument that Christ wished such burdens to be borne. Answer.

27. Third part of the chapter, treating of lawful Ecclesiastical arrangements. Their foundation in the general axiom, that all things be done decently and in order. Two extremes to be avoided.

28. All Ecclesiastical arrangements to be thus tested. What Paul means by things done decently and in order.

29. Nothing decent in the Popish ceremonies. Description of true decency. Examples of Christian decency and order.

30. No arrangement decent and orderly, unless founded on the authority of God, and derived from Scripture. Charity the best guide in these matters.

31. Constitutions thus framed not to be neglected or despised.

32. Cautions to be observed in regard to such constitutions.

1 The power of the church in enacting laws. This made a source of human traditions. Impiety of these traditions.

We come now to the second part of power, which, according to them, consists in the enacting of laws, from which source innumerable traditions have arisen, to be as many deadly snares to miserable souls. For they have not been more scrupulous than the Scribes and Pharisees in laying burdens on the shoulders of others, which they would not touch with their finger (Matthew 23:4; Luke 11:16). I have elsewhere shown (Book 3, chapter 4, section 4-7) how cruel murder they commit by their doctrine of auricular confession. The same violence is not apparent in other laws, but those, which seem most tolerable press tyrannically on the conscience. I say nothing as to the mode in which they adulterate the worship of God, and rob God himself, who is the only Lawgiver, of His right. The power we have now to consider is whether it is lawful for the Church to bind laws upon the conscience. In this discussion, civil order is not touched; but the only point considered is, how God may be duly worshipped according to the rule, which He has prescribed, and how our spiritual liberty, with reference to God, may remain unimpaired.

In ordinary language, the name of human traditions is given to all decrees concerning the worship of God, which men have issued without the authority of His Word. We contend against these, not against the sacred and useful constitutions of the Church, which tend to preserve discipline, or decency, or peace. Our aim is to curb the unlimited and barbarous empire usurped over souls by those who would be thought pastors of the church, but who are in fact its most cruel murderers. They say that the laws, which they enact, are spiritual, pertaining to the soul, and they affirm that they are necessary to eternal life.

But thus the Kingdom of Christ, as I lately observed, is invaded; thus the liberty, which He has given to the consciences of believers, is completely oppressed and overthrown. I say nothing as to the great impiety with which, to sanction the observance of their laws, they declare that from it they seek forgiveness of sins, righteousness and salvation, while they make the whole sum of religion and piety to consist in it. What I contend for is, that necessity ought not to be laid on consciences in matters in which Christ has made them free; and unless freed, cannot, as we have previously shown (Book 3, chapter 19), have peace with God. They must acknowledge Christ their deliverer, as their only king, and be ruled by the only law of liberty–namely, the sacred Word of the gospel–if they would retain the grace which they have once received in Christ: they must be subject to no bondage, be bound by no chains.

2 Many of the Papistical traditions not only difficult, but impossible to be observed.

These Solons, indeed, imagine that their constitutions are laws of liberty, a pleasant yoke, and a light burden: but who sees not that this is mere falsehood. They themselves, indeed, feel not the burden of their laws. Having cast off the fear of God, they securely and assiduously disregard their own laws as well as those, which are divine. Those, however, who feel any interest in their salvation, are far from thinking themselves free so long as they are entangled in these snares. We see how great caution Paul employed in this matter, not venturing to impose a fetter in anyone thing, and with good reason: he certainly foresaw how great a wound would be inflicted on the conscience if these things should be made necessary which the Lord had left free.

On the contrary, it is scarcely possible to count the constitutions, which these men have most grievously enforced, under the penalty of eternal death, and which they exact with the greatest rigor, as necessary to salvation. And while very many of them are most difficult of observance, the whole taken together are impossible; so great is the mass. How, then, possibly can those, on whom this mountain of difficulty lies, avoid being perplexed with extreme anxiety, and filled with terror? My intention here then is, to impugn constitutions of this description; constitutions enacted for the purpose of binding the conscience inwardly before God, and imposing religious duties, as if they enjoined things necessary to salvation.

3 That the question may be more conveniently explained, nature of conscience must be defined.

Many are greatly puzzled with this question, from not distinguishing, with sufficient care, between what is called the external forum and the forum of conscience (Book 3, chapter 19, section 15). Moreover, the difficulty is increased by the terms in which Paul enjoins obedience to magistrates, "not only for wrath, but also for conscience sake" (Romans 13:5); and from which it would follow, that civil laws also bind the conscience. But if this were so, nothing that we have said of spiritual government, in the last chapter, and are to say in this, would stand. To solve this difficulty, we must first understand what is meant by conscience. The definition must be derived from the etymology of the term. As when men, with the mind and intellect, apprehend the knowledge of things, they are thereby said to know, and hence the name of science or knowledge is used; so, when they have, in addition to this, a sense of the divine judgment, as a witness not permitting them to hide their sins, but bringing them as criminals before the tribunal of the judge, that sense is called conscience. For it occupies a kind of middle place between God and man, not suffering man to suppress what he knows in himself, but following him out until it bring him to conviction. This is what Paul means, when he says that conscience bears witness, "our thoughts the meanwhile accusing or else excusing each other" (Romans 2:15). Simple knowledge, therefore, might exist in a man shut up, and therefore the sense which sits men before the judgment seat of God has been placed over him as a sentinel, to observe and spy out all his secrets, that nothing may remain buried in darkness. Hence, the old proverb, Conscience is a thousand witnesses. For this reason, Peter also uses the "answer of a good conscience towards God" (1 Peter 3:21); for tranquility of mind, when, persuaded of the grace of Christ, we with boldness present ourselves before God. And the author of the Epistle to the Hebrews says, that we have "no more conscience of sins," that we are freed or acquitted, so that sin no longer accuses us. (See Hebrews 10:2.)

4 Definition of conscience explained. Examples in illustration of the definition.

Wherefore, as works have respect to men, so conscience bears reference to God; and hence a good conscience is nothing but inward integrity of heart. In this sense, Paul says, "the end of the commandment is charity out of a pure heart, and of a good conscience, and of faith unfeigned" (1 Timothy 1:5). He afterwards, in the same chapter, shows how widely it differs from intellect, saying, the, "some having put away" a good conscience, "concerning faith have made shipwreck." For by these words he intimates that it is a living inclination to worship God, a sincere desire to live piously and holily. Sometimes, indeed, it is extended to men also, as when Paul declares, "Herein do I exercise myself, to have always a conscience void of offense toward God, and toward men" (Acts 24:16). But this is said, because the benefits of a good conscience flow forth and reach even to men. Properly speaking, however, it respects God alone, as I have already said. Hence, a law may be said to bind the conscience when it simply binds a man without referring to men, or taking them into account. For example, God enjoins us not only to keep our mind chaste and pure from all lust, but prohibits every kind of obscenity in word, and all external lasciviousness. This law my conscience is bound to observe, though there were not another man in the world. Thus he who behaves intemperately not only sins by setting a bad example to his brethren, but stands convicted in his conscience before God. Another rule holds in the case of things, which are in themselves indifferent. For we ought to abstain when they give offense, but conscience is free. Thus Paul says of meat consecrated to idols, "If any man say unto you, This is offered in sacrifice unto idols, eat not for his sake that showed it, and for conscience sake;" "conscience, I say, not thine own, but of the other" (1 Corinthians 10:28, 29). A believer would sin, if, after being warned, he should still eat such kind of meat. But, however necessary abstinence may be in respect of a brother, as prescribed by the Lord, conscience ceases not to retain its liberty. We see how the law, while binding the external work, leaves the conscience free.

5 Paul's doctrine of submission to magistrates for conscience sake, gives no countenance to the Popish doctrine of the obligation of traditions.

Let us now return to human laws. If they are imposed for forming a religious obligation, as if the observance of them was in itself necessary, we say that the restraint thus laid on the conscience is unlawful. Our consciences have not to do with men but with God only. Hence, the common distinction between the earthly forum and the forum of conscience. When the whole world was enveloped in the thickest darkness of ignorance, it was still held (like a small ray of light which remained unextinguished) that conscience was superior to all human judgments. Although this, which was acknowledged in word, was afterwards violated in fact, yet God was pleased that there should even then exist an attestation to liberty, exempting the conscience from the tyranny of man. But we have not yet explained the difficulty, which arises from the words of Paul. For if we must obey princes not only from fear of punishment but for conscience sake, it seems to follow, that the laws of princes have dominion over the conscience. If this is true, the same thing must be affirmed of ecclesiastical laws. I answer, that the first thing to be done here is to distinguish between the genus and the species. For though individual laws do not reach the conscience, yet we are bound by the general command of God, which enjoins us to submit to magistrates. And this is the point on which Paul's discussion turns–viz. that magistrates are to be honored, because they are ordained of God. (See Romans 13:1.) Meanwhile, he does not at all teach that the laws enacted by them reach to the internal government of the soul, since he everywhere proclaims that the worship of God and the spiritual rule of living righteously are superior to all the decrees of men. Another thing also worthy of observation, and depending on what has been already said, is, that human laws, whether enacted by magistrates or by the Church, are necessary to be observed (I speak of such as are just and good), but do not therefore in themselves bind the conscience, because the whole necessity of observing them respects the general end, and consists not in the things commanded. Very different, however, is the case of those, which prescribe a new form of worshipping God, and introduce necessity into things that are free.

6 The question stated. A brief mode of deciding it.

Such, however, are what in the present day are called ecclesiastical constitutions by the Papacy, and are brought forward as part of the true and necessary worship of God. But as they are without number, so they form innumerable fetters to bind and ensnare the soul. Though, in expounding the law, we have adverted to this subject (see Book 3, chapter 4, section 6), yet as this is more properly the place for a full discussion of it, I will now study to give a summary of it as carefully as I can. I shall, however, omit the branch relating to the tyranny with which false bishops arrogate to themselves the right of teaching whatever they please, having already considered it as far as seemed necessary, but shall treat at length of the power which they claim of enacting laws. The pretext, then, on which our false bishops burden the conscience with new laws is, that the Lord has constituted them spiritual legislators, and given them the government of the Church. Hence, they maintain that everything which they order and prescribe must, of necessity, be observed by the Christian people, that he who violates their commands is guilty of a twofold disobedience, being a rebel both against God and the Church. Assuredly, if they were true bishops, I would give them some authority in this matter, not so much as they demand, but so much as is requisite for duly arranging the polity of the Church; but since they are anything but what they would be thought, they cannot possibly assume anything to themselves, however little, without being in excess. But as this also has been elsewhere shown, let us grant for the present, that whatever power true bishops possess justly belongs to them, still I deny that they have been set over believers as legislators to prescribe a rule of life at their own hands, or bind the people committed to them to their decrees. When I say this, I mean that they are not at all entitled to insist that whatever they devise without authority from the word of God shall be observed by the Church as matter of necessity. Since such power was unknown to the apostles, and was so often denied to the ministers of the Church by our Lord himself, I wonder how any have dared to usurp, and dare in the present day to defend it, without any precedent from the apostles, and against the manifest prohibition of God.

7 A perfect rule of life in the Law. God our only Lawgiver.

Everything relating to a perfect rule of life the Lord has so comprehended in His law, that He has left nothing for men to add to the summary there given. His object in doing this was, first, that since all rectitude of conduct consists in regulating all our actions by His will as a standard, He alone should be regarded as the master and guide of our life; and, secondly, that He might show that there is nothing which He more requires of us than obedience. For this reason James says, "He that speaketh evil of his brother, and judgeth his brother, speaketh evil of the law, and judgeth the law: There is one lawgiver, who is able to save and to destroy" (James 4:11, 12). We hear how God claims it as His own peculiar privilege to rule us by His laws. This had been said before by Isaiah, though somewhat obscurely, "The Lord is our judge, the Lord is our lawgiver, the Lord is our king; he will save us" (Isaiah 33:22). Both passages show that the power of life and death belongs to Him who has power over the soul. Nay, James clearly expresses this. This power no man may assume to himself. God, therefore, to whom the power of saving and destroying belongs, must be acknowledged as the only King of souls, or, as the words of Isaiah express it, He is our king and judge, and Lawgiver and Savior. So Peter, when he reminds pastors of their duty, exhorts them to feed the flock without lording it over the heritage (see 1 Peter 5:2), meaning by heritage the body of believers. If we duly consider that it is unlawful to transfer to man what God declares to belong only to himself, we shall see that this completely cuts off all the power claimed by those who would take it upon them to order anything in the Church without authority from the Word of God.

8 The traditions of the Papacy contradictory to the Word of God.

Moreover, since the whole question depends on this, that God being the only lawgiver, it is unlawful for men to assume that honor to themselves, it will be proper to keep in mind the two reasons for which God claims this solely for himself. The one reason is, that his will is to us the perfect rule of all righteousness and holiness, and that thus in the knowledge of it, we have a perfect rule of life. The other reason is that when the right and proper method of worshipping

Him is in question, He whom we ought to obey, and on whose will we ought to depend, alone has authority over our souls. When these two reasons are attended to, it will be easy to decide what human constitutions are contrary to the Word of the Lord. Of this description are all those which are devised as part of the true worship of God, and the observance of which is bound upon the conscience, as of necessary obligation. Let us remember then to weigh all human laws in this balance, if we would have a sure test, which will not allow us to go astray. The former reason is urged by Paul in the Epistle to the Colossians against the false apostles who attempted to lay new burdens on the churches. The second reason he more frequently employs in the Epistle to the Galatians in a similar case. In the Epistle to the Colossians, then, he maintains that the doctrine of the true worship of God is not to be sought from men, because the Lord has faithfully and fully taught us in what way He is to be worshipped. To demonstrate this, he says in the first chapter, that in the gospel is contained all wisdom, that the man of God may be made perfect in Christ. In the beginning of the second chapter, he says that all the treasures of wisdom and knowledge are hidden in Christ, and from this he concludes that believers should beware of being led away from the flock of Christ by vain philosophy, according to the constitutions of men. (See Colossians 2:10.) In the end of the chapter, he still more decisively condemns all fictitious modes of worship, which men themselves devise or receive from others, and all precepts they presume to deliver at their own hand concerning the worship of God. We hold, therefore, that all constitutions are impious in the observance of which the worship of God is pretended to be placed. The passages in the Galatians in which he insists that fetters are not to be bound on the conscience (which ought to be ruled by God alone), are sufficiently plain, especially Chapter 5. Therefore, let it suffice to refer to them.

9 Ceremonial traditions of the Papists. Their impiety. Substituted for the true worship of God.

But that the whole matter may be made plainer by examples, it will be proper, before we proceed, to apply the doctrine to our own times. The constitutions which they call ecclesiastical, and by which the Pope, with his adherents, burdens the church, we hold to be pernicious and impious, while our opponents defend them as sacred and salutary. Now there are two kinds of them, some relating to ceremonies and rites, and others more especially to discipline. Have we, then, any just cause for impugning both? Assuredly a more just cause than we could wish. First, do not their authors themselves distinctly declare that the very essence of the worship of God (so to speak) is contained in them? For what end do they bring forward their ceremonies but just that God may be worshipped by them? Nor is this done merely by error in the ignorant multitude, but with the approbation of those who hold the place of teachers. I am not now adverting to the gross abominations by which they have plotted the adulteration of all godliness, but they would not deem it to be so atrocious a crime to err in any minute tradition, did they not make the worship of God subordinate to their fictions. Since Paul then declares it intolerable that the legitimate worship of God should be subjected to the will of men, wherein do we err when we are unable to tolerate this in the present day? Especially when we are enjoined to worship God according to the elements of this world—a thing that Paul declares to be adverse to Christ. (See Colossians 2:20.) On the other hand, the mode in which they lay consciences under the strict necessity of observing whatever they enjoin is familiar. When we protest against this, we make common cause with Paul, who will on no account allow the consciences of believers to be brought under human bondage.

10 Through these ceremonies, the commandment of God made void.

Moreover, the worst of all is, that when once religion begins to be composed of such vain fictions, the perversion is immediately succeeded by the abominable depravity with which our Lord upbraids the Pharisees of making the commandment of God void through their traditions. (See Matthew 15:3.) I am unwilling to dispute with our present legislators in my own words; let them gain the victory if they can clear themselves from this accusation of Christ. But how can they do so, seeing they regard it as immeasurably more wicked to allow the year to pass without auricular confession, than to have spent it in the greatest iniquity: to have infected their tongue with a slight tasting of flesh on Friday, than to have daily polluted the whole body with whoredom: to have put their hand to honest labor on a day consecrated to some one or other of their saintlings, than to have constantly employed all their members in the greatest crimes: for a priest to be united to one in lawful wedlock, than to be engaged in a thousand adulteries: to have failed in performing a votive pilgrimage, than to have broken faith in every promise: not to have expended profusely on the monstrous, superfluous, and useless luxury of churches, than to have denied the poor in their greatest necessities: to have passed an idol without honor, than to have treated the whole human race with contumely: not to have muttered long unmeaning sentences at certain times, than never to have framed one proper prayer? What is meant by making the Word of God void by tradition, if this is not done when, recommending the ordinances of God only frigidly and perfunctorily, they nevertheless studiously and anxiously urge strict obedience to their own ordinances, as if the whole power of piety was contained in them; –when vindicating the transgression of the divine Law with trivial satisfactions, they visit the minutest violation of one of their decrees with no lighter punishment than imprisonment, exile, fire, or sword? –when neither severe nor inexorable against the despisers of God, they persecute to extremity, with implacable hatred, those who despise themselves, and so train all those whose simplicity they hold in thralldom, that they would sooner see the whole law of God subverted than one iota of what they call the precepts of the Church infringed. First, there is a grievous delinquency in this, that one condemns, judges, and casts off his neighbor for trivial matters–matters which, if the judgment of God is to decide, are free. But now, as if this were a small evil, those frivolous elements of this world, as Paul terms them in his Epistle to the Galatians (see Galatians 4:9), are deemed of more value than the heavenly oracles of God. He who is all but acquitted for adultery is judged in meat; and he to whom whoredom is permitted is forbidden to marry. This, forsooth, is all that is gained by that prevaricating obedience, which only turns away from God to the same extent that it inclines to men.

11 Some of these ceremonies are useless and childish. Their endless variety. Introduce Judaism.

There are other two grave vices, which we disapprove in these constitutions. First, They prescribe observances which are in a great measure useless, and are sometimes absurd; secondly, by the vast multitude of them, pious consciences are oppressed, and being carried back to a kind of Judaism, so cling to shadows that they cannot come to Christ. My allegation that they are useless and absurd will, I know, scarcely be credited by carnal wisdom, to which they are so pleasing, that the church seems to be altogether defaced when they are taken away. But this is just what Paul says, that they "have indeed a show of wisdom in will-worship, and humility, and neglecting of the body" (Colossians 2:23), a most salutary admonition, of which we ought never to lose sight. Human traditions, he says, deceive by an appearance of wisdom. Whence this show? Just that being framed by men, the human mind recognizes in them that which is its own, and embraces it when recognized more willingly than anything, however good, which is less suitable to its vanity. Secondly, That they seem to be a fit training to humility, while they keep the minds of men groveling on the ground under their yoke; hence they have another recommendation. Lastly, because they seem to have a tendency to curb the will of the flesh, and to subdue it by the rigor of abstinence, they seem to be wisely devised. But what does Paul say to all this? Does he pluck off those masks lest the simple should be deluded by a false pretext? Deeming it sufficient for their refutation to say that they were devices of men, he passes all these things without refutation, as things of no value. Nay, because he knew that all fictitious worship is condemned in the Church, and is the more suspected by believers, the more pleasing it is to the human mind–because he knew that this false show of outward humility differs so widely from true humility that it can be easily discerned; –finally, because he knew that this tutelage is valued at no more than bodily exercise, he wished the very things which commended human traditions to the ignorant to be regarded by believers as the refutation of them.

12 Absurdity of these ceremonies borrowed from Judaism and Paganism.

Thus, in the present day, not only the unlearned vulgar, but everyone in proportion as he is inflated by worldly wisdom, is wonderfully captivated by the glare of ceremonies, while hypocrites and silly women think that nothing can be imagined better or more beautiful. But those who thoroughly examine them, and weigh them more truly according to the rule of godliness, in regard to the value of all such ceremonies, know, first, that they are trifles of no utility; secondly, that they are impostures which delude the eyes of the spectators with empty show. I am speaking of those ceremonies which the Roman masters will have to be great mysteries, while we know by experience that they are mere mockery. Nor is it strange that their authors have gone the length of deluding themselves and others by mere frivolities, because they have taken their model partly from the dreams of the Gentiles, partly, like apes, have rashly imitated the ancient rites of the Mosaic Law, with which we have nothing more to do than with the sacrifices of animals and other similar things. Assuredly, were there no other proof, no sane man would expect any good from such an ill-assorted farrago. And the case itself plainly demonstrates that very many ceremonies have no other use than to stupefy the people rather than teach them. In like manner, to those new canons, which pervert discipline rather than preserve it, hypocrites attach much importance; but a closer examination will show that they are nothing but the shadowy and evanescent phantom of discipline.

13 Their intolerable number condemned by Augustine.

To come to the second fault, who sees not that ceremonies, by being heaped one upon another, have grown to such a multitude, that it is impossible to tolerate them in the Christian Church? Hence, it is that in ceremonies a strange mixture of Judaism is apparent, while other observances prove a deadly snare to pious minds. Augustine complained that in his time, while the precepts of God were neglected, prejudice everywhere prevailed to such an extent, that he who touched the ground barefoot during his octave was censured more severely than he who buried his wits in wine. He complained that the church, which God in mercy wished to be free, was so oppressed that the condition of the Jews was tolerable. Had that holy man fallen on our day, in what terms would he have deplored the bondage now existing? For the number is tenfold greater, and each iota is exacted a hundred times more rigidly than then. This is the usual course; when once those perverse legislators have usurped authority, they make no end of their commands and prohibitions until they reach the extreme of harshness. This Paul elegantly intimated by these words —"If ye be dead with Christ from the rudiments of the world, why, as though living in the world, are ye subject to ordinances? Touch not, taste not, handle not" (Colossians 2:20, 21). For while the word translated into Greek signifies both to eat and to touch, it is doubtless taken in the former sense, that there may not be a superfluous repetition. Here, therefore, he most admirably describes the progress of false apostles. The way in which superstition begins is this: they forbid not only to eat, but even to chew gently; after they have obtained this, they forbid even to taste. This also being yielded to them, they deem it unlawful to touch even with the finger.

14 Injury thus done to the church. They cannot be excused.

We justly condemn this tyranny in human constitutions, in consequence of which miserable consciences are strangely tormented by innumerable edicts, and the excessive exaction of them. Of the canons relating to discipline, we have spoken elsewhere (earlier here in section 12; also chapter 12). What shall I say of ceremonies, the effect of which has been, that we have almost buried Christ, and returned to Jewish figures? "Our Lord Christ bound together the society of His new people by sacraments, very few in number, most excellent in signification, most easy of observance." How widely different this simplicity is from the multitude and variety of rites in which we see the church entangled in the present day, cannot well be told. I am aware of the artifice by which some acute men excuse this perverseness. They say that there are numbers among us equally rude as any among the Israelitish people, and that for their sakes has been introduced this tutelage, which though the stronger may do without, they, however, ought not to neglect, because it is useful to weak brethren. I answer, that we are aware of what is due to the weakness of brethren, but, on the other hand, we object that the method of consulting for the weak is not to bury them under a great mass of ceremonies. It was not without cause that God distinguished between us and His ancient people, by training them like children by means of signs and figures, and training us more simply, without so much external show. Paul's words are, "The heir, as long as he is a child, is under tutors and governors" (Galatians 4:1, 2). This was the state of the Jews under the law. But we are like adults who, being freed from tutory and curatory, have no need of puerile rudiments. God certainly foresaw what kind of people He was to have in His Church and in what way they were to be governed. Now, He distinguished between the Jews and us in the way that has been described. Therefore, it is a foolish method of consulting for the ignorant to set up the Judaism, which Christ has abrogated. This dissimilitude between the ancient and His new people Christ expressed when He said to the woman of Samaria, "The hour cometh, and now is, when the true worshippers shall worship the Father in spirit and in truth" (John 4:23). This, no doubt, had always been done; but the new worshippers differ from the old in this, that while under Moses the spiritual worship of God was shadowed, and entangled by many ceremonies, these have been abolished, and worship is now more simple. Those, accordingly, who confound this distinction, subvert the order instituted and sanctioned by Christ.

Therefore, you will ask, Are no ceremonies to be given to the more ignorant, as a help to their ignorance? I do not say so; for I think that help of this description is very useful to them. All I contend for is the employment of such a measure as may illustrate, not obscure Christ. Hence, a few ceremonies have been divinely appointed, and these by no means laborious, in order that they may evince a present Christ. To the Jews a greater number were given, that they might be images of an absent Christ. In saying He was absent, I mean not in power, but in the mode of expression. Therefore, to secure due moderation, it is necessary to retain that fewness in number, facility in observance, and significance of meaning which consists in clearness. Of what use is it to say that this is not done? The fact is obvious to every eye.

15 Mislead the superstitious. Used as a kind of show and for incantation. Prostituted to gain.

I here say nothing of the pernicious opinions with which the minds of men are imbued, as that these are sacrifices by which propitiation is made to God, by which sins are expiated, by which righteousness and salvation are procured. It will be maintained that things good in themselves are not vitiated by errors of this description, since in acts expressly enjoined by God similar errors may be committed. There is nothing, however, more unbecoming than the fact, that works devised by the will of man are held in such estimation as to be thought worthy of eternal life. The works commanded by God receive a reward, because the Lawgiver himself accepts of them as marks of obedience. They do not, therefore, take their value from their own dignity or their own merit, but because God sets this high value on our obedience toward Him. I am here speaking of that perfection of works, which is commanded by God, but is not performed by men. The works of the law are accepted merely by the free kindness of God, because the obedience is infirm and defective. But as we are not here considering how far works avail without Christ, let us omit that question. I again repeat, as properly belonging to the present subject, that whatever commendation works have, they have it in respect of obedience, which alone God regards, as He testifies by the prophet, "I spake not unto your fathers, nor commanded them in the day that I brought them out of the land of Egypt, concerning burnt offerings or sacrifices: but this thing commanded I them, saying, Obey my voice" (Jeremiah 7:22). Of fictitious works he elsewhere speaks, "Wherefore do you spend your money for that which is not bread?" (Isaiah 55:2; 29:13). Again, "In vain do they worship me, teaching for doctrines the commandments of men" (Matthew 15:9). They cannot, therefore, excuse themselves from the charge of allowing wretched people to seek in these external frivolities a righteousness, which they may present to God, and by which they may stand before the celestial tribunal. Besides, it is not a fault deservedly stigmatized, that they exhibit unmeaning ceremonies as a kind of stage play or magical incantation? For it is certain that all ceremonies are corrupt and noxious which do not direct men to Christ. But the ceremonies in use in the Papacy are separated from doctrine, so that they confine men to signs altogether devoid of meaning. Lastly (as the belly is an ingenious contriver), it is clear, that many of their ceremonies have been invented by greedy priests as lures for catching money. But whatever be their origin, they are all so prostituted to filthy lucre, that a great part of them must be rescinded if we would prevent a profane and sacrilegious traffic from being carried on in the church.

16 All such traditions liable to similar objections.

Although I seem not to be delivering the general doctrine concerning human constitutions, but adapting my discourse wholly to our own age, yet nothing has been said which may not be useful to all ages. For whenever men begin the superstitious practice of worshipping God with their own fictions, all the laws enacted for this purpose forthwith degenerate into those gross abuses. For the curse which God denounces—viz. to strike those who worship Him with the doctrines of men with stupor and blindness—is not confined to anyone age, but applies to all ages. The uniform result of this blindness is that there is no kind of absurdity escaped by those who, despising the many admonitions of God, spontaneously entangle themselves in these deadly fetters. But if, without any regard to circumstances, you would simply know the character belonging at all times to those human traditions which ought to be repudiated by the Church, and condemned by all the godly, the definition which we formerly gave is clear and certain–viz. That they include all the laws enacted by men, without authority from the Word of God, for the purpose either of prescribing the mode of divine worship, or laying a religious obligation on the conscience, as enjoining things necessary to salvation. If to one or both of these are added the other evils of obscuring the clearness of the gospel by their multitude, of giving no edification, of being useless and frivolous occupations rather than true exercises of piety, of being set up for sordid ends and filthy lucre, of being difficult of observance, and contaminated by pernicious superstitions, we shall have the means of detecting the quantity of mischief which they occasion.

17 Arguments in favor of traditions answered.

I understand what their answer will be–viz. that these traditions are not from themselves, but from God. For to prevent the church from erring, it is guided by the Holy Spirit, whose authority resides in them. This being conceded, it at the same time follows, that their traditions are revelations by the Holy Spirit, and cannot be disregarded without impiety and contempt of God. And that they may not seem to have attempted anything without high authority, they will have it to be believed that a great part of their observances is derived from the apostles. For they contend, that in one instance they have a sufficient proof of what the apostles did in other cases. The instance is, when the apostles assembled in council, announced to all the Gentiles as the opinion of the council, that they should "abstain from pollution of idols, and from fornication, and from things strangled, and from blood" (Acts 15:20, 29). We have already explained, how, in order to extol themselves, they falsely assume the name of *church* (Chapter 8, section 10-13). If, in regard to the present cause, we remove all masks and glosses (a thing, indeed, which ought to be our first care, and also is our highest interest), and consider what kind of Church Christ wishes to have, that we may form and adapt ourselves to it as a standard, it will readily appear that it is not a property of the church to disregard the limits of the word of God, and wanton and luxuriate in enacting new laws. Does not the law, which was once given to the Church, endure forever? "What things soever I command you, observe to do it: thou shalt not add thereto, nor diminish from it" (Deuteronomy 12:32). And in another place, "Add thou not unto his words, lest he reprove thee, and thou be found a liar" (Proverbs 30:6).

Since they cannot deny that this was said to the Church, what else do they proclaim but their contumacy, when, notwithstanding of such prohibitions, they profess to add to the doctrine of God, and dare to intermingle their own with it? Far be it from us to assent to the falsehood by which they offer such insult to the Church. Let us understand that the name of Church is falsely pretended wherever men contend for that rash human license, which cannot confine itself within the boundaries prescribed by the Word of God, but petulantly breaks out, and has recourse to its own inventions.

In the above passage, there is nothing involved, nothing obscure, nothing ambiguous; the whole Church is forbidden to add to, or take from the Word of God, in relation to His worship and salutary precepts. But that was said merely of the Law, which was succeeded by the Prophets and the whole gospel dispensation! This I admit, but I at the same time add, that these are fulfillments of the Law, rather than additions or diminutions. Now, if the Lord does not permit anything to be added to, or taken from the ministry of Moses, though wrapped up, if I may so speak, in many folds of obscurity, until He furnishes a clearer doctrine by His servants the Prophets, and at last by His beloved Son, why should we not suppose that we are much more strictly prohibited from making any addition to the Law, the Prophets, the Psalms, and the Gospel? The Lord cannot forget himself, and it is long since He declared that nothing is so offensive to Him as to be worshipped by human inventions.

Hence, those celebrated declarations of the Prophets, which ought continually to ring in our ears, "I spake not unto your fathers, nor commanded them in the day that I brought them out of the land of Egypt, concerning burnt offerings or sacrifices; but this thing commanded I them, saying, Obey my voice, and I will be your God, and ye shall be my people: and walk ye in all the ways that I have commanded you" (Jeremiah 7:22, 23). "I earnestly protested unto your fathers, in the day that I brought them out of the land of Egypt, even unto this day, rising early and protesting, saying, Obey my voice" (Jeremiah 11:7). There are other passages of the same kind, but the most noted of all is, "Hath the Lord as great delight in burnt-offerings and sacrifices, as in obeying the voice of the Lord? Behold, to obey is better than sacrifice, and to hearken than the fat of rams. For rebellion is as the sin of witchcraft, and stubbornness is as iniquity and idolatry" (1 Samuel 15: 22, 23). It is easy, therefore, to prove, that whenever human inventions in this respect are defended by the authority of the church, they cannot be vindicated from the charge of impiety, and that the name of *church* is falsely assumed.

18 Answer continued.

For this reason we freely inveigh against that tyranny of human traditions which is haughtily obtruded upon us in the name of the church. Nor do we hold the Church in derision (as our adversaries, for the purpose of producing obloquy, unjustly accuse us), but we attribute to her the praise of obedience, than which she acknowledges to be none greater. They themselves rather are emphatically injurious to the Church, in representing her as contumacious to her Lord, when they pretend that she goes further than the Word of God allows, to say nothing of their combined impudence and malice, in continually vociferating about the power of the Church, while they meanwhile disguise both the command which the Lord has given her, and the obedience which she owes to the command. But if our wish is, as it ought to be, to agree with the Church, it is of more consequence to consider and remember the injunction that the Lord has given both to us and to the Church, to obey Him with one consent. For there can be no doubt that we shall best agree with the Church when we show ourselves obedient to the Lord in all things. But to ascribe the origin of the traditions by which the Church has hitherto been oppressed to the apostles is mere imposition, since the whole substance of the doctrine of the apostles is, that conscience must not be burdened with new observances, nor the worship of God contaminated by our inventions. Then, if any credit is to be given to ancient histories and records, what they attribute to the apostles was not only unknown to them, but was never heard by them. Nor let them pretend that most of their decrees, though not delivered in writing, were received by use and practice, being things which they could not understand while Christ was in the world, but which they learned after His ascension, by the revelation of the Holy Spirit. The meaning of that passage has been explained elsewhere (Chapter 8, section 14).

In regard to the present question, they make themselves truly ridiculous, seeing it is manifest that all those mysteries which so long were undiscovered by the apostles, are partly Jewish or Gentile observances, the former of which had anciently been promulgated among the Jews, and the latter among all the Gentiles, partly absurd gesticulations and empty ceremonies, which stupid priests, who have neither sense nor letters, can duly perform; nay, which children and mountebanks perform so appropriately, that it seems impossible to have fitter priests for such sacrifices. If there were no records, men of sense would judge from the very nature of the case, that such a mass of rites and observances did not rush into the church all at once, but crept in gradually. For though the venerable bishops, who were nearest in time to the apostles, introduced some things pertaining to order and discipline, those who came after them, and those after them again, had not enough of consideration, while they had too much curiosity and cupidity, he who came last always vying in foolish emulation with his predecessors, so as not to be surpassed in the invention of novelties. And because there was a danger that these inventions, from which they anticipated praise from posterity, might soon become obsolete, they were much more rigorous in insisting on the observance of them. This false zeal has produced a great part of the rites, which these men represent as apostolical. This history attests.

19 Illustration taken from the simple administration of the Lord's Supper, under the Apostles, and the complicated ceremonies of the Papists.

And not to become prolix, by giving a catalogue of all, we shall be contented with one example. Under the apostles, there was great simplicity in administering the Lord's Supper. Their immediate successors made some additions to the dignity of the ordinance, which are not to be disapproved. Afterwards came foolish imitators, who, by always patching various fragments together, have left us those sacerdotal vestments, which we see in the mass, those altar ornaments, those gesticulations, and whole farrago of useless observances. But they object, that in old time the persuasion was, that those things, which were done with the consent of the whole Church, proceeded from the apostles. Of this, they quote Augustine as a witness. I will give the explanation in the very words of Augustine. "Those things which are observed over the whole world we may understand to have been appointed either by the apostles themselves, or by general councils, whose authority in the Church is most beneficial, as the annual solemn celebration of our Lord's passion, resurrection, and ascension to Heaven, and of the descent of the Holy Spirit, and any other occurrence observed by the whole Church wherever it exists." In giving so few examples, who sees not that he meant to refer the observances then in use to authors deserving of faith and reverence;–observances few and sober, by which it was expedient that the order of the Church should be maintained? How widely does this differ from the view of our Roman masters, who insist that there is no paltry ceremony among them, which is not apostolical?

20 Another illustration from the use of Holy Water.

Not to be tedious, I will give only one example. Should anyone ask them where they get their holy water, they will at once answer,–from the apostles. As if I did not know who the Roman bishop is, to whom history ascribes the invention, and who, if he had admitted the apostles to his council, assuredly never would have adulterated baptism by a foreign and unseasonable symbol; although it does not seem probable to me that the origin of that consecration is so ancient as is there recorded. For when Augustine says that certain churches in his day rejected the formal imitation of Christ in the washing of feet, lest that rite should seem to pertain to baptism, he intimates that there was then no kind of washing which had any resemblance to baptism. Be this as it may, I will never admit that the apostolic spirit gave rise to that daily sign by which baptism, while brought back to remembrance, is in a manner repeated. I attach no importance to the fact, that Augustine elsewhere ascribes other things to the apostles. For as he has nothing better than conjecture, it is not sufficient for forming a judgment concerning a matter of so much moment. Lastly, though we should grant that the things which he mentions are derived from the apostolic age, there is a great difference between instituting some exercise of piety, which believers may use with a free conscience, or may abstain from if they think the observance not to be useful, and enacting a law which brings the conscience into bondage. Now, indeed, whoever is the author from whom they are derived, since we see the great abuses to which they have led, there is nothing to prevent us from abrogating them without any imputation on him, since he never recommended them in such a way as to lay us under a fixed and immovable obligation to observe them.

21 An argument in favor of traditions founded on the decision of the Apostles and elders at Jerusalem. This decision explained.

It gives them no great help, in defending their tyranny, to pretend the example of the apostles. The apostles and elders of the primitive Church, according to them, sanctioned a decree without any authority from Christ, by which they commanded all the Gentiles to abstain from meat offered to idols, from things strangled, and from blood. (See Acts 15:20.) If this was lawful for them, why should not their successors be allowed to imitate the example as often as occasion requires? Would that they would always imitate them both in this and other matters! For I am ready to prove, on valid grounds, that here nothing new has been instituted or decreed by the apostles. For when Peter declares in that council, that God is tempted if a yoke is laid on the necks of the disciples, he overthrows his own argument if he afterwards allows a yoke to be imposed on them. But it is imposed if the apostles, on their own authority, prohibit the Gentiles from touching meat offered to idols, things strangled, and blood. The difficulty remains, that they seem nevertheless to prohibit them. But this will easily be removed by attending more closely to the meaning of their decree. The first thing in order, and the chief thing in importance, is, that the Gentiles were to retain their liberty, which was not to be disturbed, and that they were not to be annoyed with the observances of the Law. As yet, the decree is all in our favor. The reservation, which immediately follows, is not a new law enacted by the apostles, but a divine and eternal command of God against the violation of charity, which does not detract one iota from that liberty. It only reminds the Gentiles how they are to accommodate themselves to their brother, and to not abuse their liberty for an occasion of offense. Let the second head, therefore, be, that the Gentiles are to use an innoxious liberty, giving no offense to the brethren. Still, however, they prescribe some certain thing–viz. they show and point out, as was expedient at the time, what those things are by which they may give offense to their brethren, that they may avoid them; but they add no novelty of their own to the eternal law of God, which forbids the offense of brethren.

22 Some things in the Papacy may be admitted for a time for the sake of weak brethren.

As in the case where faithful pastors, presiding over churches not yet well constituted, should intimate to their flocks not to eat flesh on Friday until the weak among whom they live become strong, or to work on a holiday, or any other similar things, although, when superstition is laid aside, these matters are in themselves indifferent, still, where offense is given to the brethren, they cannot be done without sin; so there are times when believers cannot set this example before weak brethren without most grievously wounding their consciences. Who but a slanderer would say that a new law is enacted by those who, it is evident, only guard against scandals, which their Master has distinctly forbidden? But nothing more than this can be said of the apostles, who had no other end in view, in removing grounds of offense, than to enforce the divine Law, which prohibits offense. It is as if they had said, The Lord hath commanded you not to hurt a weak brother; but meats offered to idols, things strangled, and blood, ye cannot eat, without offending weak brethren; we, therefore, require you, in the Word of the Lord, not to eat with offense. And to prove that the apostles had respect to this, the best witness is Paul, who writes as follows, undoubtedly according to the sentiments of the council: "As concerning, therefore, the eating of those things which are offered in sacrifice unto idols, we know that an idol is nothing in the world, and that there is none other God but one. Howbeit, there is not in every man that knowledge: for some with conscience of the idol unto this hour eat it as a thing offered unto an idol; and their conscience being weak is defiled. But take heed lest by any means this liberty of yours become a stumbling block to them that are weak" (1 Corinthians 8:4-9). Not anyone who duly considers these things will be imposed upon by the gloss, which these men employ when, as a cloak to their tyranny, they pretend that the apostles had begun by their decree to infringe the liberty of the Church. But that they may be unable to escape without confessing the accuracy of this explanation, let them tell me by what authority they have dared to abrogate this very decree. It was, it seems, because there was no longer any danger of those offenses and dissensions which the apostles wished to obviate, and they knew that the law was to be judged by its end. Seeing, therefore, the law was passed with a view to charity, there is nothing prescribed in it except as far as required by charity. In confessing that the transgression of this law is nothing but a violation of charity, do they not at the same time acknowledge that it was not some adventitious supplement to the law of God, but a genuine and simple adaptation of it to the times and manners for which it was destined?

23 Observance of the Popish traditions inconsistent with Christian liberty, torturing to the conscience, and insulting to God.

But though such laws are hundreds of times unjust and injurious to us, still they contend that they are to be heard without exception; for the thing asked of us is not to consent to errors, but only to submit to the strict commands of those set over us–commands which we are not at liberty to decline. (See 1 Peter 2:18.) But here also the Lord comes to the succor of His Word, and frees us from this bondage by asserting the liberty which He has purchased for us by His sacred Blood, and the benefit of which He has more than once attested by His Word. For the thing required of us is not (as they maliciously pretend) to endure some grievous oppression in our body, but to be tortured in our consciences, and brought into bondage: in other words, robbed of the benefits of Christ's Blood. Let us omit this, however, as if it were irrelevant to the point. Do we think it a small matter that the Lord is deprived of His Kingdom, which He so strictly claims for himself? Now, He is deprived of it as often as He is worshipped with laws of human invention, since His will is to be sole legislator of His worship. And lest anyone should consider this as of small moment, let us hear how the Lord himself estimates it. "Forasmuch as this people draw near me with their mouth, and with their lips do honor me, but have removed their heart far from me, and their fear toward me is taught by the precept of men: therefore, behold, I will proceed to do a marvelous work among the people, even a marvelous work and a wonder; for the wisdom of their wise men shall perish, and the understanding of their prudent men shall be hid" (Isaiah 29:13-14). And in another place, "But in vain do they worship me, teaching for doctrines the commandments of men" (Matthew 15:9).

And, indeed, when the children of Israel polluted themselves with manifold idolatries, the cause of the whole evil is ascribed to that impure mixture caused by their disregarding the commandments of God, and framing new modes of worship. Accordingly, sacred history relates that the new inhabitants who had been brought by the king of Assyria from Babylon to inhabit Samaria were torn and destroyed by wild beasts, because they knew not the judgment or statutes of the God of that land. (See 2 Kings 17:24-34.) Though they had done nothing wrong in ceremonies, still their empty show could not have been approved by God. Meanwhile He ceased not to punish them for the violation of His worship by the introduction of fictions alien from His Word.

Hence, it is afterwards said that, terrified by the punishment, they adopted the rites prescribed in the Law; but as they did not yet worship God purely, it is twice repeated that they feared Him and feared not. Hence, we infer that part of the reverence due to Him consists in worshipping Him simply in the way that He commands, without mingling any inventions of our own. And, accordingly, pious princes are repeatedly praised (see 2 Kings 22:1, etc.) for acting according to all His precepts, and not declining either to the right hand or the left. I go further: although there be no open manifestation of impiety in fictitious worship, it is strictly condemned by the Spirit, inasmuch as it is a departure from the command of God. The altar of Ahaz, a model of which had been brought from Damascus (see 2 Kings 16:10), might have seemed to give additional ornament to the temple. It was his intention there to offer sacrifices to God only, and to do it more splendidly than at the first ancient altar. Yet, we see how the Spirit detests the audacious attempt, for no other reasons but because human inventions are in the worship of God impure corruptions. And the more clearly the will of God has been manifested to us, the less excusable is our petulance in attempting anything. Accordingly, the guilt of Manasses is aggravated by the circumstance of having erected a new altar at Jerusalem, of which the Lord said, "In Jerusalem will I put my name" (2 Kings 22:3, 4), because the authority of God was thereby professedly rejected.

24 All human inventions in religion displeasing to God. Reason. Confirmed by an example.

Many wonder why God threatens so sternly that He will bring astonishment on the people who worship Him with the commandments of men, and declares that it is in vain to worship Him with the commandments of men. But if they would consider what it is in the matter of religion, that is, of heavenly wisdom, to depend on God alone, they would, at the same time, see that it is not on slight grounds the Lord abominates perverse service of this description, which is offered Him at the caprice of the human will. For although there is some show of humility in the obedience of those who obey such laws in worshipping God, yet they are by no means humble, since they prescribe to Him the very laws which they observe. This is the reason that Paul would have us so carefully to beware of being deceived by the traditions of men, and what is called "voluntary worship," worship devised by men without sanction from God. Thus it is, indeed: we must be fools in regard to our own wisdom and all the wisdom of men, in order that we may allow Him alone to be wise. This course is by no means observed by those who seek to approve themselves to Him by paltry observances of man's devising, and against His will obtrude upon Him a prevaricating obedience that is yielded to men. This is the course, which has been pursued for several ages, is within our own recollection, and is still pursued in the present day in those places in which the power of the creature is more than that of the Creator, where religion (if religion it deserves to be called) is polluted with more numerous and absurd superstitions than ever Paganism was. For what could human sense produce but things carnal and fatuous, and savoring of their authors?

25 An argument founded on the examples of Samuel and Menoah. Answer.

When the patrons of superstition cloak them by pretending that Samuel sacrificed in Ramath, and though he did so contrary to the Law, yet pleased God (see 1 Samuel 7:17), it is easy to answer that he did not set up a second altar in opposition to the only true one. Rather, as the place for the Ark of the Covenant had not been fixed, he sacrificed in the town where he dwelt, as being the most convenient. It certainly never was the intention of the holy prophet to make any innovation in sacred things, about which the Lord had so strictly forbidden addition or diminution. The case of Manoah I consider to have been extraordinary and special. He, though a private man, offered sacrifice to God, and did it not without approbation, because he did it not from a rash movement of his own mind, but by divine inspiration. (See Judges 13:19.) How much God abominates all the devices of men in His worship, we have a striking proof in the case of one not inferior to Manoah–viz. Gideon, whose ephod brought ruin not only on himself and his family, but on the whole people. (See Judges 8:27.) In short, every adventitious invention, by which men desire to worship God, is nothing else than a pollution of true holiness.

26 Argument that Christ wished such burdens to be borne. Answer.

Why then, they ask, did Christ say that the intolerable burdens, imposed by Scribes and Pharisees, were to be borne? (See Matthew 23:23.) Nay, rather, why did He say in another place that we were to beware of the leaven of the Pharisees? (See Matthew 16:6.) Meaning by leaven, as the Evangelist Matthew explains it, whatever of human doctrine is mingled with the pure Word of God. What can be plainer than that we are enjoined to shun and beware of their whole doctrine? From this it is most certain, that in the other passage our Lord never meant that the consciences of His people were to be harassed by the mere traditions of the Pharisees. And the words themselves, unless when wrested, have no such meaning. Our Lord, indeed, beginning to inveigh against the manners of the Pharisees, first instructs His hearers simply, that though they saw nothing to follow in the lives of the Pharisees, they should not, however, cease to do what they verbally taught when they sat in the seat of Moses, that is, to expound the Law. All He meant, therefore, was to guard the common people against being led by the bad example of their teachers to despise doctrine. But as some are not at all moved by reason, and always require authority, I will quote a passage from Augustine, in which the very same thing is expressed. "The Lord's sheepfold has persons set over it, of whom some are faithful, others hirelings. Those who are faithful are true shepherds; learn, however, that hirelings also are necessary. For many in the Church, pursuing temporal advantages, preach Christ, and the voice of Christ is heard by them, and the sheep follow not a hireling, but the shepherd by means of a hireling. Learn that hirelings were pointed out by the Lord himself. The Scribes and Pharisees, says he, sit in Moses' seat;

what they tell you, do, but what they do, do ye not. What is this but to say, Hear the voice of the shepherd by means of hirelings? Sitting in the chair, they teach the Law of God, and therefore God teaches by them; but if they choose to teach their own, hear not, do not."

27 Third part of the chapter, treating of lawful Ecclesiastical arrangements. Their foundation in the general axiom, that all things be done decently and in order. Two extremes to be avoided.

But as very many ignorant persons, on hearing that it is impious to bind the conscience, and vain to worship God with human traditions, apply one blot to all the laws by which the order of the Church is established, it will be proper to obviate their error. Here, indeed, the danger of mistake is great: for it is not easy to see at first sight how widely the two things differ. But I will, in a few words, make the matter so clear, that no one will be imposed upon by the resemblance. First, then, let us understand that if in every human society some kind of government is necessary to insure the common peace and maintain concord, if in transacting business some form must always be observed, which public decency, and hence humanity itself, require us not to disregard, this ought especially to be observed in churches, which are best sustained by a constitution in all respects well ordered, and without which concord can have no existence. Wherefore, if we would provide for the safety of the Church, we must always carefully attend to Paul's injunction, that all things be done decently and in order. (See 1 Corinthians 14:40.) But seeing there is such diversity in the manners of men, such variety in their minds, such repugnance in their judgments and dispositions, no policy is sufficiently firm unless fortified by certain laws, nor can any rite be observed without a fixed form. So far, therefore, are we from condemning the laws, which conduce to this, that we hold that the removal of them would unnerve the Church, deface and dissipate it entirely. For Paul's injunction, that all things be done decently and in order, cannot be observed unless order and decency be secured by the addition of ordinances, as a kind of bonds. In these ordinances, however, we must always attend to the exception, that they must not be thought necessary to salvation, nor lay the conscience under a religious obligation; they must not be compared to the worship of God, nor substituted for piety.

28 All Ecclesiastical arrangements to be thus tested. What Paul means by things done decently and in order.

We have, therefore, a most excellent and sure mark to distinguish between those impious constitutions (by which, as we have said, true religion is overthrown, and conscience subverted) and the legitimate observances of the Church, if we remember that one of two things, or both together, are always intended–viz. that in the sacred assembly of the faithful, all things may be done decently, and with becoming dignity, and that human society may be maintained in order by certain bonds of moderation and humanity. For when a law is understood to have been made for the sake of public decency, there is no room for the superstition into which those fall who measure the worship of God by human inventions. On the other hand, when a law is known to be intended for common use, that false idea of its obligation and necessity, which gives great alarm to the conscience, when traditions are deemed necessary to salvation, is overthrown; since nothing here is sought but the maintenance of charity by a common office. But it may be proper to explain more clearly what is meant by the decency that Paul commends, and also what is comprehended under order. And the object of decency is, partly that by the use of rites, which produce reverence in sacred matters, we may be excited to piety, and partly that the modesty and gravity which ought to be seen in all honorable actions may here especially be conspicuous. In order, the first thing is, that those who preside know the law and rule of right government, while those who are governed be accustomed to obedience and right discipline. The second thing is, that by duly arranging the state of the Church, provision be made for peace and tranquility.

29 Nothing decent in the Popish ceremonies. Description of true decency. Examples of Christian decency and order.

We shall not, therefore, give the name of decency to that which only ministers an empty pleasure: such, for example, as is seen in that theatrical display which the Papists exhibit in their public service, where nothing appears but a mask of useless splendor, and luxury without any fruit. But we give the name of decency to that which, suited to the reverence of sacred mysteries, forms a fit exercise for piety, or at least gives an ornament adapted to the action, and is not without fruit, but reminds believers of the great modesty, seriousness, and reverence, with which sacred things ought to be treated. Moreover, ceremonies, in order to be exercises of piety, must lead us directly to Christ. In like manner, we shall not make order consist in that nugatory pomp which gives nothing but evanescent splendor, but in that arrangement which removes all confusion, barbarism, contumacy, all turbulence and dissension. Of the former class we have examples (see 1 Corinthians 11:5, 21), where Paul says, that profane entertainments must not be intermingled with the sacred Supper of the Lord; that women must not appear in public uncovered. And there are many other things which we have in daily practice, such as praying on our knees, and with our head uncovered, administering the sacraments of the Lord, not sordidly, but with some degree of dignity; employing some degree of solemnity in the burial of our dead, and so forth. In the other class are the hours set apart for public prayer, sermon, and solemn services; during sermon, quiet and silence, fixed places, singing of hymns, days set apart for the celebration of the Lord's Supper, the prohibition of Paul against women teaching in the Church, and such like. To the same list especially may be referred those things which preserve discipline, as catechizing, ecclesiastical censures, excommunication, fasting, etc. Thus all ecclesiastical constitutions, which we admit to be sacred and salutary, may be reduced to two heads, the one relating to rites and ceremonies, the other to discipline and peace.

30 No arrangement decent and orderly, unless founded on the authority of God, and derived from Scripture. Charity the best guide in these matters.

But as there is here a danger, on the one hand, lest false bishops should thence derive a pretext for their impious and tyrannical laws, and, on the other, lest some, too apt to take alarm, should, from fear of the above evils, leave no place for laws, however holy, it may here be proper to declare, that I approve of those human constitutions only which are founded on the authority of God, and derived from Scripture, and are therefore altogether divine. Let us take, for example, the bending of the knee that is made in public prayer. It is asked, whether this is a human tradition, which anyone is at liberty to repudiate or neglect? I say that it is human, and that at the same time it is divine. It is of God, inasmuch as it is a part of that decency, the care and observance of which is recommended by the apostle; and it is of men, inasmuch as it specially determines what was indicated in general, rather than expounded.

From this one example, we may judge what is to be thought of the whole class—viz. that the whole sum of righteousness, and all the parts of divine worship, and everything necessary to salvation, the Lord has faithfully comprehended, and clearly unfolded, in His sacred oracles, so that in them He alone is the only Master to be heard. But as in external discipline and ceremonies, He has not been pleased to prescribe every particular that we ought to observe. (He foresaw that this depended on the nature of the times, and that one form would not suit all ages.) In them, we must have recourse to the general rules that He has given, employing them to test whatever the necessity of the Church may require to be enjoined for order and decency. Lastly, as He has not delivered any express command, because things of this nature are not necessary to salvation, and for the edification of the Church, should be accommodated to the varying circumstances of each age and nation, it will be proper, as the interest of the Church may require, to change and abrogate the old, as well as to introduce new forms. I confess, indeed, that we are not to innovate rashly or incessantly, or for trivial causes. Charity is the best judge of what tends to hurt or to edify: if we allow her to be guide, all things will be safe.

31 Constitutions thus framed not to be neglected or despised.

Things which have been appointed according to this rule, it is the duty of the Christian people to observe with a free conscience indeed, and without superstition, but also with a pious and ready inclination to obey. They are not to hold them in contempt, nor pass them by with careless indifference, far less openly to violate them in pride and contumacy. You will ask, What liberty of conscience will there be in such cautious observances? Nay, this liberty will admirably appear when we shall hold that these are not fixed and perpetual obligations to which we are astricted, but external rudiments for human infirmity, which, though we do not all need, we, however, all use, because we are bound to cherish mutual charity towards each other. This we may recognize in the examples given above. What? Is religion placed in a woman's bonnet, so that it is unlawful for her to go out with her head uncovered? Is her silence fixed by a decree that cannot be violated without the greatest wickedness? Is there any mystery in bending the knee, or in burying a dead body, which cannot be omitted without a crime? By no means. For should a woman require to make such haste in assisting a neighbor that she has not time to cover her head, she sins not in running out with her head uncovered. And there are some occasions on which it is not less seasonable for her to speak than on others to be silent. Nothing, moreover, forbids him who, from disease, cannot bend his knees, to pray standing. In fine, it is better to bury a dead man quickly, than from want of grave clothes, or the absence of those who should attend the funeral, to wait until it rot away unburied. Nevertheless, in those matters the custom and institutions of the country, in short, humanity and the rules of modesty itself, declare what is to be done or avoided. Here, if any error is committed through imprudence or forgetfulness, no crime is perpetrated; but if this is done from contempt, such contumacy must be disapproved.

In like manner, it is of no consequence what the days and hours are, what the nature of the edifices, and what psalms are sung on each day. But it is proper that there should be certain days and stated hours, and a place fit for receiving all, if any regard is had to the preservation of peace. For what a seedbed of quarrels will confusion in such matters be, if everyone is allowed at pleasure to alter what pertains to common order. Not all will be satisfied with the same course if matters, placed on debatable ground, are left to the determination of individuals. But if anyone here becomes clamorous, and would be wiser than he ought, let him consider how he will approve his moroseness to the Lord. Paul's answer ought to satisfy us, "If any man seem to be contentious, we have no such custom, neither the churches of God."

32 Cautions to be observed in regard to such constitutions.

Moreover, we must use the utmost diligence to prevent any error from creeping in which may either taint or sully this pure use. In this we shall succeed, if whatever observances we use are manifestly useful and very few in number; especially if to this is added the teaching of a faithful pastor, which may prevent access to erroneous opinions. The effect of this procedure is that in all these matters, each retains his freedom, and yet at the same time voluntarily subjects it to a kind of necessity, as far as the decency of which we have spoken or charity demands. Next, that in the observance of these things we may not fall into any superstition, nor rigidly require too much from others, let us not imagine that the worship of God is improved by a multitude of ceremonies: let not church despise church because of a difference in external discipline. Lastly, instead of here laying down any perpetual law for ourselves, let us refer the whole end and use of observances to the edification of the Church, at whose request let us without offense allow not only something to be changed, but even observances which were formerly in use to be inverted. For the present age is a proof that the nature of times allows that certain rites, not otherwise impious or unbecoming, may be abrogated according to circumstances. Such was the ignorance and blindness of former times; with such erroneous ideas and pertinacious zeal did churches formerly cling to ceremonies, that they can scarcely be purified from monstrous superstitions without the removal of many ceremonies which were formerly established, not without cause, and which in themselves are not chargeable with any impiety.

Chapter 11

OF THE JURISDICTION OF THE CHURCH, AND THE ABUSES OF IT, AS EXEMPLIFIED IN THE PAPACY.

This chapter may be conveniently comprehended under two heads—I. Ecclesiastical jurisdiction, its necessity, origin, description, and essential parts—viz. the sacred ministry of the Word, and discipline of excommunication, of which the aim, use, and abuse are explained, sections 1-8. II. Refutation of the arguments advanced by Papists in defense of the tyranny of Pontiffs, the right of both swords, imperial pomp and dignity, foreign jurisdiction, and immunity from civil jurisdiction, sections 9-16.

Sections

1. The power of the Church in regard to jurisdiction. The necessity, origin, and nature of this jurisdiction. The power of the keys to be considered in two points of view. The first view expounded.

2. Second view expounded. How the Church binds and looses in the way of discipline. Abuse of the keys in the Papacy.

3. The discipline of excommunication of perpetual endurance. Distinction between civil and ecclesiastical power.

4. The perpetual endurance of the discipline of excommunication confirmed. Duly ordered under the Emperors and Christian magistrates.

5. The aim and use of ecclesiastical jurisdiction in the primitive Church. Spiritual power was kept entirely distinct from the power of the sword.

6. Spiritual power was not administered by one individual, but by a lawful consistory. Gradual change. First, the clergy alone interfered in the judicial proceedings of the Church. The bishop afterwards appropriated them to himself.

7. The bishops afterwards transferred the rights thus appropriated to their officials, and converted spiritual jurisdiction into a profane tribunal.

8. Recapitulation. The Papal power confuted. Christ wished to debar the ministers of the Word from civil rule and worldly power.

9. Objections of the Papists. A. By this external splendor, the glory of Christ is displayed. B. It does not interfere with the duties of their calling. Both objections answered.

10. The commencement and gradual progress of the Papistical tyranny. Causes, A. Curiosity; B. Ambition; C. Violence; D. Hypocrisy; E. Impiety.

11. Last cause, the mystery of iniquity, and the Satanic fury of Antichrist usurping worldly dominion. The Pope claims both swords.

12. The pretended donation of Constantine. Its futility exposed.

13. When, and by what means, the Roman Pontiffs attained to imperial dignity. Hildebrand its founder.

14. By what acts they seized on Rome and other territories. Disgraceful rapacity.

15. Claim of immunity from civil jurisdiction. Contrast between this pretended immunity and the moderation of the early bishops.

16. What end the early bishops aimed at in steadfastly resisting civil encroachment.

1 The power of the Church in regard to jurisdiction. The necessity, origin, and nature of this jurisdiction. The power of the keys to be considered in two points of view. The first view expounded.

It remains to consider the third, and, indeed, when matters are well arranged, the principal part of ecclesiastical power, which, as we have said, consists in jurisdiction. Now, the whole jurisdiction of the Church relates to discipline, of which we are shortly to treat. For as no city or village can exist without a magistrate and government, so the Church of God, as I have already taught, but am again obliged to repeat, needs a kind of spiritual government. This is altogether distinct from civil government, and is so far from impeding or impairing it, that it rather does much to aid and promote it. Therefore, this power of jurisdiction is, in one word, nothing but the order provided for the preservation of spiritual polity. To this end, there were established in the Church from the first, tribunals, which might take cognizance of morals, animadvert on vices, and exercise the office of the keys. This order is mentioned by Paul in the First Epistle to the Corinthians under the name of governments (see 1 Corinthians 12:28): in like manner, in the Epistle to the Romans, when he says, "He that ruleth with diligence" (Romans 12:8). For he is not addressing magistrates, none of whom were then Christians, but those who were joined with pastors in the spiritual government of the Church. In the Epistle to Timothy, also, he mentions two kinds of presbyters, some who labor in the Word, and others who do not perform the office of preaching, but rule well. (See 1 Timothy 5:17.)

By this latter class, there is no doubt that he means those who were appointed to the inspection of manners, and the whole use of the keys. For the power of which we speak wholly depends on the keys, which Christ bestowed on the Church in the eighteenth chapter of Matthew, where he orders, that those who despise private admonition should be sharply rebuked in public, and if they persist in their contumacy, be expelled from the society of believers.

Moreover, those admonitions and corrections cannot be made without investigation, and hence the necessity of some judicial procedure and order. Wherefore, if we would not make void the promise of the keys, and abolish altogether excommunication, solemn admonitions, and everything of that description, we must, of necessity, give some jurisdiction to the Church.

Let the reader observe that we are not here treating of the general authority of doctrine, as in Matthew 21 and John 20, but maintaining that the right of the Sanhedrim is transferred to the fold of Christ. Until that time, the power of government had belonged to the Jews. This Christ establishes in His Church, in as far as it was a pure institution, and with a heavy sanction. Thus, it behooved to be, since the judgment of a poor and despised Church might otherwise be spurned by rash and haughty men.

And lest it occasion any difficulty to the reader, that Christ in the same words makes a considerable difference between the two things; it will here be proper to explain. There are two passages, which speak of binding and loosing. The one is Matthew 16, where Christ, after promising that He will give the keys of the kingdom of Heaven to Peter, immediately adds, "Whatsoever thou shalt bind on Earth shall be bound in Heaven; and whatsoever thou shalt loose on Earth shall be loosed in Heaven" (Matthew 16:19). These words have the very same meaning as those in the Gospel of John, where, being about to send forth the disciples to preach, after breathing on them, He says, "Whose soever sins ye remit, they are remitted unto them; and whose soever sins ye retain, they are retained" (John 20:23).

I will give an interpretation, not subtle, not forced, not wrested, but genuine, natural, and obvious. This command concerning remitting and retaining sins, and that promise made to Peter concerning binding and loosing, ought to be referred to nothing but the ministry of the Word. When the Lord committed it to the apostles, He, at the same time, provided them with this power of binding and loosing. For what is the sum of the gospel, but just that all being the slaves of sin and death are loosed and set free by the redemption which is in Christ Jesus, while those who do not receive and acknowledge Christ as a deliverer and redeemer are condemned and doomed to eternal chains? When the Lord delivered this message to His apostles, to be carried by them into all nations in order to prove that it was His own message and proceeded from Him, He honored it with this distinguished testimony, and that as an admirable confirmation both to the apostles themselves and to all those to whom it was to come. It was of importance that the apostles should have a constant and complete assurance of their preaching, which they were not only to exercise with infinite labor, anxiety, molestation, and peril, but ultimately to seal with their blood. That they might know that it was not vain or void, but full of power and efficacy

It was of importance, I say, that amidst all their anxieties, dangers, and difficulties, they might feel persuaded that they were doing the work of God; that though the whole world withstood and opposed them, they might know that God was for them; that not having Christ the author of their doctrine bodily present on the Earth, they might understand that He was in Heaven to confirm the truth of the doctrine which He had delivered to them.

On the other hand, it was necessary that their hearers should be most certainly assured that the doctrine of the gospel was not the word of the apostles, but of God himself–not a voice rising from the Earth, but descending from Heaven. For such things as the forgiveness of sins, the promise of eternal life, and message of salvation, cannot be in the power of man. Christ therefore testified, that in the preaching of the gospel the apostles only acted ministerially; that it was He who, by their mouths as organs, spoke and promised all; that, therefore, the forgiveness of sins which they announced was the true promise of God; the condemnation which they pronounced, the certain judgment of God. This attestation was given to all ages, and remains firm, rendering all certain and secure, that the Word of the gospel, by whomsoever it may be preached, is the very Word of God, promulgated at the supreme tribunal, written in the Book of Life, ratified firm and fixed in Heaven. We now understand that the power of the keys is simply the preaching of the gospel in those places, and as far as men are concerned, it is not so much power as ministry. Properly speaking, Christ did not give this power to men but to His Word, of which He made men the ministers.

2 Second view expounded. How the Church binds and looses in the way of discipline. Abuse of the keys in the Papacy.

The other passage, in which binding and loosing are mentioned, is in the eighteenth chapter of Matthew, where Christ says, "If he shall neglect to hear them, tell it unto the Church: but if he neglect to hear the Church, let him be unto thee as an heathen man and a publican. Verily I say unto you, Whatsoever ye shall bind on earth shall be bound in heaven; and whatsoever ye shall loose on earth shall be loosed in heaven" (Matthew 18:17 18). This passage is not altogether similar to the former, but is to be understood somewhat differently. But in saying that they are different, I do not mean that there is not much affinity between them. First, they are similar in this, that they are both general statements, that there is always the same power of binding and loosing (namely, by the Word of God), the same command, the same promise. They differ in this: the former passage relates specially to the preaching, which the ministers of the Word perform, and the latter relates to the discipline of excommunication, which has been committed to the Church. Now, the Church binds him whom she excommunicates, not by plunging him into eternal ruin and despair, but condemning his life and manners, and admonishing him, that, unless he repents, he is condemned. She looses him whom she receives into communion, because she makes him a partaker of the unity, which she has in Christ Jesus. Let no one, therefore, contumaciously despise the judgment of the Church, or account it a small matter that he is condemned by the suffrages of the faithful. The Lord testifies that such judgment of the faithful is nothing else than the promulgation of His own sentence, and that what they do on Earth is ratified in Heaven. For they have the Word of God, by which they condemn the perverse; they have the Word by which they take back the penitent into favor. Now, they cannot err nor disagree with the judgment of God, because they judge only according to the law of God, which is not an uncertain or worldly opinion, but the holy will of God, an oracle of Heaven. On these two passages, which I think I have briefly, as well as familiarly and truly expounded, these madmen, without any discrimination, as they are borne along by their spirit of giddiness, attempt to found at one time confession, at another excommunication, at another jurisdiction, at another the right of making laws, at another indulgences. The former passage they adduce for rearing up the primacy of the Roman See. So well known are the keys to those who have thought proper to fit them with locks and doors, that you would say their whole life had been spent in the mechanic art.

3 The discipline of excommunication of perpetual endurance. Distinction between civil and ecclesiastical power.

Some, in imagining that all these things were temporary, as magistrates were still strangers to our profession of religion, are led astray, by not observing the distinction and dissimilarity between ecclesiastical and civil power. For the Church has not the right of the sword to punish or restrain, has no power to coerce, neither prison nor other punishments, which the magistrate is wont to inflict. Then the object in view is not to punish the sinner against his will, but to obtain a profession of penitence by voluntary chastisement. The two things, therefore, are widely different, because neither does the Church assume anything to herself which is proper to the magistrate, nor is the magistrate competent to what is done by the Church. This will be made clearer by an example. Does anyone get intoxicated? In a well-ordered city, his punishment will be imprisonment. Has he committed whoredom? The punishment will be similar, or rather more severe. Thus, satisfaction will be given to the laws, the magistrates, and the external tribunal. But the consequence will be, that the offender will give no signs of repentance, but will rather fret and murmur. Will the Church not here interfere? Such persons cannot be admitted to the Lord's Supper without doing injury to Christ and His sacred institution. Reason demands that he, who, by a bad example, gives offense to the Church, shall remove the offense, which he has caused by a formal declaration of repentance. The reason adduced by those who take a contrary view is frigid. Christ, they say, gave this office to the Church when there were no magistrates to execute it. But it often happens that the magistrate is negligent, nay, sometimes himself requires to be chastised, as was the case with the Emperor Theodosius. Moreover, the same thing may be said regarding the whole ministry of the Word. Now, therefore, according to that view, let pastors cease to censure manifest iniquities, let them cease to chide, accuse, and rebuke. For there are Christian magistrates who ought to correct these things by the laws and the sword. But as the magistrate ought to purge the Church of offenses by corporal punishment and coercion, so the minister ought, in his turn, to assist the magistrate in diminishing the number of offenders. Thus, they ought to combine their efforts, the one being not an impediment but a help to the other.

4 The perpetual endurance of the discipline of excommunication confirmed. Duly ordered under the Emperors and Christian magistrates.

And indeed, on attending more closely to the Words of Christ, it will readily appear that the state and order of the Church there described is perpetual, not temporary. For it would be incongruous that those who refuse to obey our admonitions should be transferred to the magistrate—a course, however, which would be necessary if he were to succeed to the place of the Church. Why should the promise, "Verily I say unto you, What thing soever ye shall bind on Earth," be limited to one, or to a few years? Moreover, Christ has here made no new enactment, but followed the custom always observed in the Church of His ancient people, thereby intimating, that the Church cannot dispense with the spiritual jurisdiction, which existed from the beginning. This has been confirmed by the consent of all times. For when emperors and magistrates began to assume the Christian name, spiritual jurisdiction was not forthwith abolished, but was only so arranged as not in any respect to impair civil jurisdiction, or be confounded with it. And justly. For the magistrate, if he is pious, will have no wish to exempt himself from the common subjection of the children of God, not the least part of which is to subject himself to the Church, judging according to the Word of God; so far is it from being his duty to abolish that judgment. For, as Ambrose says, "What more honorable title can an emperor have than to be called a son of the Church? A good emperor is within the Church, not above the Church." Those, therefore, who to adorn the magistrate strip the Church of this power, not only corrupt the sentiment of Christ by a false interpretation, but pass no light condemnation on the many holy bishops who have existed since the days of the apostles, for having on a false pretext usurped the honor and office of the civil magistrate.

5 The aim and use of ecclesiastical jurisdiction in the primitive Church. Spiritual power was kept entirely distinct from the power of the sword.

But, on the other hand, it will be proper to see what was anciently the true use of ecclesiastical discipline, and how great the abuses which crept in, that we may know what of ancient practice is to be abolished, and what restored, if we would, after overthrowing the kingdom of Antichrist, again set up the true Kingdom of Christ. First, the object in view is to prevent the occurrence of scandals, and when they arise, to remove them. In the use two things are to be considered: first, that this spiritual power be altogether distinct from the power of the sword; secondly, that it be not administered at the will of one individual, but by a lawful consistory. (See 1 Corinthians 5:4.) Both were observed in the purer times of the Church. For holy bishops did not exercise their power by fine, imprisonment, or other civil penalties, but as became them, employed the Word of God only. For the severest punishment of the Church, and her last thunderbolt, is excommunication, which is not used unless in necessity. This, moreover, requires neither violence nor physical force, but is contented with the might of the Word of God. In short, the jurisdiction of the ancient Church was nothing else than (if I may so speak) a practical declaration of what Paul teaches concerning the spiritual power of pastors. "The weapons of our warfare are not carnal, but mighty through God to the pulling down of strongholds; casting down imaginations, and every high thing that exalteth itself against the knowledge of God, and bringing into captivity every thought to the obedience of Christ; and having in a readiness to revenge all disobedience" (2 Corinthians 10:4-6). As this is done by the preaching of doctrine, so in order that doctrine may not be held in derision, those who profess to be of the household of faith ought to be judged according to the doctrine that is taught. Now this cannot be done without connecting with the office of the ministry a right of summoning those who are to be privately admonished or sharply rebuked, a right, moreover, of keeping back from the communion of the Lord's Supper, those who cannot be admitted without profaning this high ordinance. Hence, when Paul elsewhere asks, "What have I to do to judge them also that are without?" (1 Corinthians 5:12), he makes the members of the Church subject to censures for the correction of their vices, and intimates the existence of tribunals from which no believer is exempted.

6 Spiritual power was not administered by one individual, but by a lawful consistory. Gradual change. First, the clergy alone interfered in the judicial proceedings of the Church. The bishop afterwards appropriated them to himself.

This power, as we have already stated, did not belong to an individual who could exercise it as he pleased, but belonged to the consistory of elders, which was in the Church what a council is in a city. Cyprian, when mentioning those by whom it was exercised in his time, usually associates the whole clergy with the bishop. In another place, he shows that though the clergy presided, the people, at the same time, were not excluded from cognizance, for he thus writes: "From the commencement of my bishopric, I determined to do nothing without the advice of the clergy, nothing without the consent of the people." But the common and usual method of exercising this jurisdiction was by the council of presbyters, of whom, as I have said, there were two classes. Some were for teaching; others were only censors of manners. This institution gradually degenerated from its primitive form, so that, in the time of Ambrose, the clergy alone had cognizance of ecclesiastical causes. Of this he complains in the following terms: "The ancient synagogue, and afterwards the Church, had elders, without whose advice nothing was done: this has grown obsolete, by whose fault I know not, unless it be by the sloth, or rather the pride, of teachers, who would have it seem that they only are somewhat" (Ambrose citing 1 Timothy 5). We see how indignant this holy man was because the better state was in some degree impaired, and yet the order, which then existed, was at least tolerable. What, then, had he seen those shapeless ruins, which exhibit no trace of the ancient edifice? How would he have lamented? First, contrary to what was right and lawful; the bishop appropriated to himself what was given to the whole Church. For this is just as if the consul had expelled the senate, and usurped the whole empire. For as he is superior in rank to the others, so the authority of the consistory is greater than that of one individual. It was, therefore, a gross iniquity, when one man, transferring the common power to himself, paved the way for tyrannical license, robbed the Church of what was its own, suppressed and discarded the consistory ordained by the Spirit of Christ.

7 The bishops afterwards transferred the rights thus appropriated to their officials, and converted spiritual jurisdiction into a profane tribunal.

But as evil always produces evil, the bishops, disdaining this jurisdiction as a thing unworthy of their care, devolved it on others. Hence, the appointment of officials to supply their place. I am not now speaking of the character of this class of persons; all I say is that they differ in no respect from civil judges. And yet, they call it spiritual jurisdiction, though all the litigation relates to worldly affairs. Were there no other evil in this, how can they presume to call a litigious forum a church court? But there are admonitions; there is excommunication. God is mocked in this way. Does some poor man owe a sum of money? He is summoned. If he appears, he is found liable. When found liable, if he does not pay, he is admonished. After the second admonition, the next step is excommunication. If he appears not, he is admonished to appear; if he delays, he is admonished, and by-and-by excommunicated. I ask, is there any resemblance whatever between this and the institution of Christ, or ancient custom or ecclesiastical procedure? But there, too, vices are censured. Whoredom, lasciviousness, drunkenness, and similar iniquities, they not only tolerate, but by a kind of tacit approbation encourage and confirm, and that not among the people only, but also among the clergy. Out of many, they summon a few, either that they may not seem to wink too strongly, or that they may mulct them in money. I say nothing of the plunder, rapine, peculation, and sacrilege, which are there committed. I say nothing of the kind of persons who are for the most part appointed to the office. It is enough, and more than enough, that when the Romanists boast of their spiritual jurisdiction, we are ready to show that nothing is more contrary to the procedure instituted by Christ, that it has no more resemblance to ancient practice than darkness has to light.

8 Recapitulation. The Papal power confuted. Christ wished to debar the ministers of the Word from civil rule and worldly power.

Although we have not said all that might here be adduced, and even what has been said is only briefly glanced, I trust enough has been said to leave no man in doubt that the spiritual power on which the Pope plumes himself, with all his adherents, is impious contradiction of the Word of God, and unjust tyranny against His people. Under the name of spiritual power, I include both their audacity in framing new doctrines, by which they led the miserable people away from the genuine purity of the Word of God, the iniquitous traditions by which they ensnared them, and the pseudo-ecclesiastical jurisdiction that they exercise by suffragans and officials. For if we allow Christ to reign amongst us, the whole of that domination cannot but immediately tumble and fall. The right of the sword, which they also claim for themselves, not being exercised against consciences, does not fall to be considered in this place. Here, however, it is worth while to observe, that they are always like themselves, there being nothing which they less resemble than that which they would be thought to be–viz. pastors of the Church. I speak not of the vices of particular men, but of the common wickedness, and, consequently, the pestiferous nature of the whole order, which is thought to be mutilated if not distinguished by wealth and haughty titles. If in this matter we seek the authority of Christ, there can be no doubt that He intended to debar the ministers of His Word from civil domination and worldly power when He said, "The princes of the Gentiles exercise dominion over them, and they that are great exercise authority upon them. But it shall not be so among you" (Matthew 20:25, 26). For He intimates not only that the office of pastor is distinct from the office of prince, but that the things differ so widely that they cannot be united in the same individual. Moses indeed held both (Exodus 18:16); but, first, this was the effect of a rare miracle; and, secondly, it was temporary, until matters should be better arranged. For when a certain form is prescribed by the Lord, the civil government is left to Moses, and he is ordered to resign the priesthood to his brother. And justly, for it is more than nature can do, for one man to bear both burdens. This has in all ages been carefully observed in the Church. Never did any bishop, so long as any true appearance of a church remained, think of usurping the right of the sword: so that, in the age of Ambrose, it was a common proverb, that emperors longed more for the priesthood than priests for imperial power. For the expression, which he afterwards adds, was fixed in all minds, Palaces belong to the emperor, churches to the priest.

9 Objections of the Papists. A. By this external splendor, the glory of Christ is displayed. B. It does not interfere with the duties of their calling. Both objections answered.

But after a method was devised by which bishops might hold the title, honor, and wealth of their office without burden and solicitude, that they might be left altogether idle, the right of the sword was given them, or rather, they themselves usurped it. With what pretext will they defend this effrontery? Was it the part of bishops to entangle themselves with the cognizance of causes and the administration of states and provinces, and embrace occupations so very alien to them—of bishops, who require so much time and labor in their own office, that though they devote themselves to it diligently and entirely, without distraction from other avocations, they are scarcely sufficient? But such is their perverseness, that they hesitate not to boast that in this way the dignity of Christ's Kingdom is duly maintained, and they, at the same time, are not withdrawn from their own vocation. In regard to the former allegation, if it is a comely ornament of the sacred office, that those holding it be so elevated as to become formidable to the greatest monarchs, they have ground to expostulate with Christ, who in this respect has grievously curtailed their honor. For what, according to their view, can be more insulting than these words, "The kings of the Gentiles exercise authority over them"? "But ye shall not be so" (Luke 22:25, 26). And yet, He imposes no harder law on His servants than He had previously laid on himself. "Who," says He, "made me a judge or divider over you?" (Luke 12:14) We see that He unreservedly refuses the office of judging; and this He would not have done if the thing had been in accordance with His office. To the subordination to which the Lord thus reduced himself, will His servants not submit? The other point I wish they would prove by experience as easily as they allege it. But as it seemed to the apostles not good to leave the Word of God and serve tables, so these men are thereby forced to admit, though they are unwilling to be taught, that it is not possible for the same person to be a good bishop and a good prince. For if those who, in respect of the largeness of the gifts with which they were endued, were able for much more numerous and weighty cares than any who have come after them, confessed that they could not serve the ministry of the Word and of tables, without giving way under the burden, how are these, who are no men at all when compared with the apostles, possibly to surpass them a hundred times in diligence? The very attempt is most impudent and audacious presumption. Still we see the thing done; with what success is plain. The result could not but be that they have deserted their own functions, and removed to another camp.

10 The commencement and gradual progress of the Papistical tyranny. Causes, A. Curiosity; B. Ambition; C. Violence; D. Hypocrisy; E. Impiety.

There can be no doubt that this great progress has been made from slender beginnings. They could not reach so far at one step, but at one time by craft and wily art, secretly raised themselves before anyone foresaw what was to happen; at another time, when occasion offered, by means of threats and terror, extorted some increase of power from princes; at another time, when they saw princes disposed to give liberally, they abused their foolish and inconsiderate facility. The godly in ancient times, when any dispute arose, in order to escape the necessity of a lawsuit, left the decision to the bishop, because they had no doubt of his integrity. The ancient bishops were often greatly dissatisfied at being entangled in such matters, as Augustine somewhere declares; but lest the parties should rush to some contentious tribunal, unwillingly submitted to the annoyance. These voluntary decisions, which altogether differed from forensic strife, these men have converted into ordinary jurisdiction. As cities and districts. When for some time pressed with various difficulties, betook themselves to the patronage of the bishops, and threw themselves on their protection, these men have, by a strange artifice, out of patrons made themselves masters. That they have seized a good part by the violence of faction cannot be denied. The princes, again, who spontaneously conferred jurisdiction on bishops, were induced to it by various causes. Though their indulgence had some appearance of piety, they did not by this preposterous liberality consult in the best manner for the interests of the Church, whose ancient and true discipline they thus corrupted, nay, to tell the truth, completely abolished. Those bishops, who abuse the goodness of princes to their own advantage, gave more than sufficient proof by this one specimen of their conduct, that they were not at all true bishops. Had they had one spark of the apostolic spirit, they would doubtless have answered in the words of Paul, "The weapons of our warfare are not carnal," but spiritual (2 Corinthians 10:4). But hurried away by blind cupidity, they lost themselves, and posterity, and the Church.

11 Last cause, the mystery of iniquity, and the Satanic fury of Antichrist usurping worldly dominion. The Pope claims both swords.

At length the Roman Pontiff, not content with moderate districts, laid hands first on kingdoms, and thereafter on empire. And that he may on some pretext or other retain possession, secured by mere robbery, he boasts at one time that he holds it by divine right, at another, he pretends a donation from Constantine, at another, some different title. First, I answer with Bernard, "Be it that on some ground or other he can claim it, it is not by apostolic right. For Peter could not give what he had not, but what he had he gave to his successors–viz. care of the churches. But when our Lord and Master says that He was not appointed a judge between two, the servant and disciple ought not to think it unbecoming not to be judge of all." Bernard is spearing of civil judgments, for he adds, "Your power then is in sins, not in rights of property, since for the former and not the latter you received the keys of the Kingdom of Heaven. Which of the two seems to you the higher dignity, the forgiving of sins or the dividing of lands? There is no comparison. These low earthly things have for their judges the kings and princes of the Earth. Why do you invade the territories of others?" etc. He addresses Pope Eugenius, "You are made superior for what? Not to domineer, I presume. Let us therefore remember, however highly we think of ourselves, that a ministry is laid upon us, not a dominion given to us. Learn that you have need of a slender rod, not of a scepter, to do the work of a prophet." Again, "It is plain that the apostles are prohibited to exercise dominion. Go you, therefore, and dare to usurp for yourself, either apostleship with dominion, or dominion with apostleship." Immediately after he says, "The apostolic form is this; dominion is interdicted, ministry is enjoined." Though Bernard speaks thus, and so speaks as to make it manifest to all that he speaks truth, nay, though without a word the thing itself is manifest, the Roman Pontiff was not ashamed at the Council of Arles to decree that the supreme right of both swords belonged to him of divine right.

12 The pretended donation of Constantine. Its futility exposed.

As far as pertains to the donation of Constantine, those who are moderately versant in the history of the time have no need of being told, that the claim is not only fabulous but also absurd. But to say nothing of history, Gregory alone is a fit and most complete witness to this effect. For wherever he speaks of the emperor, he calls him His Most Serene Lord, and himself his unworthy servant. Again, in another passage he says, "Let not our Lord in respect of worldly power be too soon offended with priests, but with excellent consideration, on account of him whose servants they are, let him while ruling them also pay them due reverence." We see how in a common subjection he desires to be accounted one of the people. For he there pleads not another's but his own cause. Again, "I trust in Almighty God that He will give long life to pious rulers, and place us under your hand according to His mercy." I have not adduced these things here from any intention thoroughly to discuss the question of Constantine's donation, but only to show my readers by the way, how childishly the Romanists tell lies when they attempt to claim an earthly empire for their Pontiff. The more vile the impudence of Augustine Steuchus, who, in so desperate a cause, presumed to lend his labor and his tongue to the Roman Pontiff. Valla, as was easy for a man of learning and acuteness to do, had completely refuted this fable. And yet, as he was little versant in ecclesiastical affairs, he had not said all that was relevant to the subject. Steuchus breaks in, and scatters his worthless quibbles, trying to bury the clear light. And certainly, he pleads the cause of his master not less frigidly than some wit might, under pretence of defending the same view, support that of Valla. But the cause is a worthy one, which the Pope may well hire such patrons to defend; equally worthy are the hired ravers whom the hope of gain may deceive, as was the case with Eugubinus.

13 When, and by what means, the Roman Pontiffs attained to imperial dignity. Hildebrand its founder.

Should anyone ask at what period this fictitious empire began to emerge, five hundred years have not yet elapsed since the Roman Pontiffs were under subjection to the emperors, and no pontiff was elected without the emperor's authority. An occasion of innovating on this order was given to Gregory VII by Henry IV, a giddy and rash man, of no prudence, great audacity, and a dissolute life. When he had the whole bishoprics of Germany in his court partly for sale, and partly exposed to plunder, Hildebrand, who had been provoked by him, seized the plausible pretext for asserting his claim. As his cause seemed good and pious, it was viewed with great favor, while Henry was generally hated by the princes because of the insolence of his government. At length Hildebrand, who took the name of Gregory VII, an impure and wicked man, betrayed his sinister intentions. On this, he was deserted by many who had joined him in his conspiracy. He gained this much, however, that his successors were not only able to shake off the yoke with impunity, but also to bring the emperors into subjection to them. Moreover, many of the subsequent emperors were more like Henry than Julius Caesar. These it was not difficult to overcome while they sat at home sluggish and secure, instead of vigorously exerting themselves, as was most necessary, by all legitimate means to repress the cupidity of the pontiffs. We see what color there is for the grand donation of Constantine, by which the Pope pretends that the western empire was given to him.

14 By what acts they seized on Rome and other territories Disgraceful rapacity.

Meanwhile, the pontiff ceased not, either by fraud, or by perfidy, or by arms, to invade the dominions of others. Rome itself, which was then free, they, about a hundred and thirty years ago, reduced under their power. At length they obtained the dominion, which they now possess, and to retain or increase which, now for two hundred years (they had begun before they usurped the dominion of the city) they have so troubled the Christian world that they have almost destroyed it. Formerly, in the time of Gregory, the guardians of ecclesiastical property seized upon lands, which they considered to belong to the Church, and, after the manner of the exchequer, affixed their seals in attestation of their claim, Gregory having assembled a council of bishops, and bitterly inveighed against that profane custom, asked whether they would not anathematize the churchman who, of his own accord, attempted to seize some possession by the inscription of a title, and in like manner, the bishop who should order it to be done, or not punish it when done without his order. All pronounced the anathema. If it is a crime deserving of anathema for a churchman to claim a property by the inscription of a title–then, now that for two hundred years, the pontiffs meditate nothing but war and bloodshed, the destruction of armies, the plunder of cities, the destruction or overthrow of nations, and the devastation of kingdoms, only that they may obtain possession of the property of others–what anathemas can sufficiently punish such conduct? Surely, it is perfectly obvious that the very last thing they aim at is the glory of Christ. For were they spontaneously to resign every portion of secular power that they possess, no peril to the glory of God, no peril to sound doctrine, no peril to the safety of the Church ensues; but they are borne blind and headlong by a lust for power, thinking that nothing can be safe unless they rule, as the prophet says, "with force and with cruelty" (Ezekiel 34:4).

15 Claim of immunity from civil jurisdiction. Contrast between this pretended immunity and the moderation of the early bishops.

To jurisdiction is annexed the immunity claimed by the Romish clergy. They deem it unworthy of them to answer before a civil judge in personal causes; and consider both the liberty and dignity of the Church to consist in exemption from ordinary tribunals and laws. But the ancient bishops, who otherwise were most resolute in asserting the rights of the Church, did not think it any injury to themselves and their order to act as subjects. Pious emperors also, as often as there was occasion, summoned clergy to their tribunals, and met with no opposition. For Constantine, in a letter to the Nicomedians, thus speaks: "Should any of the bishops unadvisedly excite tumult, his audacity shall be restrained by the minister of God, that is, by my executive." Valentinian says, "Good bishops throw no obloquy on the power of the emperor, but sincerely keep the commandments of God, the great King, and obey our laws." This was unquestionably the view then entertained by all. Ecclesiastical causes, indeed, were brought before the episcopal court; as when a clergyman had offended, but not against the laws, he was only charged by the Canons; and instead of being cited before the civil court, had the bishop for his judge in that particular case.

In like manner, when a question of faith was agitated, or one that properly pertained to the Church, cognizance was left to the Church. In this sense the words of Ambrose are to be understood: "Your father, of august memory, not only replied verbally, but enacted by law, that, in a question of faith, the judge should be one who was neither unequal from office, nor incompetent from the nature of his jurisdiction." Again, "If we attend to the Scriptures, or to ancient examples, who can deny that in a question of faith, a question of faith, I say, bishops are wont to judge Christian emperors, not emperors to judge bishops?" Again, "I would have come before your consistory, O emperor, would either the bishops or the people have allowed me to come: they say that a question of faith should be discussed in the Church before the people." He maintains, indeed, that a spiritual cause, that is, one pertaining to religion, is not to be brought before the civil court, where worldly disputes are agitated. His firmness in this respect is justly praised by all. And yet, though he has a good cause, he goes so far as to say, that if it comes to force and violence, he will yield. "I will not desert the post committed to me, but, if forced, I will not resist: prayers and tears are our weapons."

Let us observe the singular moderation of this holy man, his combination of prudence, magnanimity, and boldness. Justina, the mother of the emperor, unable to bring him over to the Arian party, sought to drive him from the government of the Church. And this would have been the result had he, when summoned, gone to the palace to plead his cause. He maintains, therefore, that the emperor is not fit to decide such a controversy. This both the necessity of the times, and the very nature of the thing, demanded. He thought it would be better for him to die than consent to transmit such an example to posterity; and yet if violence is offered, he thinks not of resisting. For he says, it is not the part of a bishop to defend the faith and rights of the Church by arms. But in all other causes, he declares himself ready to do whatever the emperor commands. "If he asks tribute, we deny it not: the lands of the Church pay tribute. If he asks lands, he has the power of evicting them; none of us interposes." Gregory speaks in the same manner. "I am not ignorant of the mind of my most serene lord: he is not wont to interfere in sacerdotal causes, lest he may in some degree burden himself with our sins." He does not exclude the emperor generally from judging priests, but says that there are certain causes, which he ought to leave to the ecclesiastical tribunal.

16 What end the early bishops aimed at in steadfastly resisting civil encroachment.

And hence, all that these holy men sought by this exception was, to prevent irreligious princes from impeding the Church in the discharge of her duty, by their tyrannical caprice and violence. They did not disapprove when princes interposed their authority in ecclesiastical affairs, provided this was done to preserve, not to disturb, the order of the Church, to establish, not to destroy discipline. For, seeing the Church has not, and ought not to wish to have, the power of compulsion (I speak of civil coercion), it is the part of pious kings and princes to maintain religion by laws, edicts, and sentences. In this way, when the emperor Maurice had commanded certain bishops to receive their neighboring colleagues, who had been expelled by the Barbarians, Gregory confirms the order, and exhorts them to obey. He himself, when admonished by the same emperor to return to a good understanding with John, Bishop of Constantinople, endeavors to show that he is not to be blamed; but so far from boasting of immunity from the secular forum, rather promises to comply as far as conscience would permit: he at the same time says, that Maurice had acted as became a religious prince, in giving these commands to priests.

Chapter 12

OF THE DISCIPLINE OF THE CHURCH, AND ITS PRINCIPAL USE IN CENSURES AND EXCOMMUNICATION.

This chapter consists of two parts:—I. The first part of ecclesiastical discipline, which respects the people, and is called common, consists of two parts, the former depending on the power of the keys, which is considered, sections 1-14; the latter consisting in the appointment of times for fasting and prayer, sections 14-21. II. The second part of ecclesiastical discipline relating to the clergy, sections 22-28.

Sections

1. Of the power of the keys, or the common discipline of the Church. Necessity and very great utility of this discipline.

2. Its various degrees. A. Private admonition. B. Rebukes before witnesses. C. Excommunication.

3. Different degrees of delinquency. Modes of procedure in both kinds of chastisement.

4. Delicts to be distinguished from flagitious wickedness. The last to be more severely punished.

5. Ends of this discipline. A. That the wicked may not, by being admitted to the Lord's Table, put insult on Christ. B. That they may not corrupt others. C. That they themselves may repent.

6. In what way sins public as well as secret are to be corrected. Trivial and grave offenses.

7. No person, not even the sovereign, exempted from this discipline. By whom and in what way it ought to be exercised.

8. In what spirit discipline is to be exercised. In what respect some of the ancient Christians exercised it too rigorously. This done more from custom than in accordance with their own sentiments. This shown from Cyprian, Chrysostom, and Augustine.

9. Moderation to be used, not only by the whole Church, but by each individual member.

10. Our Savior's words concerning binding and loosing wrested if otherwise understood. Difference between anathema and excommunication. Anathema rarely if ever to be used.

11. Excessive rigor to be avoided, as well by private individuals as by pastors.

12. In this respect, the Donatists erred most grievously, as do also the Anabaptists in the present day. Portraiture by Augustine.

13. Moderation especially to be used when not a few individuals, but the great body of the people, have gone astray.

14. A second part of common discipline relating to fasting, prayer, and other holy exercises. These used by believers under both dispensations. To what purposes applied. Of Fasting.

15. Three ends of fasting. The first refers more especially to private fasting. Second and third ends.

16. Public fasting and prayer appointed by pastors on any great emergency.

17. Examples of this under the Law.

18. Fasting consists chiefly in three things—viz. time, the quality, and sparing use of food.

19. To prevent superstition, three things to be inculcated. A. The heart to be rent, not the garments. B. Fasting not to be regarded as a meritorious work or kind of divine worship. C. Abstinence must not be immoderately extolled.

20. Owing to an excess of this kind, the observance of Lent was established. This superstitious observance refuted by three arguments. It was indeed used by the ancients, but on different grounds.

21. Laws afterwards made to regulate the choice of food. Various abuses even in the time of Jerome. Practically there is no common ecclesiastical discipline in the Papacy.

22. The second part of discipline having reference to the clergy. What its nature, and how strict it formerly was. How miserably neglected in the present day. An example, which may suit the Papists.

23. Of the celibacy of priests, in which Papists place the whole force of ecclesiastical discipline. This impious tyranny refuted from Scripture. An objection of the Papists disposed of.

24. An argument for the celibacy of priests answered.

25. Another argument answered.

26. Another argument answered.

27. An argument drawn from the commendation of virginity as superior to marriage. Answer.

28. The subject of celibacy concluded. This error not favored by all ancient writers.

1 Of the power of the keys, or the common discipline of the Church. Necessity and very great utility of this discipline.

The discipline of the Church, the consideration of which has been deferred until now, must be briefly explained, that we may be able to pass to other matters. Now discipline depends in a very great measure on the power of the keys and on spiritual jurisdiction. That this may be more easily understood, let us divide the Church into two principal classes–viz. clergy and people. The term clergy I use in the common acceptation for those who perform a public ministry in the Church. We shall speak first of the common discipline to which all ought to be subject, and then proceed to the clergy, who have besides that common discipline one peculiar to themselves. But as some, from hatred of discipline, are averse to the very name, for their sake we observe: If no society, nay, no house with even a moderate family, can be kept in a right state without discipline, much more necessary is it in the Church, whose state ought to be the best ordered possible. Hence, as the saving doctrine of Christ is the life of the Church, so discipline is its sinews; owing to it that the members of the Body adhere together, each in its own place. Wherefore, all who either wish that discipline were abolished, or who impede the restoration of it, whether they do this of design or through thoughtlessness, certainly aim at the complete devastation of the Church. For what will be the result if everyone is allowed to do as he pleases? But this must happen if to the preaching of the gospel are not added private admonition, correction, and similar methods of maintaining doctrine, and not allowing it to become lethargic. Discipline, therefore, is a kind of curb to restrain and tame those who war against the doctrine of Christ, or it is a kind of stimulus by which the indifferent are aroused; sometimes, also, it is a kind of fatherly rod, by which those who have made some more grievous lapse are chastised in mercy with the meekness of the spirit of Christ. Since, then, we already see some beginnings of a fearful devastation in the Church from the total want of care and method in managing the people, necessity itself cries aloud that there is need of a remedy. Now the only remedy is this that Christ enjoins, and the pious have always had in use.

2 Its various degrees. A. Private admonition. B. Rebukes before witnesses. C. Excommunication.

The first foundation of discipline is to provide for private admonition; that is, if anyone does not do his duty spontaneously, or behaves insolently, or lives not quite honestly, or commits something worthy of blame, he must allow himself to be admonished; and everyone must study to admonish his brother when the case requires. Here especially is there occasion for the vigilance of pastors and presbyters, whose duty is not only to preach to the people, but to exhort and admonish from house to house, whenever their hearers have not profited sufficiently by general teaching; as Paul shows, when he relates that he taught "publicly, and from house to house," and testifies that he is "pure from the blood of all men," because he had not shunned to declare "all the counsel of God" (Acts 20:20, 26, 27). Then does doctrine obtain force and authority, not only when the minister publicly expounds to all what they owe to Christ, but has the right and means of exacting this from those whom he may observe to be sluggish or disobedient to his doctrine. Should anyone either perversely reject such admonitions, or by persisting in his faults, show that he contemns them, the injunction of Christ is, that after he has been a second time admonished before witnesses, he is to be summoned to the bar of the Church, which is the consistory of elders, and there admonished more sharply, as by public authority, that if he reverence the Church he may submit and obey. (See Matthew 18:15, 17.) If even in this way he is not subdued, but persists in his iniquity, he is then, as a despiser of the Church, to be debarred from the society of believers.

3 Different degrees of delinquency. Modes of procedure in both kinds of chastisement.

Put as our Savior is not there speaking of secret faults merely, we must attend to the distinction that some sins are private, others public or openly manifest. Of the former, Christ says to every private individual, "go and tell him his fault between thee and him alone" (Matthew 18:15). Of open sins, Paul says to Timothy, "Those that sin rebuke before all, that others also may fear" (1 Timothy 5:20). Our Savior had previously used the words, "If thy brother shall trespass against thee" This clause, unless you would be captious, you cannot understand otherwise than, if this happens in a manner known to yourself, others not being privy to it. The injunction, which Paul gave to Timothy to rebuke those openly who sin openly, he himself followed with Peter. (See Galatians 2:14.) For when Peter sinned to give public offense, he did not admonish him apart, but brought him forward in face of the Church. The legitimate course, therefore, will be to proceed in correcting secret faults by the steps mentioned by Christ, and in open sins, accompanied with public scandal, to proceed at once to solemn correction by the Church.

4 Delicts to be distinguished from flagitious wickedness. The last to be more severely punished.

Another distinction to be attended to is, that some sins are mere delinquencies, others crimes and flagrant iniquities. In correcting the latter, it is necessary to employ not only admonition or rebuke, but a sharper remedy, as Paul shows when he not only verbally rebukes the incestuous Corinthian, but punishes him with excommunication, as soon as he was informed of his crime. (See 1 Corinthians 5:4.) Now then, we begin better to perceive how the spiritual jurisdiction of the Church, which animadverts on sins according to the Word of the Lord, is at once the best help to sound doctrine, the best foundation of order, and the best bond of unity. Therefore, when the Church banishes from its fellowship open adulterers, fornicators, thieves, robbers, the seditious, the perjured, false witnesses, and others of that description; likewise the contumacious, who, when duly admonished for lighter faults, hold God and His tribunal in derision, instead of arrogating to itself anything that is unreasonable, it exercises a jurisdiction which it has received from the Lord. Moreover, lest anyone should despise the judgment of the Church, or count it a small matter to be condemned by the suffrages of the faithful, the Lord has declared that it is nothing else than the promulgation of His own sentence, and that that which they do on Earth is ratified in Heaven. For they act by the Word of the Lord in condemning the perverse, and by the Word of the Lord in taking the penitent back into favor. (See John 20:23.) Those, I say, who trust that churches can long stand without this bond of discipline are mistaken, unless, indeed, we can with impunity dispense with a help which the Lord foresaw would be necessary. And, indeed, the greatness of the necessity will be better perceived by its manifold uses.

5 Ends of this discipline. A. That the wicked may not, by being admitted to the Lord's Table, put insult on Christ. B. That they may not corrupt others. C. That they themselves may repent.

There are three ends to which the Church has respect in thus correcting and excommunicating. The first is, that God may not be insulted by the name of Christians being given to those who lead shameful and flagitious lives, as if His holy Church were a combination of the wicked and abandoned. For because the Church is the Body of Christ, she cannot be defiled by such fetid and putrid members, without bringing some disgrace on her Head. Therefore, that there may be nothing in the Church to bring disgrace on His sacred name, those whose turpitude might throw infamy on the name must be expelled from His family. And here regard must be had to the Lord's Supper, which might be profaned by a promiscuous admission. For it is most true, that he who is entrusted with the dispensation of it, if he knowingly and willingly admits any unworthy person whom he ought and is able to repel, is as guilty of sacrilege as if he had cast the Lord's body to dogs. Wherefore, Chrysostom bitterly inveighs against priests, who, from fear of the great, dare not keep anyone back. He says, "Blood will be required at your hands. If you fear man, he will mock you, but if you fear God, you will be respected also by men. Let us not tremble at faces, purple, or diadems; our power here is greater. Assuredly I will sooner give up my body to death, and allow my blood to be shed, than be a partaker of that pollution." Therefore, lest this most sacred mystery should be exposed to ignominy, great selection is required in dispensing it, and this cannot be except by the jurisdiction of the Church. A second end of discipline is, that the good may not, as usually happens, be corrupted by constant communication with the wicked. For such is our proneness to go astray, that nothing is easier than to seduce us from the right course by bad example. To this use of discipline, the apostle referred when he commanded the Corinthians to discard the incestuous man from their society. "A little leaven leaveneth the whole lump" (1 Corinthians 5:6) And so much danger did he foresee here, that he prohibited them from keeping company with such persons. "If any man that is called a brother be a fornicator, or covetous, or an idolater, or a railer, or a drunkard, or an extortioner; with such an one, no not to eat" (1 Corinthians 5:11). A third end of discipline is that the sinner may be ashamed, and begin to repent of his turpitude.

Hence, it is for their interest also that their iniquity should be chastised, that whereas they would have become more obstinate by indulgence, they may be aroused by the rod. This the apostle intimates when he thus writes: "If any man obey not our word by this epistle, note that man, and have no company with him, that he may be ashamed" (2 Thessalonians 3:14). Again, when he says that he had delivered the Corinthian to Satan, "that the spirit may be saved in the day of the Lord Jesus" (1 Corinthians 5:5); that is, as I interpret it, he gave him over to temporal condemnation, that he might be made safe for eternity. And he says that he gave him over to Satan because the devil is without the Church, as Christ is in the Church. Some interpret this of a certain infliction on the flesh, but this interpretation seems to me most improbable.

6 In what way sins public as well as secret are to be corrected. Trivial and grave offenses.

These being the ends proposed, it remains to see in what way the Church is to execute this part of discipline, which consists in jurisdiction. And, first, let us remember the division above laid down, that some sins are public, others private or secret. Public are those, which are done not before one or two witnesses, but openly, and to the offense of the whole Church. By secret, I mean not such as are altogether concealed from men, such as those of hypocrites (for these fall not under the judgment of the Church), but those of an intermediate description, which are not without witnesses, and yet are not public. The former class requires not the different steps, which Christ enumerates; but whenever anything of the kind occurs, the Church ought to do her duty by summoning the offender, and correcting him according to his fault. In the second class, the matter comes not before the Church, unless there is contumacy, according to the rule of Christ. In taking cognizance of offenses, it is necessary to attend to the distinction between delinquencies and flagrant iniquities. In lighter offenses, there is not so much occasion for severity, but verbal chastisement is sufficient, and that gentle and fatherly, so as not to exasperate or confound the offender, but to bring him back to himself, so that he may rather rejoice than be grieved at the correction. Flagrant iniquities require a sharper remedy. It is not sufficient verbally to rebuke him who, by some open act of evil example, has grievously offended the Church; but he ought for a time to be denied the communion of the Supper, until he gives proof of repentance. Paul does not merely administer a verbal rebuke to the Corinthian, but discards him from the Church, and reprimands the Corinthians for having borne with him so long. (See 1 Corinthians 5:5.) This was the method observed by the ancient and purer Church, when legitimate government was in vigor. When anyone was guilty of some flagrant iniquity, and thereby caused scandal, he was first ordered to abstain from participation in the sacred Supper, and thereafter to humble himself before God, and testify his penitence before the Church. There were, moreover, solemn rites, which, as indications of repentance, were wont to be prescribed to those who had lapsed. When the penitent had thus made satisfaction to the Church, he was received into favor by the laying on of hands. This admission often receives the name of peace from Cyprian, who briefly describes the form. "They act as penitents for a certain time, next they come to confession, and receive the right of communion by the laying on of hands of the bishop and clergy." Although the bishop with the clergy thus superintended the restoration of the penitent, the consent of the people was at the same time required, as he elsewhere explains.

7 No person, not even the sovereign, exempted from this discipline. By whom and in what way it ought to be exercised.

So far was anyone from being exempted from this discipline, that even princes submitted to it in common with their subjects; and justly, since it is the discipline of Christ, to whom all scepters and diadems should be subject. Thus Theodosius, when excommunicated by Ambrose, because of the slaughter perpetrated at Thessalonica, laid aside all the royal insignia with which he was surrounded, and publicly in the Church bewailed the sin into which he had been betrayed by the fraud of others, with groans and tears imploring pardon. Great kings should not think it a disgrace to them to prostrate themselves suppliantly before Christ, the King of kings; nor ought they to be displeased at being judged by the Church. For seeing they seldom hear anything in their courts but mere flattery, the more necessary is it that the Lord should correct them by the mouth of His priests. Nay, they ought rather to wish the priests not to spare them, in order that the Lord may spare. I here say nothing as to those by whom the jurisdiction ought to be exercised, because it has been said elsewhere (Chapter 11, sections 5, 6). I only add, that the legitimate course to be taken in excommunication, as shown by Paul, is not for the elders alone to act apart from others, but with the knowledge and approbation of the Church, so that the body of the people, without regulating the procedure, may, as witnesses and guardians, observe it, and prevent the few from doing anything capriciously. Throughout the whole procedure, in addition to invocation of the name of God, there should be a gravity bespeaking the presence of Christ, and leaving no room to doubt that He is presiding over His own tribunal.

8 In what spirit discipline is to be exercised. In what respect some of the ancient Christians exercised it too rigorously. This done more from custom than in accordance with their own sentiments. This shown from Cyprian, Chrysostom, and Augustine.

It ought not, however, to be omitted, that the Church, in exercising severity, ought to accompany it with the spirit of meekness. For, as Paul enjoins, we must always take care that he on whom discipline is exercised be not "swallowed up with overmuch sorrow" (2 Corinthians 2:7): for in this way, instead of cure there would be destruction. The rule of moderation will be best obtained from the end contemplated. For the object of excommunication being to bring the sinner to repentance and remove bad examples, in order that the name of Christ may not be evil spoken of, nor others tempted to the same evil courses: if we consider this, we shall easily understand how far severity should be carried, and at what point it ought to cease. Therefore, when the sinner gives the Church evidence of his repentance, and by this evidence does what in him lies to obliterate the offense, he ought not on any account to be urged further. If he is urged, the rigor now exceeds due measure. In this respect it is impossible to excuse the excessive austerity of the ancients, which was altogether at variance with the injunction of our Lord, and strangely perilous. For when they enjoined a formal repentance, and excluded from communion for three, or four, or seven years, or for life, what could the result be, but either great hypocrisy or very great despair? In like manner, when not anyone who had again lapsed was admitted to a second repentance, but ejected from the Church, to the end of his life, this was neither useful nor agreeable to reason. Whosoever, therefore, looks at the matter with sound judgment, will here regret a want of prudence. Here, however, I rather disapprove of the public custom, than blame those who complied with it. Some of them certainly disapproved of it, but submitted to what they were unable to correct. Cyprian, indeed, declares that it was not with his own will he was thus rigorous. He says, "Our patience, facility, and humanity are ready to all who come. I wish all to be brought back into the Church: I wish all our fellow soldiers to be contained within the camp of Christ and the mansions of God the Father. I forgive all; I disguise much; from an earnest desire of collecting the brotherhood, I do not minutely scrutinize all the faults, which have been committed against God. I myself often err, by forgiving offenses more than I ought. Those returning in repentance, and those confessing their sins with simple and humble satisfaction, I embrace with prompt and full delight." Chrysostom, who is somewhat more severe, still speaks thus: "If God is so kind, why should His priest wish to appear austere?" We know, moreover, how indulgently Augustine treated the Donatists; not hesitating to admit any who returned from schism to their bishopric, as soon as they declared their repentance. But, as a contrary method had prevailed, they were compelled to follow it, and give up their own judgment.

9 Moderation to be used, not only by the whole Church, but by each individual member.

But as the whole Body of the Church are required to act thus mildly, and not to carry their rigor against those who have lapsed to an extreme, but rather to act charitably towards them, according to the precept of Paul, so every private individual ought proportionately to accommodate himself to this clemency and humanity. Such as have, therefore, been expelled from the Church, it belongs not to us to expunge from the number of the elect, or to despair of, as if they were already lost. We may lawfully judge them aliens from the Church, and so aliens from Christ, but only during the time of their excommunication. If then, also, they give greater evidence of petulance than of humility, still let us commit them to the judgment of the Lord, hoping better of them in future than we see at present, and not ceasing to pray to God for them. And (to sum up in one word) let us not consign to destruction their person, which is in the hand, and subject to the decision, of the Lord alone; but let us merely estimate the character of each man's acts according to the law of the Lord. In following this rule, we abide by the divine judgment rather than give any judgment of our own. Let us not arrogate to ourselves greater liberty in judging, if we would not limit the power of God, and give the law to His mercy. Whenever it seems good to Him, the worst are changed into the best; aliens are engrafted, and strangers are adopted into the Church. This the Lord does, that He may disappoint the thoughts of men, and confound their rashness; a rashness which, if not curbed, would usurp a power of judging to which it has no title.

10 Our Savior's Words concerning binding and loosing wrested if otherwise understood. Difference between anathema and excommunication. Anathema rarely if ever to be used.

For when our Savior promises that what His servants bound on Earth should be bound in Heaven (see Matthew 18:18), He confines the power of binding to the censure of the Church, which does not consign those who are excommunicated to perpetual ruin and damnation, but assures them, when they hear their life and manners condemned, that perpetual damnation will follow if they do not repent. Excommunication differs from anathema in this, that the latter completely excluding pardon, dooms and devotes the individual to eternal destruction, whereas the former rather rebukes and animadverts upon his manners; and although it also punishes, it is to bring him to salvation, by forewarning him of his future doom. If it succeeds, reconciliation and restoration to communion are ready to be given. Moreover, anathema is rarely if ever to be used. Hence, though ecclesiastical discipline does not allow us to be on familiar and intimate terms with excommunicated persons, still we ought to strive by all possible means to bring them to a better mind, and recover them to the fellowship and unity of the Church: as the apostle also says, "Yet count him not as an enemy, but admonish him as a brother" (2 Thessalonians 3:15). If this humanity be not observed in private as well as public, the danger is, that our discipline shall degenerate into destruction.

11 Excessive rigor to be avoided, as well by private individuals as by pastors.

Another special requisite to moderation of discipline is, as Augustine discourses against the Donatists, that private individuals must not, when they see vices less carefully corrected by the Council of Elders, immediately separate themselves from the Church; nor must pastors themselves, when unable to reform all things which need correction to the extent which they could wish, cast up their ministry, or by unwonted severity throw the whole Church into confusion. What Augustine says is perfectly true: "Whoever corrects what he can, by rebuking it, or without violating the bond of peace, excludes what he cannot correct, or unjustly condemns while he patiently tolerates what he is unable to exclude without violating the bond of peace, is free and exempted from the curse." He elsewhere gives the reason. "Every pious reason and mode of ecclesiastical discipline ought always to have regard to the unity of the Spirit in the bond of peace. This the apostle commands us to keep by bearing mutually with each other. If it is not kept, the medicine of discipline begins to be not only superfluous, but even pernicious, and therefore ceases to be medicine." "He who diligently considers these things, neither in the preservation of unity neglects strictness of discipline, nor by intemperate correction bursts the bond of society." He confesses, indeed, that pastors ought not only to exert themselves in removing every defect from the Church, but that every individual ought to his utmost do so. Nor does he disguise the fact that he who neglects to admonish, accuse, and correct the bad, although he neither favors them nor sins with them, is guilty before the Lord. If he conducts himself as though he can exclude them from partaking of the Supper, and he does not, then the sin is no longer that of other men, but his own. Only he would have that prudence used which our Lord also requires, "lest while ye gather up the tares, ye root up also the wheat with them" (Matthew 13:29). Hence, he infers from Cyprian, "Let a man then mercifully correct what he can; what he cannot correct, let him bear patiently, and in love bewail and lament."

12 In this respect, the Donatists erred most grievously, as do also the Anabaptists in the present day. Portraiture by Augustine.

This he says on account of the moroseness of the Donatists, who, when they saw faults in the Church which the bishops indeed rebuked verbally, but did not punish with excommunication (because they did not think that anything would be gained in this way), bitterly inveighed against the bishops as traitors to discipline, and by an impious schism separated themselves from the flock of Christ. Similar, in the present day, is the conduct of the Anabaptists, who, acknowledging no assembly of Christ unless conspicuous in all respects for angelic perfection, under pretence of zeal overthrow everything that tends to edification. Augustine says, "Such not from hatred of other men's iniquity, but zeal for their own disputes, ensnaring the weak by the credit of their name, attempt to draw them entirely away, or at least to separate them; swollen with pride, raving with petulance, insidious in calumny, turbulent in sedition. That it may not be seen how void they are of the light of truth, they cover themselves with the shadow of a stern severity: the correction of a brother's fault, which in Scripture is enjoined to be done with moderation, without impairing the sincerity of love or breaking the bond of peace, they pervert to sacrilegious schism and purposes of excision. Thus Satan transforms himself into an angel of light (see 2 Corinthians 11:14) when, under pretext of a just severity, he persuades to savage cruelty, desiring nothing more than to violate and burst the bond of unity and peace; because, when it is maintained, all his power of mischief is feeble, his wily traps are broken, and his schemes of subversion vanish."

13 Moderation especially to be used when not a few individuals, but the great body of the people, have gone astray.

One thing Augustine specially commends–viz. that if the contagion of sin has seized the multitude, mercy must accompany living discipline. "For counsels of separation are vain, sacrilegious, and pernicious, because of impiety and pride, and do more to disturb the weak good than to correct the wicked proud." This, which he enjoins on others, he himself faithfully practiced. For, writing to Aurelius, Bishop of Carthage, he complains that drunkenness, which is so severely condemned in Scripture, prevails in Africa with impunity, and advises a council of bishops to be called to provide a remedy. He immediately adds, "In my opinion, such things are not removed by rough, harsh, and imperious measures, but more by teaching than commanding, more by admonishing than threatening. For thus ought we to act with a multitude of offenders. Severity is to be exercised against the sins of a few." He does not mean, however, that the bishops were to wink or be silent because they are unable to punish public offenses severely, as he himself afterwards explains. But he wishes to temper the mode of correction, to give soundness to the body rather than cause destruction. And, accordingly, he thus concludes: "Wherefore, we must on no account neglect the injunction of the apostle, to separate from the wicked, when it can be done without the risk of violating peace, because he did not wish it to be done otherwise (1 Corinthians 5:13); we must also endeavor, by bearing with each other, to keep the unity of the Spirit in the bond of peace" (Ephesians 4:2).

14 A second part of common discipline relating to fasting, prayer, and other holy exercises. These used by believers under both dispensations. To what purposes applied. Of Fasting.

The remaining part of discipline, which is not, strictly speaking, included in the power of the keys, is when pastors, according to the necessity of the times, exhort the people either to fasting and solemn prayer, or to other exercises of humiliation, repentance, and faith, the time, mode, and form of these not being prescribed by the Word of God, but left to the judgment of the Church. As the observance of this part of discipline is useful, so it was always used in the Church, even from the days of the apostles. Indeed, the apostles themselves were not its first authors, but borrowed the example from the Law and Prophets. For we there see, that as often as any weighty matter occurred the people were assembled, and supplication and fasting appointed. In this, therefore, the apostles followed a course that was not new to the people of God, and which they foresaw would be useful. A similar account is to be given of the other exercises by which the people may either be aroused to duty, or kept in duty and obedience. We everywhere meet with examples in Sacred History, and it is unnecessary to collect them. In general, we must hold that whenever any religious controversy arises, which either a council or ecclesiastical tribunal behooves to decide; whenever a minister is to be chosen; whenever, in short, any matter of difficulty and great importance is under consideration: on the other hand, when manifestations of the divine anger appear, as pestilence, war, and famine, the sacred and salutary custom of all ages has been for pastors to exhort the people to public fasting and extraordinary prayer. Should anyone refuse to admit the passages, which are adduced from the Old Testament, as being less applicable to the Christian Church, it is clear that the apostles also acted thus; although, concerning prayer, I scarcely think anyone will be found to stir the question. Let us, therefore, make some observations on fasting, since very many, not understanding what utility there can be in it, judge it not to be very necessary, while others reject it altogether as superfluous. Where its use is not well known it is easy to fall into superstition.

15 Three ends of fasting. The first refers more especially to private fasting. Second and third ends.

A holy and lawful fast has three ends in view. We use it either to mortify and subdue the flesh, that it may not wanton, or to prepare the better for prayer and holy meditation; or to give evidence of humbling ourselves before God, when we would confess our guilt before Him. The first end is not very often regarded in public fasting, because all have not the same bodily constitution, nor the same state of health, and hence it is more applicable to private fasting. The second end is common to both, for this preparation for prayer is requisite for the whole Church, as well as for each individual member. The same thing may be said of the third. For it sometimes happens that God smites a nation with war or pestilence, or some kind of calamity. In this common chastisement, it behooves the whole people to plead guilty, and confess their guilt. Should the hand of the Lord strike anyone in private, then the same thing is to be done by himself alone, or by his family. The thing, indeed, is properly a feeling of the mind. But when the mind is effected, as it ought, it cannot but give vent to itself in external manifestation, especially when it tends to the common edification, that all, by openly confessing their sin, may render praise to the divine justice, and by their example mutually encourage each other.

16 Public fasting and prayer appointed by pastors on any great emergency.

Hence, fasting, as it is a sign of humiliation, has a more frequent use in public than among private individuals, although as we have said, it is common to both. In regard, then, to the discipline of which we now treat, whenever supplication is to be made to God on any important occasion, it is befitting to appoint a period for fasting and prayer. Thus when the Christians of Antioch laid hands on Barnabas and Paul, that they might the better recommend their ministry, which was of so great importance, they joined fasting and prayer. (See Acts 13:3.) Thus, these two apostles afterwards, when they appointed ministers to churches, were wont to use prayer and fasting. (See Acts 14:23.) In general, the only object, which they had in fasting, was to render themselves more alert and disencumbered for prayer. We certainly experience that after a full meal the mind does not so rise toward God as to be borne along by an earnest and fervent longing for prayer, and perseverance in prayer. In this sense is to be understood the saying of Luke concerning Anna, that she "served God with fasting and prayers, night and day" (Luke 2:37). For he does not place the worship of God in fasting, but intimates that in this way the holy woman trained herself to assiduity in prayer. Such was the fast of Nehemiah, when with more intense zeal he prayed to God for the deliverance of his people. (See Nehemiah 1:4.) For this reason Paul says, that married believers do well to abstain for a season (see 1 Corinthians 7:5), that they may have greater freedom for prayer and fasting, when by joining prayer to fasting, by way of help, he reminds us it is of no importance in itself, save in so far as it refers to this end. Again, when in the same place he enjoins spouses to render due benevolence to each other, it is clear that he is not referring to daily prayer, but prayers that require more than ordinary attention.

17 Examples of this under the Law.

On the other hand, when pestilence begins to stalk abroad, or famine or war, or when any other disaster seems to impend over a province and people (see Esther 4:16), then also it is the duty of pastors to exhort the Church to fasting, that she may suppliantly deprecate the Lord's anger. For when He makes danger appear, He declares that He is prepared and in a manner armed for vengeance. In like manner, therefore, as persons accused were anciently wont, in order to excite the commiseration of the judge, to humble themselves suppliantly with long beard, disheveled hair, and coarse garments, so when we are charged before the divine tribunal, to deprecate His severity in humble raiment is equally for His glory and the public edification, and useful and salutary to ourselves. And that this was common among the Israelites we may infer from the words of Joel. For when he says, "Blow the trumpet in Zion, sanctify a fast, call a solemn assembly," etc. (Joel 2:15), he speaks as of things received by common custom. A little before he had said that the people were to be tried for their wickedness, and that the day of judgment was at hand, and he had summoned them as criminals to plead their cause: then he exclaims that they should hasten to sackcloth and ashes, to weeping and fasting; that is, humble themselves before God with external manifestations. The sackcloth and ashes, indeed, were perhaps more suitable for those times, but the assembly, and weeping and fasting, and the like, undoubtedly belong, in an equal degree, to our age, whenever the condition of our affairs so requires. For seeing it is a holy exercise both for men to humble themselves, and confess their humility, why should we in similar necessity use this less than did those of old? We read not only that the Israelitish Church, formed and constituted by the Word of God, fasted in token of sadness, but the Ninevites also, whose only teaching had been the preaching of Jonah. Why, therefore, should not we do the same? But it is an external ceremony, which, like other ceremonies, terminated in Christ. Nay, in the present day it is an admirable help to believers, as it always was, and a useful admonition to arouse them, lest by too great security and sloth they provoke the Lord increasingly when they are chastened by His rod. Accordingly, when our Savior excuses His apostles for not fasting, He does not say that fasting was abrogated, but reserves it for calamitous times, and conjoins it with mourning. "The days will come when the bridegroom shall be taken from them" (Matthew 9:35; Luke 5:34).

18 Fasting consists chiefly in three things—viz. time, the quality, and sparing use of food.

But that there may be no error in the name, let us define what fasting is; for we do not understand by it simply a restrained and sparing use of food, but something else. The life of the pious should be tempered with frugality and sobriety, to exhibit, as much as may be, a kind of fasting during the whole course of life. But there is another temporary fast, when we retrench somewhat from our accustomed mode of living, either for one day or a certain period, and prescribe to ourselves a stricter and severer restraint in the use of that ordinary food. This consists in three things–viz. the time, the quality of food, and the sparing use of it. By the time I mean, that while fasting we are to perform those actions for the sake of which the fast is instituted. For example, when a man fasts because of solemn prayer, he should engage in it without having taken food. The quality consists in putting all luxury aside, and, being contented with common and meaner food, so as not to excite our palate by dainties. In regard to quantity, we must eat more lightly and sparingly, only for necessity and not for pleasure.

19 To prevent superstition, three things to be inculcated. A. The heart to be rent, not the garments. B. Fasting not to be regarded as a meritorious work or kind of divine worship. C. Abstinence must not be immoderately extolled.

But the first thing always to be avoided is, the encroachment of superstition, as formerly happened, to the great injury of the Church. It would have been much better to have had no fasting at all, than have it carefully observed, but at the same time corrupted by false and pernicious opinions, into which the world is always falling, unless pastors obviate them by the greatest fidelity and prudence. The first thing is constantly to urge the injunction of Joel, "Rend your heart, and not your garments" (Joel 2:13). That is, remind the people that fasting in itself is not of great value in the sight of God, unless accompanied with internal affection of the heart, true dissatisfaction with sin and with one's self, true humiliation, and true grief, from the fear of God; nay, that fasting is useful for no other reason than because it is added to these as an inferior help. There is nothing that God more abominates than when men endeavor to cloak themselves by substituting signs and external appearance for integrity of heart. Accordingly, Isaiah inveighs most bitterly against the hypocrisy of the Jews, in thinking that they had satisfied God when they had merely fasted, whatever might be the impiety and impure thoughts that they cherished in their hearts. "Is it such a fast that I have chosen?" (Isaiah 58:5). See also, what follows. The fast of hypocrites is, therefore, not only useless and superfluous fatigue, but the greatest abomination. Another evil akin to this, and greatly to be avoided, is, to regard fasting as a meritorious work and species of divine worship. For seeing it is a thing, which is in itself indifferent, and has no importance except because of those ends to which it ought to have respect, it is a most pernicious superstition to confound it with the works enjoined by God, and which are necessary in themselves without reference to anything else. Such was anciently the dream of the Manichees, in refuting whom Augustine clearly shows, that fasting is to be estimated entirely by those ends which I have mentioned, and cannot be approved by God, unless in so far as it refers to them. Another error, not indeed so impious, but perilous, is to exact it with greater strictness and severity as one of the principal duties, and extol it with such extravagant encomiums as to make men imagine that they have done something admirable when they have fasted. In this respect, I dare not entirely excuse ancient writers from having sown some seeds of superstition, and given occasion to the tyranny, which afterwards arose. We sometimes meet with sound and prudent sentiments on fasting, but we also always meet with extravagant praises, lauding it as one of the cardinal virtues.

20 Owing to an excess of this kind, the observance of Lent was established. This superstitious observance refuted by three arguments. It was indeed used by the ancients, but on different grounds.

Then, the superstitious observance of Lent had everywhere prevailed: for both the vulgar imagined that they thereby perform some excellent service to God, and pastors commended it as a holy imitation of Christ. But it is plain that Christ did not fast to set an example to others, but, by thus commencing the preaching of the gospel, meant to prove that His doctrine was not of men, but had come from Heaven. And it is strange how men of acute judgment could fall into this gross delusion, which so many clear reasons refute: for Christ did not fast repeatedly (which He must have done had He meant to lay down a law for an anniversary fast), but once only, when preparing for the promulgation of the gospel. Nor does He fast after the manner of men, as He would have done had He meant to invite men to imitation; He rather gives an example, by which He may raise all to admire rather than study to imitate Him. In short, the nature of His fast is not different from that which Moses observed when he received the law at the hand of the Lord (Exodus 24:18; 34:28). For, because that miracle was performed in Moses to establish the law, it behooved not to be omitted in Christ, lest the gospel should seem inferior to the law. But from that day, it never occurred to anyone, under pretence of imitating Moses, to set up a similar form of fast among the Israelites. Nor did any of the holy prophets and fathers follow it, though they had inclination and zeal enough for all pious exercises; for though it is said of Elijah that he passed forty days without meat and drink (1 Kings 19:8), this was merely in order that the people might recognize that he was raised up to maintain the law, from which almost the whole of Israel had revolted. It was therefore merely false zeal, replete with superstition, which set up a fast under the title and pretext of imitating Christ; although there was then a strange diversity in the mode of the fast, as is related by Cassiodorus in the ninth book of the *History of Socrates*: "The Romans," says he, "had only three weeks, but their fast was continuous, except on the Lord's day and the Sabbath. The Greeks and Illyrians had, some six, others seven, but the fast was at intervals. Nor did they differ less in the kind of food: some used only bread and water, others added vegetables; others had no objection to fish and fowls; others made no difference in their food." Augustine also makes mention of this difference in his latter epistle to Januarius.

21 Laws afterwards made to regulate the choice of food. Various abuses even in the time of Jerome. Practically there is no common ecclesiastical discipline in the Papacy.

Worse times followed. To the absurd zeal of the vulgar were added rudeness and ignorance in the bishops, lust of power, and tyrannical rigor. Impious laws were passed, binding the conscience in deadly chains. The eating of flesh was forbidden, as if a man were contaminated by it. Sacrilegious opinions were added, one after another, until all became an abyss of error. And that no kind of depravity might be omitted, they began, under a most absurd pretence of abstinence, to make a mock of God; for in the most exquisite delicacies they seek the praise of fasting: no dainties now suffice; never was there greater abundance or variety or savor of food. In this splendid display, they think that they serve God. I do not mention that at no time do those who would be thought the holiest of them wallow more foully. In short, the highest worship of God is to abstain from flesh, and, with this reservation, to indulge in delicacies of every kind. On the other hand, it is the greatest impiety, impiety scarcely to be expiated by death, for anyone to taste the smallest portion of bacon or rancid flesh with his bread. Jerome, writing to Nepotian, relates, that even in his day there were some who mocked God with such follies: those who would not even put oil in their food caused the greatest delicacies to be procured from every quarter; nay, that they might do violence to nature, abstained from drinking water, and caused sweet and costly potions to be made for them, which they drank, not out of a cup, but a shell. What was then the fault of a few is now common among all the rich: they do not fast for any other purpose than to feast more richly and luxuriously. But I am unwilling to waste many words on a subject as to which there can be no doubt. All I say is, that, as well in fasts as in all other parts of discipline, the Papists are so far from having anything right, anything sincere, anything duly framed and ordered, that they have no occasion to plume themselves as if anything was left them that is worthy of praise.

22 The second part of discipline having reference to the clergy. What its nature, and how strict it formerly was. How miserably neglected in the present day. An example, which may suit the Papists.

We come now to the second part of discipline, which relates specially to the clergy. It is contained in the canons, which the ancient bishops framed for themselves and their order: for instance, let no clergyman spend his time in hunting, in gaming, or in feasting; let none engage in usury or in trade; let none be present at lascivious dances, and the like. Penalties also were added to give a sanction to the authority of the canons, that none might violate them with impunity. With this view, each bishop was entrusted with the superintendence of his own clergy, that he might govern them according to the canons, and keep them to their duty. For this purpose, certain annual visitations and synods were appointed, that if anyone was negligent in his office he might be admonished; if anyone sinned, he might be punished according to his fault.

The bishops also had their provincial synods once—anciently twice—a year, by which they were tried, if they had done anything contrary to their duty. For if any bishop had been too harsh or violent with his clergy, there was an appeal to the synod, though only one individual complained. The severest punishment was deposition from office, and exclusion, for a time, from communion. But as this was the uniform arrangement, no synod rose without fixing the time and place of the next meeting. To call a universal council belonged to the emperor alone, as all the ancient summoning testifies. As long as this strictness was in force, the clergy demanded no more in word from the people than they performed in act and by example; nay, they were more strict against themselves than the vulgar; and, indeed, it is becoming that the people should be ruled by a kindlier, and, if I may so speak, laxer discipline; that the clergy should be stricter in their censures, and less indulgent to themselves than to others.

How this whole procedure became obsolete, it is needless to relate, since, in the present day, nothing can be imagined more lawless and dissolute than this order, whose licentiousness is so extreme that the whole world is crying out. I admit that, in order not to seem to have lost all sight of antiquity, they, by certain shadows, deceive the eyes of the simple; but these no more resemble ancient customs than the mimicry of an ape resembles what men do by reason and counsel. There is a memorable passage in Xenophon, in which he mentions that when the Persians had shamefully degenerated from the customs of their ancestors, and had fallen away from an austere mode of life to luxury and effeminacy, they still, to hide the disgrace, were sedulously observant of ancient rites. For while, in the time of Cyrus, sobriety and temperance so flourished that no Persian was required to wipe his nose, and it was even deemed disgraceful to do so, it remained with their posterity, as a point of religion, not to remove the mucus from the nostril, though they were allowed to nourish within, even to putridity, those fetid humors which they had contracted by gluttony.

In like manner, according to the ancient custom, it was unlawful to use cups at table; but it was tolerable to swallow wine to make it necessary to be carried off drunk. It was enjoined to use only one meal a day: this these good successors did not abrogate, but they continued their surfeit from midday to midnight. To finish the day's march, fasting, as the law enjoined it, was the uniform custom; but in order to avoid lassitude, the allowed and usual custom was to limit the march to two hours. As often as the degenerate Papists obtrude their rules, that they may show their resemblance to the holy fathers, this example will serve to expose their ridiculous imitation. Indeed, no painter could paint them more to the life.

23 Of the celibacy of priests, in which Papists place the whole force of ecclesiastical discipline. This impious tyranny refuted from Scripture. An objection of the Papists disposed of.

In one thing they are more than rigid and inexorable–in not permitting priests to marry. It is of no consequence to mention with what impunity whoredom prevails among them, and how, trusting to their vile celibacy, they have become callous to all kinds of iniquity. The prohibition, however, clearly shows how pestiferous all traditions are, since this one has not only deprived the Church of fit and honest pastors, but has introduced a fearful sink of iniquity, and plunged many souls into the gulf of despair. Certainly, when marriage was interdicted to priests, it was done with impious tyranny, not only contrary to the Word of God, but contrary to all justice. First, men had no title whatever to forbid what God had left free; secondly, it is too clear to make it necessary to give any lengthened proof that God has expressly provided in His Word that this liberty shall not be infringed. I omit Paul's injunction, in numerous passages, that a bishop is the husband of one wife; but what could be stronger than his declaration, that in the latter days there would be impious men "forbidding to marry"? (1 Timothy 4:3). Such persons he calls not only impostors, but devils. We have therefore a prophecy, a sacred oracle of the Holy Spirit, intended to warn the Church from the outset against perils, and declaring that the prohibition of marriage is a doctrine of devils. They think that they get finely off when they wrest this passage, and apply it to Montanus, the Tatians, the Encratites, and other ancient heretics. These (they say) alone condemned marriage; we by no means condemn it, but only deny it to the ecclesiastical order, in whom we think it not befitting. As if, even granting that this prophecy was primarily fulfilled in those heretics, it is not applicable also to themselves; or, as if one could listen to the childish quibble that they do not forbid marriage, because they do not forbid it to all. This is just as if a tyrant were to contend that a law is not unjust because its injustice presses only on a part of the state.

24 An argument for the celibacy of priests answered.

They object that there ought to be some distinguishing mark between the clergy and the people; as if the Lord had not provided the ornaments, in which priests ought to excel. Thus they charge the apostle with having disturbed the ecclesiastical order, and destroyed its ornament, when, in drawing the picture of a perfect bishop, he presumed to set down marriage among the other endowments which he required of them. I am aware of the mode in which they expound this–viz. that no one was to be appointed a bishop who had a second wife. This interpretation, I admit, is not new; but its unsoundness is plain from the immediate context, which prescribes the kind of wives whom bishops and deacons ought to have. Paul enumerates marriage among the qualities of a bishop; those men declare that, in the ecclesiastical order, marriage is an intolerable vice; and, indeed, not content with this general vituperation, they term it, in their canons, the uncleanness and pollution of the flesh. Let everyone consider with himself from what forge these things have come. Christ deigns so to honor marriage as to make it an image of His sacred union with the Church. What greater eulogy could be pronounced on the dignity of marriage? How, then, dare they have the effrontery to give the name of unclean and polluted to that, which furnishes a bright representation of the spiritual grace of Christ?

25 Another argument answered.

Though their prohibition is thus clearly repugnant to the Word of God, they, however, find something in the Scriptures to defend it. The Levitical priests, as often as their ministerial course returned, behooved to keep apart from their wives, that they might be pure and immaculate in handling sacred things; and it would be therefore very indecorous that our sacred things, which are more noble, and are ministered every day, should be handled by those who are married: as if the evangelical ministry were of the same character as the Levitical priesthood. These, as types, represented Christ, who, as Mediator between God and men, was, by His own spotless purity, to reconcile us to the Father. But as sinners could not in every respect exhibit a type of His holiness, that they might, however, shadow it forth by certain lineaments, they were enjoined to purify themselves beyond the manner of men when they approached the sanctuary, inasmuch as they then properly prefigured Christ appearing in the tabernacle, an image of the heavenly tribunal, as pacificators, to reconcile men to God. As ecclesiastical pastors do not sustain this character in the present day, the comparison is made in vain. Wherefore the apostle declares distinctly, without reservation, "Marriage is honorable in all, and the bed undefiled; but whoremongers and adulterers God will judge" (Hebrews 13:4). And the apostles showed, by their own example, that marriage is not unbefitting the holiness of any function, however excellent; for Paul declares that they not only retained their wives, but led them about with them. (See 1 Corinthians 9:5.)

26 Another argument answered.

Then how great the effrontery when, in holding forth this ornament of chastity as a matter of necessity, they throw the greatest obloquy on the primitive Church, which, while it abounded in admirable divine erudition, excelled more in holiness. For if they pay no regard to the apostles (they habitually scorned them), what, I ask, will they make of all the ancient fathers, who, it is certain, not only tolerated marriage in the episcopal order, but also approved it? They, forsooth, encouraged a foul profanation of sacred things when the mysteries of the Lord were thus irregularly performed by them. In the Council of Nice, indeed, there was some question of proclaiming celibacy: as there are never wanting little men of superstitious minds, who are always devising some novelty as a means of gaining admiration for themselves. What was resolved? The opinion of Paphnutius was adopted, who pronounced legitimate conjugal intercourse to be chastity. The marriage of priests, therefore, continued sacred, and was neither regarded as a disgrace, nor thought to cast any stain on their ministry.

27 An argument drawn from the commendation of virginity as superior to marriage. Answer.

In the times, which succeeded, a too superstitious admiration of celibacy prevailed. Hence, always, unmeasured encomiums were pronounced on virginity, so that it became the vulgar belief that scarcely any virtue was to be compared to it. And although marriage was not condemned as impurity, yet, its dignity was lessened, and its sanctity obscured; so that he who did not refrain from it was deemed not to have a mind strong enough to aspire to perfection. Hence, those canons which enacted, first, that those who had attained the priesthood should not contract marriage; and, secondly, that none should be admitted to that order but the unmarried, or those who, with the consent of their wives, renounced the marriage bed. These enactments, as they seemed to procure reverence for the priesthood, were, I admit, received even in ancient times with great applause. But if my opponents plead antiquity, my first answer is, that both under the apostles, and for several ages after, bishops were at liberty to have wives: that the apostles themselves, and other pastors of primitive authority who succeeded them, had no difficulty in using this liberty, and that the example of the primitive Church ought justly to have more weight than allow us to think that what was then received and used with commendation is either illicit or unbecoming. My second answer is, that the age, which, from an immoderate affection for virginity, began to be less favorable to marriage, did not bind a law of celibacy on the priests, as if the thing were necessary in itself, but gave a preference to the unmarried over the married. My last answer is, that they did not exact this so rigidly as to make continence necessary and compulsory on those who were unfit for it. For while the strictest laws were made against fornication, it was only enacted with regard to those who contracted marriage that they should be superseded in their office.

28 The subject of celibacy concluded. This error not favored by all ancient writers.

Therefore, as often as the defenders of this new tyranny appeal to antiquity in defense of their celibacy, so often should we call upon them to restore the ancient chastity of their priests, to put away adulterers and whoremongers, not to allow those whom they deny an honorable and chaste use of marriage, to rush with impunity into every kind of lust, to bring back that obsolete discipline by which all licentiousness is restrained, and free the Church from the flagitious turpitude by which it has long been deformed. When they have conceded this, they will next require to be reminded not to represent as necessary that which, being in itself free, depends on the utility of the Church. I do not, however, speak thus as if I thought that on any condition whatever effect should be given to those canons which lay a bond of celibacy on the ecclesiastical order, but that the better hearted may understand the effrontery of our enemies in employing the name of antiquity to defame the holy marriage of priests. Concerning the Fathers, whose writings are still in existence, none of them, when they spoke their own mind, with the exception of Jerome, thus malignantly detracted from the honor of marriage. We will be contented with a single passage from Chrysostom, because he being a special admirer of virginity, cannot be thought to be more lavish than others in praise of matrimony. Chrysostom thus speaks: "The first degree of chastity is pure virginity; the second, faithful marriage. Therefore, a chaste love of matrimony is the second species of virginity."

Chapter 13

OF VOWS. THE MISERABLE ENTANGLEMENTS CAUSED BY VOWING RASHLY.

This chapter consists of two parts–I. Of vows in general, sections 1-8. II. Of monastic vows, and especially of the vow of celibacy, sections 8-21.

Sections

1. Some general principles with regard to the nature of vows. Superstitious errors not only of the heathen, but of Christians, in regard to vows.

2. Three points to be considered with regard to vows. First, to whom the vow is made—viz. to God. Nothing to be vowed to Him but what He himself requires.

3. Second, who we are that vow. We must measure our strength, and have regard to our calling. Fearful errors of the Popish clergy by not attending to this. Their vow of celibacy.

4. Third point to be attended to—viz. the intention with which the vow is made. Four ends in vowing. Two of them refer to the past, and two to the future. Examples and use of the former class.

5. End of vows, which refer to the future.

6. The doctrine of vows in general. Common vow of Christians in Baptism, etc. This vow sacred and salutary. Particular vows how to be tested.

7. Great prevalence of superstition with regard to vows.

8. Vows of monks. Contrast between ancient and modern monasticism.

9. Portraiture of the ancient monks by Augustine.

10. Degeneracy of modern monks. A. Inconsiderate rigor. B. Idleness. C. False boast of perfection.

11. This idea of monastic perfection refuted.

12. Arguments for monastic perfection. First argument answered.

13. Second argument answered.

14. Absurdity of representing the monastic profession as a second baptism.

15. Corrupt manners of monks.

16. Some defects in ancient monasticism.

17. General refutation of monastic vows.

18. Refutation continued.

19. Refutation continued.

20. Do such vows of celibacy bind the conscience? This question answered.

21. Those who abandon the monastic profession for an honest living, unjustly accused of breaking their faith.

1 Some general principles with regard to the nature of vows. Superstitious errors not only of the heathen, but of Christians, in regard to vows.

It is indeed deplorable that the Church, whose freedom was purchased by the inestimable price of Christ's blood, should have been thus oppressed by a cruel tyranny, and almost buried under a huge mass of traditions; but, at the same time, the private infatuation of each individual shows, that not without just cause has so much power been given from above to Satan and his ministers. It was not enough to neglect the command of Christ, and bear any burdens, which false teachers might please to impose, but each individual behooved to have his own peculiar burdens, and thus sink deeper by digging his own cavern. This has been the result when men set about devising vows, by which a stronger and closer obligation might be added to common ties. Having already shown that the worship of God was vitiated by the audacity of those who, under the name of pastors, domineered in the Church when they ensnared miserable souls by their iniquitous laws, it will not be out of place here to advert to a kindred evil, to make it appear that the world, in accordance with its depraved disposition, has always thrown every possible obstacle in the way of the helps by which it ought to have been brought to God. Moreover, that the very grievous mischief introduced by such vows may be more apparent, let the reader attend to the principles formerly laid down.

First, we showed (Book 2, chapter 8, section 5) that everything requisite for the ordering of a pious and holy life is comprehended in the law. Secondly, we showed that the Lord, the better to dissuade us from devising new works, included the whole of righteousness in simple obedience to His will. If these positions are true, it is easy to see that not all fictitious worship, which we ourselves devise for serving God, is in the least degree acceptable to Him, how pleasing soever it may be to us. And, unquestionably, in many passages the Lord not only openly rejects, but grievously abhors such worship.

Hence, arises a doubt with regard to vows, which are made without any express authority from the Word of God; in what light are they to be viewed? Can they be duly made by Christian men, and to what extent are they binding? What is called a promise among men is a vow when made to God. Now, we promise to men either things that we think will be acceptable to them, or things that we in duty owe them. Much more careful, therefore, ought we to be in vows which are directed to God, with whom we ought to act with the greatest seriousness. Here superstition has in all ages strangely prevailed; men at once, without judgment and without choice, vowing to God whatever came into their minds, or even rose to their lips.

Hence, the foolish vows, nay, monstrous absurdities, by which the heathen insolently sported with their gods. Would that Christians had not imitated them in this their audacity! Nothing, indeed, could be less becoming; but it is obvious that for some ages nothing has been more usual than this misconduct–the whole body of the people everywhere despising the Law of God, and burning with an insane zeal of vowing according to any dreaming notion which they had formed. I have no wish to exaggerate invidiously, or particularize the many grievous sins, which have here been committed; but it seemed right to advert to it in passing, that it may the better appear, that when we treat of vows we are not by any means discussing a superfluous question.

2 Three points to be considered with regard to vows. First, to whom the vow is made—viz. to God. Nothing to be vowed to Him but what He himself requires.

If we would avoid error in deciding what vows are legitimate, and what preposterous, three things must be attended to–viz. who he is to whom the vow is made; who we are that make it; and, lastly, with what intention we make it. In regard in the first, we should consider that we have to do with God, whom our obedience so delights, that He abominates all will-worship, how specious and splendid soever it be in the eyes of men. (See Colossians 2:23.) If all will-worship, which we devise without authority, is abomination to God, it follows that no worship can be acceptable to Him save that which is approved by His Word. Therefore, we must not arrogate such license to ourselves as to presume to vow anything to God without evidence of the estimation in which He holds it. For the doctrine of Paul, that whatsoever is not of faith is sin (see Romans 14:23), while it extends to all actions of every kind, certainly applies with peculiar force in the case where the thought is immediately turned towards God. Nay, if in the minutest matters (Paul was then speaking of the distinction of meats) we err or fall, where the sure light of faith shines not before us, how much more modesty ought we to use when we attempt a matter of the greatest weight? For in nothing ought we to be more serious than in the duties of religion. In vows, then, our first precaution must be, never to proceed to make any vow without having previously determined in our conscience to attempt nothing rashly. And we shall be safe from the danger of rashness when we have God going before, and dictating from His Word what is good, and what is useless.

3 Second, who we are that vow. We must measure our strength, and have regard to our calling. Fearful errors of the Popish clergy by not attending to this. Their vow of celibacy.

In the second point, which we have mentioned as requiring consideration, is implied, that we measure our strength, that we attend to our vocation so as not to neglect the blessing of liberty which God has conferred upon us. For he who vows what is not within his means, or is at variance with his calling, is rash, while he who contemns the beneficence of God in making Him Lord of all things, is ungrateful. When I speak thus, I mean not that anything is so placed in our hand, that, leaning on our own strength, we may promise it to God. For in the Council of Arausica (Chapter 11), it was most truly decreed, that nothing is duly vowed to God save what we have received from His hand, since all things, which are offered to Him, are merely His gifts. But seeing that some things are given to us by the goodness of God, and others withheld by His justice, every man should have respect to the measure of grace bestowed on him, as Paul enjoins. (See Romans 12:3; 1 Corinthians 12:11.)

All then I mean here is, that your vows should be adapted to the measure which God by His gifts prescribes to you, lest by attempting more than He permits, you arrogate too much to yourself, and fall headlong. For example, when the assassins, of whom mention is made in the Acts, vowed "that they would neither eat nor drink until they had killed Paul" (see Acts 23:12), though it had not been an impious conspiracy, it would still have been intolerably presumptuous, as subjecting the life and death of a man to their own power. Thus, Jephthah suffered for his folly, when with precipitate fervor he made a rash vow. (See Judges 11:30.)

Of this class, the first place of insane audacity belongs to celibacy. Priests, monks, and nuns, forgetful of their infirmity, are confident of their fitness for celibacy. But by what oracle have they been instructed that the chastity, which they vow to the end of life, they will be able through life to maintain? They hear the voice of God concerning the universal condition of mankind, "It is not good that the man should be alone" (Genesis 2:18). They understand, and I wish they did not feel that the sin remaining in us is armed with the sharpest stings. How can they presume to shake off the common feelings of their nature for a whole lifetime, seeing the gift of continence is often granted for a certain time, as occasion requires? In such perverse conduct they must not expect God to be their helper; let them rather remember the words, "Ye shall not tempt the Lord your God" (Deuteronomy 6:16). But it is to tempt the Lord to strive against the nature implanted by Him, and to spurn His present gifts as if they did not appertain to us. This they not only do, but marriage, which God did not think it unbecoming His majesty to institute, which He pronounced honorable in all, which Christ our Lord sanctified by His presence, and which He deigned to honor with His first miracle, they presume to stigmatize as pollution, so extravagant are the terms in which they eulogize every kind of celibacy; as if in their own life they did not furnish a clear proof that celibacy is one thing and chastity another.

This life, however, they most impudently style angelical, thereby offering no slight insult to the angels of God, to whom they compare whoremongers and adulterers, and something much worse and fouler still. And, indeed, there is here very little occasion for argument, since they are abundantly refuted by fact. For we plainly see the fearful punishments with which the Lord avenges this arrogance and contempt of His gifts from overweening confidence. More hidden crimes I spare through shame; what is known of them is too much.

Beyond all controversy, we ought not to vow anything which will hinder us in fulfilling our vocation; as if the father of a family were to vow to leave his wife and children, and undertake other burdens; or one who is fit for a public office should, when elected to it, vow to live private. But the meaning of what we have said as to not despising our liberty may occasion some difficulty if not explained. Wherefore, understand it briefly thus: Since God has given us dominion over all things, and so subjected them to us that we may use them for our convenience, we cannot hope that our service will be acceptable to God if we bring ourselves into bondage to external things, which ought to be subservient to us. I say this, because some aspire to the praise of humility, for entangling themselves in a variety of observances from which God for good reason wished us to be entirely free. Hence, if we would escape this danger, let us always remember that we are by no means to withdraw from the economy that God has appointed in the Christian Church.

4 Third point to be attended to—viz. the intention with which the vow is made. Four ends in vowing. Two of them refer to the past, and two to the future. Examples and use of the former class.

I come now to my third position–viz. that if you would approve your vow to God, the mind in which you undertake it is of great moment. For seeing that God looks not to the outward appearance but to the heart, the consequence is, that according to the purpose which the mind has in view, the same thing may at one time please and be acceptable to Him, and at another be most displeasing. If you vow abstinence from wine, as if there were any holiness in so doing, you are superstitious; but if you have some end in view which is not perverse, no one can disapprove. Now, as far as I can see, there are four ends to which our vows may be properly directed; two of these, for the sake of order, I refer to the past, and two to the future. To the past belong vows by which we either testify our gratitude toward God for favors received, or in order to deprecate His wrath, inflict punishment on ourselves for faults committed. The former, let us if you please call acts of thanksgiving; the latter, acts of repentance. Of the former class, we have an example in the tithes which Jacob vowed (see Genesis 28:20), if the Lord would conduct him safely home from exile; and also in the ancient peace offerings which pious kings and commanders, when about to engage in a just war, vowed that they would give if they were victorious, or, at least, if the Lord would deliver them when pressed by some greater difficulty. Thus are to be understood all the passages in the Psalms which speak of vows. (See Psalm 22:26; 56:13; 116:14,18.)

Similar vows may also be used by us in the present day, whenever the Lord has rescued us from some disaster or dangerous disease, or other peril. For it is not abhorrent from the office of a pious man thus to consecrate a votive offering to God as a formal symbol of acknowledgment that he may not seem ungrateful for His kindness. The nature of the second class it will be sufficient to illustrate merely by one familiar example. Should anyone, from gluttonous indulgence, have fallen into some iniquity, there is nothing to prevent him, with the view of chastising his intemperance, from renouncing all luxuries for a certain time, and in doing so, from employing a vow for the purpose of binding himself more firmly. And yet, I do not lay down this as an invariable law to all who have similarly offended; I merely show what may be lawfully done by those who think that such a vow will be useful to them. Thus while I hold it lawful so to vow, I at the same time leave it free.

5 End of vows, which refer to the future.

The vows, which have reference to the future, tend partly, as we have said, to render us more cautious, and partly to act as a kind of stimulus to the discharge of duty. A man sees that he is so prone to a certain vice, that in a thing which is otherwise not bad he cannot restrain himself from forthwith falling into evil: he will not act absurdly in cutting off the use of that thing for some time by a vow. If, for instance, one should perceive that this or that bodily ornament brings him into peril, and yet allured by cupidity he eagerly longs for it, what can he do better than by throwing a curb upon himself, that is, imposing the necessity of abstinence, free himself from all doubt? In like manner, should one be oblivious or sluggish in the necessary duties of piety, why should he not, by forming a vow, both awaken his memory and shake off his sloth? In both, I confess, there is a kind of tutelage, but inasmuch as they are helps to infirmity, they are used not without advantage by the ignorant and imperfect. Hence, we hold that vows which have respect to one of these ends, especially in external things, are lawful, provided they are supported by the approbation of God, are suitable to our calling, and are limited to the measure of grace bestowed upon us.

6 The doctrine of vows in general. Common vow of Christians in Baptism, etc. This vow sacred and salutary. Particular vows how to be tested.

It is not now difficult to infer what view on the whole ought to be taken of vows. There is one vow common to all believers, which taken in baptism we confirm and sanction by our Catechism, and partaking of the Lord's Supper. For the sacraments are a kind of mutual contracts by which the Lord conveys His mercy to us, and by it eternal life, while we in our turn promise Him obedience. The formula, or at least substance, of the vow is that renouncing Satan we bind ourselves to the service of God, to obey His holy commands, and no longer follow the depraved desires of our flesh. It cannot be doubted that this vow, which is sanctioned by Scripture, nay, is exacted from all the children of God, is holy and salutary. There is nothing against this in the fact that no man in this life yields that perfect obedience to the law, which God requires of us. This stipulation being included in the covenant of grace, comprehending forgiveness of sins and the spirit of holiness, the promise which we there make is combined both with entreaty for pardon and petition for assistance. It is necessary, in judging of particular vows, to keep the three former rules in remembrance: from them anyone will easily estimate the character of each single vow. Do not suppose, however, that I so commend the vows, which I maintain to be holy that I would have them made every day. For though I dare not give any precept as to time or number, yet if anyone will take my advice, he will not undertake any but what are sober and temporary. If you are always launching out into numerous vows, the whole solemnity will be lost by the frequency, and you will readily fall into superstition. If you bind yourself by a perpetual vow, you will have great trouble and annoyance in getting free, or, worn out by length of time, you will at length make bold to break it.

7 Great prevalence of superstition with regard to vows.

It is now easy to see under how much superstition the world has labored in this respect for several ages. One vowed that he would be abstemious, as if abstinence from wine were in itself an acceptable service to God. Another bound himself to fast, another to abstain from flesh on certain days, which he had vainly imagined to be more holy than other days. Things much more boyish were vowed though not by boys. For it was accounted great wisdom to undertake votive pilgrimages to holy places, and sometimes to perform the journey on foot, or with the body half naked, that the greater merit might be acquired by the greater fatigue. These and similar things, for which the world has long bustled with incredible zeal, if tried by the rules which we formerly laid down, will be discovered to be not only empty and nugatory, but full of manifest impiety. Be the judgment of the flesh what it may, there is nothing which God more abhors than fictitious worship. To these are added pernicious and damnable notions, hypocrites, after performing such frivolities, thinking that they have acquired no ordinary righteousness, placing the substance of piety in external observances, and despising all others who appear less careful about them.

8 Vows of monks. Contrast between ancient and modern monasticism.

It is of no use to enumerate all the separate forms. But as monastic vows are held in great veneration, because they seem to be approved by the public judgment of the Church, I will say a few words concerning them. And, first, lest anyone defend the monachism of the present day on the ground of the long prescription, it is to be observed, that the ancient mode of living in monasteries was very different. The persons who retired to them were those who wished to train themselves to the greatest austerity and patience. The discipline practiced by the monks then resembled that which the Lacedemonians are said to have used under the laws of Lycurgus, and was even much more rigorous. They slept on the ground; their drink was water; their food bread, herbs, and roots; and their chief luxuries, oil and pulse. They abstained from more delicate food and care of the body. These things might seem hyperbolical were they not vouched by experienced eyewitnesses, as Gregory Nazianzen, Basil, and Chrysostom. By such rudimentary training, they prepared themselves for greater offices. For of the fact that monastic colleges were then a kind of seminaries of the ecclesiastical order, both those whom we lately named are very competent witnesses (they were all brought up in monasteries, and thence called to the episcopal office), as well as several other great and excellent men of their age. Augustine also shows that in his time the monasteries were wont to furnish the Church with clergy. For he thus addresses the monks of the island of Capri: "We exhort you, brethren in the Lord, to keep your purpose, and persevere to the end; and if at any time our mother Church requires your labor, you will neither undertake it with eager elation, nor reject it from the blandishment of sloth, but with meek hearts obey God. You will not prefer your own ease to the necessities of the Church. Had no good men been willing to minister to her when in travail, it would have been impossible for you to be born." He is speaking of the ministry by which believers are spiritually born again. In like manner, he says to Aurelius, "It is both an occasion of lapse to them, and a most unbecoming injury to the clerical order, if the deserters of monasteries are elected to the clerical warfare, since from those who remain in the monastery our custom is to appoint to the clerical office only the better and more approved. Unless, perhaps, as the vulgar say, A bad chorister is a good symphonist, so, in like manner, it will be jestingly said of us, A bad monk is a good clergyman. There will be too much cause for grief if we stir up monks to such ruinous pride, and deem the clergy deserving of so grave an affront, seeing that sometimes a good monk scarcely makes a good clerk; he may have sufficient continence, but be deficient in necessary learning." From these passages, it appears that pious men were wont to prepare for the government of the Church by monastic discipline, that thus they might be more apt and better trained to undertake the important office: not that all attained to this object, or even aimed at it, since the great majority of monks were illiterate men. Those who were fit would be selected.

9 Portraiture of the ancient monks by Augustine.

Augustine, in two passages in particular, gives a portraiture of the form of ancient monasticism. The one is in his book, *De Moribus*

Ecclesiæ Catholicæ (On the Manners of the Catholic Church), where he maintains the holiness of that profession against the calumnies of the Manichees; the other in a treatise, entitled, *De Opere Monachorum (On the Work of Monks)*, where he inveighs against certain degenerate monks who had begun to corrupt that institution. I will here give a summary of what he there delivers, and, as far as I can, in his own words: "Despising the allurements of this world, and congregated in common for a most chaste and most holy life, they pass their lives together, spending their time in prayer, reading, and discourse, not swollen with pride, not turbulent through petulance, not livid with envy. No one possesses anything of his own: no one is burdensome to any man. They labor with their hands in things by which the body may be fed, and the mind not withdrawn from God. The fruit of their labor they hand over to those whom they call deans. Those deans, disposing of the whole with great care, render an account to one whom they call father. These fathers, who are not only of the purest morals, but most distinguished for divine learning, and noble in all things, without any pride, consult those whom they call their sons, though the former have full authority to command, and the latter a great inclination to obey. At the close of the day, they assemble each from his cell, and without having broken their fast, to hear their father, and to the number of three thousand at least (he is speaking of Egypt and the East) they assemble under each father. Then the body is refreshed, so far as suffices for safety and health, everyone curbing his concupiscence so as not to be profuse in the scanty and very mean diet, which is provided. Thus, they not only abstain from flesh and wine for subduing lust, but from those things, which provoke the appetite of the stomach and gullet more readily, from seeming to some more refined. In this way the desire of exquisite dainties, in which there is no flesh, is wont to be absurdly and shamefully defended. Any surplus, after necessary food (and the surplus is very great from the labor of their hands and the frugality of their meals), is carefully distributed to the needy, the more carefully that it was not procured by those who distribute. For they never act with the view of having abundance for themselves, but always act with the view of allowing no superfluity to remain with them." Afterwards describing their austerity, of which he had himself seen instances both at Milan and elsewhere, he says, "Meanwhile, no one is urged to austerities which he is unable to bear: no one is obliged to do what he declines, nor condemned by the others, whom he acknowledges himself too weak to imitate. For they remember how greatly charity is commended: they remember that to the pure all things are pure. (See Titus 1:15.) Wherefore, all their vigilance is employed, not in rejecting kinds of food as polluted, but in subduing concupiscence, and maintaining brotherly love. They remember, "Meats for the belly, and the belly for meats ..." (1 Corinthians 6:13). Many, however strong, abstain because of the weak. In many this is not the cause of action; they take pleasure in sustaining themselves on the meanest and least expensive food.

Hence, the very persons who in health restrain themselves, decline not in sickness to use what their health requires. Many do not drink wine, and yet do not think themselves polluted by it, for they most humanely cause it to be given to the more sickly, and to those whose health requires it; and some who foolishly refuse, they fraternally admonish, lest by vain superstition they sooner become more weak than more holy. Thus, they sedulously practice piety, while they know that bodily exercise is only for a short time. Charity especially is observed: their food is adapted to charity, their speech to charity, their dress to charity, and their looks to charity. They go together, and breathe only charity: they deem it as unlawful to offend charity as to offend God; if anyone opposes it, he is cast out and shunned; if anyone offends it, he is not permitted to remain one day." Since this holy man appears in these words to have exhibited the monastic life of ancient times as in a picture, I have thought it right to insert them here, though somewhat long, because I perceive that I would be considerably longer if I collected them from different writers, however compendious I might study to be.

10 Degeneracy of modern monks. A. Inconsiderate rigor. B. Idleness. C. False boast of perfection.

Here, however, I had no intention to discuss the whole subject. I only wished to show, by the way, what kind of monks the early Church had, and what the monastic profession then was, that from the contrast sound readers might judge how great the effrontery is of those who allege antiquity in support of present monkism. Augustine, while tracing out a holy and legitimate monasticism, would keep away all rigorous exaction of those things, which the word of the Lord has left free. But in the present day, nothing is more rigorously exacted. For they deem it an inexpiable crime if anyone deviates in the least degree from the prescribed form in color or species of dress, in the kind of food, or in other frivolous and frigid ceremonies. Augustine strenuously contends that it is not lawful for monks to live in idleness on other men's means. He denies that any such example was to be found in his day in a well-regulated monastery. Our monks place the principal part of their holiness in idleness. For if you take away their idleness, where will that contemplative life be which they glory that they excel all others, and make a near approach to the angels? Augustine, in fine, requires a monasticism, which may be nothing else than a training and assistant to the offices of piety, which are recommended to all Christians. What? When he makes charity its chief and almost its only rule, do we think he praises that combination by which a few men, bound to each other, are separated from the whole body of the Church? Nay, he wishes them to set an example to others of preserving the unity of the Church. So different is the nature of present monachism in both respects, that it would be difficult to find anything so dissimilar, not to say contrary. For our monks, not satisfied with that piety, on the study of which alone Christ enjoins His followers to be intent, imagine some new kind of piety, by aspiring to which they are more perfect than all other men.

11 This idea of monastic perfection refuted.

If they deny this, I should like to know why they honor their own order only with the title of perfection, and deny it to all other divine callings. I am aware of the sophistical solution that their order is not so called because it contains perfection in itself, but because it is the best of all for acquiring perfection. When they would extol themselves to the people; when they would lay a snare for rash and ignorant youth; when they would assert their privileges and exalt their own dignity to the disparagement of others, they boast that they are in a state of perfection. When they are too closely pressed to be able to defend this vain arrogance, they betake themselves to the subterfuge that they have not yet obtained perfection, but that they are in a state in which they aspire to it more than others; meanwhile, the people continue to admire as if the monastic life alone were angelic, perfect, and purified from every vice. Under this pretence, they ply a gainful traffic, while their moderation lies buried in a few volumes. Who sees not that this is intolerable trifling? But let us treat with them as if they ascribed nothing more to their profession than to call it a state for acquiring perfection. Surely, by giving it this name, they distinguish it by a special mark from other modes of life. And who will allow such honor to be transferred to an institution of which not one syllable is said in approbation, while all the other callings of God are deemed unworthy of the same, though not only commanded by His sacred lips, but adorned with distinguished titles? And how great the insult offered to God, when some device of man is preferred to all the modes of life, which He has ordered, and by His testimony approved?

12 Arguments for monastic perfection. First argument answered.

But let them say I calumniated them when I declared that they were not contented with the rule prescribed by God. Still, though I were silent, they more than sufficiently accuse themselves; for they plainly declare that they undertake a greater burden than Christ has imposed on His followers, since they promise that they will keep evangelical counsels regarding the love of enemies, the suppression of vindictive feelings, and abstinence from swearing, counsels to which Christians are not commonly astricted. In this, what antiquity can they pretend? None of the ancients ever thought of such a thing: all with one voice proclaim that not one syllable proceeded from Christ, which it is not necessary to obey. And the very things, which these worthy expounders pretend that Christ only counseled, they uniformly declare, without any doubt, that He expressly enjoined. But as we have shown above, that this is a most pestilential error, let it suffice here to have briefly observed that monasticism, as it now exists, founded on an idea which all pious men ought to execrate—namely, the pretence that there is some more perfect rule of life than that common rule which God has delivered to the whole Church. Whatever is built on this foundation cannot but be abominable.

13 Second argument answered.

But they produce another argument for their perfection, and deem it invincible. Our Lord said to the young man who put a question to Him concerning the perfection of righteousness, "If thou wilt be perfect, go and sell that thou hast, and give to the poor" (Matthew 19:21). Whether they do so, I do not now dispute. Let us grant for the present that they do. They boast, then, that they have become perfect by abandoning their all. If the sum off perfection consists in this, what is the meaning of Paul's doctrine, that though a man should give all his goods to feed the poor, and have not charity, he is nothing? (See 1 Corinthians 13:3.) What kind of perfection is that which, if charity be wanting, is with the individual himself reduced to nothing? Here they must of necessity answer that it is indeed the highest, but is not the only work of perfection. But here again Paul interposes; and hesitates not to declare that charity, without any renunciation of that sort, is the "bond of perfectness" (Colossians 3:14). If it is certain that there is no disagreement between the scholar and the master, and the latter clearly denies that the perfection of a man consists in renouncing all his goods, and on the other hand asserts that perfection may exist without it, we must see in what sense we should understand the words of Christ, "If thou wilt be perfect, go and sell that thou hast." Now, there will not be the least obscurity in the meaning if we consider (this ought to be attended to in all our Savior's discourses) to whom the words are addressed. (See Luke 10:25.) A young man asks by what works he shall enter into eternal life. Christ, as He was asked concerning works, refers him to the law. And justly, for, considered in itself, it is the way of eternal life, and its inefficacy to give eternal life is owing to our depravity. By this answer, Christ declared that He did not deliver any other rule of life than that which had formerly been delivered in the law of the Lord. Thus He both bore testimony to the divine law, that it was a doctrine of perfect righteousness, and at the same time met the calumnious charge of seeming, by some new rule of life, to incite the people to revolt from the law.

The young man, who was not ill disposed, but was puffed up with vain confidence, answers that he had observed all the precepts of the law from his youth. It is certain that he was immeasurably distant from the goal, which he boasted of having reached. Had his boast been true, he would have wanted nothing of absolute perfection. For it has been demonstrated above, that the law contains in it a perfect righteousness. This is even obvious from the fact, that the observance of it is called the way to eternal life. To show him how little progress he had made in that righteousness which he too boldly answered that he had fulfilled, it was right to bring before him his besetting sin. Now, while he abounded in riches, he had his heart set upon them. Therefore, because he did not feel this secret wound, it is probed by Christ: "Go," says He, "and sell that thou hast." Had he been as good a keeper of the law as he supposed, he would not have gone away sorrowful on hearing these words. For he who loves God with his whole heart, not only regards everything which wars with his love as dross, but hates it as destruction (Philippians 3:8).

Therefore, when Christ orders a rich miser to leave all that he has, it is the same as if he had ordered the ambitious to renounce all his honors, the voluptuous all his luxuries, the unchaste all the instruments of his lust. Thus consciences, which are not reached by any general admonition, are to be recalled to a particular feeling of their particular sin. In vain, therefore, do they wrest that special case to a general interpretation, as if Christ had decided that the perfection of man consists in the abandonment of his goods, since He intended nothing more by the expression than to bring a youth who was out of measure satisfied with himself to feel his sore condition, and so understand that he was still at a great distance from that perfect obedience of the law which he falsely ascribed to himself. I admit that this passage was ill understood by some of the Fathers; and hence arose an affectation of voluntary poverty, those only being thought blest who abandoned all earthly goods, and in a state of destitution devoted themselves to Christ. But I am confident that, after my exposition, no good and reasonable man will have any dubiety here as to the mind of Christ.

14 Absurdity of representing the monastic profession as a second baptism.

Still there was nothing with the Fathers less intended than to establish that kind of perfection, which was afterwards fabricated by cowled monks, in order to rear up a species of double Christianity. For yet the sacrilegious dogma was not broached, which compares the profession of monasticism to baptism, nay, plainly asserts that it is the form of a second baptism. Who can doubt that the Fathers with their whole hearts abhorred such blasphemy? Then what need is there to demonstrate, by words, that the last quality, which Augustine mentions as belonging to the ancient monks–viz. that they in all things accommodated themselves to charity–is most alien from this new profession? The thing itself declares that all who retire into monasteries withdraw from the Church. For how? Do they not separate themselves from the legitimate society of the faithful, by acquiring for themselves a special ministry and private administration of the sacraments? What is meant by destroying the communion of the Church if this is not? And to follow out the comparison with which I began, and at once close the point, what resemblance have they in this respect to the ancient monks? These, though they dwelt separately from others, had not a separate Church; they partook of the sacraments with others, they attended public meetings, and were then a part of the people. But what have those men done in erecting a private altar for themselves but broken the bond of unity? For they have excommunicated themselves from the whole body of the Church, and contemned the ordinary ministry by which the Lord has been pleased that peace and charity should be preserved among His followers. Wherefore I hold that as many monasteries as there are in the present day, so many conventicles are there of schismatics, who have disturbed ecclesiastical order, and been cut off from the legitimate society of the faithful. And that there might be no doubt as to their separation; they have given themselves the various names of factions. They have not been ashamed to glory in that which Paul so execrates, that he is unable to express his detestation too strongly. Unless, indeed, we suppose that Christ was not divided by the Corinthians, when one teacher set himself above another (see 1 Corinthians 1:12, 13; 3:4); and that now no injury is done to Christ when, instead of Christians, we hear some called Benedictines, others Franciscans, others Dominicans, and so called, that while they affect to be distinguished from the common body of Christians, they proudly substitute these names for a religious profession.

15 Corrupt manners of monks.

The differences, which I have hitherto pointed out, between the ancient monks and those of our age, are not in manners, but in profession. Hence, let my readers remember that I have spoken of monachism rather than of monks; and marked, not the vices which cleave to a few, but vices which are inseparable from the very mode of life. Concerning manners, of what use is it to particularize and show how great the difference? This much is certain, that there is no order of men more polluted by all kinds of vicious turpitude; nowhere do faction, hatred, party spirit, and intrigue, more prevail. In a few monasteries, indeed, they live chastely, if we are to call it chastity, where lust is so far repressed as not to be openly infamous; still you will scarcely find one in ten, which is not rather a brothel than a sacred abode of chastity. But how frugally they live? Just like swine wallowing in their sties. But lest they complain that I deal too unmercifully with them, I go no further; although anyone who knows the case will admit, that in the few things which I have said, I have not spoken in the spirit of an accuser. Augustine though he testifies, that the monks excelled so much in chastity, yet complains that there were many vagabonds, who, by wicked arts and impostures, extracted money from the more simple, plying a shameful traffic, by carrying about the relics of martyrs, and vending any dead man's bones for relics, bringing ignominy on their order by many similar iniquities. As he declares that he had seen none better than those who had profited in monasteries, so he laments that he had seen none worse than those who had backslidden in monasteries. What would he say were he, in the present day, to see now almost all monasteries overflowing, and in a manner bursting, with numerous deplorable vices? I say nothing but what is notorious to all; and yet this charge does not apply to all without a single exception; for, as the rule and discipline of holy living was never so well framed in monasteries as that there were not always some drones very unlike the others; so I hold that, in the present day, monks have not so completely degenerated from that holy antiquity as not to have some good men among them; but these few lie scattered up and down among a huge multitude of wicked and dishonest men, and are not only despised, but even petulantly assailed, sometimes even treated cruelly by the others, who, according to the Milesian proverb, think they ought to have no good man among them.

16 Some defects in ancient monasticism.

By this contrast between ancient and modern monasticism, I trust I have gained my object, which was to show that our cowled monks falsely pretend the example of the primitive Church in defense of their profession; since they differ no less from the monks of that period than apes do from men. Meanwhile I disguise not that even in that ancient form which Augustine commends, there was something which little pleases me. I admit that they were not superstitious in the external exercises of a more rigorous discipline, but I say that they were not without a degree of affectation and false zeal. It was a fine thing to cast away their substance, and free themselves from all worldly cares; but God sets more value on the pious management of a household, when the head of it, discarding all avarice, ambition, and other lusts of the flesh, makes it his purpose to serve God in some particular vocation. It is fine to philosophize in seclusion, far away from the intercourse of society; but it ill accords with Christian meekness for anyone, as if in hatred of the human race, to fly to the wilderness and to solitude, and at the same time desert the duties, which the Lord has especially commanded. Were we to grant that there was nothing worse in that profession; there is certainly no small evil in its having introduced a useless and perilous example into the Church.

17 General refutation of monastic vows.

Now, then, let us see the nature of the vows by which the monks of the present day are initiated into this famous order. First, as their intention is to institute a new and fictitious worship with a view to gain favor with God, I conclude from what has been said above, that everything, which they vow, is abomination to God. Secondly, I hold that as they frame their own mode of life at pleasure, without any regard to the calling of God, or to His approbation, the attempt is rash and unlawful; because their conscience has no ground on which it can support itself before God; and "whatsoever is not of faith is sin" (Romans 14:23).

Moreover, I maintain that in astricting themselves to many perverse and impious modes of worship, such as are exhibited in modern monasticism, they consecrate themselves not to God but to the devil. For why should the prophets have been permitted to say that the Israelites sacrificed their sons to devils and not to God (see Deuteronomy 32:17; Psalm 106:37), merely because they had corrupted the true worship of God by profane ceremonies; and we not be permitted to say the same thing of monks who, along with the cowl, cover themselves with the net of a thousand impious superstitions? Then what is their species of vows? They offer God a promise of perpetual virginity, as if they had previously made a compact with Him to free them from the necessity of marriage. They cannot allege that they make this vow trusting entirely to the grace of God; for, seeing He declares this a special gift not given to all (see Matthew 19:11), no man has a right to assume that the gift will be his. Let those who have it use it; and if at any time they feel the infirmity of the flesh, let them have recourse to the aid of Him by whose power alone, they can resist. If this avails not, let them not despise the remedy, which is offered to them. If the faculty of continence is denied, the voice of God distinctly calls upon them to marry. By continence, I mean not merely that by which the body is kept pure from fornication, but that by which the mind keeps its chastity untainted. For Paul enjoins caution not only against external lasciviousness, but also burning of mind. (See 1 Corinthians 7:9.) It has been the practice (they say) from the remotest period, for those who wished to devote themselves entirely to God, to bind themselves by a vow of continence. I confess that the custom is ancient, but I do not admit that the age when it commenced was so free from every defect that all that was then done is to be regarded as a rule.

Moreover, the inexorable rigor of holding that after the vow is conceived there is no room for repentance, crept in gradually. This is clear from Cyprian. "If virgins have dedicated themselves to Christian faith, let them live modestly and chastely, without pretence. Thus strong and stable, let them wait for the reward of virginity. But if they will not, or cannot persevere, it is better to marry, than by their faults to fall into the fire." In the present day, with what invectives would they not lacerate anyone who should seek to temper the vow of continence by such an equitable course? Those, therefore, have wandered far from the ancient custom who not only use no moderation, and grant no pardon when anyone proves unequal to the performance of his vow, but shamelessly declare that it is a more heinous sin to cure the intemperance of the flesh by marriage, than to defile body and soul by whoredom.

18 Refutation continued.

But they still insist and attempt to show that this vow was used in the days of the apostles, because Paul says that widows who marry after having once undertaken a public office "cast off their first faith" (1 Timothy 5:12). I by no means deny that widows who dedicated themselves and their labors to the Church, at the same time came under an obligation of perpetual celibacy, not because they regarded it in the light of a religious duty, as afterwards began to be the case, but because they could not perform their functions unless they had their time at their own command, and were free from the nuptial tie. But if, after giving their pledge, they began to look to a new marriage, what else was this but to shake off the calling of God? It is not strange, therefore, when Paul says that by such desires they grow wanton against Christ. In further explanation he afterwards adds, that by not performing their promises to the Church, they violate and nullify their first faith given in baptism; one of the things contained in this first faith being, that everyone should correspond to His calling. Unless you choose rather to interpret that, having lost their modesty, they afterwards cast off all care of decency, prostituting themselves to all kinds of lasciviousness and pertness, leading licentious and dissolute lives, than which nothing can less become Christian women. I am much pleased with this exposition. Our answer then is, that those widows who were admitted to a public ministry came under an obligation of perpetual celibacy, and hence we easily understand how, when they married, they threw off all modesty, and became more insolent than became Christian women that in this way they not only sinned by violating the faith given to the Church, but revolted from the common rule of pious women.

But, first, I deny that they had any other reason for professing celibacy than just because marriage was altogether inconsistent with the function which they undertook. Hence, they bound themselves to celibacy only as far as the nature of their function required.

Secondly, I do not admit that they were bound to celibacy in such a sense that it was not better for them to marry than to suffer by the incitements of the flesh, and fall into uncleanness.

Thirdly, I hold that what Paul enjoined was in the common case free from danger, because he orders the selection to be made from those who, contented with one marriage, had already given proof of continence. Our only reason for disapproving of the vow of celibacy is that it is improperly regarded as an act of worship, and is rashly undertaken by persons who have not the power of keeping it.

19 Refutation continued.

But what ground can there be for applying this passage to nuns? For deaconesses were appointed, not to soothe God by chanting or unintelligible murmurs, and spend the rest of their time in idleness; but to perform a public ministry of the Church toward the poor, and to labor with all zeal, assiduity, and diligence, in offices of charity. They did not vow celibacy, that they might thereafter exhibit abstinence from marriage as a kind of worship rendered to God, but only that they might be freer from encumbrance in executing their office. In fine, they did not vow on attaining adolescence, or in the bloom of life, and so afterwards learn, by too late experience, over what a precipice they had plunged themselves, but after they were thought to have surmounted all danger, they took a vow not less safe than holy. But not to press the two former points, I say that it was unlawful to allow women to take a vow of continence before their sixtieth year, since the apostle admits such only, and enjoins the younger to marry and beget children. Therefore, it is impossible, on any ground, to excuse the deduction, first of twelve, then of twenty, and, lastly, of thirty years. Still less possible is it to tolerate the case of miserable girls, who, before they have reached an age at which they can know themselves, or have any experience of their character, are not only induced by fraud, but compelled by force and threats, to entangle themselves in these accursed snares. I will not enter at length into a refutation of the other two vows. This only I say, that besides involving (as matters stand in the present day) not a few superstitions, they seem to be purposely framed in such a manner, as to make those who take them mock God and men. But lest we should seem, with too malignant feeling, to attack every particular point, we will be contented with the general refutation, which has been given above.

20 Do such vows of celibacy bind the conscience? This question answered.

The nature of the vows, which are legitimate and acceptable to God, I think I have sufficiently explained. Yet, because some ill-informed and timid consciences, even when a vow displeases, and is condemned, nevertheless hesitate as to the obligation, and are grievously tormented, shuddering at the thought of violating a pledge given to God, and, on the other hand, fearing to sin more by keeping it, we must here come to their aid, and enable them to escape from this difficulty. And to take away all scruple at once, I say that all vows not legitimate, and not duly conceived, as they are of no account with God, should be regarded by us as null. For if, in human contracts, those promises only are binding in which he with whom we contract wishes to have us bound, it is absurd to say that we are bound to perform things which God does not at all require of us, especially since our works can only be right when they please God, and have the testimony of our consciences that they do please Him. For it always remains fixed, that "whatsoever is not of faith is sin" (Romans 14:23). By this Paul means, that any work undertaken in doubt is vicious, because at the root of all good works lies faith, which assures us that they are acceptable to God. Therefore, if Christian men may not attempt anything without this assurance, why, if they have undertaken anything rashly through ignorance, may they not afterwards be freed, and desist from their error? Since vows rashly undertaken are of this description, they not only oblige not, but must necessarily be rescinded. What, then, when they are not only of no estimation in the sight of God, but are even an abomination, as has already been demonstrated? It is needless further to discuss a point, which does not require it. To appease pious consciences, and free them from all doubt, this one argument seems to me sufficient–viz. that all works whatsoever which flow not from a pure fountain, and are not directed to a proper end, are repudiated by God, and so repudiated, that He no less forbids us to continue than to begin them. Hence, it follows, that vows dictated by error and superstition are of no weight with God, and ought to be abandoned by us.

21 Those who abandon the monastic profession for an honest living, unjustly accused of breaking their faith.

He who understands this solution is furnished with the means of repelling the calumnies of the wicked against those who withdraw from monasticism to some honest kind of livelihood. They are grievously charged with having perjured themselves, and broken their faith, because they have broken the bond (vulgarly supposed to be indissoluble) by which they had bound themselves to God and the Church. But I say, first, there is no bond when that which man confirms God abrogates; and, secondly, even granting that they were bound when they remained entangled in ignorance and error, now, since they have been enlightened by the knowledge of the truth, I hold that they are, at the same time, free by the grace of Christ. For if such is the efficacy of the Cross of Christ, that it frees us from the curse of the divine law by which we were held bound, how much more must it rescue us from extraneous chains, which are nothing but the wily nets of Satan? There can be no doubt, therefore, that all on whom Christ shines with the light of His gospel, he frees from all the snares in which they had entangled themselves through superstition. At the same time, they have another defense if they were unfit for celibacy. For if an impossible vow is certain destruction to the soul, which God wills to be saved and not destroyed, it follows that it ought by no means to be adhered to. Now, how impossible the vow of continence is to those who have not received it by special gift, we have shown, and experience, even were I silent, declares: while the great obscenity with which almost all monasteries teem is a thing not unknown. If any seem more decent and modest than others, they are not, however, chaste. The sin of unchastity urges, and lurks within. Thus it is that God, by fearful examples, punishes the audacity of men, when, unmindful of their infirmity, they, against nature, affect that which has been denied to them, and despising the remedies which the Lord has placed in their hands, are confident in their ability to overcome the disease of incontinence by contumacious obstinacy. For what other name can we give it, when a man, admonished of his need of marriage, and of the remedy with which the Lord has thereby furnished, not only despises it, but binds himself by an oath to despise it?

Chapter 14

OF THE SACRAMENTS.

This chapter consists of two principal parts—I. Of sacraments in general. The sum of the doctrine stated, sections 1-6. Two classes of opponents to be guarded against—viz. those who undervalue the power of the sacraments, sections 7-13; and those who attribute too much to the sacraments, sections 14-17. II. Of the sacraments in particular, both of the Old and the New Testament. Their scope and meaning. Refutation of those who have either too high or too low ideas of the sacraments.

Sections

1. *Of the sacraments in general. A sacrament defined.*
2. *Meaning of the word sacrament.*
3. *Definition explained. Why God seals His promises to us by sacraments.*
4. *The word, which ought to accompany the element, that the sacrament may be complete.*
5. *Error of those who attempt to separate the Word, or promise of God, from the element.*
6. *Why sacraments are called Signs of the Covenant.*
7. *They are such signs, though the wicked should receive them, but are signs of grace only to believers.*
8. *Objections to this view answered.*
9. *No secret virtue in the sacraments. Their whole efficacy depends on the inward operation of the Spirit.*
10. *Objections answered. Illustrated by a simile.*
11. *Of the increase of faith by the preaching of the Word.*
12. *In what way, and how far, the sacraments are confirmations of our faith.*
13. *Some regard the sacraments as mere signs. This view refuted.*

14. Some again attribute too much to the sacraments. Refutation.

15. Refutation confirmed by a passage from Augustine.

16. Previous views more fully explained.

17. The matter of the sacrament always present when the sacrament is duly administered.

18. Extensive meaning of the term sacrament.

19. The ordinary sacraments in the Church. How necessary they are.

20. The sacraments of the Old and of the New Testament. The end of both the same —viz. to lead us to Christ.

21. This apparent in the sacraments of the Old Testament.

22. Apparent also in the sacraments of the New Testament.

23. Impious doctrine of the Schoolmen as to the difference between the Old and the New Testaments.

24. Scholastic objection answered.

25. Another objection answered.

26. Sacraments of the New Testament sometimes excessively extolled by early Theologians. Their meaning explained.

1 Of the sacraments in general. A sacrament defined.

Akin to the preaching of the gospel, we have another help to our faith in the sacraments, in regard to which, it greatly concerns us that some sure doctrine should be delivered, informing us both of the end for which they were instituted, and of their present use. First, we must attend to what a sacrament is. It seems to me, then, a simple and appropriate definition to say, that it is an external sign, by which the Lord seals on our consciences His promises of good will toward us, in order to sustain the weakness of our faith, and we in our turn testify our piety towards Him, both before himself, and before angels as well as men. We may also define more briefly by calling it a testimony of the divine favor toward us, confirmed by an external sign, with a corresponding attestation of our faith towards Him. You may make your choice of these definitions, which in meaning differ not from that of Augustine, which defines a sacrament to be a visible sign of a sacred thing, or a visible form of an invisible grace, but does not contain a better or surer explanation. As its brevity makes it somewhat obscure, and thereby misleads the more illiterate, I wished to remove all doubt, and make the definition fuller by stating it at greater length.

2 Meaning of the word sacrament.

The reason that the ancients used the term in this sense is not obscure. The old interpreter, whenever he wished to render the Greek term for "sacraments" into Latin, especially when it was used with reference to divine things, used the word sacramentum. Thus, in Ephesians, "Having made known unto us the mystery (sacramentum) of his will." Again, "If ye have heard of the dispensation of the grace of God, which is given me to you-wards, how that by revelation he made known unto me the mystery" (sacramentum) (Ephesians 1:9; 3:2). In the Colossians, "Even the mystery which hath been hid from ages and from generations, but is now made manifest to his saints, to whom God would make known what is the riches of the glory of this mystery" (sacramentum) (Colossians 1:26). Also in the First Epistle to Timothy, "Without controversy, great is the mystery (sacramentum) of godliness: God was manifest in the flesh" (1 Timothy 3:16). He was unwilling to use the word arcanum (secret), lest the word should seem beneath the magnitude of the thing meant. When the thing, therefore, was sacred and secret, he used the term sacramentum. In this sense, it frequently occurs in ecclesiastical writers. And it is well known, that what the Latins call sacramenta, the Greeks call mysteries." The sameness of meaning removes all dispute. Hence, it is that the term was applied to those signs, which gave an august representation of things spiritual and sublime. This is also observed by Augustine, "It would be tedious to discourse of the variety of signs; those which relate to divine things are called sacraments."

3 Definition explained. Why God seals His promises to us by sacraments.

From the definition which we have given, we perceive that there never is a sacrament without an antecedent promise, the sacrament being added as a kind of appendix, with the view of confirming and sealing the promise, and giving a better attestation, or rather, in a manner, confirming it. In this way God provides first for our ignorance and sluggishness, and, secondly, for our infirmity; and yet, properly speaking, it does not so much confirm His Word as establish us in the faith of it. For the truth of God is in itself sufficiently stable and certain, and cannot receive a better confirmation from any other quarter than from itself. But as our faith is slender and weak, so if it be not propped up on every side, and supported by all kinds of means, it is forthwith shaken and tossed to and fro, wavers, and even falls. And here, indeed, our merciful Lord, with boundless condescension, so accommodates himself to our capacity, that seeing how from our animal nature we are always creeping on the ground, and cleaving to the flesh, having no thought of what is spiritual, and not even forming an idea of it, He declines not by means of these earthly elements to lead us to himself, and even in the flesh to exhibit a mirror of spiritual blessings. For, as Chrysostom says, "Were we incorporeal, He would give us these things in a naked and incorporeal form. Now because our souls are implanted in bodies, He delivers spiritual things under things visible. Not that the qualities which are set before us in the sacraments are inherent in the nature of the things, but God gives them this signification."

4 The Word, which ought to accompany the element, that the sacrament may be complete.

This is commonly expressed by saying that a sacrament consists of the word and the external sign. By the Word we ought to understand not one which, muttered without meaning and without faith, by its sound merely, as by a magical incantation, has the effect of consecrating the element, but one which, preached, makes us understand what the visible sign means. The thing, therefore, which was frequently done, under the tyranny of the Pope, was not free from great profanation of the mystery, for they deemed it sufficient if the priest muttered the formula of consecration, while the people, without understanding, looked stupidly on. Nay, this was done for the express purpose of preventing any instruction from thereby reaching the people: for all was said in Latin to illiterate hearers. Superstition afterwards was carried to such a height, that the consecration was thought not to be duly performed except in a low grumble, which few could hear. Very different is the doctrine of Augustine concerning the sacramental word. "Let the Word be added to the element, and it will become a sacrament. For whence can there be so much virtue in water as to touch the body and cleanse the heart, unless by the agency of the Word, and this not because it is said, but because it is believed? For even in the Word the transient sound is one thing, the permanent power another. This is the word of faith which we preach says the Apostle" (Romans 10:8).

Hence, in the Acts of the Apostles, we have the expression, "Purify their hearts by faith" (Acts 15:9). And the Apostle Peter says, "The like figure whereunto even baptism doth now save us (not the putting away of the filth of the flesh, but the answer of a good conscience)" (1 Peter 3:21). "This is the word of faith which we preach: by which word doubtless baptism also, in order that it may be able to cleanse, is consecrated." You see how he requires preaching to the production of faith. And we need not labor to prove this, since there is not the least room for doubt as to what Christ did, and commanded us to do, as to what the apostles followed, and a purer Church observed. Nay, it is known that, from the very beginning of the world, whenever God offered any sign to the holy Patriarchs, it was inseparably attached to doctrine, without which our senses would gaze bewildered on an unmeaning object. Therefore, when we hear mention made of the sacramental Word, let us understand the promise which, proclaimed aloud by the minister, leads the people by the hand to that to which the sign tends and directs us.

5 Error of those who attempt to separate the Word, or promise of God, from the element.

Nor are those to be listened to who oppose this view with a more subtle than solid dilemma. They argue thus: Either we know that the Word of God, which precedes the sacrament, is the true will of God, or we do not know it. If we know it, we learn nothing new from the sacrament, which succeeds. If we do not know it, we cannot learn it from the sacrament, whose whole efficacy depends on the Word. Our brief reply is: The seals which are affixed to diplomas, and other public deeds, are nothing considered in themselves, and would be affixed to no purpose if nothing was written on the parchment, and yet this does not prevent them from sealing and confirming when they are appended to writings. It cannot be alleged that this comparison is a recent fiction of our own, since Paul himself used it, terming circumcision a seal (Romans 4:11), where he expressly maintains that the circumcision of Abraham was not for justification, but was an attestation to the covenant, by the faith of which he had been previously justified. And how, pray, can anyone be greatly offended when we teach that the promise is sealed by the sacrament, since it is plain, from the promises themselves, that one promise confirms another? The clearer any evidence is, the fitter is it to support our faith. But sacraments bring with them the clearest promises, and, when compared with the Word, have this peculiarity, that they represent promises to the life, as if painted in a picture. Nor ought we to be moved by an objection founded on the distinction between sacraments and the seals of documents–viz. that since both consist of the carnal elements of this world, the former cannot be sufficient or adequate to seal the promises of God, which are spiritual and eternal, though the latter may be employed to seal the edicts of princes concerning fleeting and fading things. But the believer, when the sacraments are presented to his eye, does not stop short at the carnal spectacle, but by the steps of analogy, which I have indicated, rises with pious consideration to the sublime mysteries which lie hidden in the sacraments.

6 Why sacraments are called Signs of the Covenant.

As the Lord calls His promises covenants (see Genesis 6:18; 9:9; 17:2), and sacraments signs of the covenants, so something similar may be inferred from human covenants. What could the slaughter of a hog effect, unless words were interposed or rather preceded? Swine are often killed without any interior or occult mystery. What could be gained by pledging the right hand, since hands are frequently joined in giving battle? But when words have preceded, then by such symbols of covenant sanction is given to laws, though previously conceived, digested, and enacted by words. Sacraments, therefore, are exercises, which confirm our faith in the Word of God; and because we are carnal, they are exhibited under carnal objects, that thus they may train us in accommodation to our sluggish capacity, just as nurses lead children by the hand. And hence, Augustine calls a sacrament a visible Word), because it represents the promises of God as in a picture, and places them in our view in a graphic bodily form. We might refer to other similitudes, by which sacraments are more plainly designated, as when they are called the pillars of our faith. For just as a building stands and leans on its foundation, and yet is rendered more stable when supported by pillars, so faith leans on the Word of God as its proper foundation, and yet when sacraments are added leans more firmly, as if resting on pillars. Or we may call them mirrors, in which we may contemplate the riches of the grace, which God bestows upon us. For then, as has been said, He manifests himself to us in as far as our dullness can enable us to recognize Him, and testifies His love and kindness to us more expressly than by Word.

7 They are such signs, though the wicked should receive them, but are signs of grace only to believers.

It is irrational to contend that sacraments are not manifestations of divine grace toward us, because they are held forth to the ungodly also, who, however, so far from experiencing God to be more propitious to them, only incur greater condemnation. By the same reasoning, the gospel will be no manifestation of the grace of God, because it is spurned by many who hear it; nor will Christ himself be a manifestation of grace, because of the many by whom He was seen and known, very few received Him. Something similar may be seen in public enactments. A great part of the body of the people deride and evade the authenticating seal, though they know it was employed by their sovereign to confirm His will. Others trample it under foot, as a matter by no means appertaining to them. Others even execrate it, so that, seeing the condition of the two things to be alike, the appropriateness of the comparison, which I made above, ought to be more readily allowed. It is certain, therefore, that the Lord offers us His mercy and a pledge of His grace, both in His sacred Word and in the sacraments. But it is not apprehended except by those who receive the Word and sacraments with firm faith. In like manner as Christ, though offered and held forth for salvation to all, is not, however, acknowledged and received by all. Augustine, when intending to intimate this, said that the efficacy of the Word is produced in the sacrament, not because it is spoken, but because it is believed. Hence, Paul, addressing believers, includes communion with Christ, in the sacraments, as when he says, "As many of you as have been baptized into Christ have put on Christ" (Galatians 3:27). Again, "For by one Spirit we are all baptized into one body" (1 Corinthians 12:13).

But when he speaks of a preposterous use of the sacraments, he attributes nothing more to them than to frigid, empty figures; thereby intimating, that however the ungodly and hypocrites may, by their perverseness, either suppress, or obscure, or impede the effect of divine grace in the sacraments, that does not prevent them, where and whenever God is so pleased, from giving a true evidence of communion with Christ, or prevent them from exhibiting, and the Spirit of God from performing, the very thing which they promise. We conclude, therefore, that the sacraments are truly termed evidences of divine grace, and seals of the good will, which He entertains toward us. They, by sealing it to us, sustain, nourish, confirm, and increase our faith. The objections usually urged against this view are frivolous and weak. They say that our faith, if it is good, cannot be made better; for there is no faith save that which leans firmly and undividedly on the mercy of God. It had been better for the objectors to pray, with the apostles, "Lord, increase our faith" (Luke 17:5), than confidently to maintain a perfection of faith which none of the sons of men ever attained, none ever shall attain, in this life. Let them explain what kind of faith his was who said, "Lord, I believe; help thou mine unbelief" (Mark 9:24). That faith, though only commenced, was good, and might, by the removal of the unbelief, be made better. But there is no better argument to refute them than their own consciousness. For if they confess themselves sinners (this, whether they will or not, they cannot deny), then they must of necessity impute this very quality to the imperfection of their faith.

8 Objections to this view answered.

But Philip, they say, replied to the eunuch who asked to be baptized, "If thou believest with all thine heart thou mayest" (Acts 8:37). What room is there for a confirmation of baptism when faith fills the whole heart? I, in my turn, ask them, Do they not feel that a good part of their heart is void of faith–do they not perceive new additions to it every day? There was one who boasted that he grew old while learning. Thrice miserable, then, are we Christians if we grow old without making progress, we whose faith ought to advance through every period of life until it grow up into a perfect man (Ephesians 4:13). In this passage, therefore, to believe with the whole heart, is not to believe Christ perfectly, but only to embrace Him sincerely with heart and soul—not to be filled with Him, but with ardent affection to hunger and thirst, and sigh after Him. It is usual in Scripture to say that a thing is done with the whole heart, when it is done sincerely and cordially. Of this description are the following passages: "With my whole heart have I sought thee" (Psalm 119:10); "I will confess unto thee with my whole heart," etc. In like manner, when the fraudulent and deceitful are rebuked, it is said, "with flattering lips, and with a double heart, do they speak" (Psalm 12:2). The objectors next add: "If faith is increased by means of the sacraments, the Holy Spirit is given in vain, seeing it is His office to begin, sustain, and consummate our faith." I admit, indeed, that faith is the proper and entire work of the Holy Spirit, enlightened by whom we recognize God and the treasures of His grace, and without whose illumination our mind is so blind that it can see nothing, so stupid that it has no relish for spiritual things. But for the one divine blessing which they proclaim we count three. For, first, the Lord teaches and trains us by His Word. Next, He confirms us by His sacraments. Lastly, He illumines our mind by the light of His Holy Spirit, and opens up an entrance into our hearts for His Word and sacraments, which would otherwise only strike our ears, and fall upon our sight, but by no means, affect us inwardly.

9 No secret virtue in the sacraments. Their whole efficacy depends on the inward operation of the Spirit.

Wherefore, with regard to the increase and confirmation of faith, I would remind the reader (though I think I have already expressed it in unambiguous terms), that in assigning this office to the sacraments, it is not as if I thought that there is a kind of secret efficacy perpetually inherent in them, by which they can of themselves promote or strengthen faith, but because our Lord has instituted them for the express purpose of helping to establish and increase our faith. The sacraments duly perform their office only when accompanied by the Spirit, the internal Master, whose energy alone penetrates the heart, stirs up the affections, and procures access for the sacraments into our souls. If He is wanting, the sacraments can avail us no more than the sun shining on the eyeballs of the blind, or sounds uttered in the ears of the deaf. Wherefore, in distributing between the Spirit and the sacraments, I ascribe the whole energy to Him, and leave only a ministry to them; this ministry, without the agency of the

Spirit, is empty and frivolous, but when He acts within, and exerts His power, it is replete with energy. It is now clear in what way, according to this view, a pious mind is confirmed in faith by means of the sacraments–viz. in the same way in which the light of the sun is seen by the eye, and the sound of the voice heard by the ear; the former of which would not be at all affected by the light unless it had a pupil on which the light might fall; nor the latter reached by any sound, however loud, were it not naturally adapted for hearing. But if it is true, as has been explained, that in the eye it is the power of vision, which enables it to see the light, and in the ear the power of hearing, which enables it to perceive the voice, and that in our hearts it is the work of the Holy Spirit to commence, maintain, cherish, and establish faith, then it follows, both that the sacraments do not avail one iota without the energy of the Holy Spirit. Yet, in hearts previously taught by that preceptor, there is nothing to prevent the sacraments from strengthening and increasing faith. There is only this difference, that the faculty of seeing and hearing is naturally implanted in the eye and ear, whereas, Christ acts in our minds above the measure of nature by special grace.

10 Objections answered. Illustrated by a simile.

In this way, also, we dispose of certain objections by which some anxious minds are annoyed. If we ascribe either an increase or confirmation of faith to creatures, injustice is done to the Spirit of God, who alone ought to be regarded as its author. But we do not rob Him of the merit of confirming and increasing faith; nay, rather, we maintain that that which confirms and increases faith, is nothing else than the preparing of our minds by His internal illumination to receive that confirmation which is set forth by the sacraments. But if the subject is still obscure, it will be made plain by the following similitude: Were you to begin to persuade a person by word to do something, you would think of all the arguments by which he may be brought over to your view, and in a manner compelled to serve your purpose. But nothing is gained if the individual himself possesses not a clear and acute judgment, by which he may be able to weigh the value of your arguments; if, moreover, he is not of a docile disposition and ready to listen to doctrine; if, in fine, he has no such idea of your faith and prudence as in a manner to prejudice him in your favor, and secure his assent. For there are many obstinate spirits who are not to be bent by any arguments; and where faith is suspected, or authority contemned, little progress is made even with the docile.

On the other hand, when opposite feelings exist, the result will be, that the person whose interests you are consulting will acquiesce in the very counsels which he would otherwise have derided. The same work is performed in us by the Spirit. That the Word may not fall upon our ear, or the sacraments be presented to our eye in vain, He shows that it is God who there speaks to us, softens our obdurate hearts, and frames them to the obedience which is due to His Word; in short, transmits those external words and sacraments from the ear to the soul. Both word and sacraments, therefore, confirm our faith, bringing under view the kind intentions of our heavenly Father, in the knowledge of which the whole assurance of our faith depends, and by which its strength is increased; and the Spirit also confirms our faith when, by engraving that assurance on our minds, He renders it effectual. Meanwhile, it is easy for the Father of lights, in like manner, as He illumines the bodily eye by the rays of the sun, to illumine our minds by the sacraments, as by a kind of intermediate brightness.

11 Of the increase of faith by the preaching of the Word.

This property our Lord showed to belong to the external Word, when, in the parable, He compared it to seed. (See Matthew 13:4; Luke 8:15.) For as the seed, when it falls on a deserted and neglected part of the field, can do nothing but die, but when thrown into ground properly labored and cultivated, will yield a hundred fold; so the Word of God, when addressed to any stubborn spirit, will remain without fruit, as if thrown upon the barren waste, but when it meets with a soul which the hand of the heavenly Spirit has subdued, will be most fruitful. But if the case of the seed and of the Word is the same, and from the seed corn can grow and increase, and attain to maturity, why may not faith also take its beginning, increase, and completion from the Word? Both things are admirably explained by Paul in different passages. For when he would remind the Corinthians how God had given effect to his labors, he boasts that he possessed the ministry of the Spirit (see 1 Corinthians 2:4), just as if his preaching were inseparably connected with the power of the Holy Spirit, in inwardly enlightening the mind, and stimulating it. But in another passage, when he would remind them what the power of the Word is in itself, when preached by man, he compares ministers to husbandmen, who, after they have expended labor and industry in cultivating the ground, have nothing more that they can do. For what would ploughing, and sowing, and watering avail, unless that which was sown should, by the kindness of Heaven, vegetate? Wherefore he concludes, that he that planteth, and he that watereth is nothing, but that the whole is to be ascribed to God, who alone gives the increase. The apostles, therefore, exert the power of the Spirit in their preaching, inasmuch as God uses them as instruments, which He has ordained for the unfolding of His spiritual grace. Still, however, we must not lose sight of the distinction, but remember what man is able of himself to do, and what is peculiar to God.

12 In what way, and how far, the sacraments are confirmations of our faith.

The sacraments are confirmations of our faith in such a sense, that the Lord, sometimes, when He sees meet to withdraw our assurance of the things which He had promised in the sacraments, takes away the sacraments themselves. When He deprives Adam of the gift of immortality, and expels him from the garden, "lest he put forth his hand and take also of the tree of life, and live forever" (Genesis 3:22). What is this we hear? Could that fruit have restored Adam to the immortality from which he had already fallen? By no means. It is just as if He had said, Lest he indulge in vain confidence, if allowed to retain the symbol of my promise, let that be withdrawn which might give him some hope of immortality. On this ground, when the apostle urges the Ephesians to remember, that they "were without Christ, being aliens from the commonwealth of Israel, and strangers from the covenants of promise, having no hope, and without God in the world" (Ephesians 2:12), he says that they were not partakers of circumcision. He thus intimates metonymically, that all were excluded from the promise who had not received the badge of the promise. To the other objection–viz. that when so much power is attributed to creatures, the glory of God is bestowed upon them, and thereby impaired–it is obvious to reply, that we attribute no power to the creatures. All we say is, that God uses the means and instruments which He sees to be expedient, in order that all things may be subservient to His glory, He being the Lord and disposer of all. Therefore, as by bread and other aliment He feeds our bodies, as by the sun He illumines, and by fire gives warmth to the world, and yet bread, sun, and fire are nothing, save inasmuch as they are instruments under which He dispenses His blessings to us; so in like manner He spiritually nourishes our faith by means of the sacraments, whose only office is to make His promises visible to our eye, or rather, to be pledges of His promises. And as it is our duty in regard to the other creatures which the divine liberality and kindness has destined for our use, and by whose instrumentality He bestows the gifts of His goodness upon us, to put no confidence in them, nor to admire and extol them as the causes of our mercies; so neither ought our confidence to be fixed on the sacraments, nor ought the glory of God to be transferred to them, but passing beyond them all, our faith and confession should rise to Him who is the Author of the sacraments and of all things.

13 Some regard the sacraments as mere signs. This view refuted.

There is nothing in the argument which some found on the very term sacrament. This term, they say, while it has many significations in approved authors, has only one which is applicable to signs–namely, when it is used for the formal oath which the soldier gives to his commander on entering the service. For as by that military oath recruits bind themselves to be faithful to their commander, and make a profession of military service; so, by our signs we acknowledge Christ to be our commander, and declare that we serve under His standard. They add similitude, in order to make the matter more clear. As the toga distinguished the Romans from the Greeks, who wore the pallium; and as the different orders of Romans were distinguished from each other by their peculiar insignia; e.g., the senatorial from the equestrian by purple, and crescent shoes, and the equestrian from the plebeian by a ring, so we wear our symbols to distinguish us from the profane. But it is sufficiently clear from what has been said above, that the ancients, in giving the name of sacraments to signs, had not at all attended to the use of the term by Latin writers, but had, for the sake of convenience, given it this new signification, as a means of simply expressing sacred signs. But were we to argue more subtlety, we might say that they seem to have given the term this signification in a manner analogous to that in which they employ the term faith in the sense in which it is now used. For while faith is truth in performing promises, they have used it for the certainty or firm persuasion which is had of the truth. In this way, while a sacrament is the act of the soldier when he vows obedience to his commander, they made it the act by which the commander admits soldiers to the ranks. For in the sacraments the Lord promises that He will be our God, and we that we will be His people. But we omit such subtleties, since I think I have shown by arguments abundantly plain, that all which ancient writers intended was to intimate, that sacraments are the signs of sacred and spiritual things. The similitudes, which are drawn from external objects (chapter 15, section 1), we indeed admit; but we approve not, that that which is a secondary thing in sacraments is by them made the first, and indeed the only thing. The first thing is that they may contribute to our faith in God; the secondary, that they may attest our confession before men. These similitudes are applicable to the secondary reason. Let it therefore remain a fixed point, that mysteries would be frigid (as has been seen) were they not helps to our faith, and adjuncts annexed to doctrine for the same end and purpose.

14 Some again attribute too much to the sacraments. Refutation.

On the other hand, it is to be observed, that as these objectors impair the force, and altogether overthrow the use of the sacraments, so there are others who ascribe to the sacraments a kind of secret virtue, which is nowhere said to have been implanted in them by God. By this error, the more simple and unwary are perilously deceived, while they are taught to seek the gifts of God where they cannot possibly be found, and are insensibly withdrawn from God, to embrace instead of His truth mere vanity. For the schools of the Sophists have taught with general consent that the sacraments of the new law, in other words, those now in use in the Christian Church, justify, and confer grace, provided only that we do not interpose the obstacle of mortal sin. It is impossible to describe how fatal and pestilential this sentiment is, and the more so, that for many ages it has, to the great loss of the Church, prevailed over a considerable part of the world. It is plainly of the devil: for, first, in promising a righteousness without faith, it drives souls headlong on destruction; secondly, in deriving a cause of righteousness from the sacraments, it entangles miserable minds, already of their own accord too much inclined to the Earth, in a superstitious idea, which makes them acquiesce in the spectacle of a corporeal object rather than in God himself. I wish we had not such experience of both evils as to make it altogether unnecessary to give a lengthened proof of them. For what is a sacrament received without faith, but most certain destruction to the Church? For, seeing that nothing is to be expected beyond the promise, and the promise no less denounces wrath to the unbeliever than offers grace to the believer, it is an error to suppose that anything more is conferred by the sacraments than is offered by the Word of God, and obtained by true faith. From this another thing follows–viz. that assurance of salvation does not depend on participation in the sacraments, as if justification consisted in it. This, which is treasured up in Christ alone, we know to be communicated, not less by the preaching of the gospel than by the seal of the sacrament, and may be completely enjoyed without this seal. So true is it, as Augustine declares, that there may be invisible sanctification without a visible sign, and, on the other hand, a visible sign without true sanctification. For, as he elsewhere says, "Men put on Christ, sometimes to the extent of partaking in the sacrament, and sometimes to the extent of holiness of life." The former may be common to the good and the bad; the latter is peculiar to the good.

15 Refutation confirmed by a passage from Augustine.

Hence, the distinction, if properly understood, repeatedly made by Augustine between the sacrament and the matter of the sacrament. For he does not mean merely that the figure and truth are therein contained, but that they do not so cohere as not to be separable, and that in this connection it is always necessary to distinguish the thing from the sign, so as not to transfer to the one what belongs to the other. Augustine speaks of the separation when he says that in the elect alone the sacraments accomplish what they represent. Again, when speaking of the Jews, he says, "Though the sacraments were common to all, the grace was not common: yet grace is the virtue of the sacraments. Thus, too, the laver of regeneration is now common to all, but the grace by which the members of Christ are regenerated with their head is not common to all." Again, in another place, speaking of the Lord's Supper, he says, "We also this day receive visible food; but the sacrament is one thing, the virtue of the sacrament another. Why is it that many partake of the altar and die, and die by partaking? For even the cup of the Lord was poison to Judas, not because he received what was evil, but being wicked he wickedly received what was good." A little after, he says, "The sacrament of this thing, that is, of the unity of the body and blood of Christ, is in some places prepared every day, in others at certain intervals at the Lord's table, which is partaken by some unto life, by others unto destruction. But the thing itself, of which there is a sacrament, is life to all, and destruction to none who partake of it." Some time before he had said, "He who may have eaten shall not die, but he must be one who attains to the virtue of the sacrament, not to the visible sacrament; who eats inwardly, not outwardly; who eats with the heart, and not with the teeth." Here you are uniformly told that a sacrament is so separated from the reality by the unworthiness of the partaker, that nothing remains but an empty and useless figure. Now, in order that you may have not a sign devoid of truth, but the thing with the sign, the Word, which is included in it, must be apprehended by faith. Thus, as far as by means of the sacraments you will profit in the communion of Christ, will you derive advantage from them.

16 Previous views more fully explained.

If this is obscure from brevity, I will explain it more at length. I say that Christ is the matter, or, if you rather choose it, the substance of all the sacraments, since in Him they have their whole solidity, and out of Him promise nothing. Hence, the less toleration is due to the error of Peter Lombard, who distinctly makes them causes of the righteousness and salvation of which they are parts (Sent. Lib. 4 Dist. 1). Bidding adieu to all other causes of righteousness, which the wit of man devises, our duty is to hold by this only. In so far, therefore, as we are assisted by their instrumentality in cherishing, confirming, and increasing the true knowledge of Christ, so as both to possess Him more fully, and enjoy Him in all His richness, so far are they effectual in regard to us. This is the case when that which is there offered is received by us in true faith. Therefore, you will ask, Do the wicked, by their ingratitude, make the ordinance of God fruitless and void? I answer, that what I have said is not to be understood as if the power and truth of the sacrament depended on the condition or pleasure of him who receives it. That which God instituted continues firm, and retains its nature, however men may vary; but since it is one thing to offer, and another to receive, there is nothing to prevent a symbol, consecrated by the Word of the Lord, from being truly what it is said to be, and preserving its power, though it may at the same time confer no benefit on the wicked and ungodly. This question is well solved by Augustine in a few words: "If you receive carnally, it ceases not to be spiritual, but it is not spiritual to you." But as Augustine shows in the above passages that a sacrament is a thing of no value if separated from its truth; so also, when the two are conjoined, he reminds us that it is necessary to distinguish, in order that we may not cleave too much to the external sign. "As it is servile weakness to follow the latter, and take the signs for the thing signified, so to interpret the signs as of no use is an extravagant error." He mentions two faults which are here to be avoided; the one when we receive the signs as if they had been given in vain, and by malignantly destroying or impairing their secret meanings, prevent them from yielding any fruit—the other, when by not raising our minds beyond the visible sign, we attribute to it blessings which are conferred upon us by Christ alone, and that by means of the Holy Spirit, who makes us to be partakers of Christ, external signs assisting if they invite us to Christ; whereas, when wrested to any other purpose, their whole utility is overthrown.

17 The matter of the sacrament always present when the sacrament is duly administered.

Wherefore, let it be a fixed point, that the office of the sacraments differs not from the Word of God; and this is to hold forth and offer Christ to us, and, in Him, the treasures of heavenly grace. They confer nothing, and avail nothing, if not received in faith, just as wine and oil, or any other liquor, however large the quantity which you pour out, will run away and perish unless there be an open vessel to receive it. When the vessel is not open, though it may be sprinkled all over, it will nevertheless remain entirely empty. We must be aware of being led into a kindred error by the terms, somewhat too extravagant, which ancient Christian writers have employed in extolling the dignity of the sacraments. We must not suppose that there is some latent virtue inherent in the sacraments by which they, in themselves, confer the gifts of the Holy Spirit upon us, in the same way in which wine is drunk out of a cup, since the only office divinely assigned them is to attest and ratify the benevolence of the Lord towards us; and they avail no further than accompanied by the Holy Spirit to open our minds and hearts, and make us capable of receiving this testimony, in which various distinguished graces are clearly manifested. For the sacraments, as we lately observed (Chapter 13, section 6; and Chapter14, sections 6, 7), are to us what messengers of good news are to men, or earnests in ratifying pacts. They do not of themselves bestow any grace, but they announce and manifest it, and, like earnests and badges, give a ratification of the gifts, which the divine liberality has bestowed upon us.

The Holy Spirit, whom the sacraments do not bring promiscuously to all, but whom the Lord specially confers on His people, brings the gifts of God along with Him, makes way for the sacraments, and causes them to bear fruit. But though we deny not that God, by the immediate agency of His Spirit, countenances His own ordinance, preventing the administration of the sacraments, which He has instituted from being fruitless and vain, still we maintain that the internal grace of the Spirit, as it is distinct from the external ministration, ought to be viewed and considered separately. God, therefore, truly performs whatever He promises and figures by signs; nor are the signs without effect, for they prove that He is their true and faithful author. The only question here is, whether the Lord works by proper and intrinsic virtue (as it is called), or resigns His office to external symbols. We maintain that whatever organs He employs detract nothing from his primary operation. In this doctrine of the sacraments, their dignity is highly extolled, their use plainly shown, their utility sufficiently proclaimed, and moderation in all things duly maintained; so that nothing is attributed to them, which ought not to be attributed, and nothing denied them, which they ought to possess.

Meanwhile, we get rid of that fiction by which the cause of justification and the power of the Holy Spirit are included in elements as vessels and vehicles, and the special power, which was overlooked, is distinctly explained. Here, also, we ought to observe, that what the minister figures and attests by outward action, God performs inwardly, lest that which God claims for himself alone should be ascribed to mortal man. This Augustine is careful to observe: "How does both God and Moses sanctify? Not Moses for God, but Moses by visible sacraments through his ministry, God by invisible grace through the Holy Spirit. Herein is the whole fruit of visible sacraments; for what do these visible sacraments avail without that sanctification of invisible grace?"

18 Extensive meaning of the term sacrament.

The term sacrament, in the view we have hitherto taken of it, includes, generally, all the signs which God ever commanded men to use, that He might make them sure and confident of the truth of His promises. These He was pleased sometimes to place in natural objects—sometimes to exhibit in miracles. Of the former class we have an example, in His giving the Tree of Life to Adam and Eve, as an earnest of immortality, that they might feel confident of the promise as often as they ate of the fruit. Another example was, when He gave the bow in the cloud to Noah and his posterity, as a memorial that He would not again destroy the Earth by a flood. These were to Adam and Noah as sacraments: not that the Tree could give Adam and Eve the immortality, which it could not give to itself; or the bow (which is only a reflection of the solar rays on the opposite clouds) could have the effect of confining the waters; but they had a mark engraved on them by the Word of God, to be proofs and seals of His covenant. The tree was previously a tree and the bow a bow; but when they were inscribed with the Word of God, a new form was given to them; they began to be what they previously were not.

Lest anyone suppose that these things were said in vain, the bow is even in the present day a witness to us of the covenant, which God made with Noah. As often as we look upon it, we read this promise from God, that the Earth will never be destroyed by a flood. Wherefore, if any philosophizer, to deride the simplicity of our faith, shall contend that the variety of colors arises naturally from the rays reflected by the opposite cloud, let us admit the fact; but, at the same time, deride his stupidity in not recognizing God as the Lord and governor of nature, who, at His pleasure, makes all the elements subservient to His glory. If He had impressed memorials of this description on the sun, the stars, the Earth, and stones, they would all have been to us as sacraments. For why is the shapeless and the coined silver not of the same value, seeing they are the same metal? Just because the former has nothing but its own nature, whereas the latter, impressed with the public stamp, becomes money, and receives a new value. And shall the Lord not be able to stamp

His creatures with His Word, that things, which were formerly bare elements, may become sacraments?

Examples of the second class were given when He showed light to Abraham in the smoking furnace (see Genesis 15:17), when He covered the fleece with dew while the ground was dry; and, on the other hand, when the dew covered the ground while the fleece was untouched, to assure Gideon of victory (see Judges 6:37); also, when He made the shadow go back ten degrees on the dial, to assure Hezekiah of his recovery. (See 2 Kings 20:9; Isaiah 38:7.) These things, which were done to assist and establish their faith, were also sacraments.

19 The ordinary sacraments in the Church. How necessary they are.

But my present purpose is to discourse especially of those sacraments which the Lord has been pleased to institute as ordinary sacraments in His Church, to bring up His worshippers and servants in one faith, and the confession of one faith. For, to use the words of Augustine, "In no name of religion, true or false, can men be assembled, unless united by some common use of visible signs or sacraments." Our most merciful Father, foreseeing this necessity, from the very first appointed certain exercises of piety to His servants; these, Satan, by afterwards transferring to impious and superstitious worship, in many ways corrupted and depraved. Hence, those initiations of the Gentiles into their mysteries and other degenerate rites. Yet, although they were full of error and superstition, they were, at the same time, an indication that men could not be without such external signs of religion. But, as they were neither founded on the Word of God, nor bore reference to that truth which ought to be held forth by all signs, they are unworthy of being named when mention is made of the sacred symbols which were instituted by God, and have not been perverted from their end–viz. to be helps to true piety. And they consist not of simple signs, like the rainbow and the Tree of Life, but of ceremonies, or (if you prefer it) the signs here employed are ceremonies. But since, as has been said above, they are testimonies of grace and salvation from the Lord, so, in regard to us, they are marks of profession by which we openly swear by the name of God, binding ourselves to be faithful to Him. Hence, Chrysostom somewhere shrewdly gives them the name of pacts, by which God enters into covenant with us, and we become bound to holiness and purity of life, because a mutual stipulation is here interposed between God and us. For as God there promises to cover and efface any guilt and penalty which we may have incurred by transgression, and reconciles us to himself in His only begotten Son, so we, in our turn, oblige ourselves by this profession to the study of piety and righteousness. And hence it may be justly said, that such sacraments are ceremonies, by which God is pleased to train His people, first, to excite, cherish, and strengthen faith within; and, secondly, to testify our religion to men.

20 The sacraments of the Old and of the New Testament. The end of both the same—viz. to lead us to Christ.

Now these have been different at different times, according to the dispensation, which the Lord has seen, meet to employ in manifesting himself to men. Circumcision was enjoined on Abraham and his posterity, and to it would be afterwards added purifications and sacrifices, and other rites of the Mosaic Law. These were the sacraments of the Jews even until the advent of Christ. After these were abrogated, the two sacraments of Baptism and the Lord's Supper, which the Christian Church now employs, were instituted. I speak of those, which were instituted, for the use of the whole Church. For the laying on of hands, by which the ministers of the Church are initiated into their office, though I have no objection to its being called a sacrament, I do not number among ordinary sacraments. The place to be assigned to the other commonly reputed sacraments we shall see by and by. Still the ancient sacraments had the same end in view as our own–viz. to direct and almost lead us by the hand to Christ, or rather, were like images to represent Him and hold Him forth to our knowledge. But as we have already shown that sacraments are a kind of seals of the promises of God, so let us hold it as a most certain truth, that no divine promise has ever been offered to man except in Christ, and that hence when they remind us of any divine promise, they must of necessity exhibit Christ. Hence, that heavenly pattern of the tabernacle and legal worship which was shown to Moses in the mount. There is only this difference, that while the former shadowed forth a promised Christ while He was still expected, the latter bear testimony to Him as already come and manifested.

21 This apparent in the sacraments of the Old Testament.

When these things are explained singly and separately, they will be much clearer. Circumcision was a sign by which the Jews were reminded that whatever comes of the seed of man–in other words, the whole nature of man–is corrupt, and requires to be cut off. Moreover, it was a proof and memorial to confirm them in the promise made to Abraham, of a seed in whom all the nations of the Earth should be blessed, and from whom they themselves were to look for a blessing. That saving seed, as we are taught by Paul (see Galatians 5:16), was Christ, in whom alone they trusted to recover what they had lost in Adam. Wherefore circumcision was to them what Paul says it was to Abraham–viz. a sign of the righteousness of faith (see Romans 9:11):–viz. a seal by which they were more certainly assured that their faith in waiting for the Lord would be accepted by God for righteousness. But we shall have a better opportunity elsewhere (Chapter 16, sections 3, 4) of following out the comparison between circumcision and baptism. Their washings and purifications placed under their eye the uncleanness, defilement, and pollution with which they were naturally contaminated, and promised another laver in which all their impurities might be wiped and washed away. This laver was Christ, washed by whose blood we bring His purity into the sight of God, that He may cover all our defilements. The sacrifices convicted them of their unrighteousness, and at the same time taught that there was a necessity for paying some satisfaction to the justice of God; and that, therefore, there must be some High Priest, some mediator between God and man, to satisfy God by the shedding of blood, and the immolation of a victim, which might suffice for the remission of sins. The High Priest was Christ: He shed His own blood, He was himself the victim; for in obedience to the Father, He offered himself to death, and by this obedience abolished the disobedience by which man had provoked the indignation of God. (See Philippians 2:8; Romans 5:19.)

22 Apparent also in the sacraments of the New Testament.

In regard to our sacraments, they present Christ the more clearly to us; the more familiarly He has been manifested to man. Ever since

He was exhibited by the Father, truly as He had been promised. For Baptism testifies that we are washed and purified, the Supper of the Eucharist that we are redeemed. Ablution is figured by water, satisfaction by blood. Both are found in Christ, who, as John says, "came by water and blood;" that is, to purify and redeem. Of this, the Spirit of God also is a witness. Nay, there are three witnesses in one, water, Spirit, and blood. In the water and blood, we have an evidence of purification and redemption, but the Spirit is the primary witness who gives us a full assurance of this testimony. This sublime mystery was illustriously displayed on the Cross of Christ, when water and blood flowed from His sacred side (see John 19:34); which, for this reason, Augustine justly termed the fountain of our sacraments. Of these, we shall shortly treat at greater length. There is no doubt that, it you compare time with time, the grace of the Spirit is now more abundantly displayed. For this forms part of the glory of the Kingdom of Christ, as we gather from several passages, and especially from the seventh chapter of John. In this sense are we to understand the words of Paul, that the law was "a shadow of good things to come, but the body is of Christ" (Colossians 2:17). His purpose is not to declare the inefficacy of those manifestations of grace in which God was pleased to prove His truth to the patriarchs, just as He proves it to us in the present day in Baptism and the Lord's Supper, but to contrast the two, and show the great value of what is given to us, that no one may think it strange that by the advent of Christ the ceremonies of the law have been abolished.

23 Impious doctrine of the Schoolmen as to the difference between the Old and the New Testaments.

The Scholastic dogma (to glance at it in passing), by which the difference between the sacraments of the old and the new dispensation is made so great, that the former did nothing but shadow forth the grace of God, while the latter actually confer that it, must be altogether exploded. Since the apostle speaks in no higher terms of the one than of the other, when he says that the fathers ate of the same spiritual food, and explains that that food was Christ (see 1 Corinthians 10:3), who will presume to regard as an empty sign that which gave a manifestation to the Jews of true communion with Christ? And the state of the case, which the apostle is there treating, militates strongly for our view. For to guard against confiding in a frigid knowledge of Christ, an empty title of Christianity and external observances, and thereby daring to contemn the judgment of God, he exhibits signal examples of divine severity in the Jews, to make us aware that if we indulge in the same vices, the same punishments which they suffered are impending over us. Now, to make the comparison appropriate, it was necessary to show that there is no inequality between us and them in those blessings in which he forbade us to glory. Therefore, he first makes them equal to us in the sacraments, and leaves us not one iota of privilege, which could give us hopes of impunity. Nor can we justly attribute more to our baptism than he elsewhere attributes to circumcision, when he terms it a seal of the righteousness of faith. (See Romans 4:11.) Whatever, therefore, is now exhibited to us in the sacraments, the Jews formerly received in theirs–viz. Christ, with His spiritual riches. The same efficacy, which ours possess, they experienced in theirs–viz. that they were seals of the divine favor toward them in regard to the hope of eternal salvation. Had the objectors been sound expounders of the Epistle to the Hebrews, they would not have been so deluded, but reading therein that sins were not expiated by legal ceremonies, nay, that the ancient shadows were of no importance to justification, they overlooked the contrast which is there drawn, and fastening on the single point, that the law in itself was of no avail to the worshipper, thought that they were mere figures, devoid of truth. The purpose of the apostle is to show that there is nothing in the ceremonial law until we arrive at Christ, on whom alone the whole efficacy depends.

24 Scholastic objection answered.

But they will found on what Paul says of the circumcision of the letter, and object that it is in no esteem with God; that it confers nothing, and is empty; that passages such as these seem to set it far beneath our baptism. But by no means. For the very same thing might justly be said of baptism. Indeed, it is said; first by Paul himself, when he shows that God regards not the external ablution by which we are initiated into religion, unless the mind is purified inwardly, and maintains its purity to the end; and, secondly, by Peter, when he declares that the reality of baptism consists not in external ablution, but in the testimony of a good conscience. But it seems that in another passage he speaks with the greatest contempt of circumcision made with hands, when he contrasts it with the circumcision made by Christ. I answer that not even in that passage is there anything derogatory to its dignity. Paul is there disputing against those who insisted upon it as necessary, after it had been abrogated. He therefore admonishes believers to lay aside ancient shadows, and cleave to truth. These teachers, he says, insist that your bodies shall be circumcised. But you have been spiritually circumcised both in soul and body. You have, therefore, a manifestation of the reality, and this is far better than the shadow. Still anyone might have answered, that the figure was not to be despised because they had the reality, since among the Fathers also was exemplified that putting off of the old man of which he was speaking, and yet to them external circumcision was not superfluous. This objection he anticipates, when he immediately adds, that the Colossians were buried together with Christ by baptism, thereby intimating that baptism is now to Christians what circumcision was to those of ancient times; and that the latter, therefore, could not be imposed on Christians without injury to the former.

25 Another objection answered.

But there is more difficulty in explaining the passage which follows, and which I lately quote–viz. that all the Jewish ceremonies were shadows of things to come, but the Body is of Christ. (See Colossians 2:17.) The most difficult point of all, however, is that which is discussed in several chapters of the Epistle to the Hebrews–namely, that the blood of beasts did not reach to the conscience; that the law was a shadow of good things to come, but not the very image of the things (Hebrews 10:1); that worshippers under the Mosaic ceremonies obtained no degree of perfection, and so forth. I repeat what I have already hinted, that Paul does not represent the ceremonies as shadowy because they had nothing solid in them, but because their completion was in a manner suspended until the manifestation of Christ.

Again, I hold that the words are to be understood not of their efficiency, but rather of the mode of significance. For until Christ was manifested in the flesh, all signs shadowed Him as absent, however He might inwardly exert the presence of His power, and consequently of His person on believers. But the most important observation is that in all these passages Paul does not speak simply but by way of reply. He was contending with false apostles, who maintained that piety consisted in mere ceremonies, without any respect to Christ; for their refutation, it was sufficient merely to consider what effect ceremonies have in themselves. This, too, was the scope of the author of the Epistle to the Hebrews. Let us remember, therefore, that he is here treating of ceremonies not taken in their true and native signification, but when wrested to a false and vicious interpretation, not of the legitimate use, but of the superstitious abuse of them. What wonder, then, if ceremonies, when separated from Christ, are devoid of all virtue? All signs become null when the thing signified is taken away. Thus Christ, when addressing those who thought that manna was nothing more than food for the body, accommodates his language to their gross opinion, and says, that he furnished a better food, one, which fed souls for immortality.

But if you require a clearer solution, the substance comes to this: First, the whole apparatus of ceremonies under the Mosaic Law, unless directed to Christ, is evanescent and null. Secondly, these ceremonies had such respect to Christ, that they had their fulfillment only when Christ was manifested in the flesh. Lastly, at His advent they behooved to disappear, just as the shadow vanishes in the clear light of the sun. But I now touch more briefly on the point, because I defer the future consideration of it until I come to the place where I intend to compare baptism with circumcision.

26 Sacraments of the New Testament sometimes excessively extolled by early Theologians. Their meaning explained.

Those wretched sophists are perhaps deceived by the extravagant eulogiums on our signs which occur in ancient writers: for instance, the following passage of Augustine: "The sacraments of the old law only promised a Savior, whereas ours give salvation." Not perceiving that these and similar figures of speech are hyperbolical, they too have promulgated their hyperbolical dogmas, but in a sense altogether alien from that of ancient writers. For Augustine means nothing more than in another place where he says, "The sacraments of the Mosaic Law foretold Christ, ours announce Him." And again, "Those were promises of things to be fulfilled, these indications of the fulfillment;" as if he had said, Those figured Him when He was still expected, ours, now that He has arrived, exhibit Him as present. Moreover, with regard to the mode of signifying, he says, as he also elsewhere indicates, "The Law and the Prophets had sacraments foretelling a thing future, the sacraments of our time attest that what they foretold as to come has come."

His sentiments concerning the reality and efficacy, he explains in several passages, as when he says, "The sacraments of the Jews were different in the signs, alike in the things signified; different in the visible appearance, alike in spiritual power." Again, "In different signs there was the same faith: it was thus in different signs as in different words, because the words change the sound according to times, and yet words are nothing else than signs. The Fathers drank of the same spiritual drink, but not of the same corporeal drink. See then, how, while faith remains, signs vary. There the rock was Christ; to us that is Christ which is placed on the altar. They as a great sacrament drank of the water flowing from the rock: believers know what we drink. If you look at the visible appearance there was a difference; if at the intelligible signification, they drank of the same spiritual drink." Again, "In this mystery their food and drink are the same as ours; the same in meaning, not in form, for the same Christ was figured to them in the rock; to us He has been manifested in the flesh" (Psalm 77).

We grant that in this respect, there is some difference. Both testify that the paternal kindness of God and the graces of the Spirit are offered us in Christ, but ours more clearly and splendidly. In both there is an exhibition of Christ, but in ours, it is more full and complete, in accordance with that distinction between the Old and New Testaments of which we have discoursed above. And this is the meaning of Augustine (whom we quote more frequently, as being the best and most faithful witness of all antiquity), where he says that after Christ was revealed, sacraments were instituted, fewer in number, but of more august significance and more excellent power. It is here proper to remind the reader that all the trifling talk of the sophists concerning the opus operatum is not only false, but repugnant to the very nature of sacraments, which God appointed in order that believers, who are void and in want of all good, might bring nothing of their own, and simply beg. Hence, it follows, that in receiving them they do nothing, which deserves praise, and that in this action (which in respect of them is merely passive) no work can be ascribed to them.

Chapter 15

OF BAPTISM.

There are two parts of this chapter–I. Dissertation on the two ends of Baptism, sections 1-13. II. The second part may be reduced to four heads. Of the use of Baptism, sections 14, 15. Of the worthiness or unworthiness of the minister, sections 16-18. Of the corruptions by which this sacrament was polluted, section 19. To whom reference is had in the dispensation, sections 20-22.

Sections

1. Baptism defined. Its primary object. This consists of three things. First thing in Baptism—viz. to attest the forgiveness of sins.

2. Passages of Scripture proving the forgiveness of sins.

3. Forgiveness not only of past but also of future sins. This is no encouragement to license in sin.

4. Refutation of those who share forgiveness between Baptism and Repentance.

5. Second thing in Baptism—viz. to teach that we are engrafted into Christ for mortification and newness of life.

6. Third thing in Baptism—viz. to teach us that we are united to Christ to be partakers of all His blessings. Second and third things conspicuous in the baptism both of John and the apostles.

7. Identity of the baptism of John and the apostles.

8. An objection to this refuted.

9. The benefits of baptism typified to the Israelites by the passage of the Red Sea and the pillar of cloud.

10. Objection of those who imagine that there is some kind of perfect renovation after baptism. Original depravity remains after baptism. Its existence in infants. The elect after baptism are righteous in this life only by imputation.

11. Original corruption trying to the pious during the whole course of their lives. They do not, on this account, seek a license for sin. They rather walk more cautiously and safely in the ways of the Lord.

12. The trouble occasioned by corruption, shown by the example and testimony of the Apostle Paul.

13. Another end of baptism is to serve as our confession to men.

14. Second part of the chapter. Of baptism as a confirmation of our faith.

15. This illustrated by the examples of Cornelius and Paul. Of the use of baptism as a confession of faith.

16. Baptism not affected by the worthiness or unworthiness of the minister. Hence, no necessity to rebaptize those who were baptized under the Papacy.

17. Nothing in the argument that those so baptized remained some years blind and unbelieving. The promise of God remains firm. God, in inviting the Jews to repentance, does not enjoin them to be again circumcised.

18. No ground to allege that Paul rebaptized certain of John's disciples. The baptism of John. What it is to be baptized in the name of Christ.

19. The corruptions introduced into baptism. The form of pure Christian baptism. Immersion or sprinkling should be left free.

20. To whom the dispensation of baptism belongs. Not to private individuals or women, but to the ministers of the Church. Origin of the baptism of private individuals and women. An argument in favor of it refuted.

21. Exploded also by Tertullian and Epiphanius.

22. Objection founded on the case of Zipporah. Answer. Children dying before baptism not excluded from Heaven, provided the want of it was not caused by negligence or contempt.

1 Baptism defined. Its primary object. This consists of three things. First thing in Baptism—viz. to attest the forgiveness of sins.

Baptism is the initiatory sign by which we are admitted to the fellowship of the Church, that being engrafted into Christ we may be accounted children of God. Moreover, the end for which God has given it (this I have shown to be common to all mysteries) is, first, that it may be conducive to our faith in Him; and, secondly, that it may serve the purpose of a confession among men. The nature of both institutions we shall explain in order. Baptism contributes to our faith three things, which require to be treated separately. The first object, therefore, for which it is appointed by the Lord, is to be a sign and evidence of our purification, or (better to explain my meaning) it is a kind of sealed instrument by which He assures us that all our sins are so deleted, covered, and effaced, that they will never come into His sight, never be mentioned, never imputed. For it is His will that all who have believed, be baptized for the remission of sins. Hence, those who have thought that baptism is nothing else than the badge and mark by which we profess our religion before men, in the same way as soldiers attest their profession by bearing the insignia of their commander, having not attended to what was the principal thing in baptism; and this is, that we are to receive it in connection with the promise, "He that believeth and is baptized shall be saved" (Mark 16:16).

2 Passages of Scripture proving the forgiveness of sins.

In this sense is to be understood the statement of Paul, that "Christ loved the Church, and gave himself for it, that he might sanctify and cleanse it with the washing of water by the word" (Ephesians 5:25, 26); and again, "not by works of righteousness which we have done, but according to his mercy he saved us, by the washing of regeneration and renewing of the Holy Ghost" (Titus 3:5). Peter also says, "baptism also doth now save us" (1 Peter 3:21). For he did not mean to intimate that our ablution and salvation are perfected by water, or that water possesses in itself the virtue of purifying, regenerating, and renewing; nor does he mean that it is the cause of salvation, but only that the knowledge and certainty of such gifts are perceived in this sacrament. This the words themselves evidently show. For Paul connects together the Word of Life and baptism of water, as if he had said, by the gospel the message of our ablution and sanctification is announced; by baptism, this message is sealed. And Peter immediately subjoins, that that baptism is "not the putting away of the filth of the flesh, but the answer of a good conscience toward God, which is of faith." Nay, the only purification which baptism promises is by means of the sprinkling of the blood of Christ, who is figured by water from the resemblance to cleansing and washing. Who, then, can say that we are cleansed by that water which certainly attests that the blood of Christ is our true and only laver? So that we cannot have a better argument to refute the hallucination of those who ascribe the whole to the virtue of water than we derive from the very meaning of baptism, which leads us away as well from the visible element which is presented to our eye, as from all other means, that it may fix our minds on Christ alone.

3 Forgiveness not only of past but also of future sins. This is no encouragement to license in sin.

Nor is it to be supposed that baptism is bestowed only with reference to the past, so that, in regard to new lapses into which we fall after baptism, we must seek new remedies of expiation in other so-called sacraments, just as if the power of baptism had become obsolete. To this error, in ancient times, it was owing that some refused to be initiated by baptism until their life was in extreme danger, and they were drawing their last breath, that they might thus obtain pardon for all the past. Against this preposterous precaution, ancient bishops frequently inveigh in their writings. We ought to consider that at whatever time we are baptized, we are washed and purified once for the whole of life. Wherefore, as often as we fall, we must recall the remembrance of our baptism, and thus fortify our minds, to feel certain and secure of the remission of sins. For though, when once administered, it seems to have passed, it is not abolished by subsequent sins. For the purity of Christ was therein offered to us, always is in force, and is not destroyed by any stain: it wipes and washes away all our defilements. Nor must we hence assume a license of sinning for the future (there is certainly nothing in it to countenance such audacity), but this doctrine is intended only for those who, when they have sinned, groan under their sins burdened and oppressed, that they may have wherewith to support and console themselves, and not rush headlong into despair. Thus, Paul says that Christ was made a propitiation for us for the remission of sins that are past. (See Romans 3:25.) By this, he denies not that constant and perpetual forgiveness of sins is thereby obtained even until death: he only intimates that it is designed by the Father for those poor sinners who, wounded by remorse of conscience, sigh for the physician. To these the mercy of God is offered. Those who, from hopes of impunity, seek a license for sin, only provoke the wrath and justice of God.

4 Refutation of those who share forgiveness between Baptism and Repentance.

I know it is a common belief that forgiveness, which at our first regeneration we receive by baptism alone, is after baptism procured by means of penitence and the keys (see Chapter 19, section 17). But those who entertain this fiction err from not considering that the power of the keys, of which they speak, so depends on baptism, that it ought not on any account to be separated from it. The sinner receives forgiveness by the ministry of the Church, in other words, not without the preaching of the gospel. And of what nature is this preaching? That we are washed from our sins by the blood of Christ. And what is the sign and evidence of that washing if it be not baptism? We see, then, that that forgiveness has reference to baptism. This error had its origin in the fictitious sacrament of penance, on which I have already touched. What remains will be said at the proper place. There is no wonder if men who, from the grossness of their minds, are excessively attached to external things, have here also betrayed the defect–if not contented with the pure institution of God, they have introduced new helps devised by themselves, as if baptism were not itself a sacrament of penance. But if repentance is recommended during the whole of life, the power of baptism ought to have the same extent. Wherefore, there can be no doubt that all the godly may, during the whole course of their lives, whenever they are vexed by a consciousness of their sins, recall the remembrance of their baptism, that they may thereby assure themselves of that sole and perpetual ablution which we have in the blood of Christ.

5 Second thing in Baptism—viz. to teach that we are engrafted into Christ for mortification and newness of life.

Another benefit of baptism is that it shows us our mortification in Christ and new life in Him. "Know ye not," says the apostle, "that as many of us as were baptized into Jesus Christ, were baptized into His death? Therefore we are buried with Him by baptism into death," that we "should walk in newness of life" (Romans 6:3, 4). By these words, he not only exhorts us to imitation of Christ, as if he had said that we are admonished by baptism, in like manner as Christ died, to die to our lusts, and as He rose, to rise to righteousness; but he traces the matter much higher, that Christ by baptism has made us partakers of His death, engrafting us into it. And as the twig derives substance and nourishment from the root, to which it is attached, so those who receive baptism with true faith truly feel the efficacy of Christ's death in the mortification of their flesh, and the efficacy of His resurrection in the quickening of the Spirit. On this, he founds his exhortation, that if we are Christians we should be dead unto sin, and alive unto righteousness. He elsewhere uses the same argument–viz. that we are circumcised, and put off the old man, after we are buried in Christ by baptism. (See Colossians 2:12.) And in this sense, in the passage, which we formerly quoted, he calls it "the washing of regeneration, and renewing of the Holy Ghost" (Titus 3:5). We are promised, first, the free pardon of sins and imputation of righteousness; and, secondly, the grace of the Holy Spirit, to form us again to newness of life.

6 Third thing in Baptism—viz. to teach us that we are united to Christ to be partakers of all His blessings. Second and third things conspicuous in the baptism both of John and the apostles.

The last advantage which our faith receives from baptism is its assuring us not only that we are engrafted into the death and life of Christ, but so united to Christ himself as to be partakers of all His blessings. For He consecrated and sanctified baptism in His own body, that He might have it in common with us as the firmest bond of union and fellowship which He deigned to form with us; and hence Paul proves us to be the sons of God, from the fact that we put on Christ in baptism. (See Galatians 3:27.) Thus, we see the fulfillment of our baptism in Christ, whom for this reason we call the proper object of baptism. Hence, it is not strange that the apostles are said to have baptized in the name of Christ, though they were enjoined to baptize in the name of the Father and Spirit also. (See Acts 8:16; 19:5; Matthew 28:19.) For all the divine gifts held forth in baptism are found in Christ alone. And yet, he who baptizes into Christ cannot but at the same time invoke the name of the Father and the Spirit. For we are cleansed by His blood, just because our gracious Father, of His incomparable mercy, willing to receive us into favor, appointed Him Mediator to effect our reconciliation with himself. Regeneration we obtain from His death and resurrection only, when sanctified by His Spirit we are imbued with a new and spiritual nature. Wherefore we obtain, and in a manner distinctly perceive, in the Father the cause, in the Son the matter, and in the Spirit the effect of our purification and regeneration. Thus first John baptized, and thus afterwards the apostles by the baptism of repentance for the remission of sins, understanding by the term repentance, regeneration, and by the remission of sins, ablution.

7 Identity of the baptism of John and the apostles.

This makes it perfectly certain that the ministry of John was the very same as that which was afterwards delegated to the apostles. For the different hands by which baptism is administered do not make it a different baptism, but sameness of doctrine proves it the same. John and the apostles agreed in one doctrine. Both baptized unto repentance, both for remission of sins, and both in the name of Christ, from whom repentance and remission of sins proceed. John pointed to Him as the Lamb of God who taketh away the sins of the world (see John 1:29), thus describing Him as the victim accepted of the Father, the propitiation of righteousness, and the author of salvation. What could the apostles add to this confession? Wherefore, let no one be perplexed because ancient writers labor to distinguish the one from the other. Their views ought not to be in such esteem with us as to shake the certainty of Scripture. For who would listen to Chrysostom denying that remission of sins was included in the baptism of John (reference to Matthew 1:14), rather than to Luke asserting, on the contrary, that John preached "the baptism of repentance for the remission of sins"? (Luke 3:3). Nor can we admit Augustine's subtlety: that by the baptism of John sins were forgiven in hope, but by the baptism of Christ are forgiven in reality. For seeing the Evangelist clearly declares that John in his baptism promised the remission of sins, why detract from this eulogium when no necessity compels it? Should anyone ask what difference the Word of God makes, he will find it to be nothing more than that John baptized in the name of Him who was to come, the apostles in the name of Him who was already manifested. (See Luke 3:16; Acts 19:4.)

8 An objection to this refuted.

This fact, that the gifts of the Spirit would be more liberally poured out after the resurrection of Christ, does not go to establish a diversity of baptisms. For baptism, administered by the apostles while he was still on the earth, was called His baptism, and yet the Spirit was not poured out in larger abundance on it than on the baptism of John. Nay, not even after the ascension did the Samaritans receive the Spirit above the ordinary measure of former believers, until Peter and John were sent to lay hands on them. (See Acts 8:14-17.) I imagine that the thing, which imposed on ancient writers, and made them say that the one baptism was only a preparative to the other, was, because they read that those who had received the baptism of John were again baptized by Paul. (See Acts 19:3-5; Matthew 3:11.) How greatly they are mistaken in this will be most clearly explained in its own place. Why, then, did John say that he baptized with water, but there was one coming who would baptize with the Holy Ghost and with fire? This may be explained in a few words. He did not mean to distinguish the one baptism from the other, but he contrasted his own person with the person of Christ, saying, that while he was a minister of water, Christ was the giver of the Holy Spirit, and would declare this virtue by a visible miracle on the day on which He would send the Holy Spirit on the apostles, under the form of tongues of fire. What greater boast could the apostles make, and what greater those who baptize in the present day? For they are only ministers of the external sign, whereas Christ is the Author of internal grace, as those same ancient writers uniformly teach, and, in particular, Augustine, who, in his refutation of the Donatists, founds chiefly on this axiom, Whoever it is that baptizes, Christ alone presides.

9 The benefits of baptism typified to the Israelites by the passage of the Red Sea and the pillar of cloud.

The things which we have said, both of mortification and ablution, were adumbrated among the people of Israel, who, for that reason, are described by the apostle as having been baptized in the cloud and in the sea. (See 1 Corinthians 10:2.) Mortification was figured when the Lord, vindicating them from the hand of Pharaoh and from cruel bondage, paved a way for them through the Red Sea, and drowned Pharaoh himself and their Egyptian foes, who were pressing close behind, and threatening them with destruction. For in this way also He promises us in baptism, and shows by a given sign that we are led by His might, and delivered from the captivity of Egypt, that is, from the bondage of sin, that our Pharaoh is drowned; in other words, the devil, although he ceases not to try and harass us. But as that Egyptian was not plunged into the depth of the sea, but cast out upon the shore, still alarmed the Israelites by the terror of his look, though he could not hurt them, so our enemy still threatens, shows his arms and is felt, but cannot conquer. The cloud was a symbol of purification. (See Numbers 9:18.) For as the Lord then covered them by an opposite cloud, and kept them cool, that they might not faint or pine away under the burning rays of the sun; so in baptism we perceive that we are covered and protected by the blood of Christ, lest the wrath of God, which is truly an intolerable flame, should lie upon us. Although the mystery was then obscure, and known to few, yet as there is no other method of obtaining salvation than in those two graces, God was pleased that the ancient fathers, whom He had adopted as heirs, should be furnished with both badges.

10 Objection of those who imagine that there is some kind of perfect renovation after baptism. Original depravity remains after baptism. Its existence in infants. The elect after baptism are righteous in this life only by imputation.

It is now clear how false the doctrine is which some long ago taught, and others still persist in, that by baptism we are exempted and set free from original sin, and from the corruption which was propagated by Adam to all his posterity, and that we are restored to the same righteousness and purity of nature which Adam would have had if he had maintained the integrity in which he was created. This class of teachers never understands what is meant by original sin, original righteousness, or the grace of baptism. Now, it has been previously shown (see Book 2, chapter 1, section 8), that original sin is the depravity and corruption of our nature, which first makes us liable to the wrath of God, and then produces in us works which Scripture terms the works of the flesh. (See Galatians 5:19.) The two things, therefore, must be distinctly observed—viz. that we are vitiated and perverted in all parts of our nature, and then, on account of this corruption, are justly held to be condemned and convicted before God, to whom nothing is acceptable but purity, innocence, and righteousness. And hence, even infants bring their condemnation with them from their mother's womb; for although they have not yet brought forth the fruits of their unrighteousness, they have its seed included in them. Nay, their whole nature is a seed of sin, and, therefore, cannot but be odious and abominable to God. Believers become assured by baptism, that this condemnation is entirely withdrawn from them, since (as has been said) the Lord by this sign promises that a full and entire remission has been made, both of the guilt, which was imputed to us, and the penalty incurred by the guilt. They also apprehend righteousness, but such righteousness as the people of God can obtain in this life—viz. by imputation only, God, in His mercy, regarding them as righteous and innocent.

11 Original corruption trying to the pious during the whole course of their lives. They do not, on this account, seek a license for sin. They rather walk more cautiously and safely in the ways of the Lord.

Another point is, that this corruption never ceases in us, but constantly produces new fruits—viz. those works of the flesh which we previously described, just as a burning furnace perpetually sends forth flame and sparks, or a fountain is ever pouring out water. Men's concupiscence never wholly dies or is extinguished until, freed by death from the body of death, they have altogether laid aside their own nature. (See Book 3, chapter 3, sections 10-13.) Baptism, indeed, tells us that our Pharaoh is drowned and sin mortified, not so, however, as no longer to exist, or give no trouble, but only so as not to have dominion. For as long as we live shut up in this prison of the body, the remains of sin dwell in us, but if we faithfully hold the promise which God has given us in baptism, they will neither rule nor reign. But let no man deceive himself, let no man look complacently on his disease, when he hears that sin always dwells in us. When we say so, it is not in order that those who are otherwise too prone to sin may sleep securely in their sins, but only that those who are tried and stung by the flesh may not faint and despond. Let them rather reflect that they are still on the way, and think that they have made great progress when they feel that their concupiscence is somewhat diminished from day to day, until they shall have reached the point at which they aim—viz. the final death of the flesh; a death which shall be completed at the termination of this mortal life. Meanwhile, let them cease not to contend strenuously, and animate themselves to further progress, and press on to complete victory. Their efforts should be stimulated by the consideration, that after a lengthened struggle much still remains to be done. We ought to hold that we are baptized for the mortification of our flesh, which is begun in baptism, is prosecuted every day, and will be finished when we depart from this life to go to the Lord.

12 The trouble occasioned by corruption, shown by the example and testimony of the Apostle Paul.

Here, we say nothing more than the Apostle Paul expounds most clearly in the sixth and seventh chapters of the Epistle to the Romans. He had discoursed of free justification, but as some wicked men thence inferred that they were to live as they listed, because their acceptance with God was not procured by the merit of works, he adds, that all who are clothed with the righteousness of Christ are at the same time regenerated by the Spirit, and that we have an earnest of this regeneration in baptism. Hence, he exhorts believers not to allow sin to reign in their members. And because he knew that there is always some infirmity in believers, lest they should be cast down on this account, he adds, for their consolation, that they are not under the law. Again, as there may seem a danger that Christians might grow presumptuous because they were not under the yoke of the law, he shows what the nature of the abrogation is, and at the same time, what the use of the law is. This question he had already postponed a second time. The substance is that we are freed from the rigor of the law in order that we may adhere to Christ, and that the office of the law is to convince us of our depravity, and make us confess our impotence and wretchedness. Moreover, as this malignity of nature is not so easily apparent in a profane man who, without fear of God, indulges his passions, he gives an example in the regenerate man, in other words, in himself. He therefore says that he had a constant struggle with the remains of his flesh, and was kept in miserable bondage, to be unable to devote himself entirely to the obedience of the divine law. Hence, he is forced to groan and exclaim, "O wretched man that I am! Who shall deliver me from the body of this death?" (Romans 7:24). But if the children of God are kept captive in prison as long as they live, they must necessarily feel very anxious at the thought of their danger, unless their fears are allayed. For this single purpose, then, he subjoins the consolation, that there is "now no condemnation to them which are in Christ Jesus" (Romans 8:1). Hence, he teaches that those whom the Lord has once admitted into favor, engrafted into communion with Christ, and received into the fellowship of the Church by baptism, are freed from guilt and condemnation while they persevere in the faith of Christ, though they may be beset by sin and thus bear sin about with them. If this is the simple and genuine interpretation of Paul's meaning, we cannot think that there is anything strange in the doctrine, which he here delivers.

13 Another end of baptism is to serve as our confession to men.

Baptism serves as our confession before men, inasmuch as it is a mark by which we openly declare that we wish to be ranked among the people of God, by which we testify that we concur with all Christians in the worship of one God and in one religion; by which, in short, we publicly assert our faith, so that not only do our hearts breathe, but our tongues also, and all the members of our body, in every way they can, proclaim the praise of God. In this way, as is meet, everything we have is made subservient to the glory of God, which ought everywhere to be displayed, and others are stimulated by our example to the same course. To this Paul referred when he asked the Corinthians whether or not they had been baptized in the name of Christ (see 1 Corinthians 1:13); intimating, that by the very circumstance of having been baptized in His name, they had devoted themselves to Him, had sworn and bound themselves in allegiance to Him before men, so that they could no longer confess any other than Christ alone, unless they would abjure the confession which they had made in baptism.

14 Second part of the chapter. Of baptism as a confirmation of our faith.

Now that the end to which the Lord had regard in the institution of baptism has been explained, it is easy to judge in what way we ought to use and receive it. For inasmuch as it is appointed to elevate, nourish, and confirm our faith, we are to receive it as from the hand of its author, being firmly persuaded that it is himself who speaks to us by means of the sign; that it is himself who washes and purifies us, and effaces the remembrance of our faults; that it is himself who makes us the partakers of His death, destroys the kingdom of Satan, subdues the power of concupiscence, nay, makes us one with himself, that being clothed with Him we may be accounted the children of God. These things, I say, we ought to feel as truly and certainly in our mind as we see our body washed, immersed, and surrounded with water. For this analogy or similitude furnishes the surest rule in the sacraments–viz. that in corporeal things, we are to see spiritual, just as if they were actually exhibited to our eye, since the Lord has been pleased to represent them by such figures; not that such graces are included and bound in the sacrament, so as to be conferred by its efficacy, but only that by this badge the Lord declares to us that He is pleased to bestow all these things upon us. Nor does He merely feed our eyes with bare show; He leads us to the actual object, and effectually performs what He figures.

15 This illustrated by the examples of Cornelius and Paul. Of the use of baptism as a confession of faith.

We have a proof of this in Cornelius the centurion, who, after he had been previously endued with the graces of the Holy Spirit, was baptized for the remission of sins, not seeking a fuller forgiveness from baptism, but a surer exercise of faith; nay, an argument for assurance from a pledge. It will, perhaps, be objected, Why did Ananias say to Paul that he washed away his sins by baptism (see Acts 22:16), if sins are not washed away by the power of baptism? I answer, we are said to receive, procure, and obtain, whatever according to the perception of our faith is exhibited to us by the Lord, whether He then attests it for the first time, or gives additional confirmation to what He had previously attested. All then that Ananias meant to say was, Be baptized, Paul, that you may be assured that your sins are forgiven you. In baptism, the Lord promises forgiveness of sins: receive it, and be secure. I have no intention, however, to detract from the power of baptism. I would only add to the sign the substance and reality, inasmuch as God works by external means. But from this sacrament, as from all others, we gain nothing, unless in so far as we receive in faith. If faith is wanting, it will be an evidence of our ingratitude, by which we are proved guilty before God, for not believing the promise there given. In so far as it is a sign of our confession, we ought thereby to testify that we confide in the mercy of God and are pure through the forgiveness of sins which Christ Jesus has procured for us; that we have entered into the Church of God; that with one consent of faith and love we may live in concord with all believers. This last was Paul's meaning, when he said, "by one Spirit are we all baptized into one body" (1 Corinthians 12:13).

16 Baptism not affected by the worthiness or unworthiness of the minister. Hence, no necessity to rebaptize those who were baptized under the Papacy.

Moreover, if we have rightly determined that a sacrament is not to be estimated by the hand of him by whom it is administered, but is to be received as from the hand of God himself, from whom it undoubtedly proceeded, we may hence infer that its dignity neither gains nor loses by the administrator. And, just as among men, when a letter has been sent, if the hand and seal is recognized, it is not of the least consequence who or what the messenger was; so it ought to be sufficient for us to recognize the hand and seal of our Lord in His sacraments, let the administrator be who he may. This confutes the error of the Donatists, who measured the efficacy and worth of the sacrament by the dignity of the minister. Such in the present day are our Catabaptists, who deny that we are duly baptized, because we were baptized in the Papacy by wicked men and idolaters; hence, they furiously insist on anabaptism. Against these absurdities we shall be sufficiently fortified if we reflect that by baptism we were initiated not into the name of any man, but into the name of the Father, and the Son, and the Holy Spirit; and, therefore, that baptism is not of man, but of God, by whomsoever it may have been administered. Be it that those who baptized us were most ignorant of God and all piety, or were despisers, still they did not baptize us into a fellowship with their ignorance or sacrilege, but into the faith of Jesus Christ, because the name which they invoked was not their own but God's, nor did they baptize into any other name. But if baptism was of God, it certainly included in it the promise of forgiveness of sin, mortification of the flesh, quickening of the Spirit, and communion with Christ. Thus, it did not harm the Jews that they were circumcised by impure and apostate priests. It did not nullify the symbol to make it necessary to repeat it. It was enough to return to its genuine origin. The objection that baptism ought to be celebrated in the assembly of the godly does not prove that it loses its whole efficacy because it is partly defective. When we show what ought to be done to keep baptism pure and free from every taint, we do not abolish the institution of God though idolaters may corrupt it. Circumcision was anciently vitiated by many superstitions, and yet ceased not to be regarded as a symbol of grace; nor did Josiah and Hezekiah, when they assembled out of all Israel those who had revolted from God, call them to be circumcised anew.

17 Nothing in the argument that those so baptized remained some years blind and unbelieving. The promise of God remains firm. God, in inviting the Jews to repentance, does not enjoin them to be again circumcised.

Then, again, when they ask us what faith for several years followed our baptism, that they may thereby prove that our baptism was in vain, since it is not sanctified unless the Word of the Promise is received with faith, our answer is, that being blind and unbelieving, we for a long time did not hold the promise, which was given us in baptism, but that still the promise, as it was of God, always remained fixed, and firm, and true. Although all men should be false and perfidious, yet God ceases not to be true (see Romans 3:3, 4); though all were lost, Christ remains safe. We acknowledge, therefore, that at that time baptism profited us nothing, since in us the offered promise, without which baptism is nothing, lay neglected. Now, when by the grace of God we begin to repent, we accuse our blindness and hardness of heart in having been so long ungrateful for His great goodness. But we do not believe that the promise itself has vanished, we rather reflect thus: God in baptism promises the remission of sins, and will undoubtedly perform what He has promised to all believers. That promise was offered to us in baptism; let us therefore embrace it in faith. In regard to us, indeed, it was long buried because of unbelief; now, therefore, let us with faith receive it. Wherefore, when the Lord invites the Jewish people to repentance, He gives no injunction concerning another circumcision, though (as we have said) they were circumcised by a wicked and sacrilegious hand, and had long lived in the same impiety. All He urges is conversion of heart. For how much soever the covenant might have been violated by them, the symbol of the covenant always remained, according to the appointment of the Lord, firm and inviolable. Solely, therefore, on the condition of repentance, were they restored to the covenant, which God had once made with them in circumcision, though this, which they had received at the hand of a covenant breaking priest, they had themselves as much as in them lay polluted and extinguished.

18 No ground to allege that Paul rebaptized certain of John's disciples. The baptism of John. What it is to be baptized in the name of Christ.

But they seem to think the weapon, which they brandish, irresistible, when they allege that Paul rebaptized those who had been baptized with the baptism of John. (See Acts 19:3,5.) For if, by our confession, the baptism of John was the same as ours, then, in like manner as those who had been improperly trained, when they learned the true faith, were rebaptized into it, ought that baptism which was without true doctrine to be accounted as nothing, and hence we ought to be baptized anew into the true religion with which we are now, for the first time, imbued? It seems to some that it was a foolish imitator of John, who, by a former baptism, had initiated them into vain superstition. This, it is thought, may be conjectured from the fact, that they acknowledge their entire ignorance of the Holy Spirit, an ignorance in which John never would have left his disciples. But it is not probable that the Jews, even though they had not been baptized at all, would have been destitute of all knowledge of the Spirit, who is celebrated in so many passages of Scripture. Their answer, therefore, that they knew not whether there was a Spirit, must be understood as if they had said, that they had not yet heard whether or not the gifts of the Spirit, as to which Paul questioned them, were given to the disciples of Christ.

I grant that John's was a true baptism, and one and the same with the baptism of Christ. But I deny that they were rebaptized. What then is meant by the words, "They were baptized in the name of the Lord Jesus"? Some interpret that they were only instructed in sound doctrine by Paul; but I would rather interpret more simply, that the baptism of the Holy Spirit, in other words, the visible gifts of the Holy Spirit, were given by the laying on of hands. These are sometimes designated under the name of baptism. Thus, on the day of Pentecost, the apostles are said to have remembered the words of the Lord concerning the baptism of the Spirit and of fire. And Peter relates that the same words occurred to him when he saw these gifts poured out on Cornelius and his family and kindred. There is nothing repugnant to this interpretation in its being afterwards added, "When Paul had laid his hands upon them, the Holy Ghost came on them" (Acts 19:6). For Luke does not narrate two different things, but follows the form of narrative common to the Hebrews, who first give the substance, and then explain more fully. This anyone may perceive from the mere context. For he says, "When they heard this they were baptized in the name of the Lord Jesus. And when Paul laid his hands upon them, the Holy Ghost came on them."

In this last sentence is described what the nature of the baptism was. But if ignorance vitiates a former, and requires to be corrected by a second baptism, the apostles should first have been rebaptized, since for more than three full years after their baptism they had scarcely received any slender portion of purer doctrine. Then so numerous being the acts of ignorance, which by the mercy of God are daily, corrected in us, what rivers would suffice for so many repeated baptisms?

19 The corruptions introduced into baptism. The form of pure Christian baptism. Immersion or sprinkling should be left free.

The force, dignity, utility, and end of the sacrament must now, if I mistake not, be sufficiently clear. In regard to the external symbol, I wish the genuine institution of Christ had been maintained as fit to repress the audacity of men. As if to be baptized with water, according to the precept of Christ, had been a contemptible thing, a benediction, or rather incantation, was devised to pollute the true consecration of water. There was afterwards added the taper and chrism, while exorcism was thought to open the door for baptism. Though I am aware of how ancient the origin of this adventitious farrago is, still it is lawful for me and all the godly to reject whatever men have presumed to add to the institution of Christ. When Satan saw that by the foolish credulity of the world his impostures were received almost without objection at the commencement of the gospel, he proceeded to grosser mockery: hence, spittle and other follies, to the open disgrace of baptism, were introduced with unbridled license. From our experience of them, let us learn that there is nothing holier, or better, or safer, than to be contented with the authority of Christ alone.

How much better, therefore, is it to lay aside all theatrical pomp, which dazzles the eyes of the simple, and dulls their minds, and when anyone is to be baptized to bring him forward and present him to God, the whole Church looking on as witnesses, and praying over him; to recite the Confession of Faith, in which the catechumen has been instructed, explain the promises which are given in baptism, then baptize in the name of the Father, and the Son, and the Holy Spirit, and conclude with prayer and thanksgiving. In this way, nothing which is appropriate would be omitted, and the one ceremony, which proceeded from its divine Author, would shine forth most brightly, not being buried or polluted by extraneous observances. Whether the person baptized is to be wholly immersed, and that whether once or thrice, or whether he is only to be sprinkled with water, is not of the least consequence: churches should be at liberty to adopt either, according to the diversity of climates, although it is evident that the term baptize means to immerse, and that this was the form used by the primitive Church.

20 To whom the dispensation of baptism belongs. Not to private individuals or women, but to the ministers of the Church. Origin of the baptism of private individuals and women. An argument in favor of it refuted.

It is here also pertinent to observe, that it is improper for private individuals to take upon themselves the administration of baptism; for it, as well as the dispensation of the Supper, is part of the ministerial office. For Christ did not give command to any men or women whatever to baptize, but to those whom He had appointed apostles. And when, in the administration of the Supper, He ordered His disciples to do what they had seen Him do (he having done the part of a legitimate dispenser), He doubtless meant that in this they should imitate His example. The practice which has been in use for many ages, and even almost from the very commencement of the Church, for laics to baptize, in danger of death, when a minister could not be present in time, cannot, it appears to me, be defended on sufficient grounds. Even the early Christians who observed or tolerated this practice were not clear whether it would be rightly done. This doubt is expressed by Augustine when he says, "Although a laic have given baptism when compelled by necessity, I know not whether anyone can piously say that it ought to be repeated. For if it is done without any necessity compelling it, it is usurpation of another's office; but if necessity urges, it is either no fault, or a venial one." With regard to women, it was decreed, without exception, in the Council of Carthage, that they were not to presume to baptize at all. But there is a danger that he who is sick may be deprived of the gift of regeneration if he dies without baptism! By no means. Our children, before they are born, God declares that He adopts for His own when He promises that He will be a God to us and to our seed after us. In this promise, their salvation is included. None will dare to offer such an insult to God as to deny that He is able to give effect to His promise. How much evil has been caused by the dogma, ill expounded, that baptism is necessary to salvation, few perceive, and therefore think caution the less necessary. For when the opinion prevails that all are lost who happen not to be dipped in water, our condition becomes worse than that of God's ancient people, as if His grace were more restrained than under the Law. In that case, Christ will be thought to have come not to fulfill, but to abolish the promises, since the promise, which was then effectual in itself to confer salvation before the eighth day, would not now be effectual without the help of a sign.

21 Exploded also by Tertullian and Epiphanius.

What the custom was before Augustine's day is gathered, first, from Tertullian, who says, that a woman is not permitted to speak in the Church, nor yet to teach, or baptize, or offer, that she may not claim to herself any office of the man, not to say of the priest. Of the same thing, we have a sufficient witness in Epiphanius, when he upbraids Marcian with giving permission to women to baptize. I am aware of the answer given by those who take an opposite view–viz. that common use is very different from an extraordinary remedy used under the pressure of extreme necessity–but since he declares it mockery to allow women to baptize, and makes no exception, it is sufficiently plain that the corruption is condemned as inexcusable on any pretext. In his Third Book, also, when he says that it was not even permitted to the holy mother of Christ, he makes no reservation.

22 Objection founded on the case of Zipporah. Answer. Children dying before baptism not excluded from Heaven, provided the want of it was not caused by negligence or contempt.

The example of Zipporah (see Exodus 4:25) is irrelevantly quoted. Because the angel of God was appeased after she took a stone and circumcised her son, it is erroneously inferred that her act was approved by God. Were it so, we must say that God was pleased with a worship, which Gentiles brought from Assyria, and set up in Samaria. But other valid reasons prove that what a foolish woman did is ignorantly drawn into a precedent. Were I to say that there was something special in the case, making it unfit for a precedent–and especially as we nowhere read that the command to circumcise was specially given to priests, the cases of baptism and circumcision are different–I should give a sufficient refutation. For the Words of Christ are plain: "Go ye, therefore, and teach all nations, baptizing them" (Matthew 28:19). Since He appointed the same persons to be preachers of the Gospel, and dispensers of baptism–and in the Church, "no man taketh this honor unto himself," as the apostle declares (see Hebrews 5:4), "but he that is called of God, as was Aaron"–anyone who baptizes without a lawful call usurps another's office. Paul declares, that whatever we attempt with a dubious conscience, even in the minutest matters, as in meat and drink, is sin. (See Romans 14:23.) Therefore, in baptism by women, the sin is the greater, when it is plain that the rule delivered by Christ is violated, seeing we know it to be unlawful to put asunder what God has joined. But all this I pass; only I would have my readers to observe, that the last thing intended by Zipporah was to perform a service to God. Seeing her son in danger, she frets and murmurs, and, not without indignation, throws down the foreskin on the ground; thus upbraiding her husband, and taking offense at God. In short, it is plain that her whole procedure is dictated by passion: she complains both against her husband and against God, because she is forced to spill the blood of her son. We may add, that however well she might have conducted herself in all other respects, yet her presumption is inexcusable in this, in circumcising her son while her husband is present, and that husband not a mere private individual, but Moses, the chief prophet of God, than whom no greater ever arose in Israel. This was no more allowable in her, than it would be for women in the present day under the eye of a bishop. But this controversy will at once be disposed of when we maintain, that children who happen to depart this life before an opportunity of immersing them in water, are not excluded from the Kingdom of Heaven.

Now, it has been seen, that unless we admit this position, great injury is done to the covenant of God, as if in itself it would be weak, whereas its effect depends neither on baptism nor any accessories. The sacrament is afterwards added as a kind of seal, not to give efficacy to the promise, as if in itself invalid, but merely to confirm it to us. Hence, it follows, that the children of believers are not baptized, in order that though formerly aliens from the Church, they may then, for the first time, become children of God, but rather are received into the Church by a formal sign, because, in virtue of the promise, they previously belonged to the Body of Christ.

Hence, if, in omitting the sign, there is neither sloth, nor contempt, nor negligence, we are safe from all danger. By far the better course, therefore, is to pay such respect to the ordinance of God as not to seek the sacraments in any other quarter than where the Lord has deposited them. When we cannot receive them from the Church, the grace of God is not so inseparably annexed to them that we cannot obtain it by faith, according to His Word.

Chapter 16

PAEDOBAPTISM. ITS ACCORDANCE WITH THE INSTITUTION OF CHRIST, AND THE NATURE OF THE SIGN.

Divisions of this chapter—I. Confirmation of the orthodox doctrine of Paedobaptism, sections 1-9. II. Refutation of the arguments which the Anabaptists urge against Paedobaptism, sections 10-30. III. Special objections of Servetus refuted, sections 31, 32.

Sections

1. *Paedobaptism. The consideration of the question necessary and useful. Paedobaptism of divine origin.*

2. *This demonstrated from a consideration of the promises. These explain the nature and validity of Paedobaptism.*

3. *Promises annexed to the symbol of water cannot be better seen than in the institution of circumcision.*

4. *The promise and thing figured in circumcision and baptism one and the same. The only difference in the external ceremony.*

5. *Hence, the baptism of the children of Christian parents as competent as the circumcision of Jewish children. An objection founded on a stated day for circumcision refuted.*

6. *An argument for Paedobaptism founded on the covenant which God made with Abraham. An objection disposed of. The grace of God not diminished by the advent of Christ.*

7. *Argument founded on Christ's invitation to children. Objection answered.*

8. *Objection, that no infants were baptized by the apostles. Answer. Objection, that Paedobaptism is a novelty. Answer.*

9. *Twofold use and benefit of Paedobaptism. In respect, A. Of parents. B. Of children baptized.*

10 Second part of the chapter, stating the arguments of Anabaptists. Alleged dissimilitude between baptism and circumcision. First answer.

11. Second answer. The covenant in baptism and circumcision not different.

12. Third answer.

13. Infants, both Jewish and Christian, comprehended in the covenant.

14. Objection considered.

15. The Jews being comprehended in the covenant, no substantial difference between baptism and circumcision.

16. Another argument of the Anabaptists considered.

17. Argument that children are not fit to understand baptism, and therefore should not be baptized.

18. Answer continued.

19. Answer continued.

20. Answer continued.

21. Answer continued.

22. Argument, that baptism being appointed for the remission of sins, infants, not having sinned, ought not to be baptized. Answer.

23. Argument against Paedobaptism, founded on the practice of the apostles. Answer.

24. Answer continued.

25. Argument founded on a saying of our Lord to Nicodemus. Answer.

26. Error of those who adjudge all who die unbaptized to eternal destruction.

27. Argument against Paedobaptism, founded on the precept and example of our Savior, in requiring instruction to precede baptism. Answer.

28. Answer continued.

29. Answer continued.

30. Argument, that there is no stronger reason for giving baptism to children than for giving them the Lord's Supper. Answer.

31. Last part of the chapter, refuting the arguments of Servetus.

32. Why Satan so violently assails Paedobaptism.

1 Paedobaptism. The consideration of the question necessary and useful. Paedobaptism of divine origin.

But since, in this age, certain frenzied spirits have raised, and even now continue to raise, great disturbance in the Church because of Paedobaptism, I cannot avoid here, by way of appendix, adding something to restrain their fury. Should anyone think me more prolix than the subject is worth, let him reflect that, in a matter of the greatest moment, so much is due to the peace and purity of the Church, that we should not fastidiously object to whatever may be conducive to both. I may add, that I will study so to arrange this discussion, that it will tend, in no small degree, still further to illustrate the subject of baptism. The argument by which Paedobaptism is assailed is, no doubt, specious–viz. that it is not founded on the institution of God, but was introduced merely by human presumption and depraved curiosity, and afterwards, by a foolish facility, rashly received in practice; whereas a sacrament has not a thread to hang upon, if it rest not on the sure foundation of the Word of God. But what if, when the matter is properly attended to, it should be found that a calumny is falsely and unjustly brought against the holy ordinance of the Lord? First, then, let us inquire into its origin. Should it appear to have been devised merely by human rashness, let us abandon it, and regulate the true observance of baptism entirely by the will of the Lord; but should it be proved by no means destitute of His sure authority, let us beware of discarding the sacred institutions of God, and thereby insulting their Author.

2 This demonstrated from a consideration of the promises. These explain the nature and validity of Paedobaptism.

In the first place, then, it is a well-known doctrine, and one as to which all the pious are agreed–that the right consideration of signs does not lie merely in the outward ceremonies, but depends chiefly on the promise and the spiritual mysteries, to typify which the ceremonies themselves are appointed. He, therefore, who would thoroughly understand the effect of baptism–its object and true character–, must not stop short at the element and corporeal object. But look forward to the divine promises, which are therein offered to us, and rise to the internal secrets, which are therein represented. He who understands these has reached the solid truth, and, so to speak, the whole substance of baptism, and will thence perceive the nature and use of outward sprinkling. On the other hand, he who passes them by in contempt, and keeps his thoughts entirely fixed on the visible ceremony, will neither understand the force, nor the proper nature of baptism, nor comprehend what is meant, or what end is gained by the use of water. This is confirmed by passages of Scripture too numerous and too clear to make it necessary here to discuss them more at length. It remains, therefore, to inquire into the nature and efficacy of baptism, as evinced by the promises therein given. Scripture shows, first, that it points to that cleansing from sin which we obtain by the blood of Christ; and, secondly, to the mortification of the flesh which consists in participation in His death, by which believers are regenerated to newness of life, and thereby to the fellowship of Christ. To these general heads may be referred all that the Scriptures teach concerning baptism, with this addition, that it is also a symbol to testify our religion to men.

3 Promises annexed to the symbol of water cannot be better seen than in the institution of circumcision.

Now, since prior to the institution of baptism, the people of God had circumcision in its stead, let us see how far these two signs differ, and how far they resemble each other. In this way it will appear what analogy there is between them. When the Lord enjoins Abraham to observe circumcision (see Genesis 17:10), he premises that He would be a God unto him and to his seed, adding, that in himself was a perfect sufficiency of all things, and that Abraham might reckon on His hand as a fountain of every blessing. These words include the promise of eternal life, as our Savior interprets when He employs it to prove the immortality and resurrection of believers: "God," says He, "is not the God of the dead, but of the living" (Matthew 22:32). Hence, too, Paul, when showing to the Ephesians how great the destruction was from which the Lord had delivered them, seeing that they had not been admitted to the covenant of circumcision, infers that at that time they were aliens from the covenant of promise, without God, and without hope (see Ephesians 2:12), all these being comprehended in the covenant. Now, the first access to God, the first entrance to immortal life, is the remission of sins. Hence, it follows, that this corresponds to the promise of our cleansing in baptism. The Lord afterwards covenants with Abraham, that he is to walk before him in sincerity and innocence of heart: this applies to mortification or regeneration. And lest any should doubt whether circumcision were the sign of mortification, Moses explains more clearly elsewhere when he exhorts the people of Israel to circumcise the foreskin of their heart, because the Lord had chosen them for His own people, out of all the nations of the Earth. As the Lord, in choosing the posterity of Abraham for His people, commands them to be circumcised, so Moses declares that they are to be circumcised in heart, thus explaining what is typified by that carnal circumcision. Then, lest anyone should attempt this in his own strength, he shows that it is the work of divine grace. All this is so often inculcated by the prophets, that there is no occasion here to collect the passages, which everywhere occur. We have, therefore, a spiritual promise given to the Fathers in circumcision, similar to that which is given to us in baptism, since it figured to them both the forgiveness of sins and the mortification of the flesh. Besides, as we have shown that Christ, in whom both of these reside, is the foundation of baptism, so must He also be the foundation of circumcision. For He is promised to Abraham, and in him all nations are blessed. To seal this grace, the sign of circumcision is added.

4 The promise and thing figured in circumcision and baptism one and the same. The only difference in the external ceremony.

There is now no difficulty in seeing wherein the two signs agree, and wherein they differ. The promise, in which we have shown that the power of the signs consists, is one in both–viz. the promise of the paternal favor of God, of forgiveness of sins, and eternal life. And the thing figured is one and the same–viz. regeneration. The foundation on which the completion of these things depends is one in both. Wherefore, there is no difference in the internal meaning, from which the whole power and peculiar nature of the sacrament is to be estimated. The only difference, which remains, is in the external ceremony, which is the least part of it, the chief part consisting in the promise and the thing signified. Hence, we may conclude, that everything applicable to circumcision applies also to baptism, excepting always the difference in the visible ceremony. To this analogy and comparison, we are led by that rule of the apostle, in which he enjoins us to bring every interpretation of Scripture to the analogy of faith. (See Romans 12:3, 6.) And certainly, in this matter the truth may almost be felt. For just as circumcision, which was a kind of badge to the Jews, assuring them that they were adopted as the people and family of God, was their first entrance into the Church, while they, in their turn, professed their allegiance to God, so now we are initiated by baptism, so as to be enrolled among His people, and at the same time swear unto His name. Hence, it is incontrovertible, that baptism has been substituted for circumcision, and performs the same office.

5 Hence, the baptism of the children of Christian parents as competent as the circumcision of Jewish children. An objection founded on a stated day for circumcision refuted.

Now, if we are to investigate whether or not baptism is justly given to infants, will we not say that the man trifles, or rather is delirious, who would stop short at the element of water, and the external observance, and not allow his mind to rise to the spiritual mystery? If reason is listened to, it will undoubtedly appear that baptism is properly administered to infants as a thing due to them. The Lord did not anciently bestow circumcision upon them without making them partakers of all the things signified by circumcision. He would have deluded his people with mere imposture, had he quieted them with fallacious symbols: the very idea is shocking. He distinctly declares that the circumcision of the infant will be instead of a seal of the promise of the covenant. But if the covenant remains firm and fixed, it is no less applicable to the children of Christians in the present day, than to the children of the Jews under the Old Testament. Now, if they are partakers of the thing signified, how can they be denied the sign? If they obtain the reality, how can they be refused the figure? The external sign is so united in the sacrament with the Word, that it cannot be separated from it: but if they can be separated, to which of the two shall we attach the greater value? Surely, when we see that the sign is subservient to the Word, we shall say that it is subordinate, and assign it the inferior place. Since, then, the Word of baptism is destined for infants, why should we deny them the sign, which is an appendage of the Word? This one reason, could no other be furnished, would be amply sufficient to refute all gainsayers. The objection, that there was a fixed day for circumcision, is a mere quibble. We admit that we are not now, like the Jews, tied down to certain days; but when the Lord declares, that though he prescribes no day, yet He is pleased that infants shall be formally admitted to His covenant, what more do we ask?

6 An argument for Paedobaptism founded on the covenant which God made with Abraham. An objection disposed of. The grace of God not diminished by the advent of Christ.

Scripture gives us a still clearer knowledge of the truth. For it is most evident that the covenant, which the Lord once made with Abraham, is not less applicable to Christians now than it was anciently to the Jewish people, and therefore that Word has no less reference to Christians than to Jews. Unless, indeed, we imagine that Christ, by His advent, diminished, or curtailed the grace of the Father–an idea not free from execrable blasphemy. Wherefore, both the children of the Jews, because, when made heirs of that covenant, they were separated from the heathen, were called a holy seed, and for the same reason the children of Christians, or those who have only one believing parent, are called holy, and, by the testimony of the apostle, differ from the impure seed of idolaters. Then, since the Lord, immediately after the covenant was made with Abraham, ordered it to be sealed in infants by an outward sacrament, how can it be said that Christians are not to attest it in the present day, and seal it in their children? Let it not be objected, that the only symbol by which the Lord ordered His covenant to be confirmed was that of circumcision, which was long ago abrogated. It is easy to answer, that, in accordance with the form of the old dispensation, He appointed circumcision to confirm His covenant, but that it being abrogated, the same reason for confirmation still continues, a reason which we have in common with the Jews.

Hence, it is always necessary carefully to consider what is common to both, and wherein they differed from us. The covenant is common, and the reason for confirming it is common. The mode of confirming it is so far different, that they had circumcision, instead of which we now have baptism. Otherwise, if the testimony by which the Jews were assured of the salvation of their seed is taken from us, the consequence will be, that, by the advent of Christ, the grace of God, which was formerly given to the Jews, is more obscure and less perfectly attested to us. If this cannot be said without extreme insult to Christ, by whom the infinite goodness of the Father has been more brightly and benignly than ever shed upon the Earth, and declared to men, it must be confessed that it cannot be more confined, and less clearly manifested, than under the obscure shadows of the law.

7 Argument founded on Christ's invitation to children. Objection answered.

Hence, our Lord Jesus Christ, to give an example from which the world might learn that He had come to enlarge rather than to limit the grace of the Father, kindly takes the little children in His arms, and rebukes His disciples for attempting to prevent them from, coming (Matthew 19:13), because they were keeping those to whom the Kingdom of Heaven belonged away from Him, through whom alone there is access to Heaven. But it will be asked, What resemblance is there between baptism and our Savior embracing little children? He is not said to have baptized, but to have received, embraced, and blessed them; and, therefore, if we would imitate His example, we must give infants the benefit of our prayers, not baptize them. But let us attend to the act of our Savior a little more carefully than these men do. For we must not lightly overlook the fact, that our Savior, in ordering little children to be brought to Him, adds the reason, " of such is the Kingdom of Heaven." And He afterwards testifies His good will by act, when He embraces them, and with prayer and benediction commends them to His Father. If it is right that children should be brought to Christ, why should they not be admitted to baptism, the symbol of our communion and fellowship with Christ? If the Kingdom of Heaven is theirs, why should they be denied the sign by which access is opened to the Church, that being admitted into it they may be enrolled among the heirs of the heavenly Kingdom? How unjust were we to drive away those whom Christ invites to himself, to spoil those whom He adorns with His gifts, to exclude those whom He spontaneously admits. But if we insist on discussing the difference between our Savior's act and baptism, in how much higher esteem shall we hold baptism (by which we testify that infants are included in the divine covenant), than the taking up, embracing, laying hands on children, and praying over them, acts by which Christ, when present, declares both that they are His, and are sanctified by Him. By the other cavils by which the objectors endeavor to evade this passage, they only betray their ignorance: they quibble that, because our Savior says, "Suffer little children to come," they must have been several years old, and fit to come. But they are called by the Evangelists a term that denotes infants still at their mothers' breasts. The term "come" is used simply for "approach."

See the quibbles to which men are obliged to have recourse when they have hardened themselves against the truth! There is nothing more solid in their allegation, that the Kingdom of Heaven is not assigned to children, but to those like children, since the expression is, "of such," not "of themselves." If this is admitted, what will be the reason, which our Savior employs to show that they are not strangers to Him from nonage? When He orders that little children shall be allowed to come to Him, nothing is plainer than that mere infancy is meant. Lest this should seem absurd, He adds, "Of such is the Kingdom of Heaven." But if infants must necessarily be comprehended, the expression, "of such," clearly shows that infants themselves, and those like them, are intended.

8 Objection, that no infants were baptized by the apostles. Answer. Objection, that Paedobaptism is a novelty. Answer.

Everyone must now see that Paedobaptism, which receives such strong support from Scripture, is by no means of human invention. Nor is there anything plausible in the objection that we nowhere read of even one infant having been baptized by the hands of the apostles. For although this is not expressly narrated by the Evangelists, yet as they are not expressly excluded when mention is made of any baptized family (see Acts 16:15, 32), what man of sense will argue from this that they were not baptized? If such kinds of argument were good, it would be necessary, in like manner, to interdict women from the Lord's Supper, since we do not read that they were ever admitted to it in the days of the apostles. But here we are contented with the rule of faith. For when we reflect on the nature of the ordinance of the Lord's Supper, we easily judge who the persons are to whom the use of it is to be communicated. The same we observe in the case of baptism. For, attending to the end for which it was instituted, we clearly perceive that it is not less applicable to children than to those of more advanced years, and that, therefore, they cannot be deprived of it without manifest fraud to the will of its divine Author. The assertion which they disseminate among the common people, that a long series of years elapsed after the resurrection of Christ, during which Paedobaptism was unknown, is a shameful falsehood, since there is no writer, however ancient, who does not trace its origin to the days of the apostles.

9 Twofold use and benefit of Paedobaptism. In respect, A. Of parents. B. Of children baptized.

It remains briefly to indicate what benefit redounds from the observance, both to believers who bring their children to the Church to be baptized, and to the infants themselves, to whom the sacred water is applied, that no one may despise the ordinance as useless or superfluous: though anyone who would think of ridiculing baptism under this pretence, would also ridicule the divine ordinance of circumcision: for what can they adduce to impugn the one, that may not be retorted against the other? Thus, the Lord punishes the arrogance of those who forthwith condemn whatever their carnal sense cannot comprehend. But God furnishes us with other weapons to repress their stupidity. His holy institution, from which we feel that our faith derives admirable consolation, deserves not to be called superfluous. For the divine symbol communicated to the child, as with the impress of a seal, confirms the promise given to the godly parent, and declares that the Lord will be a God not to him only, but to his seed; not merely visiting him with His grace and goodness, but his posterity also to the thousandth generation. When the infinite goodness of God is thus displayed, it, in the first place, furnishes most ample materials for proclaiming His glory, and fills pious breasts with no ordinary joy, urging them more strongly to love their affectionate Parent, when they see that, on their account, He extends His care to their posterity. I am not moved by the objection, that the promise ought to be sufficient to confirm the salvation of our children. It has seemed otherwise to God, who, seeing our weakness, has herein been pleased to condescend to it. Let those, then, who embrace the promise of mercy to their children, consider it as their duty to offer them to the Church, to be sealed with the symbol of mercy, and animate themselves to surer confidence, on seeing with the bodily eye the covenant of the Lord engraved on the bodies of their children. On the other hand, children derive some benefit from their baptism, when, being engrafted into the body of the Church, they are made an object of greater interest to the other members. Then when they have grown up, they are thereby strongly urged to an earnest desire of serving God, who has received them as sons by the formal symbol of adoption, before, from nonage, they were able to recognize Him as their Father. In fine, we ought to stand greatly in awe of the denunciation, that God will take vengeance on everyone who despises to impress the symbol of the covenant on His child (see Genesis 17:15), such contempt being a rejection, and abjuration of the offered grace.

10 Second part of the chapter, stating the arguments of Anabaptists. Alleged dissimilitude between baptism and circumcision. First answer.

Let us now discuss the arguments by which some furious madmen cease not to assail this holy ordinance of God. And, first, feeling themselves pressed beyond measure by the resemblance between baptism and circumcision, they contend that there is a wide difference between the two signs, that the one has nothing in common with the other. They maintain that the things meant are different, that the covenant is altogether different, and that the persons included under the name of children are different. When they first proceed to the proof, they pretend that circumcision was a figure of mortification, not of baptism. This we willingly concede to them, for it admirably supports our view, in support of which the only proof we use is, that baptism and circumcision are signs of mortification. Hence, we conclude that the one was substituted for the other, baptism representing to us the very thing which circumcision signified to the Jews. In asserting a difference of covenant, with what barbarian audacity do they corrupt and destroy Scripture? And that not in one passage only, but so as not to leave any passage safe and entire. The Jews they depict as so carnal as to resemble brutes more than men, representing the covenant, which was made with them as reaching no further than a temporary life, and the promises, which were given to them as dwindling down into present and corporeal blessings. If this dogma is received, what remains but that the Jewish nation was overloaded for a time with divine kindness (just as swine are gorged in their sty), that they might at last perish eternally? Whenever we quote circumcision and the promises annexed to it, they answer, that circumcision was a literal sign, and that its promises were carnal.

11 Second answer. The covenant in baptism and circumcision not different.

Certainly, if circumcision was a literal sign, the same view must be taken of baptism, since, in the second chapter to the Colossians, the apostle makes the one to be not a whit more spiritual than the other. For he says that in Christ, we "are circumcised with the circumcision made without hands, in putting off the body of the sins of the flesh, by the circumcision of Christ." In explanation of his sentiment he immediately adds, that we are "buried with him in baptism." What do these words mean, but just that the truth and completion of baptism is the truth and completion of circumcision, since they represent one thing? For his object is to show that baptism is the same thing to Christians, that circumcision formerly was to the Jews. Now, since we have already clearly shown that the promises of both signs, and the mysteries which are represented by them, agree, we shall not dwell on the point longer at present. I would only remind believers to reflect, without anything being said by me, whether that is to be regarded as an earthly and literal sign, which has nothing heavenly or spiritual under it. But lest they should blind the simple with their smoke, we shall, in passing, dispose of one objection by which they cloak this most impudent falsehood. It is absolutely certain that the original promises comprehending the covenant which God made with the Israelites under the old dispensation were spiritual, and had reference to eternal life, and were, of course, in like manner spiritually received by the Fathers, that they might thence entertain a sure hope of immortality, and aspire to it with their whole soul. Meanwhile, we are far from denying that He testified His kindness to them by carnal and earthly blessings, though we hold that by these the hope of spiritual promises was confirmed. In this manner, when He promised eternal blessedness to His servant Abraham, He, in order to place a manifest indication of favor before His eye, added the promise of possession of the land of Canaan. In the same way we should understand all the terrestrial promises, which were given to the Jewish nation, the spiritual promise, as the head to which the others bore reference, always holding the first place. Having handled this subject fully when treating of the difference between the old and the new dispensations, I now only glance at it.

12 Third answer.

Under the appellation of children, the difference they observe is this, that the children of Abraham, under the old dispensation, were those who derived their origin from his seed, but that the appellation is now given to those who imitate his faith, and therefore that carnal infancy, which was engrafted into the fellowship of the covenant by circumcision, typified the spiritual children of the new covenant, who are regenerated by the Word of God to immortal life. In these words we indeed discover a small spark of truth, but these giddy spirits err grievously in this, that laying hold of whatever comes first to their hand, when they ought to proceed further, and compare many things together, they obstinately fasten upon one single word. Hence, it cannot but happen that they are every now and then deluded, because they do not exert themselves to obtain a full knowledge of any subject. We certainly admit that the carnal seed of Abraham for a time held the place of the spiritual seed, which is engrafted into him by faith. (See Galatians 4:28; Romans 4:12.) For we are called his sons, though we have no natural relationship with him. But if they mean, as they not obscurely show, that the spiritual promise was never made to the carnal seed of Abraham, they are greatly mistaken. We must, therefore, take a better aim, one to which we are directed by the infallible guidance of Scripture. The Lord therefore promises to Abraham that he shall have a seed in whom all the nations of the earth will be blessed, and at the same time assures him that He will be a God both to him and his seed. All who in faith receive Christ as the author of the blessing are the heirs of this promise, and accordingly are called the children of Abraham.

13 Infants, both Jewish and Christian, comprehended in the covenant.

Although, after the resurrection of Christ, the boundaries of the Kingdom began to be extended far and wide into all nations indiscriminately, so that, according to the declaration of Christ, believers were collected from all quarters to sit down with Abraham, Isaac, and Jacob, in the Kingdom of Heaven (see Matthew 8:11), still, for many ages before, the Jews had enjoyed this great mercy.

And as He had selected them (while passing by all other nations) to be for a time the depositaries of His favor, He designated them as His peculiar purchased people. (See Exodus 19:5.) In attestation of this kindness, he appointed circumcision, by which symbol the Jews were taught that God watched over their safety, and they were thereby raised to the hope of eternal life. For what can ever be wanting to him whom God has once taken under His protection? Wherefore the apostle, to prove that the Gentiles, as well as the Jews, were the children of Abraham, speaks in this way: "Faith was reckoned to Abraham for righteousness. How was it then reckoned? when he was in circumcision, or in uncircumcision? Not in circumcision, but in uncircumcision. And he received the sign of circumcision, a seal of the righteousness of the faith which he had yet being uncircumcised; that he might be the father of all them that believe, though they be not circumcised: that righteousness might be imputed to them also: and the father of circumcision to them who are not of the circumcision only, but who also walk in the steps of that faith of our father Abraham, which he had yet being uncircumcised" (Romans 4:9-12).

Do we not see that both are made equal in dignity? For, to the time appointed by the divine decree, he was the father of circumcision. But when, as the apostle elsewhere writes (see Ephesians 2:14), the wall of partition which separated the Gentiles from the Jews was broken down, to them, also, access was given to the Kingdom of God, and he became their father, and that without the sign of circumcision, its place being supplied by baptism. In saying expressly that Abraham was not the father of those who were of the circumcision only, his object was to repress the superciliousness of some who, laying aside all regard to godliness, plumed themselves on mere ceremonies. In like manner, today, we may refute the vanity of those who, in baptism, seek nothing but water.

14 Objection considered.

But in opposition to this is produced a passage from the Epistle to the Romans, in which the apostle says, that those who are of the flesh are not the children of Abraham, but that those only who are the children of promise are considered as the seed. (See Romans 9.) For he seems to insinuate, that carnal relationship to Abraham, which we think of some consequence, is nothing. But we must attend carefully to the subject which the apostle is there treating. His object being to show to the Jews that the goodness of God was not restricted to the seed of Abraham, nay, that of itself it contributes nothing, produces, in proof of the fact, the cases of Ishmael and Esau. These being rejected, just as if they had been strangers, although, according to the flesh, they were the genuine offspring of Abraham, the blessing resides in Isaac and Jacob. This proves what he afterwards affirms–viz. that salvation depends on the mercy which God bestows on whomsoever He pleases, but that the Jews have no ground to glory or plume themselves on the name of the covenant, unless they keep the law of the covenant, that is, obey the word. On the other hand, after casting down their vain confidence in their origin, because he was aware that the covenant, which had been made with the posterity of Abraham, could not properly prove fruitless, he declares that due honor should still be paid to the carnal relationship to Abraham, in consequence of which, the Jews were the primary and native heirs of the gospel, unless in so far as they were, for their ingratitude, rejected as unworthy, and yet rejected so as not to leave their nation utterly destitute of the heavenly blessing.

For this reason, though they were rebellious breakers of the covenant, he styles them holy (such respect does he pay to the holy generation which God had honored with his sacred covenant), while we, in comparison of them, are termed posthumous, or abortive children of Abraham not by nature, but by adoption, just as if a twig were broken from its own tree, and engrafted on another stock. Therefore, that they might not be defrauded of their privilege, it was necessary that the gospel should first be preached to them. For they are the firstborn in the family of God. The honor due, on this account, must therefore be paid them, until they have rejected the offer, and, by their ingratitude, caused it to be transferred to the Gentiles. Nor, however great the contumacy with which they persist in warring against the gospel, are we therefore to despise them. We must consider, that in respect of the promise, the blessing of God still resides among them; and, as the apostle testifies, will never entirely depart from them, seeing that "the gifts and calling of God are without repentance" (Romans 11:29).

15 The Jews being comprehended in the covenant, no substantial difference between baptism and circumcision.

Such is the value of the promise given to the posterity of Abraham, –such the balance in which it is to be weighed. Hence, though we have no doubt that in distinguishing the children of God from bastards and foreigners, that the election of God reigns freely, we, at the same time, perceive that He was pleased specially to embrace the seed of Abraham with His mercy, and, for the better attestation of it, to seal it by circumcision. The case of the Christian Church is entirely of the same description, for as Paul there declares that the Jews are sanctified by their parents, so he elsewhere says that the children of Christians derive sanctification from their parents. Hence, it is inferred, that those who are chargeable with impurity are justly separated from others. Now, who can have any doubt as to the falsehood of their subsequent averment–viz. that the infants who were formerly circumcised only typified the spiritual infancy, which is produced by the regeneration of the Word of God? When the apostle says, "Jesus Christ was a minister of the circumcision for the truth of God, to confirm the promises made unto the fathers" (Romans 15:8), he does not philosophize subtlety, as if he had said, Since the covenant made with Abraham has respect unto his seed, Christ, in order to perform and discharge the promise made by the Father, came for the salvation of the Jewish nation. Do you see how he considers that, after the resurrection of Christ, the promise is to be fulfilled to the seed of Abraham, not allegorically, but literally, as the words express?

To the same effect is the declaration of Peter to the Jews: "The promise is unto you and to your children" (Acts 2:39); and in the next chapter, he calls them the children of the covenant, that is, heirs. Not widely different from this is the other passage of the apostle, above quoted, in which he regards and describes circumcision performed on infants as an attestation to the communion, which they have with Christ. And, indeed, if we listen to the absurdities of those men, what will become of the promise by which the Lord, in the second commandment of his law, engages to be gracious to the seed of his servants for a thousand generations? Shall we here have recourse to allegory? This would be the merest quibble. Shall we say that it has been abrogated? In this way, we should do away with the law, which Christ came not to destroy, but to fulfill, inasmuch as it turns to our everlasting good. Therefore, let it be without controversy, that God is so good and liberal to His people, and that He is pleased, as a mark of His favor, to extend their privileges to the children born to them.

16 Another argument of the Anabaptists considered.

The distinctions, which these men attempt to draw between baptism and circumcision, are not only ridiculous, and void of all semblance of reason, but at variance with each other. For, when they affirm that baptism refers to the first day of spiritual contest, and circumcision to the eighth day, mortification being already accomplished, they immediately forget the distinction, and change their song, representing circumcision as typifying the mortification of the flesh, and baptism as a burial, which is given to none but those who are already dead. What are these giddy contradictions but frenzied dreams? According to the former view, baptism ought to precede circumcision; according to the latter, it should come after it. It is not the first time we have seen the minds of men wander back and forth when they substitute their dreams for the infallible Word of God. We hold, therefore, that their former distinction is a mere imagination. Were we disposed to make an allegory of the eighth day, theirs would not be the proper mode of it.

It would be much better with the early Christians to refer the number eight to the resurrection, which took place on the eighth day, and on which we know that newness of life depends, or to the whole course of the present life, during which, mortification ought to be in progress, only terminating when life itself terminates; although it would seem that God intended to provide for the tenderness of infancy by deferring circumcision to the eighth day, as the wound would have been more dangerous if inflicted immediately after birth.

How much more rational is the declaration of Scripture, that we, when already dead, are buried by baptism (see Romans 6:4); since it distinctly states, that we are buried into death that we may thoroughly die, and thenceforth aim at that mortification? Equally ingenious is their cavil, that women should not be baptized if baptism is to be made conformable to circumcision. For if it is most certain that the sanctification of the seed of Israel was attested by the sign of circumcision, it cannot be doubted that it was appointed alike for the sanctification of males and females. But though the right could only be performed on males, yet the females were, through them, partners and associates in circumcision. Wherefore, disregarding all such quibbling distinctions, let us fix on the very complete resemblance between baptism and circumcision, as seen in the internal office, the promise, the use, and the effect.

17 Argument that children are not fit to understand baptism, and therefore should not be baptized.

They seem to think they produce their strongest reason for denying baptism to children, when they allege, that they are yet unfit, from nonage, to understand the mystery which is there sealed–viz. spiritual regeneration, which is not applicable to earliest infancy. Hence, they infer that children are only to be regarded as sons of Adam until they have attained an age fit for the reception of the second birth. But all this is directly opposed to the truth of God. For if they are to be accounted sons of Adam, they are left in death, since, in Adam, we can do nothing but die. On the contrary, Christ bids them be brought to Him. Why so? Because He is life. Therefore, that He may quicken them, He makes them partners with himself; whereas these men would drive them away from Christ, and adjudge them to death. For if they pretend that infants do not perish when they are accounted the sons of Adam, the error is more than sufficiently confuted by the testimony of Scripture. (See 1 Corinthians 15:22.) For seeing it declares that in Adam all die, it follows, that no hope of life remains unless in Christ. Therefore, that we may become heirs of life, we must communicate with Him.

Again, seeing it is elsewhere written that we are all by nature the children of wrath (see Ephesians 2:3), and conceived in sin (see Psalm 51:5), of which condemnation is the inseparable attendant, we must part with our own nature before we have any access to the Kingdom of God. And what can be clearer than the expression, "Flesh and blood cannot inherit the kingdom of God"? (1 Corinthians 15:50.) Therefore, let everything that is our own be abolished (this cannot be without regeneration), and then we shall perceive this possession of the Kingdom. In fine, if Christ speaks truly when He declares that He is life, we must necessarily be engrafted into Him by whom we are delivered from the bondage of death. But how, they ask, are infants regenerated, when not possessing knowledge of either good or evil? We answer, that the work of God, though beyond the reach of our capacity, is not therefore null. Moreover, infants who are to be saved (and that some are saved at this age is certain) must, without question, be previously regenerated by the Lord. For if they bring innate corruption with them from their mother's womb, they must be purified before they can be admitted into the Kingdom of God, into which shall not enter anything that defileth.

(See Revelation 21:27.) If they are born sinners, as David and Paul affirm, they must either remain unaccepted and hated by God, or be justified. And why do we ask more, when the Judge himself publicly declares, that "except a man be born again, he cannot see the kingdom of God" (John 3:3)?

But to silence this class of objectors, God gave, in the case of John the Baptist, whom He sanctified from his mother's womb (Luke 1:15), a proof of what he might do in others. They gain nothing by the quibble to which they here resort–viz. that this was only once done, and therefore it does not forthwith follow that the Lord always acts thus with infants. That is not the mode in which we reason. Our only object is to show, that they unjustly and malignantly confine the power of God within limits, within which it cannot be confined. As little weight is due to another subterfuge. They allege that, by the usual phraseology of Scripture, "from the womb," has the same meaning as "from childhood." But it is easy to see that the angel had a different meaning when he announced to Zacharias that the child not yet born would be filled with the Holy Spirit. Instead of attempting to give a law to God, let us hold that He sanctifies whom He pleases, in the way in which He sanctified John, seeing that His power is not impaired.

18 Answer continued.

And, indeed, Christ was sanctified from earliest infancy, that He might sanctify His elect in himself at any age, without distinction. For as He, in order to wipe away the guilt of disobedience that had been committed in our flesh, assumed that very flesh, so that in it He might, on our account and in our stead, perform a perfect obedience, so He was conceived by the Holy Spirit, that, completely pervaded with His holiness in the flesh that He had assumed, He might transfuse it into us. If in Christ we have a perfect pattern of all the graces, which God bestows on all His children, in this instance we have a proof that the age of infancy is capable of receiving sanctification. This, at least, we set down as incontrovertible, that none of the elect is called away from the present life without being previously sanctified and regenerated by the Spirit of God. As to their objection that, in Scripture, the Spirit acknowledges no sanctification save that from incorruptible seed, that is, the Word of God, they erroneously interpret Peter's words, in which he comprehends only believers who had been taught by the preaching of the gospel. (See 1 Peter 1:23.) We confess, indeed, that the Word of the Lord is the only seed of spiritual regeneration; but we deny the inference that, therefore, the power of God cannot regenerate infants. This is as possible and easy for Him, as it is wondrous and incomprehensible to us. It would be dangerous to deny that the Lord is able to furnish them with the knowledge of himself in any way He pleases.

19 Answer continued.

But faith, they say, cometh by hearing, the use of which infants have not yet obtained, nor can they be fit to know God, being, as Moses declares, without the knowledge of good and evil (Deuteronomy 1:39). But they observe not that where the apostle makes hearing the beginning of faith, he is only describing the usual economy and dispensation which the Lord is wont to employ in calling His people, and not laying down an invariable rule, for which no other method can be substituted. Many He certainly has called and endued with the true knowledge of himself, by internal means, by the illumination of the Spirit, without the intervention of preaching. But since they deem it very absurd to attribute any knowledge of God to infants, whom Moses makes void of the knowledge of good and evil, let them tell me where the danger lies if they are said now to receive some part of that grace, of which they are to have the full measure shortly after. For if fullness of life consists in the perfect knowledge of God, since some of those whom death hurries away in the first moments of infancy pass into life eternal, they are certainly admitted to behold the immediate presence of God. Those, therefore, whom the Lord is to illumine with the full brightness of His light, why may He not, if He so pleases, irradiate at present with some small beam, especially if He does not remove their ignorance, before He delivers them from the prison of the flesh? I would not rashly affirm that they are endued with the same faith which we experience in ourselves, or have any knowledge at all resembling faith (this I would rather leave undecided); but I would somewhat curb the stolid arrogance of those men who, as with inflated cheeks, affirm or deny whatever suits them.

20 Answer continued.

In order to gain a stronger footing here, they add, that baptism is a sacrament of penitence and faith, and as neither of these is applicable to tender infancy, we must beware of rendering its meaning empty and vain, by admitting infants to the communion of baptism. But these darts are directed more against God then against us; since the fact that circumcision was a sign of repentance is completely established by many passages of Scripture. (See Jeremiah 4:4.)

Thus, Paul terms it a seal of the righteousness of faith. (See Romans 4:11.) Let God, then, be demanded why He ordered circumcision to be performed on the bodies of infants? For baptism and circumcision being here in the same case, they cannot give anything to the latter without conceding it to the former. If they recur to their usual evasion, that, by the age of infancy, spiritual infants were then figured, we have already closed this means of escape against them. We say, then, that since God imparted circumcision, the sign of repentance and faith, to infants, it should not seem absurd that they are now made partakers of baptism, unless men choose to clamor against an institution of God. But as in all His acts, so here also, enough of wisdom and righteousness shines forth to repress the slanders of the ungodly. For although infants, at the moment when they were circumcised, did not comprehend what the sign meant, still they were truly circumcised for the mortification of their corrupt and polluted nature–a mortification at which they afterwards aspired when adults. In fine, the objection is easily disposed of by the fact, that children are baptized for future repentance and faith. Though these are not yet formed in them, yet the seed of both lies hid in them by the secret operation of the Spirit.

This answer at once overthrows all the objections, which are twisted against us out of the meaning of baptism; for instance, the title by which Paul distinguishes it when he terms it the "washing of regeneration and renewing" (Titus 3:5). Hence, they argue, that it is not to be given to any but to those who are capable of such feelings. But we, on the other hand, may object that neither ought circumcision, which is designated regeneration, to be conferred on any but the regenerate. In this way, we shall condemn a divine institution. Thus, as we have already hinted, all the arguments, which tend to shake circumcision, are of no force in assailing baptism. Nor can they escape by saying, that everything which rests on the authority of God is absolutely fixed, though there should be no reason for it, but that this reverence is not due to Paedobaptism, nor other similar things which are not recommended to us by the express Word of God. They always remain caught in this dilemma. The command of God to circumcise infants was either legitimate and exempt from cavil, or deserved reprehension. If there was nothing incompetent or absurd in it, no absurdity can be shown in the observance of Paedobaptism.

21 **Answer continued.**

The charge of absurdity with which they attempt to stigmatize it, we thus dispose of. If those on whom the Lord has bestowed His election, after receiving the sign of regeneration, depart this life before they become adults, He, by the incomprehensible energy of His Spirit, renews them in the way, which He alone sees to be expedient. Should they reach an age when they can be instructed in the meaning of baptism, they will thereby be animated to greater zeal for renovation, the badge of which they will learn that they received in earliest infancy, in order that they might aspire to it during their whole lives. To the same effect are the two passages in which Paul teaches that we are buried with Christ by baptism. (See Romans 6:4; Colossians 2:12.) For by this he means not that he who is to be initiated by baptism must have previously been buried with Christ; he simply declares the doctrine which is taught by baptism, and that to those already baptized: so that the most senseless cannot maintain from this passage that it ought to precede baptism. In this way, Moses and the prophets reminded the people of the thing meant by circumcision, which however infants received. To the same effect, Paul says to the Galatians, "As many of you as have been baptized into Christ have put on Christ" (Galatians 3:27). Why so? That they might thereafter live to Christ, to whom previously they had not lived. And though, in adults, the receiving of the sign ought to follow the understanding of its meaning, yet, as will shortly be explained, a different rule must be followed with children. No other conclusion can be drawn from a passage in Peter, on which they strongly found. He says, that baptism is "not the putting away of the filth of the flesh, but the answer of a good conscience toward God by the resurrection of Jesus Christ" (1 Peter 3:21). From this they contend that nothing is left for Paedobaptism, which becomes mere empty smoke, as being altogether at variance with the meaning of baptism.

But the delusion, which misleads them, is that they would always have the thing to precede the sign in the order of time. For the truth of circumcision consisted in the same answer of a good conscience; but if the truth must necessarily have preceded, infants would never have been circumcised by the command of God. But he himself, showing that the answer of a good conscience forms the truth of circumcision, and, at the same time, commanding infants to be circumcised, plainly intimates that, in their case, circumcision had reference to the future. Wherefore, nothing more of present effect is to be required in Paedobaptism, than to confirm and sanction the covenant, which the Lord has made with them. The other part of the meaning of the sacrament will follow at the time which God himself has provided.

22 Argument, that baptism being appointed for the remission of sins, infants, not having sinned, ought not to be baptized. Answer.

Everyone must, I think, clearly perceive that all arguments of this stamp are mere perversions of Scripture. The other remaining arguments akin to these we shall cursorily examine. They object that baptism is given for the remission of sins. When this is conceded, it strongly supports our view; for, seeing we are born sinners, we stand in need of forgiveness and pardon from the very womb. Moreover, since God does not preclude this age from the hope of mercy, but rather gives assurance of it, why should we deprive it of the sign, which is much inferior to the reality? The arrow, therefore, which they aim at us, we throw back upon themselves. Infants receive forgiveness of sins; therefore, they are not to be deprived of the sign. They adduce the passage from the Ephesians, that Christ gave himself for the Church, "that he might sanctify and cleanse it with the washing of water by the word" (Ephesians 5:26). Nothing could be quoted more appropriate than this to overthrow their error: it furnishes us with an easy proof. If, by baptism, Christ intends to attest the ablution by which He cleanses His Church, it would seem not equitable to deny this attestation to infants, who are justly deemed part of the Church, seeing they are called heirs of the Heavenly kingdom. For Paul comprehends the whole Church when he says that it was cleansed by the washing of water. In like manner, from his expression in another place, that by baptism we are engrafted into the body of Christ (see 1 Corinthians 7:13), we infer, that infants, whom He enumerates among His members, are to be baptized, in order that they may not be dissevered from His body. See the violent onset, which they make with all their engines on the bulwarks of our faith.

23 Argument against Paedobaptism, founded on the practice of the apostles. Answer.

They now come down to the custom and practice of the apostolic age, alleging that there is no instance of anyone having been admitted to baptism without a previous profession of faith and repentance. For when Peter is asked by his hearers, who were pricked in their heart, "What shall we do?" his advice is, "Repent and be baptized, every one of you, in the name of Jesus Christ, for the remission of sins" (Acts 2:37, 38). In like manner, when Philip was asked by the eunuch to baptize him, he answered, "If thou believest with all thine heart, thou mayest." Hence, they think they can make out that baptism cannot be lawfully given to anyone without previous faith and repentance. If we yield to this argument, the former passage, in which there is no mention of faith, will prove that repentance alone is sufficient, and the latter, which makes no requirement of repentance, that there is need only of faith. They will object, I presume, that the one passage helps the other, and that both, therefore, are to be connected. I, in my turn, maintain that these two must be compared with other passages, which contribute somewhat to the solution of this difficulty. The meanings of many passages of Scripture depend on their peculiar positions. Of this, we have an example in the present instance. Those to whom these things are said by Peter and Philip are of an age fit to aim at repentance, and receive faith. We strenuously insist that such men are not to be baptized unless their conversion and faith are discerned, at least in as far as human judgment can ascertain it. But it is perfectly clear that infants must be placed in a different class. For when anyone formerly joined the religious communion of Israel, he behooved to be taught the covenant, and instructed in the law of the Lord, before he received circumcision, because he was of a different nation; in other words, an alien from the people of Israel, with whom the covenant, which circumcision sanctioned, had been made.

24 Answer continued.

Thus the Lord, when He chose Abraham for himself, did not commence with circumcision, in the meanwhile concealing what He meant by that sign, but first announced that He intended to make a covenant with him, and, after his faith in the promise, made him partaker of the sacrament. Why does the sacrament come after faith in Abraham, and precede all intelligence in his son Isaac? It is right that he, who, in adult age, is admitted to the fellowship of a covenant by one from whom he had hitherto been alienated, should previously learn its conditions; but it is not so with the infant born to him. He, according to the terms of the promise, is included in the promise by hereditary right from his mother's womb.

Or, to state the matter more briefly and more clearly, If the children of believers, without the help of understanding, are partakers of the covenant, there is no reason that they should be denied the sign, because they are unable to swear to its stipulations. This undoubtedly is the reason that the Lord sometimes declares that the children born to the Israelites are begotten and born to Him. (See Ezekiel 16:20; 23:37.) For He undoubtedly gives the place of sons to the children of those, to whose seed He has promised that He will be a Father. But the child descended from unbelieving parents is deemed an alien to the covenant until he is united to God by faith.

Hence, it is not strange that the sign is withheld when the thing signified would be vain and fallacious. In that view, Paul says that the Gentiles, so long as they were plunged in idolatry, were strangers to the covenant. (See Ephesians 2:11.) The whole matter may, if I mistake not, be thus briefly and clearly expounded: Those who, in adult age, embrace the faith of Christ, having hitherto been aliens from the covenant, are not to receive the sign of baptism without previous faith and repentance. These alone can give them access to the fellowship of the covenant, whereas children, deriving their origin from Christians, as they are immediately on their birth received by God as heirs of the covenant, are also to be admitted to baptism. To this we must refer the narrative of the Evangelist, that those who were baptized by John confessed their sins. (See Matthew 3:6.) This example, we hold, ought to be observed in the present day. Were a Turk to offer himself for baptism, we would not at once perform the rite without receiving a confession, which was satisfactory to the Church.

25 Argument founded on a saying of our Lord to Nicodemus. Answer.

Another passage which they adduce is from the third chapter of John, where our Savior's words seem to them to imply that a present regeneration is required in baptism, "Except a man be born of water, and of the Spirit, he cannot enter into the kingdom of God" (John 3:5). See, they say, how baptism is termed regeneration by the lips of our Lord himself, and on what pretext, therefore, with what consistency is baptism given to those who, it is perfectly obvious, are not at all capable of regeneration? First, they are in error in imagining that there is any mention of baptism in this passage, merely because the word water is used.

Nicodemus, after our Savior had explained to him the corruption of nature and the necessity of being born again, kept dreaming of a corporeal birth, and hence our Savior intimates the mode in which God regenerates us–viz. by water and the Spirit; in other words, by the Spirit, who, in irrigating and cleansing the souls of believers, operates in the manner of water. By "water and the Spirit," therefore, I simply understand the Spirit, which is water. Nor is the expression new. It perfectly accords with that which is used in the third chapter of Matthew, "He that cometh after me is mightier than I." And, "He shall baptize you with the Holy Ghost, and with fire" (Matthew 3:11). Therefore, as to baptize with the Holy Spirit and fire is to confer the Holy Spirit, who, in regeneration, has the office and nature of fire, so to be born again of water and of the Spirit is nothing else than to receive that power of the Spirit, which has the same effect on the soul that water has on the body.

I know that a different interpretation is given, but I have no doubt that this is the genuine meaning, because our Savior's only purpose was to teach, that all who aspire to the Kingdom of Heaven must lay aside their own disposition. And yet were we disposed to imitate these men in their mode of caviling, we might easily, after conceding what they wish, reply to them, that baptism is prior to faith and repentance, since, in this passage, our Savior mentions it before the Spirit. This certainly must be understood of spiritual gifts, and if they follow baptism, I have gained all I contend for. But, caviling aside, the simple interpretation to be adopted is that which I have given—viz. that no man, until renewed by living water, that is, by the Spirit, can enter the Kingdom of God.

26 Error of those who adjudge all who die unbaptized to eternal destruction.

This, moreover, plainly explodes the fiction of those who consign all the unbaptized to eternal death. Let us suppose, then, that, as they insist, baptism is administered to adults only. What will they make of a youth who, after being imbued duly and properly with the rudiments of piety, while waiting for the day of baptism, is unexpectedly carried off by sudden death? The promise of our Lord is clear, "He that heareth my word, and believeth on him that sent me, hath everlasting life, and shall not come into condemnation, but is passed from death unto life" (John 5:24). We nowhere read of His having condemned him who was not yet baptized. I would not be understood as insinuating that baptism may be contemned with impunity. So far from excusing this contempt, I hold that it violates the covenant of the Lord. The passage only serves to show, that we must not deem baptism so necessary as to suppose that everyone who has lost the opportunity of obtaining it has forthwith perished. By assenting to their fiction, we should condemn all, without exception, whom any accident may have prevented from procuring baptism, how much soever they may have been endued with the faith by which Christ himself is possessed.

Moreover, as they hold, baptism is necessary to salvation. In denying it to infants, they consign them all to eternal death. Let them now consider what kind of agreement they have with the words of Christ, who says, "of such is the kingdom of heaven" (Matthew 19:14). And though we were to concede everything to them, in regard to the meaning of this passage, they will extract nothing from it, until they have previously overthrown the doctrine, which we have already established concerning the regeneration of infants.

27 Argument against Paedobaptism, founded on the precept and example of our Savior, in requiring instruction to precede baptism. Answer.

But they boast of having their strongest bulwark in the very institution of baptism, which they find in the last chapter of Matthew, where Christ, sending His disciples into the entire world, commands them to teach and then baptize. Then, in the last chapter of Mark, it is added, "He that believeth, and is baptized, shall be saved" (Mark 16:16). What more (they say) do we ask, since the Words of Christ distinctly declare, that teaching must precede baptism, and assign to baptism the place next to faith? Of this arrangement, our Lord himself gave an example, in choosing not to be baptized until His thirtieth year. In how many ways do they here entangle themselves, and betray their ignorance! They err more than childishly in this, that they derive the first institution of baptism from this passage, whereas Christ, from the commencement of His ministry, had ordered it to be administered by the apostles. There is no ground, therefore, for contending that the law and rule of baptism is to be sought from these two passages as containing the first institution. But to indulge them in their error, how nerveless is this mode of arguing? Were I disposed to evasion, I have not only a place of escape, but a wide field to expatiate in. For when they cling so desperately to the order of the words, insisting that because it is said, "Go, preach and baptize," and again, "Whosoever believes and is baptized," they must preach before baptizing, and believe before being baptized, why may not we in our turn object, that they must baptize before teaching the observance of those things which Christ commanded, because it is said, "Baptize, teaching whatsoever I have commanded you"? The same thing we observed in the other passage in which Christ speaks of the regeneration of water and of the Spirit. For if we interpret as they insist, then baptism must take precedence of spiritual regeneration, because it is first mentioned. Christ teaches that we are to be born again, not of the Spirit and of water, but of water and of the Spirit.

28 Answer continued.

This unassailable argument, in which they confide so much, seems already to be considerably shaken; but as we have sufficient protection in the simplicity of truth, I am unwilling to evade the point by paltry subtleties. Let them, therefore, have a solid answer. The command here given by Christ relates principally to the preaching of the gospel: to it, baptism is added as a kind of appendage. Then He merely speaks of baptism as far as the dispensation of it is subordinate to the function of teaching. For Christ sends His disciples to publish the gospel to all nations of the world, that by the doctrine of salvation they may gather men, who were previously lost, into His kingdom.

But who or what are those men? It is certain that mention is made only of those who are fit to receive His doctrine. He subjoins, that such, after being taught, were to be baptized, adding the promise, whosoever believeth and is baptized, shall be saved. Is there one syllable about infants in the whole discourse? What, then, is the form of argument with which they assail us? Those who are of adult age are to be instructed and brought to the faith before being baptized, and therefore it is unlawful to make baptism common to infants. They cannot, at the very utmost, prove any other thing out of this passage, than that the gospel must be preached to those who are capable of hearing it before they are baptized; for of such only the passage speaks. From this let them, if they can, throw an obstacle in the way of baptizing infants.

29 Answer continued.

But I will make their fallacies palpable even to the blind, by a very plain similitude. Should anyone insist that infants are to be deprived of food, on the presence that the apostle permits none to eat but those who labor (2 Thessalonians 3:10), would he not deserve to be scouted by all? Why so? Because that which was said of a certain class of men, and a certain age, he wrests and applies to all indifferently. The dexterity of these men in the present instance is not greater. That which everyone sees to be intended for adult age merely, they apply to infants, subjecting them to a rule, which was laid down only for those of riper years. With regard to the example of our Savior, it gives no countenance to their case. He was not baptized before his thirtieth year. This is indeed true, but the reason is obvious; that He then determined to lay the solid foundation of baptism by His preaching, or rather to confirm the foundation, which John had previously laid. Therefore, when He was pleased with His doctrine to institute baptism, that He might give the greater authority to His institution, He sanctified it in His own person, and that at the most befitting time, namely, the commencement of His ministry. In fine, they can prove nothing more than that baptism received its origin and commencement with the preaching of the gospel. But if they are pleased to fix upon the thirtieth year, why do they not observe it, but admit anyone to baptism according to the view, which they may have formed of His proficiency? Nay, even Servetus, one of their masters, although he resolutely insisted on this period, had begun to act the prophet in his twenty-first year; as if any man could be tolerated in arrogating to himself the office of a teacher in the Church before he was a member of the Church.

30 Argument, that there is no stronger reason for giving baptism to children than for giving them the Lord's Supper. Answer.

At length they object, that there is not greater reason for admitting infants to baptism than to the Lord's Supper, to which, however, they are never admitted: as if Scripture did not in every way draw a wide distinction between them. In the early Church indeed, the Lord's Supper was frequently given to infants, as appears from Cyprian and Augustine, but the practice justly became obsolete. For if we attend to the peculiar nature of baptism, it is a kind of entrance and initiation into the Church, by which we are ranked among the people of God, a sign of our spiritual regeneration, by which we are again born to be children of God.

On the contrary, the Supper is intended for those of riper years, who, having passed the tender period of infancy, are fit to bear solid food. This distinction is very clearly pointed out in Scripture. For there, as far as regards baptism, the Lord makes no selection of age, whereas He does not admit all to partake of the Supper, but confines it to those who are fit to discern the body and blood of the Lord, to examine their own conscience, to show forth the Lord's death, and understand its power. Can we wish anything clearer than what the apostle says, when he thus exhorts, "Let a man examine himself, and so let him eat of that bread, and drink of that cup" (1 Corinthians 11:28)?

Examination, therefore, must precede, and this it would be vain to expect from infants. Again, "He that eateth and drinketh unworthily, eateth and drinketh damnation to himself, not discerning the Lord's body." If they cannot partake worthily without being able duly to discern the sanctity of the Lord's body, why should we stretch out poison to our young children instead of vivifying food? Then what is our Lord's injunction? "Do this in remembrance of me." And what inference does the apostle draw from this? "As often as ye eat this bread, and drink this cup, ye do show the Lord's death until he come."

How, pray, can we require infants to commemorate any event of which they have no understanding; how require them "to show forth the Lord's death," of the nature and benefit of which they have no idea? Nothing of the kind is prescribed by baptism. Wherefore, there is the greatest difference between the two signs. This also we observe in similar signs under the old dispensation. Circumcision, which, as is well known, corresponds to our baptism, was intended for infants, but the Passover, for which the Supper is substituted, did not admit all kinds of guests promiscuously, but was duly eaten only by those who were of an age sufficient to ask the meaning of it. (See Exodus 12:26.) Had these men the least particle of soundness in their brain, would they be thus blind as to a matter so very clear and obvious?

31 Last part of the chapter, refuting the arguments of Servetus.

Though I am unwilling to annoy the reader with the series of conceits, which Servetus, not the least among the Anabaptists, nay, the great honor of this crew, when girding himself for battle, deemed, when he adduced them, to be specious arguments, it will be worth while briefly to dispose of them. He pretends that as the symbols of Christ are perfect, they require persons who are perfect, or at least capable of perfection. But the answer is plain. The perfection of baptism, which extends even to death, is improperly restricted to one moment of time; moreover, perfection, in which baptism invites us to make continual progress during life, is foolishly exacted by him all at once. He objects, that the symbols of Christ were appointed for remembrance, that everyone may remember that he was buried together with Christ. I answer, that what he coined out of his own brain does not need refutation, nay, that which he transfers to baptism properly belongs to the Supper, as appears from Paul's words, "Let a man examine himself," words similar to which are nowhere used with reference to baptism. Whence we infer, that those who from nonage are incapable of examination are duly baptized. His third point is that all who believe not in the Son remain in death, the wrath of God abideth on them (John 3:36); and, therefore, infants who are unable to believe lie under condemnation. I answer, that Christ does not there speak of the general guilt in which all the posterity of Adam are involved, but only threatens the despisers of the gospel, who proudly and contumaciously spurn the grace which is offered to them. But this has nothing to do with infants.

At the same time, I meet him with the opposite argument. Everyone whom Christ blesses is exempted from the curse of Adam, and the wrath of God. Therefore, seeing it is certain that infants are blessed by Him, it follows that they are freed from death. He next falsely quotes a passage, which is nowhere found: "Whosoever is born of the Spirit, hears the voice of the Spirit." Though we should grant that such a passage occurs in Scripture, all he can extract from it is that believers, according as the Spirit works in them, are framed to obedience. But that which is said of a certain number, it is illogical to apply to all alike. His fourth objection is, as that which precedes is animal (see 1 Corinthians 15:46), we must wait the full time for baptism, which is spiritual.

But while I admit that all the posterity of Adam, born of the flesh, bear their condemnation with them from the womb, I hold that this is no obstacle to the immediate application of the divine remedy. Servetus cannot show that by divine appointment, several years must elapse before the new spiritual life begins. Paul's testimony is that though lost by nature, the children of believers are holy by supernatural grace. He afterwards brings forward the allegory that David, when going up into Mount Zion, took with him neither the blind nor the lame, but vigorous soldiers. (See 2 Samuel 5:8.) But what if I meet this with the parable in which God invites to the heavenly feast the lame and the blind? In what way will Servetus disentangle this knot?

I ask, moreover, whether the lame and the maimed had not previously served with David? But it is superfluous to dwell longer on this argument, which, as the reader will learn from the sacred history, is founded on mere misquotation. He adds another allegory–viz. that the apostles were fishers of men, not of children.

I ask, then, What does our Savior mean when He says that in the net are caught all kinds of fishes? (See Matthew 9:19; 13:47.) But as I have no pleasure in sporting with allegory, I answer, that when the office of teaching was committed to the apostles, they were not prohibited from baptizing infants. Moreover, I should like to know why, when the Evangelist uses a Greek term, which comprehends the whole human race without exception, he denies that infants are included.

His seventh argument is that since spiritual things accord with spiritual (see 1 Corinthians 2:13), infants, not being spiritual, are unfit for baptism. It is plain how perversely he wrests this passage of Paul. It relates to doctrine. The Corinthians, pluming themselves excessively on a vain acuteness, Paul rebukes their folly, because they still require to be imbued with the first rudiments of heavenly doctrine. Who can infer from this that baptism is to be denied to infants, whom, when begotten of the flesh, the Lord consecrates to himself by gratuitous adoption? His objection, that if they are new men, they must be fed with spiritual food, is easily obviated. By baptism, they are admitted into the fold of Christ, and the symbol of adoption is sufficient for them, until they grow up and become fit to bear solid food. Therefore, we must wait for the time of examination, which God distinctly demands in the sacred Supper.

His next objection is that Christ invites all His people to the sacred Supper. But as it is plain that He admits those only who are prepared to celebrate the commemoration of His death, it follows that infants, whom He honored with His embrace, remain in a distinct and peculiar position until they grow up, and yet are not aliens. When he objects, that it is strange why the infant does not partake of the Supper, I answer, that souls are fed by other food than the external eating of the Supper, and that accordingly Christ is the food of infants, though they partake not of the symbol. The case is different with baptism, by which the door of the Church is thrown open to them.

He again objects that a good householder distributes meat to his household in due season. (See Matthew 24:45.) This I willingly admit; but how will he define the time of baptism, to prove that it is not seasonably given to infants? He, moreover, adduces Christ's command to the apostles to make haste, because the fields are already white to the harvest (John 4:35). Our Savior only means that the apostles, seeing the present fruit of their labor, should bestir themselves with more alacrity to teach. Who will infer from this, that harvest only is the fit time for baptism?

His eleventh argument is that in the primitive Church, Christians and disciples were the same, but we have already seen that he argues unskillfully from the part to the whole. The name of disciple is given to men of full age, who had already been taught and assumed the name of Christ, just as the Jews behooved to be disciples under the Law of Moses. Still none could rightly infer from this that infants, whom the Lord declared to be of His household, were strangers. Moreover, he alleges that all Christians are brethren, and that infants cannot belong to this class, so long as we exclude them from the Supper.

But I return to my position. First, not any are heirs of the Kingdom of Heaven except those who are the members of Christ; and, secondly, the embracing of Christ was the true badge of adoption, in which infants are joined in common with adults, and that temporary abstinence from the Supper does not prevent them from belonging to the body of the Church. The thief on the cross, when converted, became the brother of believers, though he never partook of the Lord's Supper.

Servetus afterwards adds, that no man becomes our brother unless by the Spirit of adoption, who is only conferred by the hearing of faith. I answer, that he always falls back into the same paralogism, because he preposterously applies to infants what is said only of adults. Paul there teaches that the ordinary way in which God calls His elect, and brings them to the faith, is by raising up faithful teachers, and thus stretching out His hand to them by their ministry and labors. Who will presume from this to give the law to God, and say that He may not engraft infants into Christ by some other secret method?

He objects, that Cornelius was baptized after receiving the Holy Spirit; but how absurdly he would convert a single example into a general rule, is apparent from the case of the Eunuch and the Samaritans, in regard to whom the Lord observed a different order, baptism preceding the gifts of the Holy Spirit. The fifteenth argument is more than absurd. He says that we become gods by regeneration, but that they are gods to whom the Word of God is sent (see John 10:35; 2 Peter 1:4), a thing not possible to infant children. The attributing of deity to believers is one of his ravings, which this is not the proper place to discuss; but it betrays the utmost effrontery to wrest the passage in the psalm (Psalm 82:6) to a meaning so alien to it. Christ says that kings and magistrates are called gods by the prophet, because they perform an office divinely appointed them. This dexterous interpreter transfers what is addressed by special command to certain individuals to the doctrine of the gospel, to exterminate infants from the Church. Again, he objects, that infants cannot be regarded as new men, because they are not begotten by the Word.

But what I have said again and again I now repeat, that, for regenerating us, doctrine is an incorruptible seed, if indeed we are fit to perceive it; but when, from nonage, we are incapable of being taught, God takes His own methods of regenerating.

He afterwards returns to his allegories, and says, that under the law, the sheep and the goat were not offered in sacrifice the moment they were dropt. (See Exodus 12:5.) Were I disposed to deal in figures, I might obviously reply, first, that all the first-born, on opening the matrix, were sacred to the Lord (see Exodus 13:12); and, secondly, that a lamb of a year old was to be sacrificed: whence it follows, that it was not necessary to wait for mature age, the young and tender offspring having been selected by God for sacrifice. He contends, moreover, that none could come to Christ but those who were previously prepared by John, as if John's ministry had not been temporary. But, to omit this, assuredly there was no such preparation in the children whom Christ took up in His arms and blessed. Wherefore, let us have done with his false principle. He at length calls in the assistance of Trismegistus and the Sybils, to prove that sacred ablutions are fit only for adults. See how honorably he thinks of Christian baptism, when he tests it by the profane rites of the Gentiles, and will not have it administered except in the way pleasing to Trismegistus.

We defer more to the authority of God, who has seen it meet to consecrate infants to himself, and initiate them by a sacred symbol, the significance of which they are unable from nonage to understand. We do not think it lawful to borrow from the expiations of the Gentiles, in order to change, in our baptism, that eternal and inviolable law which God enacted in circumcision.

His last argument is that if infants, without understanding, may be baptized, baptism may be mimicked and jestingly administered by boys in sport. Here let him plead the matter with God, by whose command circumcision was common to infants before they received understanding. Was it, then, a fit matter for ridicule or boyish sport, to overthrow the sacred institution of God? But no wonder these reprobate spirits, as if they were under the influence of frenzy, introduce the grossest absurdities in defense of their errors, because God, by this spirit of giddiness, justly avenges their pride and obstinacy. I trust I have made it apparent how feebly Servetus has supported his friends the Anabaptists.

32 Why Satan so violently assails Paedobaptism.

No sound man, I presume, can now doubt how rashly the Church is disturbed by those who excite quarrels and disturbances because of Paedobaptism. For it is of importance to observe what Satan means by all this craft—viz. to rob us of the singular blessing of confidence and spiritual joy, which is hence to be derived, and in so far to detract from the glory of the divine goodness. For how sweet is it to pious minds to be assured not only by word, but even by ocular demonstration, that they are so much in favor with their heavenly Father, that He interests himself in their prosperity! Here we may see how He acts towards us as a most provident parent, not ceasing to care for us even after our death, but consulting and providing for our children. Ought not our whole heart to be stirred up within us, as David's was (see Psalm 48:11), to bless His name for such a manifestation of goodness? Doubtless the design of Satan in assaulting Paedobaptism with all his forces is to keep out of view, and gradually efface, that attestation of divine grace which the promise itself presents to our eyes. In this way, not only would men be impiously ungrateful for the mercy of God, but be less careful in training their children to piety. For it is no slight stimulus to us to bring them up in the fear of God, and the observance of His law, when we reflect, that from their birth they have been considered and acknowledged by Him as His children. Wherefore, if we would not maliciously obscure the kindness of God, let us present to Him our infants, to whom He has assigned a place among His friends and family, that is, the members of the Church.

Chapter 17

OF THE LORD'S SUPPER, AND THE BENEFITS CONFERRED BY IT.

This chapter is divided into two principal heads.–I. The first part shows what it is that God exhibits in the Holy Supper, sections 1-4; and then in what way and how far it becomes ours, sections 5-11. II. The second part is chiefly occupied with a refutation of the errors which superstition has introduced in regard to the Lord's Supper. And, first, Transubstantiation is refuted, sections 12-15. Next, Consubstantiation and Ubiquity, sections 16-19. Thirdly, It is shown that the institution itself is opposed to those hyperbolical doctors, sections 20-25. Fourth, The orthodox view is confirmed by other arguments derived from Scripture, sections 26-27. Fifth, The authority of the Fathers is shown to support the same view. Sixth, The presence for which opponents contend is overthrown, and another presence established, sections 29-32. Seventh, What the nature of our communion ought to be, sections 33, 34. Eighth, The adoration introduced by opponents refuted. For what end the Lord's Supper was instituted, sections 35-39. Lastly, The examination of communicants is considered, sections 40-42. Of the external rites to be observed. Of frequent communion in both kinds. Objections refuted, sections 43-50.

Sections

1. Why the Holy Supper was instituted by Christ. The knowledge of the sacrament, how necessary. The signs used. Why there are no others appointed.

2. The manifold uses and advantages of this sacrament to the pious.

3. The Lord's Supper exhibits the great blessings of redemption, and even Christ himself. This even evident from the words of the institution. The thing specially to be considered in them. Congruity of the signs and the things signified.

4. The chief parts of this sacrament.

5. How Christ, the Bread of Life, is to be received by us. Two faults to be avoided. The receiving of it must bear reference both to faith and the effect of faith. What is meant by eating Christ. In what sense Christ is the bread of life.

6. This mode of eating confirmed by the authority of Augustine and Chrysostom.

7. It is not sufficient, while omitting all mention of flesh and blood, to recognize this communion merely as spiritual. It is impossible fully to comprehend it in the present life.

8. In explanation of it, it may be observed: A. There is no life at all save in Christ. B. Christ has life in a twofold sense; first, in himself, as He is God; and, secondly, by transfusing it into the flesh which He assumed, that He might thereby communicate life to us.

9. This confirmed from Cyril, and by a familiar example. How the flesh of Christ gives life, and what is the nature of our communion with Christ.

10. No distance of place can impede it. In the Supper, it is not presented as an empty symbol, but, as the apostle testifies, we receive the reality. Objection, that the expression is figurative. Answer. A sure rule with regard to the sacraments.

11. Conclusion of the first part of the chapter. The sacrament of the Supper consists of two parts—viz. corporeal signs, and spiritual truth. These comprehend the meaning, matter, and effect. Christ truly exhibited to us by symbols.

12. Second part of the chapter, reduced to nine heads. The transubstantiation of the Papists considered and refuted. Its origin and absurdity. Why it should be exploded.

13. Transubstantiation as feigned by the Schoolmen. Refutation. The many superstitions introduced by their error.

14. The fiction of transubstantiation why it was invented contrary to Scripture, and the consent of antiquity. The term of transubstantiation never used in the early Church. Objection. Answer.

15. The error of transubstantiation favored by the consecration, which was a kind of magical incantation. The bread is not a sacrament to itself, but to those who receive it. The changing of the rod of Moses into a serpent gives no countenance to Popish transubstantiation. No resemblance between it and the words of institution in the Supper. Objection. Answer.

16. Refutation of consubstantiation, whence the idea of ubiquity.

17. This ubiquity confounds the natures of Christ. Subtleties answered.

18. Absurdities connected with consubstantiation. Candid exposition of the orthodox view.

19. The nature of the true presence of Christ in the Supper. The true and substantial communion of the body and blood of the Lord. This orthodox view assailed by turbulent spirits.

20. This view vindicated from their calumnies. The words of the institution explained in opposition to the glosses of transubstantiators and consubstantiators. Their subterfuges and absurd blasphemies.

21. Why the name of the thing signified is given to the sacramental symbols. This illustrated by passages of Scripture; also by a passage of Augustine.

22. Refutation of an objection founded on the words, This is. Objection answered.

23. Other objections answered.

24. Other objections answered. No question here as to the omnipotence of God.

25. Other objections answered.

26. The orthodox view further confirmed. A. By a consideration of the reality of Christ's body. B. From our Savior's declaration that He would always be in the world. This confirmed by the exposition of Augustine.

27. Refutation of the sophisms of the Ubiquitists. The evasion of visible and invisible presence refuted.

28. The authority of Fathers not in favor of these errors as to Christ's presence. Augustine opposed to them.

29. Refutation of the invisible presence maintained by opponents. Refutation from Tertullian, from a saying of Christ after His resurrection, from the definition of a true body, and from different passages of Scripture.

30. Ubiquity refuted by various arguments.

31. The imaginary presence of Transubstantiators, Consubstantiators, and Ubiquitists, contrasted with the orthodox doctrine.

32. The nature of our Savior's true presence explained. The mode of it incomprehensible.

33. Our communion in the blood and flesh of Christ. Spiritual not oral, and yet real. Erroneous view of the Schoolmen.

34. This view not favored by Augustine. How the wicked eat the body of Christ. Cyril's sentiments as to the eating of the body of Christ.

35. Absurdity of the adoration of sacramental symbols.

36. This adoration condemned. A. By Christ himself. B. By the Council of Nice. C. By ancient custom. D. By Scripture. This adoration is mere idolatry.

37. This adoration inconsistent with the nature and institution of the sacrament. Ends for which the sacrament was instituted.

38. Ends for which the sacrament was instituted.

39. True nature of the sacrament, contrasted with the Popish observance of it.

40. Nature of an unworthy approach to the Lord's Table. The great danger of it. The proper remedy in serious self-examination.

41. The spurious examination introduced by the Papists. Refutation.

42. The nature of Christian examination.

43. External rites in the administration of the Supper. Many of them indifferent.

44. Duty of frequent communion. This proved by the practice of the Church in its purer state, and by the canons of the early bishops.

45. Frequent communion in the time of Augustine. The neglect of it censured by Chrysostom.

46. The Popish injunction to communicate once a year an execrable invention.

47. Communion in one kind proved to be an invention of Satan.

48. Subterfuges of the Papists refuted.

49. The practice of the early Church further considered.

50. Conclusion.

1 Why the Holy Supper was instituted by Christ. The knowledge of the sacrament, how necessary. The signs used. Why there are no others appointed.

After God has once received us into His family, it is not that He may regard us in the light of servants, but of sons, performing the part of a kind and anxious parent, and providing for our maintenance during the whole course of our lives. And, not contented with this, He has been pleased by a pledge to assure us of His continued liberality. To this end, He has given another sacrament to His Church by the hand of his only begotten Son–viz. a spiritual feast, at which Christ testifies that He himself is living bread (John 6:51), on which our souls feed for a true and blessed immortality. Now, as the knowledge of this great mystery is most necessary, and, in proportion to its importance, demands an accurate exposition, and Satan, in order to deprive the Church of this inestimable treasure, long ago introduced first mists and then darkness to obscure its light, and stirred up strife and contention to alienate the minds of the simple from a relish for this sacred food, and in our age, also, has tried the same artifice, I will proceed, after giving a simple summary adapted to the capacity of the ignorant, to explain those difficulties by which Satan has tried to ensnare the world. First, then, the signs are bread and wine, which represent the invisible food, which we receive from the body and blood of Christ. For as God, regenerating us in baptism, engrafts us into the fellowship of His Church, and makes us His by adoption, so we have said that He performs the office of a provident parent, in continually supplying the food by which He may sustain and preserve us in the life to which He has begotten us by His word. Moreover, Christ is the only food of our soul, and, therefore, our heavenly Father invites us to Him, that, refreshed by communion with Him, we may always gather new vigour until we reach the heavenly immortality.

But as this mystery of the secret union of Christ with believers is incomprehensible by nature, He exhibits its figure and image in visible signs adapted to our capacity, nay, by giving earnests and badges, He makes it as certain to us as if it were seen by the eye; the familiarity of the similitude giving it access to minds however dull, and showing that souls are fed by Christ just as the corporeal life is sustained by bread and wine. We now, therefore, understand the end which this mystical benediction has in view–viz. to assure us that the body of Christ was once sacrificed for us, so that we may now eat it, and, eating, feel within ourselves the efficacy of that one sacrifice, –that His blood was once shed for us so as to be our perpetual drink. This is the force of the promise which is added, "Take, eat; this is my body, which is broken for you" (Matthew 26:26, etc.). The body which was once offered for our salvation we are enjoined to take and eat, that, while we see ourselves made partakers of it, we may safely conclude that the virtue of that death will be efficacious in us. Hence, He terms the cup the covenant in His blood. For the covenant which He once sanctioned by His blood He in a manner renews, or rather continues, in so far as regards the confirmation of our faith, as often as He stretches forth His sacred blood as drink to us.

2 The manifold uses and advantages of this sacrament to the pious.

Pious souls can derive great confidence and delight from this sacrament, as being a testimony that they form one body with Christ, so that everything, which is His, they may call their own. Hence, it follows, that we can confidently assure ourselves that eternal life, of which He himself is the heir, is ours, and that the Kingdom of Heaven, into which He has entered, can no more be taken from us than from Him. On the other hand, we cannot be condemned for our sins, from the guilt of which He absolves us, because He has been pleased that these should be imputed to himself as if they were His own. This is the wondrous exchange made by His boundless goodness. Having become with us the Son of Man, He has made us with himself sons of God. By His own descent to the Earth, He has prepared our ascent to Heaven. Having received our mortality, He has bestowed on us His immortality. Having undertaken our weakness, He has made us strong in His strength. Having submitted to our poverty, He has transferred to us His riches. Having taken upon himself the burden of unrighteousness with which we were oppressed, He has clothed us with his righteousness.

3 The Lord's Supper exhibits the great blessings of redemption, and even Christ himself. This even evident from the words of the institution. The thing specially to be considered in them. Congruity of the signs and the things signified.

To all these things, we have a complete attestation in this sacrament, enabling us certainly to conclude that they are as truly exhibited to us as if Christ were placed in bodily presence before our view, or handled by our hands. For these are words, which can never lie nor deceive–"Take, eat, drink. This is my body, which is broken for you: this is my blood, which is shed for the remission of sins." In bidding us take, He intimates that it is ours. In bidding us eat, He intimates that it becomes one substance with us, affirming that His body was broken and His blood was shed for us, He shows that both were not so much His own as ours. He took and laid down both, not for His own advantage, but for our salvation. And we ought carefully to observe, that the chief, and almost the whole energy of the sacrament, consists in these words, "It is broken for you; it is shed for you." It would not be of much importance to us that the body and blood of the Lord are now distributed, had they not once been set forth for our redemption and salvation. Wherefore they are represented under bread and wine, that we may learn that they are not only ours, but intended to nourish our spiritual life; that is, as we formerly observed, by the corporeal things which are produced in the sacrament, we are by a kind of analogy conducted to spiritual things. Thus, when bread is given as a symbol of the body of Christ, we must immediately think of this similitude. As bread nourishes, sustains, and protects our bodily life, so the body of Christ is the only food to invigorate and keep alive the soul. When we behold wine set forth as a symbol of blood, we must think that such use as wine serves to the body, the same is spiritually bestowed by the blood of Christ; and the use is to foster, refresh, strengthen, and exhilarate. For if we duly consider what profit we have gained by the breaking of His sacred body, and the shedding of His blood, we shall clearly perceive that these properties of bread and wine, agreeably to this analogy, most appropriately represent it when they are communicated to us.

4 The chief parts of this sacrament.

Therefore, it is not the principal part of a sacrament simply to hold forth the body of Christ to us without any higher consideration, but rather to seal and confirm that promise by which He testifies that His flesh is meat indeed, and His blood drink indeed, nourishing us unto life eternal. By these, He affirms that He is the bread of life, of which, whosoever shall eat, shall live forever–I say, to seal and confirm that promise, and in order to do so, it sends us to the Cross of Christ, where that promise was performed and fulfilled in all its parts. For we do not eat Christ duly and savingly unless as crucified, while with lively apprehension we perceive the efficacy of His death. When He called himself the bread of life, He did not take that appellation from the sacrament, as some perversely interpret. But such as He was given to us by the Father, such He exhibited himself when becoming partaker of our human mortality, He made us partakers of his divine immortality. When offering himself in sacrifice, he took our curse upon himself, that he might cover us with his blessing, when by His death He devoured and swallowed up death, when in His resurrection He raised our corruptible flesh, which He had put on, to glory and incorruption.

5 How Christ, the Bread of Life, is to be received by us. Two faults to be avoided. The receiving of it must bear reference both to faith and the effect of faith. What is meant by eating Christ. In what sense Christ is the bread of life.

It only remains that the whole become ours by application. This is done by means of the gospel, and more clearly by the sacred Supper, where Christ offers himself to us with all His blessings, and we receive Him in faith. The sacrament, therefore, does not make Christ become for the first time the bread of life; but, while it calls to remembrance that Christ was made the bread of life that we may constantly eat Him, it gives us a taste and relish for that bread, and makes us feel its efficacy. For it assures us, first, that whatever Christ did or suffered was done to give us life; and, secondly, that this quickening is eternal; by it we are ceaselessly nourished, sustained, and preserved in life. For as Christ would not have not been the bread of life to us if He had not been born, if He had not died and risen again; so He could not now be the bread of life, were not the efficacy and fruit of His nativity, death, and resurrection, eternal. All this Christ has elegantly expressed in these words, "The bread that I will give is my flesh, which I will give for the life of the world" (John 6:51). Doubtlessly, He intimates that His body will be as bread in regard to the spiritual life of the soul, because it was to be delivered to death for our salvation, and that He extends it to us for food when He makes us partakers of it by faith. Wherefore He once gave himself, that He might become bread, when He gave himself to be crucified for the redemption of the world; and He gives himself daily, when in the word of the gospel, He offers himself to be partaken by us, inasmuch as He was crucified, when He seals that offer by the sacred mystery of the Supper, and when He accomplishes inwardly what He externally designates. Moreover, two faults are here to be avoided. We must neither, by setting too little value on the signs, dissever them from their meanings to which they are in some degree annexed, nor by immoderately extolling them, seem somewhat to obscure the mysteries themselves. That Christ is the bread of life by which believers are nourished unto eternal life, no man is so utterly devoid of religion as not to acknowledge. But not all are agreed as to the mode of partaking of Him. For there are some who define the eating of the flesh of Christ, and the drinking of His blood, to be, in one word, nothing more than believing in Christ himself. But Christ seems to me to have intended to teach something more express and more sublime in that noble discourse, in which He recommends the eating of his flesh–viz. that we are quickened by the true partaking of Him, which He designated by the terms eating and drinking, lest anyone should suppose that the life which we obtain from Him is obtained by simple knowledge. For as it is not the sight but the eating of bread that gives nourishment to the body, so the soul must partake of Christ truly and thoroughly, that by His energy it may grow up into spiritual life.

Meanwhile, we admit that this is nothing else than the eating of faith, and that no other eating can be imagined. But there is this difference between their mode of speaking and mine. According to them, to eat is merely to believe. On the other hand, I maintain that the flesh of Christ is eaten by believing, because it is made ours by faith, and that that eating is the effect and fruit of faith; or, if you will have it more clearly, according to them, eating is faith, whereas it rather seems to me to be a consequence of faith. The difference is little in words, but not little in reality. For, although the apostle teaches that Christ dwells in our hearts by faith (Ephesians 3:17), no one will interpret that dwelling to be faith. All see that it explains the admirable effect of faith, because believers have Christ dwelling in them. In this way, the Lord was pleased: by calling himself the bread of life, not only to teach that our salvation is treasured up in the faith of His death and resurrection, but also, by virtue of true communication with Him, His life passes into us and becomes ours, just as bread when taken for food gives vigour to the body.

6 This mode of eating confirmed by the authority of Augustine and Chrysostom.

When Augustine, whom they claim as their patron, wrote, that we eat by believing, all he meant was to indicate that that eating is of faith, and not of the mouth. This I deny not; but I at the same time add, that by faith we embrace Christ, not as appearing at a distance, but as uniting himself to us, He being our head, and we His members. I do not absolutely disapprove of that mode of speaking; I only deny that it is a full interpretation, if they mean to define what it is to eat the flesh of Christ. I see that Augustine repeatedly used this form of expression, as when he said, " Unless ye eat the flesh of the Son of Man" is a figurative expression enjoining us to have communion with our Lord's passion, and sweetly and usefully to treasure in our memory that His flesh was crucified and wounded for us. Also, when he says, "These three thousand men who were converted at the preaching of Peter (Acts 2:41), by believing, drank the blood which they had cruelly shed." But in very many other passages, he admirably commends faith for this, that by means of it our souls are not less refreshed by the communion of the blood of Christ, than our bodies with the bread, which they eat. The very same thing is said by Chrysostom, "Christ makes us His body, not by faith only, but in reality." He does not mean that we obtain this blessing from any other quarter than from faith: he only intends to prevent anyone from thinking of mere imagination when he hears the name of faith. I say nothing of those who hold that the Supper is merely a mark of external profession, because I think I sufficiently refuted their error when I treated of the sacraments in general (Chapter 14, section 13). Only let my readers observe that when the cup is called the covenant in blood (Luke 22:20), the promise, which tends to confirm faith, is expressed. Hence, it follows, that unless we have respect to God, and embrace what He offers, we do not make a right use of the sacred Supper.

7 It is not sufficient, while omitting all mention of flesh and blood, to recognize this communion merely as spiritual. It is impossible fully to comprehend it in the present life.

I am not satisfied with the view of those who, while acknowledging that we have some kind of communion with Christ, only make us partakers of the Spirit, omitting all mention of flesh and blood. As if it were said to no purpose at all, that His flesh is meat indeed, and His blood is drink indeed; that we have no life unless we eat that flesh and drink that blood; and so forth. Therefore, if it is evident that full communion with Christ goes beyond their description, which is too confined, I will attempt briefly to show how far it extends, before proceeding to speak of the contrary vice of excess. For I shall have a longer discussion with these hyperbolical doctors, who, according to their gross ideas, fabricate an absurd mode of eating and drinking, and transfigure Christ, after divesting Him of His flesh, into a phantom: if, indeed, it be lawful to put this great mystery into words, a mystery which I feel, and therefore freely confess that I am unable to comprehend with my mind, so far am I from wishing anyone to measure its sublimity by my feeble capacity. Nay, I rather exhort my readers not to confine their apprehension within those too narrow limits, but to attempt to rise much higher than I can guide them. For whenever this subject is considered, after I have done my utmost, I feel that I have spoken far beneath its dignity. And though the mind is more powerful in thought than the tongue in expression, it too is overcome and overwhelmed by the magnitude of the subject. All then that remains is to break forth in admiration of the mystery, which plainly neither the mind can comprehend, nor the tongue express. I will, however, give a summary of my view as I best can, not doubting its truth, and therefore trusting that it will not be disapproved by pious breasts.

8 In explanation of it, it may be observed, —A. There is no life at all save in Christ. B. Christ has life in a twofold sense; first, in himself, as He is God; and, secondly, by transfusing it into the flesh which He assumed, that He might thereby communicate life to us.

First of all, we are taught by the Scriptures that Christ was from the beginning the living Word of the Father, the fountain and origin of life, from which all things should always receive life. Hence, John at one time calls Him the Word of Life and at another says, that in

Him was life, intimating that He, even then pervading all creatures, instilled into them the power of breathing and living. He afterwards adds, that the life was at length manifested, when the Son of God, assuming our nature, exhibited himself in bodily form to be seen and handled. For although He previously diffused His virtue into the creatures, yet as man, because alienated from God by sin, had lost the communication of life, and saw death on every side impending over Him, He behooved, in order to regain the hope of immortality, to be restored to the communion of that Word. How little confidence can it give you, to know that the Word of God, from which you are at the greatest distance, contains within himself the fullness of life, whereas in yourself, in whatever direction you turn, you see nothing but death? But ever since that fountain of life began to dwell in our nature, He no longer lies hidden at a distance from us, but exhibits himself openly for our participation. Nay, the very flesh in which He resides He makes vivifying to us, that by partaking of it we may feed for immortality. "I," says He, "am that bread of life;" "I am the living bread which came down from heaven;" "And the bread that I will give is my flesh, which I will give for the life of the world" (John 6:48, 51). By these words He declares, not only that He is life, inasmuch as He is the eternal Word of God who came down to us from Heaven, but, by coming down, gave vigour to the flesh which He assumed, that a communication of life to us might thence emanate. Hence, too, He adds, that His flesh is meat indeed, and that His blood is drink indeed: by this food, believers are reared to eternal life. The pious, therefore, have admirable comfort in this, that they now find life in their own flesh. For they not only reach it by easy access, but have it spontaneously set forth before them. Let them only throw open the door of their hearts that they may take it into their embrace, and they will obtain it.

9 This confirmed from Cyril, and by a familiar example. How the flesh of Christ gives life, and what the nature of our communion is with Christ.

The flesh of Christ, however, has not such power in itself as to make us live, because by its own first condition it was subject to mortality, and even now, when endued with immortality, lives not by itself. Still it is properly said to be life giving, as it is pervaded with the fullness of life for transmitting it to us. In this sense, I understand our Savior's words as Cyril interprets them, "As the Father hath life in himself, so hath he given to the Son to have life in himself" (John 5:26). For there properly He is speaking not of the properties, which He possessed with the Father from the beginning, but of those with which he was invested in the flesh in which He appeared. Accordingly, He shows that in His humanity also fullness of life resides, so that everyone who communicates in His flesh and blood, at the same time enjoys the participation of life. The nature of this may be explained by a familiar example. As water is at one time drunk out of the fountain, at another drawn, at another led away by conduits to irrigate the fields, and yet does not flow forth of itself for all these uses, but is taken from its source, which, with perennial flow, always sends forth a new and sufficient supply; so the flesh of Christ is like a rich and inexhaustible fountain, which transfuses into us the life flowing forth from the Godhead into itself. Now, who sees not that the communion of the flesh and blood of Christ is necessary to all who aspire to the heavenly life? Hence, those passages of the apostle: The Church is the "body" of Christ; His "fullness." He is "the head," "from whence the whole body fitly joined together, and compacted by that which every joint supplieth," "maketh increase of the body" (Ephesians 1:23; 4:15,16). Our bodies are the "members of Christ" (1 Corinthians 6:15). We perceive that not all these things can possibly take place unless He adheres to us wholly in body and spirit. But the very close connection, which unites us to His flesh, He illustrated with still more splendid epithets, when He said that we "are members of his body, of his flesh, and of his bones" (Ephesians 5:30). At length, to testify that the matter is too high for utterance, He concludes with exclaiming, "This is a great mystery" (Ephesians 5:32). It would be, therefore, extreme infatuation not to acknowledge the communion of believers with the body and blood of the Lord, a communion that the apostle declares to be so great that he chooses to marvel at it rather than to explain it.

10 No distance of place can impede it. In the Supper, it is not presented as an empty symbol, but, as the apostle testifies, we receive the reality. Objection, that the expression is figurative. Answer. A sure rule with regard to the sacraments.

The sum is that the flesh and blood of Christ feed our souls just as bread and wine maintain and support our corporeal life. There would be no aptitude in the sign, if our souls did not find their nourishment in Christ. This could not be, if did not Christ truly form one with us, and refresh us by the eating of his flesh, and the drinking of his blood. But though it seems an incredible thing that the flesh of Christ, while at such a distance from us in respect of place, should be food to us, let us remember how far the secret virtue of the Holy Spirit surpasses all our conceptions, and how foolish it is to wish to measure its immensity by our feeble capacity. Therefore, what our mind does not comprehend let faith conceive–viz. that the Spirit truly unites things separated by space. That sacred communion of flesh and blood by which Christ transfuses His life into us, just as if it penetrated our bones and marrow, He testifies and seals in the Supper, and that not by presenting a vain or empty sign, but by there exerting an efficacy of the Spirit by which He fulfills what He promises. And truly, the thing there signified He exhibits and offers to all who sit down at that spiritual feast, although it is beneficially received by believers only who receive this great benefit with true faith and heartfelt gratitude. For this reason the apostle said, "The cup of blessing which we bless, is it not the communion of the blood of Christ? The bread which we break, is it not the communion of the body of Christ?" (1 Corinthians 10:16). There is no ground to object that the expression is figurative, and gives the sign the name of the thing signified.

I admit, indeed, that the breaking of bread is a symbol, not the reality. But this being admitted, we duly infer from the exhibition of the symbol that the thing itself is exhibited. For unless we would charge God with deceit, we will never presume to say that, Be holds forth an empty symbol. Therefore, if by the breaking of bread the Lord truly represents the partaking of Bis body, there ought to be no doubt whatever that he truly exhibits and performs it. The rule, which the pious ought always to observe, is, whenever they see the symbols instituted by the Lord, to think and feel surely persuaded that the truth of the thing signified is also present. For why does the Lord put the symbol of His body into your hands, but just to assure you that you truly partake of Him? If this is true, let us feel as much assured that the visible sign is given us in seal of an invisible gift as that His body itself is given to us.

11 Conclusion of the first part of the chapter. The sacrament of the Supper consists of two parts—viz. corporeal signs, and spiritual truth. These comprehend the meaning, matter, and effect. Christ is truly exhibited to us by symbols.

I hold then (as has always been received in the Church, and is still taught by those who feel aright), that the sacred mystery of the Supper consists of two things–the corporeal signs, which, presented to the eye, represent invisible things in a manner adapted to our weak capacity, and the spiritual truth, which is at once figured and exhibited by the signs. When attempting familiarly to explain its nature, I am accustomed to set down three things–the thing meant, the matter, which depends on it, and the virtue or efficacy consequent upon both. The thing meant consists in the promises, which are in a manner included in the sign. By the matter, or substance, I mean Christ, with his death and resurrection. By the effect, I understand redemption, justification, sanctification, eternal life, and all other benefits, which Christ bestows upon us. Moreover, though all these things have respect to faith, I leave no room for the cavil, that when I say Christ is conceived by faith, I mean that he is only conceived by the intellect and imagination. He is offered by the promises, not that we may stop short at the sight or mere knowledge of him, but that we may enjoy true communion with him. And, indeed, I see not how anyone can expect to have redemption and righteousness in the cross of Christ, and life in his death, without trusting first to true communion with Christ himself. Those blessings could not reach us, did not Christ previously make himself ours. I say then, that in the mystery of the Supper, by the symbols of bread and wine, Christ and his body and blood are truly exhibited to us. In them, he fulfilled all obedience in order to procure righteousness for us– first that we might become one body with him; and, secondly, that being made partakers of his substance, we might feel the result of this fact in the participation of all his blessings.

12 Second part of the chapter, reduced to nine heads. The transubstantiation of the Papists considered and refuted. Its origin and absurdity. Why it should be exploded.

I now come to the hyperbolical mixtures which superstition has introduced. Here Satan has employed all his wiles, withdrawing the minds of men from heaven, and imbuing them with the perverse error that Christ is annexed to the element of bread. And, first, we are not to dream of such a presence of Christ in the sacrament as the artificers of the Romish court have imagined, as if the body of Christ, locally present, were to be taken into the hand, and chewed by the teeth, and swallowed by the throat. This was the form of Palinode, which Pope Nicholas dictated to Berengarius, in token of his repentance, a form expressed in terms so monstrous, that the author of the Gloss exclaims, that there is danger, if the reader is not particularly cautious, that he will be led by it into a worse heresy than was that of Berengarius. Peter Lombard, though he labors much to excuse the absurdity, rather inclines to a different opinion. As we cannot at all doubt that it is bounded according to the invariable rule in the human body, and is contained in heaven, where it was once received, and will remain until it return to judgment, so we deem it altogether unlawful to bring it back under these corruptible elements, or to imagine it everywhere present. And, indeed, there is no need of this, in order to our partaking of it, since the Lord by his Spirit bestows upon us the blessing of being one with him in soul, body, and spirit. The bond of that connection, therefore, is the Spirit of Christ, who unites us to him, and is a kind of channel by which everything that Christ is and has is derived to us. For if we see that the sun, in sending forth its rays upon the earth, to generate, cherish, and invigorate its offspring, in a manner transfuses its substance into it, why should the radiance of the Spirit be less in conveying to us the communion of his flesh and blood? Wherefore the Scripture, when it speaks of our participation with Christ, refers its whole efficacy to the Spirit. Instead of many, one passage will suffice. Paul, in the Epistle to the Romans (Romans 8:9-11), shows that the only way in which Christ dwells in us is by his Spirit. By this, however, he does not take away that communion of flesh and blood of which we now speak, but shows that it is owing to the Spirit alone that we possess Christ wholly, and have him abiding in us.

13 Transubstantiation as feigned by the Schoolmen. Refutation. The many superstitions introduced by their error.

The Schoolmen, horrified at this barbarous impiety, speak more modestly, though they do nothing more than amuse themselves with more subtle delusions. They admit that Christ is not contained in the sacrament circumscriptively, or in a bodily manner, but they afterwards devise a method, which they themselves do not understand, and cannot explain to others. It, however, comes to this, that Christ may be sought in what they call the species of bread. What? When they say that the substance of bread is converted into

Christ, do they not attach him to the white color, which is all they leave of it? But they say, that though contained in the sacrament, he still remains in heaven, and has no other presence there than that of abode. But, whatever be the terms in which they attempt to make a gloss, the sum of all is, that that which was formerly bread, by consecration becomes Christ: so that Christ thereafter lies hid under the color of bread. This they are not ashamed distinctly to express. For Lombard's words are, "The body of Christ, which is visible in itself, lurks and lies covered after the act of consecration under the species of bread." Thus, the figure of the bread is nothing but a mask, which conceals the view of the flesh from our eye. But there is no need of many conjectures to detect the snare, which they intended to lay by these words, since the thing itself speaks clearly. It is easy to see how great is the superstition under which not only the vulgar but the leaders also, have labored for many ages, and still labor, in Popish Churches. Little solicitous as to true faith (by which alone we attain to the fellowship of Christ, and become one with him), provided they have his carnal presence, which they have fabricated without authority from the word, they think he is present. Hence, we see that all, which they have gained by their ingenious subtlety, is to make bread to be regarded as God.

14 The fiction of transubstantiation why invented contrary to Scripture, and the consent of antiquity. The term of transubstantiation never used in the early Church. Objection. Answer.

Hence, proceeded that fictitious transubstantiation for which they fight more fiercely in the present day than for all the other articles of their faith. For the first architects of local presence could not explain how the body of Christ could be mixed with the substance of bread, without forthwith meeting with many absurdities. Hence, it was necessary to have recourse to the fiction, that there is a conversion of the bread into body, not that properly instead of bread it becomes body, but that Christ, in order to conceal himself under the figure, reduces the substance to nothing. It is strange that they have fallen into such a degree of ignorance, nay, of stupor, as to produce this monstrous fiction not only against Scripture, but also against the consent of the ancient Church. I admit, indeed, that some of the ancients occasionally used the term conversion, not that they meant to do away with the substance in the external signs, but to teach that the bread devoted to the sacrament was widely different from ordinary bread, and was now something else. All clearly and uniformly teach that the sacred Supper consists of two parts, an earthly and a heavenly. The earthly they without dispute interpret to be bread and wine. Certainly, whatever they may pretend, it is plain that antiquity, which they often dare to oppose to the clear word of God, gives no countenance to that dogma. It is not so long since it was devised; indeed, it was unknown not only to the better ages, in which a purer doctrine still flourished, but after that, purity was considerably impaired.

There is no early Christian writer who does not admit in distinct terms that the sacred symbols of the Supper are bread and wine, although, as has been said, they sometimes distinguish them by various epithets in order to recommend the dignity of the mystery. For when they say that a secret conversion takes place at consecration, so that it is now something other than bread and wine, their meaning, as I already observed, is not that these are annihilated, but that they are to be considered in a different light from common food, which is only intended to feed the body, whereas in the former the spiritual food and drink of the mind are exhibited. This we do not deny. But, say our opponents, if there is conversion, one thing must become another. If they mean that something becomes different from what it was before, I assent. If they will wrest it in support of their fiction, let them tell me of what kind of change they are sensible in baptism. For here, also, the Fathers make out a wonderful conversion, when they say that out of the corruptible element is made the spiritual laver of the soul, and yet no one denies that it remains water. But say they, there is no such expression in Baptism as that in the Supper, This is my body; as if we were treating of these words, which have a meaning sufficiently clear, and not rather of that term conversion, which ought not to mean more in the Supper than in Baptism.

Have done, then, with those quibbles upon words, which betray nothing but their silliness. The meaning would have no congruity, unless the truth, which is there figured, had a living image in the external sign. Christ wished to testify by an external symbol that his flesh was food. If he exhibited merely an empty show of bread, and not true bread, where is the analogy or similitude to conduct us from the visible thing to the invisible? For, in order to make all things consistent, the meaning cannot extend to more than this: that we are fed by the species of Christ's flesh, just as in the case of baptism. If the figure of water deceived the eye, it would not be to us a sure pledge of our ablution; nay, the fallacious spectacle would rather throw us into doubt. The nature of the sacrament is therefore overthrown, if in the mode of signifying the earthly sign corresponds not to the heavenly reality; and, accordingly, the truth of the mystery is lost if true bread does not represent the true body of Christ. I repeat, since the Supper is nothing but a conspicuous attestation to the promise contained in the sixth chapter of John–viz. that Christ is the bread of life, who came down from heaven, that visible bread must intervene in order for that spiritual bread to be figured, unless we would destroy all the benefits with which God here favors us for the purpose of sustaining our infirmity. Then on what ground could Paul infer that we are all one bread, and one body in partaking together of that one bread, if only the semblance of bread, and not the natural reality, remained?

15 The error of transubstantiation favored by the consecration, which was a kind of magical incantation. The bread is not a sacrament to itself, but to those who receive it. The changing of the rod of Moses into a serpent gives no countenance to Popish transubstantiation. No resemblance between it and the words of institution in the Supper. Objection. Answer.

They could not have been so shamefully deluded by the impostures of Satan had they not been fascinated by the erroneous idea that the body of Christ included under the bread is transmitted by the bodily mouth into the belly. The cause of this brutish imagination was that consecration had the same effect with them as magical incantation. They overlooked the principle, that bread is a sacrament to none but those to whom the word is addressed, just as the water of baptism is not changed in itself, but begins to be to us what it formerly was not, as soon as the promise is annexed. This will better appear from the example of a similar sacrament. The water gushing from the rock in the desert was to the Israelites a badge and sign of the same thing that is figured to us in the Supper by wine. For Paul declares that they drank the same spiritual drink (1 Corinthians 10:4). But the water was common to the herds and flocks of the people. Hence, it is easy to infer, that in the earthly elements, when employed for a spiritual use, no other conversion takes place than in respect of men, inasmuch as they are to them seals of promises. Moreover, since it is the purpose of God, as I have repeatedly inculcated, to raise us up to himself by fit vehicles, those who indeed call us to Christ, but to Christ lurking invisibly under bread, impiously, by their perverseness, defeat this object.

It is impossible for the mind of man to disentangle itself from the immensity of space, and ascend to Christ even above the heavens. What nature denied them, they attempted to gain by a noxious remedy. Remaining on the earth, they felt no need of a celestial proximity to Christ. Such was the necessity, which impelled them to transfigure the body of Christ. In the age of Bernard, though a harsher mode of speech had prevailed, transubstantiation was not yet recognized. And in all previous ages, the similitude in the mouths of all was that a spiritual reality was conjoined with bread and wine in this sacrament. As to the terms, they think they answer acutely, though they adduce nothing relevant to the case in hand. The rod of Moses (they say), when turned into a serpent, though it acquires the name of a serpent, still retains its former name, and is called a rod; and thus, according to them, it is equally probable that though the bread passes into a new substance, it is still called by catachresis, and not inaptly, what it still appears to the eye to be. But what resemblance, real or apparent, do they find between an illustrious miracle and their fictitious illusion, of which no eye on the earth is witness? The magi by their impostures had persuaded the Egyptians, that they had a divine power above the ordinary course of nature to change created beings. Moses comes forth, and after exposing their fallacies, shows that the invincible power of God is on his side, since his rod swallows up all the other rods. But as that conversion was visible to the eye, we have already observed, that it has no reference to the case. Shortly after, the rod visibly resumed its form.

It may be added, that we know not whether this was an extemporary conversion of substance. For we must attend to the illusion to the rods of the magicians, which the prophet did not choose to term serpents, lest he might seem to insinuate a conversion which had no existence, because those impostors had done nothing more than blind the eyes of the spectators. But what resemblance is there between that expression and the following? "The bread which we break;"–"As often as ye eat this bread;"–"They communicated in the breaking of bread;" and so forth. It is certain that the eye only was deceived by the incantation of the magicians. The matter is more doubtful with regard to Moses, by whose hand it was not more difficult for God to make a serpent out of a rod, and again to make a rod out of a serpent, than to clothe angels with corporeal bodies, and a little after unclothe them. If the case of the sacrament were at all akin to this, there might be some color for their explanation. Let it, therefore, remain fixed that there is no true and fit promise in the Supper, that the flesh of Christ is truly meat, unless there is a correspondence in the true substance of the external symbol. But as one error gives rise to another, a passage in Jeremiah has been so absurdly wrested, to prove transubstantiation, that it is painful to refer to it. The prophet complains that wood was placed in his bread, intimating that by the cruelty of his enemies his bread was infected with bitterness, as David by a similar figure complains, "They gave me also gall for my meat: and in my thirst they gave me vinegar to drink" (Psalm 69:21). These men would allegorize the expression to mean, that the body of Christ was nailed to the wood of the cross. But some of the Fathers thought so! As if we ought not rather to pardon their ignorance and bury the disgrace, than to add impudence, and bring them into hostile conflict with the genuine meaning of the prophet.

16 Refutation of consubstantiation, whence the idea of ubiquity.

Some, who see that the analogy between the sign and the thing signified cannot be destroyed without destroying the truth of the sacrament, admit that the bread of the Supper is truly the substance of an earthly and corruptible element, and cannot suffer any change in itself, but must have the body of Christ included under it. If they would explain this to mean, that when the bread is held forth in the sacrament, an exhibition of the body is annexed, because the truth is inseparable from its sign, I would not greatly object. But because fixing the body itself in the bread, they attach to it a ubiquity contrary to its nature, and by adding under the bread, will have it that it lies hid under it, I must employ a short time in exposing their craft, and dragging them forth from their concealments. Here, however, it is not my intention professedly to discuss the whole case; I mean only to lay the foundations of a discussion, which will afterwards follow in its own place. They insist, then, that the body of Christ is invisible and immense, so that it may be hid under bread, because they think that there is no other way by which they can communicate with him than by his descending into the bread, though they do not comprehend the mode of descent by which he raises us up to himself. They employ all the colors they possibly can, but after they have said all, it is sufficiently apparent that they insist on the local presence of Christ. How so? Because they cannot conceive any other participation of flesh and blood than that which consists either in local conjunction and contact, or in some gross method of enclosing.

17 This ubiquity confounds the natures of Christ. Subtleties answered.

Some, in order obstinately to maintain the error, which they have once rashly adopted, hesitate not to assert that the dimensions of Christ's flesh are not more circumscribed than those of heaven and earth. His birth as an infant, his growth, his extension on the cross, and his confinement in the sepulcher were effected, they say, by a kind of dispensation, that he might perform the offices of being born, of dying, and of other human acts. His being seen with his wonted bodily appearance after the resurrection, his ascension into heaven, and his appearance after his ascension to Stephen and Paul were the effect of the same dispensation, that it might be made apparent to the eye of man that he was constituted King in heaven. What is this but to call forth Marcion from his grave? For there cannot be a doubt that the body of Christ, if so constituted, was a ghost or was ghostlike. Some employ a rather more subtle evasion, That the body which is given in the sacrament is glorious and immortal, and that, therefore, there is no absurdity in its being contained under the sacrament in various places, or in no place, and in no form. But, I ask, what did Christ give to his disciples the day before he suffered? Do not the words say that he gave the mortal body, which was to be delivered shortly after? But, say they, he had previously manifested his glory to the three disciples on the mount (Matthew 17:2). This is true; but his purpose was to give them for the time a taste of immortality. Still they cannot find there a twofold body, but only the one, which he had assumed, arrayed in new glory. When he distributed his body in the first Supper, the hour was at hand in which he was "stricken, smitten of God, and afflicted" (Isaiah 53:4). So far was he from intending at that time to exhibit the glory of his resurrection. And here what a door is opened to Marcion, if the body of Christ was seen humble and mortal in one place, glorious and immortal in another! And yet, if their opinion is well founded, the same thing happens every day, because they are forced to admit that the body of Christ, which is in itself visible, lurks invisibly under the symbol of bread. And yet, those who send forth such monstrous dogmas, so far from being ashamed at the disgrace, assail us with virulent invectives for not subscribing to them.

18 Absurdities connected with consubstantiation. Candid exposition of the orthodox view.

But if the body and blood of Christ are attached to the bread and wine, then the one must necessarily be dissevered from the other. For as the bread is given separately from the cup, so the body, united to the bread, must be separated from the blood, included in the cup. For since they affirm that the body is in the bread, and the blood is in the cup, while the bread and wine are, in regard to space, at some distance from each other, they cannot, by any quibble, evade the conclusion that the body must be separated from the blood. Their usual pretence–viz. that the blood is in the body, and the body again in the blood, by what they call concomitance, is more than frivolous, since the symbols in which they are included are thus distinguished. But if we are carried to heaven with our eyes and minds, that we may there behold Christ in the glory of his kingdom, as the symbols invite us to him in his integrity, so, under the symbol of bread, we must feed on his body, and under the symbol of wine, drink separately of his blood, and thereby have the full enjoyment of him. For though he withdrew his flesh from us, and with his body ascended to heaven, he, however, sits at the right hand of the Father; that is, he reigns in power and majesty, and the glory of the Father. This kingdom is not limited by any intervals of space, nor circumscribed by any dimensions. Christ can exert his energy wherever he pleases, in earth and heaven, can manifest his presence by the exercise of his power, can always be present with his people, breathing into them his own life, can live in them, sustain, confirm, and invigorate them, and preserve them safe, just as if he were with them in the body; in fine, can feed them with his own body, communion with which he transfuses into them. After this manner, the body and blood of Christ are exhibited to us in the sacrament.

19 The nature of the true presence of Christ in the Supper. The true and substantial communion of the body and blood of the Lord. This orthodox view assailed by turbulent spirits.

The presence of Christ in the Supper we must hold to be such as neither affixes him to the element of bread, nor encloses him in bread, nor circumscribes him in any way (this would obviously detract from his celestial glory); and it must, moreover, be such as neither divests him of his just dimensions, nor dissevers him by differences of place, nor assigns to him a body of boundless dimensions, diffused through heaven and earth. All these things are clearly repugnant to his true human nature. Let us never allow ourselves to lose sight of the two restrictions. First, Let there be nothing derogatory to the heavenly glory of Christ. This happens whenever he is brought under the corruptible elements of this world, or is affixed to any earthly creatures. Secondly, Let no property be assigned to his body inconsistent with his human nature. This is done when it is either said to be infinite, or made to occupy a variety of places at the same time. But when these absurdities are discarded, I willingly admit anything which helps to express the true and substantial communication of the body and blood of the Lord, as exhibited to believers under the sacred symbols of the Supper, understanding that they are received not by the imagination or intellect merely, but are enjoyed in reality as the food of eternal life. For the odium with which this view is regarded by the world, and the unjust prejudice incurred by its defense, there is no cause, unless it is in the fearful fascinations of Satan. What we teach on the subject is in perfect accordance with Scripture, contains nothing absurd, obscure, or ambiguous, is not unfavorable to true piety and solid edification; in short, has nothing in it to offend, save that, for some ages, while the ignorance and barbarism of sophists reigned in the Church, the clear light and open truth were unbecomingly suppressed. And yet, as Satan, by means of turbulent spirits, is still exerting himself to the utmost to bring dishonor on this doctrine by all kinds of calumny and reproach, it is right to assert and defend it with the greatest care.

20 This view vindicated from their calumnies. The words of the institution explained in opposition to the glosses of transubstantiators and consubstantiators. Their subterfuges and absurd blasphemies.

Before we proceed further, we must consider the ordinance itself, as instituted by Christ, because the most plausible objection of our opponents is, that we abandon his words. To free ourselves from the obloquy with which they thus load us, the fittest course will be to begin with an interpretation of the words. Three Evangelists and Paul relate that our Savior took bread, and after giving thanks, brake it, and gave it to his disciples, saying, Take, eat: this is my body which is given or broken for you. Of the cup, Matthew and Mark say, "This is my blood of the new testament, which is shed for many for the remission of sins" (Matthew 26:26; Mark 14:22). Luke and Paul say, "This cup is the new testament in my blood" (Luke 22:20; 1 Corinthians 11:25). The advocates of transubstantiation insist, that by the pronoun, this, is denoted the appearance of bread, because the whole complexion of our Savior's address is an act of consecration, and there is no substance which can be demonstrated. But if they adhere so religiously to the words, inasmuch as that which our Savior gave to his disciples he declared to be his body, there is nothing more alien from the strict meaning of the words than the fiction, that what was bread is now body. What Christ takes into his hands, and gives to the apostles, he declares to be his body; but he had taken bread, and, therefore, who sees not that what is given is still bread? Hence, nothing can be more absurd than to transfer what is affirmed of bread to the species of bread. Others, in interpreting the particle is, as equivalent to being transubstantiated, have recourse to a gloss, which is forced and violently wrested. They have no ground, therefore, for pretending that they are moved by a reverence for the words. The use of the term is, for being converted into something else, is unknown to every tongue and nation. With regard to those who leave the bread in the Supper, and affirm that it is the body of Christ, there is great diversity among them.

Those who speak more modestly, though they insist upon the letter, This is my body, afterwards abandon this strictness, and observe that it is equivalent to saying that the body of Christ is with the bread, in the bread, and under the bread. To the reality, which they affirm, we have already adverted, and will by-and-by, at greater length. I am not only considering the words by which they say they are prevented from admitting that the bread is called body, because it is a sign of the body. But if they shun everything like metaphor, why do they leap from the simple demonstration of Christ to modes of expression, which are widely different? For there is a great difference between saying that the bread is the body, and that the body is with the bread. But seeing it impossible to maintain the simple proposition that the bread is the body, they endeavored to evade the difficulty by concealing themselves under those forms of expression. Others, who are bolder, hesitate not to assert that, strictly speaking, the bread is body, and in this way prove that they are truly of the letter. If it is objected that the bread, therefore, is Christ, and, being Christ, is God, –they will deny it, because the words of Christ do not expressly say so. But they gain nothing by their denial, since all agree that the whole Christ is offered to us in the Supper. It is intolerable blasphemy to affirm, without figure, a fading and corruptible element, that it is Christ. I now ask them, if they hold the two propositions to be identical, Christ is the Son of God, and Bread is the body of Christ. If they concede that they are different (and this, whether they will or not, they will be forced to do), let them tell wherein is the difference. All, which they can adduce, is, I presume, that the bread is called body in a sacramental manner.

Hence, it follows, that the words of Christ are not subject to the common rule, and ought not to be tested grammatically. I ask all these rigid and obstinate exactors of the letter, whether, when Luke and Paul call the cup the testament in blood, they do not express the same thing as in the previous clause, when they call bread the body? There certainly was the same solemnity in the one part of the mystery as in the other, and, as brevity is obscure, the longer sentence better elucidates the meaning. As often, therefore, as they contend, from the one expression, that the bread is body, I will adduce an apt interpretation from the longer expression, that it is a testament in the body. What? Can we seek for surer or more faithful expounders than Luke and Paul? I have no intention, however, to detract, in any respect, from the communication of the body of Christ, which I have acknowledged. I only meant to expose the foolish perverseness with which they carry on a war of words. The bread I understand, on the authority of Luke and Paul, to be the body of Christ, because it is a covenant in the body. If they impugn this, their quarrel is not with me, but with the Spirit of God. However often they may repeat, that reverence for the words of Christ will not allow them to give a figurative interpretation to what is spoken plainly, the pretext cannot justify them in thus rejecting all the contrary arguments, which we adduce. Meanwhile, as I have already observed, it is proper to attend to the force of what is meant by a testament in the body and blood of Christ. The covenant, ratified by the sacrifice of death, would not avail us without the addition of that secret communication, by which we are made one with Christ.

21 Why the name of the thing signified is given to the sacramental symbols. This illustrated by passages of Scripture; also by a passage of Augustine.

It remains, therefore, to hold, that because of the affinity, which the things signified, have with their signs, the name of the thing itself is given to the sign figuratively, indeed, but very appropriately. I say nothing of allegories and parables, lest it should be alleged that I am seeking subterfuges, and slipping out of the present question. I say that the expression, which is uniformly used in Scripture, when the sacred mysteries are treated of, is metonymical. For you cannot otherwise understand the expressions, that circumcision is a "covenant"—that the lamb is the Lord's "Passover"—that the sacrifices of the law are expiations—that the rock from which the water flowed in the desert was Christ, —unless you interpret them metonymically." Nor is the name merely transferred from the superior to the inferior. On the contrary, the name of the visible sign is given to the thing signified, as when God is said to have appeared to Moses in the bush; the Ark of the Covenant is called God, and the face of God, and the dove is called the Holy Spirit. For although the sign differs essentially from the thing signified, the latter being spiritual and heavenly, the former corporeal and visible, —yet, as it not only figures the thing which it is employed to represent as a naked and empty badge, but also truly exhibits it, why should not its name be justly applied to the thing? But if symbols humanly devised, which are images of absent, rather than marks of present things, and of which they are very often most fallacious types, are sometimes honored with their names, —with much greater reason do the institutions of God borrow the names of things, of which they always bear a sure, and by no means fallacious signification, and have the reality annexed to them. So great, then, is the similarity, and so close the connection between the two, that it is easy to pass from the one to the other.

Let our opponents, therefore, cease to indulge their mirth in calling us Tropists, when we explain the sacramental mode of expression according to the common use of Scripture. For, while the sacraments agree in many things, there is also, in this metonymy, a certain community in all respects between them. As, therefore, the apostle says that the rock from which spiritual water flowed forth to the Israelites was Christ (1 Corinthians 10:4), and was thus a visible symbol under which that spiritual drink was truly perceived, though not by the eye, so the body of Christ is now called bread, inasmuch as it is a symbol under which our Lord offers us the true eating of his body.

Lest anyone should despise this as a novel invention, the view which Augustine took and expressed was the same: "Had not the sacraments a certain resemblance to the things of which they are sacraments, they would not be sacraments at all. And from this resemblance, they generally have the names of the things themselves. This, as the sacrament of the body of Christ, is, after a certain manner, the body of Christ, and the sacrament of Christ is the blood of Christ; so the sacrament of faith is faith." He has many similar passages, which it would be superfluous to collect, as that one may suffice.

I need only remind my readers, that the same doctrine is taught by that holy man in his Epistle to Evodius. Where Augustine teaches that nothing is more common than metonymy in mysteries, it is a frivolous quibble to object that there is no mention of the Supper. Were this objection sustained, it would follow that we are not entitled to argue from the genus to the species; e.g., every animal is endued with motion; and, therefore, the horse and the ox are endued with motion. Indeed, longer discussion is rendered unnecessary by the words of the Saint himself, where he says, that when Christ gave the symbol of his body, he did not hesitate to call it his body. He elsewhere says, "Wonderful was the patience of Christ in admitting Judas to the feast, in which he committed and delivered to the disciples the symbol of his body and blood."

22 Refutation of an objection founded on the words, "This is." Objection answered.

Should any morose person, shutting his eyes to everything else, insist upon the expression, "This is," as distinguishing this mystery from all others, the answer is easy. They say that the substantive verb is so emphatic, as to leave no room for interpretation. Though I should admit this, I answer, that the substantive verb occurs in the words of Paul (1 Corinthians 10:16), where he calls the bread the communion of the body of Christ. But communion is something different from the body itself. Nay, when the sacraments are treated of, the same word occurs: "My covenant shall be in your flesh for an everlasting covenant" (Genesis 17:13). "This is the ordinance of the Passover" (Exodus 12:43). To say no more, when Paul declares that the rock was Christ (1 Corinthians 10:4), why should the substantive verb, in that passage, be deemed less emphatic than in the discourse of Christ? When John says, "The Holy Ghost was not yet given, because that Jesus was not yet glorified" (John 7:39), I should like to know what is the force of the substantive verb? If the rule of our opponents is rigidly observed, the eternal essence of the Spirit will be destroyed, as if he had only begun to be after the ascension of Christ. Let them tell me, in fine, what is meant by the declaration of Paul, that baptism is "the washing of regeneration, and renewing of the Holy Ghost" (Titus 3:5); though it is certain that to many it was of no use. But they cannot be more effectually refuted than by the expression of Paul, that the Church is Christ. For, after introducing the similitude of the human body, he adds, "So also is Christ" (1 Corinthians 7:12), when he means not the only begotten Son of God in himself, but in his members. I think I have now gained this much, that all men of sense and integrity will be disgusted with the calumnies of our enemies, when they give out that we discredit the words of Christ; though we embrace them not less obediently than they do, and ponder them with greater reverence. Nay, their supine security proves that they do not greatly care what Christ meant, provided it furnishes them with a shield to defend their obstinacy, while our careful investigation should be an evidence of the authority which we yield to Christ. They invidiously pretend that human reason will not allow us to believe what Christ uttered with his sacred mouth; but how naughtily they endeavor to fix this odium upon us, I have already, in a great measure, shown, and will still show more clearly. Nothing, therefore, prevents us from believing Christ speaking, and from acquiescing in everything to which he intimates his assent. The only question here is whether it is unlawful to inquire into the genuine meaning.

23 Other objections answered.

Those worthy masters, to show that they are of the letter, forbid us to deviate, in the least, from the letter. On the contrary, when Scripture calls God a man of war, as I see that the expression would be too harsh if not interpreted, I have no doubt that the similitude is taken from man. And, indeed, the only pretext which enabled the Anthropomorphites to annoy the orthodox Fathers was by fastening on the expressions, "The eyes of God see;" "It ascended to his ears;" "His hand is stretched out;" "The earth is his footstool;" and exclaimed, that God was deprived of the body which Scripture assigns to him. Were this rule admitted, complete barbarism would bury the whole light of faith. What monstrous absurdities shall fanatical men not be able to extract, if they are allowed to urge every knotty point in support of their dogmas? Their objection that it is not probable that when Christ was providing special comfort for the apostles in adversity, he spoke enigmatically or obscurely, –supports our view. For, had it not occurred to the apostles that the bread was called the body figuratively, as being a symbol of the body; the extraordinary nature of the thing would doubtless have filled them with perplexity. For, at this very period, John relates, that the slightest difficulties perplexed them (John 14:5, 8; 16:17).

They debate, among themselves, how Christ is to go to the Father, and not understanding that the things which were said referred to the heavenly Father, raise a question as to how he is to go out of the world until they shall see him? How, then, could they have been so ready to believe what is repugnant to all reason–viz. that Christ was seated at table under their eye, and yet was contained invisible under the bread? As they attest their consent by eating this bread without hesitation, it is plain that they understood the words of Christ in the same sense as we do, considering what ought not to seem unusual when mysteries are spoken of, that the name of the thing signified was transferred to the sign. There was therefore to the disciples, as there is to us, clear and sure consolation, not involved in any enigma; and the only reason that certain persons reject our interpretation is, because they are blinded by a delusion of the devil to introduce the darkness of enigma, instead of the obvious interpretation of an appropriate figure.

Besides, if we insist strictly on the words, our Savior will be made to affirm erroneously something of the bread different from the cup. He calls the bread body, and the wine blood. There must either be confusion in terms, or there must be a division separating the body from the blood. Nay, "This is my body," may be as truly affirmed of the cup as of the bread; and it may in turn be affirmed that the bread is the blood. If they answer, that we must look to the end or use for which symbols were instituted, I admit it: but still they will not disencumber themselves of the absurdity which their error drags along with it–viz. that the bread is blood, and the wine is body. Then I know not what they mean when they concede that bread and body are different things, and yet maintain that the one is predicated of the other, properly and without figure, as if one were to say that a garment is different from a man, and yet is properly called a man. Still, as if the victory depended on obstinacy and invective, they say that Christ is charged with falsehood, when it is attempted to interpret his words. It will now be easy for the reader to understand the injustice which is done to us by those carpers at syllables, when they possess the simple with the idea that we bring discredit on the words of Christ; words which, as we have shown, are madly perverted and confounded by them, but are faithfully and accurately expounded by us.

24 Other objections answered. No question here as to the omnipotence of God.

This infamous falsehood cannot be completely wiped away without disposing of another charge. They give out that we are so wedded to human reason, that we attribute nothing more to the power of God than the order of nature admits, and common sense dictates. From these wicked calumnies, I appeal to the doctrine which I have delivered, –a doctrine which makes it sufficiently clear that I by no means measure this mystery by the capacity of human reason, or subject it to the laws of nature. I ask whether it is from physics we have learned that Christ feeds our souls from heaven with his flesh, just as our bodies are nourished by bread and wine. How has flesh this virtue of giving life to our souls? All will say that it is not done naturally. Not more agreeable is it to human reason to hold that the flesh of Christ penetrates to us, to be our food. In short, everyone who may have tasted our doctrine will be carried away with admiration of the secret power of God. But these worthy zealots fabricate for themselves a miracle, and think that without it God himself and his power vanish away. I would again admonish the reader carefully to consider the nature of our doctrine, whether it depends on common apprehension, or whether, after having surmounted the world on the wings of faith, it rises to heaven. We say that Christ descends to us, as well by the external symbol as by his Spirit, that he may truly quicken our souls by the substance of his flesh and blood. He, who does not feel that in these few words are many miracles, is more than stupid; since nothing is more contrary to nature than to derive the spiritual and heavenly life of the soul from flesh, which received its origin from the earth, and was subjected to death, nothing more incredible than that things separated by the whole space between heaven and earth should, notwithstanding of the long distance, not only be connected, but united, so that souls receive aliment from the flesh of Christ.

Let preposterous men, then, cease to assail us with the vile calumny, that we malignantly restrict the boundless power of God. They either foolishly err, or wickedly lie. The question here is not, "What could God do?" But rather, "What has he been pleased to do?" We affirm that he has done what pleased him, and it pleased him that Christ should be in all respects like his brethren, "yet without sin" (Hebrews 4:15). What is our flesh? Is it not that which consists of certain dimensions? Is confined within a certain place? Is touched and seen? And why, say they, may not God make the same flesh occupy several different places, so as not to be confined to any particular place, and so as to have neither measure nor species? Fool! Why do you require the power of God to make a thing to be at the same time flesh and not flesh? It is just as if you were to insist on his making light to be at the same time light and darkness. He wills light to be light, darkness to be darkness, flesh to be flesh. True, when he so chooses, he will convert darkness into light, and light into darkness: but when you insist that there shall be no difference between light and darkness, what do you but pervert the order of the divine wisdom? Flesh must therefore be flesh, and spirit, spirit; each under the law and condition on which God has created them. Now, the condition of flesh is that it should have one certain place, its own dimensions, and its own form. On that condition, Christ assumed the flesh, to which, as Augustine declares, he gave incorruption and glory, but without destroying its nature and reality.

25 Other objections answered.

They object that they have the word by which the will of God has been openly manifested; that is if we permit them to banish from the Church the gift of interpretation, which should throw light upon the word. I admit that they have the word, but just as the Anthropomorphites of old had it, when they made God corporeal, just as Marcion and the Manichees had it when they made the body of Christ celestial or ghostlike. They quoted the passages, "The first man is of the earth, earthy; the second man is the Lord from heaven" (1 Corinthians 15:47): Christ "made himself of no reputation, and took upon him the form of a servant, and was made in the likeness of men" (Philippians 2:7). But these vain boasters think that there is no power of God unless they fabricate a monster in their own brains, by which the whole order of nature is subverted. This rather is to circumscribe the power of God, to attempt to try, by our fictions, what he can do. From this word, they have assumed that the body of Christ is visible in heaven, and yet lurks invisible on the earth under innumerable bits of bread. They will say that this is rendered necessary, in order that the body of Christ may be given in the Supper. In other words, because they have been pleased to extract a carnal eating from the words of Christ, carried away by their own prejudice, they have found it necessary to coin this subtlety, which is wholly repugnant to Scripture.

That we detract, in any respect, from the power of God, is so far from being true, that our doctrine is the loudest in extolling it. But as they continue to charge us with robbing God of his honor, in rejecting what, according to common apprehension, it is difficult to believe, though it had been promised by the mouth of Christ. I answer, as I lately did, that in the mysteries of faith we do not consult common apprehension, but, with the placid docility and spirit of meekness, which James recommends (James 1:21), receive the doctrine, which has come from heaven. Wherein they perniciously err, I am confident that we follow a proper moderation.

On hearing the words of Christ, "This is my body," they imagine a miracle most remote from his intention; and when, from this fiction, the grossest absurdities arise, having already, by their precipitate haste, entangled themselves with snares, they plunge themselves into the abyss of the divine omnipotence, that, in this way, they may extinguish the light of truth. Hence, the supercilious moroseness. We have no wish to know how Christ is hid under the bread: we are satisfied with his own words, "This is my body." We again study, with no less obedience than care, to obtain a sound understanding of this passage, as of the whole of Scripture. We do not, with preposterous fervor, rashly and without choice, lay hold on whatever first presents itself to our minds. Rather, after careful meditation, we embrace the meaning, which the Spirit of God suggests.

Trusting to him, we look down, as from a height, on whatever opposition may be offered by earthly wisdom. Nay, we hold our minds captive, not allowing one word of murmur, and humble them, that they may not presume to gainsay. In this way, we have arrived at that exposition of the words of Christ, which all who are moderately versant in Scripture know to be perpetually used with regard to the sacraments. Still, in a matter of difficulty, we deem it not unlawful to inquire, after the example of the blessed Virgin, "How shall this be?" (Luke 1:34).

26 The orthodox view further confirmed. A. By a consideration of the reality of Christ's body. B. From our Savior's declaration that he would always be in the world. This confirmed by the exposition of Augustine.

But as nothing will be more effectual to confirm the faith of the pious than to show them that the doctrine which we have laid down is taken from the pure word of God, and rests on its authority, I will make this plain with as much brevity as I can. The body with which Christ rose is declared, not by Aristotle, but by the Holy Spirit, to be finite, and to be contained in heaven until the last day. I am aware of how confidently our opponents evade the passages, which are quoted, to this effect. Whenever Christ says that he will leave the world and go away (John 14:2, 28), they reply that that departure was nothing more than a change of mortal state. Were this so, Christ would not substitute the Holy Spirit, to supply, as they express it, the defect of his absence, since he does not succeed in place of him, nor, on the other hand, does Christ himself descend from the heavenly glory to assume the condition of a mortal life. Certainly, the advent of the Spirit and the ascension of Christ are set against each other, and hence it necessarily follows that Christ dwells with us according to the flesh, in the same way as that in which he sends his Spirit.

Moreover, he distinctly says that he would not always be in the world with his disciples (Matthew 26:11). This saving, also, they think they admirably dispose of, as if it were a denial by Christ that he would always be poor and mean, or liable to the necessities of a fading life. But this is plainly repugnant to the context, since reference is made not to poverty and want, or the wretched condition of an earthly life, but to worship and honor. The disciples were displeased with the anointing by Mary, because they thought it a superfluous and useless expenditure, akin to luxury, and would therefore have preferred that the price which they thought wasted should have been expended on the poor. Christ answers, that he will not be always with them to receive such honor.

No different exposition is given by Augustine, whose words are by no means ambiguous. When Christ says, "Me ye have not always," he spoke of his bodily presence. In regard to his majesty, in regard to his providence, in regard to his ineffable and invisible grace, is fulfilled what he said: "Lo, I am with you always, even unto the end of the world" (Matthews 28:20); but in regard to the flesh which the Word assumed–in regard to that which was born of the Virgin–in regard to that which was apprehended by the Jews, nailed to the tree, suspended on the cross, wrapped in linen clothes, laid in the tomb, and manifested in the resurrection, –"Me ye have not always." Why? Since he conversed with his disciples in bodily presence for forty days, and, going out with them, ascended, while they saw but followed not. He is not here, for he sits there, at the right hand of the Father. And yet, he is here: for the presence of his majesty is not withdrawn. Otherwise, as regards the presence of his majesty, we have Christ always; while, in regard to his bodily presence, it was rightly said, "Me ye have not always."

In respect of bodily presence, the Church had him for a few days: now she holds him by faith, but sees him not with the eye. Here, he makes him present with us in three ways–in majesty, providence, and ineffable grace; under which I comprehend that wondrous communion of his body and blood, provided we understand that it is effected by the power of the Holy Spirit, and not by that fictitious enclosing of his body under the element, since our Lord declared that he had flesh and bones which could be handled and seen. Going away, and ascending, intimate, not that he had the appearance of one going away and ascending, but that he truly did what the words express. Some one will ask, Are we then to assign a certain region of heaven to Christ? I answer with Augustine, that this is a curious and superfluous question, provided we believe that he is in heaven.

27 Refutation of the sophisms of the Ubiquitists. The evasion of visible and invisible presence refuted.

What? Does not the very name of ascension, so often repeated, intimate removal from one place to another? This they deny, because by height, according to them, the majesty of empire only is denoted. But what was the very mode of ascending? Was he not carried up while the disciples looked on? Do not the Evangelists clearly relate that he was carried into heaven? These acute Sophists reply that a cloud intervened, and took him out of their sight, to teach the disciples that he would not afterwards be visible in the world. As if he ought not rather to have vanished in a moment, to make them believe in his invisible presence, or the cloud to have gathered around him before he moved a step. When he is carried aloft into the air, and the interposing cloud shows that he is no more to be sought on earth, we safely infer that his dwelling now is in the heavens, as Paul also asserts, bidding us look for him from thence (Philippians 3:20). For this reason, the angels remind the disciples that it is vain to keep gazing up into heaven, because Jesus, who was taken up, would come in like manner, as they had seen him ascend. Here the adversaries of sound doctrine escape, as they think, by the ingenious quibble, that he will come in visible form, though he never departed from the earth, but remained invisible among his people. As if the angels had insinuated a two-fold presence, and not simply made the disciples eyewitnesses of the ascent, that no doubt might remain. It was just as if they had said, By ascending to heaven, while you looked on, he has asserted his heavenly power: it remains for you to wait patiently until he again arrives to judge the world. He has not entered into heaven to occupy it alone, but to gather you and all the pious along with him.

28 The authority of Fathers not in favor of these errors as to Christ's presence. Augustine opposed to them.

Since the advocates of this spurious dogma are not ashamed to honor it with the suffrages of the ancients, and especially of Augustine, how perverse they are in the attempt I will briefly explain. Pious and learned men have collected the passages, and therefore I am unwilling to plead a concluded cause: anyone who wishes may consult their writings. I will not even collect from Augustine what might be pertinent to the matter, but will be contented to show briefly, that without all controversy he is wholly ours. The pretence of our opponents, when they would wrest him from us, that throughout his works the flesh and blood of Christ are said to be dispensed in the Supper–namely, the victim once offered on the cross, is frivolous, seeing he, at the same time, calls it either the eucharist or sacrament of the body. But it is unnecessary to go far to find the sense in which he uses the terms flesh and blood, since he himself explains, saying that the sacraments receive names from their similarity to the things which they designate; and that, therefore, the sacrament of the body is after a certain manner the body. With this agrees another well-know passage, "The Lord hesitated not to say, This is my body, when he gave the sign." They again object that Augustine says distinctly that the body of Christ falls upon the earth, and enters the mouth.

But this is in the same sense in which he affirms that it is consumed, for he conjoins both at the same time. There is nothing repugnant to this in his saying that the bread is consumed after the mystery is performed: for he had said a little before, "As these things are known to men, when they are done by men they may receive honor as being religious, but not as being wonderful." His meaning is not different in the passage, which our opponents too rashly appropriate to themselves–viz. that Christ in a manner carried himself in his own hands, when he held out the mystical bread to his disciples. For by interposing the expression, in a manner, he declares that he was not really or truly included under the bread. Nor is it strange, since he elsewhere plainly contends that bodies could not be without particular localities, and being nowhere, would have no existence. It is a paltry cavil that he is not there treating of the Supper, in which God exerts a special power.

The question had been raised as to the flesh of Christ, and the holy man professedly replying, says, "Christ gave immortality to his flesh, but did not destroy its nature. In regard to this form, we are not to suppose that it is everywhere diffused: for we must beware not to rear up the divinity of the man, to take away the reality of the body. It does not follow that that which is in God is everywhere as God." He immediately subjoins the reason, "One person is God and man, and both one Christ, everywhere, inasmuch as he is God, and in heaven, inasmuch as he is man." How careless would it have been not to except the mystery of the Supper, a matter so grave and serious, if it were in any respect adverse to the doctrine, which he was handling? And yet, if anyone will attentively read what follows shortly after, he will find that under that general doctrine the Supper also is comprehended, that Christ, the only begotten Son of God, and also Son of man, is everywhere wholly present as God: in the temple of God, that is, in the Church, as an inhabiting God, and in some place in heaven, because of the dimensions of his real body.

We see how, in order to unite Christ with the Church, he does not bring his body out of heaven. This he certainly would have done had the body of Christ not been truly our food, unless when included under the bread. Elsewhere, explaining how believers now possess Christ, he says, "You have him by the sign of the cross, by the sacrament of baptism, by the meat and drink of the altar" (Tract. in Joann. 50). How rightly he enumerates a superstitious rite, among the symbols of Christ's presence, I dispute not; but in comparing the presence of the flesh to the sign of the cross, he sufficiently shows that he has no idea of a twofold body of Christ, one lurking concealed under the bread, and another sitting visible in heaven. If there is any need of explanation, it is immediately added, "In respect of the presence of his majesty, we have Christ always: in respect of the presence of his flesh, it is rightly said, 'Me ye have not always.'" They object that he also adds, "In respect of ineffable and invisible grace is fulfilled what was said by him, 'I am with you always, even to the end of the world.'" But this is nothing in their favor. For it is at length restricted to his majesty, which is always opposed to body, while the flesh is expressly distinguished from grace and virtue.

The same antithesis elsewhere occurs, when he says "Christ left the disciples in bodily presence, that he might be with them in spiritual presence." Here it is clear that the essence of the flesh is distinguished from the virtue of the Spirit, which conjoins us with Christ, when, in respect of space, we are at a great distance from him. He repeatedly uses the same mode of expression, as when he says, "He is to come to the quick and the dead in bodily presence, according to the rule of faith and sound doctrine: for in spiritual presence he was to come to them, and to be with the whole Church in the world until its consummation. Therefore, this discourse is directed to believers, whom he had begun already to save by corporeal presence, and whom he was to leave in corporeal absence, that by spiritual presence he might preserve them with the Father." By corporeal to understand visible is mere trifling, since he both opposes his body to his divine power, and by adding, that he might "preserve them with the Father," clearly expresses that he sends his grace to us from heaven by means of the Spirit.

29 Refutation of the invisible presence maintained by opponents Refutation from Tertullian, from a saying of Christ after his resurrection, from the definition of a true body, and from different passages of Scripture.

Since they put so much confidence in his hiding-place of invisible presence, let us see how well they conceal themselves in it. First, they cannot produce a syllable from Scripture to prove that Christ is invisible; but they take for granted what no sound man will admit, that the body of Christ cannot be given in the Supper, unless covered with the mask of bread. This is the very point in dispute; so far is it from occupying the place of the first principle. And while they thus prate, they are forced to give Christ a twofold body, because, according to them, it is visible in itself in heaven, but in the Supper is invisible, by a special mode of dispensation. The beautiful consistency of this may easily be judged, both from other passages of Scripture, and from the testimony of Peter. Peter says that the heavens must receive, or contain Christ, until he comes again (Acts 3:21). These men teach that he is in every place, but without form. They say that it is unfair to subject a glorious body to the ordinary laws of nature. But this answer draws along with it the delirious dream of Servetus, which all pious minds justly abhor, that his body was absorbed by his divinity.

I do not say that this is their opinion; but if it is considered one of the properties of a glorified body to fill all things in an invisible manner, it is plain that the corporeal substance is abolished, and no distinction is left between his Godhead and his human nature. Again, if the body of Christ is so multiform and diversified, that it appears in one place, and in another is invisible, where is there anything of the nature of body with its proper dimensions, and where is its unity?

Far more correct is Tertullian, who contends that the body of Christ was natural and real, because its figure is set before us in the mystery of the Supper, as a pledge and assurance of spiritual life. And certainly, Christ said of his glorified body, "Handle me, and see; for a spirit hath not flesh and bones, as ye see me have" (Luke 24:30). Here, by the lips of Christ himself, the reality of his flesh is proved, by its admitting of being seen and handled. Take these away, and it will cease to be flesh. They always betake themselves to their lurking-place of dispensation, which they have fabricated. But it is our duty so to embrace what Christ absolutely declares, as to give it an unreserved assent. He proves that he is not a phantom, because he is visible in his flesh. Take away what he claims as proper to the nature of his body, and must not a new definition of body be devised? Then, however they may turn themselves about, they will not find any place for their fictitious dispensation in that passage, in which Paul says, that "our conversation is in heaven; from whence we look for the Savior, the Lord Jesus Christ: who shall change our vile body, that it may be fashioned like unto his glorious body" (Philippians 3:20, 21). We are not to hope for conformity to Christ in these qualities, which they ascribe to him as a body, without bounds, and invisible. They will not find anyone so stupid as to be persuaded of this great absurdity. Let them not, therefore, set it down as one of the properties of Christ's glorious body, that it is, at the same time, in many places, and in no place.

In short, let them either openly deny the resurrection of his flesh, or admit that Christ, when invested with celestial glory, did not lay aside his flesh, but is to make us, in our flesh, his associates, and partakers of the same glory, since we are to have a common resurrection with him. For what does Scripture throughout deliver more clearly than that, as Christ assumed our flesh when he was born of the Virgin, and suffered in our true flesh when he made satisfaction for us, so on rising again he resumed the same true flesh, and carried it with him to heaven? The hope of our resurrection, and ascension to heaven, is that Christ rose again and ascended, and, as Tertullian says, "Carried an earnest of our resurrection along with him into heaven." Moreover, how weak and fragile would this hope be, had not this very flesh of ours in Christ been truly raised up, and entered into the kingdom of heaven. But the essential properties of a body are to be confined by space, to have dimension and form. Have done, then, with that foolish fiction, which affixes the minds of men, as well as Christ, to bread. For to what end this occult presence under the bread, save that those who wish to have Christ conjoined with them may stop short at the symbol? But our Lord himself wished us to withdraw not only our eyes, but all our senses, from the earth, forbidding the woman to touch him until he had ascended to the Father (John 20:17). When he sees Mary, with pious reverential zeal, hastening to kiss his feet, there could be no reason for his disapproving and forbidding her to touch him before he had ascended to heaven, unless he wished to he sought nowhere else.

The objection, that he afterwards appeared to Stephen, is easily answered. It was not necessary for our Savior to change his place, as he could give the eyes of his servant a power of vision, which could penetrate to heaven. The same account is to be given of the case of Paul. The objection, that Christ came forth from the closed sepulcher, and came in to his disciples while the doors were shut (Matthew 28:6; John 20:19), gives no better support to their error. For as the water, just as if it had been a solid pavement, furnished a path to our Savior when he walked on it (Matthew 14), so it is not strange that the hard stone yielded to his step; although it is more probable that the stone was removed at his command, and forthwith, after giving him a passage, returned to its place. To enter while the doors were shut, was not so much to penetrate through solid matter, as to make a passage for himself by divine power, and stand in the midst of his disciples in a most miraculous manner. They gain nothing by quoting the passage from Luke, in which it is said, that

Christ suddenly vanished from the eyes of the disciples, with whom he had journeyed to Emmaus (Luke 24:31). In withdrawing from their sight, he did not become invisible; he only disappeared. Thus, Luke declares that, on the journeying with them, he did not assume a new form, but that " their eyes were holden." But these men not only transform Christ that he may live on the earth, but pretend that there is another elsewhere of a different description. In short, by thus trifling, they, not in direct terms indeed, but by a circumlocution, make a spirit of the flesh of Christ; and, not contented with this, give him properties altogether opposite. Hence, it necessarily follows that he must be twofold.

30 Ubiquity refuted by various arguments.

Granting what they absurdly talk of the invisible presence, it will still be necessary to prove the immensity, without which it is vain to attempt to include Christ under the bread. Unless the body of Christ can be everywhere without any boundaries of space, it is impossible to believe that he is hid in the Supper under the bread. Hence, they have been under the necessity of introducing the monstrous dogma of ubiquity. But it has been demonstrated by strong and clear passages of Scripture, first, that it is bounded by the dimensions of the human body; and, secondly, that its ascension into heaven made it plain that it is not in all places, but on passing to a new one, leaves the one formerly occupied. The promise to which they appeal, "I am with you always, even to the end of the world," is not to be applied to the body. First, then, a perpetual connection with Christ could not exist, unless he dwells in us corporeally, independently of the use of the Supper; and, therefore, they have no good ground for disputing so bitterly concerning the words of Christ, in order to include him under the bread in the Supper. Secondly, the context proves that Christ is not speaking at all of his flesh, but promising the disciples his invincible aid to guard and sustain them against all the assaults of Satan and the world. For, in appointing them to a difficult office, he confirms them by the assurance of his presence, that they might neither hesitate to undertake it, nor be timorous in the discharge of it, as if he had said that his invincible protection would not fail them.

Unless we would throw everything into confusion, must it not be necessary to distinguish the mode of presence? And, indeed, some, to their great disgrace, choose rather to betray their ignorance than give up one iota of their error. I speak not of Papists, whose doctrine is more tolerable or at least more modest; but some are so hurried away by contention as to say that because of the union of natures in Christ, wherever his divinity is, there his flesh, which cannot be separated from it, is also; as if that union formed a kind of medium of the two natures, making him to be neither God nor man. So held Eutyches, and after him Servetus. But it is clearly gathered from Scripture that the one person of Christ is composed of two natures, but so that each has its peculiar properties unimpaired. That Eutyches was justly condemned; they will not have the hardihood to deny. It is strange that they attend not to the cause of condemnation–viz. that destroying the distinction between the natures, and insisting only on the unity of person, he converted God into man and man into God. What madness, then, is it to confound heaven with earth, sooner than not withdraw the body of Christ from its heavenly sanctuary?

In regard to the passages, which they adduce, "No man has ascended up to heaven, but he that came down from heaven, even the Son of man which is in heaven" (John 3:13); "The only begotten Son, who is in the bosom of the Father, he hath declared him" (John 1:18), they betray the same stupidity, scouting the communion of properties, which not without reason was formerly invented by holy Fathers. Certainly, when Paul says of the princes of this world that they "crucified the Lord of glory" (1 Corinthians 2:8), he means not that he suffered anything in his divinity, but that Christ, who was rejected and despised, and suffered in the flesh, was likewise God and the Lord of glory. In this way, both the Son of man was in heaven because he was also Christ; and he who, according to the flesh, dwelt as the Son of man on earth, was God in heaven. For this reason, he is said to have descended from heaven in respect of his divinity, not that his divinity quitted heaven to conceal itself in the prison of the body, but because, although he filled all things, it yet resided in the humanity of Christ corporeally, that is, naturally, and in an ineffable manner. There is a trite distinction in the schools, which I hesitate not to quote. Although the whole Christ is everywhere, yet not everything, which is in him, is everywhere.

I wish the Schoolmen had duly weighed the force of this sentence, as it would have obviated their absurd fiction of the corporeal presence of Christ. Therefore, while our whole Mediator is everywhere, he is always present with his people, and in the Supper exhibits his presence in a special manner; yet so, that while he is wholly present, not everything which is in him is present, because, as has been said, in his flesh he will remain in heaven until he come to judgment.

31 The imaginary presence of Transubstantiators, Consubstantiators, and Ubiquitists, contrasted with the orthodox doctrine.

They are greatly mistaken in imagining that there is no presence of the flesh of Christ in the Supper, unless it is placed in the bread. They thus leave nothing for the secret operation of the Spirit, which unites Christ himself to us. Christ does not seem to them to be present unless He descends to us, as if we did not equally gain His presence when He raises us to himself. The only question, therefore, is as to the mode, they placing Christ in the bread, while we deem it unlawful to draw him down from heaven. Which of the two is more correct, let the reader judge. Only have done with the calumny that Christ is withdrawn from his Supper if he lurks not under the covering of bread. For seeing this mystery is heavenly, there is no necessity to bring Christ on the earth that he may be connected with us.

32 The nature of our Savior's true presence explained. The mode of it incomprehensible.

Now, should anyone ask me as to the mode, I will not be ashamed to confess that it is too high a mystery either for my mind to comprehend or my words to express; and to speak more plainly, I rather feel than understand it. The truth of God, therefore, in which I can safely rest, I here embrace without controversy. He declares that His flesh is the meat, His blood the drink, of my soul; I give my soul to Him to be fed with such food. In His sacred Supper, He bids me take, eat, and drink His body and blood under the symbols of bread and wine. I have no doubt that He will truly give and I receive. Only, I reject the absurdities, which appear to be unworthy of the heavenly majesty of Christ and are inconsistent with the reality of His human nature. Since they must also be repugnant to the Word of God, which teaches both that Christ was received into the glory of the heavenly kingdom, so as to be exalted above all the circumstances of the world (Luke 24:26), and no less carefully ascribes to Him the properties belonging to a true human nature. This ought not to seem incredible or contradictory to reason, because, as the whole Kingdom of Christ is spiritual, so whatever he does in his Church is not to be tested by the wisdom of this world. Or, to use the words of Augustine, "This mystery is performed by man like the others, but in a divine manner, and on Earth, but in a heavenly manner." Such, I say, is the corporeal presence, which the nature of the sacrament requires and is here displayed in such power and efficacy that it not only gives our minds undoubted assurance of eternal life, but also secures the immortality of our flesh, since it is now quickened by His immortal flesh, and in a manner shines in His immortality. Those who are carried beyond this with their hyperboles, do nothing more by their extravagancies than obscure the plain and simple truth.

If anyone is not yet satisfied, I would have him here to consider with himself that we are speaking of the sacrament, every part of which ought to have reference to faith. Now by participation of the body, as we have explained, we nourish faith not less richly and abundantly than do those who drag Christ himself from heaven. Still I am free to confess that I repudiate the mixture or transfusion of the flesh of Christ with our soul, which they teach. It is enough for us that Christ, out of the substance of His flesh, breathes life into our souls, nay, diffuses His own life into us, though the real flesh of Christ does not enter us. I may add, that there can be no doubt that the analogy of faith by which Paul enjoins us to test every interpretation of Scripture, is clearly with us in this matter. Let those who oppose a truth so clear, consider to what standard of faith they conform themselves: "Every spirit that confesseth not that Jesus Christ is come in the flesh is not of God" (1 John 4:3; 2 John 7). These men, though they disguise the fact or perceive it not, rob Him of His flesh.

33 Our communion in the blood and flesh of Christ. Spiritual not oral, and yet real. Erroneous view of the Schoolmen.

The same view must be taken of communion, which, according to them, has no existence unless they swallow the flesh of Christ under the bread. But no slight insult is offered to the Spirit if we refuse to believe that it is by His incomprehensible agency that we communicate in the body and blood of Christ. Nay, if the nature of the mystery, as delivered to us, and known to the ancient Church for four hundred years, had been considered, as it deserves, there was more than enough to satisfy us; the door would have been shut against many disgraceful errors. These have kindled up fearful dissensions, by which the Church, both anciently and in our own times, has been miserably vexed; curious men insisting on an extravagant mode of presence to which Scripture gives no countenance. And for a matter thus foolishly and rashly devised they keep up turmoil, as if the including of Christ under the bread were, so to speak, the beginning and end of piety.

It was of primary importance to know how the body of Christ once delivered to us becomes ours, and how we become partakers of His shed blood, because this is to possess the whole of Christ crucified, to enjoy all His blessings. But overlooking these points, in which there was so much importance, nay, neglecting and almost suppressing them, they occupy themselves only with this one perplexing question, How is the body of Christ hidden under the bread, or under the appearance of bread? They falsely pretend that all which we teach concerning spiritual eating is opposed to true and what they call real eating, since we have respect only to the mode of eating. This, according to them, is carnal, since they include Christ under the bread, but according to us is spiritual, inasmuch as the sacred agency of the Spirit is the bond of our union with Christ. Not better founded is the other objection that we attend only to the fruit or effect which believers receive from eating the flesh of Christ. We formerly said that Christ himself is the matter of the Supper, and that the effect follows from this, that by the sacrifice of His death our sins are expiated, by His blood we are washed, and by His resurrection we are raised to the hope of life in heaven.

But a foolish imagination, of which Lombard was the author, perverts their minds, while they think that the sacrament is the eating of the flesh of Christ. His words are, "The sacrament and not the thing are the forms of bread and wine; the sacrament and the thing are the flesh and blood of Christ; the thing and not the sacrament is His mystical flesh." Again a little after, "The thing signified and contained is the proper flesh of Christ; the thing signified and not contained is His mystical body." To His distinction between the flesh of Christ and the power of nourishing which it possesses, I assent. But His maintaining it to be a sacrament, and a sacrament contained under the bread, is an error not to be tolerated.

Hence, has arisen that false interpretation of sacramental eating, because it was imagined that even the wicked and profane, however much alienated from Christ, eat His body. But the very flesh of Christ in the mystery of the Supper is no less a spiritual matter than eternal salvation. Whence we infer, that all who are devoid of the Spirit of

Christ can no more eat the flesh of Christ than drink wine that has no savor. Certainly, Christ is shamefully lacerated, when His body, as lifeless and without any vigour, is prostituted to unbelievers. This is clearly repugnant to His words, "He that eateth my flesh, and drinketh my blood, dwelleth in me, and I in him" (John 6:56). They object that He is not there speaking of sacramental eating.

This I admit, provided they will not always stumble on this stone, that His flesh itself is eaten without any benefit. I should like to know how they confine it after they have eaten. Here, in my opinion, they will find no outlet. But they object, that the ingratitude of man cannot in any respect detract from, or interfere with, faith in the promises of God.

I admit and hold that the power of the sacrament remains entire, however the wicked may labor with all their might to annihilate it. Still, it is one thing to be offered, another to be received. Christ gives this spiritual food and holds forth this spiritual drink to all. Some eat eagerly; others superciliously reject it. Will their rejection cause the meat and drink to lose their nature? They will say that this similitude supports their opinion–viz. that the flesh of Christ, though it is without taste, is still flesh.

But I deny that it can be eaten without the taste of faith, or (if it is more agreeable to speak with Augustine), I deny that men carry away more from the sacrament than they collect in the vessel of faith. Thus nothing is detracted from the sacrament, nay, its reality and efficacy remain unimpaired, although the wicked, after externally partaking of it, go away empty. If, again, they object, that it derogates from the expression, "This is my body." If the wicked receive corruptible bread and nothing besides, it is easy to answer that God wills not that His truth should be recognized in the mere reception, but in the constancy of His goodness, while He is prepared to perform, nay, liberally offers to the unworthy what they reject. The integrity of the sacrament, an integrity, which the whole world cannot violate, lies here, that the flesh and blood of Christ are not less truly given to the unworthy than to the elect believers of God; and yet it is true, that just as the rain falling on the hard rock runs away because it cannot penetrate, so the wicked by their hardness repel the grace of God, and prevent it from reaching them.

We may add that it is no more possible to receive Christ without faith, than it is for seed to germinate in the fire. They ask how Christ can have come for the condemnation of some, unless they unworthily receive Him; but this is absurd, since we nowhere read that they bring death upon themselves by receiving Christ unworthily, but by rejecting Him. They are not aided by the parable in which Christ says that the seed, which fell among thorns, sprung up, but was afterwards choked (Matthew 13:7), because He is there speaking of the effect of a temporary faith, which those who place Judas in this respect on a footing with Peter, do not think necessary to the eating of the flesh and the drinking of the blood of Christ. Nay, their error is refuted by the same parable, when Christ says that some seed fell upon the wayside, and some on stony ground, and yet neither took root.

Hence, it follows that the hardness of believers is an obstacle, which prevents Christ from reaching them. All who would have our salvation to be promoted by this sacrament will find nothing more appropriate than to conduct believers to the fountain, that they may draw life from the Son of God. The dignity is amply enough commended when we hold, that it is a help by which we may be engrafted into the body of Christ, or, already engrafted, may be more and more united to Him, until the union is completed in Heaven. They object that Paul could not have made them guilty of the body and blood of the Lord if they had not partaken of them (1 Corinthians 11:7). I answer that they were not condemned for having eaten, but only for having profaned the ordinance by trampling under foot the pledge, which they ought to have reverently received, the pledge of sacred union with God.

34 This view not favored by Augustine. How the wicked eat the body of Christ. Cyril's sentiments as to the eating of the body of Christ.

Moreover, as among ancient writers, Augustine especially maintained this head of doctrine, that the grace figured by the sacraments is not impaired or made void by the infidelity or malice of men, it will be useful to prove clearly from his words how ignorantly and erroneously those who cast forth the body of Christ to be eaten by dogs, wrest them to their present purpose. Sacramental eating, according to them, is that by which the wicked receive the body and blood of Christ without the agency of the Spirit, or any gracious effect. Augustine, on the contrary, prudently pondering the expression, "Whoso eateth my flesh, and drinketh my blood, hath eternal life " (John 6:54), says: "That is the virtue of the sacrament, and not merely the visible sacrament: the sacrament of him who eats inwardly, not of him who eats outwardly, or merely with the teeth." Hence, he at length concludes that the sacrament of the unity of the body and blood of Christ in the Lord's Supper is set before some for life, before others for destruction, while the matter itself, of which it is the sacrament, is to all for life and to none for destruction, whoever may have been the partaker. Lest anyone should here cavil that by thing is not meant body, but the grace of the Spirit, which may be separated from it, he dissipates these myths by the antithetical epithets, Visible and Invisible. For the body of Christ cannot be included under the former.

Hence, it follows, that unbelievers communicate only in the visible symbol; and the better to remove all doubt, after saying that this bread requires an appetite in the inner man, he adds, "Moses, and Aaron, and Phinehas, and many others who ate manna, pleased God. Why? Because the visible food they understood spiritually, hungered for spiritually, tasted spiritually, and feasted on spiritually. We, too, in the present day, have received visible food: but the sacrament is one thing, the virtue of the sacrament is another." A little after, he says: "And hence, he who remains not in Christ, and in whom Christ remains not, without doubt neither spiritually eats his flesh, nor drinks his blood, though with his teeth he may carnally and visibly press the symbol of his body and blood." Again, we are told that the visible sign is opposed to spiritual eating. This refutes the error that the invisible body of Christ is sacramentally eaten in reality, although not spiritually. We are told, also, that nothing is given to the impure and profane beyond the visible taking of the sign.

Hence, his celebrated saying, that the other disciples ate bread, which was the Lord, whereas Judas ate the bread of the Lord. By this, he clearly excludes unbelievers from participation in his body and blood. He has no other meaning when he says, "Why do you wonder that the bread of Christ was given to Judas, though he consigned him to the devil, when you see, on the contrary, that a messenger of the devil was given to Paul to perfect him in Christ?" He indeed says elsewhere that the bread of the Supper was the body of Christ to those to whom Paul said, "He that eateth and drinketh unworthily, eateth and drinketh damnation to himself; and that it does not follow that they received nothing because they received unworthily." But in what sense he says this, he explains more fully in another passage. For undertaking professedly to explain how the wicked and profane, who profess the faith of Christ, but deny Him in acts; eat the body of Christ; and, indeed, refuting the opinion of some who thought that they ate not only sacramentally, but really, he says: "Neither can they be said to eat the body of Christ, because they are not to be accounted among the members of Christ. For, not to mention other reasons, they cannot be at the same time the members of Christ and the members of a harlot. In fine, when Christ himself says, "He that eateth my flesh, and drinketh my blood, dwelleth in me, and I in him" (John 6:56), he shows what it is to eat the body of Christ, not sacramentally, but in reality. It is to abide in Christ, that Christ may abide in him. For it is just as if he had said, Let not him who abides not in me, and in whom I abide not, say or think that he eats my body or drinks my blood." Let the reader attend to the antithesis between eating sacramentally and eating really, and there will be no doubt.

The same thing he confirms not less clearly in these words: "Prepare not the jaws, but the heart; for which alone the Supper is appointed. We believe in Christ when we receive him in faith: in receiving, we know what we think: we receive a small portion, but our heart is filled: it is not therefore that which is seen, but that which is believed, that feeds." Here, also, he restricts what the wicked take to be the visible sign, and shows that the only way of receiving Christ is by faith. So, also, in another passage, declaring distinctly that the good and the bad communicate by signs, he excludes the latter from the true eating of the flesh of Christ. For had they received the reality, he would not have been altogether silent as to a matter, which was pertinent to the case.

In another passage, speaking of eating, and the fruit of it, he thus concludes: "Then will the body and blood of Christ be life to each, if that which is visibly taken in the sacrament is in reality spiritually eaten, spiritually drunk." Let those, therefore, who make unbelievers partakers of the flesh and blood of Christ, if they would agree with Augustine, set before us the visible body of Christ, since, according to him, the whole truth is spiritual. And certainly, his words imply that sacramental eating, when unbelief excludes the entrance of the reality, is oly equivalent to visible or external eating. But if the body of Christ may be truly and yet not spiritually eaten, what could he mean when he elsewhere says: "Ye are not to eat this body which you see, nor to drink the blood which will be shed by those who are to crucify me? I have committed a certain sacrament to you: it is the spiritual meaning which will give you life." He certainly meant not to deny that the body offered in the Supper is the same as that which Christ offered in sacrifice; but he adverted to the mode of eating–viz. that the body, though received into the celestial glory, breathes life into us by the secret energy of the Spirit.

I admit, indeed, that he often uses the expression, "that the body of Christ is eaten by unbelievers;" but he explains himself by adding, "in the sacrament." And he elsewhere speaks of a spiritual eating, in which our teeth do not chew grace. And, lest my opponents should say that I am trying to overwhelm them with the mass of my quotations, I would ask how they get over this one sentence: "In the elect alone, the sacraments effect what they figure." Certainly, they will not venture to deny, that by the bread in the Supper, the body of Christ is figured.

Hence, it follows, that the reprobate are not allowed to partake of it. That Cyril did not think differently is clear from these words: "As one in pouring melted wax on melted wax mixes the whole together, so it is necessary, when one receives the body and blood of the Lord, to be conjoined with Him, that Christ may be found in him, and he in Christ." From these words, I think it plain that there is no true and real eating by those who only eat the body of Christ sacramentally, seeing the body cannot be separated from its virtue, and that the promises of God do not fail, though, while he ceases not to rain from Heaven, rocks and stones are not penetrated by the moisture.

35 Absurdity of the adoration of sacramental symbols.

This consideration will easily dissuade us from that carnal adoration which some men have, with perverse temerity, introduced into the sacrament, reasoning thus with themselves: If it is body, then it is also soul and divinity which go along with the body, and cannot be separated from it; and, therefore, Christ must there be adored. First, if we deny their pretended concomitance, what will they do? For, as they chiefly insist on the absurdity of separating the body of Christ from His soul and divinity, what sane and sober man can persuade himself that the body of Christ is Christ? They think that they completely establish this by their syllogisms. But since Christ speaks separately of His body and blood, without describing the mode of His presence, how can they in a doubtful matter arrive at the certainty, which they wish? What then? If their consciences are at any time exercised with some more grievous apprehension, will they forthwith set them free and dissolve the apprehensions by their syllogisms? In other words, when they see that no certainty is to be obtained from the Word of God, in which alone our minds can rest and without which they go astray the very first moment when they begin to reason, when they see themselves opposed by the doctrine and practice of the apostles, and that they are supported by no authority but their own, how will they feel?

To such feelings, other sharp stings will be added. What? Was it a matter of little moment to worship God under this form without any express injunction? In a matter relating to the true worship of God, were we thus lightly to act without one Word of Scripture? Had all their thoughts been kept in due subjection to the Word of God, they certainly would have listened to what he himself has said, "Take, eat, and drink," and obeyed the command by which he enjoins us to receive the sacrament, not worship it. Those who receive, without adoration, as commanded by God, are secure that they deviate not from the command. In commencing any work, nothing is better than this security. They have the example of the apostles, of whom we read not that they prostrated themselves and worshipped, but that they sat down, took, and ate. They have the practice of the apostolic Church, where, as Luke relates, believers communicated not in adoration, but in the breaking of bread (Acts 2:42). They have the doctrine of the apostles as taught to the Corinthian Church by Paul, who declares that what he delivered he had received of the Lord (1 Corinthians 11:23).

36 This adoration condemned. A. By Christ himself. B. By the Council of Nice. C. By ancient custom. D. By Scripture. This adoration is mere idolatry.

The object of these remarks is to lead pious readers to reflect how dangerous it is in matters of such difficulty to wander from the simple Word of God to the dreams of our own brain. What has been said above should free us from all scruple in this matter. That the pious soul may duly apprehend Christ in the sacrament, it must rise to heaven. But if the office of the sacrament is to aid the infirmity of the human mind, assisting it in rising upwards, so as to perceive the height of spiritual mysteries, those who stop short at the external sign stray from the right path of seeking Christ. What then? Can we deny that the worship is superstitious when men prostrate themselves before bread that they may therein worship Christ? The Council of Nice undoubtedly intended to meet this evil when it forbade us to give humble heed to the visible signs. And for no other reason was it formerly the custom, before consecration, to call aloud upon the people to raise their hearts, sursum corda.

Scripture itself, also, besides carefully narrating the ascension of Christ, by which He withdrew His bodily presence from our eye and company, that it might make us abandon all carnal thoughts of Him, whenever it makes mention of Him, enjoins us to raise our minds upwards and seek Him in heaven, seated at the right hand of the Father (Colossians 3:2). According to this rule, we should rather have adored Him spiritually in the heavenly glory, than devised that perilous species of adoration replete with gross and carnal ideas of God. Those, therefore, who devised the adoration of the sacrament, not only dreamed it of themselves, without any authority from Scripture, where no mention of it can be shown (it would not have been omitted, had it been agreeable to God); but, disregarding Scripture, forsook the living God, and fabricated a god for themselves, after the lust of their own hearts. For what is idolatry if it is not to worship the gifts instead of the giver? Here the sin is twofold. The honor robbed from God is transferred to the creature, and God is dishonored by the pollution and profanation of His own goodness, while His holy sacrament is converted into an execrable idol. Let us, on the contrary, that we may not fall into the same pit, wholly confine our eyes, ears, hearts, minds, and tongues, to the sacred doctrine of God. For this is the school of the Holy Spirit, that best of masters, in which such progress is made, that while nothing is to be acquired anywhere else, we must willingly be ignorant of whatever is not there taught.

37 This adoration inconsistent with the nature and institution of the sacrament. Ends for which the sacrament was instituted.

Then, as superstition, when once it has passed the proper bounds, has no end to its errors, men went much further; for they devised rites altogether alien from the institution of the Supper, and to such a degree that they paid divine honors to the sign. They say that their veneration is paid to Christ. First, if this were done in the Supper, I would say that that adoration only is legitimate which stops not at the sign, but rises to Christ sitting in Heaven. Now, under what pretext do they say that they honor Christ in that bread, when they have no promise of this nature? They consecrate the host, as they call it, and carry it about in solemn show, and formally exhibit it to be admired, reverenced, and invoked. I ask by what virtue they think it duly consecrated. They will quote the words, "This is my body."

I, on the contrary, will object, that it was at the same time said, "Take, eat." Nor will I count the other passage as nothing; for I hold that since the promise is annexed to the command, the former is so included under the latter, that it cannot possibly be separated from it. This will be made clearer by an example. God gave a command when He said, "Call upon me," and added a promise, "I will deliver thee" (Psalm 50:15). Should anyone invoke Peter or Paul, and found on this promise, will not all exclaim that he does it in error? And what else, pray, do those do who, disregarding the command to eat, fasten on the mutilated promise, "This is my body," that they may pervert it to rites alien from the institution of Christ? Let us remember, therefore, that this promise has been given to those who observe the command connected with it, and that those who transfer the sacrament to another end have no countenance from the Word of God. We formerly showed how the mystery of the sacred Supper contributes to our faith in God.

But since the Lord not only reminds us of this great gift of his goodness, as we formerly explained, but passes it from hand to hand, and urges us to recognize it, he, at the same time, admonishes us not to be ungrateful for the kindness thus bestowed, but rather to proclaim it with such praise as is meet, and celebrate it with thanksgiving. Accordingly, when He delivered the institution of the sacrament to the apostles, He taught them to do it in remembrance of Him, which Paul interprets, "to show forth His death" (1 Corinthians 11:26). And this is, that all should publicly and with one mouth confess that all our confidence of life and salvation is placed in our Lord's death, that we ourselves may glorify Him by our confession, and by our example excite others also to give Him glory.

Here, again, we see what the aim of the sacrament is–namely, to keep us in remembrance of Christ's death. When we are ordered to show forth the Lord's death until He come again, all that is meant is, that we should, with confession of the mouth, proclaim what our faith has recognized in the sacrament–viz. that the death of Christ is our life. This is the second use of the sacrament, and relates to outward confession.

38 Ends for which the sacrament was instituted.

Thirdly, The Lord intended it to be a kind of exhortation, than which no other could urge or animate us more strongly, both to purity and holiness of life, and also to charity, peace, and concord. For the Lord there communicates His body, so that He may become altogether one with us, and we with him. Moreover, since He has only one body of which He makes us all to be partakers, we must necessarily, by this participation, all become one body. This unity is represented by the bread, which is exhibited in the sacrament. As it is composed of many grains, so mingled together, that one cannot be distinguished from another; so ought our minds to be so cordially united, as not to allow of any dissension or division. This I prefer giving in the words of Paul: "The cup of blessing which we bless, is it not the communion of the blood of Christ? The bread which we break, is it not the communion of the body of Christ? For we being many, are one bread and one body, for we are all partakers of that one bread" (1 Corinthians 10:15, 16).

We shall have profited admirably in the sacrament if the thought shall have been engraved on our minds, that none of our brethren is hurt, despised, rejected, injured, or in any way offended, without our, at the same time, hurting, despising, and injuring Christ; that we cannot have dissension with our brethren, without at the same time dissenting from Christ; that we cannot love Christ without loving our brethren; that the same care we take of our own body we ought to take of that of our brethren, who are members of our body; that as no part of our body suffers pain without extending to the other parts, so every evil which our brother suffers ought to excite our compassion. Wherefore Augustine appropriately often terms this sacrament the bond of charity. What stronger stimulus could be employed to excite mutual charity, than when Christ, presenting himself to us, not only invites us by His example to give and devote ourselves mutually to each other, but inasmuch as He makes himself common to all, also makes us all to be one in Him.

39 True nature of the sacrament, contrasted with the Popish observance of it.

This most admirably confirms what I elsewhere said—viz. that there cannot be a right administration of the Supper without the Word. Any utility, which we derive from the Supper, requires the Word. Whether we are to be confirmed in faith, exercised in confession, or aroused to duty, there is need of preaching. Nothing, therefore, can be more preposterous than to convert the Supper into a dumb action. This is done under the tyranny of the Pope, the whole effect of consecration being made to depend on the intention of the priest, as if it in no way concerned the people, to whom especially the mystery ought to have been explained. This error has originated from not observing that those promises by which consecration is effected are intended, not for the elements themselves, but for those who receive them. Christ does not address the bread and tell it to become His body, but bids His disciples eat, and promises them the communion of His body and blood. And, according to the arrangement, which Paul makes, the promises are to be offered to believers along with the bread and the cup. Thus, indeed, it is. We are not to imagine some magical incantation, and think it sufficient to mutter the words, as if they were heard by the elements; but we are to regard those words as a living sermon, which is to edify the hearers, penetrate their minds, being impressed and seated in their hearts, and exert its efficacy in the fulfillment of that which it promises. For these reasons, it is clear that the setting apart of the sacrament, as some insist, that an extraordinary distribution of it may be made to the sick, is useless. They will either receive it without hearing the words of the institution read, or the minister will conjoin the true explanation of the mystery with the sign. In the silent dispensation, there is abuse and defect. If the promises are narrated, and the mystery is expounded, that those who are to receive may receive with advantage, it cannot be doubted that this is the true consecration. What then becomes of that other consecration, the effect of which reaches even to the sick? But those who do so have the example of the early Church. I confess it; but in so important a matter, where error is so dangerous, nothing is safer than to follow the truth.

40 Nature of an unworthy approach to the Lord's Table The great danger of it. The proper remedy in serious self-examination.

Moreover, as we see that this sacred bread of the Lord's Supper is spiritual food, is sweet and savory, not less than salutary, to the pious worshippers of God, on tasting which they feel that Christ is their life, are disposed to give thanks, and exhorted to mutual love; so, on the other hand, it is converted into the most noxious poison to all whom it does not nourish and confirm in the faith, nor urge to thanksgiving and charity. For, just as corporeal food, when received into a stomach subject to morbid humors, becomes itself vitiated and corrupted, and rather hurts than nourishes, so this spiritual food also, if given to a soul polluted with malice and wickedness, plunges it into greater ruin, not indeed by any defect in the food, but because to the "defiled and unbelieving is nothing pure" (Titus 1:15), however much it may be sanctified by the blessing of the Lord. For, as Paul says, "Whosoever shall eat this bread, and drink this cup of the Lord, unworthily, shall be guilty of the body and blood of the Lord;" "eateth and drinketh damnation to himself, not discerning the Lord's body" (1 Corinthians 11:27, 29).

For men of this description, who without any spark of faith, without any zeal for charity, rush forward like swine to seize the Lord's Supper, do not at all discern the Lord's body. For, inasmuch as they do not believe that body to be their life, they put every possible affront upon it, stripping it of all its dignity, and profane and contaminate it by so receiving; inasmuch as while alienated and estranged from their brethren, they dare to mingle the sacred symbol of Christ's body with their dissensions. No thanks to them if the body of Christ is not rent and torn to pieces. Wherefore they are justly held guilty of the body and blood of the Lord, which, with sacrilegious impiety, they so vilely pollute. By this unworthy eating, they bring judgment on themselves. For while they have no faith in Christ, yet, by receiving the sacrament, they profess to place their salvation only in Him, and abjure all other confidence.

Wherefore they themselves are their own accusers; they bear witness against themselves; they seal their own condemnation. Next being divided and separated by hatred and ill will from their brethren, that is, from the members of Christ, they have no part in Christ, and yet they declare that the only safety is to communicate with Christ, and be united to him.

For this reason Paul commands a man to examine himself before he eats of that bread, and drinks of that cup (l Corinthians 11:28). By this, as I understand, he means that each individual should descend into himself, and consider, first, whether, with inward confidence of heart, he leans on the salvation obtained by Christ, and with confession of the mouth, acknowledges it; and, secondly, whether with zeal for purity and holiness he aspires to imitate Christ; whether, after His example, he is prepared to give himself to his brethren, and to hold himself in common with those with whom he has Christ in common; whether, as he himself is regarded by Christ, he in his turn regards all his brethren as members of his body, or, like his members, desires to cherish, defend, and assist them, not that the duties of faith and charity can now be perfected in us, but because it behooves us to contend and seek, with all our heart, daily to increase our faith.

41 The spurious examination introduced by the Papists Refutation.

In seeking to prepare for eating worthily, men have often dreadfully harassed and tortured miserable consciences, and yet have not attained the end. They have said that those eat worthily who are in a state of grace. Being in a state of grace, they have interpreted to be pure and free from all sin. By this definition, all the men that ever have been, and are upon the Earth, were debarred from the use of this sacrament. For if we are to seek our worthiness from ourselves, it is all over with us, only despair and fatal ruin await us. Though we struggle to the utmost, we will not only make no progress, but then be most unworthy after we have labored most to make ourselves worthy. To cure this ulcer, they have devised a mode of procuring worthiness–viz. after having, as far as we can, made an examination, and taken an account of all our actions, to expiate our unworthiness by contrition, confession, and satisfaction. Of the nature of this expiation, we have spoken at the proper place (Book 3, chapter 4, sections 2, 17, 27). As far as regards our present object, I say that such things give poor and evanescent comfort to alarmed and downcast consciences, struck with terror at their sins. For if the Lord, by His prohibition, admits none to partake of His Supper but the righteous and innocent, every man would require to be cautious before feeling secure of that righteousness of his own which he is told that God requires. But how are we to be assured that those who have done what in them lay have discharged their duty to God? Even were we assured of this, who would venture to assure himself that he had done what in him lay? Thus, there being no certain security for our worthiness, access to the Supper would always be excluded by the fearful interdict, "He that eateth and drinketh unworthily, eateth and drinketh damnation to himself."

42 The nature of Christian examination.

It is now easy to judge what is the nature, and who is the author, of that doctrine which prevails in the Papacy, and which, by its inhuman austerity, deprives and robs wretched sinners, oppressed with sorrow and trembling, of the consolation of this sacrament, a sacrament in which all that is delightful in the Gospel was set before them. Certainly, the devil could have no shorter method of destroying men than by thus infatuating them, and so excluding them from the taste and savor of this food with which their most merciful Father in Heaven had been pleased to feed them. Therefore, lest we should rush over such a precipice, let us remember that this sacred feast is medicine to the sick, comfort to the sinner, and bounty to the poor; while to the healthy, the righteous, and the rich, if any such could be found, it would be of no value. For while Christ is therein given us for food, we perceive that without Him we fail, pine, and waste away, just as hunger destroys the vigour of the body. Next, as He is given for life, we perceive that without Him we are certainly dead. Wherefore, the best and only worthiness, which we can bring to God, is to offer him our own vileness, and, if I may so speak, unworthiness, that his mercy may make us worthy; to despond in ourselves, that we may be consoled in him; to humble ourselves, that we may be elevated by him; to accuse ourselves, that we may be justified by him; to aspire, moreover, to the unity which he recommends in the Supper; and, as he makes us all one in himself, to desire to have all one soul, one heart, one tongue.

If we ponder and meditate on these things, we may be shaken, but will never be overwhelmed by such considerations as these, how shall we, who are devoid of all good, polluted by the defilements of sin, and half dead, worthily eat the body of the Lord? We shall rather consider that we, who are poor, are coming to a benevolent giver, sick to a physician, sinful to the author of righteousness, in fine, dead to Him who gives life; that worthiness which is commanded by God, consists especially in faith, which places all things in Christ, nothing in ourselves, and in charity, charity which, though imperfect, it may be sufficient to offer to God, that he may increase it, since it cannot be fully rendered. Some, concurring with us in holding that worthiness consists in faith and charity, have widely erred in regard to the measure of worthiness, demanding a perfection of faith to which nothing can be added, and a charity equivalent to that which Christ manifested towards us. And in this way, just as the other class, they debar all men from access to this sacred feast. For, were their view well founded, everyone who receives must receive unworthily, since all, without exception, are guilty, and chargeable with imperfection. And certainly it would be too stupid, not to say idiotic, to require to the receiving of the sacrament a perfection, which would render the sacrament vain and superfluous, because it was not instituted for the perfect, but for the infirm and weak, to stir up, excite, stimulate, and exercise the feeling of faith and charity, and at the same time, correct the deficiency of both.

43 External rites in the administration of the Supper. Many of them indifferent.

In regard to the external form of the ordinance, whether or not believers are to take into their hands and divide among themselves, or each is to eat what is given to him: whether they are to return the cup to the deacon or hand it to their neighbor; whether the bread is to be leavened or unleavened, and the wine to be red or white, is of no consequence. These things are indifferent, and left free to the Church, though it is certain that it was the custom of the ancient Church for all to receive into their hand. And Christ said, "Take this, and divide it among yourselves" (Luke 22:17). History relates that leavened and ordinary bread was used before the time of Alexander the Bishop of Rome, who was the first that was delighted with unleavened bread: for what reason I see not, unless it was to draw the wondering eyes of the populace by the novelty of the spectacle, more than to train them in sound religion. I appeal to all who have the least zeal for piety, whether they do not evidently perceive both how much more brightly the glory of God is here displayed, and how much more abundant spiritual consolation is felt by believers than in these rigid and histrionic follies, which have no other use than to impose on the gazing populace. They call it restraining the people by religion, when, stupid and infatuated, they are drawn hither and thither by superstition. Should anyone choose to defend such inventions by antiquity, I am aware how ancient is the use of chrism and exorcism in baptism, and how, not long after the age of the apostles, the Supper was tainted with adulteration; such, indeed, is the forwardness of human confidence, which cannot restrain itself, but is always sporting and wantoning in the mysteries of God. But let us remember that God sets so much value on obedience to His word, that, by it, He would have us to judge His angels and the whole world.

All this mass of ceremonies being abandoned, the sacrament might be celebrated in the most becoming manner, if it were dispensed to the Church very frequently, at least once a week. The commencement should be with public prayer; next, a sermon should be delivered: then the minister, having placed bread and wine on the table, should read the institution of the Supper. He should next explain the promises which are therein given; and, at the same time, keep back from communion all those who are debarred by the prohibition of the Lord. He should afterwards pray that the Lord, with the kindness with which He has bestowed this sacred food upon us, would also form and instruct us to receive it with faith and gratitude; and, as we are of ourselves unworthy, would make us worthy of the feast by His mercy. Here, either a psalm should be sung, or something read, while the faithful, in order, communicate at the sacred feast, the minister breaking the bread, and giving it to the people. The Supper being ended, an exhortation should be given to sincere faith, and confession of faith, to charity, and lives becoming Christians. Lastly, thanks should be offered, and the praises of God should be sung. This being done, the Church should be dismissed in peace.

44 Duty of frequent communion. This proved by the practice of the Church in its purer state, and by the canons of the early bishops.

What we have hitherto said of the sacrament abundantly shows that it was not instituted to be received customarily once a year, but that all Christians might have it in frequent use, and frequently call to mind the sufferings of Christ, thereby sustaining and confirming their faith: stirring themselves up to sing the praises of God and to proclaim His goodness; cherishing and testifying towards each other that mutual charity, the bond of which they see in the unity of the body of Christ. As often as we communicate in the symbol of our Savior's body, as if a pledge were given and received, we mutually bind ourselves to all the offices of love, that none of us may do anything to offend his brother, or omit anything by which he can assist him when necessity demands, and opportunity occurs. That such was the practice of the Apostolic Church we are informed by Luke in the Acts, when he says, "They continued steadfastly in the apostles' doctrine and fellowship, and in breaking of bread, and in prayers" (Acts 2:42). Thus, we ought always to provide that no meeting of the Church is held without the Word, prayer, the dispensation of the Supper, and alms. We may gather from Paul that this was the order observed by the Corinthians, and it is certain that this was the practice many ages after. Hence, by the ancient canons, which are attributed to Anacletus and Calixtus, after the consecration was made, all were to communicate who did not wish to be without the pale of the Church. And in those ancient canons, which bear the name of Apostolical, it is said that those who continue not to the end, and partake not of the sacred communion, are to be corrected, as causing disquiet to the Church. In the Council of Antioch it was decreed, that those who enter the Church, hear the Scriptures, and abstain from communion, are to be removed from the Church until they amend their fault. And although, in the first Council of Tholouse, this was mitigated, or at least stated in milder terms, yet there also it was decreed, that those who after hearing the sermon, never communicated, were to be admonished, and if they still abstained after admonition, were to be excluded.

45 Frequent communion in the time of Augustine. The neglect of it censured by Chrysostom.

By these enactments, holy men wished to retain and ensure the use of frequent communion, as handed down by the apostles themselves; and which, while it was most salutary to believers, they saw gradually falling into desuetude by the negligence of the people. Of his own age, Augustine testifies: "The sacrament of the unity of our Lord's body is, in some places, provided daily, and in others at certain intervals, at the Lord's table; and at that table some partake to life, and others to destruction." And in the first Epistle to Januarius, he says, "Some communicate daily in the body and blood of the Lord; others receive it on certain days: in some places, not a day intervenes on which it is not offered: in others, it is offered only on the Sabbath and the Lord's Day: in others, on the Lord's Day only." But since, as we have said, the people were sometimes remiss, holy men urged them with severe rebukes, that they might not seem to connive at their sluggishness. Of this, we have an example in Chrysostom, on the Epistle to the Ephesians. "It was not said to him who dishonored the feast, Why have you not taken your seat? But, How camest thou in?" (Matthew 22:12). Whoever partakes not of the sacred rites is wicked and impudent in being present: should anyone who was invited to a feast come in, wash his hands, take his seat, and seem to prepare to eat, and thereafter taste nothing, would he not, I ask, insult both the feast and the entertainer? So you, standing among those who prepare themselves by prayer to take the sacred food, profess to be one of the number by the mere fact of your not going away, and yet you do not partake, –would it not have been better not to have made your appearance? I am unworthy, you say. Then neither were you worthy of the communion of prayer, which is the preparation for taking the sacred mystery."

46 The Popish injunction to communicate once a year an execrable invention.

Most assuredly, the custom, which prescribes communion once a year, is an invention of the devil, by what instrumentality soever it may have been introduced. They say that Zephyrinus was the author of the decree, though it is not possible to believe that it was the same as we now have it. It may be that as times were then, he did not, by his ordinance, consult ill for the Church. For there cannot be a doubt that at that time the sacred Supper was dispensed to the faithful at every meeting; nor can it be doubted that a great part of them communicated. But as it scarcely ever happened that all could communicate at the same time, and it was necessary that those, who were mingled with the profane and idolaters, should testify their faith by some external symbol, this holy man, with a view to order and government, had appointed that day, that on it the whole of Christendom might give a confession of their faith by partaking of the Lord's Supper. The ordinance of Zephyrinus, which was otherwise good, posterity perverted, when they made a fixed law of one communion in the year. The consequence is that almost all, when they have once communicated, as if they were discharged as to all the rest of the year, sleep on secure. It ought to have been far otherwise. Each week, at least, the table of the Lord ought to have been spread for the company of Christians, and the promises declared on which we might then spiritually feed. No one, indeed, ought to be forced, but all ought to be exhorted and stimulated; the torpor of the sluggish, also, ought to be rebuked, that all, like persons famishing, should come to the feast. It was not without cause, therefore, I complained, at the outset, that this practice had been introduced by the wile of the devil; a practice which, in prescribing one day in the year, makes the whole year one of sloth. We see, indeed, that this perverse abuse had already crept in by the time of Chrysostom; but we, also, at the same time, see how much it displeased him. For he complains in bitter terms, in the passage which I lately quoted, that there is so great an inequality in this matter, that they did not approach often, at other times of the year, even when prepared, but only at Easter, though unprepared. Then he exclaims, "O custom! O presumption! In vain, then, is the daily oblation made: in vain do we stand at the altar. There is none who partakes along with us." So far is he from having approved the practice by interposing his authority to it.

47 Communion in one kind proved to be an invention of Satan.

From the same forge proceeded another constitution, which snatched or robbed a half of the Supper from the greater part of the people of God—namely, the symbol of blood, which, interdicted to laics and profane (such are the titles which they give to God's heritage), became the peculiar possession of a few shaven and anointed individuals. The edict of the eternal God is that all are to drink. This an upstart dares to antiquate and abrogate by a new and contrary law, proclaiming that all are not to drink. And that such legislators may not seem to fight against their God without any ground, they make a pretext of the dangers which might happen if the sacred cup were given indiscriminately to all: as if these had not been observed and provided for by the eternal wisdom of God. Then they reason acutely, forsooth, that the one is sufficient for the two. For if the body is, as they say, the whole Christ, who cannot be separated from His body, then the blood includes the body by concomitance. Here we see how far our sense accords with God, when to any extent whatever it begins to rage and wanton with loosened reins. The Lord, pointing to the bread, says, "This is my body." Then pointing to the cup, He calls it His blood. The audacity of human reason objects and says, the bread is the blood, the wine is the body, as if the Lord had without reason distinguished His body from His blood, both by words and signs; and it had ever been heard that the body of Christ or the blood is called God and man. Certainly, if He had meant to designate himself wholly, He might have said, It is I, according to the Scriptural mode of expression, and not, "This is my body," "This is my blood." But wishing to succor the weakness of our faith, he placed the cup apart from the bread, to show that he suffices not less for drink than for food. Now, if one part be taken away, we can only find the half of the elements in what remains. Therefore, though it was true, as they pretend, that the blood is in the bread, and, on the other hand, the body in the cup, by concomitance, yet they deprive the pious of that confirmation of faith which Christ delivered as necessary. Bidding adieu, therefore, to their subtleties, let us retain the advantage, which, by the ordinance of Christ, is obtained by a double pledge.

48 Subterfuges of the Papists refuted.

I am aware, indeed, how the ministers of Satan, whose usual practice is to hold the Scriptures in derision, here cavil. First, they allege that from a simple fact we are not to draw a rule, which is to be perpetually obligatory on the Church. But they state an untruth when they call it a simple fact. For Christ not only gave the cup, but appointed that the apostles should do so in future. For His words contain the command, "Drink ye all of it." And Paul relates that it was so done, and recommends it as a fixed institution. Another subterfuge is that the apostles alone were admitted by Christ to partake of this sacred Supper, because He had already selected and chosen them to the priesthood. I wish they would answer the five following questions, which they cannot evade, and which easily refute them and their lies. First, by what oracle was this solution so much at variance with the Word of God revealed to them? Scripture mentions twelve who sat down with Jesus, but it does not so derogate from the dignity of Christ as to call them priests. Of this appellation, we shall afterwards speak in its own place. Although He then gave to twelve, He commanded them to "do this;" in other words, to distribute thus among themselves. Secondly, Why during that purer age, from the days of the apostles downward for a thousand years, did all, without exception, partake of both symbols? Did the primitive Church not know who the guests were whom Christ would have admitted to His Supper? It would be the most shameless impudence to carp and quibble here. We have existing, ecclesiastical histories; we have the writings of the Fathers, which furnish clear proof of this fact.

"The flesh," says Tertullian, "feeds on the body and blood of Christ, that the soul may be satiated by God." "How," says Ambrose to Theodosius, "will you receive the sacred body of the Lord with such hands? How will you have the boldness to put the cup of precious blood to your lips?" Jerome speaks of "the priests who perform the Eucharist and distribute the Lord's blood to the people." Chrysostom says, "Not as under the ancient law the priest ate a part and the people a part, but one body and one cup is set before all. All the things which belong to the Eucharist are common to the priest and the people." The same thing is attested by Augustine in numerous passages.

49 The practice of the early Church further considered.

But why dispute about a fact, which is perfectly notorious? Look at all Greek and Latin writers. Passages of the same kind everywhere occur. Nor did this practice fall into desuetude so long as there was one particle of integrity in the Church. Gregory, whom you may with justice call the last Bishop of Rome, says that it was observed in his age. "What the blood of the Lamb is you have learned, not by hearing, but by drinking it. His blood is poured into the mouths of the faithful." Nay, four hundred years after His death, when all things had degenerated, the practice remained. Nor was it regarded as the custom merely, but as an inviolable law. Reverence for the divine institution was then maintained, and they had no doubt of its being sacrilege to separate what the Lord had joined. For Gelasius thus speaks: "We find that some taking only the portion of the sacred body, abstain from the cup. Undoubtedly let those persons, as they seem entangled by some strange superstition, either receive the whole sacrament, or be debarred from the whole. For the division of this mystery is not made without great sacrilege." Reasons were given by Cyprian, which surely ought to weigh with Christian minds. "How," says he, "do we teach or incite them to shed their blood in confessing Christ, if we deny His blood to those who are to serve; or how do we make them fit for the cup of martyrdom, if we do not previously admit them by right of communion in the Church, to drink the cup of the Lord?" The attempt of the Canonists to restrict the decree of Gelasius to priests is a cavil too puerile to deserve refutation.

50 Conclusion.

Thirdly, why did our Savior say of the bread simply, "Take, eat," and of the cup, "drink ye all of it," as if He had purposely intended to provide against the wile of Satan? Fourthly, If, as they will have it, the Lord honored priests only with His Supper, what man would ever have dared to call strangers, whom the Lord had excluded, to partake of it, and to partake of a gift which he had not in his power, without any command from Him who alone could give it? Nay, what presumption do they show in the present day in distributing the symbol of Christ's body to the common people, if they have no command or example from the Lord? Fifthly, Did Paul lie when he said to the Corinthians, "I have received of the Lord that which also I delivered unto you?" (1 Corinthians 11:23). The thing delivered, he afterwards declares to be, that all should communicate promiscuously in both symbols. But if Paul received of the Lord that all were to be admitted without distinction, let those who drive away almost the whole people of God see from whom they have received, since they cannot now pretend to have their authority from God, with whom there is not "yea and nay" (2 Corinthians 1:19, 20). And yet, these abominations they dare to cloak with the name of the Church, and defend under this pretence, as if those Antichrists were the Church who so licentiously trample under foot, waste, and abrogate the doctrine and institutions of Christ, or as if the Apostolic Church, in which religion flourished in full vigour, were not the Church.

Chapter 18

OF THE POPISH MASS. HOW IT NOT ONLY PROFANES, BUT ANNIHILATES THE LORD'S SUPPER.

The principal heads of this chapter are, –I. The abomination of the Mass, section 1. Its manifold impiety included under five heads, sections 2-7. Its origin described, sections 8, 9. II. Of the name of sacrifice, which the ancients gave to the holy Supper, sections 10-12. An apposite discussion on sacrifice, refuting the arguments of the Papists for the sacrifice of the Mass, sections 13-18. III. A summary of the doctrine of the Christian Church respecting sacraments, paving the way for the subsequent discussion of the five sacraments, falsely so called, sections 19, 20.

Sections

1. The chief of all the abominations set up in opposition to the Lord's Supper is the Papal Mass. A description of it.

2. Its impiety is five-fold. A. Its intolerable blasphemy in substituting priests to Him the only Priest. Objections of the Papists answered.

3. Impiety of the Mass continued. B. It overthrows the Cross of Christ by setting up an altar. Objections answered.

4. Other objections answered.

5. Impiety of the Mass continued. C. It banishes the remembrance of Christ's death. It crucifies Christ afresh. Objections answered.

6. Impiety of the Mass continued. D. It robs us of the benefit of Christ's death.

7. Impiety of the Mass continued. E. It abolishes the Lord's Supper. In the Supper, the Father offers Christ to us; in the Mass, priestlings offer Christ to the Father. The Supper is a sacrament common to all Christians; the Mass confined to one priest.

8. The origin of the Mass. Private masses an impious profanation of the Supper.

9. This abomination unknown to the purer Church. It has no foundation in the Word of God.

10. Second part of the chapter. Some of the ancients call the Supper a sacrifice, but not propitiatory, as the Papists do the Mass. This proved by passages from Augustine.

11. Some of the ancients seem to have declined too much to the shadows of the law.

12. Great distinction to be made between the Mosaic sacrifices and the Lord's Supper, which is called a eucharistic sacrifice. Same rule in this discussion.

13. The terms sacrifice and priest. Different kinds of sacrifices. A. Propitiatory. B. Eucharistic. None propitiatory but the death of Christ.

14. The Lord's Supper not properly called a propitiatory sacrifice, still less can the Popish Mass be so called. Those who mutter over the mass cannot be called priests.

15. Their vanity proved even by Plato.

16. To the eucharistic class of sacrifice belong all offices of piety and charity. This species of sacrifice has no connection with the appeasing of God.

17. Prayer, thanksgiving, and other exercises of piety, called sacrifices. In this sense, the Lord's Supper called the eucharist. In the same sense, all believers are priests.

18. Conclusion. Names given to the Mass.

19. Last part of the chapter, recapitulating the views, which ought to be held concerning baptism and the Lord's Supper. Why the Lord's Supper is, and Baptism is not, repeated.

20. Christians should be contented with these two sacraments. They are abolished by the sacraments decreed by men.

1 The chief of all the abominations set up in opposition to the Lord's Supper is the Papal Mass. A description of it.

By these and similar inventions, Satan has attempted to adulterate and envelop the sacred Supper of Christ as with thick darkness, that its purity might not be preserved in the Church. But the head of this horrid abomination was, when he raised a sign by which it was not only obscured and perverted, but altogether obliterated and abolished, vanished away and disappeared from the memory of man—namely, when, with most pestilential error, he blinded almost the whole world into the belief that the mass was a sacrifice and oblation for obtaining the remission of sins. I say nothing as to the way in which the sounder Schoolmen at first received this dogma. I leave them with their puzzling subtleties, which, however they may be defended by caviling, are to be repudiated by all good men, because, all they do is to envelop the brightness of the Supper in great darkness.

Bidding adieu to them, therefore, let my readers understand that I am here combating that opinion with which the Roman Antichrist and his prophets have imbued the whole world— viz. that the mass is a work by which the priest who offers Christ, and the others who in the oblation receive him, gain merit with God, or that it is an expiatory victim by which they regain the favor of God. And this is not merely the common opinion of the vulgar, but the very act has been so arranged as to be a kind of propitiation, by which satisfaction is made to God for the living and the dead. This is also expressed by the words employed, and the same thing may be inferred from daily practice. I am aware how deeply this plague has struck its roots; under what a semblance of good it conceals its true character, bearing the name of Christ before it, and making many believe that under the single name of Mass is comprehended the whole sum of faith. But when it shall have been most clearly proved by the word of God, that this mass, however glossed and splendid, offers the greatest insult to Christ, suppresses and buries His Cross, consigns His death to oblivion, takes away the benefit that it was designed to convey, enervates and dissipates the sacrament, by which the remembrance of His death was retained, will its roots be so deep that this most powerful axe, the Word of God, will not cut it down and destroy it? Will any semblance be so specious that this light will not expose the lurking evil?

2 Its impiety is five-fold. A. Its intolerable blasphemy in substituting priests to Him the only Priest. Objections of the Papists answered.

Let us show, therefore, as was proposed in the first place, that in the mass, intolerable blasphemy and insult are offered to Christ. For He was not appointed Priest and Pontiff by the Father for a time merely, as priests were appointed under the Old Testament. Since their life was mortal, their priesthood could not be immortal, and hence there was need of successors, who might always be substituted in the room of the dead. But Christ being immortal, had not the least occasion to have a vicar substituted for Him. Wherefore He was appointed by His Father a priest forever, after the order of Melchizedek, that He might eternally exercise a permanent priesthood. This mystery had been typified long before in Melchizedek, whom Scripture, after once introducing as the priest of the living God, never afterwards mentions, as if he had had no end of life. In this way, Christ is said to be a priest after His order. But those who sacrifice daily must necessarily give the charge of their oblations to priests, whom they surrogate as the vicars and successors of Christ. By this surrogacy, they not only rob Christ of His honor, and take from Him the prerogative of an eternal priesthood, but attempt to remove Him from the right hand of His Father, where he cannot sit immortal without being an eternal priest. Nor let them allege that their priestlings are not substituted for Christ, as if He were dead, but are only substitutes in that eternal priesthood, which therefore ceases not to exist. The words of the apostle are too stringent to leave them any means of evasion–viz. "They truly were many priests, because they were not suffered to continue by reason of death: but this man, because he continueth ever, hath an unchangeable priesthood" (Hebrews 7:23, 24).

Yet, such is their dishonesty, that to defend their impiety they arm themselves with the example of Melchizedek. As he is said to have "brought forth (obtulisse) bread and wine" (Genesis 14:18), they infer that it was a prelude to their mass, as if there was any resemblance between him and Christ in the offering of bread and wine. This is too silly and frivolous to need refutation. Melchizedek gave bread and wine to Abraham and his companions, that he might refresh them when worn out with the march and the battle. What has this to do with sacrifice? The humanity of the holy king is praised by Moses: these men absurdly coin a mystery of which there is no mention. They, however, put another gloss upon their error, because it is immediately added, he was "priest of the most high God." I answer, that they erroneously wrest to bread and wine what the apostle refers to blessing. "This Melchizedek, king of Salem, priest of the most high God, who met Abraham," "and blessed him." Hence, the same apostle (and a better interpreter cannot be desired) infers his excellence. "Without all contradiction, the less is blessed of the better." But if the oblation of Melchizedek were a figure of the sacrifice of the mass, I ask, would the apostle, who goes into the minutest details, have forgotten a matter so grave and serious? Now, however they quibble, it is in vain for them to attempt to destroy the argument which is adduced by the apostle himself–viz. that the right and honor of the priesthood has ceased among mortal men, because Christ, who is immortal, is the one perpetual priest.

3 Impiety of the Mass continued. B. It overthrows the Cross of Christ by setting up an altar. Objections answered.

Another iniquity chargeable on the mass is, that it sinks and buries the Cross and passion of Christ. This much, indeed, is most certain, –the Cross of Christ is overthrown the moment an altar is erected. For if, on the Cross, He offered himself in sacrifice that He might sanctify us forever, and purchase eternal redemption for us, undoubtedly the power and efficacy of His sacrifice continues without end. Otherwise, we should not think more honorably of Christ than of the oxen and calves, which were sacrificed under the law, the offering of which is proved to have been weak and inefficacious because often repeated. Wherefore, it must be admitted, either that the sacrifice, which Christ offered on the Cross, wanted the power of eternal cleansing, or that He performed this once forever by His one sacrifice.

Accordingly, the apostle says, "Now once in the end of the world hath He appeared to put away sin by the sacrifice of himself." Again: "By the which act we are sanctified through the offering of the body of Jesus Christ once for all." Again: "For by one offering He hath perfected forever them that are sanctified." To this He subjoins the celebrated passage: "Now, where remission of these is, there is no more offering for sin."

The same thing Christ intimated by His latest voice, when, on giving up the ghost, he exclaimed, "It is finished." We are accustomed to observe the last words of the dying as oracular. Christ, when dying, declares, that by His one sacrifice is perfected and fulfilled whatever was necessary to our salvation. To such a sacrifice, whose perfection He so clearly declared, shall we, as if it were imperfect, presume daily to append innumerable sacrifices? Since the sacred Word of God not only affirms, but proclaims and protests, that this sacrifice was once accomplished, and remains eternally in force, do not those who demand another, charge it with imperfection and weakness? But to what tends the mass, which has been established, that a hundred thousand sacrifices may be performed every day, but just to bury and suppress the passion of our Lord, in which He offered himself to His Father as the only victim? Who but a blind man does not see that it was satanic audacity to oppose a truth so clear and transparent?

I am aware of the impostures by which the father of lies is wont to cloak his fraud–viz. that the sacrifices are not different or various, but that the one sacrifice is repeated. Such smoke is easily dispersed. The apostle, during his whole discourse, contends not only that there are no other sacrifices, but that that one was once offered, and is no more to be repeated. The more subtle try to make their escape by a still narrower loophole–viz. that it is not repetition, but application. But there is no more difficulty in confuting this sophism also. For Christ did not offer himself once, in the view that His sacrifice should be daily ratified by new oblations, but that by the preaching of the Gospel and the dispensation of the sacred Supper, the benefit of it should be communicated to us. Thus Paul says, that "Christ, our passover, is sacrificed for us," and bids us "keep the feast" (1 Corinthians 5:7, 8). The method, I say, in which the Cross of Christ is duly applied to us is when the enjoyment is communicated to us, and we receive it with true faith.

4 Other objections answered.

But it is worthwhile to hear on what other foundation besides they rear up their sacrifice of the mass. To this end, they drag in the prophecy of Malachi, in which the Lord promises, "in every place incense shall be offered unto my name, and a pure offering" (Malachi 1:11). As if it were new or unusual for the prophets, when they speak of the calling of the Gentiles, to designate the spiritual worship of God to which they call them, by the external rites of the law, more familiarly to intimate to the men of their age that they were to be called into the true fellowship of religion, just as in general they are wont to describe the truth which has been exhibited by the Gospel by the types of their own age. Thus they use going up to Jerusalem for conversion to the Lord, the bringing of all kinds of gifts for the adoration of God—dreams and visions for the more ample knowledge with which believers were to be endued in the Kingdom of Christ. The passage they quote from Malachi resembles one in Isaiah, in which the prophet speaks of three altars to be erected in Assyria, Egypt, and Judea.

First, I ask, whether or not they grant that this prophecy is fulfilled in the Kingdom of Christ. Secondly, Where are those altars, or when were they ever erected? Thirdly, Do they suppose that a single temple is destined for a single kingdom, as was that of Jerusalem? If they ponder these things, they will confess, I think, that the prophet, under types adapted to his age, prophesied concerning the propagation of the spiritual worship of God over the whole world. This is the answer, which we give them; but, as obvious examples everywhere occur in the Scripture, I am not anxious to give a longer enumeration. Although they are miserably deluded in this also, that they acknowledge no sacrifice but that of the mass, whereas in truth believers now sacrifice to God and offer Him a pure offering, of which we shall speak by-and-by.

5 Impiety of the Mass continued. C. It banishes the remembrance of Christ's death. It crucifies Christ afresh. Objections answered.

I now come to the third part of the mass, in regard to which, we are to explain how it obliterates the true and only death of Christ, and drives it from the memory of men. For as among men, the confirmation of a testament depends upon the death of the testator, so also the testament by which He has bequeathed to us remission of sins and eternal righteousness, our Lord has confirmed by His death. Those who dare to make any change or innovation on this testament deny His death, and hold it as of no moment. Now, what is the mass but a new and altogether different testament? What? Does not each mass promise a new forgiveness of sins, a new purchase of righteousness, so that now there are as many testaments as there are masses? Therefore, let Christ come again, and, by another death, make this New Testament; or rather, by innumerable deaths, ratify the innumerable testaments of the mass. Said I not true, then, at the outset, that the only true death of Christ is obliterated by the mass?

For what is the direct aim of the mass but just to put Christ again to death, if that were possible? For, as the apostle says, "Where a testament is, there must also of necessity be the death of the testator" (Hebrews 9:16). The novelty of the mass bears, on the face of it, to be a testament of Christ, and therefore demands His death.

Besides, it is necessary that the victim, which is offered, be slain and immolated. If Christ is sacrificed at each mass, He must be cruelly slain every moment in a thousand places. This is not my argument, but the apostle's: "Nor yet that He should offer himself often;" "for then must He often have suffered since the foundation of the world" (Hebrews 9:25, 26).

I admit that they are ready with an answer, by which they even charge us with calumny; for they say that we object to them what they never thought, and could not even think. We know that the life and death of Christ are not at all in their hand. Whether they mean to slay Him, we regard not: our intention is only to show the absurdity consequent on their impious and accursed dogma. This I demonstrate from the mouth of the apostle. Though they insist a hundred times that this sacrifice is bloodless, I will reply, that it depends not on the will of man to change the nature of sacrifice, for in this way the sacred and inviolable institution of God would fall. Hence, it follows, that the principle of the apostle stands firm, "without shedding of blood is no remission" (Hebrews 9:22).

6 Impiety of the Mass continued. D. It robs us of the benefit of Christ's death.

The fourth property of the mass, which we are to consider, is that it robs us of the benefit, which redounded to us from the death of Christ, while it prevents us from recognizing it and thinking of it. For who can think that he has been redeemed by the death of Christ when he sees a new redemption in the mass? Who can feel confident that his sins have been remitted when he sees a new remission? It will not do to say that the only ground on which we obtain forgiveness of sins in the mass is, because it has been already purchased by the death of Christ. For this is just equivalent to saying that we are redeemed by Christ on the condition that we redeem ourselves. For the doctrine which is disseminated by the ministers of Satan, and which, in the present day, they defend by clamor, fire, and sword, is, that when we offer Christ to the Father in the mass, we, by this work of oblation, obtain remission of sins, and become partakers of the sufferings of Christ.

What is now left for the sufferings of Christ, but to be an example of redemption, that we may thereby learn to be our own redeemers? Christ himself, when He seals our assurance of pardon in the Supper, does not bid His disciples stop short at that act, but sends them to the sacrifice of His death, intimating that the Supper is the memento, or, as it is commonly expressed, the memorial from which they may learn that the expiatory victim, by which God was to be appeased, was to be offered only once. For it is not sufficient to hold that Christ is the only victim, without adding that His is the only immolation, in order that our faith may be fixed to His Cross.

7 Impiety of the Mass continued. E. It abolishes the Lord's Supper. In the Supper, the Father offers Christ to us; in the Mass, priestlings offer Christ to the Father. The Supper is a sacrament common to all Christians; the Mass confined to one priest.

I come now to the crowning point–viz. that the sacred Supper, on which the Lord left the memorial of His passion formed and engraved, was taken away, hidden, and destroyed, when the mass was erected. While the supper itself is a gift of God, which was to be received with thanksgiving, the sacrifice of the mass pretends to give a price to God to be received as satisfaction. As widely as giving differs from receiving, does sacrifice differ from the sacrament of the Supper. But herein does the wretched ingratitude of man appear, – that when the liberality of the divine goodness ought to have been recognized, and thanks returned, he makes God to be his debtor. The sacrament promised that by the death of Christ we were not only restored to life once, but constantly quickened, because all the parts of our salvation were then completed.

The sacrifice of the mass uses a very different language–viz. that Christ must be sacrificed daily, in order that He may lend something to us. The Supper was to be dispensed at the public meeting of the Church, to remind us of the communion by which we are all united in Christ Jesus. This communion the sacrifice of the mass dissolves, and tears asunder. For after the heresy prevailed, that there behooved to be priests to sacrifice for the people, as if the Supper had been handed over to them, it ceased to be communicated to the assembly of the faithful according to the command of the Lord. Entrance has been given to private masses, which more resemble a kind of excommunication than that communion ordained by the Lord, when the priestling, about to devour his victim apart, separates himself from the whole body of the faithful. That there may be no mistake, I call it a private mass whenever there is no partaking of the Lord's Supper among believers, though, at the same time, a great multitude of persons may be present.

8 The origin of the Mass. Private masses an impious profanation of the Supper.

The origin of the name of Mass I have never been able certainly to ascertain. It seems probable that it was derived from the offerings, which were collected. Hence, the ancients usually speak of it in the plural number. But without raising any controversy as to the name, I hold that private masses are diametrically opposed to the institution of Christ, and are, therefore, an impious profanation of the sacred Supper. For what did the Lord enjoin? Was it not to take and divide amongst ourselves? What does Paul teach as to the observance of this command? Is it not that the breaking of bread is the communion of body and blood? (1 Corinthians 10:16). Therefore, when one person takes without distributing, where is the resemblance? But that one acts in the name of the whole Church. By what command? Is it not openly to mock God when one privately seizes for himself what ought to have been distributed among a number? But as the words, both of our Savior and of Paul, are sufficiently clear, we must briefly conclude, that wherever there is no breaking of bread for the communion of the faithful, there is no Supper of the Lord, but a false and preposterous imitation of the Supper. But false imitation is adulteration. Moreover, the adulteration of this high ordinance is not without impiety. In private masses, therefore, there is an impious abuse. And, as in religion, one fault always begets another. After that custom of offering without communion once crept in, they began gradually to make innumerable masses in all the separate corners of the churches, and to draw the people hither and thither, when they ought to have formed one meeting, and thus recognized the mystery of their unity. Let them now go and deny their idolatry when they exhibit the bread in their masses, that it may be adored for Christ. In vain do they talk of those promises of the presence of Christ, which, however they may be understood, were certainly not given that impure and profane men might form the body of Christ as often as they please, and for whatever abuse they please; but that believers, while, with religious observance, they follow the command of Christ in celebrating the Supper, might enjoy the true participation of it.

9 This abomination unknown to the purer Church. It has no foundation in the Word of God.

We may add that this perverse course was unknown to the purer Church. For however the more impudent among our opponents may attempt to gloss the matter, it is certain that all antiquity is opposed to them, as has been above demonstrated in other instances, and may be more surely known by the diligent reading of the Fathers. But before I conclude, I ask our missal doctors, seeing they know that obedience is better than sacrifice, and God commands us to listen to His voice rather than to offer sacrifice (1 Samuel 15:22), –how they can believe this method of sacrificing to be pleasing to God, since it is certain that He does not command it, and they cannot support it by one syllable of Scripture? Besides, when they hear the apostle declaring that "no man taketh this honor to himself, but he that is called of God, as was Aaron," so also Christ glorified not himself to be made an High Priest, but He that said unto Him, "Thou art my Son: this day have I begotten thee" (Hebrews 5:4, 5). They must either prove God to be the author and founder of their priesthood, or confess that there is no honor from God in an office, into which, without being called, they have rushed with wicked temerity. They cannot produce one iota of Scripture in support of their priesthood. And must not the sacrifices be vain, since they cannot be offered without a priest?

10 Second part of the chapter. Some of the ancients call the Supper a sacrifice, but not propitiatory, as the Papists do the Mass. This proved by passages from Augustine.

Should anyone here obtrude concise sentences of the ancients, and contend, or their authority, that the sacrifice which is performed in the Supper is to be understood differently from what we have explained it, let this be our brief reply, –that if the question relates to the approval of the fiction of sacrifice, as imagined by Papists in the mass, there is nothing in the Fathers to countenance the sacrilege.

They indeed use the term sacrifice, but they, at the same time, explain that they mean nothing more than the commemoration of that one true sacrifice which Christ, our only sacrifice (as they themselves everywhere proclaim), performed on the cross.

"The Hebrews," says Augustine "in the victims of beasts which they offered to God, celebrated the prediction of the future victim which Christ offered: Christians now celebrate the commemoration of a finished sacrifice by the sacred oblation and participation of the body of Christ." Here he certainly teaches the same doctrine which is delivered at greater length in the Treatise on Faith, addressed to Peter the deacon, whoever may have been the author. The words are, "Hold most firmly, and have no doubt at all, that the Only begotten became incarnate for us, that He offered himself for us, an offering and sacrifice to God for a sweet-smelling savor; to whom, with the Father and the Holy Spirit, in the time of the Old Testament, animals were sacrificed, and to whom now, with the Father and the Holy Spirit (with whom there is one Godhead), the holy Church, throughout the whole world, ceases not to offer the sacrifice of bread and wine. For, in those carnal victims, there was a typifying of the flesh of Christ, which He himself was to offer for our sins, and of the blood, which He was to shed for the forgiveness of sins. But in that sacrifice there is thanksgiving and commemoration of the flesh of Christ which He offered for us, and of the blood which He shed for us."

Hence, Augustine himself, in several passages explains that it is nothing else than a sacrifice of praise. In short, you will find in his writings, passim, that the only reason for which the Lord's Supper is called a sacrifice is, because it is a commemoration, an image, a testimonial of that singular, true, and only sacrifice by which Christ expiated our guilt. For there is a memorable passage in *De Trinitate* where, after discoursing of the only sacrifice, he thus concludes, "Since, in a sacrifice, four things are considered–viz. to whom it is offered, by whom, what and for whom, the same one true Mediator, reconciling us to God by the sacrifice of peace, remains one with Him to whom He offered, made himself one with those for whom He offered, is himself the one who offered, and the one thing which He offered." Chrysostom speaks to the same effect. They so strongly claim the honor of the priesthood for Christ alone, that Augustine declares it would be equivalent to Antichrist for anyone to make a bishop to be an intercessor between God and man.

11 Some of the ancients seem to have declined too much to the shadows of the law.

And yet we deny not that in the Supper the sacrifice of Christ is so vividly exhibited as almost to set the spectacle of the Cross before our eyes, just as the apostle says to the Galatians, that Jesus Christ had been evidently set forth before their eyes, when the preaching of the Cross was delivered to them (Galatians 3:1). But because I see that those ancient writers have wrested this commemoration to a different purpose than was accordant to the divine institution (the Supper somehow seemed to them to present the appearance of a repeated, or at least renewed, immolation), nothing can be safer for the pious than to rest satisfied with the pure and simple ordinance of God, whose Supper it is said to be, just because His authority alone ought to appear in it. Seeing that they retained a pious and orthodox view of the whole ordinance–and I cannot discover that they wished to derogate in the least from the one sacrifice of the Lord–I cannot charge them with any impiety, and yet I think they cannot be excused from having erred somewhat in the mode of action. They imitated the Jewish mode of sacrificing more closely than either Christ had ordained, or the nature of the Gospel allowed. The only thing, therefore, for which they may be justly censured is, that preposterous analogy that, not contented with the simple and genuine institution of Christ, they declined too much to the shadows of the law.

12 Great distinction to be made between the Mosaic sacrifices and the Lord's Supper, which is called a eucharistic sacrifice. Same rule in this discussion.

Any who will diligently consider, will perceive that the Word of the Lord makes this distinction between the Mosaic sacrifices and our eucharist–that while the former represented to the Jewish people the same efficacy of the death of Christ which is now exhibited to us in the Supper, yet the form of representation was different. There the Levitical priests were ordered to typify the sacrifice, which Christ was to accomplish. A victim was placed to act as a substitute for Christ himself. An altar was erected on which it was to be sacrificed. The whole, in short, was so conducted as to bring under the eye an image of the sacrifice, which was to be offered to God in expiation. But now that the sacrifice has been performed, the Lord has prescribed a different method to us–viz. to transmit the benefit of the sacrifice offered to Him by his Son to His believing people. The Lord, therefore, has given us a table at which we may feast, not an altar on which a victim may be offered; He has not consecrated priests to sacrifice, but ministers to distribute a sacred feast. The more sublime and holy this mystery is, the more religiously and reverently ought it to be treated. Nothing, therefore, is safer than to banish all the boldness of human sense, and adhere solely to what Scripture delivers. And certainly, if we reflect that it is the Supper of the Lord and not of men, why do we allow ourselves to be turned aside one nail's-breadth from Scripture, by any authority of man or length of prescription? Accordingly, the apostle, in desiring completely to remove the vices which had crept into the Church of Corinth, as the most expeditious method, recalls them to the institution itself, showing that thence a perpetual rule ought to be derived.

13 The terms sacrifice and priest. Different kinds of sacrifices. A. Propitiatory. B. Eucharistic. None propitiatory but the death of Christ.

Lest any quarrelsome person should raise a dispute with us as to the terms sacrifice and priest, I will briefly explain what in the whole of this discussion we mean by sacrifice and what by priest. Some, on what rational ground I see not, extend the term sacrifice to all sacred ceremonies and religious acts. We know that by the uniform use of Scripture, the several Greek translations for "sacrifice" include everything whatever that is offered to God. Wherefore, we ought to distinguish, but so that the distinction may derive its analogy from the sacrifices of the Mosaic Law, under whose shadows the Lord was pleased to represent to His people the whole reality of sacrifices. Though these were various in form, they may all be referred to two classes. For either an oblation for sin was made by a certain species of satisfaction, by which the penalty was redeemed before God, or it was a symbol and attestation of religion and divine worship, at one time in the way of supplication to demand the favor of God; at another, by way of thanksgiving, to testify gratitude to God for benefits received; at another, as a simple exercise of piety, to renew the sanction of the covenant, to which latter branch, burnt-offerings, and libations, oblations, first fruits, and peace offerings, referred. Hence, let us also distribute them into two classes. The other class, with the view of explaining, consists of the veneration and worship, which believers both owe and render to God.

Or, if you prefer it, it can be interpreted as exhibited to God by none but those who, enriched with His boundless benefits, offer themselves and all their actions to Him in return. The other class let us call propitiatory or expiatory. A sacrifice of expiation is one whose object is to appease the wrath of God, to satisfy His justice, and thereby wipe and wash away the sins, by which the sinner being cleansed and restored to purity, may return to favor with God. Hence, the name given in the Law to the victims, which were offered in expiation of sin (Exodus 29:36); not that they were adequate to regain the favor of God and wipe away guilt, but because they typified the true sacrifice of this nature, which was at length performed in reality by Christ alone; by Him alone, because no other could, and once, because the efficacy and power of the one sacrifice performed by Christ is eternal, as He declared by His voice, when He said, "It is finished;" that is, that everything necessary to regain the favor of the Father, to procure forgiveness of sins, righteousness, and salvation, that all this was performed and consummated by His one oblation, and that hence nothing was wanting. No place was left for another sacrifice.

14 The Lord's Supper not properly called a propitiatory sacrifice, still less can the Popish Mass be so called. Those who mutter over the mass cannot be called priests.

Wherefore, I conclude, that it is an abominable insult and intolerable blasphemy, as well against Christ as the sacrifice, which, by His death, He performed for us on the Cross, for anyone to think of repeating the oblation, of purchasing the forgiveness of sins, of propitiating God, and obtaining justification. But what else is done in the mass than to make us partakers of the sufferings of Christ by means of a new oblation? And that there might be no limit to their extravagance, they have deemed it little to say, that it properly becomes a common sacrifice for the whole Church, without adding, that it is at their pleasure to apply it specially to this one or that, as they choose; or rather, to anyone who is willing to purchase their merchandise from them for a price paid. Moreover, as they could not come up to the estimate of Judas, still that they in some way might refer to their author they make the resemblance to consist in the number. He sold for thirty pieces of silver: they, according to the French method of computation, sell for thirty pieces of brass. He did it once: they as often as a purchaser is met with. We deny that they are priests in this sense–namely, that by such oblations they intercede with God for the people, that by propitiating God they make expiation for sins. Christ is the only Pontiff and Priest of the New Testament: to Him all priestly offices were transferred, and in Him, they closed and terminated. Even had Scripture made no mention of the eternal priesthood of Christ, yet, as God, after abolishing those ancient sacrifices, appointed no new priest, the argument of the apostle remains invincible, "No man taketh this honor unto himself, but he that is called of God, as was Aaron" (Hebrews 5:4). How, then, can those sacrilegious men, who by their own account are murderers of Christ, dare to call themselves the priests of the living God?

15 Their vanity proved even by Plato.

There is a most elegant passage in the second book of Plato's *Republic*. Speaking of ancient expiations, and deriding the foolish confidence of wicked and iniquitous men, who thought that by them, as a kind of veils, they concealed their crimes from the gods; and, as if they had made a pact with the gods, indulged themselves more securely, he seems accurately to describe the use of the expiation of the mass, as it exists in the world in the present day. All know that it is unlawful to defraud and circumvent another. To do injustice to widows, to pillage pupils, to molest the poor, to seize the goods of others by wicked arts, to get possession of any man's succession by fraud and perjury, to oppress by violence and tyrannical terror, all admit to be impious. How then do so many, as if assured of impunity dare to do all those things? Undoubtedly, if we duly consider, we will find that the only thing, which gives them so much courage, is, that by the sacrifice of the mass as a price paid, they trust that they will satisfy God, or at least will easily find a means of transacting with Him. Plato next proceeds to deride the gross stupidity of those who think by such expiations to redeem the punishments, which they must otherwise suffer after death. And what is meant by anniversaries and the greater part of masses in the present day, but just that those who through life have been the most cruel tyrants, or most rapacious plunderers, or adepts in all kinds of wickedness, may, as if redeemed at this price, escape the fire of purgatory?

16 To the eucharistic class of sacrifice belong all offices of piety and charity. This species of sacrifice has no connection with the appeasing of God.

Under the other kind of sacrifice, which we have called eucharistic, are included all the offices of charity, by which, while we embrace our brethren, we honor the Lord himself in His members; in fine, all our prayers, praises, thanksgivings, and every act of worship which we perform to God. All these depend on the greater sacrifice with which we dedicate ourselves, soul and body, to be a holy temple to the Lord. For it is not enough that our external acts be framed to obedience, but we must dedicate and consecrate first ourselves, and, secondly, all that we have, so that all which is in us may be subservient to His glory, and be stirred up to magnify it. This kind of sacrifice has nothing to do with appeasing God, with obtaining remission of sins, with procuring justification, but is wholly employed in magnifying and extolling God, since it cannot be grateful and acceptable to God unless at the hand of those who, having received forgiveness of sins, have already been reconciled and freed from guilt. This is so necessary to the Church, that it cannot be dispensed with. Therefore, it will endure forever, so long as the people of God shall endure, as we have already seen above from the prophet. For in this sense we may understand the prophecy, "From the rising of the sun, even unto the going down of the same, my name shall be great among the Gentiles; and in every place incense shall be offered unto my name, and a pure offering: for my name shall be great among the heathen, said the Lord of hosts" (Malachi 1:11); so far are we from doing away with this sacrifice. Thus, Paul beseeches us by the mercies of God, to present our bodies "a living sacrifice, holy, acceptable unto God," our "reasonable service" (Romans 12:1). Here he speaks very significantly when he adds, that this service is reasonable, for he refers to the spiritual mode of worshipping God, and tacitly opposes it to the carnal sacrifices of the Mosaic Law. Thus to do good and communicate are called sacrifices with which God is well pleased (Hebrews 13:16). Thus, the kindness of the Philippians in relieving Paul's want is called "an odor of a sweet smell, a sacrifice acceptable, well pleasing to God" (Philippians 4:18); and thus all the good works of believers are called spiritual sacrifices.

17 Prayer, thanksgiving, and other exercises of piety, called sacrifices. In this sense, the Lord's Supper called the eucharist. In the same sense, all believers are priests.

And why do I enumerate? This form of expression is constantly occurring in Scripture. Nay, even while the people of God were kept under the external tutelage of the law, the prophets clearly expressed that under these carnal sacrifices there was a reality, which is common both to the Jewish people and the Christian Church. For this reason David prayed, "Let my prayer ascend forth before thee as incense" (Psalm 141:2). And Hosea gives the name of "calves of the lips" (Hosea 14:3) to thanksgivings, which David elsewhere calls "sacrifices of praise;" the apostle, imitating him, speaks of offering "the sacrifice of praise," which he explains to mean, "the fruit of our lips, giving thanks to His name" (Hebrews 13:15). This kind of sacrifice is indispensable in the Lord's Supper, in which, while we show forth His death, and give Him thanks, we offer nothing but the sacrifice of praise. From this office of sacrificing, all Christians are called "a royal priesthood," because by Christ we offer that sacrifice of praise of which the apostle speaks, the fruit of our lips, giving thanks to His name (1 Pet. 2:9; Hebrews 13:15). We do not appear with our gifts in the presence of God without an intercessor. Christ is our Mediator, by whose intervention we offer ourselves and our all to the Father. He is our High Priest, who, having entered into the upper sanctuary, opens up an access for us. He is the altar on which we lay our gifts, that whatever we do attempt, we may attempt in Him. He it is, I say, who "hath made us kings and priests unto God and His Father" (Revelation 1:6).

18 Conclusion. Names given to the Mass.

What remains but for the blind to see, the deaf to hear, children even to perceive this abomination of the mass, which, held forth in a golden cup, has so intoxicated all the kings and nations of the Earth, from the highest to the lowest; so struck them with stupor and giddiness, that, duller than the lower animals, they have placed the vessel of their salvation in this fatal vortex. Certainly, Satan never employed a more powerful engine to assail and storm the Kingdom of Christ. This is the Helen for whom the enemies of the truth in the present day fight with so much rage, fury, and atrocity; and truly the Helen with whom they commit spiritual whoredom, the most execrable of all. I am not here laying my little finger on those gross abuses by which they might pretend that the purity of their sacred mass is profaned; on the base traffic which they ply; the sordid gain which they make; the rapacity with which they satiate their avarice. I only indicate, and that in few and simple terms, how very sacred the sanctity of the mass is, how well it has for several ages deserved to be admired and held in veneration! It would be a greater work to illustrate these great mysteries as they deserve, and I am unwilling to meddle with their obscene impurities, which are daily before the eyes and faces of all, that it may be understood that the mass, taken in the most choice form in which it can be exhibited, without any appendages, teems from head to foot with all kinds of impiety, blasphemy, idolatry, and sacrilege.

19 Last part of the chapter, recapitulating the views, which ought to be held concerning baptism and the Lord's Supper. Why the Lord's Supper is, and Baptism is not, repeated.

My readers have here a compendious view of all that I have thought it of importance to know concerning these two sacraments, which have been delivered to the Christian Church, to be used from the beginning of the new dispensation to the end of the world, Baptism being a kind of entrance into the Church, an initiation into the faith, and the Lord's Supper the constant aliment by which Christ spiritually feeds his family of believers. Wherefore, as there is but one God, one faith, one Christ, one Church, which is His body, so Baptism is one, and is not repeated. But the Supper is always dispensed, to intimate, that those who are once allured into the Church are constantly fed by Christ. Besides these two, no other has been instituted by God, and no other ought to be recognized by the assembly of the faithful. That sacraments are not to be instituted and set up by the will of men, is easily understood by him who remembers what has been above with sufficient plainness expounded –viz. that the sacraments have been appointed by God to instruct us in His promise, and testify His goodwill towards us; and who, moreover, considers, that the Lord has no counselor (Isaiah 40:13; Romans 11:34); who can give us any certainty as to His will, or assure us how He is disposed towards us, what He is disposed to give, and what to deny? From this it follows, that no one can set forth a sign which is to be a testimonial of His will, and of some promise. He alone can give the sign, and bear witness to himself. I will express it more briefly, perhaps in homelier, but also in clearer terms, –There never can be a sacrament without a promise of salvation. Not all men collected into one can, of themselves, give us any promise of salvation, and, therefore, they cannot, of themselves, give out and set up a sacrament.

20 Christians should be contented with these two sacraments. They are abolished by the sacraments decreed by men.

With these two, therefore, let the Christian Church be contented, and not only not admit or acknowledge any third at present, but not even desire or expect it even until the end of the world. For though to the Jews were given, besides his ordinary sacraments, others differing somewhat according to the nature of the times (as the manna, the water gushing from the rock, the brazen serpent, and the like), by this variety they were reminded not to stop short at such figures, the state of which could not be durable, but to expect from God something better, to endure without decay and without end. Our case is very different. To us Christ has been revealed. In Him are hidden all the treasures of wisdom and knowledge (Colossians 2:3), in such richness and abundance, that to ask or hope for any new addition to these treasures is truly to offend God and provoke Him against us. It behooves us to hunger after Christ only, to seek Him, look to Him, learn of Him, and learn again, until the arrival of the great day on which the Lord will fully manifest the glory of his kingdom, and exhibit himself as he is to our admiring eye (1 John 3:2). And, for this reason, this age of ours is designated in Scripture by the last hour, the last days, the last times, that no one may deceive himself with the vain expectation of some new doctrine or revelation. Our heavenly Father, who "at sundry times, and in divers manners, spake in time past unto the fathers by the prophets, hath in these last days spoken unto us" by His beloved Son, who alone can manifest, and, in fact, has fully manifested, the Father, in so far as is of importance to us, while we now see Him through a mirror. Now, since men have been denied the power of making new sacraments in the Church of God, it would be to be wished, that in those which are of God, there should be the least possible admixture of human invention. For just as when water is infused, the wine is diluted, and when leaven is put in, the whole mass is leavened, so the purity of the ordinances of God is impaired, whenever man makes any addition of his own. And yet, we see how far the sacraments as at present used have degenerated from their genuine purity. There is everywhere more than enough of pomp, ceremony, and gesticulation, while no account is taken, or mention made, of the Word of God, without which, even the sacraments themselves are not sacraments. Nay, in such a crowd, the very ceremonies ordained by God cannot raise their head, but lie oppressed. In Baptism, as we have elsewhere justly complained, how little is seen of that which alone ought to shine and be conspicuous there, I mean Baptism itself? The Supper was altogether buried when it was turned into the Mass. The utmost is, that it is seen once a year, but in a garbled, mutilated, and lacerated form.

Chapter 19

OF THE FIVE SACRAMENTS, FALSELY SO CALLED. THEIR SPURIOUSNESS PROVED, AND THEIR TRUE CHARACTER EXPLAINED.

There are two divisions of this chapter, –I. A general discussion of these five sacraments, sections 1-3. II. A special consideration of each. 1. Of Confirmation, sections 4-13. 2. Of Penance, sections 14-17. 3. Of Extreme Unction, sections 18-21. 4. Of Order, in which the seven so-called sacraments have originated, sections 22-23. 5. Of Marriage, sections 34-37.

Sections

1. Connection of the present discussion with that concerning Baptism and the Lord's Supper. Impiety of the popish teachers in attributing more to human rites than to the ordinances of God.

2. Men cannot institute sacraments. Necessary to keep up a distinction between sacraments and other ceremonies.

3. Seven sacraments not to be found in ecclesiastical writers. Augustine, who may represent all the others, acknowledged two sacraments only.

4. Nature of confirmation in ancient times. The laying on of hands.

5. This kind of confirmation afterwards introduced. It is falsely called a sacrament.

6. Popish argument for confirmation answered.

7. Argument confirmed by the example of Christ. Absurdity and impiety of Papists in calling their oil the oil of salvation.

8. Papistical argument, that Baptism cannot be complete without Confirmation. Answered.

9. Argument, that without confirmation we cannot be fully Christians. Answer.

10. Argument, that the Unction in confirmation is more excellent than Baptism. Answer.

11. Answer continued. Argument, that confirmation has greater virtue.

12. Argument from the practice of antiquity. Augustine's view of confirmation.

13. The ancient confirmation very praiseworthy. Should be restored in churches in the present day.

14. Of Penitence. Confused and absurd language of the Popish doctors. Imposition of hands in ancient times. This made by the Papists a kind of foundation of the sacrament of Penance.

15. Disagreement among Papists themselves, as to the grounds on which penance is regarded as a sacrament.

16. More plausibility in calling the absolution of the priest, than in calling penance a sacrament.

17. Penance not truly a sacrament. Baptism the sacrament of penitence.

18. Extreme Unction described. No foundation for it in the words of James.

19. No better ground for making this unction a sacrament, than any of the other symbols mentioned in Scripture.

20. Insult offered by this unction to the Holy Spirit. It cannot be a sacrament, as it was not instituted by Christ, and has no promise annexed to it.

21. No correspondence between the unction enjoined by James and the anointing of the Papists.

22. Of ecclesiastical orders. Two points for discussion. Absurdities here introduced. Whether ecclesiastical order is a sacrament. Papists not agreed as to holy orders.

23. Insult to Christ in attempting to make Him their colleague.

24. The greater part of these orders empty names implying no certain office. Popish exorcists.

25. Absurdity of the tonsure.

26. The Judaizing nature of the tonsure. Why Paul shaved his head in consequence of a vow.

27. Origin of this clerical tonsure as given by Augustine. Absurd ceremonies in consecrating Doorkeepers, Readers, Exorcists, and Acolytes.

28. Of the higher class of orders called Holy Orders. Insult offered to Christ when ministers are regarded as priests. Holy orders have nothing of the nature of a sacrament.

29. Absurd imitation of our Savior in breathing on His apostles.

30. Absurdity of the anointing employed.

31. Imposition of hands. Absurdity of, in Papistical ordination.

32. Ordination of deacons. Absurd forms of Papists.

33. Of sub-deacons.

34. Marriage not a sacrament.

35. Nothing in Scripture to countenance the idea that marriage is a sacrament.

36. Origin of the notion that marriage is a sacrament.

37. Practical abuses from this erroneous idea of marriage. Conclusion.

1 Connection of the present discussion with that concerning Baptism and the Lord's Supper. Impiety of the popish teachers in attributing more to human rites than to the ordinances of God.

The above discourse concerning the sacraments might have the effect, among the docile and sober-minded, of preventing them from indulging their curiosity, or from embracing, without authority from the word, any other sacraments than those two, which they know to have been instituted by the Lord. But since the idea of seven sacraments, almost common in the mouths of all, and circulated in all schools and sermons, by mere antiquity, has struck its roots and is even now seated in the minds of men, I thought it might be worth while to give a separate and closer consideration of the other five, which are vulgarly classed with the true and genuine sacraments of the Lord, and, after wiping away every gloss, to hold them up to the view of the simple, that they may see what their true nature is, and how falsely they have hitherto been regarded as sacraments. Here, at the outset, I would declare to all the pious, that I engage not in this dispute about a word for love of wrangling, but am induced, by weighty causes, to impugn the abuse of it. I am aware that Christians are the masters of words, as they are of all things, and that, therefore, they may at pleasure adapt words to things, provided a pious meaning is retained, though there should be some impropriety in the mode of expression. All this I concede, though it was better to make words subordinate to things than things to words. But in the name of sacrament, the case is different. For those who set down seven sacraments, at the same time give this definition to all–viz. that they are visible forms of invisible grace; and at the same time, make them all vehicles of the Holy Spirit, instruments for conferring righteousness, causes of procuring grace. Accordingly, the Master of Sentences himself denies that the sacraments of the Mosaic Law are properly called by this name, because they exhibited not what they figured.

Is it tolerable, I ask, that the symbols which the Lord has consecrated with His own lips, which He has distinguished by excellent promises, should be regarded as no sacraments, and that, meanwhile, this honor should be transferred to those rites which men have either devised of themselves, or at least observe without any express command from God? Therefore, let them either change the definition, or refrain from this use of the word, which may afterwards give rise to false and absurd opinions. Extreme unction, they say, is a figure and cause of invisible grace, because it is a sacrament. If we cannot possibly admit the inference, we must certainly meet them on the subject of the name, that we may not receive it on terms, which may furnish occasion for such an error. On the other hand, when they prove it a sacrament, they add the reason, because it consists of the external sign and the word. If we find neither command nor promise, what else can we do than protest against it?

2 Men cannot institute sacraments. Necessary to keep up a distinction between sacraments and other ceremonies.

It now appears that we are not quarreling about a word, but raising a not unnecessary discussion as to the reality. Accordingly, we most strenuously maintain what we formerly confirmed by invincible argument, that the power of instituting a sacrament belongs to God alone, since a sacrament ought, by the sure promise of God, to raise up and comfort the consciences of believers, which could never receive this assurance from men. A sacrament ought to be a testimony of the good will of God toward us. Of this no man or angel can be witness, since God has no counselor (Isaiah 40:13; Romans 11:34). He himself alone, with legitimate authority, testifies of himself to us by His Word. A sacrament is a seal of attestation or promise of God. Now, it could not be sealed by corporeal things, or the elements of this world, unless they were confirmed and set apart for this purpose by the will of God. Man, therefore, cannot institute a sacrament, because it is not in the power of man to make such divine mysteries lurk under things so abject. The Word of God must precede to make a sacrament to be a sacrament, as Augustine most admirably shows. Moreover, it is useful to keep up some distinction between sacraments and other ceremonies, if we would not fall into many absurdities. The apostles prayed on their bended knees; therefore, our knees may not be bent without a sacrament (Acts 9:20; 20:36). The disciples are said to have prayed toward the east; thus looking at the east is a sacrament. Paul would have men in every place to lift up pure hands (1 Timothy 2:8). It is repeatedly stated that the saints prayed with uplifted hands. Therefore, let the outstretching of hands also become a sacrament. In short, let all the gestures of saints pass into sacraments, though I should not greatly object to this, provided it was not connected with those greater inconveniences.

3 Seven sacraments not to be found in ecclesiastical writers. Augustine, who may represent all the others, acknowledged two sacraments only.

If they would press us with the authority of the ancient Church, I say that they are using a gloss. This number seven is nowhere found in the ecclesiastical writers, nor is it well ascertained at what time it crept in. I confess, indeed, that they sometimes use freedom with the term *sacrament*, but what do they mean by it? All ceremonies, external writs, and exercises of piety. But when they speak of those signs, which ought to be testimonies of the divine favor toward us, they are contented with those two, Baptism and the Eucharist. Lest anyone suppose that this is falsely alleged by me, I will here give a few passages from Augustine. "First, I wish you to hold that the principle point in this discussion is, that our Lord Jesus Christ (as He himself says in the Gospel) has placed us under a yoke which is easy, and a burden which is light. Hence, He has knit together the society of His new people by sacraments, very few in number, most easy of observance, and most excellent in meaning; such is baptism consecrated by the name of the Trinity: such is the communion of the body and blood of the Lord, and any other, if recommended in the canonical Scriptures." Again, "After the resurrection of our Lord, our Lord himself, and apostolic discipline, appointed, instead of many, a few signs, and these most easy of performance, most august in meaning, most chaste in practice; such is baptism and the celebration of the body and blood of the Lord." Why does He here make no mention of the sacred number, I mean seven? Is it probable that He would have omitted it if it had then been established in the Church, especially seeing He is otherwise more curious in observing numbers than might be necessary? Nay, when He makes mention of Baptism and the Supper, and is silent as to others, does He not sufficiently intimate that these two ordinances excel in special dignity, and that other ceremonies sink down to an inferior place? Wherefore, I say, that those sacramentary doctors are not only unsupported by the word of God, but also by the consent of the early Church, however much they may plume themselves on the pretence that they have this consent. But let us now come to particulars.

OF CONFIRMATION

4 Nature of confirmation in ancient times. The laying on of hands.

It was anciently customary for the children of Christians, after they had grown up, to appear before the bishop to fulfill that duty which was required of such adults as presented themselves for baptism. These sat among the catechumens until they were duly instructed in the mysteries of the faith, and could make a confession of it before bishop and people. The infants, therefore, who had been initiated by baptism, not having then given a confession of faith to the Church, were again, toward the end of their boyhood, or on adolescence, brought forward by their parents, and were examined by the bishop in terms of the Catechism which was then in common use. In order that this act, which otherwise justly required to be grave and holy, might have more reverence and dignity, the ceremony of laying on of hands was also used. Thus the boy, on his faith being approved, was dismissed with a solemn blessing. Ancient writers often make mention of this custom. Pope Leo says, "If anyone returns from heretics, let him not be baptized again, but let that which was there wanting to him—viz. the virtue of the Spirit, be conferred by the laying on of the hands of the bishop." Our opponents will here exclaim that the name of sacrament is justly given to that by which the Holy Spirit is conferred. But Leo elsewhere explains what he means by these words: "Let not him who was baptized by heretics be rebaptized, but be confirmed by the laying on of hands with the invocation of the Holy Spirit, because he received only the form of baptism without sanctification." Jerome also mentions it (*Contra Luciferian*). Now though I deny not that Jerome is somewhat under delusion when he says that the observance is apostolical, he is, however, very far from the follies of these men. And he softens the expression when he adds, that this benediction is given to bishops only, more in honor of the priesthood than from any necessity of law. This laying on of hands, which is done simply by way of benediction, I commend, and would like to see restored to its pure use in the present day.

5 This kind of confirmation afterwards introduced. It is falsely called a sacrament.

A later age having almost obliterated the reality, introduced a kind of fictitious confirmation as a divine sacrament. They feigned that the virtue of confirmation consisted in conferring the Holy Spirit, for increase of grace, on him who had been prepared in baptism for righteousness, and in confirming for contest those who in baptism were regenerated to life. This confirmation is performed by unction, and the following form of words: "I sign thee with the sign of the holy cross, and confirm thee with the chrism of salvation, in the name of the Father, and of the Son, and of the Holy Spirit." All fair and venerable. But where is the Word of God, which promises the presence of the Holy Spirit here? Not one iota can they allege. How will they assure us that their chrism is a vehicle of the Holy Spirit? We see oil that is a thick and greasy liquid, but nothing more. "Let the word be added to the element," says Augustine, "and it will become a sacrament." Let them, I say, produce this word if they would have us to see anything more in the oil than oil. But if they would show themselves to be ministers of the sacraments, as they ought, there would be no room for further dispute. The first duty of a minister is not to do anything without a command. Come, then, and let them produce some command for this ministry, and I will not add a word. If they have no command, they cannot excuse their sacrilegious audacity. For this reason our Savior interrogated the Pharisees as to the baptism of John, "Was it from heaven, or of men?" (Matthew 21:25). If they had answered, Of men, he held them confessed that it was frivolous and vain; if Of Heaven, they were forced to acknowledge the doctrine of John. Accordingly, not to be too contumelious to John, they did not venture to say that it was of men. Therefore, if confirmation is of men, it is proved to be frivolous and vain; if they would persuade us that it is of Heaven, let them prove it.

6 Popish argument for confirmation answered.

They indeed defend themselves by the example of the apostles, who, they presume, did nothing rashly. In this, they are right, nor would they be blamed by us if they showed themselves to be imitators of the apostles. But what did the apostles do? Luke narrates (Acts 8:15, 17), that the apostles who were at Jerusalem, when they heard that Samaria had received the Word of God, sent thither Peter and John, that Peter and John prayed for the Samaritans, that they might receive the Holy Spirit, who had not yet come upon any of them, they having only been baptized in the name of Jesus; that after prayer they laid their hands upon them, and that by this laying on of hands the Samaritans received the Holy Spirit. Luke repeatedly mentions this laying on of hands. I hear what the apostles did, that is, they faithfully executed their ministry. It pleased the Lord that those visible and admirable gifts of the Holy Spirit, which He then poured out upon His people, should be administered and distributed by His apostles by the laying on of hands. I think that there was no deeper mystery under this laying on of hands, but I interpret that this kind of ceremony was used by them to intimate, by the outward act, that they commended to God, and offered Him on whom they laid hands. Did this ministry, which the apostles then performed, still remain in the Church, it would also behoove us to observe the laying on of hands: but since that gift has ceased to be conferred, to what end is the laying on of hands? Assuredly, the Holy Spirit is still present with the people of God; without His guidance and direction, the

Church of God cannot subsist. For we have a promise of perpetual duration, by which Christ invites the thirsty to come to Him, that they may drink living water (John 7:37). But those miraculous powers and manifest operations, which were distributed by the laying on of hands, have ceased. They were only for a time. For it was right that the new preaching of the Gospel, the new Kingdom of Christ, should be signalized and magnified by unwonted and unheard-of miracles. When the Lord ceased from these, He did not forthwith abandon His Church, but intimated that the magnificence of His kingdom, and the dignity of His word, had been sufficiently manifested. In what respect then can these stage-players say that they imitate the apostles? The object of the laying on of hands was that the evident power of the Holy Spirit might be immediately exerted. This they effect not. Why then do they claim to themselves the laying on of hands, which is indeed said to have been used by the apostles, but altogether to a different end?

7 Argument confirmed by the example of Christ. Absurdity and impiety of Papists in calling their oil the oil of salvation.

The same account is to be given were anyone to insist that the breathing of our Lord upon His disciples (John 20:22) is a sacrament by which the Holy Spirit is conferred. But the Lord did this once for all, and did not also wish us to do it. In the same way, also, the apostles laid their hands, agreeably to that time at which it pleased the Lord that the visible gifts of the Spirit should be dispensed in answer to their prayers; not that posterity might, as those apes do, mimic the empty and useless sign without the reality. But if they prove that they imitate the apostles in the laying on of hands (though in this they have no resemblance to the apostles, except it be in manifesting some absurd false zeal), where did they get their oil, which they call the oil of salvation? Who taught them to seek salvation in oil? Who taught them to attribute to it the power of strengthening? Was it Paul, who draws us far away from the elements of this world, and condemns nothing more than clinging to such observances? This I boldly declare, not of myself, but from the Lord: Those who call oil the oil of salvation abjure the salvation which is in Christ, deny Christ, and have no part in the kingdom of God. Oil for the belly, and the belly for oil, but the Lord will destroy both. For all these weak elements, which perish even in the using, have nothing to do with the Kingdom of God, which is spiritual, and will never perish. What, then, some one will say, do you apply the same rule to the water by which we are baptized, and the bread and wine under which the Lord's Supper is exhibited? I answer, that in the sacraments of divine appointment, two things are to be considered: the substance of the corporeal thing which is set before us, and the form which has been impressed upon it by the Word of God, and in which its whole force lies. In as far, then, as the bread, wine, and water, which are presented to our view in the sacraments, retain their substance, Paul's declaration applies, "meats for the belly, and the belly for meats: but God shall destroy both it and them" (l Corinthians 6:13). For they pass and vanish away with the fashion of this world. But in as far as they are sanctified by the word of God to be sacraments, they do not confine us to the flesh, but teach truly and spiritually.

8 Papistical argument, that Baptism cannot be complete without Confirmation. Answered.

But let us make a still closer inspection, and see how many monsters this greasy oil fosters and nourishes. Those anointers say that the Holy Spirit is given in baptism for righteousness, and in confirmation, for increase of grace, that in baptism we are regenerated for life, and in confirmation, equipped for contest. And, accordingly, they are not ashamed to deny that baptism can be duly completed without confirmation. How nefarious! Are we not, then, buried with Christ by baptism, and made partakers of His death, that we may also be partners of His resurrection? This fellowship with the life and death of Christ, Paul interprets to mean the mortification of our flesh, and the quickening of the Spirit, our old man being crucified in order that we may walk in newness of life (Romans 6:6). What is it to be equipped for contest, if this is not? But if they deemed it as nothing to trample on the Word of God, why did they not at least reverence the Church, to which they would be thought to be in everything so obedient? What heavier charge can be brought against their doctrine than the decree of the Council of Melita? "Let him who says that baptism is given for the remission of sins only, and not in aid of future grace, be anathema." When Luke, in the passage that we have quoted, says that the Samaritans were only "baptized in the name of the Lord Jesus" (Acts 8:16), but had not received the Holy Spirit, he does not say absolutely that those who believed in Christ with the heart and confessed Him with the mouth were not endued with any gift of the Spirit. He means receiving of the Spirit by which miraculous power and visible graces were received. Thus, the apostles are said to have received the Spirit on the day of Pentecost (Acts 2:4), whereas Christ had long before said to them, "It is not ye that speak, but the Spirit of your Father which speaketh in you" (Matthew 10:20). Ye who are of God see the malignant and pestiferous wile of Satan. What was truly given in baptism is said to be falsely given in the confirmation of it, that he may stealthily lead away the unwary from baptism. Who can now doubt that this doctrine, which dissevers the proper promises of baptism from baptism, and transfers them elsewhere, is a doctrine of Satan? We have discovered on what foundation this famous unction rests. The Word of God says that as many as have been baptized into Christ, have put on Christ with His gifts (Galatians 3:27). The word of the anointers says that they received no promise in baptism to equip them for contest. The former is the word of truth; the latter must be the word of falsehood. I can define this baptism more truly than they themselves have hitherto defined it– viz. that it is a noted insult to baptism, the use of which it obscures–nay, abolishes: that it is a false suggestion of the devil, which draws us away from the truth of God; or, if you prefer it, that it is oil polluted with a lie of the devil, deceiving the minds of the simple by shrouding them in darkness.

9 Argument, that without confirmation we cannot be fully Christians. Answer.

They add, moreover, that all believers ought, after baptism, to receive the Holy Spirit by the laying on of hands, that they may become complete Christians, inasmuch as there never can be a Christian who has not been *chrismed* by episcopal confirmation. These are their exact words. I thought that everything pertaining to Christianity was prescribed and contained in Scripture. Now I see that the true form of religion must be sought and learned elsewhere than in Scripture. Divine wisdom, heavenly truth, and the whole doctrine of Christ only begin the Christian; it is the oil that perfects him. By this sentence are condemned all the apostles and the many martyrs who, it is absolutely certain, were never chrismed, the oil not yet being made, besmeared with which, they might fulfill all the parts of Christianity, or rather become Christians, which, as yet, they were not. Though I would be silent, they abundantly refute themselves. How small the proportion of the people whom they anoint after baptism! Why, then, do they allow among their flock so many half Christians, whose imperfection they might easily remedy? Why, with such supine negligence, do they allow them to omit what cannot be omitted without grave offense? Why do they not more rigidly insist on a matter so necessary, that, without it, salvation cannot be obtained unless, perhaps, when the act has been anticipated by sudden death? When they allow it to be thus licentiously despised, they tacitly confess that it is not of the importance, which they pretend.

10 Argument, that the Unction in confirmation is more excellent than Baptism. Answer.

Lastly, they conclude that this sacred unction is to be held in greater veneration than baptism, because the former is specially administered by the higher order of priests, whereas the latter is dispensed in common by all priests whatever. What can you here say, but that they are plainly mad in thus pluming themselves on their own inventions, while, in comparison with these, they carelessly contemn the sacred ordinances of God? Sacrilegious mouth! Dare you oppose oil merely polluted with your fetid breath, and charmed by your muttered words, to the sacrament of Christ, and compare it with water sanctified by the Word of God? But even this was not enough for your improbity: you must also prefer it. Such are the responses of the Holy See, such the oracles of the apostolic tripod. But some of them have begun to moderate this madness, which, even in their own opinion, was carried too far. It is to be held in greater veneration, they say, not perhaps because of the greater virtue and utility which it confers, but because it is given by more dignified persons, and in a more dignified part of the body, the forehead; or because it gives a greater increase of virtue, though baptism is more effectual for forgiveness. But do they not, by their first reason, prove themselves Donatists, who estimate the value of the sacrament by the dignity of the minister? Grant, however, that confirmation may be called more dignified from the dignity of the bishop's hand, still should anyone ask how this great prerogative was conferred on the bishops, what reason can they give but their own caprice? The right was used only by the apostles, who alone dispensed the Holy Spirit. Are bishops alone apostles? Are they apostles at all? However, let us grant this also; why do they not, on the same grounds, maintain that the sacrament of blood in the Lord's Supper is to be touched only by bishops? Their reason for refusing it to laics is that it was given by our Lord to the apostles only. If to the apostles only, why not infer then to bishops only? But in that place, they make the apostles simple Presbyters, whereas here another vertigo seizes them, and they suddenly elect them bishops. Lastly, Ananias was not an apostle, and yet Paul was sent to him to receive his sight, to be baptized and filled with the Holy Spirit (Acts 9:17). I will add, though cumulatively, if, by divine right, this office was peculiar to bishops, why have they dared to transfer it to plebeian Presbyters, as we read in one of the Epistles of Gregory?

11 Answer continued. Argument, that confirmation has greater virtue.

How frivolous, inept, and stolid the other reason, that their confirmation is worthier than the baptism of God, because in confirmation it is the forehead that is besmeared with oil, and in baptism the cranium. As if baptism were performed with oil, and not with water! I take all the pious to witness, whether it be not the one aim of these miscreants to adulterate the purity of the sacraments by their leaven. I have said elsewhere, that what is of God in the sacraments, can scarcely be got a glimpse of among the crowd of human inventions. If any did not then give me credit for the fact, let them now give it to their own teachers. Here, passing over water, and making it of no estimation, they set a great value on oil alone in baptism. We maintain, against them, that in baptism also the forehead is sprinkled with water, in comparison with which, we do not value your oil one straw, whether in baptism or in confirmation. But if anyone alleges that oil is sold for more, I answer, that by this accession of value any good, which might otherwise be in it, is vitiated, so far is it from being lawful fraudulently to vend this most vile imposture. They betray their impiety by the third reason, when they pretend that a greater increase of virtue is conferred in confirmation than in baptism. By the laying on of hands, the apostles dispensed the visible gifts of the Spirit. In what respect does the oil of these men prove its fecundity? But have done with these guides, who cover one sacrilege with many acts of sacrilege. It is a Gordian knot, which it is better to cut than to lose so much labor in untying.

12 Argument from the practice of antiquity. Augustine's view of confirmation.

When they see that the Word of God and everything like plausible argument fails them, they pretend, as usual, that the observance is of the highest antiquity and is confirmed by the consent of many ages. Even were this true, they gain nothing by it. A sacrament is not of Earth, but of Heaven; not of men, but of God only. They must prove God to be the author of their confirmation, if they would have it to be regarded as a sacrament. But why obtrude antiquity, seeing that ancient writers, whenever they would speak precisely, nowhere mention more than two sacraments? Were the bulwark of our faith to be sought from men, we have an impregnable citadel in this, that the fictitious sacraments of these men were never recognized as sacraments by ancient writers. They speak of the laying on of hands, but do they call it a sacrament? Augustine distinctly affirms that it is nothing but prayer. Let them not here yelp out one of their vile distinctions, that the laying on of hands to which Augustine referred was not the confirmatory, but the curative or reconciliatory. His book is extant and in men's hands; if I wrest it to any meaning different from that which Augustine himself wrote it, they are welcome not only to load me with reproaches after their wonted manner, but to spit upon me. He is speaking of those who returned from schism to the unity of the Church. He says that they have no need of a repetition of baptism, for the laying on of hands is sufficient, that the Lord may bestow the Holy Spirit upon them by the bond of peace. But as it might seem absurd to repeat laying on of hands more than baptism, he shows the difference: "What," he asks, "is the laying on of hands but prayer over the man?" That this is his meaning is apparent from another passage, where he says, "Because of the bond of charity, which is the greatest gift of the Holy Spirit, without which all the other holy qualities which a man may possess are ineffectual for salvation, the hand is laid on reformed heretics."

13 The ancient confirmation very praiseworthy. Should be restored in churches in the present day.

I wish we could retain the custom, which, as I have observed, existed in the early Church, before this abortive mask of a sacrament appeared. It would not be such a confirmation as they pretend, one which cannot even be named without injury to baptism, but catechizing by which those in boyhood, or immediately beyond it, would give an account of their faith in the face of the Church. And the best method of catechizing would be, if a form were drawn up for this purpose, containing, and briefly explaining, the substance of almost all the heads of our religion, in which the whole body of the faithful ought to concur without controversy. A boy of ten years of age would present himself to the Church, to make a profession of faith, would be questioned on each head, and give answers to each. If he was ignorant of any point, or did not well understand it, he would be taught. Thus, while the whole Church looked on and witnessed, he would profess the one true sincere faith with which the body of the faithful, with one accord, worship one God. Were this discipline in force in the present day, it would undoubtedly whet the sluggishness of certain parents, who carelessly neglect the instruction of their children, as if it did not at all belong to them, but who could not then omit it without public disgrace; there would be greater agreement in faith among the Christian people, and not so much ignorance and rudeness; some persons would not be so readily carried away by new and strange dogmas; in fine, it would furnish all with a methodical arrangement of Christian doctrine.

OF PENITENCE.

14 Of Penitence. Confused and absurd language of the Popish doctors. Imposition of hands in ancient times. This made by the Papists a kind of foundation of the sacrament of Penance.

The next place they give to Penitence, of which they discourse so confusedly and unmethodically, that consciences cannot derive anything certain or solid from their doctrine. In another place (Book 3, chapters 3 and 4), we have explained at length, first, what the Scriptures teach concerning repentance, and, secondly, what these men teach concerning it. All we have now to advert to is the grounds of that opinion of it as a sacrament, which has long prevailed in schools and churches. First, however, I will speak briefly of the rite of the early Church, which those men have used as a pretext for establishing their fiction. By the order observed in public repentance, those who had performed the satisfactions imposed upon them were reconciled by the formal laying on of hands. This was the symbol of absolution by which the sinner himself regained his confidence of pardon before God, and the Church was admonished to lay aside the remembrance of the offense, and kindly receive him into favor. This Cyprian often terms *to give peace*. In order that the act might have more weight and estimation with the people, it was appointed that the authority of the bishop should always be interposed. Hence, the decree of the second Council of Carthage, "No presbyter may publicly at mass reconcile a penitent;" and another, of the Council of Arausica, "Let those who are departing this life, at the time of penitence, be admitted to communion without the reconciliatory laying on of hands; if they recover from the disease, let them stand in the order of penitents, and after they have fulfilled their time, receive the reconciliatory laying on of hands from the bishop." Again, in the third Council of Carthage, "A presbyter may not reconcile a penitent without the authority of the bishop." The object of all these enactments was to prevent the strictness, which they wished to be observed in that matter, from being lost by excessive laxity. Accordingly, they wished cognizance to be taken by the bishop, who, it was probable, would be more circumspect in examining. Although Cyprian somewhere says that not the bishop only laid hands, but also the whole clergy. For he thus speaks, "They do penitence for a proper time; next they come to communion, and receive the right of communion by the laying on of the hands of the bishop and clergy." Afterwards, in process of time, the matter came to this, that they used the ceremony in private absolutions also without public penitence.

Hence, the distinction in Gratian between public and private reconciliation. I consider that ancient observance of which Cyprian speaks to have been holy and salutary to the Church, and I could wish it restored in the present day. The more modern form, though I dare not disapprove, or at least strongly condemn, I deem to be less necessary. Be this as it may, we see that the laying on of hands in penitence was a ceremony ordained by men, not by God, and is to be ranked among indifferent things, and external exercises, which indeed are not to be despised, but occupy an inferior place to those which have been recommended to us by the Word of the Lord.

15 Disagreement among Papists themselves, as to the grounds on which penance is regarded as a sacrament.

The Romanists and Schoolmen, whose wont it is to corrupt all things by erroneous interpretation, anxiously labor to find a sacrament here, and it cannot seem wonderful, for they seek a thing where it is not. At best, they leave the matter involved, undecided, uncertain, confused, and confounded by the variety of opinions. Accordingly, they say one of two things. External penitence is a sacrament, and, if so, ought to be regarded as a sign of internal penitence, such as contrition of heart, which will be the matter of the sacrament. Or they say that both together make a sacrament: not two, but one complete. They make the distinction that the external is the sacrament merely. The internal is the matter and the sacrament, whereas the forgiveness of sins is the matter only, and not the sacrament. Let those who remember the definition of a sacrament, which we have given above, test by it that which they say is a sacrament, and it will be found that it is not an external ceremony appointed by God for the confirmation of our faith. But if they allege that my definition is not a law, which they are necessarily bound to obey, let them hear Augustine, whom they pretend to regard as a saint. "Visible sacraments were instituted for the sake of carnal men, that by the ladder of sacraments they may be conveyed from those things which are seen by the eye, to those which are perceived by the understanding." Do they themselves see, or can they show to others, anything like this in that which they call the sacrament of penance? In another passage, he says, "It is called a sacrament, because in it one thing is seen, another thing is understood. What is seen has bodily appearance, what is understood has spiritual fruit." These things in no way apply to the sacrament of penance, as they feign it; there, there is no bodily form to represent spiritual fruit.

16 More plausibility in calling the absolution of the priest, than in calling penance a sacrament.

And (to dispatch these beasts in their own arena) if any sacrament is sought here, would it not have been much more plausible to maintain that the absolution of the priest is a sacrament, than penitence either external or internal? For it might obviously have been said that it is a ceremony to confirm our faith in the forgiveness of sins, and that it has the promise of the keys, as they describe them: "Whatsoever ye shall bind or loose on earth, shall be bound or loosed in heaven." But some one will object that to most of those who are absolved by priests nothing of the kind is given by the absolution, whereas, according to their dogma, the sacraments of the new dispensation ought to effect what they figure. This is ridiculous. As in the eucharist, they make out a twofold eating—a sacramental, which is common to the good and bad alike, and a spiritual, which is proper only to the good; why should they not also pretend that absolution is given in two ways? And yet, I have never been able to understand what they meant by their dogma. How much it is at variance with the truth of God, we showed when we formally discussed that subject. Here I only wish to show that no scruple should prevent them from giving the name of a sacrament to the absolution of the priest. For they might have answered by the mouth of Augustine, that there is a sanctification without a visible sacrament, and a visible sacrament without internal sanctification. Again, that in the elect alone sacraments effect what they figure. Again, that some put on Christ so far as the receiving of the sacrament, and others so far as sanctification; that the former is done equally by the good and the bad, the latter by the good only. Surely, they were more deluded than children and blind in the full light of the sun when they toiled with so much difficulty, and perceived not a matter so plain and obvious to every man.

17 Penance not truly a sacrament. Baptism the sacrament of penitence.

Lest they become elated, however, whatever be the part in which they place the sacrament, I deny that it can justly be regarded as a sacrament. First, there exists not to this effect any special promise of God, which is the only ground of a sacrament. Secondly, whatever ceremony is here used is a mere invention of man, whereas, as has already been shown, the ceremonies of sacraments can only be appointed by God. Their fiction of the sacrament of penance, therefore, was falsehood and imposture. This fictitious sacrament they adorned with the befitting eulogium, that it was the second plank in the case of shipwreck, because if anyone had, by sin, injured the garment of innocence received in baptism, he might repair it by penitence. This was a saying of Jerome. Let it be whose it may, as it is plainly impious, it cannot be excused if understood in this sense; as if baptism were effaced by sin and were not to be recalled to the mind of the sinner whenever he thinks of the forgiveness of sins, that he may thereby recollect himself, regain courage, and be confirmed in the belief that he shall obtain the forgiveness of sins, which was promised him in baptism. What Jerome said harshly and improperly–viz. that baptism, which is fallen from by those who deserve to be excommunicated from the Church, is repaired by penitence, these worthy expositors wrest to their own impiety. You will speak most correctly, therefore, if you call baptism the sacrament of penitence, seeing it is given to those who aim at repentance to confirm their faith and seal their confidence. But lest you should think this our invention, it appears that besides being conformable to the words of Scripture, it was generally regarded in the early Church as an indubitable axiom. For in the short Treatise on Faith addressed to Peter, and bearing the name of Augustine, it is called, *The Sacrament of Faith and Repentance*. But why have recourse to doubtful writings, as if anything can be required more distinct than the statement of the Evangelist, that John preached "the baptism of repentance for the remission of sins"? (Mark 1:4; Luke 3:3).

OF EXTREME UNCTION, SO CALLED.

18 Extreme Unction described. No foundation for it in the words of James.

The third fictitious sacrament is Extreme Unction, which is performed only by a priest, and, as they express it, *in extremis*, with oil consecrated by the bishop and with these words: "By this holy unction and His most tender mercy, may God forgive you whatever sin you have committed, by the eye, the ear, the smell, the touch, the taste." They pretend that there are two virtues in it–the forgiveness of sins and relief of bodily disease, if so expedient; if not expedient, the salvation of the soul. For they say, that the institution was set down by James, whose words are, "Is any sick among you? Let him send for the elders of the Church; and let them pray over him, anointing him with oil in the name of the Lord; and the prayer of faith shall save the sick, and the Lord shall raise him up: and if he have committed sins, they shall be forgiven him" (James 5:14). The same account is here to be given of this unction as we lately gave of the laying on of hands; in other words, it is mere hypocritical stageplay, by which, without reason or result, they would resemble the apostles.

Mark relates that the apostles, on their first mission, agreeably to the command, which they had received of the Lord, raised the dead, cast out devils, cleansed lepers, healed the sick, and, in healing, used oil. He says, they "anointed with oil many that were sick, and healed them" (Mark 6:13). To this James referred when he ordered the presbyters of the Church to be called to anoint the sick. That no deeper mystery lay under this ceremony will easily be perceived by those who consider how great liberty both our Lord and His apostles used in those external things. Our Lord, when about to give sight to the blind man, spat on the ground, and made clay of the spittle; some He cured by a touch, others by a word. In like manner, the apostles cured some diseases by word only, others by touch, and others by anointing. But it is probable that neither this anointing nor any of the other things were used at random.

I admit this; not, however, that they were instruments of the cure, but only symbols to remind the ignorant whence this great virtue proceeded, and prevent them from ascribing the praise to the apostles. To designate the Holy Spirit and his gifts by oil is trite and common (Psalm 45:8). But the gift of hearing disappeared with the other miraculous powers, which the Lord was pleased to give for a time, that it might render the new preaching of the Gospel forever wonderful. Therefore, even were we to grant that anointing was a sacrament of those powers, which were then administered by the hands of the apostles, it pertains not to us, to whom no such powers have been committed.

19 No better ground for making this unction a sacrament, than any of the other symbols mentioned in Scripture.

And what better reason have they for making a sacrament of this unction, than of any of the other symbols which are mentioned in Scripture? Why do they not dedicate some pool of Siloam, into which, at certain seasons the sick may plunge themselves? That, they say, were done in vain. Certainly not more in vain than unction. Why do they not lay themselves on the dead, seeing that Paul, in raising up the dead youth, lay upon him? Why is not clay made of dust and spittle a sacrament? The other cases were special, but this is commanded by James. In other words, James spoke agreeably to the time when the Church still enjoyed this blessing from God. They affirm, indeed, that there is still the same virtue in their unction, but we experience differently. Let no man now wonder that they have with so much confidence deluded souls which they knew to be stupid and blind, because deprived of the Word of God, that is, of His light and life, seeing they blush not to attempt to deceive the bodily perceptions of those who are alive, and have all their senses about them. They make themselves ridiculous, therefore, by pretending that they are endued with the gift of healing. The Lord, doubtless, is present with His people in all ages, and cures their sicknesses as often as there is need, not less than formerly; and yet He does not exert those manifest powers, nor dispense miracles by the hands of apostles, because that gift was temporary, and owing, in some measure, to the ingratitude of men, immediately ceased.

20 Insult offered by this unction to the Holy Spirit. It cannot be a sacrament, as it was not instituted by Christ, and has no promise annexed to it.

Wherefore, as the apostles, not without cause, openly declared, by the symbol of oil, that the gift of healing committed to them was not their own, but the power of the Holy Spirit; so, on the other hand, these men insult the Holy Spirit by making his power consist in a filthy oil of no efficacy. It is just as if one were to say that all oil is the power of the Holy Spirit, because it is called by that name in Scripture, and that every dove is the Holy Spirit, because he appeared in that form. Let them see to this: it is sufficient for us that we perceive, with absolute certainty, that their unction is no sacrament, as it is neither a ceremony appointed by God, nor has any promise. For when we require, in a sacrament, these two things, that it be a ceremony appointed by God, and have a promise from God, we at the same time demand that that ceremony be delivered to us, and that that promise have reference to us. No man contends that circumcision is now a sacrament of the Christian Church, although it was both an ordinance of God, and had his promise annexed to it, because it was neither commanded to us, nor was the promise annexed to it given us on the same condition. The promise, of which they vaunt so much in unction, as we have clearly demonstrated, and they themselves show by experience, has not been given to us. The ceremony behooved to be used only by those who had been endued with the gift of healing, not by those murderers, who do more by slaying and butchering than by curing.

21 No correspondence between the unction enjoined by James and the anointing of the Papists.

Even were it granted that this precept of unction, which has nothing to do with the present age, were perfectly adapted to it, they will not even thus have advanced much in support of their unction, with which they have hitherto besmeared us. James would have all the sick to be anointed: these men besmear, with their oil, not the sick, but half-dead carcasses, when life is quivering on the lips, or, as they say, *in extremis*. If they have a present cure in their sacrament, with which they can either alleviate the bitterness of disease, or at least give some solace to the soul, they are cruel in never curing in time. James would have the sick man to be anointed by the elders of the Church. They admit no anointer but a priestling. When they interpret the elders of James to be priests, and allege that the plural number is used for honor, the thing is absurd, as if the Church had at that time abounded with swarms of priests, so that they could set out in long procession, bearing a dish of sacred oil. James, in ordering simply that the sick be anointed, seems to me to mean no other anointing than that of common oil, nor is any other mentioned in the narrative of Mark. These men deign not to use any oil but that which has been consecrated by a bishop, that is warmed with much breath, charmed by much muttering, and saluted nine times on bended knee, Thrice Hail, holy oil! Thrice Hail, holy chrism! Thrice Hail, holy balsam! From whom did they derive these exorcisms? James says that when the sick man shall have been anointed with oil and prayer shall have been made over him, if he has committed sins, they shall be forgiven him—viz. that his guilt being forgiven, he shall obtain a mitigation of the punishment, not meaning that sins are effaced by oil, but that the prayers by which believers commended their afflicted brother to God would not be in vain. These men are impiously false in saying that sins are forgiven by their sacred, that is, abominable unction. See how little they gain, even when they are allowed to abuse the passage of James as they list. And to save us the trouble of a laborious proof, their own annals relieve us from all difficulty; for they relate that Pope Innocent, who presided over the church of Rome in the age of Augustine, ordained, that not elders only, but all Christians, should use oil in anointing, in their own necessity, or in that of their friends. Our authority for this is Sigebert, in his Chronicles.

OF ECCLESIASTICAL ORDERS.

22 **Of ecclesiastical orders. Two points for discussion. Absurdities here introduced. Whether ecclesiastical order is a sacrament. Papists not agreed as to holy orders.**

The fourth place in their catalogue is held by the sacrament of Orders, one so prolific, as to beget of itself seven lesser sacraments. It is very ridiculous that, after affirming that there are seven sacraments, when they begin to count, they make out thirteen. It cannot be alleged that they are one sacrament, because they all tend to one priesthood, and are a kind of steps to the same thing. For while it is certain that the ceremonies in each are different, and they themselves say that the graces are different, no man can doubt that if their dogmas are admitted, they ought to be called seven sacraments. And why debate it as a doubtful matter, when they themselves plainly and distinctly declare that they are seven?

First, then, we shall glance at them in passing, and show to how many absurdities they introduce us when they would recommend their orders to us as sacraments; and, secondly, we shall see whether the ceremony, which churches use in ordaining ministers, ought at all to be called a sacrament. They make seven ecclesiastical orders, or degrees, which they distinguish by the title of a sacrament. These are Doorkeepers, Readers, Exorcists, Acolytes, Subdeacons, Deacons, and Priests. And they say that they are seven, because of the seven kinds of graces of the Holy Spirit with which those who are promoted to them ought to be endued. This grace is increased and more liberally accumulated on promotion. The mere number has been consecrated by a perversion of Scripture, because they think they read in Isaiah that there are seven gifts of the Holy Spirit, whereas truly not more than six are mentioned by Isaiah, who, however, meant not to include all in that passage. For, in other passages are mentioned the spirit of life, of sanctification, of the adoption of sons, as well as there, the spirit of wisdom and understanding, the spirit of counsel and might, the spirit of knowledge, and of the fear of the Lord. Although others who are more acute make not seven orders, but nine, in imitation, as they say, of the Church triumphant. But among these, also, there is a contest; because some insist that the clerical tonsure is the first order of all, and the episcopate the last, while others, excluding the tonsure, class the office of archbishop among the orders.

Isiodorus distinguishes differently, for he makes Psalmists and Readers different. To the former, he gives the charge of chanting; to the latter, that of reading the Scriptures for the instruction of the common people. And this distinction is observed by the canons. In this great variety, what would they have us to follow or to avoid? Shall we say that there are seven orders? So the master of the school teaches, but the most illuminated doctors determine otherwise. On the other hand, they are at variance among themselves. Besides, the most sacred canons call us in a different direction. Such, indeed, is the concord of men when they discuss divine things apart from the word of God.

23 Insult to Christ in attempting to make Him their colleague.

But the crowning folly of all is that in each of these they make Christ their colleague. First, they say he performed the office of Doorkeeper when, with a whip of small cords, he drove the buyers and sellers from the temple. He intimates that he is a Doorkeeper when He says, "I am the door." He assumed the office of Reader, when He read Isaiah in the synagogue. He performed the office of Exorcist when, touching the tongue and ears of the deaf and dumb man with spittle, He restored his hearing. He declared that he was an Acolyte by the words, "He that followeth me shall not walk in darkness." He performed the office of Subdeacon, when, girding himself with a towel, He washed the feet of his disciples. He acted the part of a Deacon, when He distributed His body and blood in the Supper. He performed the part of a Priest, when, on the Cross, He offered himself in sacrifice to the Father. As these things cannot be heard without laughter, I wonder how they could have been written without laughter, if, indeed, they were men who wrote them. But their most notable subtlety is that in which they speculate on the name of Acolyte, calling him Ceroferarius—a magical term, I presume, one certainly unknown to all nations and tongues, in Greek, meaning simply *attendant*. Were I to stop and seriously refute these things, I might myself justly be laughed at, so frivolous are they and ludicrous.

24 The greater part of these orders empty names implying no certain office. Popish exorcists.

Still, lest they should be able to impose on silly women, their vanity must be exposed in passing. With great pomp and solemnity they elect their readers, psalmists, doorkeepers, acolytes, to perform those services which they give in charge, either to boys, or at least to those whom they call laics. Who, for the most part, lights the tapers, who pours wine and water from the pitcher, but a boy or some mean person among laics, who gains his bread by so doing? Do not the same persons chant? Do they not open and shut the doors of Churches? Who ever saw, in their churches, either an acolyte or doorkeeper performing his office? Nay, when he who as a boy performed the office of acolyte, is admitted to the order of acolyte, he ceases to be the very thing he begins to be called, so that they seem professedly to wish to cast away the office when they assume the title. See why they hold it necessary to be consecrated by sacraments, and to receive the Holy Spirit! It is just to do nothing. If they pretend that this is the defect of the times, because they neglect and abandon their offices, let them, at the same time, confess that today there is not in the Church any use or benefit of these sacred orders, which they wondrously extol, and that their whole Church is full of anathema, since the tapers and flagons, which none are worthy to touch but those who have been consecrated acolytes, she allows to be handled by boys and profane persons; since her chants, which ought to be heard only from consecrated lips, she delegates to children. And to what end, pray, do they consecrate exorcists? I hear that the Jews had their exorcists, but I see they were so called from the exorcisms, which they practiced (Acts 19:13). Who ever heard of those fictitious exorcists having given one specimen of their profession? It is pretended that power has been given them to lay their hands on energumens, catechumens, and demoniacs, but they cannot persuade demons that they are endued with such power, not only because demons do not submit to their orders, but even command themselves. Scarcely will you find one in ten who is not possessed by a wicked spirit. All, then, which they babble about their paltry orders, is a compound of ignorant and stupid falsehoods. Of the ancient acolytes, doorkeepers, and readers, we have spoken when explaining the government of the Church. All that we here proposed was to combat that novel invention of a sevenfold sacrament in ecclesiastical orders of which we nowhere read except among silly raving Sorbonnists and Canonists.

25 Absurdity of the tonsure.

Let us now attend to the ceremonies that they employ. And first, all whom they enroll among their militia they initiate into the clerical status by a common symbol. They shave them on the top of the head, that the crown may denote regal honor, because clergy ought to be kings in governing themselves and others. Peter thus speaks of them: "Ye are a chosen generation, a royal priesthood, a holy nation, a peculiar people" (1 Peter 2:9). But it was sacrilege in them to arrogate to themselves alone what is given to the whole Church, and proudly to glory in a title of which they had robbed the faithful. Peter addresses the whole Church: these men wrest it to a few shaven crowns, as if it had been said to them alone, Be ye holy: as if they alone had been purchased by the blood of Christ: as if they alone had been made by Christ kings and priests unto God. Then they assign other reasons. The top of the head is bared, that their mind may be shown to be free, with unveiled face, to behold the glory of God; or that they may be taught to cut off the vices of the eye and the lip. Or the shaving of the head is the laying aside of temporal things, while the circumference of the crown is the remnants of good which are retained for support. Everything is in figure, because forsooth, the veil of the temple is not yet rent. Accordingly, persuaded that they have excellently performed their part because they have figured such things by their crown, they perform none of them in reality. How long will they delude us with such masks and impostures? The clergy, by shaving off some hair, intimate that they have cast away abundance of temporal good—that they contemplate the glory of God—that they have mortified concupiscence of the ear and the eye: but no class of men is more rapacious, more stupid, more libidinous. Why do they not rather exhibit true sanctity, than give a hypocritical semblance of it in false and lying signs?

26 The Judaizing nature of the tonsure. Why Paul shaved his head in consequence of a vow.

Moreover, when they say that the clerical crown has its origin and nature from the Nazarenes, what else do they say than that their mysteries are derived from Jewish ceremonies, or rather are mere Judaism? When they add that Priscilla, Aquila, and Paul himself, after they had taken a vow, shaved their head that they might be purified, they betray their gross ignorance. For we nowhere read this of Priscilla, while, with regard to Aquila, it is uncertain, since that tonsure may refer equally well to Paul as to Aquila (Acts 18:18). But not to leave them in possession of what they ask—viz. that they have an example in Paul, it is to be observed, to the more simple, that Paul never shaved his head for any sanctification, but only in subservience to the weakness of brethren. Vows of this kind I am accustomed to call vows of charity, not of piety; in other words, vows not undertaken for divine worship, but only in deference to the infirmity of the weak, as he himself says, that to the Jews he became a Jew (1 Corinthians 9:20). This, therefore, he did, and that once and for a short time, that he might accommodate himself for a little to the Jews. When these men would, for no end, imitate the purifications of the Nazarenes (Numbers 6:18), what else do they than set up a new, while they improperly affect to rival the ancient Judaism? In the same spirit the Decretal Epistle was composed, which enjoins the clergy, after the apostle, not to nourish their hair, but to shave it all round; as if the apostle, in showing what is comely for all men, had been solicitous for the spherical tonsure of the clergy. Hence, let my readers consider what kind of force or dignity there can be in the subsequent mysteries, to which this is the introduction.

27 Origin of this clerical tonsure as given by Augustine. Absurd ceremonies in consecrating Doorkeepers, Readers, Exorcists, and Acolytes.

Whence the clerical tonsure had its origin, is abundantly clear from Augustine alone. While in that age none wore long hair but the effeminate, and those who affected an unmanly beauty and elegance, it was thought to be of bad example to allow the clergy to do so. They were therefore enjoined either to cut or shave their hair, that they might not have the appearance of effeminate indulgence. And so common was the practice, that some monks, to appear more sanctimonious than others by a notable difference in dress, let their locks hang loose. But when hair returned to use, and some nations, which had always worn long hair, as France, Germany, and England, embraced Christianity; it is probable that the clergy everywhere shaved the head, that they might not seem to affect ornament. At length, in a more corrupt age, when all ancient customs were either changed, or had degenerated into superstition, seeing no reason for the clerical tonsure (they had retained nothing but a foolish imitation), they betook themselves to mystery, and now superstitiously obtrude it upon us in support of their sacrament. The Doorkeepers, on consecration, receive the keys of the Church, by which it is understood that the custody of it is committed to them;

the Readers receive the Holy Bible; the Exorcists, forms of exorcism which they use over the possessed and catechumens; the Acolytes, tapers and the flagon. Such are the ceremonies, which, it would seem, possess so much secret virtue, that they cannot only be signs and badges, but even causes of invisible grace. For this, according to their definition, they demand, when they would have them to be classed among sacraments. But to dispatch the matter in a few words, I say that it is absurd for schools and canons to make sacraments of those minor orders, since, even by the confession of those who do so, they were unknown to the primitive Church, and were devised many ages after. But sacraments as containing a divine promise ought not to be appointed, either by angels or men, but by God only, to whom alone it belongs to give the promise.

28 Of the higher class of orders called Holy Orders. Insult offered to Christ when ministers are regarded as priests. Holy orders have nothing of the nature of a sacrament.

There remain the three orders, which they call major. Of these, what they call the subdeaconate was transferred to this class, after the crowd of minor began to be prolific. But as they think they have authority for these from the Word of God, they honor them especially with the name of Holy Orders. Let us see how they wrest the ordinances of God to their own ends. We begin with the order of presbyter or priest. To these two names they give one meaning, understanding by them, those to whom, as they say, it pertains to offer the sacrifice of Christ's body and blood on the altar, to frame prayers, and bless the gifts of God. Hence, at ordination, they receive the patena with the host, as symbols of the power conferred upon them of offering sacrifices to appease God, and their hands are anointed, this symbol being intended to teach that they have received the power of consecrating. But of the ceremonies afterwards. Of the thing itself, I say that it is so far from having, as they pretend, one particle of support from the Word of God, that they could not more wickedly corrupt the order, which he has appointed. And first, it ought to be held as confessed (this we maintained when treating of the Papal Mass), that all are injurious to Christ who call themselves priests in the sense of offering expiatory victims. He was constituted and consecrated Priest by the Father, with an oath, after the order of Melchisedek, without end and without successor (Psalm 110:4;

Hebrews 5:6; 7:3). He once offered a victim of eternal expiation and reconciliation, and now having entered the sanctuary of Heaven, He intercedes for us. In Him, we all are priests, but to offer praise and thanksgiving, in fine, ourselves, and all that is ours, to God. It was peculiar to Him alone to appease God and expiate sins by His oblation. When these men usurp it to themselves, what follows, but that they have an impious and sacrilegious priesthood? It is certainly wicked over much to dare to distinguish it with the title of sacrament.

In regard to the true office of presbyter, which was recommended to us by the lips of Christ, I willingly give it that place. For in it there is a ceremony, which, first, is taken from the Scriptures; and, secondly, is declared by Paul to be not empty or superfluous, but to be a faithful symbol of spiritual grace (1 Timothy 4:14). My reason for not giving a place to the third is that it is not ordinary or common to all believers, but is a special rite for a certain function. But while this honor is attributed to the Christian ministry, Popish priests may not plume themselves upon it. Christ ordered dispensers of His Gospel and His sacred mysteries to be ordained, not sacrificers to be inaugurated, and His command was to preach the Gospel and feed the flock, not to immolate victims. He promised the gift of the Holy Spirit, not to make expiation for sins, but duly to undertake and maintain the government of the Church (Matthew 28:19; Mark 16:15; John 21:15).

29 Absurd imitation of our Savior in breathing on His apostles.

With the reality, the ceremonies perfectly agree. When our Lord commissioned the apostles to preach the Gospel, He breathed upon them (John 20:22). By this symbol, He represented the gift of the Holy Spirit, which He bestowed upon them. This breathing these worthy men have retained; and, as they were bringing the Holy Spirit from their throat, mutter over their priestlings, "Receive the Holy Spirit." Accordingly, they omit nothing that they do not preposterously mimic. I say not in the manner of players (who have art and meaning in their gestures), but like apes that imitate at random without selection. We observe, say they, the example of the Lord. But the Lord did many things, which He did not intend to be examples to us. Our Lord said to His disciples, "Receive the Holy Spirit" (John 20:22). He said also to Lazarus, "Lazarus, come forth" (John 11:43). He said to the paralytic, "Rise, take up thy bed, and walk" (John 5:8). Why do they not say the same to all the dead and paralytic? He gave a specimen of His divine power when, in breathing on the apostles, He filled them with the gift of the Holy Spirit. If they attempt to do the same, they rival God, and do all but challenge Him to the contest. But they are very far from producing the effect, and only mock Christ by that absurd gesture. Such, indeed, is the effrontery of some, that they dare to assert that the Holy Spirit is conferred by them; but what truth there is in this, we learn from experience, which cries aloud that all who are consecrated priests, of horses become asses, and of fools, madmen. And yet it is not here that I am contending against them; I am only condemning the ceremony itself, which ought not to be drawn into a precedent, since it was used as the special symbol of a miracle, so far is it from furnishing them with an example for imitation.

30 Absurdity of the anointing employed.

But from whom, pray, did they receive their unction? They answer, that they received it from the sons of Aaron, from whom also their order derived its origin. Thus, they constantly choose to defend themselves by perverse examples, rather than confess that any of their rash practices is of their own devising. Meanwhile, they observe not that in professing the successors of the sons of Aaron, they are injurious to the priesthood of Christ, which alone was adumbrated and typified by all ancient priesthoods. In Him, therefore, they were all concluded and completed, in him they ceased, as we have repeatedly said, and as the Epistle to the Hebrews, unaided by any gloss, declares. But if they are so much delighted with Mosaic ceremonies, why do they not hurry oxen, calves, and lambs, to their sacrifices? They have, indeed, a great part of the ancient tabernacle, and of the whole Jewish worship. The only thing wanted to their religion is, that they do not sacrifice oxen and calves. Who sees not that this practice of unction is much more pernicious than circumcision, especially when to it is added superstition and a Pharisaical opinion of the merit of the work? The Jews placed their confidence of justification in circumcision; these men look for spiritual gifts in unction. Therefore, in desiring to be rivals of the Levites, they become apostates from Christ, and discard themselves from the pastoral office.

31 Imposition of hands. Absurdity of, in Papistical ordination.

It is, if you please, the sacred oil, which impresses an indelible character. As if oil could not be washed away by sand and salt, or if it sticks the closer, with soap. But that character is spiritual. What has oil to do with the soul? Have they forgotten what they quote from Augustine: that if the word be withdrawn from the water, there will be nothing but water, but that it is owing to the word that it is a sacrament? What word can they show in their oil? Is it because Moses was commanded to anoint the sons of Aaron? (Exodus 30:30). But he there receives command concerning the tunic, the ephod, the breastplate, the miter, the crown of holiness with which Aaron was to be adorned; and concerning the tunics, belts, and miters, which his sons were to wear. He receives command about sacrificing the calf, burning its fat, about cutting and burning rams, about sanctifying ear-rings and vestments with the blood of one of the rams, and innumerable other observances. Having passed over all these, I wonder why the unction of oil alone pleases them. If they delight in being sprinkled, why are they sprinkled with oil rather than with blood? They are attempting, forsooth, an ingenious device; they are trying, by a kind of patchwork, to make one religion out of Christianity, Judaism, and Paganism. Their unction, therefore, is without savor; it wants salt, that is, the Word of God. There remains the laying on of hands, which, though I admit it to be a sacrament in true and legitimate ordination, I do deny to have any such place in this fable, where they neither obey the command of Christ, nor look to the end to which the promise ought to lead us. If they would not have the sign denied them, they must adapt it to the reality to which it is dedicated.

32 Ordination of deacons. Absurd forms of Papists.

As to the order of the diaconate, I would raise no dispute, if the office which existed under the apostles, and a purer Church, were restored to its integrity. But what resemblance to it do we see in their fictitious deacons? I speak not of the men, lest they should complain that I am unjustly judging their doctrine by the vices of those who profess it; but I contend that those, whom their doctrine declares to us, derive no countenance from those deacons whom the apostolic Church appointed. They say that it belongs to their deacons to assist the priests, and minister at all the things, which are done in the sacraments, as in baptism, in chrism, the patena, and chalice, to bring the offerings and lay them on the altar, to prepare and dress the table of the Lord, to carry the cross, announce and read out the Gospel and epistle to the people. Is there here one word about the true office of deacon? Let us now attend to the appointment. The bishop alone lays hands on the deacon who is ordained; he places the prayer-book and stole upon his left shoulder, that he may understand that he has received the easy yoke of the Lord, in order that he may subject to the fear of the Lord everything pertaining to the left side: he gives him a text of the Gospel, to remind him that he is its herald. What have these things to do with deacons? But they act just as if one were to say he was ordaining apostles, when he was only appointing persons to kindle the incense, clean the images, sweep the churches, set traps for mice, and put out dogs. Who can allow this class of men to be called apostles, and to be compared with the very apostles of Christ? After this, let them not pretend that those whom they appoint to mere stage-play are deacons. Nay, they even declare, by the very name, what the nature of the office is. For they call them Levites, and wish to trace their nature and origin to the sons of Levi. As far as I am concerned, they are welcome, provided they do not afterwards deck themselves in borrowed feathers.

33 Of sub-deacons.

What use is there in speaking of subdeacons? For, whereas in fact they anciently had the charge of the poor, they attribute to them some kind of nugatory function, as carrying the chalice and patena, the pitcher with water, and the napkin to the altar, pouring out water for the hands, etc. Then, by the offerings, which they are said to receive and bring in, they mean those, which they swallow up, as if they had been destined to anathema. There is an admirable correspondence between the office and the mode of inducting to it–viz. receiving from the bishop the patena and chalice, and from the archdeacon the pitcher with water, the manual, and trumpery of this kind. They call upon us to admit that the Holy Spirit is included in these frivolities. What pious man can be induced to grant this? But to have done at once, we may conclude the same of this as of the others, and there is no need to repeat at length what has been explained above. To the modest and docile (it is such I have undertaken to instruct), it will be enough that there is no sacrament of God, unless where a ceremony is shown annexed to a promise, or rather where a promise is seen in a ceremony. Here there is not one syllable of a certain promise, and it is vain, therefore, to seek for a ceremony to confirm the promise. On the other hand, we read of no ceremony appointed by God in regard to those usages, which they employ, and, therefore, there can be no sacrament.

OF MARRIAGE.

34 Marriage not a sacrament.

The last of all is marriage, which, while all admit it to be an institution of God, no man ever saw to be a sacrament, until the time of Gregory. And would it ever have occurred to the mind of any sober man? It is a good and holy ordinance of God. And agriculture, architecture, shoemaking, and shaving, are lawful ordinances of God; but they are not sacraments. For in a sacrament, the thing required is not only that it be a work of God, but that it be an external ceremony appointed by God to confirm a promise. That there is nothing of the kind in marriage, even children can judge. But it is a sign, they say, of a sacred thing, that is, of the spiritual union of Christ with the Church. If by the term sign they understand a symbol set before us by God to assure us of our faith, they wander widely from the mark. If they mean merely a sign because it has been employed as a similitude, I will show how acutely they reason. Paul says, "One star differeth from another star in glory. So also is the resurrection of the dead" (1 Corinthians 15:41, 42). Here is one sacrament. Christ says, "The kingdom of heaven is like to a grain of mustard-seed" (Matthew 13:13). Here is another sacrament. Again, "The kingdom of heaven is like unto leaven" (Matthew 13:13). Here is a third sacrament. Isaiah says, "He shall feed his flock like a shepherd" (Isaiah 40:11). Here is a fourth sacrament. In another passage he says, "The Lord shall go forth as a mighty man" (Isaiah 42:13). Here is a fifth sacrament. And where will be the end or limit? Everything in this way will be a sacrament. All the parables and similitudes in Scripture will be so many sacraments. Nay, even theft will be a sacrament, seeing it is written, "The day of the Lord so cometh as a thief in the night" (1 Thessalonians 5:2). Who can tolerate the ignorant garrulity of these sophists? I admit, indeed, that whenever we see a vine, the best thing is to call to mind what our Savior says, "I am the true vine, and my father is the husbandman." " I am the vine, ye are the branches" (John 15:1, 5). And whenever we meet a shepherd with his flock, it is good to remember, "I am the good shepherd, and know my sheep, and am known of mine" (John 10:14). But any man who would class such similitudes with sacraments should be sent to bedlam.

35 Nothing in Scripture to countenance the idea that marriage is a sacrament.

They adduce the words of Paul, by which they say that the name of a sacrament is given to marriage, "He that loveth his wife loveth himself. For no man ever yet hated his own flesh; but nourisheth and cherisheth it, even as the Lord the Church: for we are members of His body, of His flesh, and of His bones. For this cause shall a man leave his father and mother, and shall be joined unto his wife, and they two shall be one flesh. This is a great mystery: but I speak concerning Christ and the Church" (Ephesians 5:28, 32). To treat Scripture thus is to confound heaven and earth. Paul, in order to show husbands how they ought to love their wives, sets Christ before them as an example. As He shed his bowels of affection for the Church, which He has espoused to himself, so He would have everyone to feel affected toward his wife. Then he adds, "He that loveth his wife loveth himself," "even as the Lord the Church." Moreover, to show how Christ loved the Church as himself, nay, how He made himself one with His spouse the Church, He applies to her what Moses relates that Adam said of himself. For after Eve was brought into his presence, knowing that she had been formed out of his side, he exclaimed, "This is now bone of my bones, and flesh of my flesh" (Genesis 2:23). That all this was spiritually fulfilled in Christ, and in us, Paul declares, when He says, that we are members of His body, of His flesh, and of His bones, and so one flesh with Him. At length he breaks out into the exclamation, "This is a great mystery;" and lest anyone should be misled by the ambiguity, he says, that he is not speaking of the connection between husband and wife, but of the spiritual marriage of Christ and the Church. And truly it is a great mystery that Christ allowed a rib to be taken from himself, of which we might be formed; that is, that when He was strong, He was pleased to become weak, that we might be strengthened by His strength, and should no longer live ourselves, but He live in us (Galatians 2:20).

36 Origin of the notion that marriage is a sacrament.

The thing that misled them was the term *sacrament*. But, was it right that the whole Church should be punished for the ignorance of these men? Paul called it a mystery. When the Latin interpreter might have abandoned this mode of expression as uncommon to Latin ears, or converted it into "secret," he preferred calling it *sacramentum*, but in no other sense than the Greek term that was used by Paul. Let them go now and clamor against skill in languages, their ignorance of which leads them most shamefully astray in a matter easy and obvious to everyone. But why do they so strongly urge the term sacrament in this one passage and in others pass it by with neglect? For both in the First Epistle to Timothy (1 Timothy 3:9, 16), and in the Epistle to the Ephesians, it is used by the Vulgate interpreter, and in every instance, for mystery. Let us, however, pardon them this lapse, though liars ought to have good memories. Marriage being thus recommended by the title of a sacrament, can it be anything but vertiginous levity afterwards to call it uncleanness, and pollution, and carnal defilement? How absurd is it to debar priests from a sacrament! If they say that they debar not from a sacrament but from carnal connection, they will not thus escape me. They say that this connection is part of the sacrament, and thereby figures the union, which we have with Christ in conformity of nature, inasmuch as it is by this connection that husband and wife become one flesh. Although, some have here found two sacraments, the one of God and the soul, in bridegroom and bride, another of Christ and the Church, in husband and wife. Be this as it may, this connection is a sacrament from which no Christian can lawfully be debarred, unless, indeed, the sacraments of Christians accord so ill that they cannot stand together. There is also another absurdity in these dogmas. They affirm that in a sacrament, the gift of the Holy Spirit is conferred; this connection they hold to be a sacrament, and yet they deny that in it the Holy Spirit is ever present.

37 Practical abuses from this erroneous idea of marriage. Conclusion.

And, that they might not delude the Church in this matter merely, what a long series of errors, lies, frauds, and iniquities have they appended to one error? So that you may say they sought nothing but a hidingplace for abominations when they converted marriage into a sacrament. When once they obtained this, they appropriated to themselves the cognizance of conjugal causes: as the thing was spiritual, it was not to be intermeddled with by profane judges. Then they enacted laws by which they confirmed their tyranny, –laws partly impious toward God, partly fraught with injustice toward men; such as, that marriages contracted between minors, without the consent of their parents, should be valid; that no lawful marriages can be contracted between relations within the seventh degree, and that such marriages, if contracted, should be dissolved. Moreover, they frame degrees of kindred contrary to the laws of all nations, and even the polity of Moses, and enact that a husband who has repudiated an adulteress may not marry again–that spiritual kindred cannot be joined in marriage–that marriage cannot be celebrated from Septuagesimo to the Octaves of Easter, three weeks before the nativity of John, nor from Advent to Epiphany, and innumerable others too tedious to mention. We must now get out of their mire, in which our discourse has stuck longer than our inclination. Methinks, however, that much has been gained if I have, in some measure, deprived these asses of their lion's skin.

Chapter 20

OF CIVIL GOVERNMENT.

This chapter consists of two principal heads, –I. General discourse on the necessity, dignity, and use of Civil Government, in opposition to the frantic proceedings of the Anabaptists, sections 1-3. II. A special exposition of the three leading parts of which Civil Government consists, sections 4-32.

The first part treats of the function of Magistrates, whose authority and calling is proved, sections 4-7. Next, the three Forms of civil government are added, section 8. Thirdly, Consideration of the office of the civil magistrate in respect of piety and righteousness. Here, of rewards and punishments–viz. punishing the guilty, protecting the innocent, repressing the seditious, managing the affairs of peace and war, sections 9-13. The second part treats of Laws, their utility, necessity, form, authority, constitution, and scope, sections 14-16. The last part relates to the People, and explains the use of laws, courts, and magistrates, to the common society of Christians, sections 17-21. Deference which private individuals owe to magistrates, and how far obedience ought to be carried, sections 22-32.

Sections

1. Last part of the whole work, relating to the institution of Civil Government. The consideration of it necessary. A. To refute the Anabaptists. B. To refute the flatterers of princes. C. To excite our gratitude to God. Civil government not opposed to Christian liberty. Civil government to be distinguished from the spiritual Kingdom of Christ.

2. Objections of the Anabaptists. A. That civil government is unworthy of a Christian man. B. That it is diametrically repugnant to the Christian profession. Answer.

3. The answer confirmed. Discourse reduced to three heads, A. Of Laws. B. Of Magistrates. 3. Of the People.

4. The office of Magistrates approved by God. A. They are called Gods. B. They are ordained by the wisdom of God. Examples of pious Magistrates.

5. Civil government appointed by God for Jews, not Christians. This objection answered.

6. Divine appointment of Magistrates. Effect which this ought to have on Magistrates themselves.

7. This consideration should repress the fury of the Anabaptists.

8. Three forms of civil government, Monarchy, Aristocracy, Democracy. Impossible absolutely to say which is best.

9. Of the duty of Magistrates. Their first care the preservation of the Christian religion and true piety. This proved.

10. Objections of Anabaptists to this view. These answered.

11. Lawfulness of War.

12 Objection, that the lawfulness of war is not taught in Scripture. Answer.

13. Right of exacting tribute and raising revenues.

14. Of Laws, their necessity and utility. Distinction between the Moral, Ceremonial, and Judicial Law of Moses.

15. Sum and scope of the Moral Law. Of the Ceremonial and Judicial Law. Conclusion.

16. All Laws should be just. Civil Law of Moses: how far in force, and how far abrogated.

17. Of the People, and of the use of laws as respects individuals.

18. How far litigation lawful.

19. Refutation of the Anabaptists, who condemn all judicial proceedings.

20. Objection, that Christ forbids us to resist evil. Answer.

21. Objection, that Paul condemns lawsuits absolutely. Answer.

22. Of the respect and obedience due to Magistrates.

23. Same subject continued.

24. How far submission due to tyrants.

25. Same continued.

26. Proof from Scripture.
27. Proof continued.
28. Objections answered.
29. Considerations to curb impatience under tyranny.
30. Considerations considered.
31. General submission due by private individuals.
32. Obedience due only in so far as compatible with the Word of God.

1 Last part of the whole work, relating to the institution of Civil Government. The consideration of it necessary. A. To refute the Anabaptists. B. To refute the flatterers of princes. C. To excite our gratitude to God. Civil government not opposed to Christian liberty. Civil government to be distinguished from the spiritual Kingdom of Christ.

Having shown above that there is a twofold government in man and having fully considered the one which, placed in the soul or inward man, relates to eternal life, we are here called to say something of the other, which pertains only to civil institutions and the external regulation of manners. For although this subject seems from its nature to be unconnected with the spiritual doctrine of faith, which I have undertaken to treat, it will appear as we proceed, that I have properly connected them, nay, that I am under the necessity of doing so, especially while, on the one hand, frantic and barbarous men are furiously endeavoring to overturn the order established by God, and, on the other, the flatterers of princes, extolling their power without measure, hesitate not to oppose it to the government of God. Unless we meet both extremes, the purity of the faith will perish. We may add, that it in no small degree concerns us to know how kindly God has here consulted for the human race, that pious zeal may the more strongly urge us to testify our gratitude. And first, before entering on the subject itself, it is necessary to attend to the distinction which we formerly laid down (Book 3, Chapter 19, section 16, et supra, Chapter 10), lest, as often happens to many, we imprudently confound these two things, the nature of which is altogether different. For some, on hearing that liberty is promised in the Gospel, a liberty that acknowledges no king and no magistrate among men, but looks to Christ alone, think that they can receive no benefit from their liberty so long as they see any power placed over them.

Accordingly, they think that nothing will be safe until the whole world is changed into a new form, when there will be neither courts, nor laws, nor magistrates, nor anything of the kind to interfere, as they suppose, with their liberty. But he who knows to distinguish between the body and the soul, between the present fleeting life and that which is future and eternal, will have no difficulty in understanding that the spiritual Kingdom of Christ and civil government are things very widely separated. Seeing, therefore, it is a Jewish vanity to seek and include the Kingdom of Christ under the elements of this world, let us, considering, as Scripture clearly teaches, that the blessings, which we derive from Christ, are spiritual, remember to confine the liberty, which is promised and offered to us in Him within its proper limits. For why is it that the very same apostle who bids us "stand fast in the liberty wherewith Christ hath made us free, and be not again entangled with the yoke of bondage" (Galatians 5:1), in another passage forbids slaves to be solicitous about their state (1 Corinthians 7:21), unless it be that spiritual liberty is perfectly compatible with civil servitude? In this sense, the following passages are to be understood: "There is neither Jew nor Greek, there is neither bond nor free, there is neither male nor female" (Galatians 3:28). Again, "There is neither Greek nor Jew, circumcision nor uncircumcision, barbarian, Scythian, bond nor free: but Christ is all and in all" (Colossians 3:11). It is thus intimated, that it matters not what your condition is among men, nor under what laws you live, since in them the Kingdom of Christ does not at all consist.

2 Objections of the Anabaptists. A. That civil government is unworthy of a Christian man. B. That it is diametrically repugnant to the Christian profession. Answer.

Still, the distinction does not go so far as to justify us in supposing that the whole scheme of civil government is matter of pollution, with which Christian men have nothing to do. Fanatics, indeed, delighting in unbridled license, insist and vociferate that after we are dead by Christ to the elements of this world, and have been translated into the Kingdom of God to sit among the celestials, it is unworthy of us and far beneath our dignity to be occupied with those profane and impure cares, which relate to matters alien from a Christian man.

To what end, they say, are laws without courts and tribunals? But what has a Christian man to do with courts? Nay, if it is unlawful to kill, what have we to do with laws and courts? But as we lately taught that that kind of government is distinct from the spiritual and internal Kingdom of Christ, so we ought to know that they are not adverse to each other. The former, in some measure, begins the heavenly Kingdom in us, even now upon Earth, and in this mortal and evanescent life commences immortal and incorruptible blessedness, while to the latter it is assigned, so long as we live among men, to foster and maintain the external worship of God, to defend sound doctrine and the condition of the Church, to adapt our conduct to human society, to form our manners to civil justice, to conciliate us to each other, to cherish common peace and tranquility. All these I confess to be superfluous, if the Kingdom of God, as it now exists within us, extinguishes the present life. But if it is the will of God that while we aspire to true piety we are pilgrims upon the Earth, and if such pilgrimage stands in need of such aids, those who take them away from man rob him of his humanity. As to their allegation that there ought to be such perfection in the Church of God that her guidance should suffice for law, they stupidly imagine her to be such as she never can be found in the community of men. For while the insolence of the wicked is so great, and their iniquity so stubborn, that it can scarcely be curbed by any severity of laws, what do we expect would be done by those whom force can scarcely repress from doing ill, were they to see perfect impunity for their wickedness?

3 The answer confirmed. Discourse reduced to three heads, A. Of Laws. B. Of Magistrates. 3. Of the People.

But we shall have a fitter opportunity of speaking of the use of civil government. All we wish to be understood at present is, that it is perfect barbarism to think of exterminating it, its use among men being not less than that of bread and water, light and air, while its dignity is much more excellent. Its object is not merely, like those things, to enable men to breathe, eat, drink, and be warmed (though it certainly includes all these, while it enables them to live together); this, I say, is not its only object, but it is, that no idolatry, no blasphemy against the name of God, no calumnies against His truth, nor other offenses to religion, break out and be disseminated among the people; that the public quiet be not disturbed, that every man's property be kept secure, that men may carry on innocent commerce with each other, that honesty and modesty be cultivated; in short, that a public form of religion may exist among Christians, and humanity among men. Let no one be surprised that I now attribute the task of constituting religion aright to human polity, though I seem above to have placed it beyond the will of man, since I no more than formerly allow men at pleasure to enact laws concerning religion and the worship of God, when I approve of civil order which is directed to this end–viz. to prevent the true religion, which is contained in the law of God, from being with impunity openly violated and polluted by public blasphemy. But the reader, by the help of a perspicuous arrangement, will better understand what view is to be taken of the whole order of civil government, if we treat of each of its parts separately. Now these are three: The Magistrate, who is president and guardian of the laws; the Laws, according to which he governs; and the People, who are governed by the laws and obey the magistrate. Let us consider first, What is the function of the magistrate? Is it a lawful calling approved by God? What is the nature of his duty? What the extent of his power? Secondly, What are the laws by which Christian polity is to be regulated? And, lastly, What is the use of laws as regards the people? And, What obedience is due to the magistrate?

4 The office of Magistrates approved by God. A. They are called gods. B. They are ordained by the wisdom of God. Examples of pious Magistrates.

With regard to the function of magistrates, the Lord has not only declared that He approves and is pleased with it, but, moreover, has strongly recommended it to us by the very honorable titles which He has conferred upon it. To mention a, few. When those who bear the office of magistrate are called gods, let no one suppose that there is little weight in that appellation. It is thereby intimated that they have a commission from God, that they are invested with divine authority, and, in fact, represent the person of God, as whose substitutes they in a manner act. This is not a quibble of mine, but is the interpretation of Christ. "If Scripture," says He, "called them gods, to whom the Word of God came." What is this but that the business was committed to them by God, to serve Him in their office, and (as Moses and Jehoshaphat said to the judges whom they were appointing over each of the cities of Judah) to exercise judgment, not for man, but for God? To the same effect Wisdom affirms, by the mouth of Solomon, "By me kings reign, and princes decree justice. By me princes rule, and nobles, even all the judges of the earth" (Proverbs 8:15, 16). For it is just as if it had been said, that it is not owing to human perverseness that supreme power on Earth is lodged in kings and other governors, but by Divine Providence, and the holy decree of Him to whom it has seemed good so to govern the affairs of men, since He is present, and also presides in enacting laws and exercising judicial equity. This Paul also plainly teaches when he enumerates offices of rule among the gifts of God, which, distributed variously, according to the measure of grace, ought to be employed by the servants of Christ for the edification of the Church (Romans 12:8). In that place, however, he is properly speaking of the senate of grave men who were appointed in the primitive Church to take charge of public discipline. This office, in the Epistle to the Corinthians, he calls in Greek, "governments" (1 Corinthians 12:28). Still, as we see that civil power has the same end in view, there can be no doubt that he is recommending every kind of just government. He speaks much more clearly, when he comes to a proper discussion of the subject. For he says that "there is no power but of God: the powers that be are ordained of God;" that rulers are the ministers of God, "not a terror to good works, but to the evil" (Romans 13:1, 3). To this we may add the examples of saints, some of whom held the offices of kings, as David, Josiah, and Hezekiah; others of governors, as Joseph and Daniel; others of civil magistrates among a free people, as Moses, Joshua, and the Judges. Their functions were expressly approved by the Lord. Wherefore no man can doubt that civil authority is, in the sight of God, not only sacred and lawful, but the most sacred, and by far the most honorable, of all stations in mortal life.

5 Civil government appointed by God for Jews, not Christians. This objection answered.

Those who are desirous to introduce anarchy object that, though anciently kings and judges presided over a rude people, yet that, in the present day, that servile mode of governing does not at all accord with the perfection which Christ brought with His Gospel. Herein they betray not only their ignorance, but their devilish pride, arrogating to themselves a perfection of which not even a hundredth part is seen in them. But be they what they may, the refutation is easy. For when David says, "Be wise now therefore, O ye kings: be instructed, ye judges of the earth;" "Kiss the Son, lest he be angry" (Psalm 2:10, 12), he does not order them to lay aside their authority and return to private life, but to make the power with which they are invested subject to Christ, that He may rule over all. In like manner, when Isaiah predicts of the Church, "Kings shall be thy nursing-fathers, and their queens thy nursing-mothers" (Isaiah 49:23), he does not bid them abdicate their authority; he rather gives them the honorable appellation of patrons of the pious worshippers of God; for the prophecy refers to the advent of Christ. I intentionally omit very many passages that occur throughout Scripture, and especially in the Psalms, in which the due authority of all rulers is asserted. The most celebrated passage of all is that in which Paul, admonishing Timothy, that prayers are to be offered up in the public assembly for kings, subjoins the reason, "that we may lead a quiet and peaceable life in all godliness and honesty" (1 Timothy 2:2). In these words, he recommends the condition of the Church to their protection and guardianship.

6 Divine appointment of Magistrates. Effect which this ought to have on Magistrates themselves.

This consideration ought to be constantly present to the minds of magistrates, since it is fitted to furnish a strong stimulus to the discharge of duty, and also afford singular consolation, smoothing the difficulties of their office, which are certainly numerous and weighty. What zeal for integrity, prudence, meekness, continence, and innocence, ought to sway those who know that they have been appointed ministers of the divine justice! How will they dare to admit iniquity to their tribunal, when they are told that it is the throne of the living God? How will they venture to pronounce an unjust sentence with that mouth which they understand to be an ordained organ of divine truth? With what conscience will they subscribe impious decrees with that hand which they know has been appointed to write the acts of God? In a word, if they remember that they are the vicegerents of God, it behooves them to watch with all care, diligence, and industry, that they may in themselves exhibit a kind of image of the Divine Providence, guardianship, goodness, benevolence, and justice. And let them constantly keep the additional thought in view, that if a curse is pronounced on him that "doeth the work of the Lord deceitfully," a much heavier curse must lie on him who deals deceitfully in a righteous calling. Therefore, when Moses and Jehoshaphat would urge their judges to the discharge of duty, they had nothing by which they could more powerfully stimulate their minds than the consideration to which we have already referred, —"Take heed what ye do: for ye judge not for man, but for the Lord, who is with you in the judgment. Wherefore now let the fear of the Lord be upon you; take heed and do it: for there is no iniquity with the Lord our God, nor respect of persons, nor taking of gifts" (2 Corinthians 19:6, 7, compared with Deuteronomy 1:16, etc.). And in another passage it is said, "God standeth in the congregation of the mighty; he judgeth among the gods" (Psalm 82:1; Isaiah 3:14), that they may be animated to duty when they hear that they are the ambassadors of God, to whom they must one day render an account of the province committed to them. This admonition ought justly to have the greatest effect upon them; for if they sin in any respect, not only is injury done to the men whom they wickedly torment, but they also insult God himself, whose sacred tribunals they pollute. On the other hand, they have an admirable source of comfort when they reflect that they are not engaged in profane occupations, unbefitting a servant of God, but in a most sacred office, inasmuch as they are the ambassadors of God.

7 This consideration should repress the fury of the Anabaptists.

In regard to those who are not debarred by all these passages of Scripture from presuming to inveigh against this sacred ministry, as if it were a thing abhorrent from religion and Christian piety, what else do they than assail God himself, who cannot but be insulted when His servants are disgraced? These men not only speak evil of dignities, but would not even have God to reign over them (1 Samuel 7:7). For if this was truly said of the people of Israel, when they declined the authority of Samuel, how can it be less truly said in the present day of those who allow themselves to break loose against all the authority established by God? But it seems that when our Lord said to His disciples, "The kings of the gentiles exercise lordship over them; and they that exercise authority upon them are called benefactors. But ye shall not be so: but he that is greatest among you, let him be as the younger; and he that is chief; as he that doth serve" (Luke 22:25, 26). By these words, He prohibited all Christians from becoming kings or governors. Dexterous expounders! A dispute had arisen among the disciples as to which of them should be greatest. To suppress this vain ambition, our Lord taught them that their ministry was not like the power of earthly sovereigns, among whom one greatly surpasses another. What, I ask, is there in this comparison disparaging to royal dignity? Nay, what does it prove at all unless that the royal office is not the apostolic ministry? Besides, though among magisterial offices themselves there are different forms, there is no difference in this respect, that they are all to be received by us as ordinances of God. For Paul includes all together when he says that "there is no power but of God," and that which was by no means the most pleasing of all, was honored with the highest testimonial–I mean the power of one. This, as carrying with it the public servitude of all (except the one to whose despotic will all is subject), was anciently disrelished by heroic and more excellent natures. But Scripture, to obviate these unjust judgments, affirms expressly that it is by divine wisdom that "kings reign," and gives special command "to honor the king" (1 Peter 2:17).

8 Three forms of civil government, Monarchy, Aristocracy, Democracy. Impossible absolutely to say which is best.

And certainly it would be a very idle occupation for private men to discuss what would be the best form of polity in the place where they live, seeing these deliberations cannot have any influence in determining any public matter. Then the thing itself could not be defined absolutely without rashness, since the nature of the discussion depends on circumstances. And if you compare the different states with each other, without regard to circumstances, it is not easy to determine which of these has the advantage in point of utility, so equal are the terms on which they meet. Monarchy is prone to tyranny. In an aristocracy, again, the tendency is not less to the faction of a few; while in popular ascendancy there is the strongest tendency to sedition. When these three forms of government, of which philosophers treat, are considered in themselves, I am far from denying that the form, which greatly surpasses the others, is aristocracy: either pure or modified by popular government, not indeed in itself, but because it very rarely happens that kings so rule themselves as never to dissent from what is just and right, or are possessed of so much acuteness and prudence as always to see correctly. Owing, therefore, to the vices or defects of men, it is safer and more tolerable when several bear rule, that they may thus mutually assist, instruct, and admonish each other, and should anyone be disposed to go too far, the others are censors and masters to curb his excess. This has already been proved by experience and confirmed by the authority of the Lord himself, when He established an aristocracy bordering on popular government among the Israelites, keeping them under that as the best form, until He exhibited an image of the Messiah in David. And as I willingly admit that there is no kind of government happier than where liberty is framed with becoming moderation, and duly constituted so as to be durable, so I deem those very happy who are permitted to enjoy that form, and I admit that they do nothing at variance with their duty when they strenuously and constantly labor to preserve and maintain it. Nay, even magistrates ought to do their utmost to prevent the liberty, of which they have been appointed guardians, from being impaired, far less violated. If in this they are sluggish or little careful, they are perfidious traitors to their office and their country.

But should those to whom the Lord has assigned one form of government, take it upon them anxiously to long for a change, the wish would not only be foolish and superfluous, but very pernicious. If you fix your eyes not on one state merely, but look around the world, or at least direct your view to regions widely separated from each other, you will perceive that Divine Providence has not, without good cause, arranged that different countries should be governed by different forms of polity. For as only elements of unequal temperature adhere together, so in different regions a similar inequality in the form of government is best. All this, however, is said unnecessarily to those to whom the will of God is a sufficient reason. For if it has pleased Him to appoint kings over kingdoms, and senates or burgomasters over free states, whatever be the form which He has appointed in the places in which we live, our duty is to obey and submit.

9 Of the duty of Magistrates. Their first care the preservation of the Christian religion and true piety. This proved.

The duty of magistrates, its nature, as described by the Word of God, and the things in which it consists, I will here indicate in passing. That it extends to both tables of the law, did Scripture not teach, we might learn from profane writers; for no man has discoursed of the duty of magistrates, the enacting of laws, and the common weal, without beginning with religion and divine worship. Thus, all have confessed that no polity can be successfully established unless piety is its first care, and that those laws are absurd which disregard the rights of God, and consult only for men. Seeing then that among philosophers religion holds the first place, and that the same thing has always been observed with the universal consent of nations, Christian princes and magistrates may be ashamed of their heartlessness if they make it not their care. We have already shown that this office is specially assigned them by God, and indeed it is right that they exert themselves in asserting and defending the honor of Him whose vicegerents they are, and by whose favor they rule. Hence, in Scripture holy kings are especially praised for restoring the worship of God when corrupted or overthrown, or for taking care that religion flourished under them in purity and safety.

On the other hand, the sacred history sets down anarchy among the vices, when it states that there was no king in Israel, and, therefore, everyone did as he pleased (Judges 21:25). This rebukes the folly of those who would neglect the care of divine things, and devote themselves merely to the administration of justice among men, as if God had appointed rulers in His own name to decide earthly controversies, and omitted what was of far greater moment, His own pure worship as prescribed by His law. Such views are adopted by turbulent men, who, in their eagerness to make all kinds of innovations with impunity, would fain get rid of all the vindicators of violated piety.

In regard to the second table of the law, Jeremiah addresses rulers, "Thus saith the Lord, Execute ye judgment and righteousness, and deliver the spoiled out of the hand of the oppressor: and do no wrong, do no violence to the stranger, the fatherless, nor the widow, neither shed innocent blood" (Jeremiah 22:3). To the same effect is the exhortation in the Psalm, "Defend the poor and fatherless; do justice to the afflicted and needy. Deliver the poor and needy; rid them out of the hand of the wicked" (Psalm 82:3, 4). Moses also declared to the princes whom he had substituted for himself, "Hear the causes between your brethren, and judge righteously between every man and his brother, and the stranger that is with him. Ye shall not respect persons in judgment; but ye shall hear the small as well as the great: ye shall not be afraid of the face of man, for the judgment is God's" (Deuteronomy 1:16). I say nothing as to such passages as these, "He shall not multiply horses to himself, nor cause the people to return to Egypt;" "neither shall he multiply wives to himself; neither shall he greatly multiply to himself silver and gold;" "he shall write him a copy of this law in a book;" "and it shall be with him, and he shall read therein all the days of his life, that he may learn to fear the Lord his God;" "that his heart be not lifted up above his brethren" (Deuteronomy 17:16-20). In here explaining the duties of magistrates, my exposition is intended not so much for the instruction of magistrates themselves, as to teach others why there are magistrates, and to what end they have been appointed by God.

We say, therefore, that they are the ordained guardians and vindicators of public innocence, modesty, honor, and tranquility, so that it should be their only study to provide for the common peace and safety. Of these things, David declares that he will set an example when he shall have ascended the throne. "A froward [disobedient] heart shall depart from me: I will not know a wicked person. Whoso privily [privately] slandereth [insults or maligns] his neighbor, him will I cut off: him that hath an high look and a proud heart will not I suffer. Mine eyes shall be upon the faithful of the land, that they may dwell with me: he that walketh in a perfect way, he shall serve me" (Psalm 101:4-6). But as rulers cannot do this unless they protect the good against the injuries of the bad, and give aid and protection to the oppressed, they are armed with power to curb manifest evildoers and criminals, by whose misconduct the public tranquility is disturbed or harassed. For we have full experience of the truth of Solon's saying, that all public matters depend on reward and punishment; that where these are wanting, the whole discipline of states totters and falls to pieces. For in the minds of many the love of equity and justice grows cold, if due honor be not paid to virtue, and the licentiousness of the wicked cannot be restrained, without strict discipline and the infliction of punishment. The two things are comprehended by the prophet when he enjoins kings and other rulers to execute "judgment and righteousness" (Jeremiah 21:12; 22:3). It is righteousness (justice) to take charge of the innocent, to defend and avenge them, and set them free: it is judgment to withstand the audacity of the wicked, to repress their violence, and punish their faults.

10 Objections of Anabaptists to this view. These answered.

But here a difficult, and, as it seems, a perplexing question arises. If all Christians are forbidden to kill, and the prophet predicts concerning the holy mountain of the Lord, that is, the Church, "They shall not hurt or destroy," how can magistrates be at once pious and yet shedders of blood? But if we understand that the magistrate, in inflicting punishment, acts not of himself, but executes the very judgments of God, we shall be disencumbered of every doubt. The law of the Lord forbids to kill; but, that murder may not go unpunished, the Lawgiver himself puts the sword into the hands of His ministers, that they may employ it against all murderers. It belongs not to the pious to afflict and hurt; but to avenge the afflictions of the pious, at the command of God, is neither to afflict nor hurt. I wish it could always be present to our mind, that nothing is done here by the rashness of man, but all in obedience to the authority of God. When it is the guide, we never stray from the right path, unless, indeed, divine justice is to be placed under restraint, and not allowed to take punishment on crimes. But if we dare not give the law to it, why should we bring a charge against its ministers? "He beareth not the sword in vain," says Paul, "for he is the minister of God, a revenger to execute wrath on him that doeth evil" (Romans 13:4).

Wherefore, if princes and other rulers know that nothing will be more acceptable to God than their obedience, let them give themselves to this service if they are desirous to improve their piety, justice, and integrity to God. This was the feeling of Moses when, recognizing himself as destined to deliver his people by the power of the Lord, he laid violent hands on the Egyptian, and afterwards took vengeance on the people for sacrilege, by slaying three thousand of them in one day. This was the feeling of David also, when, towards the end of his life, he ordered his son Solomon to put Joab and Shimei to death. Hence, also, in an enumeration of the virtues of a king, one is to cut off the wicked from the Earth, and banish all workers of iniquity from the City of God.

To the same effect is the praise, which is bestowed on Solomon, "Thou lovest righteousness, and hatest wickedness." How is it that the meek and gentle temper of Moses becomes so exasperated, that, besmeared and reeking with the blood of his brethren, he runs through the camp making new slaughter? How is it that David, who, during his whole life, showed so much mildness, almost at his last breath, leaves with his son the bloody testament, not to allow the grey hairs of Joab and Shimei to go to the grave in peace? Both, by their sternness, sanctified the hands, which they would have polluted by showing mercy, inasmuch as they executed the vengeance committed to them by God.

Solomon says, "It is an abomination to kings to commit wickedness; for the throne is established by righteousness." Again, "A king that sitteth in the throne of judgment, scattereth away all evil with his eyes." Again, "A wise king scattereth the wicked, and bringeth the wheel over them." Again, "Take away the dross from the silver, and there shall come forth a vessel for the finer. Take away the wicked men from before the king, and his throne shall be established in righteousness." Again, "He that justifieth the wicked, and he that condemneth the just, even they both are an abomination to the Lord." Again, "An evil man seeketh only rebellion, therefore an evil messenger shall be sent against him." Again, "He that saith unto the wicked, Thou art righteous; him shall the people curse, nations shall abhor him."

Now, if it is true justice in them to pursue the guilty and impious with drawn sword, to sheath the sword, and keep their hands pure from blood, while nefarious men wade through murder and slaughter, so far from redounding to the praise of their goodness and justice, would be to incur the guilt of the greatest impiety; provided always they eschew reckless and cruel asperity, and that tribunal which may be justly termed a rock on which the accused must founder. For I am not one of those who would either favor an unseasonable severity, or think that any tribunal could be accounted just that is not presided over by mercy, that best and surest counselor of kings, and, as Solomon declares, "upholder of the throne" (Proverbs 20:28). This, as was truly said by one of old, should be the primary endowment of princes. The magistrate must guard against both extremes; he must neither, by excessive severity, rather wound than cure, nor by a superstitious affectation of clemency, fall into the most cruel inhumanity, by giving way to soft and dissolute indulgence to the destruction of many. It was well said by one under the empire of Nerva, It is indeed a bad thing to live under a prince with whom nothing is lawful, but a much worse to live under one with whom all things are lawful.

11 Lawfulness of War.

As it is sometimes necessary for kings and states to take up arms in order to execute public vengeance, the reason assigned furnishes us with the means of estimating how far the wars, which are thus undertaken, are lawful. For if power has been given them to maintain the tranquility of their subjects, repress the seditious movements of the turbulent, assist those who are violently oppressed, and animadvert on crimes, can they use it more opportunely than in repressing the fury of him who disturbs both the ease of individuals and the common tranquility of all; who excites seditious tumult, and perpetrates acts of violent oppression and gross wrongs? If it becomes them to be the guardians and maintainers of the laws, they must repress the attempts of all alike by whose criminal conduct the discipline of the laws is impaired. Nay, if they justly punish those robbers whose injuries have been afflicted only on a few, will they allow the whole country to be robbed and devastated with impunity? Since it makes no difference whether it is by a king or by the lowest of the people that a hostile and devastating inroad is made into a district over which they have no authority, all alike are to be regarded and punished as robbers. Natural equity and duty, therefore, demand that princes be armed not only to repress private crimes by judicial inflictions, but to defend the subjects committed to their guardianship whenever they are hostilely assailed. Such even the Holy Spirit, in many passages of Scripture, declares to be lawful.

12 Objection, that the lawfulness of war is not taught in Scripture. Answer.

But if it is objected, that in the New Testament there is no passage or example teaching that war is lawful for Christians, I answer, first, that the reason for carrying on war, which anciently existed, still exists in the present day, and that, on the other hand, there is no ground for debarring magistrates from the defense of those under them; and, secondly, that in the Apostolical writings we are not to look for a distinct exposition of those matters, their object being not to form a civil polity, but to establish the spiritual Kingdom of Christ; lastly, that there also it is indicated, in passing, that our Savior, by his advent, made no change in this respect. For (to use the words of Augustine) "if Christian discipline condemned all wars, when the soldiers ask counsel as to the way of salvation, they would have been told to cast away their arms, and withdraw altogether from military service. Whereas it was said (Luke 3:14), Concuss no one, do injury to no one, be contented with your pay. Those whom he orders to be contented with their pay he certainly does not forbid to serve."

But all magistrates must here be particularly cautious not to give way, in the slightest degree, to their passions. Or rather, whether punishments are to be inflicted, they must not be borne headlong by anger or hurried away by hatred, or burn with implacable severity.

They must, as Augustine says, "Even pity a common nature in him in whom they punish an individual fault;" or whether they have to take up arms against an enemy, that is, an armed robber, they must not readily catch at the opportunity, nay, they must not take it when offered, unless compelled by the strongest necessity. For if we are to do far more than that heathen demanded, who wished war to appear as desired peace, assuredly all other means must be tried before having recourse to arms.

In fine, in both cases, they must not allow themselves to be carried away by any private feeling, but be guided solely by regard for the public. Acting otherwise, they wickedly abuse their power, which was given them, not for their own advantage, but for the good and service of others. On this right of war depends the right of garrisons, leagues, and other civil munitions. By garrisons, I mean those which are stationed in states for defense of the frontiers; by leagues, the alliances which are made by neighboring princes, on the ground that if any disturbance arise within their territories, they will mutually assist each other, and combine their forces to repel the common enemies of the human race; under civil munitions, I include everything pertaining to the military art.

13 Right of exacting tribute and raising revenues.

Lastly, we think it proper to add, that taxes and imposts are the legitimate revenues of princes, which they are chiefly to employ in sustaining the public burdens of their office. These, however, they may use for the maintenance of their domestic state, which is in a manner combined with the dignity of the authority which they exercise. Thus we see that David, Hezekiah, Josiah, Jehoshaphat, and other holy kings, Joseph also, and Daniel, in proportion to the office which they sustained, without offending piety, expended liberally of the public funds; and we read in Ezekiel, that a very large extent of territory was assigned to kings (Ezekiel 48:21). In that passage, indeed, he is depicting the spiritual Kingdom of Christ, but still he borrows his representation from lawful dominion among men. Princes, however, must remember, in their turn, that their revenues are not so much private chests as treasuries of the whole people (this Paul testifies, Roman 13:6), which they cannot, without manifest injustice, squander or dilapidate; or rather, that they are almost the blood of the people, which it would be the harshest inhumanity not to spare. They should also consider that their levies and contributions, and other kinds of taxes, are merely subsidies of the public necessity, and that it is tyrannical rapacity to harass the poor people with them without cause. These things do not stimulate princes to profusion and luxurious expenditure (there is certainly no need to inflame the passions, when they are already, of their own accord, inflamed more than enough), but seeing it is of the greatest consequence that, whatever they venture to do, they should do with a pure conscience, it is necessary to teach them how far they can lawfully go, lest, by impious confidence, they incur the divine displeasure. Nor is this doctrine superfluous to private individuals, that they may not rashly and petulantly stigmatize the expenditure of princes, though it should exceed the ordinary limits.

14 Of Laws, their necessity and utility. Distinction between the Moral, Ceremonial, and Judicial Law of Moses.

It states, the thing next in importance to the magistrates is laws, the strongest sinews of government, or, as Cicero calls them after Plato, the soul, without which, the office of the magistrate cannot exist; just as, on the other hand, laws have no vigour without the magistrate. Hence, nothing could be said more truly than that, the law is a dumb magistrate, the magistrate a living law. As I have undertaken to describe the laws by which Christian polity is to be governed, there is no reason to expect from me a long discussion on the best kind of laws. The subject is of vast extent, and belongs not to this place. I will only briefly observe, in passing, what the laws are which may be piously used with reference to God, and duly administered among men. This I would rather have passed in silence, were I not aware that many dangerous errors are here committed. For there are some who deny that any commonwealth is rightly framed which neglects the Law of Moses, and is ruled by the common law of nations. How perilous and seditious these views are, let others see: for me it is enough to demonstrate that they are stupid and false. We must attend to the well known division which distributes the whole law of God, as promulgated by Moses, into the moral, the ceremonial, and the judicial law, and we must attend to each of these parts, in order to understand how far they do, or do not, pertain to us.

Meanwhile, let no one be moved by the thought that the judicial and ceremonial laws relate to morals. For the ancients who adopted this division, though they were aware that the two latter classes had to do with morals, did not give them the name of moral, because they might be changed and abrogated without affecting morals. They give this name especially to the first class, without which, true holiness of life and an immutable rule of conduct cannot exist.

15 Sum and scope of the Moral Law. Of the Ceremonial and Judicial Law. Conclusion.

The moral law, then (to begin with it), being contained under two heads, the one of which simply enjoins us to worship God with pure faith and piety. The other, to embrace men with sincere affection, is the true and eternal rule of righteousness prescribed to the men of all nations and of all times, who would frame their life agreeably to the will of God. For His eternal and immutable will is that we are all to worship Him and mutually love one another. The ceremonial law of the Jews was a tutelage by which the Lord was pleased to exercise the childhood of that people, until the fullness of the time should come when He was fully to manifest His wisdom to the world, and exhibit the reality of those things which were then adumbrated by figures (Galatians 3:24; 4:4). The judicial law, given them as a kind of polity, delivered certain forms of equity and justice, by which they might live together innocently and quietly. And as that exercise in ceremonies properly pertained to the doctrine of piety, inasmuch as it kept the Jewish Church in the worship and religion of God, yet was still distinguishable from piety itself, so the judicial form, though it looked only to the best method of preserving that charity which is enjoined by the eternal law of God, was still something distinct from the precept of love itself. Therefore, as ceremonies might be abrogated without interfering with piety, so, also, when these judicial arrangements are removed, the duties and precepts of charity can remain perpetual.

But if it is true that each nation has been left at liberty to enact the laws which it judges to be beneficial, still these are always to be tested by the rule of charity, so that while they vary in form, they must proceed on the same principle. Those barbarous and savage laws, for instance, which conferred honor on thieves, allowed the promiscuous intercourse of the sexes, and other things even fouler and more absurd, I do not think entitled to be considered as laws, since they are not only altogether abhorrent to justice, but to humanity and civilized life.

16 All Laws should be just. Civil Law of Moses: how far in force, and how far abrogated.

What I have said will become plain if we attend, as we ought, to two things connected with all laws–viz. the enactment of the law, and the equity on which the enactment is founded and rests. Equity, as it is natural, cannot be the same in all, and therefore ought to be proposed by all laws, according to the nature of the thing enacted. As constitutions have some circumstances on which they partly depend, there is nothing to prevent their diversity, provided they all alike aim at equity as their end. Now, as it is evident that the law of God which we call moral, is nothing else than the testimony of natural law, and of that conscience which God has engraved on the minds of men, the whole of this equity of which we now speak is prescribed in it. Hence, it alone ought to be the aim, the rule, and the end of all laws. Wherever laws are formed after this rule, directed to this aim, and restricted to this end, there is no reason that they should be disapproved by us, however much they may differ from the Jewish law, or from each other. The law of God forbids to steal. The punishment appointed for theft in the civil polity of the Jews may be seen in Exodus 22. Very ancient laws of other nations punished theft by exacting the double of what was stolen, while subsequent laws made a distinction between theft manifest and not manifest. Other laws went the length of punishing with exile, or with branding, while others made the punishment capital. Among the Jews, the punishment of the false witness was to "do unto him as he had thought to have done with his brother" (Deuteronomy 19:19). In some countries, the punishment is infamy, in others hanging, in others crucifixion. All laws alike avenge murder with blood, but the kinds of death are different. In some countries, adultery was punished more severely, in others more leniently.

Yet, we see that amidst this diversity they all tend to the same end. For they all with one mouth declare against those crimes, which are condemned by the eternal law of God–viz. murder, theft, adultery, and false witness, though they agree not as to the mode of punishment. This is not necessary, nor even expedient. There may be a country, which, if murder were not visited with fearful punishments, would instantly become a prey to robbery and slaughter. There may be an age requiring that the severity of punishments should be increased. If the state is in troubled condition, those things from which disturbances usually arise must be corrected by new edicts. In time of war, civilization would disappear amid the noise of arms, were not men overawed by an unwonted severity of punishment. In sterility, in pestilence, were not stricter discipline employed, all things would grow worse. One nation might be more prone to a particular vice, were it not most severely repressed. How malignant were it, and invidious of the public good, to be offended at this diversity, which is admirably adapted to retain the observance of the divine law. The allegation, that insult is offered to the law of God enacted by Moses, where it is abrogated, and other new laws are preferred to it, is most absurd. Others are not preferred when they are more approved, not absolutely, but from regard to time and place, and the condition of the people, or when those things are abrogated which were never enacted for us. The Lord did not deliver it by the hand of Moses to be promulgated in all countries, and to be everywhere enforced; but having taken the Jewish nation under his special care, patronage, and guardianship, he was pleased to be specially its legislator, and as became a wise legislator, he had special regard to it in enacting laws.

17 Of the People, and of the use of laws as respects individuals.

It now remains to see, as was proposed in the last place, what use the common society of Christians derives from laws, judicial proceedings, and magistrates. With this is connected another question –viz. What difference ought private individuals to pay to magistrates, and how far ought obedience to proceed? To very many it seems that among Christians the office of magistrate is superfluous, because they cannot piously implore his aid, inasmuch as they are forbidden to take revenge, cite before a judge, or go to law. But when Paul, on the contrary, clearly declares that he is the minister of God to us for good (Romans 13:4), we thereby understand that he was so ordained of God, that, being defended by his hand and aid against the dishonesty and injustice of wicked men, we may live quiet and secure. But if he would have been appointed over us in vain, unless we were to use his aid, it is plain that it cannot be wrong to appeal to it and implore it. Here, indeed, I have to do with two classes of men. For there are very many who boil with such a rage for litigation, that they never can be quiet with themselves unless they are fighting with others. Lawsuits they prosecute with the bitterness of deadly hatred and with an insane eagerness to hurt and revenge, and they persist in them with implacable obstinacy, even to the ruin of their adversary. Meanwhile, that they may be thought to do nothing but what is legal, they use this pretext of judicial proceedings as a defense of their perverse conduct. But if it is lawful for brother to litigate with brother, it does not follow that it is lawful to hate him, and obstinately pursue him with a furious desire to do him harm.

18 How far litigation lawful.

Let such persons then understand that judicial proceedings are lawful to him who makes a right use of them; and the right use, both for the pursuer and for the defender, is for the latter to sist himself on the day appointed, and, without bitterness, urge what he can in his defense, but only with the desire of justly maintaining his right; and for the pursuer, when undeservedly attacked in his life or fortunes, to throw himself upon the protection of the magistrate, state his complaint, and demand what is just and good; while, far from any wish to hurt or take vengeance far from bitterness or hatred far from the ardor of strife, he is rather disposed to yield and suffer somewhat than to cherish hostile feelings towards his opponent. On the contrary, when minds are filled with malevolence, corrupted by envy, burning with anger, breathing revenge, or, in fine, so inflamed by the heat of the contest, that they, in some measure, lay aside charity, the whole pleading, even of the most just cause, cannot but be impious. For it ought to be an axiom among all Christians, that no plea, however equitable, can be rightly conducted by anyone who does not feel as kindly towards his opponent as if the matter in dispute were amicably transacted and arranged. Some one, perhaps, may here break in and say, that such moderation in judicial proceedings is so far from being seen, that an instance of it would be a kind of prodigy. I confess that in these times, it is rare to meet with an example of an honest litigant; but the thing itself, untainted by the accession of evil, ceases not to be good and pure. When we hear that the assistance of the magistrate is a sacred gift from God, we ought the more carefully to beware of polluting it by our fault.

19 Refutation of the Anabaptists, who condemn all judicial proceedings.

Let those who distinctly condemn all judicial distinction know that they repudiate the holy ordinance of God, and one of those gifts, which to the pure are pure, unless they would charge Paul with a crime, because he repelled the calumnies of his accusers. He exposed their craft and wickedness, and, at the tribunal, claimed for himself the privilege of a Roman citizen, appealing, when necessary, from the governor to Caesar's judgment seat. There is nothing contrary to this in the prohibition, which binds all Christians to refrain from revenge, a feeling, which we drive far away from all Christian tribunals. For whether the action be of a civil nature, the one who takes the right course is the one who, with innocuous simplicity, commits his cause to the judge as the public protector without any thought of returning evil for evil (which is the feeling of revenge). If the action is of a graver nature, directed against a capital offense, the accuser required is not one who comes into court, carried away by some feeling of revenge or resentment from some private injury, but one whose only object is to prevent the attempts of some bad men to injure others. But if you take away the vindictive mind, you offend in no respect against that command that forbids Christians to indulge revenge. But they are not only forbidden to thirst for revenge, they are also enjoined to wait for the hand of the Lord, who promises that He will be the avenger of the oppressed and afflicted. But those who call upon the magistrate to give assistance to themselves or others anticipate the vengeance of the heavenly Judge. By no means, for we are to consider that the vengeance of the magistrate is the vengeance not of man, but of God, which, as Paul says, He exercises by the ministry of man for our good (Romans 13:8).

20 Objection, that Christ forbids us to resist evil. Answer.

No more are we at variance with the words of Christ, who forbids us to resist evil, and adds, "Whosoever shall smite thee on thy right cheek, turn to him the other also. And if any man will sue thee at the law, and take away thy coat, let him have thy cloak also" (Matthew 5:39, 40). He would have the minds of His followers to be so abhorrent to everything like retaliation, that they would sooner allow the injury to be doubled than desire to repay it. From this patience, we do not dissuade them. For verily, Christians were to be a class of men born to endure affronts and injuries, and be exposed to the iniquity, imposture, and derision of abandoned men, and not only so, but were to be tolerant of all these evils; that is, so composed in the whole frame of their minds, that, on receiving one offense, they were to prepare themselves for another, promising themselves nothing during the whole of life but the endurance of a perpetual cross. Meanwhile, they must do good to those who injure them, and pray for those who curse them, and (this is their only victory) strive to overcome evil with good (Romans 12:20, 21). Thus affected, they will not seek eye for eye, and tooth for tooth (as the Pharisees taught their disciples to long for vengeance), but (as we are instructed by Christ), they will allow their body to be mutilated, and their goods to be maliciously taken from them, prepared to remit and spontaneously pardon those injuries the moment they have been inflicted. This equity and moderation, however, will not prevent them, with entire friendship for their enemies, from using the aid of the magistrate for the preservation of their goods, or, from zeal for the public interest, to call for the punishment of the wicked and pestilential man, whom they know nothing will reform but death. All these precepts are truly expounded by Augustine, as tending to prepare the just and pious man patiently to sustain the malice of those whom he desires to become good, that he may thus increase the number of the good, not add himself to the number of the bad by imitating their wickedness. Moreover, it pertains more to the preparation of the heart which is within, than to the work which is done openly, that patience and good will may be retained within the secret of the heart, and that may be done openly which we see may do good to those to whom we ought to wish well.

21 **Objection, that Paul condemns lawsuits absolutely. Answer.**

The usual objection, that lawsuits are universally condemned by Paul (1 Corinthians 6:6) is false. It may easily be understood from his words, that a rage for litigation prevailed in the Church of Corinth to such a degree, that they exposed the Gospel of Christ, and the whole religion which they professed, to the calumnies and cavils of the ungodly. Paul rebukes them, first for traducing the Gospel to unbelievers by the intemperance of their dissensions; and, secondly, for so striving with each other while they were brethren. For so far were they from bearing injury from another, that they greedily coveted each other's effects, and voluntarily provoked and injured them. He inveighs, therefore, against that madness for litigation, and not absolutely against all kinds of disputes. He declares it to be altogether a vice or infirmity that they do not submit to the loss of their effects, rather than strive, even to contention, in preserving them; in other words, seeing they were so easily moved by every kind of loss, and on every occasion, however slight, ran off to the forum and to law-suits, he says, that in this way they showed that they were of too irritable a temper, and not prepared for patience. Christians should always feel disposed rather to give up part of their right than to go into court, out of which they can scarcely come without a troubled mind, a mind inflamed with hatred of their brother. But when one sees that his property, the want of which he would grievously feel, he is able, without any loss of charity, to defend, if he should do so, he offends in no respect against that passage of Paul. In short, as we said at first, every man's best adviser is charity. Everything in which we engage without charity, and all the disputes which carry us beyond it, are unquestionably unjust and impious.

22 Of the respect and obedience due to Magistrates.

The first duty of subjects towards their rulers is to entertain the most honorable views of their office, recognizing it as a delegated jurisdiction from God, and on that account receiving and reverencing them as the ministers and ambassadors of God. For you will find some who show themselves very obedient to magistrates, and would be unwilling that there should be no magistrates to obey, because they know this is expedient for the public good, and yet the opinion which those persons have of magistrates is, that they are a kind of necessary evils. But Peter requires something more of us when he says, "Honor the king" (1 Peter 2:17); and Solomon, when he says, "My son, fear thou the Lord and the king" (Proverbs 24:21). For, under the term honor, the former includes a sincere and candid esteem, and the latter, by joining the king with God, shows that he is invested with a kind of sacred veneration and dignity. We have also the remarkable injunction of Paul, "Be subject not only for wrath, but also for conscience sake" (Romans 13:5). By this he means, that subjects, in submitting to princes and governors, are not to be influenced merely by fear (just as those submit to an armed enemy who see vengeance ready to be executed if they resist), but because the obedience which they yield is rendered to God himself, inasmuch as their power is from God. I speak not of the men as if the mask of dignity could cloak folly, or cowardice, or cruelty, or wicked or flagitious manners, and thus acquire for vice the praise of virtue; but

I say that the station itself is deserving of honor and reverence, and that those who rule should, in respect of their office, be held by us in esteem and veneration.

23 Same subject continued.

From this, a second consequence is, that we must with ready minds prove our obedience to them, whether in complying with edicts, or in paying tribute, or in undertaking public offices and burdens, which relate to the common defense, or in executing any other orders. "Let every soul," says Paul, "be subject unto the higher powers." "Whosoever, therefore, resisteth the power, resisteth the ordinance of God" (Romans 13:1, 2). Writing to Titus, he says, "Put them in mind to be subject to principalities and powers, to obey magistrates, to be ready to every good work" (Titus 3:1). Peter also says, "Submit yourselves to every human creature" (or rather, as I understand it, "ordinance of man"), "for the Lord's sake: whether it be to the king, as supreme; or unto governors, as unto them that are sent by him for the punishment of evil-doers, and for the praise of them that do well" (1 Peter 2:13). Moreover, to testify that they do not feign subjection, but are sincerely and cordially subject, Paul adds, that they are to commend the safety and prosperity of those under whom they live to God. "I exhort, therefore," says he, "that, first of all, supplications, prayers, intercessions, and giving of thanks, be made for all men; for kings, and for all that are in authority: that we may lead a quiet and peaceable life in all godliness and honesty" (1 Timothy 2:1, 2). Let no man here deceive himself, since we cannot resist the magistrate without resisting God. For, although an unarmed magistrate may seem to be despised with impunity, yet God is armed, and will signally avenge this contempt. Under this obedience, I comprehend the restraint which private men ought to impose on themselves in public, not interfering with public business, or rashly encroaching on the province of the magistrate, or attempting anything at all of a public nature. If it is proper that anything in a public ordinance should be corrected, let them not act tumultuously, or put their hands to a work where they ought to feel that their hands are tied, but let them leave it to the cognizance of the magistrate, whose hand alone here is free. My meaning is, let them not dare to do it without being ordered. For when the command of the magistrate is given, they too are invested with public authority. For as, according to the common saying, the eyes and ears of the prince are his counselors, so one may not improperly say that those who, by his command, have the charge of managing affairs, are his hands.

24 How far submission due to tyrants.

But as we have hitherto described the magistrate who truly is what he is called–viz. the father of his country, and (as the Poet speaks) the pastor of the people, the guardian of peace, the president of justice, the vindicator of innocence, he is justly to be deemed a madman who disapproves of such authority. And since in almost all ages, we see that some princes, careless about all their duties on which they ought to have been intent, live without solicitude in luxurious sloth. Others, bent on their own interest, venally prostitute all rights, privileges, judgments, and enactments. Others pillage poor people of their money, and afterwards squander it in insane largesse. Others act as mere robbers, pillaging houses, violating matrons, and slaying the innocent. Many cannot be persuaded to recognize such persons for princes, whose command, as far as lawful, they are bound to obey. For while in this unworthy conduct, and among atrocities so alien, not only from the duty of the magistrate, but also of the man, they behold no appearance of the image of God, which ought to be conspicuous in the magistrate, while they see not a vestige of that minister of God, who was appointed to be a praise to the good and a terror to the bad, they cannot recognize the ruler whose dignity and authority Scripture recommends to us. And, undoubtedly, the natural feeling of the human mind has always been not less to assail tyrants with hatred and execration, than to look up to just kings with love and veneration.

25 Same continued.

But if we have respect to the Word of God, it will lead us further, and make us subject not only to the authority of those princes who honestly and faithfully perform their duty toward us, but all princes, by whatever means they have so become, although there is nothing they less perform than the duty of princes. For though the Lord declares that a ruler to maintain our safety is the highest gift of His beneficence, and prescribes to rulers themselves their proper sphere, He at the same time declares, that of whatever description they may be, they derive their power from none but Him. Those, indeed, who rule for the public good, are true examples and specimens of His beneficence, while those who domineer unjustly and tyrannically are raised up by Him to punish the people for their iniquity. Still all alike possess that sacred majesty with which He has invested lawful power. I will not proceed further without subjoining some distinct passages to this effect. We need not labor to prove that an impious king is a mark of the Lord's anger, since I presume no one will deny it, and that this is not less true of a king than of a robber who plunders your goods, an adulterer who defiles your bed, and an assassin who aims at your life, since all such calamities are classed by Scripture among the curses of God. But let us insist at greater length in proving what does not so easily fall in with the views of men, that even an individual of the worst character, one most unworthy of all honor, if invested with public authority, receives that illustrious divine power which the Lord has by His Word devolved on the ministers of His justice and judgment, and that, accordingly, in so far as public obedience is concerned, he is to be held in the same honor and reverence as the best of kings.

26 Proof from Scripture.

And, first, I would have the reader carefully to attend to that Divine Providence which, not without cause, is so often set before us in Scripture, and that special act of distributing kingdoms, and setting up as kings whomsoever he pleases. In Daniel it is said, "He changeth the times and the seasons: he removeth kings, and setteth up kings" (Daniel 2:21, 37). Again, "That the living may know that the Most High ruleth in the kingdom of men, and giveth it to whomsoever he will" (Daniel 4:17, 25). Similar sentiments occur throughout Scripture, but they abound particularly in the prophetical books. It is well known what kind of king Nebuchadnezzar, who stormed Jerusalem, was. He was an active invader and devastator of other countries. Yet, the Lord declares in Ezekiel that he had given him the land of Egypt as his hire for the devastation, which he had committed. Daniel also said to him, "Thou, O king, art a king of kings: for the God of heaven hath given thee a kingdom, power, and strength, and glory. And wheresoever the children of men dwell, the beasts of the field and the fowls of the heaven hath he given into thine hand, and hath made thee ruler over them all" (Daniel 2:37, 38). Again, he says to his son Belshazzar, "The most high God gave Nebuchadnezzar thy father a kingdom, and majesty, and glory, and honor: and for the majesty that he gave him, all people, nations, and languages, trembled and feared before him" (Daniel 5:18, 19).

When we hear that the king was appointed by God, let us, at the same time, call to mind those heavenly edicts as to honoring and fearing the king, and we shall have no doubt that we are to view the most iniquitous tyrant as occupying the place with which the Lord has honored him. When Samuel declared to the people of Israel what they would suffer from their kings, he said, "This will be the manner of the king that shall reign over you: He will take your sons, and appoint them for himself, for his chariots, and to be his horsemen; and some shall run before his chariots. And he will appoint him captains over thousands, and captains over fifties; and will set them to ear his ground, and to reap his harvest, and to make his instruments of war, and instruments of his chariots. And he will take your daughters to be confectioneries, to be cooks, and to be bakers. And he will take your fields, and your vineyards, and your olive yards, even the best of them, and give them to his servants. And he will take the tenth of your seed, and of your vineyards, and give to his officers, and to his servants. And he will take your menservants, and your maidservants, and your goodliest young men, and your asses, and put them to his work. He will take the tenth of your sheep: and ye shall be his servants" (1 Samuel 8:11-17).

Certainly, these things could not be done legally by kings, whom the law trained most admirably to all kinds of restraint. But it was called justice in regard to the people, because they were bound to obey and could not lawfully resist: as if Samuel had said, To such a degree will kings indulge in tyranny, which it will not be for you to restrain. The only thing remaining for you will be to receive their commands, and be obedient to their words.

27 Proof continued.

But the most remarkable and memorable passage is in Jeremiah. Though it is rather long, I am not indisposed to quote it, because it most clearly settles this whole question. "I have made the earth, the man and the beast that are upon the ground, by my great power, and by my outstretched arm, and have given it unto whom it seemed meet unto me. And now have I given all these lands into the hand of Nebuchadnezzar the king of Babylon, my servant: and the beasts of the field have I given him also to serve him. And all nations shall serve him, and his son, and his son's son, until the very time of his land come: and then many nations and great kings shall serve themselves of him. And it shall come to pass, that the nation and kingdom which will not serve the same Nebuchadnezzar the king of Babylon, and that will not put their neck under the yoke of the king of Babylon, that nation will I punish, saith the Lord, with the sword, and with famine, and with pestilence, until I have consumed them by his hand" (Jeremiah 27:5-8). Therefore, "bring your necks under the yoke of the king of Babylon, and serve him and his people, and live" (verse 12). We see how great obedience the Lord was pleased to demand for this dire and ferocious tyrant, for no other reason than just that he held the kingdom. In other words, the divine decree had placed him on the throne of the kingdom, and admitted him to regal majesty, which could not be lawfully violated. If we constantly keep before our eyes and minds the fact that even the most iniquitous kings are appointed by the same decree, which establishes all regal authority, we will never entertain the seditious thought that a king is to be treated according to his deserts, and that we are not bound to act the part of good subjects to him who does not in his turn act the part of a king to us.

28 Objections answered.

It is vain to object, that that command was specially given to the Israelites. For we must attend to the ground on which the Lord places it–"I have given the kingdom to Nebuchadnezzar; therefore serve him and live." Let us doubt not that on whomsoever the kingdom has been conferred, him we are bound to serve. Whenever God raises anyone to royal honor, He declares it His pleasure that he should reign. To this effect, we have general declarations in Scripture. Solomon says–"For the transgression of a land, many are the princes thereof" (Proverbs 28:2). Job says–"He looseth the bond of kings, and girdeth their loins with a girdle" (Job 12:18). This being confessed, nothing remains for us but to serve and live.

There is in Jeremiah another command in which the Lord thus orders His people–"Seek the peace of the city whither I have caused you to be carried away captives, and pray unto the Lord for it: for in the peace thereof shall ye have peace" (Jeremiah 29:7). Here the Israelites, plundered of all their property, torn from their homes, driven into exile, thrown into miserable bondage, are ordered to pray for the prosperity of the victor, not as we are elsewhere ordered to pray for our persecutors, but that his kingdom may be preserved in safety and tranquility, that they too may live prosperously under him. Thus David, when already king elect by the ordination of God, and anointed with his holy oil, though causelessly and unjustly assailed by Saul, holds the life of one who was seeking his life to be sacred, because the Lord had invested him with royal honor. "The Lord forbid that I should do this thing unto my master, the Lord's anointed, to stretch forth mine hand against him, seeing he is the anointed of the Lord." "Mine eyes spare thee; and I said, I will not put forth mine hand against my lord; for he is the Lord's anointed" (1 Samuel 24:6, 11). Again, –"Who can stretch forth his hand against the Lord's anointed, and be guiltless"? "As the Lord liveth the Lord shall smite him, or his day shall come to die, or he shall descend into battle, and perish. The Lord forbid that I should stretch forth mine hand against the Lord's anointed" (l Samuel 24:9-11).

29 Considerations to curb impatience under tyranny.

This feeling of reverence, and even of piety, we owe to the utmost to all our rulers, be their characters what they may. This I repeat the oftener, that we may learn not to consider the individuals themselves, but hold it to be enough that by the will of the Lord they sustain a character on which He has impressed and engraved inviolable majesty. But rulers, you will say, owe mutual duties to those under them. This I have already confessed. But if from this you conclude that obedience is to be returned to none but just governors, you reason absurdly. Husbands are bound by mutual duties to their wives, and parents to their children. Should husbands and parents neglect their duty; should the latter be harsh and severe to the children whom they are enjoined not to provoke to anger, and by their severity harass them beyond measure; should the former treat with the greatest contumely the wives whom they are enjoined to love and to spare as the weaker vessels; would children be less bound in duty to their parents, and wives to their husbands? They are made subject to the froward and undutiful. Nay, since the duty of all is not to look behind them, that is, not to inquire into the duties of one another, but to submit each to his own duty, this ought especially to be exemplified in the case of those who are placed under the power of others. Wherefore, if we are cruelly tormented by a savage, if we are rapaciously pillaged by an avaricious or luxurious, if we are neglected by a sluggish, if, in short, we are persecuted for righteousness' sake by an impious and sacrilegious prince, let us first call up the remembrance of our faults, which doubtless the Lord is chastising by such scourges. In this way, humility will curb our impatience. And let us reflect that it belongs not to us to cure these evils, that all that remains for us is to implore the help of the Lord, in whose hands are the hearts of kings, and inclinations of kingdoms. "God standeth in the congregation of the mighty; he judgeth among the gods." Before His face shall fall and be crushed all kings and judges of the Earth, who have not kissed His anointed, who have enacted unjust laws to oppress the poor in judgment, and do violence to the cause of the humble, to make widows a prey, and plunder the fatherless.

30 Considerations considered.

Herein is the goodness, power, and providence of God wondrously displayed. At one time He raises up manifest avengers from among His own servants, and gives them His command to punish accursed tyranny, and deliver His people from calamity when they are unjustly oppressed; at another time He employs, for this purpose, the fury of men who have other thoughts and other aims. Thus, He rescued His people Israel from the tyranny of Pharaoh by Moses; from the violence of Chusa, king of Syria, by Othniel; and from other bondage by other kings or judges. Thus He tamed the pride of Tyre by the Egyptians; the insolence of the Egyptians by the Assyrians; the ferocity of the Assyrians by the Chaldeans; the confidence of Babylon by the Medes and Persians, –Cyrus having previously subdued the Medes, while the ingratitude of the kings of Judah and Israel, and their impious contumacy after all His kindness, He subdued and punished, –at one time by the Assyrians, at another by the Babylonians. Not all these things, however, were done in the same way. The former class of deliverers being brought forward by the lawful call of God to perform such deeds, when they took up arms against kings, did not at all violate that majesty with which kings are invested by divine appointment, but armed from Heaven, they, by a greater power, curbed a less, just as kings may lawfully punish their own satraps. The latter class, though they were directed by the hand of God, as seemed to Him good, and did His work without knowing it, had nothing but evil in their thoughts.

31 General submission due by private individuals.

But whatever may be thought of the acts of the men themselves, the Lord by their means equally executed His own work, when He broke the bloody scepters of insolent kings, and overthrew their intolerable dominations. Let princes hear and be afraid; but let us at the same time guard most carefully against spurning or violating the venerable and majestic authority of rulers, an authority which God has sanctioned by the surest edicts, although those invested with it should be most unworthy of it, and, as far as in them lies, pollute it by their iniquity. Although the Lord takes vengeance on unbridled domination, let us not therefore suppose that that vengeance is committed to us, to whom no command has been given but to obey and suffer. I speak only of private men. For when popular magistrates have been appointed to curb the tyranny of kings (as the Ephori, who were opposed to kings among the Spartans, or Tribunes of the people to consuls among the Romans, or Demarchs to the senate among the Athenians; and perhaps there is something similar to this in the power exercised in each kingdom by the three orders, when they hold their primary diets). So far am I from forbidding these officially to check the undue license of kings, that if they connive at kings when they tyrannize and insult over the humbler of the people, I affirm that their dissimulation is not free from nefarious perfidy, because they fraudulently betray the liberty of the people, while knowing that, by the ordinance of God, they are its appointed guardians.

32 Obedience due only in so far as compatible with the word of God.

But in that obedience which we hold to be due to the commands of rulers, we must always make the exception, nay, must be particularly careful that it is not incompatible with obedience to Him to whose will the wishes of all kings should be subject, to whose decrees their commands must yield, to whose majesty their scepters must bow. And, indeed, how preposterous were it, in pleasing men, to incur the offense of Him for whose sake you obey men! The Lord, therefore, is King of kings. When He opens His sacred mouth, He alone is to be heard, instead of all and above all. We are subject to the men who rule over us, but subject only in the Lord. If they command anything against Him let us not pay the least regard to it, nor be moved by all the dignity, which they possess as magistrates–a dignity to which no injury is done when it is subordinated to the special and truly supreme power of God. On this ground Daniel denies that he had sinned in any respect against the king when he refused to obey his impious decree (Daniel 6:22), because the king had exceeded his limits, and not only been injurious to men, but, by raising his horn against God, had virtually abrogated his own power. On the other hand, the Israelites are condemned for having too readily obeyed the impious edict of the king. For, when Jeroboam made the golden calf, they forsook the temple of God, and, in submissiveness to him, revolted to new superstitions (1 Kings 12:28). With the same facility, posterity had bowed before the decrees of their kings. For this they are severely upbraided by the Prophet (Hosea 5:11).

So far is the praise of modesty from being due to that pretence by which flattering courtiers cloak themselves, and deceive the simple, when they deny the lawfulness of declining anything imposed by their kings, as if the Lord had resigned His own rights to mortals by appointing them to rule over their fellows, or as if earthly power were diminished when it is subjected to its author, before whom even the principalities of heaven tremble as suppliants.

I know the imminent peril to which subjects expose themselves by this firmness, kings being most indignant when they are contemned. As Solomon says, "The wrath of a king is as messengers of death" (Proverbs 16:14). But since Peter, one of Heaven's heralds, has published the edict, "We ought to obey God rather than men" (Acts 5:29), let us console ourselves with the thought, that we are rendering the obedience which the Lord requires, when we endure anything rather than turn aside from piety. And that our courage may not fail, Paul stimulates us by the additional consideration (1 Corinthians 7:23), that we were redeemed by Christ at the great price which our redemption cost Him, in order that we might not yield a slavish obedience to the depraved wishes of men, far less do homage to their impiety.

End of the Institutes

One Hundred Aphorisms

CONTAINING, WITHIN A NARROW COMPASS, THE SUBSTANCE AND ORDER OF THE FOUR BOOKS OF THE

Institutes of the Christian Religion

Book 1

1. The true wisdom of man consists in the knowledge of God the Creator and Redeemer.

2. This knowledge is naturally implanted in us, and the end of it ought to be the worship of God rightly performed, or reverence for the Deity accompanied by fear and love.

3. But this seed is corrupted by ignorance, whence arises superstitious worship; and by wickedness, whence arise slavish dread and hatred of the Deity.

4. It is also from another source that it is derived namely, from the structure of the whole world, and from the Holy Scriptures.

5. This structure teaches us what are the goodness, power, justice, and wisdom of God in creating all things in Heaven and Earth, and in preserving them by ordinary and extraordinary government, by which His Providence is more clearly made known. It teaches also, what are our wants, that we may learn to place our confidence in the goodness, power, and wisdom of God, to obey His commandments, to flee to Him in adversity, and to offer thanksgiving to Him for the gifts, which we enjoy.

6. By the Holy Scriptures, also, God the Creator is known. We ought to consider what these Scriptures are; that they are true, and have proceeded from the Spirit of God; which is proved by the testimony of the Holy Spirit, by the efficacy and antiquity of the Scriptures, by the certainty of the Prophecies, by the miraculous preservation of the Law, by the calling and writings of the Apostles, by the consent of the Church, and by the steadfastness of the martyrs, whence it is evident that all the principles of piety are overthrown by those fanatics who, laying aside the Scripture, fly to revelations.

7. Next, what they teach; or, what is the nature of God in himself and in the creation and government of all things.

8. The nature of God in himself is infinite, invisible, eternal, almighty; whence it follows that they are mistaken who ascribe to God a visible form. In His one essence, there are three persons, the Father, the Son, and the Holy Spirit.

9. In the creation of all things there are chiefly considered, A. Heavenly and spiritual substances, that is, angels, of which some are good and the protectors of the godly, while others are bad, not by creation, but by corruption; B. Earthly substances, and particularly man, whose perfection is displayed in soul and in body.

10. In the government of all things, the nature of God is manifested. Now His government is, in one respect, universal, by which He directs all the creatures according to the properties, which He bestowed on each when He created them.

11. In another respect, it is special; which appears in regard to contingent events, so that if any person is visited either by adversity or by any prosperous result, he ought to ascribe it wholly to God; and with respect to those things which act according to a fixed law of nature, though their peculiar properties were naturally bestowed on them, still they exert their power only so far as they are directed by the immediate hand of God.

12. It is viewed also with respect to time past and future. *Past*, that we may learn that all things happen by the appointment of God, who acts either by means, or without means, or contrary to means; so that everything which happens yields good to the godly and evil to the wicked. *Future*, to which belong human deliberations, and which

shows that we ought to employ lawful means; since that Providence on which we rely furnishes its own means.

13. Lastly, by attending to the advantage, which the godly derive from it. For we know certainly, A. That God takes care of the whole human race, but especially of His Church. B. That God governs all things by His will, and regulates them by His wisdom. C. That He has most abundant power of doing good; for in His hand are Heaven and Earth, all creatures are subject to His sway, the godly rest on His protection, and the power of hell is restrained by His authority. That nothing happens by chance, though the causes may be concealed, but by the will of God; by His secret will which we are unable to explore, but adore with reverence, and by His will which is conveyed to us in the Law and in the Gospel.

Book 2

14. The knowledge of God the Redeemer is obtained from the fall of man, and from the material cause of redemption.

15. In the fall of man, we must consider what he ought to be, and what he may be.

16. For he was created after the image of God; that is, he was made a partaker of the divine Wisdom, Righteousness, and Holiness, and, being thus perfect in soul and in body, was bound to render to God a perfect obedience to His commandments.

17. The immediate causes of the fall were–Satan, the Serpent, Eve, the forbidden fruit; the remote causes were–unbelief, ambition, ingratitude, and obstinacy. Hence, followed the obliteration of the image of God in man, who became unbelieving, unrighteous, and liable to death.

18. We must now see what he may be, in respect both of soul and of body. The understanding of the soul in divine things, that is, in the knowledge and true worship of God, is blinder than a mole; good works it can neither contrive nor perform. In human affairs, as in the liberal and mechanical arts, it is exceedingly blind and

variable. Now the will, so far as regards divine things, chooses only what is evil. So far as regards lower and human affairs, it is uncertain, wandering, and not wholly at its own disposal.

19. The body follows the depraved appetites of the soul, is liable to many infirmities, and at length to death.

20. Hence, it follows that redemption for ruined man must be sought through Christ the Mediator; because the first adoption of a chosen people, the preservation of the Church, her deliverance from dangers, her recovery after dispersions, and the hope of the godly, always depended on the grace of the Mediator. Accordingly, the law was given, that it might keep their minds in suspense until the coming of Christ; which is evident from the history of a gracious covenant frequently repeated, from ceremonies, sacrifices, and washings, from the end of adoption, and from the law of the priesthood.

21. The material cause of redemption is Christ, in whom we must consider three things; A. How He is exhibited to men; B. How He is received; C. How men are retained in His fellowship.

22. Christ is exhibited to men by the Law and by the Gospel.

23. The Law is threefold: Ceremonial, Judicial, and Moral. The use of the Ceremonial Law is repealed; its effect is perpetual. The Judicial or Political Law was peculiar to the Jews, and has been set aside, while that universal justice which is described in the Moral Law remains. The latter, or Moral Law, the object of which is to cherish and maintain godliness and righteousness, is perpetual, and is incumbent on all.

24. The use of the Moral Law is threefold. The first use shows our weakness, unrighteousness, and condemnation; not that we may despair, but that we may flee to Christ. The second is that those who are not moved by promises may be urged by the terror of threatening. The third is, that we may know what is the will of God; that we may consider it in order to obedience; that our minds may be strengthened for that purpose; and that we may be kept from falling.

25. The sum of the Law is contained in the Preface, and in the two Tables. In the Preface we observe, A. The power of God, to constrain the people by the necessity of obedience; B. A promise of

grace, by which he declares himself the God of the Church; C. A kind act, on the ground of which he charges the Jews with ingratitude, if they do not requite his goodness.

26. The first Table, which relates to the worship of God, consists of four commandments.

27. The design of the First Commandment is that God alone may be exalted in His people. To God alone, therefore, we owe adoration, trust, invocation, and thanksgiving.

28. The design of the Second Commandment is that God will not have His worship profaned by superstitious rites. It consists of two parts. The former restrains our licentious daring, that we may not subject God to our senses, or represent Him under any visible shape. The latter forbids us to worship any images on religious grounds, and, therefore, proclaims His power, which He cannot suffer to be despised, –His jealousy, for He cannot bear a partner, –His vengeance on children's children, –His mercy to those who adore His majesty.

29. The Third Commandment enjoins three things: A. That whatever our mind conceives, or our tongue utters, may have a regard to the majesty of God; B. That we may not rashly abuse His holy word and adorable mysteries for the purposes of ambition or avarice; C. That we may not throw obloquy on His works, but may speak of them with commendations of His Wisdom, Long-suffering, Power, Goodness, Justice. With these is contrasted a threefold profanation of the name of God, by perjury, unnecessary oaths, and idolatrous rites; that is, when we substitute in the place of God saints, or creatures animate or inanimate.

30. The design of the Fourth Commandment is that, being dead to our own affections and works, we may meditate on the Kingdom of God. Now there are three things here to be considered: A. A spiritual rest, when believers abstain from their own works, that God may work in them; B. That there may be a stated day for calling on the name of God, for hearing his Word, and for performing religious rites; C. That servants may have some remission from labor.

31. The Second Table, which relates to the duties of charity towards our neighbor, contains the last Six Commandments. The design of the Fifth Commandment is, that, since God takes pleasure

in the observance of His own ordinance, the degrees of dignity appointed by Him must be held inviolable. We are therefore forbidden to take anything from the dignity of those who are above us, by contempt, obstinacy, or ingratitude; and we are commanded to pay them reverence, obedience, and gratitude.

32. The design of the Sixth Commandment is that, since God has bound mankind by a kind of unity, the safety of all ought to be considered by each person; whence it follows that we are forbidden to do violence to private individuals, and are commanded to exercise benevolence.

33. The design of the Seventh Commandment is that, because God loves purity, we ought to put away from us all uncleanness. He therefore forbids adultery in mind, word, and deed.

34. The design of the Eighth Commandment is that, since injustice is an abomination to God, He requires us to render to every man what is His own. Now men steal, either by violence, or by malicious imposture, or by craft, or by sycophancy, etc.

35. The design of the Ninth Commandment is, that, since God, who is truth, abhors falsehood, He forbids calumnies and false accusations, by which the name of our neighbor is injured, –and lies, by which anyone suffers loss in his fortunes. On the other hand, He requires every one of us to defend the name and property of our neighbor by asserting the truth.

36. The design of the Tenth Commandment is, that, since God would have the whole soul pervaded by love, every desire averse to charity must be banished from our minds; and therefore every feeling, which tends to the injury of another is forbidden.

37. We have said that Christ is revealed to us by the Gospel. In addition, first, the agreement between the Gospel, or the New Testament, and the Old Testament is demonstrated: A. Because the godly, under both dispensations, have had the same hope of immortality; B. They have had the same covenant, founded not on the works of men, but on the mercy of God; C. They have had the same Mediator between God and men–Christ.

38. Next, five points of difference between the two dispensations are pointed out. A. Under the Law the heavenly inheritance was held out to them under earthly blessings; but under the Gospel, our minds are led directly to meditate upon it. B. The Old Testament, by means of figures, presented the image only, while the reality was absent; but the New Testament exhibits the present truth. C. The former, in respect of the Law, was the ministry of condemnation and death; the latter, of righteousness and life. D. The former is connected with bondage, which begets fear in the mind; the latter is connected with freedom, which produces confidence. E. The word had been confined to the single nation of the Jews; but now it is preached to all nations.

39. The sum of evangelical doctrine is, to teach, A. What Christ is; B. Why He was sent; C. In what manner He accomplished the work of redemption.

40. Christ is God and man: *God*, that He may bestow on His people righteousness, sanctification, and redemption; *Man*, because He had to pay the debt of man.

41. He was sent to perform the office, A. Of a Prophet, by preaching the truth, by fulfilling the prophecies, by teaching and doing the will of His Father; B. Of a King, by governing the whole Church and every member of it, and by defending his people from every kind of adversaries; C. Of a Priest, by offering His body as a sacrifice for sins, by reconciling God to us though His obedience, and by perpetual intercession for His people to the Father.

42. He performed the office of a Redeemer by dying for our sins, by rising again for our justification, by opening Heaven to us through His ascension, by sitting at the right hand of the Father whence He will come to judge the quick and the dead; and, therefore, He procured for us the grace of God and salvation.

Book 3

43. We receive Christ the Redeemer by the power of the Holy Spirit, who unites us to Christ; and, therefore, He is called the Spirit

of sanctification and adoption, the earnest and seal of our salvation, water, oil, a fountain, fire, the hand of God.

44. Faith is the hand of the soul, which receives, through the same efficacy of the Holy Spirit, Christ offered to us in the Gospel.

45. The general office of faith is, to assent to the truth of God, whenever, whatever, and in what manner soever He speaks; but its peculiar office is, to behold the will of God in Christ, His mercy, the promises of grace, for the full conviction of which the Holy Spirit enlightens our minds and strengthens our hearts.

46. Faith, therefore, is a steady and certain knowledge of the divine kindness towards us, which is founded on a gracious promise through Christ, and is revealed to our minds and sealed on our hearts by the Holy Spirit.

47. The effects of faith are four: A. Repentance; B. A Christian life; C. Justification; D. Prayer.

48. True repentance consists of two parts: A. Mortification, which proceeds from the acknowledgment of sin, and a real perception of the divine displeasure; B. Quickening, the fruits of which are–piety towards God, charity towards our neighbor, the hope of eternal life, holiness of life. With this true repentance is contrasted false repentance, the parts of which are, Contrition, Confession, and Satisfaction. The two former may be referred to true repentance, provided that there be contrition of heart because of the acknowledgment of sin. It must not be separated from the hope of forgiveness through Christ. The confession must be either *private* to God alone or made to the pastors of the Church willingly and for the purpose of consolation, not for the enumeration of offenses, and for introducing a torture of the conscience; or *public*, which is made to the whole Church, or to one or many persons in presence of the whole Church. What was formerly called Ecclesiastical Satisfaction, that is, what was made for the edification of the Church on account of repentance and public confession of sins, was introduced as due to God by the Sophists; whence sprung the supplements of Indulgences in this world, and the fire of Purgatory after death. But that Contrition of the Sophists, Auricular Confession (as they call

it), and the Satisfaction of actual performance are opposed to the free forgiveness of sins.

49. The two parts of a Christian life are laid down: A. The love of righteousness; that we may be holy, because God is holy, and because we are united to him, and are reckoned among His people; B. That a rule may be prescribed to us, which does not permit us to wander in the course of righteousness, and that we may be conformed to Christ. A model of this is laid down to us, which we ought to copy in our whole life. Next are mentioned the blessings of God, which it will argue extreme ingratitude if we do not requite.

50. The sum of the Christian life is denial of ourselves.

51. The ends of this self-denial are four. A. That we may devote ourselves to God as a living sacrifice. B. That we may not seek our own things, but those which belong to God and to our neighbor. C. That we may patiently bear the cross, the fruits of which are—acknowledgment of our weakness, the trial of our patience, correction of faults, more earnest prayer, and more cheerful meditation on eternal life. D. That we may know in what manner we ought to use the present life and its aids, for necessity and delight. Necessity demands that we possess all things as though we possessed them not; that we bear poverty with mildness, and abundance with moderation; that we know how to endure patiently fullness, and hunger, and want; that we pay regard to our neighbor, because we must give account of our stewardship; and that all things correspond to our calling. The delight of praising the kindness of God ought to be with us a stronger argument.

52. In considering Justification, which is the third effect of faith, the first thing that occurs is an explanation of the word. He is said to be justified who, in the judgment of God, is deemed righteous. He is justified by works, whose life is pure and blameless before God; and no such person ever existed except Christ. They are justified by faith who, shut out from the righteousness of works, receive the righteousness of Christ. Such are the elect of God.

53. Hence follows the strongest consolation; for instead of a severe Judge, we have a most merciful Father. Justified in Christ, and having peace, trusting to his power, we aim at holiness.

54. Next follows Christian liberty, consisting of three parts. A. That the consciences of believers may rise above the Law, and may forget the whole righteousness of the Law. B. That the conscience, free from the yoke of the Law, may cheerfully obey the will of God. C. That they may not be bound by any religious scruples before God about things indifferent. But here we must avoid two precipices. A. That we do not abuse the gifts of God. B. That we avoid giving and taking offense.

55. The fourth effect of faith is Prayer; in which are considered its fruits, laws, faults, and petitions.

56. The fruit of prayer is fivefold. A. When we are accustomed to flee to God, our heart is inflamed with a stronger desire to seek, love, and adore Him. B. Our heart is not a prey to any wicked desire, of which we would be ashamed to make God our witness. C. We receive His benefits with thanksgiving. D. Having obtained a gift, we more earnestly meditate on the goodness of God. E. Experience confirms to us the Goodness, Providence, and Truth of God.

57. The laws are four. A. That we should have our heart framed as becomes those who enter into converse with God; and therefore the lifting up of the hands, the raising of the heart, and perseverance, are recommended. B. That we should feel our wants. C. That we should divest ourselves of every thought of our own glory, giving the whole glory to God. D. That while we are prostrated amidst overwhelming evils, we should be animated by the sure hope of succeeding, since we rely on the command and promise of God.

58. They err who call on the Saints that are placed beyond this life. A. Because Scripture teaches that prayer ought to be offered to God alone, who alone knows what is necessary for us. He chooses to be present, because he has promised. He can do so, for He is Almighty. B. Because He requires that he is addressed in faith, which rests on his word and promise. C. Because faith is corrupted as soon as it departs from this rule. But in calling on the saints, there is no word, no promise; and therefore there is no faith; nor can the saints themselves either hear or assist.

59. The summary of prayer, which has been delivered to us by Christ the Lord, is contained in a Preface and two Tables.

60. In the Preface, the Goodness of God is conspicuous, for He is called *our Father*. It follows that we are His children, and that to seek supplies from any other quarter would be to charge God either with poverty or with cruelty; that sins ought not to hinder us from humbly imploring mercy; and that a feeling of brotherly love ought to exist amongst us. The power of God is likewise conspicuous in this Preface, for He is *in Heaven*. Hence, we infer that God is present everywhere, and that when we seek him, we ought to rise above perceptions of the body and the soul; that He is far beyond all risk of change or corruption; that He holds the whole universe in His grasp, and governs it by His power.

61. The First Table is entirely devoted to the glory of God, and contains three petitions. A. That the *name* of God, that is, His power, goodness, wisdom, justice, and truth, *may be hallowed*; that is, that men may neither speak nor think of God but with the deepest veneration. B. That God may correct, by the agency of His Spirit, all the depraved lusts of the flesh; may bring all our thoughts into obedience to His authority; may protect His children; and may defeat the attempts of the wicked. The use of this petition is threefold. (1). It withdraws us from the corruptions of the world. (2). It inflames us with the desire of mortifying the flesh. (3). It animates us to endure the cross. C. The Third petition relates not to the secret will of God, but to that which is made known by the Scriptures, and to which voluntary obedience is the counterpart.

62. The Second Table contains the three remaining petitions, which relate to our neighbors and ourselves. A. It asks everything, which the body needs in this sublunary state; for we commit ourselves to the care and providence of God, that He may feed, foster, and preserve us. B. We ask those things which contribute to the spiritual life, namely, the *forgiveness of sins*, which implies satisfaction, and to which is added a condition, that when we have been offended by deed or by word, we nevertheless forgive them their offenses against us. C. We ask *deliverance from temptations*, or, that we may be furnished with armor and defended by the Divine protection, that we may be able to obtain the victory. *Temptations* differ in their *causes*, for God, Satan, the world, and the flesh *tempt*; in their *matter*, for we are tempted, on the right hand, in respect of riches, honors,

beauty, etc., and on the left hand, in respect of poverty, contempt, and afflictions: and in their *end*, for God tempts the godly for good, but Satan, the flesh, and the world, tempt them for evil.

63. Those Four effects of faith bring us to the certainty of election, and of the final resurrection.

64. The causes of election are these. The *efficient* cause is–the free mercy of God, which we ought to acknowledge with humility and thanksgiving. The *material* cause is–Christ, the well-beloved Son. The *final* cause is–that, being assured of our salvation, because we are God's people, we may glorify Him both in this life and in the life which is to come, to all eternity. The effects are, in respect either of many persons, or of a single individual; and that by electing some, and justly reprobating others. The elect are called by the preaching of the word and the illumination of the Holy Spirit, are justified, and sanctified, that they may at length be glorified.

65. The final resurrection will take place. A. Because on any other supposition we cannot be perfectly glorified. B. Because Christ rose in our flesh. C. Because God is Almighty.

Book 4

66. God keeps us united in the fellowship of Christ by means of Ecclesiastical and Civil government.

67. In Ecclesiastical government, three things are considered. A. What is the Church? B. How is it governed? C. What is its power?

68. The Church is regarded in two points of view; as Invisible and Universal, which is the communion of saints; and as Visible and Particular. The Church is discerned by the pure preaching of the word, and by the lawful administration of the sacraments.

69. As to the government of the Church, there are five points of inquiry. A. Who rule? B. What are they? C. What is their calling? D. What is their office? E. What was the condition of the ancient Church?

70. They that rule are not Angels, but Men. In this respect, God declares His condescension towards us: we have a most excellent training to humility and obedience, and it is singularly fitted to bind us to mutual charity.

71. These are Prophets, Apostles, Evangelists, whose office was temporary; Pastors and Teachers, whose office is of perpetual duration.

72. Their calling is twofold: *internal* and *external.* The *internal* is from the Spirit of God. In the *external,* there are four things to be considered. A. What sort of persons ought to be chosen? Men of sound doctrine and holy lives. B. In what manner? With fasting and prayer. C. By whom? Immediately, by God, as Prophets and Apostles. Mediately, with the direction of the Word, by Bishops, by Elders, and by the people. D. With what rite of ordination? By the laying on of hands, the use of which is threefold. (1). That the dignity of the ministry may be commended. (2). that he who is called may know that he is devoted to god. (3). that he may believe that the Holy Spirit will not desert this holy ministry.

73. The duty of Pastors in the Church is, to preach the Word, to administer the Sacraments, to exercise Discipline.

74. The condition of the ancient Church was distributed into Presbyters, Elders, Deacons, who dispensed the funds of the Church to the Bishops, the Clergy, the poor, and for repairing churches.

75. The power of the Church is viewed in relation to Doctrine, Legislation, and Jurisdiction.

76. Doctrine respects the articles of faith, none of which must be laid down without the authority of the Word of God, but all must be directed to the glory of God and the edification of the Church. It respects also the application of the articles, which must agree with the analogy of faith.

77. Ecclesiastical laws, in precepts necessary to be observed, must be in accordance with the written word of God. In things indifferent, regard must be had to places, persons, times, with a due attention to order and decorum. Those constitutions ought to be avoided which have been laid down by pretended pastors instead of the pure worship

of God, which bind the consciences by rigid necessity, which make void a commandment of God, which are useless and trifling, which oppress the consciences by their number, which lead to theatrical display, which are considered to be propitiatory sacrifices, and which are turned to the purposes of gain.

78. Jurisdiction is twofold. (A). That which belongs to the Clergy, which was treated of under the head of Provincial and General Synods. (B). That which is common to the Clergy and the people, the design of which is twofold that scandals may be prevented, and that scandal which has arisen may be removed. The exercise of it consists in private and public admonitions, and likewise in excommunication, the object of which is threefold. (1). That the Church may not be blamed; (2). That the good may not be corrupted by intercourse with the bad; (3). That they who are excommunicated may be ashamed, and may begin to repent.

79. With regard to Times, Fasts are appointed, and Vows are made. The design of Fasts is, that the flesh may be mortified, that we may be better prepared for prayer, and that they may be evidences of humility and obedience. They consist of three things, the time, the quality, and the quantity of food. But here we must beware lest we rend our garments only, and not our hearts, as hypocrites do, lest those actions be regarded as a meritorious performance, and lest they be too rigorously demanded as necessary to salvation.

80. In Vows we must consider; A. To whom the vow is made–namely, to God. Hence, it follows that nothing must be attempted but what is approved by His Word, which teaches us what is pleasing and what is displeasing to God. B. Who it is that vows–namely, a man. We must, therefore, beware lest we disregard our liberty, or promise what is beyond our strength or inconsistent with our calling. C. What is vowed. Here regard must be had to time; to the *past*, such as a vow of thanksgiving and repentance; to the *future*, that we may afterwards be more cautious, and may be stimulated by them to the performance of duty. Hence, it is evident what opinion we ought to form respecting Popish vows.

81. In explaining the Sacraments, there are three things to be considered. A. What a sacrament is–namely, an external sign, by

which God seals on our consciences the promises of His good will towards us, in order to sustain the weakness of our faith. We in our turn testify our piety towards him. B. What things are necessary—namely, the Sign, the Thing signified, the Promise, and the general Participation. C. What is the number of them—namely, Baptism and the Lord's Supper.

82. The Sign in Baptism is water; the Thing Signified is the blood of Christ; the Promise is eternal life; the Communicants or Partakers are, adults, after making a confession of their faith, and likewise infants; for Baptism came in the place of Circumcision, and in both the mystery, promise, use, and efficacy, are the same. Forgiveness of sins also belongs to infants, and therefore it is likewise a sign of this forgiveness.

83. The end of Baptism is twofold. (A). To promote our faith towards God. For it is a sign of our washing by the blood of Christ, and of the mortification of our flesh, and the renewal of our souls in Christ. Besides, being united to Christ, we believe that we shall be partakers of all His blessings, and that we shall never fall under condemnation. (B). To serve as our confession before our neighbor, for it is a mark that we choose to be regarded as the people of God, and we testify that we profess the Christian religion, and that our desire is, that all the members of our body may proclaim the praise of God.

84. The Lord's Supper is a spiritual feast, by which we are preserved in that life into which God hath begotten us by His Word.

85. The design of the Lord's Supper is threefold. (A). To aid in confirming our faith towards God. (B). To serve as a confession before men. (C). To be an exhortation to charity.

86. We must beware lest, by undervaluing the signs, we separate them too much from their mysteries, with which they are in some measure connected; and lest, on the other hand, by immoderately extolling them, we appear to obscure the mysteries themselves.

87. The parts are two. (A). The *spiritual truth* in which the meaning is beheld consists in the promises; the *matter*, or substance, is Christ dead and risen; and the *effect* is our redemption and justification. (B). The visible signs are, bread, and wine.

88. With the Lord's Supper is contrasted the Popish Mass. A. It offers insult and blasphemy to Christ. B. It buries the Cross of Christ. C. It obliterates His death. D. It robs us of the benefits, which we obtain in Christ. E. It destroys the Sacraments in which the memorial of His death was left.

89. The Sacraments, falsely so-called, are enumerated, which are Confirmation, Penitence, Extreme Unction, Orders [which gave rise to the (seven) less and the (three) greater], and Marriage.

90. Next comes civil government, which belongs to the external regulation of manners.

91. Under this head are considered Magistrates, Laws, and the People.

92. The Magistrate is God's vicegerent, the father of his country, the guardian of the laws, the administrator of justice, the defender of the Church.

93. By these names, he is excited to the performance of duty. A. That he may walk in holiness before God, and before men may maintain uprightness, prudence, temperance, harmlessness, and righteousness. B. That by wonderful consolation it may smooth the difficulties of his office.

94. The kinds of Magistracy or Civil Government are Monarchy, Aristocracy, and Democracy.

95. As to Laws, we must see what is their constitution in regard to God and to men: and what is their equity in regard to times, places, and nations.

96. The People owe to the Magistrate, A. Reverence heartily rendered to him as god's ambassador. b. obedience or compliance with edicts, or paying taxes, or undertaking public offices and burdens. C. That love which will lead us to pray to God for His prosperity.

97. We are enjoined to obey not only good magistrates, but all who possess authority, though they may exercise tyranny; for it was not without the authority of God that they were appointed princes.

98. When tyrants reign, let us first remember our faults, which are chastised by such scourges; and, therefore, humility will restrain

our impatience. Besides, it is not in our power to remedy these evils, and all that remains for us is to implore the assistance of the Lord, in whose hand are the hearts of men and the revolutions of kingdoms.

99. In Two ways God restrains the fury of tyrants; either by raising up from among their own subjects open avengers, who rid the people of their tyranny, or by employing for that purpose the rage of men whose thoughts and contrivances are totally different, thus overturning one tyranny by means of another.

100. The obedience enjoined on subjects does not prevent the interference of any popular Magistrates whose office it is to restrain tyrants and to protect the liberty of the people. Our obedience to Magistrates ought to be such, that the obedience, which we owe to the King of kings, shall remain entire and unimpaired

A Defense of Calvinism

by
Charles Haddon Spurgeon
Author of ***Morning by Morning*** and ***Evening by Evening***

The old truth that Calvin preached, that Augustine preached, and that Paul preached is the truth that I must preach today, or else be false to my conscience and my God. I cannot shape the truth; I know of no such thing as paring off the rough edges of a doctrine. John Knox's Gospel is my Gospel. That which thundered through Scotland must thunder through England again.

It is a great thing to begin the Christian life by believing good solid doctrine. Some people have received twenty different "gospels" in as many years; how many more they will accept before they get to their journey's end, it would be difficult to predict. I thank God that He early taught me the Gospel, and I have been so perfectly satisfied with it, that I do not want to know any other. Constant change of creed is sure loss. If a tree has to be taken up two or three times a year, you will not need to build a very large loft in which to store the apples. When people are always shifting their doctrinal principles, they are not likely to bring forth much fruit to the glory of God. It is good for young believers to begin with a firm hold upon those great fundamental doctrines, which the Lord has taught in His Word. Why, if I believed what some preach about the temporary, trumpery salvation which only lasts for a time, I would scarcely be at all grateful for it; but when I know that those whom God saves He saves with an everlasting salvation, when I know that He gives to them an everlasting righteousness, when I know that He settles them on an everlasting foundation of everlasting love, and that He will bring them to His everlasting kingdom, oh, then I do wonder, and I am astonished that such a blessing as this should ever have been given to me!

Pause, my soul! adore, and wonder!
Ask, "Oh, why such love to me?"
Grace hath put me in the number
Of the Saviour's family:
Hallelujah!
Thanks, eternal thanks, to Thee.

I suppose there are some persons whose minds naturally incline towards the doctrine of free will. I can only say that mine inclines as naturally towards the doctrines of sovereign grace. Sometimes, when I see some of the worst characters in the street, I feel as if my heart must burst forth in tears of gratitude that God has never let me act as they have done! I have thought, if God had left me alone, and had not touched me by His grace, what a great sinner I should have been! I should have run to the utmost lengths of sin, dived into the very depths of evil, nor should I have stopped at any vice or folly, if God had not restrained me. I feel that I should have been a very king of sinners, if God had let me alone. I cannot understand the reason why I am saved, except upon the ground that God would have it so. I cannot, if I look ever so earnestly, discover any kind of reason in myself why I should be a partaker of Divine grace. If I am not at this moment without Christ, it is only because Christ Jesus would have His will with me, and that will was that I should be with Him where He is, and should share His glory. I can put the crown nowhere but upon the head of Him whose mighty grace has saved me from going down into the pit.

Looking back on my past life, I can see that the dawning of it all was of God, of God effectively. I took no torch with which to light the sun, but the sun enlightened me. I did not commence my spiritual life—no, I rather kicked, and struggled against the things of the Spirit: when He drew me, for a time I did not run after Him: there was a natural hatred in my soul of everything holy and good. Wooings were lost upon me-warnings were cast to the wind- thunders were despised; and as for the whispers of His love, they were rejected as being less than nothing and vanity. But, sure I am, I can say now, speaking on behalf of myself, "He only is my salvation." It was He who turned my heart, and brought me down on my knees before Him. I can in very deed, say with Doddridge and Toplady:

Grace taught my soul to pray,
And made my eyes o'erflow.

And coming to this moment, I can add:

Tis grace has kept me to this day,
And will not let me go.

Well can I remember the manner in which I learned the doctrines of grace in a single instant. Born, as all of us are by nature, an Arminian, I still believed the old things I had heard continually from the pulpit, and did not see the grace of God. When I was coming to Christ, I thought I was doing it all myself, and though I sought the Lord earnestly, I had no idea the Lord was seeking me. I do not think the young convert is at first aware of this. I can recall the very day and hour when first I received those truths in my own soul–when they were, as John Bunyan says, burnt into my heart as with a hot iron, and I can recollect how I felt that I had grown on a sudden from a babe into a man–that I had made progress in Scriptural knowledge, through having found, once for all, the clue to the truth of God. One weeknight, when I was sitting in the house of God, I was not thinking much about the preacher's sermon, for I did not believe it. The thought struck me, How did you come to be a Christian? I sought the Lord. But how did you come to seek the Lord? The truth flashed across my mind in a moment. I should not have sought Him unless there had been some previous influence in my mind to make me seek Him. I prayed, thought I, but then I asked myself, How came I to pray? I was induced to pray by reading the Scriptures. How came I to read the Scriptures? I did read them, but what led me to do so? Then, in a moment, I saw that God was at the bottom of it all, and that He was the Author of my faith, and so the whole doctrine of grace opened up to me, and from that doctrine I have not departed to this day, and I desire to make this my constant confession, "I ascribe my change wholly to God."

I once attended a service where the text happened to be, "He shall choose our inheritance for us;" and the good man who occupied the pulpit was more than a little of an Arminian. Therefore, when he commenced, he said, "This passage refers entirely to our temporal inheritance, it has nothing whatever to do with our everlasting destiny, for," said he, "we do not want Christ to choose for us in the matter of Heaven or hell. It is so plain and easy, that every man who has a grain of common sense will choose Heaven, and any person would know better than to choose hell. We have no need of any superior intelligence, or any greater Being, to choose Heaven or hell for us. It is left to our own free- will, and we have enough wisdom given us, sufficiently correct means to judge for ourselves," and therefore, as he very logically inferred, there was no necessity for Jesus Christ, or anyone, to make a choice for us. We could choose the inheritance for ourselves without any assistance. "Ah!" I thought, "but, my good brother, it may be very true that we could, but I think we should want something more than common sense before we should choose aright."

First, let me ask, must we not all of us admit an over-ruling Providence, and the appointment of Jehovah's hand, as to the means whereby we came into this world? Those men who think that, afterwards, we are left to our own free-will to choose this one or the other to direct our steps, must admit that our entrance into the world was not of our own will, but that God had then to choose for us. What circumstances were those in our power, which led us to elect certain persons to be our parents? Had we anything to do with it? Did not God himself appoint our parents, native place, and friends? Could He not have caused me to be born with the skin of the Hottentot, brought forth by a filthy mother who would nurse me in her "kraal," and teach me to bow down to Pagan gods, quite as easily as to have given me a pious mother, who would each morning and night bend her knee in prayer on my behalf? Or, might He not, if He had pleased have given me some profligate to have been my parent, from whose lips I might have early heard fearful, filthy, and obscene language? Might He not have placed me where I should have had a drunken father, who would have immured me in a very dungeon of ignorance, and brought me up in the chains of crime? Was it not God's Providence that I had so happy a lot, that both my parents were His children, and endeavored to train me up in the fear of the Lord?

John Newton used to tell a whimsical story, and laugh at it, too, of a good woman who said, in order to prove the doctrine of election, "Ah! sir, the Lord must have loved me before I was born, or else He would not have seen anything in me to love afterwards." I am sure it is true in my case; I believe the doctrine of election, because I am quite certain that, if God had not chosen me, I should never have chosen Him; and I am sure He chose me before I was born, or else He never would have chosen me afterwards; and He must have elected me for reasons unknown to me, for I never could find any reason in myself why He should have looked upon me with special love. So I am forced to accept that great Biblical doctrine. I recollect an Arminian brother telling me that he had read the Scriptures through a score or more times, and could never find the doctrine of election in them. He added that he was sure he would have done so if it had been there, for he read the Word on his knees. I said to him, "I think you read the Bible in a very uncomfortable posture, and if you had read it in your easy chair, you would have been more likely to understand it. Pray, by all means, and the more, the better, but it is a piece of superstition to think there is anything in the posture in which a man puts himself for reading: and as to reading through the Bible twenty times without having found anything about the doctrine of election, the wonder is that you found anything at all: you must have galloped through it at such a rate that you were not likely to have any intelligible idea of the meaning of the Scriptures."

If it would be marvelous to see one river leap up from the Earth full-grown, what would it be to gaze upon a vast spring from which all the rivers of the Earth. should at once come bubbling up, a million of them born at a birth? What a vision would it be! Who can conceive it. And yet the love of God is that fountain, from which all the rivers of mercy, which have ever gladdened our race-all the rivers of grace in time, and of glory hereafter-take their rise. My soul, stand thou at that sacred fountainhead, and adore and magnify, forever and ever, God, even our Father, who hath loved us! In the very beginning, when this great universe lay in the mind of God, like unborn forests in the acorn cup; long ere the echoes awoke the solitudes; before the mountains were brought forth; and long ere the light flashed through the sky, God loved His chosen creatures. Before there was any created being...when the ether was not fanned by an angel's wing, when space itself had not an existence, when there was nothing save God alone-even then, in that loneliness of Deity, and in that deep quiet and profundity, His bowels moved with love for His chosen. Their names were written on His heart, and then were they dear to His soul. Jesus loved His people before the foundation of the world-even from eternity! and when He called me by His grace, He said to me, "I have loved thee with an everlasting love: therefore with loving kindness have I drawn thee."

Then, in the fullness of time, He purchased me with His blood; He let His heart run out in one deep gaping wound for me long ere I loved Him. Yea, when He first came to me, did I not spurn Him? When He knocked at the door, and asked for entrance, did I not drive Him away, and do despite to Ms grace? Ah, I can remember that I full often did so until, at last, by the power of His effectual grace, He said, "I must, I will come in;" and then He turned my heart, and made me love Him. But even till now I should have resisted Him, had it not been for His grace. Well, then since He purchased me when I was dead in sins, does it not follow, as a consequence necessary and logical, that He must have loved me first? Did my Savior die for me because I believed on Him? No; I was not then in existence; I had then no being. Could the Savior, therefore, have died because I had faith, when I myself was not yet born? Could that have been possible? Could that have been the origin of the Savior's love towards me? Oh! no; my Saviour died for me long before I believed. "But," says someone, "He foresaw that you would have faith; and, therefore, He loved you." What did He foresee about my faith? Did He foresee that I should get that faith myself, and that I should believe on Him of myself) No; Christ could not foresee that, because no Christian man will ever say that faith came of itself without the gift and without the working of the Holy Spirit. I have met with a great many believers, and talked with them about this matter; but I never knew one who could put his hand on his heart, and say, "I believed in Jesus without the assistance of the Holy Spirit."

I am bound to the doctrine of the depravity of the human heart, because I find myself depraved in heart, and have daily proofs that in my flesh there dwelleth no good thing. If God enters into covenant with unfallen man, man is so insignificant a creature that it must be an act of gracious condescension on the Lord's part; but if God enters into covenant with sinful man, he is then so offensive a creature that it must be, on God's part, an act of pure, free, rich, sovereign grace. When the Lord entered into covenant with me, I am sure that it was all of grace, nothing else but grace. When I remember what a den of unclean beasts and birds my heart was, and how strong was my unrenewed will, how obstinate and rebellious against the sovereignty of the Divine rule, I always feel inclined to take the very lowest room in my Father's house, and when I enter Heaven, it will be to go among the less than the least of all saints, and with the chief of sinners.

The late lamented Mr. Denham has put, at the foot of his portrait, a most admirable text, "Salvation is of the Lord." That is just an epitome of Calvinism; it is the sum and substance of it. If anyone should ask me what I mean by a Calvinist, I should reply, "He is one who says, Salvation is of the Lord." I cannot find in Scripture any other doctrine than this. It is the essence of the Bible. "He only is my rock and my salvation." Tell me anything contrary to this truth, and it will be a heresy; tell me a heresy, and I shall find its essence here, that it has departed from this great, this fundamental, this rock truth, "God is my rock and my salvation." What is the heresy of Rome, but the addition of something to the perfect merits of Jesus Christ, the bringing in of the works of the flesh, to assist in our justification? And what is the heresy of Arminianism but the addition of something to the work of the Redeemer? Every heresy, if brought to the touchstone, will discover itself here. I have my own Private opinion that there is no such thing as preaching Christ and Him crucified, unless we preach what nowadays is called Calvinism. It is a nickname to call it Calvinism; Calvinism is the Gospel, and nothing else. I do not believe we can preach the Gospel, if we do not preach justification by faith, without works; nor unless we preach the sovereignty of God in His dispensation of grace; nor unless we exalt the electing, unchangeable, eternal, immutable, conquering love of Jehovah; nor do I think we can preach the Gospel, unless we base it upon the special and particular redemption of His elect and chosen people which Christ wrought out upon the Cross; nor can I comprehend a Gospel which lets saints fall away after they are called, and suffers the children of God to be burned in the fires of damnation after having once believed in Jesus. Such a Gospel I abhor.

If ever it should come to pass,
That sheep of Christ might fall away,
My fickle, feeble soul, alas!
Would fall a thousand times a day.

If one dear saint of God had perished, so might all; if one of the covenant ones be lost, so may all be; and then there is no Gospel promise true, but the Bible is a lie, and there is nothing in it worth my acceptance. I will be an infidel at once when I can believe that a saint of God can ever fall finally. If God hath loved me once, then He will love me forever. God has a mastermind; He arranged everything in His gigantic intellect long before He did it; and once having settled it, He never alters it, 'This shall be done," saith He, and the iron hand of destiny marks it down, and it is brought to pass. "This is My purpose," and it stands, nor can Earth or hell alter it. "This is My decree," saith He, "promulgate it, ye holy angels; rend it down from the gate of Heaven, ye devils, if ye can; but ye cannot alter the decree, it shall stand for ever." God altereth not His plans; why should He? He is Almighty, and therefore can perform His pleasure. Why should He? He is the All Wise, and therefore cannot have planned wrongly. Why should He? He is the everlasting God, and therefore cannot die before His plan is accomplished. Why should He change? Ye worthless atoms of Earth, ephemera of a day, ye creeping insects upon this bay leaf of existence, ye may change your plans, but He shall never, never change His. Has He told me that His plan is to save me? If so, I am forever safe.

My name from the palms of His hands
Eternity will not erase;

Impress'd on His heart it remains,
In marks of indelible grace.

I do not know how some people, who believe that a Christian can fall from grace, manage to be happy. It must be a very commendable thing in them to be able to get through a day without despair. If I did not believe the doctrine of the final perseverance of the saints, I think I should be of all men the most miserable, because I should lack any ground of comfort. I could not say, whatever state of heart I came into, that I should be like a wellspring of water, whose stream fails not; I should rather have to take the comparison of an intermittent spring, that might stop on a sudden, or a reservoir, which I had no reason to expect would always be full. I believe that the happiest of Christians and the truest of Christians are those who never dare to doubt God, but who take His Word simply as it stands, and believe it, and ask no questions, just feeling assured that if God has said it, it will be so. I bear my willing testimony that I have no reason, nor even the shadow of a reason, to doubt my Lord, and I challenge Heaven, and Earth, and hell, to bring any proof that God is untrue. From the depths of hell I call the fiends, and from this Earth I call the tried and afflicted believers, and to Heaven I appeal, and challenge the long experience of the blood-washed host, and there is not to be found in the three realms a single person who can bear witness to one fact which can disprove the faithfulness of God, or weaken His claim to be trusted by His servants. There are many things that may or may not happen, but this I know shall happen:

He shall present my soul,
Unblemish'd and complete,
Before the glory of His face,
With joys divinely great.

All the purposes of man have been defeated, but not the purposes of God. The promises of man may be broken, many of them are made to be broken, but the promises of God shall all be fulfilled. He is a promise maker, but He never was a promise breaker; He is a promise keeping God, and every one of His people shall prove it to be so. This is my grateful, personal confidence, "The Lord will perfect that which concerneth me" unworthy me, lost and ruined me. He will yet save me; and ...

I, among the blood-wash'd throng,
Shall wave the palm, and wear the crown,
And shout loud victory.

I go to a land, which the plough of Earth hath never upturned, where it is greener than earth's best pastures, and richer than her most abundant harvests ever saw. I go to a building of more gorgeous architecture than man hath ever built; it is not of mortal design; it is "a building of God, a house not made with hands, eternal in the Heavens." All I shall know and enjoy in Heaven, will be given to me by the Lord, and I shall say, when at last I appear before Him-

Grace all the work shall crown
Through everlasting days;
It lays in Heaven the topmost stone,
And well deserves the praise.

I know there are some who think it necessary to their system of theology to limit the merit of the blood of Jesus: if my theological system needed such a limitation, I would cast it to the winds. I cannot, I dare not allow the thought to find a lodging in my mind, it seems so near akin to blasphemy. In Christ's finished work I see an ocean of merit; my plummet finds no bottom, my eye discovers no shore. There must be sufficient efficacy in the blood of Christ, if God had so willed it, to have saved not only all in this world, but all in ten thousand worlds, had they transgressed their Maker's law. Once admit infinity into the matter, and limit is out of the question. Having a Divine Person for an offering, it is not consistent to conceive of limited value; bound and measure are terms inapplicable to the Divine sacrifice. The intent of the Divine purpose fixes the application of the infinite offering, but does not change it into a finite work. Think of the numbers upon whom God has bestowed His grace already. Think of the countless hosts in Heaven: if thou wert introduced there today, thou wouldst find it as easy to tell the stars, or the sands of the sea, as to count the multitudes that are before the throne even now. They have come from the East, and from the West, from the North, and from the South, and they are sitting down with Abraham, and with Isaac, and with Jacob in the Kingdom of God; and beside those in Heaven, think of the saved ones on Earth. Blessed be God, His elect on Earth are to be counted by millions, I believe, and the days are coming, brighter days than these, when there shall be multitudes upon multitudes brought to know the Savior, and to rejoice in Him. The Father's love is not for a few only, but for an exceeding great company. "A great multitude, which no man could number," will be found in Heaven. A man can reckon up to very high figures; set to work your Newtons, your mightiest calculators, and they can count great numbers, but God and God alone can tell the multitude of His redeemed. I believe there will be more in Heaven than in hell. If anyone asks me why I think so, I answer, because Christ, in everything, is to "have the pre-eminence," and I cannot conceive how He could have the pre-eminence if there are to be more in the dominions of Satan than in Paradise. Moreover, I have never read that there is to be in hell a great multitude, which no man could number. I rejoice to know that the souls of all infants, as soon as they die, speed their way to Paradise. Think what a multitude there is of them! Then there are already in Heaven unnumbered myriads of the spirits of just men made perfect ... the redeemed of all nations, and kindred, and people, and tongues up till now; and there are better times coming, when the religion of Christ shall be universal; when ...

He shall reign from pole to pole,
With illimitable sway,

... when whole kingdoms shall bow down before Him, and nations shall be born in a day, and in the thousand years of the great millennial state there will be enough saved to make up all the deficiencies of the thousands of years that have gone before. Christ shall be Master everywhere, and His praise shall be sounded in every land. Christ shall have the preeminence at last; His train shall be far larger than that which shall attend the chariot of the grim monarch of hell.

Some persons love the doctrine of universal atonement because they say, "It is so beautiful. It is a lovely idea that Christ should have died for all men; it commends itself," they say, "to the instincts of humanity; there is something in it full of joy and beauty." I admit there is, but beauty may be often associated with falsehood. There is much, which I might admire in the theory of universal redemption, but I will just show what the supposition necessarily involves. If Christ on His Cross intended to save every man, then He intended to save those who were lost before He died. If the doctrine is true, that He died for all men, then He died for some who were in hell before He came into this world, for doubtless there were even then myriads there that had been cast away because of their sins. Once again, if it was Christ's intention to save all men, how deplorably has He been disappointed, for we have His own testimony that there is a lake which burns with fire and brimstone, and into that pit of woe have been cast some of the very persons who, according to the theory of universal redemption, were bought with His blood. That seems to me a conception a thousand times more repulsive than any of those consequences, which are said to be associated with the Calvinistic and Christian doctrine of special and particular redemption.

To think that my Savior died for men who were or are in hell, seems a supposition too horrible for me to entertain. To imagine for a moment that He was the Substitute for all the sons of men, and that God, having first punished the Substitute, afterwards punished the sinners themselves, seems to conflict with all my ideas of Divine justice. That Christ should offer an atonement and satisfaction for the sins of all men, and that afterwards some of those very men should be punished for the sins for which Christ had already atoned, appears to me to be the most monstrous iniquity that could ever have been imputed to Saturn, to Janus, to the goddess of the Thugs, or to the most diabolical heathen deities. God forbid that we should ever think thus of Jehovah, the just and wise and good! There is no soul living who holds more firmly to the doctrines of grace than I do, and if any man asks me whether I am ashamed to be called a Calvinist, I answer, I wish to be called nothing but a Christian; but if you ask me, do I hold the doctrinal views which were held by John Calvin, I reply, I do in the main hold them, and rejoice to avow it. But far be it from me even to imagine that Zion contains none but Calvinistic Christians within her walls, or that there are none saved who do not hold our views.

Most atrocious things have been spoken about the character and spiritual condition of John Wesley, the modern prince of Arminians. I can only say concerning him that, while I detest many of the doctrines which he preached, yet for the man himself I have a reverence second to no Wesleyan; and if there were wanted two apostles to be added to the number of the twelve, I do not believe that there could be found two men more fit to be so added than George Whitefield and John Wesley. The character of John Wesley stands beyond all imputation for self-sacrifice, zeal, holiness, and communion with God; he lived far above the ordinary level of common Christians, and was one "of whom the world was not worthy." I believe there are multitudes of men who cannot see these truths, or, at least, cannot see them in the way in which we put them, who nevertheless have received Christ as their Saviour, and are as dear to the heart of the God of grace as the soundest Calvinist in or out of Heaven.

I do not think I differ from any of my Calvinistic brethren in what I do believe, but I differ from them in what they do not believe. I do not hold any less than they do, but I hold a little more, and, I think, a little more of the truth revealed in the Scriptures. Not only are there a few cardinal doctrines, by which we can steer our ship North, South, East, or West, but as we study the Word, we shall begin to learn something about the Northwest and Northeast, and all else that lies between the four cardinal points. The system of truth revealed in the Scriptures is not simply one straight line, but two; and no man will ever get a right view of the Gospel until he knows how to look at the two lines at once. For instance, I read in one Book of the Bible, "The Spirit and the bride say, Come. And let him that heareth say, Come. And let him that is athirst come. And whosoever will, let him take the water of life freely." Yet I am taught, in another part of the same inspired Word, that "it is not of him that willeth, nor of him that runneth, but of God that sheweth mercy." I see, in one place, God in providence presiding over all, and yet I see, and I cannot help seeing, that man acts as he pleases, and that God has left his actions, in a great measure, to his own free will. Now, if I were to declare that man was so free to act that there was no control of God over his actions, I should be driven very near to atheism; and if, on the other hand, I should declare that God so over-rules all things that man is not free enough to be responsible, I should be driven at once into Antinomianism or fatalism.

That God predestines, and yet that man is responsible, are two facts that few can see clearly. They are believed to be inconsistent and contradictory to each other. If, then, I find taught in one part of the Bible that everything is foreordained, that is true; and if I find, in another Scripture, that man is responsible for all his actions, that is true; and it is only my folly that leads me to imagine that these two truths can ever contradict each other. I do not believe they can ever be welded into one upon any earthly anvil, but they certainly shall be one in eternity. They are two lines that are so nearly parallel, that the human mind which pursues them farthest will never discover that they converge, but they do converge, and they will meet somewhere in eternity, close to the throne of God, whence all truth doth spring.

It is often said that the doctrines we believe have a tendency to lead us to sin. I have heard it asserted most positively, that those high doctrines which we love, and which we find in the Scriptures, are licentious ones. I do not know who will have the hardihood to make that assertion, when they consider that the holiest of men have been believers in them. I ask the man who dares to say that Calvinism is a licentious religion, what he thinks of the character of Augustine, or Calvin, or Whitefield, who in successive ages were the great exponents of the system of grace; or what will he say of the Puritans, whose works are full of them? Had a man been an Arminian in those days, he would have been accounted the vilest heretic breathing, but now we are looked upon as the heretics, and they as the orthodox. We have gone back to the old school; we can trace our descent from the apostles. It is that vein of free grace, running through the sermonizing of Baptists, which has saved us as a denomination. Were it not for that, we should not stand where we are today. We can run a golden line up to Jesus Christ himself, through a holy succession of mighty fathers, who all held these glorious truths; and we can ask concerning them, "Where will you find holier and better men in the world?"

No doctrine is so calculated to preserve a man from sin as the doctrine of the grace of God. Those who have called it "a licentious doctrine" did not know anything at all about it. Poor ignorant things, they little knew that their own vile stuff was the most licentious doctrine under Heaven. If they knew the grace of God in truth, they would soon see that there was no preservative from lying like a knowledge that we are elect of God from the foundation of the world. There is nothing like a belief in my eternal perseverance, and the immutability of my Father's affection, which can keep me near to Him from a motive of simple gratitude. Nothing makes a man so virtuous as belief of the truth. A lying doctrine will soon beget a lying practice. A man cannot have an erroneous belief without by-and-by having an erroneous life. I believe the one thing naturally begets the other. Of all men, those have the most disinterested piety, the most sublime reverence, the most ardent devotion, who believe that they are saved by grace, without works, through faith, and that not of themselves, it is the gift of God. Christians should take heed, and see that it always is so, lest by any means Christ should be crucified afresh, and put to an open shame.

The Five Points of Calvinism

With the possible exception of Martin Luther, no man has had greater influence on the theology of the Protestant Churches today than John Calvin. It's impossible to condense countless volumes of Biblical commentary of John Calvin down to a short summary, it is true that Calvin's most well-known teachings, set forth in *The Institutes of Christian Religion* are the often-quoted "Five Points of Calvinism."

The acronym used to help remember them is "**T.U.L.I.P.**" They are:

TOTAL DEPRAVITY OF MAN: That man's nature is basically evil, not basically good. Apart from the direct influence of God, man will never truly seek God or God's will, though he may seek the benefits of association with God.

UNCONDITIONAL ELECTION: That God sovereignly chooses or "elects" His children from before the foundation of time. God does not "look down the corridors of time to see what decision people will make"... rather, God causes them to make the decision to seek Him.

LIMITED ATONEMENT: That the death and resurrection of Christ is a substitutionary payment for the sins of only those who are God's elect children... not the entire world.

IRRESISTIBLE GRACE: That when God calls a person, His call cannot ultimately be ignored.

PERSEVERANCE OF THE SAINTS: That it is not possible for one to "lose his salvation.

Index

D

E

F

G

N

O

P

R

S

T